CARRIER

CARRIER

A Century of First-Hand Accounts of Naval Operations in War and Peace

EDITED BY JEAN HOOD

CONWAY

For Commander David 'Shorty' Hamilton

A Conway Maritime book

© Jean Hood, 2010
Foreword © Rear Admiral Simon Charlier, 2010

First published in Great Britain
in 2010 by Conway,
an imprint of Anova Books Company Limited,
10 Southcombe Street,
London W14 0RA
www.anovabooks.com
www.conwaymaritime.com

Distributed in the U.S. and Canada
by Sterling Publishing Co., Inc. 387 Park Avenue South,
New York, NY 10016-8810

British Library Cataloguing in Publication Data:
A catalogue record for this book is available from the British Library

ISBN 9781844860906

Anova Books Company Ltd is committed to respecting the intellectual
property rights of others. We have made all reasonable efforts to ensure
that the reproduction of all content on these pages is included with the
full consent of the copyright owners. If you are aware of any unintentional
omissions please contact the company directly so that any necessary
corrections may be made for future editions. Full details of all the books
can be found in the Bibliography.

Editing and design by DAG Publications Ltd
Printed by T. J. International Ltd., Cornwall

To receive regular email updates on forthcoming Conway titles,
email conway@anovabooks.com with Conway Update
in the subject field.

Endpaper illustration:
Front: USS *Langley* and USS *Ticonderoga* lead Task Group 38.3
into the anchorage at Ulithi Atoll on 12 December 1944 after
strikes in the Philippines. (CPL) Back: Sea King helicopters
landing on HMS *Invincible*, 1991. (Crown copyright)

Contents

Foreword

by Rear Admiral Simon Charlier
Chief of Staff Carrier Strike and Aviation
and Rear Admiral Fleet Air Arm

It is with a great sense of pride and privilege that I write this foreword. Having been involved in naval aviation for more than 25 years, including serving as the head of the Fleet Air Arm, I have come to know and understand the huge effort that is required at every level to make flying from the sea a success. The added dimension to aviation presented when your airfield is pitching and rolling, when the airfield you left is no longer in the same place when you return, and when you have to maintain, repair and service aircraft in a cramped hangar that is always moving demands a special type of person of the highest calibre.

Having joined my first frontline squadron as a pilot shortly after the Falklands conflict, I have spent my career flying from ships, including aircraft carriers. Initially a Wasp pilot, I later retrained to the more modern Lynx and spent this intensive period almost constantly deployed worldwide in a number of key operational environments. It was during this time that my opinions and experiences were forged and I learnt to respect maritime aviation and the unique set of circumstances and challenges that those who operate aircraft from the sea face. I have been fortunate enough to work with navies from a wide variety of different nations all across the globe, both as a pilot and as a staff officer, and more recently as the head of the Fleet Air Arm and CINC's Chief of Staff for Aviation and Carriers. Collectively, these posts represent a career that only scratches the surface of the breadth of skill and expertise that those in this book represent.

In 2009 the Royal Navy celebrated 100 years of Naval Aviation, and as we reflected on this milestone one thing stood out above all others: our people. What rings true for the Royal Navy will undoubtedly resonate in all Navies around the world that operate carriers and fly from the sea, the professionalism, ethos and commitment of this special cadre of individuals – from engineers to deck crews to pilots to those who operate the ship – is vital to ensure that this most demanding of activities is undertaken as safely and effectively as possible. But it must be remembered that life continues unabated on a carrier when not on duty, on some well-deserved down time, recreation or during port visits, and these stories are also well worth telling, and their recollections herein are enlightening!

The benefits that a carrier brings are well understood, a testament to the significant investment made by many countries to possess this formidable asset. As we look to the future, this investment continues, including by the United Kingdom, to ensure that carriers and their air power are a cornerstone of defence capability, not only to provide military firepower but also to offer immense flexibility across a number of less obvious tasks that the carrier can undertake – from humanitarian aid and assistance, to disaster relief, to diplomacy, conflict prevention, peacekeeping and international cooperation and training, the employment of a carrier and her air group is limited only by our imagination. Given the uncertain nature of the world we live in, and our inherent difficulty in being able to predict the place and nature of the next conflict, there could be no more flexible asset available in the government's defence inventory than the carrier and its air group.

The stories of those that have served on carriers throughout the decades are inspirational and heartfelt; sometimes they are full of humour, and sometimes they tell of tragedy and suffering. However, in delivering air power from the sea, each individual has a vital contribution to make, and when we fly in the maritime environment we challenge ourselves to a unique skills set, which adds a dimension to aviation and its support that is just not found ashore. The carrier has proved its worth many times, and will continue to do so, but it is only a sum of its parts. The contributions made from those within these pages are what really matters – they tell of the human interaction, the real people who have served, succeeded, overcome and sometimes suffered. Each has a unique story that deserves to be told. This book, with its evocative testimony from those who have served in operations over the years and around the world, brings together the sense of purpose, service and pride that the carrier community possesses.

I commend this book to you. Its pages contain a truly unique insight and perspective from individuals across naval aviation and support from various nations. Their experiences are brought together to form a remarkable story, full of determination, humour, professionalism and, above all, authenticity. Their exploits and recollections make a truly gripping and inspirational read.

Glossary

A/S	Anti-Submarine		below the edge of the
A25	Form to be filled in after		flight deck
	an aircraft accident	Commander	Officer responsible for
AAA	Anti Aircraft Artillery	(Flying) /	flying operations
ABAN	Aviation Boatswain's Mate	Commander (F)	
	Airman (USN)	Con	Direct the steering
ADO	Air Direction Officer	Corpsman	Member of a para-medical
AIM	Air Intercept Missile		unit in US Navy ships
Asdic	Early term for SONAR		(pronounced Core-man)
ASW	Anti-Submarine Warfare	CPO	Chief Petty Officer
AVGAS	Aviation petrol/gasoline	CVA	Attack Aircraft Carrier
Bats	Paddle-shaped objects	CVE	Escort Carrier (crews
	held by the Deck Landing		translated it as
	Control Officer		'Combustible, Vulnerable,
Batsman	Colloquial name for the		Expendable')
	Deck Landing Control	DLCO	Deck landing Control
	officer		Officer (RN), Landing
Bogey	Enemy aircraft /		Signals Officer (USN), who
	unidentified aircraft		guides a pilot for a deck
Bomb Dolly	Trolly for moving bombs		landing
Bone Dome	Helmet	(E)	Designation affixed to a
Cab	Aircraft		rank to denote
CAG	Carrier Air Group (the		Engineering branch;
	squadrons embarked on a		e.g., Lieutenant (E)
	carrier); renamed Carrier	Fantail	After end of the carrier
	Air Wing. Also used for		[USN]
	the Air Wing Commander.	FDO	Fighter Direction Officer
CAM	Catapult-Armed Merchant	Feet Wet /	Aviator speak for flying
	ship, capable of launching	Feet Dry	over sea/land
	(but not recovering) a	Fish head	Seaman officer
	fighter to deal with enemy	Flyco	Flying Control / the
	aircraft		aviation bridge from
CAOC	Combined Air Operations		which aircraft are
	Center		controlled (RN)
CAP	Combat Air Patrol	Goofers	Vantage points / people
Capitano di	Lieutenant Commander		watching deck landings
Corvetta	(Italian Navy)	GQ	General Quarters
Capitano di	Commander (Italian Navy)	Grog	Rum and water mix,
Fregata			formerly issued to sailors
Carley Float	A large life raft		in the Royal Navy
Cat	Catapult	H/F	High Frequency
Catwalk	A gallery around and	HARM	High Speed Anti-Radiation

	Missile		aircraft gun
Head(s)	Toilet(s)/bathroom	Prang	Accident
HF/DF	High-Frequency Direction Finding, used to pinpoint the location of a submarine	Primary Fly	Control, from where flying operations are managed (USN equivalent of RN's Flyco)
Huffer	Small jet engine towed round the flight deck, used for starting engines	RNAS	Royal Naval Air Service, forerunner of the Fleet Air Arm
Hydrophone	Microphone used, submerged, to detect the sound of propellers and engines of enemy ships	RAS	Refuelling at sea
		RATOG	Rocket Assisted Take-off Gear
		RCO	Radar Control Office
Jaunty	Master at Arms	RNR	Royal Naval Reserve, formed of Merchant Navy officers who served with the Royal Navy, full time, while the war lasted
Kite	Aircraft (slang)		
LCT	Landing Craft Tank		
Lieutenant de Vaisseau	Lieutenant (French Navy)		
Little (F)	Colloquial name for Lieutenant Commander (Flying)	RNVR	Royal Navy Volunteer Reserve, as above, but civilians
MFV	Motor Fishing Vessel, used to ferry stores and large bodies of men between ship and shore	Round-down	Downward-curving after-end of the flight deck
		SAM	Surface to Air Missile
		SAR	Search And Rescue
MAC ship	Merchant Aircraft Carrier; a merchant ship fitted with a flight deck in order to provide air protection to a convoy	SARBE	Search And Rescue beacon
		SDO	Signal Distribution Office
		SFO	Senior Flying Officer
		SONAR	SOund Navigation And Ranging, underwater detection system
Makee-learn	Young/youngster		
Meatball	Ball of light seen by, and guiding, the pilot using the mirror landing system	Sottotente di Vascello	Sub-Lieutenant (Italian Navy)
		Sparker	Electrical or radio technician
Monkey Island	The upper bridge		
Monkey's Fist	Knot at the end of a heaving line, giving it weight and making it easier to throw	Sponson	Platform on side of ship
		TAG	Tailored Air Group (modern)
		TAG	Telegraphist/Air Gunner (not after World War II)
OD	Officer of the Deck		
Oiler	Refuelling tanker	Target of Opportunity	Something that could be successfully attacked but has not been designated as a target
Oppo	Shipmate, friend		
PT boat	Patrol Torpedo boat		
PAN PAN PAN	Distress call of grade lower than MAYDAY (both derived from French)		
		Tenente di Vascello	Lieutenant (Italian Navy)
Plot	Operations Plotting Room	Tin fish	Torpedo
PO	Petty Officer	W/T	Wireless Telegraphy
Pom-Pom	Multi-barrelled anti-	Wings	Commander (Flying) (RN)

Introduction

The aircraft carrier is truly amazing. Even now at the end of cruise, through the rain beating on the canopy, watching different colored wands and shadows of men scurrying in and out of the darkness, I am amazed at the concept of the carrier, and the fact that it works. And it doesn't just work, it kicks butt.

— Lieutenant Barry 'Skull' W. Hull, VFA-81 Squadron (The Sunliners),
USS *Saratoga*, 1991, from a letter to his family

2010 marks the centenary of the first flight from a warship. As early as World War I, the aircraft carrier served notice that naval warfare was about to undergo a fundamental change. Since then, huge advances have been made in warship design, aviation and weapons technology to produce today's fast, elegant, functional and supremely effective fighting units. Ultimately, however, the success of a carrier depends at least as much upon the calibre of the crew and the embarked squadrons as upon the hardware and software systems. This book, therefore, is the story of the carriers told through the memories of those who served on them in both war and peace, from stokers to admirals, from pilots to engineers, from air fitters to radio operators. The eyewitness contributions are drawn from several countries, and between them they cover all types of carriers, from today's nuclear powered titans with their supersonic fighters and sophisticated ASW helicopters to the MAC ships of World War II and the seaplane-carrying converted ferries of World War I.

There are very few theatres of war in which the carrier has not played a major part, from the Arctic to the South Atlantic; from the Mediterranean to the Pacific. Carrier aircrew have sunk submarines, defended fleets, covered amphibious landings, carried out reconnaissance, attacked not just coastal targets but strategic facilities far beyond the reach of land-based aircraft or battleship guns, provided Airborne Early Warning, gathered intelligence, evacuated casualties, transported troops and equipment, offered humanitarian assistance, torpedoed capital ships and rescued downed aircrew. In addition, the ships themselves have carried commandos, evacuated citizens, brought supplies, landed and resupplied agents and flown the flag around the world. They are arguably the most versatile warship that has ever existed.

Contributors describe all the above experiences and explain how they adapted to innovations such as the introduction of new aircraft or the mirror landing system. They recall the vices and virtues of aircraft as varied as the simple Fairey Swordfish, the carrier-friendly Hellcat, the much-loved Douglas Skyraider and the revolutionary Sea Harrier. They talk, too, about their lives: the conditions on board, aspects of their job, places they visited and how they spent what little leisure they enjoyed aboard their floating airstrip. And they describe in often painful detail the carnage caused by fires or bombs that exploded in the hanger, the sadness of losing friends and the drama of abandoning ship or ditching.

The opening chapter offers a swift 'welcome' to the world of carriers and naval aviation, and thereafter the book runs chronologically through the carrier century with occasional pauses to reflect on life aboard. (It should be noted that contributions by serving personnel have been subject to official approval.) Each chapter begins with a brief introduction to place the accounts that follow in context; it is not intended to be a full account of naval operations nor of carrier and aircraft design. Many books have been written on both subjects. This book, however, is a tribute to the men, and more recently the women, of several nations who have served on carriers and often given their lives in the service of their country.

Acknowledgements

I have to begin by thanking those who generously gave up their time over the past two years to contribute their memories. They are all identified as contributors by 'Communication with the Editor', an unfortunately austere phrase that covers telephone conversations, meetings, letters and emails, but not the pleasure of the human contact. Being in touch with them has been both a privilege and the most enjoyable part of writing the book. It was a special pleasure to be able to include post-war recollections from Captain George Hunt, DSO*, DSC*, who was also one of the stars of my previous book *Submarine*. I also want to thank those who sent me material that had appeared elsewhere but to which they hold the copyright.

I am also indebted to those institutions that hold archive material, in particular the Imperial War Museum, London, whose staff in both the Sound Archive and the Department of Documents are always helpful. Copyright to many of their documents remain in private hands, and I would like to thank those individuals who gave permission for the material to be used. Despite the best efforts of myself and the Keeper of Documents, Mr R. Suddaby, it was impossible to trace every copyright holder, and we would like to hear from anyone who finds their material quoted. Very big thanks are due to the Fleet Air Arm Museum at Yeovilton, to Martha Elmore at East Carolina University's Joyner Library, who made it possible for me to quote from some first-rate material in the collection, to Karl Zingheim at the USS Midway Museum, to the Library of Congress, to Assistant Professor Heather Wade, MA, CA, at Emporia State University, The Fleet Air Arm Museum of the Royal Australian Navy and, as ever, to the National Archives.

Making contact with veterans was made possible by, in particular, the Fleet Air Arm Officers' Association, the Australian Fleet Air Arm Officers' Association, the New Zealand Fleet Air Arm Officers' Association, The Association of Naval Aviation, the numerous aircraft carrier associations that keep alive the memory of ships and people, and www.navybuddies.com. Contributors also put me in touch with their friends, and so the links were built.

Without the official support of several navies, it would have been impossible to include serving personnel. Commander Rich King, Lieutenant Commanders Adam Jones, Gavin Simmonite, DFC, and Paula Howe (Royal Navy); Lieutenant Sean P. Riordan at NAVINFO East, Sonja Hansen, and Lieutenant Commander Jim Krohne (US Navy); Contramiraglio Paolo Treu (COMFORAER) and Capitano di Corvetta Giovanni Esposito (Marina Militare); Contre-Amiral Olivier de Rostolan and Enseigne de Vaisseau Pascal Subtil (Marine Française) were all very helpful.

The assistance of the following also deserves my gratitude: Jim Verdolini, Commodore Rajan Vir, Bob Potochniak, Dr Enrico Cernuschi, Vince O'Hara, Dan

Rivers, Ken Walling, Alec Braybrooke, Peter Roalf, Bill Entwistle, David Allison, James Cummings, Captain Hiroyuki Terada, Zip Rausa, Peter Roalf, Robert Burchill, Vince Fazio, Rowland White, Terence Hetherington and Fred Lane. Among my contributors, let me single out Commander Jason Phillips, RN, for checking my translations of Italian 'pinger' jargon.

Thank you to the publishers who licensed or generously gave permission for quotations. Full details of all the published sources can be found in the Bibliography.

All authors appreciate enthusiastic and patient editors, and I am as fortunate in John Lee and Alison Moss at Conway as I am in the unwavering support of my husband George, the IT skills of our son, Adrian, and the hospitality of my London friends Judy, Peter and Sarah Greenwood. I'm also lucky to have Tony and David at DAG as the design team because they are both great naval enthusiasts.

The foreword has been kindly written by Rear Admiral Simon Charlier, RN, Chief of Staff Carrier Strike and Aviation and Rear Admiral Fleet Air Arm, at a critical period for the Royal Navy as it seeks to upgrade its aircraft carriers during the world financial crisis and the debate over the Royal Navy's future role. Conway and I are very much indebted to him for his support.

Lastly, I want to acknowledge a very special debt, to Commander David 'Shorty' Hamilton who, as well as providing some valuable memories, became my unofficial 'technical editor'. David's service in the Fleet Air Arm took place at a time of great change, and he had personal experience of those changes. His amendments, suggestions, enthusiasm and support have been, quite simply, invaluable.

A note on sources:

Sources beginning with ADM or AIR can be found in the National Archives, Kew, Surrey, England.

Joyner Library refers refers to Special Collections Department, J. Y. Joyner Library, East Carolina University, Greenville, North Carolina, USA.

IWM stands for Imperial War Museum, London.

Part One

SHIPS,
BUT NOT AS WE KNOW THEM

1
Permission to Come Aboard

Commander Bonham de Laune Faunce, HMS *Vindictive*, 1918
from the private papers of B. de Laune Faunce, IWM Reference 3181 87/3/1

I had only been in the *Neptune* about six months when I was appointed to the *Vindictive*, shortly due to commission at Harland [and] Wolff's at Belfast. From Rosyth it was a day and night journey via Stranraer and Larne and I was weary when a taxi deposited to me at a gate of the yard and the driver pointed out the ship lying just inside. Instead of the *Effingham* Class cruiser that I'd expected to see, she was a most peculiar sight in her dazzle paint. Above the upper deck level about all that was left of the cruiser design were the bridge and funnels and foremast, two 7½ inch guns amidships and one on the quarterdeck. Forward of the bridge was a high solid barn. Abaft the funnels, a flat deck covered the ship at the same height as far aft as the after gun. It dawned on me that she was an aircraft carrier. I reported to the Commander who told me to find my way round the ship and that commissioning was delayed by the flu epidemic …

Lieutenant Joe Frosio, USS *Langley*
from *Navy Times*, 14 January 1985

Joe Frosio enlisted in 1917, qualified as a pilot in 1923, and three years later faced his first carrier landing on *Langley*:

That was quite an experience. Here I was, way up in the sky looking down at something that resembled a matchbox, thinking 'I must be crazy, I'm turning back'. Well, it was funny how the whole situation turned out. The pilot in front of me was the boss man. He was in charge of the rest of us and he was consoling me, telling me not to worry about it. As it turned out, he beached his plane and I landed onboard like it was duck soup, though I was scared as hell. He was so upset that he said, 'Damn you, Frosio, you think you're so good, you go up there and land a dozen more times.' Well, he was the boss and that's what I had to do. When they sent us out on a mission, it was 'good luck, guys, see you around'. We didn't have radar or any of that fancy stuff. If you came back, fine. If you didn't … oh well.

Edward Wilson Whitley, Air Fitter, HMS *Illustrious*, 1940
IWM Sound Archive Reference 28496

Rails for hammocks, banks of lockers for your kit, long tables out from the ship's side, with forms to sit on, and a rack on the ship's side for the knives and forks and spoons and things. You went up to the galley and carted down the food and shared it out. We were all together with the air mechanics and the fabric bashers and the parachute packers … The petty officers and sergeants had a separate mess, obviously. They [the seamen] used to pull our legs. One of the problems we had [was that] we didn't work watches: we seemed to be working all the time, and we couldn't wash our overalls and get them nice and pretty and pale blue like the sailors', and they used to pull our legs for that. But they worked a completely different system, the watch-keeping system.

CPO Richard Griffin RN, 815 Squadron, HMS *Illustrious*
www.maritimequest.com

We had joined the ship on the 7th June 1940 and she sailed that night. We straight away ran into some very heavy Atlantic weather, so much so that the forward bulkheads were staved in and had to be shored up. The ship had a flared bow, making her liable to this in heavy seas. At Worthy Down, the ex R.N. lads were always ribbing me. 'Wait until you get to sea, you'll spew your ring up – ha – ha.'

As soon as the aircraft had flown on board we started to fly anti-submarine patrols. This entailed loading the A/C with 100lb A.S. bombs. Normally two of us lifted these onto the bomb racks, but Gissing, Bonner and McCauley were all comatose – seasick – leaving new entry Dick to do the loading. I was seasick too; felt bloody awful in fact, but not as bad as they were, although I was always seasick every trip.

After a few days we were all recovered; it was quite an experience for the first time being borne on those huge Atlantic rollers. We eventually arrived in the Bermudas, mostly to do on and off flying exercises.

One day it was decided that there was enough wind to operate the aircraft whilst anchored in harbour. Fine – then the wind dropped. All the Swordfish managed to land back on OK, but of the Fairey Fulmars [fighters], one tore out its arrester hook and went over the side, one crash landed on the golf course, and one went somewhere else, but where I can't recall. It was all quite relaxed. The sun was warm, we were wearing our tropical whites, there were a couple of runs ashore in Hamilton, and the war seemed a long way off. Captain Boyd cleared the lower deck and gave a little pep talk in which he expressed the view that he was looking forward to seeing bombs bounce off our 4 inch armoured deck. A bit prophetic that. Only they didn't bounce.

Ken Morris, Sick Berth Attendant, HMS *Illustrious*
from the private papers of K. Morris, IWM Reference 03/14/1

Calling up papers arrived from the Royal Navy; I was to report as a would-be coder … at HMS *Glendower* on the 29th June 1942.

HMS *Glendower* turned out not to be a ship but Billy Butlin's Holiday Camp at Pwllheli, North Wales. Here we were turned from civilians of many different occupations and characters into embryo sailors.

We were kitted out, inoculated, vaccinated and made to jump into tanks of cold water (to test our life belts). We were taught the very basics elements of seamanship, how to salute, to string and lash a hammock, march up and down with rifles, present arms and, in general, given the run-around.

As I had worked in a bank before joining up, I hoped to become a Writer or Pay Clerk in the Navy ... but the Royal Navy was having none of that and, as I wasn't even shown on their records as a Coder either, I was told to 'get in with them Probationer Sick Berth Attendants'!

I had no medical experience whatsoever, but being a quiet lad, and as everybody seemed to be senior to me, I did as I was told and 'got in with them Probationers ...'!

Six weeks later the PSBAs found themselves taken to the local RN Hospital at Stonehouse, Plymouth (HMS *Drake*):

One of the first orders was to have the hob-nails removed from our boots so as not to damage the highly polished wooded floors of the wards (pedantically called 'decks'). From then on we had six months of lectures and duties on the wards: we were instructed in bed making (Sister Tutor had a thing about neat envelope corners) general nursing, anatomy (how the body is built on a skeleton – 206 bones in all), physiology – how it all works, skin diseases (a horrible two weeks on the skin ward), lice, scabies, venereal disease (all of which I was to meet aplenty, later on) and so on.

Morris was posted to *Illustrious* at the Gladstone dock in Liverpool.

The sight of her, still in dry dock, blotches of red lead paint here and there, cables and pipes all over the place, the clatter of riveting and general noise, did nothing to lift our spirits on that grey November day. *She* wasn't the fighting ship of Taranto, Malta and the Mediterranean convoys; this was a tired old hulk, subjected to the indignities of the dockyard workers swarming over her.

Lieutenant John P. Sanderson, Torpedo Bomber Pilot, VC-10, USS *Gambier Bay*
USS *Gambier Bay* Association

Shortly after writing the following poem, Sanderson and his crew were killed during a catapult launch on 26 July 1944 off Saipan.

Carrier Life

'Carrier life is something' we've all heard people say,
'If you've missed this grand experience, get your transfer in today.'
But when it comes to flying, you can put me on the shore.
For life on a CVE is something worse than war!

They get you up at three o'clock with a whistle and a bell,
And you stand by in the ready-room just sleepier 'n hell.

Word is passed to man the planes, and you race out on the double.
Then word is passed to go below, there is no end to trouble.

You'll be sitting in the cockpit when Borries says 'fly off!'
You jam the throttle forward, and the engine starts to cough.
You go rolling down the deck, but you always feel the need,
Of just one extra knot to keep above stalling speed.

Or you're up on ASP, or combat air patrol.
Your gas is almost gone, and your belly's just a hole.
You'd like to eat, you and your plane have both been cruising lean,
But airplot says to orbit, there's a bogey on the screen.

Sometimes we're told to scramble, and you go charging to your plane,
But you sit there twenty minutes while the shrapnel falls like rain.
When the enemy is gone, the Admiral says 'Let's go!'
So you retire with your gear to the ready room below.

They put you on the catapult, and secure you in the gear,
Pilgrim sticks his finger up, and looks up with a leer.
You're drawing forty inches when Charlie points 'away!'
And you hope to hell you've power to get in the air and stay.

It's when you're landing back aboard that you find it really rough
You're high, you're fast, you're low – Christ Mac!! that's slow enough!
You're out, you're in your gear, and now Krida signals things
Like 'Hook Up, Hold your brakes! Spill your flaps, Now fold your wings!'

YES Carrier life is something, dangerous and hard.
Your wings will all turn green, and your ass will turn to lard.
Oh take us back to 'Dago', and give us stateside duty,
Where once a month we fly four hours, or maybe strop a beauty!!

Frank Skull, L.M.(E), HMS *Indomitable*
Communication with the Editor

I can still remember the day I first saw her, which was from the back of a R.N. lorry which was taking a draft of stokers to join her on 15th May 1950. I think that every man among us would have picked up his hammock, kitbag and case and walked back to the barracks if we had been given the choice. What we saw was a rusty hulk in a dry dock, with hoses and electric cables snaking all over her and being dragged by dockies who were either arc welding, riveting or hammering. Everywhere the flashes of the arc welders were visible through the pall of smoke hanging over the ship! Was this to be our home for the foreseeable future?

Making our way on board, we were directed to 133 mess, which conjured up an impression in our minds of a nice enclosed area, but making our way down the accommodation stairs we were quickly disillusioned when a mess-deck table with two benches was pointed out as our living space, one of about ten occupied by the Engine Room department. The only suggestion of any privacy were rows of lockers about five foot high around each table. I was later to find that with about sixteen men in each mess we were unable to all sit at the table together; the system relied entirely on men being absent on watch or ashore! The next morning we were awakened at six a.m. by a bugle being played over the Tannoy; had we really left the Royal Naval Barracks? After an excellent breakfast, I, together with several more, were ordered to report to the starboard boiler-room. I was about to start on ten months of the hardest, dirtiest work I have ever done!

There were two Admiralty Pattern three drum boilers in each boiler-room; the top drum stood about twelve foot high and was connected to the other two by hundreds of water tubes in the shape of a ridge tent; in the triangle in the middle were nine sprayers, which sprayed Furnace Fuel Oil when the boiler was fired up. In the meantime, our job was to squeeze into the top drum through a small oval aperture and, once inside, clean the water tubes with a rotating wire brush on a flexible drive. As we completed the first boiler-room, we did the Centre and Port boilers in succession. We next had to clean the uptakes from the boilers into the funnel and, later, the double casing which surrounded the funnel. Few people realise that there are a series of compartments six feet wide, with linking ladders, that run from bottom to top of the outside of the funnel, which act as an airspace; it was while working in these that we found that the dockies had installed a mess-deck table and two benches during the four years the *Indomitable* had stood in the dockyard after returning from war service. Judging by the depth of cigarette ends underneath, they had spent many happy hours idling their time away playing cards. Little wonder that, with the completion date of the refit drawing ever closer, it was becoming obvious that there was no chance of it being achieved. A high level meeting was held between the Admiralty and the Dockyard, at which it was decided that the dockies would work round the clock to complete on time. No one, of course, appeared to care too much that there was a couple of hundred of us living on board, and our lives would be made intolerable. From the first night, war was declared, with equipment being sabotaged and threats of G.B.H. to the user every time a dockie was unwise enough to decide it was safe to start making a noise. Soon letters were being sent to M.P.s, and when this appeared to produce no results, the national press was contacted, and when reporters started snooping around, suddenly the powers that be started to take notice and the night work was suspended; throughout all this the Officers were aware of the conditions on board and couldn't care less, as long as they lived ashore and slept peacefully in their beds at night, an attitude which I found typical of all Naval Officers throughout my nearly eight years service!

Joe Policastro, USS *Coral Sea* (CV-43)
www.usscoralsea.net

We had a little free time so I decided I would do some exploring. I descended the ladder that led to the hangar deck. I was so taken by the sight of it I started walking forward. I was so proud and happy I started whistling; it was then I heard 'Hey boot stand fast' as a chief master of arms came up to me. He said 'Square that rig' – in other words, square your hat and button up that shirt. I said 'Yes, sir'; he came right back with: 'The correct reply is aye aye, and do not call me sir; this is not boot camp – call me chief. By the way there are only two people who whistle in the navy: one is a boatswain's mate and the other is a damn fool and I know you are not a boatswain's mate. Carry on and be more aware of proper navy regs.' That was my welcome aboard and to ship's company.

James Stephens, USS *Essex*, Korea, 1952–3
Communication with the Editor

I would be awakened about 2:30 a.m. I would dress and go to the mess hall for breakfast of steak and eggs. Then I would dress in my flight suit/gear and go to the Ready Room for flight briefing by Intelligence personnel. We would receive the word to man the planes about 3:30 and would launch prior to 4 a.m. It would take about 45 minutes to climb to altitude and fly to the combat zone. We would stay in the area searching for targets of opportunity for two or more hours, depending on fuel conditions and weather. If we had not expended all ordnance prior to then, we would find a likely target such as rail lines or bridges to drop the remainder of our bombs on. Then we would proceed to the Task Force at sea and wait for the clear deck signal, and then land on the carrier. We would then go directly to debrief the mission in the Ready Room.

Bill Flink, USN ABAN, V1-F, USS *Coral Sea* (CV-43)
www.usscoralsea.net

As close as I can determine I reported to the *Coral Sea* in April 1952 from Natcenter N.A.S Jax. When I got my orders to the Coral Sea I looked on the map to find out where the Coral Sea was. Then I looked at my orders and they said to report to pier 7 N.O.B. Norfolk, Va. It was only then I began to understand *Coral Sea* was a ship. Ooooh my! I was an 18 year old raised in the little farm town of Bloomington, Illinois. The biggest floating thing I ever saw was a row boat in Miller Park.

Captain Pran Parashar, Indian Navy, INS *Vikrant*
Communication with the Editor

During 1948, I was ADC to the late Admiral of the Fleet Earl Mountbatten of Burma when he was the Governor General of India. One day he called me and said, 'Pran, I have just had Pandit ji (the Prime Minister of India) agree that the

Indian Navy should acquire an aircraft carrier. You should volunteer for flying.' Aye, aye, Sir. Hence I was amongst the initial lot of ten officers selected for training as Pilot in the UK ...

I was not Qualified in Deck landing. I had cleared it with Adm. Kirke that I would qualify in Deck landing at the first opportunity if I was to function as a Cdr (Air) of the carrier ...

I qualified in Deck Landing in 1962 at the age of 37 years in an Alizé aircraft, both Day and Night flying ... I wonder how many other aviators qualified in Deck Landing at that age. I used to fly almost every day from the deck. So much so that, at a Flight Safety Meeting with the Director of Medical Services (Navy), the Pilots complained that even on a Tuesday when I observe 24 hours fast, I fly. He however assured them that I have chocolate and keep my blood sugar level!! My counterparts in RN carriers used to feel envious of me!

Command Master Chief Kathleen A. Hansen, USS *Ronald Reagan*, 2004
Communication with the Editor

I was the Command Master Chief (CMC) of the Navy's newest aircraft carrier USS *Ronald Reagan* from March 2004 to December 2005. The *Ronald Reagan* is the largest warship in the world. It's the ninth of the *Nimitz* class aircraft carriers to be built, commissioned in July 2003. Five galleys, you might call restaurants, laundry services, medical and dental facilities, and a post office. She displaces 95,000 tons of water and has 17 decks and a flight deck that stretches 4.5 acres. Fully loaded her crew is 5,000, a floating city.

The *Kitty Hawk* was a steam turbine ship and the *Ronald Reagan* was nuclear powered (which is just a fancy way of boiling water and making steam). Besides the fact that the *Ronald Reagan* was newer than the *Kitty Hawk*, the biggest difference was working with nuclear trained personnel. They're interesting people because they're so smart.

The crew of the *Tortuga* [a Landing Ship Dock] was eight percent women; the *Pearl Harbor* [another Landing Ship Dock] was 50 percent women. The *Kitty Hawk* was 10 percent women, and the *Ronald Reagan* was between 20 to 25 percent women. After you've been doing this for so long, you don't really notice whether a sailor is male or female. Everybody's in uniform, and there's just no difference. Female sailors don't really wear a lot of make-up or worry about looking pretty; they are there to do a job. They do call me a perfume freak though: I tell them, if I can smell them before they get to me and after they leave me it's too much. There's just no need for it.

Lieutenant Barry 'Skull' W. Hull, VFA-81 Squadron (The Sunliners), USS *Saratoga*
from a letter written to his family in 1991 during the First Gulf War

Our ready room is six floors down, and we use an escalator to carry the pilots and sixty pounds of flight gear to the deck. After a few corners and knee knockers to cross I see the hatch leading outside. A few deep breaths are taken at this point because I'm about to enter another world. It's dark and dangerous and if you're not careful will kill you. That hatch is always pitch dark and seems to suck the light out of my flashlight. There is no reflection of any kind due to the dark black dirty surfaces. It reminds me of walking into a haunted house at an amusement park. What's in there? Once outside the hatch, which leads to the catwalk, if there is a moon I'll see the reflection off the water. If no moon then just lots of darkness and noise. The catwalk is one small flight of steps below the flight deck and very carefully a check is made above the rail to look for the tailpipe of a turning jet or if jets are recovering. There are fueling hoses and extra catapult wires and chocks and chains and yellow gear waiting to grab you if you're not deliberate and alert. The yellow sodium vapor lights cast an eerie glow to the men and aircraft. Looking into the lights only outlines are seen. Many times you can't tell if someone is facing you or turned away. Looking away from the lights it's reflections off goggles and more darkness. Outlines and shadows and smoky rays of light and noise and wind and steam and power and teamwork make up this strange world.

There are several hundred men topside and I search one out with a Sunliner patch so he can tell me where my jet is parked. He knows what I want and just points without my asking. Of course it's the other end of the flight deck so I start the walk. The wind is blowing twenty to thirty knots and everyone has a certain lean to them. Your flashlight gives you a small tunnel vision to see clearly and all the rest is noise and shadows. No faces, just helmets and goggles. I've gone through an entire night launch and not known who my plane captain was. It's too dark to see and too loud to talk. We know the procedures and communication is done by signals with the flashlights. Taxi directors have yellow wands, plane captains are blue and ordnance men use red ones. There is a Tomcat starting to turn up and the huffer drives by blasting my legs with hot air. That's nice on those cold days. It's a high pitch squeal that goes by on the edge of your vision. A few more steps and I begin to hear the helo blades pounding the air. The SAR guys are on deck for a pilot switch and some gas. Next out of nowhere a blue flashlight is stuck in my face and a hand stops me. The young kid points and screams so I can hear, 'Excuse me sir, but this Tom is turning, you'll have to go around'. He just saved me from walking through the exhaust blast. A nice gesture since it would have blown me over the side. But I don't even thank him. I just nod the nod and go around. He knows I appreciate it and also it's his job. One guy on each side to watch for unsuspecting jet blast victims, like me. Soon that commotion fades along with the noise of the helo and I come across another flurry of activity in the darkness. A jet is being taken to the hangar via the elevator. Twenty men standing around, all required for this operation. To avoid hitting something the eyes move constantly from the feet to head level. Tie down chains are everywhere and after tripping over one you learn quickly. Now the landing area has been cleared and fifty feet to my left a Hornet slams into the deck and startles me. Or maybe he bolters and gives everyone a light show as his hook drags down the landing area at 150 kts spewing sparks and lighting up the night, especially if he scared himself and tapped a little afterburner for mom and the kids. Now that's a real light show! Of course I try to act cool like I knew it was going to happen and it didn't scare me. Take a few deep breaths.

Ordnance men are all over loading and unloading and pushing carts around with the bombs of war. You wonder why all these men are needed up here. They are everywhere, little shadows and flashlights scurrying around in the darkness and noise. Yet everyone is essential. They all have a job and are busy. Heads are on a swivel, constantly checking six for that unseen rear collision. No one just 'hangs out' on the flight deck during launch. It's not allowed, and stupid. The steam from the cats blows by. Sometimes it completely envelopes you and vision is reduced to zero. But the wait is not long with the wind. It blows by and with glimpses of your path you make your way, carefully. Finally, after all this, and it is good for the frame of mind needed for a night hop, I shine my light onto the correct jet (the side number is what I'm looking for) and there stands my plane captain at attention ready to get to work launching this jet. He gives me a salute and it is returned with pride and usually without a word we start. If we're lucky and no jets are turning close by and we have time we'll talk about the launch and the mission and how nice it would be to go home and of course putting a bullet between Saddam's eyes. The plane captains and maintenance troops know we are compartmentalizing and most of them sense if you are in the mood to talk. Depends on the hop as to whether I can afford to relax enough to chat. Mostly now we can because we're getting good at this Red Sea stuff. Usually just prior to cranking the jets it calms down a little. It's been a while since the last launch and most of the turnaround maintenance is complete and things quiet a little. Then one half hour before launch the air boss comes over the loudspeaker and gives his spiel about getting ready. 'Gentlemen, it's time to get into the proper flight deck uniform, sleeves rolled down, helmets on and buckled, goggles pulled down, life vests on and securely fastened, let's check around the go birds for FOD, whenever you're ready gentlemen, let's crank 'em up, crank the go birds.' It gives me goose bumps to hear that. At this point if my wingman is close I'll give him a nod as we each climb into our jets. Behind me up the ladder comes the plane captain to help with the strap in. Usually a word or two, mostly he will tell me to have a safe flight. I'll thank him and then he's gone, down underneath doing plane captain things. I do my interior inspection, which is a pain due to the darkness, and hook on my faithful kneeboard. All systems checked and about that time the plane captain appears outside ready for my start signal. Usually he is toward the lights of the tower and from my perch of the cockpit all I see is the outline of a nineteen year old and the glow of his blue wands. Everyone starts at the same time and it reminds me of the Indy 500. The feel of power when all these engines come on line is tremendous. The canopy comes down with a thud and the sound of a fine piece of machinery and then slides forward and locks into place. Things quiet down tenfold and the focus begins to shift a little toward the mission, and away from the darkness and noise, and the nervousness starts to take a back seat. Canopy down gives an invincible, cozy feel. It takes about fifteen minutes for the checks to be completed and finally I give the thumbs up.

During this time my eyes are getting adjusted to the light and the initial shock of the darkness begins to ease. The chocks and chains are removed, nose wheel steering engaged, and I arm my seat. Oxygen masks are required when taxiing on the boat so that's strapped in place. Now the nervous task of the night taxi. Taxi directors (yellow shirts) are not allowed to walk when they taxi you at night. It gives us vertigo and we lose the ability to know if we're moving, or if it's him. I saw a yellow shirt walk on a pilot one night and after the guy shut down he chased that yellow shirt down and I thought he was going to kill him. Sometimes I simply can't tell how fast I'm going so I quickly glance back and forth between the yellow shirt and the side of my aircraft. It seems if you look to your side you detect the sensation of movement easier than out the front. But every so often they will taxi someone around you and you don't know he's coming. For a brief instant you experience total sheer terror because you think your brakes have failed and you are moving, not the other aircraft. Quickly you realize you're stationary and then of course you look around to make sure no one realizes just how scared you are. Hey, that would be uncool, wouldn't it? But nobody can see you anyway in the darkness.

You make your way to the catapult trying to do the takeoff checks and roger the weight board and spread your wings and make sure they're locked, etc. The yellow shirt stands on the cat and due to the steam we regularly have to stop and wait for it to clear. If you can't see him you can't follow his directions. Sometimes you can't see him but you can see his wands through the steamy mist lighting up the dark night, just like in the movies. One last big turn and we're in place. Ten men or so are underneath the jet doing final checks and hooking up the launch bar. The taxi signals now are very precise and small and accurate. We develop a cadence and rhythm with these guys and soon work well together. He turns you over to the ordies. Heart rate picks up. They arm your weapons and then pass you back. All stations check go. Heart is pretty fast now. Yellow shirt checks with the cat officer. He says go for it and the run up signal is given. Heart beats even faster. I release the brakes (the hold back keeps me still) and add full power. One last wipe of the controls and engine check. Everything ok so I lean my head back and with the flick of my thumb, turn on the lights, the night salute. Heart is screaming. Out of the corner of my eye I see the green wand and outline of the cat officer as he touches the deck, signaling launch. Time stands very still now. About five seconds later the jet lurches forward and within less than two seconds I'm doing well over 200 mph and pinned to the seat. It takes a few seconds for my eyeballs to uncage so I can read the instruments to make sure I'm climbing. You better believe most of us tap afterburner. Does it use up a little extra gas? Sure it does, so what? It's back to that Mom and the kids thing. It's a big black hole we've just entered and your life depends on flying the instruments. This is the night cat shot and guess what? The hop just began!

2
Back to the Beginning

The twentieth century dawned with the power and prestige of the world's great navies firmly invested in their ironclad battleships and heavy cruisers – metal leviathans with massive guns that dwarfed the firepower of their wooden-walled, muzzle-loading ancestors. Then in 1903 the Wright Brothers made the first flight in a heavier-than-air machine, and forty years later the battleship was all but obsolete, its place triumphantly usurped by the aircraft carrier.

An appreciation of the advantages of naval air power did not come out of the blue. As the old adage says, what can be seen can be destroyed, and for centuries the humble lookout in the crow's nest had given his ship or his fleet an advantage if he spotted the enemy before it discerned his masts on the horizon. In 1805, two years after then Rear Admiral Charles Knowles unsuccessfully proposed the use of a balloon for reconnaissance over Brest, a sniper in the rigging picked off Admiral Nelson, and Cochrane apparently used kites to drop propaganda leaflets over the French coast in 1806. The Austro-Hungarian Navy's *Volcano* can be credited with the first sea-borne aerial attack, when pilotless balloons were launched on a bombing mission against Venice in 1849 – the raid failed because the winds were unfavourable. Towed balloons and kites proved useful for tasks such as reconnaissance and mine spotting, and the Germans developed the dirigible Zeppelin, but once the Wright Brothers' feat proved to be no false dawn, naval planners began work to make ship-borne aircraft a reality. The leaders in the field were France, Britain and the USA, and as early as 1909, Clément Ader, the father of French aviation, described the ideal vessel to carry aircraft: 'These ships will be constructed to designs that are very different to those currently in use. First of all, the deck will be free of obstructions, flat, as large as possible without compromising the sailing qualities of the hull; it will look like a landing strip. The speed of the ship must be at least equal to that of the cruisers, and even greater.' Ader saw the need for a hangar accessed by lifts that were capable of handling an aircraft with its wings folded and also for space for the technicians who would carry out repairs and keep the planes ready for take-off at all times. In 1911, even before the formation of the Service Aéronautique, the French Navy had ordered the conversion, completed the following year, of the minelayer *Foudre*. The British followed with the conversion of the light cruiser HMS *Hermes*, commissioned in 1913, and in 1914 the construction* of HMS *Ark Royal*, the Royal Navy's first purpose-built seaplane carrier.

* The Navy took over the hull of a merchant ship already under construction, but the amount of changes made entitle *Ark Royal* to be called the first purpose-built carrier.

What of the men who would fly off, and eventually, on to, this new type of ship? Aviation was still in its infancy, but opportunities to learn were increasing, and in 1909 the Aero Club of Great Britain found a home at Eastchurch on the Isle of Sheppey. It was here that many of the early British naval aviators would first learn their trade, the first four officers being sent for training in 1911, a year before the formation of the Royal Flying Corps. Popularly thought of as the forerunner of the Royal Air Force alone, it initially comprised a Naval Wing and a Military Wing, plus the Central Flying School, whose task was to train the aircrew for both wings. The Naval Wing soon became independent as the Royal Naval Air Service (RNAS) and trained its own pilots.

The USA waited until 1916 before establishing its Naval Flying Corps, but some ambitious young pilots volunteered to serve with the French and British navies when World War I broke out. The US Navy had already claimed a 'first' when in 1910 a civilian pilot, Eugene Ely, actually took off from a ship. USS *Birmingham* was fitted with a wooden platform over the forecastle, and Ely flew a Curtiss pusher safely to shore. Less than two months later he proved that landing on was possible when, again in a Curtiss pusher, he successfully landed on a platform erected on the quarterdeck of the armoured cruiser USS *Pennsylvania*. Asked later in the year how long he intended to keep flying, he responded: 'Oh, I'll do like the rest of them: keep it up until I am killed.' Two weeks later, on 19 November 1911, aged 25, he became the 101st pilot to die in an air crash (though not in the cause of furthering naval aviation).

Across the Atlantic in that same year, Lieutenant Charles Samson, RN, later an RAF air commodore, was one of four Royal Navy officers given the opportunity to learn to fly. Whereas Ely had made his historic take-off from something recognisably like a flight deck, Samson made the Royal Navy's first take-off using a downward sloping track erected over the predreadnought battleship HMS *Africa*'s forward turret. He secured his place in aviation history on 2 May 1912 when he made the first take-off from a ship under way rather than anchored, HMS *Hibernia*.

New York Times, **15 November 1910**:
NORFOLK, VA. Nov. 14 – Eugene Ely, the aviator, launched his airship this afternoon from the bows of the scout cruiser *Birmingham* in the face of weather conditions little short of prohibitory, in an attempt to prove the practicability of a successful flight from ship to shore. Ely, after clearing the cruiser, lost his way in the heavy fog over the bay. The moment he discovered himself over land he effected a landing within a few miles of the Hampton Roads Yacht Club house on Willoughby Spit and about 5 miles from the point of departure. The *Birmingham*, accompanied by the torpedo boat destroyers *Roe* and *Terry*, left the navy yard at 11:30 this morning, and proceeded out into the bay. A strong wind was driving the rain in sheets when they reached the Roads, and turned to sleet. Anchoring off Fort Monroe, the vessels waited for better weather conditions. At 3:30 the sleet turned to rain, driven by a 12-mile breeze.

Ely suggested that the experiment be made, despite the rain, and at 3:32 his bi-plane rushed along the runway, and the test began. But he failed to elevate his planes properly as the bi-plane left the runway, and the rudder and propellers struck the water some yards from of the ship. There was a heavy splash and Ely was drenched. Although blinded by the water and the rain, the aviator, nevertheless, rapidly swung his machine into the air.

It was soon seen by the observers on the decks of the many crafts dotting the bay that Ely was handicapped by the driving rain and foggy conditions and he had lost his bearings. At first he headed directly out to sea. He approached the beach swerving, almost in the opposite direction from the navy yard, and quickly landed on the sands. The destroyer *Roe* was off the beach and sent a boat to him. Ely found that a blade of his propeller had been bent by the collision with the water. The impact with which his machine struck the water after its thirty-seven foot drop from the front of the cruiser caught the blade as though a heavy coarse saw had scraped its edge, and a small piece was split from the blade. But not for an instant was the speed of the aeroplane lessened, and it darted away with express train rapidity on its flight. Ely did not wait for the *Birmingham* to get into motion, which would have added to his momentum, and thus have aided him greatly, but, seizing an opportune moment between showers, he was off before those on the ship with him and on other vessels nearby, to follow him in case of need, were aware that he was ready for his flight.

The aviator said he landed because he was unable to judge his direction in the rain, which beat into his face the moment he headed toward the navy yard, and was uncertain as to the extent of the damage to his propeller. He admitted that his failure to elevate his forward plane properly in leaving the runway caused him to strike the water. A dense fog obscured everything …

Captain Washington I. Chambers, detailed by the Navy Department as Chairman of a board for aeronautical navigation, declared that the flight was more than he had anticipated, and he is confident that the time is near when all scout cruisers will be equipped with a number of aeroplanes. They would not be for battleship use, he explained, but for scout duty in connection with the work of the scout cruisers of the navy.

'When Ely flew with such ease from a standing ship,' he said, 'it showed beyond doubt that his task would have been much simpler if the *Birmingham* had been moving.'

New York Times, 19 January 1911:

SAN FRANCISCO, Cal., Jan. 18. – Eugene B. Ely today flew thirteen miles in an aeroplane, made a successful landing on the cruiser *Pennsylvania*, and an hour later rose from the cruiser and flew back to Selfridge Field, twelve miles south of San Francisco. The feat was accomplished without mishap. Not a wire or bolt of the bi-plane was injured. 'It was easy enough,' said Ely as he stepped from his seat after his return and was seized by the cheering soldiers of the Thirtieth Infantry and hoisted on their shoulders. 'I think the trick could be successfully turned nine times out of ten.'

Ely's flight had been postponed from day to day, but he decided today that atmospheric conditions were favorable. The air was hazy. It was 10:45 o'clock when he left the aviation grounds. His motor worked perfectly, and after a few circles, he headed north east, swept over the San Bruno hills and disappeared toward San Francisco. In the meantime the wireless advised the cruiser at anchor with the fleet in the bay that he would make the attempt, and final preparations were made for his reception. A wooden platform 130 feet long and fifty feet wide had been constructed over the after deck of the ship. It sloped gently aft, and across the floor were stretched ropes, with 100 pound sand bags made fast at either end. These were designed to be caught by hooks on the lower framework of the bi-plane. As a further precaution a canvas barrier was stretched across the forward end of the platform. Launches and ships' boats fully manned were put out, in the event of a mishap. Ely had installed two 7-foot pontoons under his aeroplane to float the machine in case he were forced to descend on the water, and forward he had built a hydroplane to keep the aeroplane from diving into the water.

At 10:58 o'clock the lookout on the cruiser *Pennsylvania* sighted Ely through the haze and the ship's siren roared a blast of welcome. He came on at terrific speed and circled round the fleet, dipping in salute to each ship, and came up in the wind for the stern of the *Pennsylvania*. He was flying low as he neared the ship and touched down [illegible] lightly striking the platform about forty feet from the inner end. The hooks of the aeroplane caught the ropes and stopped the bi-plane within sixty feet.

When Ely touched the deck he was going about 35 miles an hour, but so gradually was the speed checked by the dragging of the weighted ropes as they were caught in succession that he came to a standstill without damaging any part of the machine.

There was a great outburst of cheers and a rush of the officers, visitors and Sailors to greet the aviator. One of the first to reach Ely was his wife, who was on the bridge with Capt. Pond …

Exactly one hour from the time he landed on the cruiser, Ely took his seat in the machine and gave the word to let go. The aeroplane swept down the 130-foot platform at high speed, dropped off the stern with a gentle dip and then rose rapidly over the ships in the the harbor. The start was as perfect as the landing had been.

Rising to a height of 2000 feet, Ely circled over San Francisco and then headed for the aviation field. He landed there at 12:13 o-clock …

'The flight to the ship was made under almost perfect weather conditions', Ely said, 'though I encountered difficulties in approaching the *Pennsylvania*. The wind was on the cruiser's starboard side and to effect a safe landing I saw it would be unwise to alight squarely on the platform. So after circling the ships I came down, quartering the platform and with my planes pressed as fully into the wind as possible. I missed the first ropes stretched to check my momentum, but my grappling hooks caught the other strands and I was brought up gently about sixty feet from where I first touched the boards. Though I did not require the full surface of the 130-foot platform, I do not think a smaller one would be entirely safe for such an experiment. I am convinced, however, that had the ship had been in motion and sailing directly into the wind, my landing on the after deck would have been considerably easier. On my return trip I had no trouble leaving the boat – that is very simple.'

Ely had intended to land while the cruiser was underway, but Capt. Pond of the *Pennsylvania* deemed it unwise to attempt manoeuvres in the harbour.

The Times, 11 January 1912:

Yesterday afternoon in Sheerness Harbour the first aeroplane flight from a British warship was accomplished. The experiment, which was made by Lieut. C. R. Samson, R.N., of H.M.S. *Actaeon*, one of the four officers to have had a special course of instruction at the Royal Aero Club's grounds, Eastchurch, proved a complete success.

A dense fog had enveloped the Isle of Sheppey throughout the morning, but at noon the mist began to disperse and half an hour later Lieutenant Samson left the Eastchurch Aerodrome in a Short biplane and flew to Sheerness, passing over the Medway and alighting on the marshland behind the sea wall of the Cockleshell Hard, on the Isle of Grain shore. A party of bluejackets at once went to his assistance, and hauled the machine across the sea wall and the beach to a coaling lighter which had been moored off Grain in readiness to transport the aeroplane to the battleship *Africa*, from which the flight was to be made. A pinnace belonging to the *Actaeon* took the lighter in tow, and at 1.50 p.m., the bi-plane was brought alongside the *Africa*. With the aid of the derrick it was lifted on board without delay or mishap and placed on a wooden staging, which extended from the forward turret to the bows of the *Africa*, projecting a few feet over the stem of the ship.

Lieutenant Samson having tested the staging to make sure that it would stand the strain of the aeroplane running over it, the forepart of the *Africa*'s deck was speedily cleared as for action, and at 2.20 p.m., half an hour after the machine had been brought alongside, the airman made a most successful ascent. When the engine was set in motion for a preliminary test the biplane was held back by bluejackets, but, everything being found in order, Lieutenant Samson gave the signal to 'let go', and the machine ran down the staging and, passing the bows of the ship, rose steadily to a height of about 100 feet, amid the cheers of the officers and men of the *Africa* and the warships nearby. The biplane was piloted first over the destroyer *Cherwell*, and then making a graceful curve the pilot circled around the battleship at an altitude some yards below her top masts. Lieutenant Samson then rose gradually to a height of 300 feet, and, after flying up the Medway for a short distance, crossed over land again at the West Minster and flew back to the aerodrome at Eastchurch. The bi-plane had been fitted with three floats in case it should be found necessary to descend on the water during the flight.

3
World War I

At the start of World War I, the Royal Navy led the field in the development of naval aviation, but the British and French aircraft carriers that operated for the vast majority of the conflict were just that – ships that could carry aircraft, which at that time were seaplanes. These had to be hoisted out and placed on to the water by cranes and were recovered in the same way after completing their operation. This cumbersome procedure made it impossible for crews to get airborne quickly in the event of an alarm, and take-off was impossible in rough weather. Despite Ely's feat, landing on was still not possible for landplanes, and for as long as all large warships were encumbered with heavy guns and superstructures it would remain so. It was possible for a plane to take off from a small ramp erected over the gun turret of a capital ship, but that meant the whole fleet having to turn out of line into the wind in order for a reconnaissance aircraft to get airborne.

The situation was of particular concern to another of the great pioneers, Lieutenant Frederick Rutland. Exasperated by the Royal Navy's dependence on the seaplane (a term which Churchill had invented as an alternative to the clumsier 'hydro-aeroplane') he tried to convince his masters of the need for ships to be designed or converted for the operation of the faster and more manoeuvrable landplanes such as Sopwith Pups. Such ships required a flush deck 60 feet wide and 600 feet long. As an interim measure, he recommended flying a landplane off a short ramp mounted over the turret of a cruiser or battleship. To the continuing objection that the ship would have to turn out of line and into the wind, he answered – and demonstrated – that simply by turning the gun turret, rather than the whole ship, into the wind, an aeroplane could be flown off without disrupting the formation of the fleet. On completion of the patrol, the pilot would either fly to friendly land, if that were practicable, or ditch close to a destroyer so the pilot and, perhaps, the engine could be picked up. One might cavil at the risk to the aircrew, but unlike a modern fighter the World War I Shorts, Sopwiths, Bristols and Wrights were cheap, expendable contraptions.

Navies being creatures of tradition and vested interests, not everyone was enthusiastically behind the introduction of naval air power, particularly not in the Royal Navy. While Admiral Beatty could envisage the role that it might play, there were others in senior positions who remained unenthusiastic, sceptical, frustrated by the limitations that were painfully obvious, or simply hostile. Many of those who had risen to their high positions via battleship commands, and those who were working their way up from the middle ranks, were still wedded to the idea of 'the big gun', and the concept of carrier warfare was fundamentally different from all previous forms of naval operations. Crews were used to a weapons system that fired inanimate projectiles at the target. Once the trajectory had been set, the speed and movement of the ship accounted for and the firing system put into action, the human element was over. The guns fired and the shells either hit or missed the target. A carrier would fire off human beings, trust to their wit and hope to recover them.

The days of balloon observation were almost over, but not the Royal Navy appointment of 'Observer'. The specialization of Observer Officer was created in 1916 by the Royal Naval Air Service, and in 1917 the first organised 'O' course took place at Eastchurch. It was realized that aircraft could be extremely useful as the 'eyes of the fleet'. The Observer's main task was observe the movements of an enemy and transmit its course, speed and composition. He was also able to spot the fall of shot of the big ship guns, when required, and pass back corrections. Because this was to be the main use of the aeroplane, and because the pilot could well be a rating, the 'O' was designated captain of the aircraft. He was also responsible for navigation.

To boost its seaplane-carrying capacity the Royal Navy requisitioned a number of merchant ships, almost all ferries, for conversion to seaplane carriers: *Riviera*, *Engadine*, *Empress*, *Ben-My-Chree*, *Nairana*, *Manxman*, *Vindex* (ex-*Viking*), *Pegasus*, and the old ex-Cunard liner *Campania*; *Anne* and *Raven II* were German ships seized in 1914. There were even two paddle-steamers: *Brocklesby* and *Killingholme*. France's earliest carrier, *Foudre*, saw limited service during the Dardanelles campaign in 1915.

The contribution of the Allied carriers to the naval war was hardly spectacular, let alone decisive, but it served notice of things to come, pointing the way to Taranto, Matapan, Pearl Harbor and the escort carriers that took on the U-boats during World War II. Those who were part of this fledgling arm knew that, for all the limitations of the hardware at their disposal, they were writing a major chapter, not a footnote, in naval history.

Although the aerial aspect of the 1914–18 naval war was fought for the most part with seaplanes, the Royal Navy's quest for a successful landing on continued. In 1917 the forward 18-inch gun of the light battlecruiser HMS *Furious* was replaced to permit the erection of a 228-foot deck, and on 2 August one of the Royal Navy's star pilots, 25-year-old Squadron Leader Edwin Dunning, performed what was hailed as the first landing on a ship under way. But this was a brave stunt that led nowhere and had a tragic sequel within days – having the aircraft flying at the speed of the carrier, so that the flight deck crew could grab it and pull it down while the engine was cut, proved as impractical as it was dangerous.

Lieutenant Erskine Childers, DSC, RNVR, Observer, HMS *Engadine*
from the diary of Erskine Childers, DSC, RNVR, IWM Reference PP/MCR/C28, © Trinity College Library, Dublin

The first carrier raid came very early in the war, at Christmas 1914, when seaplanes were sent to bomb German Zeppelin sheds at Cuxhaven. Lieutenant Erskine Childers, author of the 1903 thriller *The Riddle of the Sands* and an accomplished yachtsman who knew that area of the North Sea, was serving as an instructor on HMS *Engadine* with Commodore Tyrwhitt's Harwich Fleet but managed to take part in the raid when offered a seat in a Canton-Unne Short flown by Flight Commander Cecil Francis Kilner of HMS *Aurora*. His account demonstrates many of the difficulties faced by those early crews, not least communications – he and his pilot communicated by passing scribbled messages to one another. (There are a few illegible words in the diary, and these are indicated by a dash.)

I began the day badly, waking with a guilty start to hear the quartermaster calling me at – when? 6AM! An hour and a half late. I shall never forget my horror and despair. The quartermaster was abject. He had forgotten to call me before – on this day of days.

'Have they started?' I shouted.

No – just hoisting out.

Through my open door I saw the [sic] all was dark though the shape of a destroyer was clearly outlined. I leapt into my boots, trousers and jacket, tumbled all my gear, already laid out, into my bag, donned helmet, goggles, seized charts and rushed to the Upper Deck. I was in good time really though without any time for breakfast or another visit to my cabin to collect a few forgotten things, my big pad, Thermos etc. I did not dare leave the deck. The dinghy was lowered and I dumped my gear into it and then jumped in myself only to be ordered out again. Another dinghy was to be mine. Soon this was lowered – with two hands in it – with appalling slowness it seemed to me and I ... cast off and turned round. The sea was calm with a heaving swell. It was still dark. *Engadine* towered above my cockle-shell. The dark shapes of *Riviera* and *Empress* could be seen not far away, and of *Arethusa* and some destroyers, and at intervals on the surrounding sea, the dim spidery forms of sea-planes at rest, expanding their wings and preparing for flight. It was very silent and queer. An occasional word of command from *Engadine* that all was well.

The sky —ly clear with — clouds and the yellow dawn just giving its first faint signs. A light air from E. I identified *Empress* and told my men to pull for her hard. Away they went, and soon we saw a sea-plane, evidently one of hers. I hoped to reach it in time but it was further than I had thought in the twilight and we seemed to make no progress (the dinghy is a miserable thing for speed). It occurred to me – 'Supposing the first signal goes and he taxies past and misses me?' On the other hand 'Supposing that there has been a hitch and he waits for me to go to him instead of coming to the *Engadine*?' 'Back to the ship' I ordered, and back they tore, I goading them on with forcible language. I was right. An order was called down. 'Lieut. Childers is to remain astern of *Engadine*.' We waited for a little, I pining for a cup of tea and a cigarette before a 3 hours flight into Germany. Then the first executive signal was made – two black balls at *Engadine*'s masthead – this meant permission to the sea-planes to taxi but not to start. I strained my eyes for Kilner. The hoarse hum of an engine was heard in the direction of *Empress*. 'Row like blazes!' I shouted to my men and out we went to meet the plane. I wanted to hail it but the noise of the engine would drown any words of mine. Suddenly it went — and then stopped. 'Is that you, Kilner' I called. 'Is that you Childers' was his reply. We rowed up to the port-side float and I jumped up on to it saying 'Happy Christmas'. 'Same to you' came back from the pilot's seat. The dinghy rowed away.

The minutes that followed were crowded. Too crowded. I lifted my bag and charts into the pilot's seat and immediately began to discuss arrangements. The main point was his scheme of action and direction for approaching the sheds, whether low and over the land from Cuxhaven or along the coast until opposite the objective, to the general line of the return journey. He wished to skirt the coast if our landfall was Cuxhaven and to return outside the Friesian Islands. The other main point was my function. Having no compass fixed, I could not control steering in any way and he of course was to be in absolute command. But he would rely on me for fixing our position by marks and giving chart courses if need be. At the outset he was going to steer 167° (S by E½), the direct line from Position II, if correct by chart, to the sheds, if situated where we had been told – two important ifs.

Meanwhile I was groping in the dark for places to stow things in, examining the interior of the observer's seat and trying first and foremost to fix the compass. Impossible – no place whatever. All I could do was to place it on the sloping floor between my sea-boots where it was useless! The second most important thing was a place for the chart – none. A wretched little dart-board and a tiny table with no rim upon which nothing at all could be placed with safety. I had to hold the chart, I hung up a pencil by a string, placed my binoculars and pocket compass on top of a bag of tools and left everything else in my linen bag or my pockets ...

The second signal had gone and the 100HP sea-planes had started and now our time came. The second black ball dropped. And off we went, slowly at first to warm the engine, then 'full out'.

Greedy for every moment of preparation, I was busy with little arrangements when 136 began to leap from swell to swell with resounding bumps. One final leap and she was free – 7.10AM. Equilibrium was steady and we began to climb fast above the sea, the engine roaring as I never heard one roar before. A saffron dawn was in the east behind great grey — of cloud and morning mist which was soon below us – my first experience of that unnatural inversion – But the day here was distinctly clear in the sense that there was no haze – only cloud.

I looked for Heligoland, and there sure enough it was in the SW, a grim grey cliff wreathed with clouds but gaining definition as we proceeded. We were rising steadily, 300 ft at 7.34. We appeared, by a rough view of it, to be taking rather too northerly a course, but this, I knew, would matter little and was far better than too easterly a course. Three other sea-planes could be seen flying far below us ahead and astern, like children's toy models with their yellow —wings.

There was little to record at first. I could enjoy the magnificent scene while keeping a sharp lookout for hostile craft and our own sea-planes. We saw one or two trawlers but the first thing of note was a message from Kilner to me calling attention to the fact that one of our seaplanes, probably Hewlett, had alighted and was damaged. Afterwards he told me that he saw the pilot out on a float and that the machine seemed to be sinking. I could not distinguish these points. A moment later we sighted two German torpedo boats steaming from the south towards this disabled sea-plane. (We fear it was Hewlett of the *Riviera* and hope the Germans picked him up alive.)

Next we saw what appeared to be a patrol of four trawlers going north on a wide front. I was now straining my eyes to pick up some marks, the Scharhorn especially which we should have sighted by now 7.45; but nothing was to be seen. On our port hand a vast and baffling mass of cloud and ahead a very black cloud with others around it. But there was little doubt as to our general situation. Southwestward vast expanses of sands were becoming visible, some just covered with water, some already above it but shining with wet. Nothing but sea on the starboard hand. Unless we were making a big eastward error (highly understandable owing to the position of Heligoland), we were clearly flying down into the deep bight west of the Scharhorn and towards the Weser River. This view was strengthened by the appearance on our port hand about 7.45 of a great flotilla of small craft, trawlers apparently, steaming out of the Elbe estuary. Two of the T.B.s passed signals upwards with a strong arc light, evidently recognition signals to discover our nationality.

The next important event was the appearance of a German airship on the port bow – we judge it to have been of the Schuette-Lauz type but are not sure – Kilner immediately rose circling round with a view to attack from above, but she too climbed instantly and more rapidly than we. At 4500 ft Kilner gave it up and we resumed our course.

Then came an interval of suspense. I strained my eyes for marks. We had been flying nearly an hour and wanted a definite lead. I had already passed a message to Kilner to ask him to fly lower as I was afraid the marks would be difficult to see at so great a height. He had complied, throttling down his engine and planing down, but the moment he put her full out again she seemed to soar like a Lark to the old height, an extraordinarily exhilarating sensation for the sense of power and vitality it conveyed.

At last came a clue. 'What beacon?' wrote Kilner on one of the rough chits we conveyed messages on. I looked right ahead and saw clearly silhouetted against gleaming land the slender fretted framework base and, the big lantern above, of the Ober Ever Sand lighthouse ...

I passed back to Kilner 'Ever Sand' (at 8.12 we sighted a Zeppelin air ship to the south-westward going north but did not pursue her) and when we were about a mile N of Meyers Legde Neu Lt house (8.14) he asked for the course, and I gave him E by S, which I calculated would bring us to the northward of the village of Cappel and of the sheds beyond that village – if they were there. It was of course a rough guess from chart, but when ruled out later that day on the big-scale chart, proved correct ...

[I] naturally left to Kilner the length of our stay over the mainland. Indeed I did not know if we might not have to descend on the land as it was, a discouraging prospect as in the intervals between the masses of fog one could see hoar-frost on the ploughed fields, and even an unfrosted field would probably smash the machine to bits.

However, on we steered, groping for a distant view. Presently a little road appeared beneath, then suddenly, the spire of a church, then a village which I took to be Cappel, then the railway. It need scarcely be said that by this time in any ordinary light we should have easily sighted the sheds which were enormous buildings. Indeed we should have sighted them some time before we entered the mainland. Nothing was to be seen. Our limit of vision was half a mile and even this was constantly interrupted by mist. We now circled Wilhelmshafen, too far, however, to distinguish. Beneath us was the fair-way of the Weser, narrowing here to a width of a little over a mile, but broadening steadily to the North, and in another minute we were traversing the vast pike-shaped Hohe Weg Sand, based upon Butjadingen, and tapering northward to a sharp point at Mellum Sand. Hohe Weg lighthouse, on the Eastern edge of the sound soon came sharp and clear into view with the storm and ice signal station beside it which I had so often indicated in my lectures as a sign which differentiates it from all other light-houses. Then the triangular form of the Mellum beacon appeared on the starboard bow and beyond it the big patch of high but desolate sand which is never covered by the tide and showed a bright fawn colour in the morning sun.

We were now between the two great estuaries of the Weser and the Jade and rapidly approaching the latter on our diagonal course. The engine had improved greatly but was now misfiring badly again and we came so low at one time that I thought Kilner was going to descend so passed him our position and warned him of the high Mellum Sand. The crisis passed, however, and up we soared once more.

It was now evident that quite a considerable fraction of the German Fleet was lying in Schillig Roads on our port hand. Many more ships were in the Weser but too far to distinguish very accurately, though we managed to note some cruisers and merchant vessels. Schillig Roads was the chief point of interest and at 7.45 or thereabouts we were leaving the Hohe Weg and passing over the coast. On our port quarter anchored in line ahead were some battleships – seven according to Kilner, five according to me. Right ahead we counted during the next few minutes a large number of vessels – three battlecruisers, a big four-funnelled cruiser, several two funnelled cruisers and a flotilla of 10 destroyers. There was also what appeared to be a big converted liner painted grey, and some merchant vessels. As soon as we were over the first ships – battle-cruisers and cruisers – we turned slightly and took a course roughly along their line. Absorbed in the strange spectacle below me – the ships looking toy models in the Serpentine* – I had not given a thought to hostilities when suddenly, just audible above the boom of the engine, I heard a slight report and saw a puff of brown and dirty white smoke directly in front of the machine.

We were under fire. I looked down to identify our assailant but it was useless. No men were visible on the decks of the ships, no smoke or flashes (though Kilner says he saw the latter occasionally). Still and tranquil in the gentle sun lay the enemy's fleet, remote, detached, as though belonging to another world. And yet most of the — on board must have been fired at us and many guns trained on us. Pop-pop-pop went the bursting shrapnel – it sounded little louder – and the plump round balls of smoke appeared and feathered away in front, behind, above. And yet we had a sense of curious unreality about the bombardment, due perhaps to the absence of noise and the apparent immobility of the assailant. It did not seem remotely possible that any shot would hit us, though some came near enough, and one could take one's notes undisturbed. We were — out of range of the big ships on the eastern side of the Roads and passing over the destroyers which, I think, did not fire. And now we were issuing from the — and striking over for Wangeroog Island to the NW and approaching Minsener Sand. The beacon was clearly visible and the curious isolated wharf by which it stands with its long arms – wharfs or training walls – stretching out to the N and NW respectively, the latter abutting on the Blaue Balje, the channel which separates Minsener Sand from the east point of Wangeroog. It was here that Gordon Shepherd had led me to expect that we should find a submarine depot, but we could see nothing of the sort.

Meanwhile, what about our own bombs? I had supposed that Kilner must have dropped them on the German warships and sent him a message asking him, but the reply was 'no'. He afterwards said that he found himself unable to get the ships into his sights and thought it useless to drop the bombs. He also wished to reserve them for the submarine depot, if discovered ...

At 9 AM we were off Wangeroog and taking our last look to the east and south of it. I particularly noticed three destroyers steaming seaward at high speed, with the view, I surmised, of going out to scout for a squadron in advance of their battle fleet. Whether their battle-fleet and cruisers were preparing for sea or not it was impossible to say. A large number of small vessels were dotted about East of Wangeroog, apparently trawlers and tugs.

We now turned west to follow the line of Friesian islands. Thinking over the matter since, I am sorry that we did not travel right over them or close to either inside or outside in order to get a close view of them, discover any ports there may be and identifying features like beacons and seeing how the villages etc

* The lake in London's Hyde Park.

appear from above. If I had known how much fuel we had left I would have suggested this course to Kilner even as late as 9.15 but we should, I think, have cut across much earlier, passing over the Minsener and between Wangeroog and the mainland.

As it was, the remainder of our journey was beautiful from the standpoint of the picturesque but of no remarkable interest. We were not far from the islands – about three miles but they were strangely obscured in a peculiar effect of light, looking a uniform dark brown, houses ...

All aircrew returned safely or were picked up. Newspapers in London and New York reported the destruction of a Zeppelin, but none of the seaplanes found the sheds, let alone hit them.

Air Commodore Eugene Louis L. Gerrard, Observer
from his unpublished memoir *The Early Days of Flying*, Woodbridge, 1947, Fleet Air Arm Museum

Infamous for the huge loss of life among the Allied infantry who died trying to land on the Gallipoli Peninsula in the spring of 1915, the Dardanelles campaign began as a naval operation in the Mediterranean after Turkey joined the Central Powers. Its aim was to break through the straits to the Black Sea in order to support the Russians, capture Constantinople, force Turkey out of the war and, by opening this second front, break the terrible deadlock on the Western Front. The Dardanelles were defended by minefields and by forts on both sides. If the Anglo-French Fleet were to force the straits, its big guns would have to put those forts out of action, and one task of the seaplanes was 'spotting' the fall of shot. Although Gerrard was shore-based during the event he describes, his comments could have been written by any of his comrades aboard the seaplane carriers that accompanied the fleet.

The Naval side ... found itself with no objective and was allotted various odd-jobs: fighter squadrons in France, anti-Zeppelin work, and all the air work in the Dardanelles. The Dardanelles was a typical Winston Churchill side-show ... Although the campaign was a failure, it was extremely interesting from our point of view. We could see the whole war in five minutes and we dabbled in everything: bombing, reconnaissance, photography, fighting and anti-submarine work. The latter was rather disappointing; I hoped to be able to see a submerged submarine, in the comparatively clear Mediterranean, but it became invisible a few feet down. Perhaps the mud of the Danube still had an influence. At least we kept them under, and perhaps away altogether. No ship was torpedoed in my time.

Our people were being annoyed by a gun which the Turks had very cleverly sited on the Asiatic side of the Straits, near ancient Troy. Our ships' guns had a very low trajectory and could not get at the thing directly, but, cleverly also, retired a few miles along the European side, and so were able to cock their muzzles up enough to get a sharp descent over the high ground in front of the target. I was spotting for the battleship [HMS *Queen Elizabeth*]: the first shot failed to clear the high ground and hit a hill called Achi Baba; I signalled 2000 yards short. The next shot hit exactly the same spot. I repeated my signal, but the next shell was on the same spot. That a battleship miss the target by more than a few yards was unthinkable: that airman must be mad. Hitherto my messages were in code; but now I sent en clair: 'you are hitting the wrong bloody continent'. That was the sort of language the Navy used to understand, the sights were duly adjusted, and soon I was able to report Target Destroyed.

Geoffrey Rylands, Navigating Officer, HMS *Ark Royal*
From the papers of G. K. Rylands, IWM reference 7466

On completion of her acceptance trials on 10 January 1915, *Ark Royal* was sent to the Dardanelles. She arrived at Tenedos on 17 February in time for the main action, which took place on 18 March.

On arrival at Tenedos the seaplanes carried in *Ark Royal* were *Daily Mail* Sopwiths,* Wrights and Shorts. The two latter were fitted with Canton-Unne engines and the Sopwiths with Gnome Mono-Soupape. On the 19th February the bombardment of the outer forts was carried out. The forts did not reply and there seemed little doubt that the guns in all of them were badly damaged. Reconnaissance flights were made by planes 172 and 136. The former flew over Kum Kale and was hit 7 times with rifle bullets. Fortunately neither the pilot nor the observer were wounded.

March 5th.
Today *Ark Royal* was ordered to send a seaplane to spot for *Queen Elizabeth*. She was lying off Gaba Tepe and intended to fire over the land at the Fort at Kilid Bahr. *Daily Mail* Sopwith number 808 was hoisted out and left with Garnett as pilot and Williamson as observer. Conditions were perfect and the plane took off without difficulty. When it had climbed to approximately 3000 ft it suddenly started to spiral downwards. It was impossible to see just what had happened, but clearly the machine was badly damaged. We turned towards the plane and increased to full speed. The machine was fluttering down like a falling leaf, and when about 200 ft from the sea something fell out and fell into the water with a large splash, and then after what seemed an interminable time the seaplane fell into the sea. It seemed certain that both the pilot and observer were killed. *Usk* reached the plane first and lowered two boats. At last we got a signal 'both picked up – both injured, one slightly one seriously'. Soon we had them on board and found that Williamson our First Lieutenant was seriously injured and Garnett was badly shaken and suffering from shock. Later it was found that Williamson had no bones broken but had dislocated his shoulder very badly and was suffering from shock. The doctors said that he very nearly died under anaesthetic. Subsequently Williamson had to be sent to

* These had been civilian planes owned by the *Daily Mail*.

Malta for treatment and under X-ray it was found that his arm had been fractured close under the shoulder joint. However, after treatment he returned to duty. The most probable cause of the accident was that the propeller fractured, flew aft and broke the main spar, but neither Garnett nor Williamson could say positively that this was the case. Immediately we had salvaged the wreckage No. 922 was sent up with Douglas as pilot and Dunning as observer, but just as they were going in over the land Douglas was shot in the leg and had to come back. Kershaw was then sent away in No. 922. He climbed to slightly over 3000 ft and did some good work and so far as he could see several hits on the Forts were obtained. Unfortunately he could not climb high enough to spot efficiently. A very unfortunate day.

March 6th – 10th.

There was some bombardment of Fort No. 8 by various ships. *Ark Royal* was underway in each day sending up seaplanes for reconnaissance flights. During the night minesweepers went up the Straits supported by destroyers and light cruisers. They did excellent work under trying conditions being under fire from rifles and machine guns and 8" guns or howitzers.

March 10th.

Ark Royal left for Xeros [Saroz] Island to carry out reconnaissance of Bulair Lines [Bolayir] from the northern side of Gallipoli peninsula. Air reconnaissance disclosed the existence of a large camp and numerous new earthworks and gun emplacements, but the guns were not then in position. The existing forts which were supposed to have heavy guns in them did not appear to be as formidable as had been reported.

Ark Royal remained in Xeros until the 10th of March 7 p.m. and was then recalled to Tenedos. We were all rather disappointed at having to leave since it seemed that there was useful work to be done in further reconnaissance and spotting for the battleships bombarding the existing forts and destroying the camps. During our absence at Xeros [mine]sweeping had continued under difficult conditions.

March 18th.

Forcing the Narrows by this method was started today. *Ark Royal* was close to Tenedos all day sending up seaplanes so we saw little or nothing from the ship of what was going on. From time to time seaplanes brought back reports that both the ships and the Forts were firing and that both were making good shooting. The last seaplane to go up said that it did not appear much damage had been done to the guns in the Forts. This report was accepted with reserve. The bombardment proceeded for about 3 hours after this report, and at the end there was no doubt that considerable damage had been done. At the end of the day we met with disaster. Both the *Ocean* and *Irresistible* struck mines and sank. One or another of the French ships *Charlemagne* or *Bouvet* was also sunk. The *Inflexible* came back with her fore submerged flat [fore flat submerged?], fore-shell room and air compressor flat flooded and the fore-magazine filling slowly. The *Gaulois* was badly holed forward and was beached on the bank between Phido and Drepano islands ... It was to be expected there would be considerable loss in forcing the Narrows, but I think three ships sunk and two badly damaged on the first day's operation is a rather more than was reasonable to expect. There is considerable uncertainty as to how much damage the Forts suffered.

It is true one cannot make omelettes without breaking eggs, but it is bad if the eggs are broken and the omelette is not made. The question is, have we done three ships' worth of damage to the Forts? Perhaps we shall hear soon ...

March 28th.

Today we were ordered to send up a seaplane to spot for *Majestic*. We got underway at 6-30 a.m. ... and sent up seaplane after seaplane, but all of them came back with something wrong. This was getting monotonous, but at 9-30 a.m. to relieve the boredom we sighted an enemy aeroplane almost overhead. It was from 6000/7000 ft. up. There was nothing much we could do about it since we had a Wright seaplane made fast astern and were stopped. Just to do something we fired a Maxim at it and just expended one belt when we saw the bomb leave the aeroplane. It fell about 100 yards ahead of the ship. We waited for the second and it seemed reasonable to suppose that he would probably score a hit since with the first bomb he had got the line right and had probably allowed for the ship going ahead. After waiting for what seemed a very long time I heard the unpleasant whistle of its close approach and it fell just 10 yards away from our port side abreast the hold. Over a long length the side is pitted and dented and bits of bomb have embedded themselves in the iron plates. A number of fragments came on to the flying deck but nobody was hit. Two pieces buried themselves in the woodwork of the wheelhouse and another piece carried away one strand of the leg of the aerial. Apparently he had no more bombs and turned away towards the mainland.

Eventually we got a seaplane off the water and it staggered around at about 400 feet over Yeni Shehr.

On 25 April Allied infantry landings began. By the end of this disastrous campaign, each side had suffered around 250,000 casualties. The Royal Navy had lost five capital ships, one destroyer and three submarines. The Australian Navy had lost one submarine, and the French Navy had lost four submarines and a capital ship with more than 1,000 men.

Air Vice Marshal Charles Edmonds, CBE, DSO, MBE, then Flight Commander HMS *Ben-My-Chree*
AIR 1/665/17/122/714

The Gallipoli campaign was the first to feature an aerial torpedo attack. In June 1915, *Ben-My-Chree* arrived in the Dardanelles, taking over from HMS *Ark Royal* whose slower speed made her vulnerable to enemy submarines. Childers was serving aboard her as an instructor, and Edmonds was his star pupil. On 12 August Edmonds took off in a Short Type 184 armed with a 14-inch torpedo:

Report of Flight
In accordance with your Operation Order No 26
Seaplane – No 842
Pilot – Flight Commander Edmonds
Armament – 14" Mark X Torpedo

Time and position at commencement of flight – Xeros Island 4.55 a.m.
Time and position at completion of flight – Xeros Island 5.45 a.m.
I climbed to 1500 feet and crossing the Isthmus of Bulair over the low land one mile to the East of Bulair, arrived over the Sea of Marmora and shaped course along the coast towards the North East.

The steamer to be attacked was lying just to the West of Injeh Burnu. There was a number of sailing craft, about twelve in all, between Injeh Burnu and Gallipoli, also a tug towing two large lighters just to the East of Injeh Burnu, all within two miles of the European shore. Opposite Dohan Aslan a navigation buoy was visible, but I cannot be certain whether this is the red conical buoy or the light buoy shown on Admiralty Chart No 1004.

Approaching Injeh Burnu, I glided down and fired my torpedo at the steamer from a height of about 15 feet and range of some 800 yards, with the sun astern of me. I noticed some flashes from the tug previously mentioned, so presumed she was firing at me and therefore kept on a westerly course, climbing rapidly. Looking back, I observed the track of the torpedo, which struck the ship abreast the mainmast, the starboard side. The explosion sent a column of water and large fragments of the ship almost as high as her masthead. The ship was of about 8000 tons displacement, painted black, with one funnel and four masts. She was lying close to the land, so cannot sink very far, but the force of the explosion was such that it is impossible for her to be of further use to the enemy. She appeared to have settled down a little by the stern when I ceased watching her.

I noticed a line of trenches running North and South about 3½ miles East of Bulair, also considerable rifle fire when in this vicinity. There were three groups of about five men in Khaki on the Exomili-Bulair road,and a small camp near the trenches mentioned above and just to the North of the road.

It is submitted that information regarding the Dohan Aslan Bank buoys and the fact that all water traffic was within two miles of the European coast, might be of use to commanding officers of HM Submarines.
(signed) Chas HK Edmonds

Unfortunately for Edmonds, his target turned out to have been beached, almost certainly as a result of having been previously torpedoed by a submarine. But as Squadron Leader Malone observed in his own report (same reference):

One cannot help looking on this operation as a forerunner of a line of development which will tend to revolutionise warfare.

Wing Commander Leopold Howard Wilkins, DSC, HMS *Campania*
from the private papers of L. Howard Wilkins DSC, IWM Reference 4182
83/17/1

In 1915 Wilkins was commissioned in the RNAS. Gaining his pilot's licence in a
month, he later became Temporary Captain (Flying), HMS *Furious*, in 1918. The
incident to which he refers took place while he was a flight lieutenant aboard HMS
Campania in the Mediterranean.

HMHS *China*
Sept 24 1916.

My dear Pater
No doubt Captain Schwann has sent you a line to say that I have had an
accident while flying. I have come off rather better than I thought I would
when the machine took charge. My passenger broke his arm and I have cut my
head above my left eye and had 10 stitches put in when on board one of our
latest battleships which picked me up – I am now in a hospital ship in bed, was
up for an hour today.

I thought it was all U.P. at first, and the amount of thought I put in during
my last 100ft vertical nosedive was wonderful. I will let you know all about the
accident when I come south as I hope to do for a rest but only for a few days.

I feel quite fit and am still very keen on flying. Would go up tomorrow if
they'd let me.

Undated letter from George Alder, HMS *Cyclops*:
Communication with the Editor

Dear Wilkins
I wonder if it were you doing those stunts over the *Cyclops* this morning? If so,
you gave us all an excellent show, with the exception of one skipper who fully
made up his mind that you had come over specially to commit suicide and
thereby mess up his quarter-deck!!! I loved those tail slides and splits and
banks etc. I can thoroughly appreciate the latter having done one once at least
10° from the horizontal!!!

Flight Commander Frederick Rutland, HMS *Engadine*
Memoir, Fleet Air Arm Museum

The value of air reconnaissance by carrier-based planes was demonstrated in 1916
at the Battle of Jutland. Frederick Rutland, then a flight lieutenant, was based
aboard HMS *Engadine*, and his Short had wireless communication. (Note that the
text of the original is not always grammatical, and no amendments have been
made.)

So we come to the eve of Jutland. I do not propose to discuss the battle here,
except insofar as it concerns aircraft. We went to sea to carry out a sweep of the

North Sea, because we had observed indications that at least a portion of the German Fleet were putting to sea. We left the Firth of Forth on the afternoon of May 30, having a rendezvous with the Grand Fleet from Scapa at the Long Forties, a point about 100 miles east of Aberdeen, but we were never to reach there, suspicious smoke reported by an advanced cruiser *Galatea*, resulted in an order to send up a seaplane to report. I got away in a Short no. 8359 ... Trewin was the observer. We got off in undisturbed water, sighted the enemy and sent in our reports. They put in some extremely accurate anti-aircraft fire, but we took little notice of this. We got our report to *Engadine*, and although it was arranged they should have then be passed by signal to the *Lion*, the battle-cruiser communications were so badly organized that she would not answer our call, but the signals were picked up by a light cruiser and passed on. Here was perhaps the turning point in the Navy's appreciation of the use to which aircraft could be used in conjunction with warships. It was to be the end of a long long pull, unfortunately, about an hour after getting away, and just when I was on my way South to sweep for the enemy battle squadron, as I had a petrol feed pipe fracture. I landed and repaired this, when the ship came up and I was ordered to hoist in. I asked permission to go on, but this was refused. We could have been of great use had we gone on again, unfortunately, as the *Engadine* could not effect communications with the *Lion*, the captain decided it was better to hoist the plane in for the moment, later the sea became too rough to hoist out planes. We had got off at sea, we had established inter-communication between plane and ship, in action, for the first time in history. It was the fault of the Navy entirely that we were not used to better effect. Their point of view was that we could not be relied upon, due to so many failures, and inability to get off at sea, except in most favourable circumstances. They would not accept us until we were 100% perfect.

The Commander-in-Chief's attitude to aircraft is exemplified in his action regarding *Campania*. She was at anchor near the seaplane station, and did not get the signal to get under way. It is difficult to understand why this was not discovered at the time, as it is usually the duty of the flagship to get a confirmation of such a general signal from all ships. Captain of *Campania* saw the fleet as they passed his anchorage and made a signal asking permission to sail. It was not until then Jellicoe knew she was not there. She was ordered to join, but by this time she was so far astern of the fleet, the Commander-in-Chief ordered her to return to port. The *Campania* was a large ship but could not maintain a speed of more than 14 knots. This was her only real disadvantage. It seems to have escaped the Commander-in-Chief that even if she were 100 miles astern, her planes could still operate with the fleet. She had one great advantage, seaplanes could be flown from her decks, she carried 14, all equipped with wireless and with the thoroughly trained wireless operators. Many of the mistakes of Jutland would have been averted had she been present. Jellicoe was not air minded one would suppose, but this is not so, he was just incapable of adding to his organization any unit that was not, as I have stated before, 100% perfect.

We kept our station on the beam of the Lion all through the action, until the advanced units of the Grand Fleet came into action, when we went to the assistance of the disabled heavy cruiser *Warrior*. We really had ringside seats, and saw the *Queen Mary* blow up with my great friend Freddie Sheath, who was the Director Officer, whose duty it was to fire all guns from the control top … The *Warrior* having come through the mist, found herself, together with her sister ships, within 5000 yards of the enemy battle cruisers. These ships opened at point blank range, and literally blew the flagship defences out of the water. Fortunately at this moment the *Warspite*, one of our latest and [finest] battleships, was struck after, and her steering gear was temporarily put out of action, with the result that she came around in a large circle which carried her between the *Warrior* and the enemy, effectively masking their fire, but not before the *Warrior* had sustained many casualties, and was on fire in several places. The enemy again disappeared and in the poor visibility and confusion, the *Warrior* came out to the westward and met the *Engadine*. As we now had no duties, we asked if we could be of assistance, and were told to stand by her. Later we took her in tow, the weather got bad during the night and in the stern of the *Warrior* sank lower in the water, as each hour passed. At daybreak it was decided that she could not possibly reach port, and preparations were made to abandon her, and take off her officers and ship's company. It looked as though we were too late, there was now a fair sea running. The *Engadine* was a Cross Channel Steamer and was fitted with huge rubbing streaks [strakes] all around the ship, to facilitate going alongside jetties. Without to these we could not have stayed alongside for the period necessary to take on board her 900 odd persons. The crew lined up as though at drill, thought that they would have to swim for it, and discarded pieces of shell that they intended to keep as souvenirs. We got alongside, by a superb piece of seamanship, and the order was given to abandon ship. Our officers and men lined the ship and grabbed each man as he came across, until he was safely inboard. Because of the large numbers, on so small a ship as ours, it was decided to get all the able bodied personnel over first, and send them below decks, thus leaving the deck clear for the wounded. Each ship had put out all the 'fenders' they could muster, and a great many of these were hazelwood, 'bundles of sticks wired together'. These were mostly broken up by the working of the two ships together, davits had been sheared from their supports, and we were holed in several places, though all holes were small. The noise of rending steel was terrific and only orders shouted in your ears could be distinguished. The wounded were passed over, and practically the last (of course they were transferred all along the ship's side and so at least six would be passing at once) stretcher was being passed over when the wounded man in it slipped out of the side and fell between the two ships.

Rutland, who had joined the navy as a 15-year old boy and studied to gain his commission before transferring to the RNAS, was promoted to flight commander for his reconnaissance at Jutland and awarded the Albert Medal, First Class, for diving into the gap between the two ships to rescue that mortally-wounded casualty.

William Hawkins, Armourer, HMS *Furious*
IWM Sound Archive Reference 19

Shortly after qualifying as an Armourer, Hawkins and three colleagues were posted to *Furious* as she was being converted from an 18,000-ton cruiser to a carrier – though not the fully flush-decked vessel envisaged by both Rutland and Clément Ader.

She had two 18" guns aboard, but the one on the foredeck had been removed to make a flight deck, and then round the taffrail [guardrail] (the edge of the ship from the bridge to the end of the foredeck) a number of slots for planks to be put in. The planks would be about 12ft long, something in the nature of 9 by 3 [nine inches wide, three inches thick]. These were to break any wind, because we were to try to land on the foredeck. When you land, you have to run into the wind, and if you get a crosswind – as subsequently proved – [it] can do a lot of damage. Of course we had an Otis lift that used to bring the planes that were stored – seaplanes; we had one or two landplanes. The seaplane was put on the lift and taken up and down as the case may be, and when it got onto the deck it was picked up by the topping lift, which is what you'd call a crane on an ordinary ship, as she was swung out and dropped onto the water ... You had to lift the plane out of the hold with the men on it and lower it into the sea and the crew had to stand on the floats in order to get the right balance.

On one occasion I remember they were doing it and the topping lift broke and the whole thing crashed into the sea ... 30 feet, I should say. The results were rather drastic really. It dumped all the men in the sea, broke the plane's floats. These chaps were [floating] about in the sea, and somebody released a flare, a sodium flare, in the sea ... A young officer got the wind up and thought there was a fire. He broke out the hoses. He was going to squirt them, when the captain came along. He just stood there quite calmly. 'Put that hose away. Get out the picket boat. Pick those men up. Bring them to Sick Bay. Sink the plane.' That's all there was to it. We picked the plane up, actually. He thought it was a write-off, because he was a sea captain.

Settling in trials ... consist of taking the ship to sea, seeing how she acts and responds, trying the guns out, seeing that men knew how to handle the guns because, you see, you get a bunch of ordinary fellows and you don't know what an action would be like: you have to be trained into this. So what they do is, they stage a mock exercise. You're all allotted to different guns. [My job] happened to be the ammunition. The ammunition for a big gun or even a small one, come to that ... is brought up from the bowels of the ship and it comes up on a hoist and is dropped into a pit in front of you which is covered over with a blanket … what they call a 'flash blanket' in case anything goes wrong, all in leather cases. The charge is taken out of that and handed to the gunner who loads the gun, and you have to go as though it was a real action. All watertight doors are sealed, no meals are served, and that goes on for about five hours, and every gun is fired. The Captain has you on the quarterdeck, as he did us, and he says: 'Now, we shall be going into action one of these days … we will never call for help and we will fight it out.' And things like that, all personal things that had to be dealt with … The first thing we had to do was to learn to fly on and off the foredeck, and that wasn't as simple as it sounds, really. I remember the Captain said 'you may as well take the revolver and blow your brains out, as try and land.'

You see, what had to happen was: the plane came into land and 'hovered'. Now, you've got to synchronise the speed of the ship with the speed of the plane, which is quite difficult. Though we're a fast oil-fuelled ship that could do 30 knots full out, a plane can go, even in those days, fairly fast: 60 mph or more … We got the pilot to hover over the ship, then we grabbed onto the undercarriage – jumped up and down and grabbed it. The next step wasn't quite so simple; it depended on the pilot, whether he figured he couldn't manage it and he opened the throttle. Or closed the throttle too quick and came down on top. And if he couldn't manage it, he opened the throttle and we let go and he went: tried again. That happened a number of times. We made one or two successful landings of a sort. I think the Admiralty could see it wasn't all that good. Squadron Leader Dunning was doing it one day and he took off and he tried to land. Now he wasn't happy about the landing, and he took off again and he crashed into the sea and it killed him. We picked him up. I'll always remember: there was quite a schermozzle about that. We put a boat of seamen out to get him in. None of them had a jack-knife, which a sailor has to carry, and they couldn't cut him free … They were raw recruits, you see. Thereon, we were under strict discipline and training for knots and how to tackle instances of that sort, 'cause half of them couldn't tie a bowline knot or a reef knot.

Flight Commander Frederick Rutland, HMS *Engadine*
Memoir, Fleet Air Arm Museum

Rutland was a true visionary, clear about what was needed for naval air power to become a force to be reckoned with and also capable of identifying problems and suggesting workable solutions. His criticism of many of the pilots sent to him for training, for example, were not aimed at the men themselves but at the system that produced them.

None of them were sailors, and I am convinced that this factor alone places them at a distinct disadvantage. It is well known that a man's familiarity with the sea breeds a contempt for its dangers. These men had to acquire the familiarity, and at the same time experience the very real danger, in those days, of flying over it. The danger from submarines was ever present, though over estimated, both in numbers and danger. In addition to that they were out of touch with the advances made in handling of planes ... Because of this, when it was decided to convert *Furious* to a seaplane carrier, it was decided to select the best pilots that could be found. The first selection was Flight Commander Dunning, and around him he collected a group of pilots who, I am sure, were second to none in the RNAS. They did nothing but exercise in both seaplanes and Sopwith Pups at Grain, for approximately three months. When *Furious* commissioned in July she had these superb pilots, and the effect on the fleet was extremely interesting. It had the effect of a rejuvenation, and raised the standard of flying to the standard obtaining on the Western Front ...

The forward turret was removed, and a forward hangar was installed. The top of this was extended to the stern of the ship, forming a flying off deck, with a length of approximately 180 feet. Eight seaplanes and 10 Pups were carried, and these were brought from the hangar to the flying deck by a lift, operated by the equipment originally fitted to work the turret, by hydraulic power. On each side of the deck was a stump derrick for hoisting all planes in and out when required. Seaplanes and Sopwith Pups both could fly off the deck. The Pups of course on their own chassis, the seaplanes on a specially constructed chassis upon which the floats rested. This chassis was developed in *Campania*; the seaplane would automatically lift out of a V-shaped device on the chassis, into which rested a pin, secured to the side of the float; as soon as it had gained flying speed it was free to lift, while the chassis would carry on until it was a few feet from the stem of the ship, when it would meet a shock absorbing buffer, and be held for there till it was released, and rolled back for the next flight. Workshops were arranged, as in other carriers; the petrol was carried in tins; it was a long time before the Admiralty was satisfied that petrol could safely be carried in bulk. The ship was 780 feet long, 68 feet beam, and had a speed of 32 knots. She arrived at Scapa for trials at the end of July, 1917 ...

Dunning had toyed with the idea of a landing a Pup on the flying deck of *Furious*. He reasoned that if a Pup could be flown at 30 knots to 35 knots, then it would be possible to sit over the flying deck at such time as the ship was steaming to produce this air speed over the flying deck, and thus there would be no relative movement between the plane and the ship, if at the right moment the plane was held by a reliable ground crew, then a method of landing would be provided. I do not know what consideration was given to the details by the ship's captain, or whether he urged Dunning to experiment, I judge by my later dealings with the captain, that he did a considerable amount of urging, in which case I do not hesitate to state that in doing so, he discarded all of the experience he must have gained in his long years at sea. A plane, when the air speed flowing past its wings approaches its take off at speed, is much like a kite in a high wind, and unless kept accurately into the wind is wholly unmanageable. I say he must have known this and should never have permitted the experiment to have been made; however it was made and with some initial success. The port stump derrick was removed, and Dunning came in, and throttled down his plane, while the ship gradually caught him up, as it were. A number of the officers were stationed at fixed positions and at a signal from Dunning, they grabbed the plane, and held it to the deck, at the same time the ship lowered speed, and he throttled down his engine. He thereby gained the honour of being the first man to land a plane on a ship under way. A day or two after this flight I met Seymour, Beatty's Flag Lieutenant, and he told me that Dunning had made this landing, and gave me details. I asked him to see Beattie upon his arrival on board, and to ask him to stop the landings until some arrangement had been made to automatically hold the plane, as soon as the wheels touched the deck.

It is quite certain that by this time a second landing had been made; this was also successful. I do not suppose any signal or telegram was sent north by Beattie, or if there was, there was not time to act upon it, for on the next day Dunning was dead. His third landing was carried out in all respects the same as the two previous ones, but somehow the plane got slightly off the wind, up went the left wing, the plane came down on one wheel, the tyre burst, and the plane was swept over the starboard side; many officers narrowly escaped being dragged over with it. I think the greatest tragedy of all was, Dunning was drowned, and not killed by the fall …

The Captain of the *Furious* was a most charming and likeable man; he however was not the man for a seaplane carrier. He would have made an ideal leader of a destroyer flotilla. He talked and generally behaved as if he knew all about flying, when in fact he was abysmally ignorant, and remained so until the end of my association with him. We gave him approximately 50 hours dual instruction, and he never learnt to fly … It was not till later that I realised he had an entirely different policy to mine. He wanted a combined fighting ship and carrier …

The method used by Dunning I discarded completely … I decided to experiment therefore with the normal approach landings, on the forward deck. This entailed flying along the port side of the ship edging in when abreast of the conning tower and straightening up just ahead of it. The plane had to be flown at its very lowest speed if it was to cease rolling before it reached the end of the flying deck. As we did not have any holding device for the plane, I decided that I would land and fly off again without being held, without losing control of my plane and without losing my engine. Actually this latter was the most difficult part, and most likely to cause trouble. I took the first plane away, and made the first attempt; six pilots went into the air at the same time. They were instructed to practice throttling down the engines, so that they had a pretty good idea of how much petrol to give it, when flying at the low speed necessary. They were told to come in, and if they could, to make a landing, but were not to stop more than a second or two, or to lose control of the plane, and then they were to fly straight off again. I came in about 4 feet above the deck, and bringing my wing tips within 2 feet of the conning tower; I then, using the thumb switch on my 'stick' blipped the engine, and regulated my petrol needle valve, and landed, only a couple of fuselage lengths from the conning tower. The air speed of the ship was approximately 25 knots. I sat there for perhaps 10–15 seconds, my tail up, and literally flying the plane, with my wheels on the ground … and flew off, landing at the aerodrome … When I arrived back on board, which was as soon as the ship came to anchor, I was met at the gangway by Admiral Phillimore and the Captain. To their inexperienced eyes, landing on the flying off deck was already an accomplished fact. Had they not seen a plane come in, and actually stop on the deck, and fly off again? And I was sorry to see the look of joy, and to receive their congratulations, for I knew that we should never land on this deck, even before I had received the reports of my pilots and seen the plotted curve of their flights.

Landing on became a practical proposition only after the removal of *Furious*'s after gun allowed the construction of a landing-on deck; the two flight decks remained divided by the central superstructure. She re-entered service in March 1918 and later that year was joined by HMS *Argus*, the world's first carrier with a continuous flight deck, and the converted cruiser, HMS *Vindictive*.

Captain Bernard Smart, DSO, RAF, HMS *Furious*
from the private papers of B. A. Smart, IWM Reference 7179 79/44/1

Smart's papers illustrate the new direction pilots would take. His lively undated letter refers to 21 August 1917, when he was in the North Sea and flying from the turret ramp of HMS *Yarmouth*.

My dearest Mother and Father

Things have been moving so rapidly these past few weeks that I am afraid when you get the latest bit of news your poor old heads will begin to ache with excitement, still you must take it as calmly as possible. The fact is I was that 'portion of our light forces' which brought down the Zep [L23] off Jutland. Doesn't it sound too good to be true, but it is so, and I have not slept a wink since – have been so bucked with myself. Sorry I couldn't let you know before, but have spent all my time since return visiting Admirals & Commodores and the big men of the fleet, and have not had a chance to get ashore or even time to write … Saw [Admiral] Beatty this morning, and he is awfully bucked and spoke very decently.

This is only a note to give you the wheeze and details will follow, but am afraid for the time being you must keep it dark, except perhaps a few of our very intimate friends on giving their word of honour not to mention it, not even to their wives. The reason is that as long as the Huns think it is brought down by gunfire, they will merely give orders to keep well clear of our warships so there will be many other chances.

Another startling piece of news is that I am appointed to the *Furious*, the very latest thing in Battle Cruisers, which was redesigned for'ard to take 'planes. Rutland is to be SFO …

On 21 July 1918, while serving on HMS *Furious*, Smart led the second flight of a successful two-flight bombing raid on the German Zeppelin sheds at Tondern. The first flight had already bombed one shed. On his return he submitted this report (ADM 1/455/15/312/44):

At 0300, being in position 'C' 56.03N 7.35E received orders to proceed with my flight, consisting of Capt. Thyne and Lieuts. Yeulet and Dawson R.A.F., to bomb Zeppelin sheds at Tondern. All the pilots were flying 150 B. R. Ship's Camels fitted with two 50lb bombs.

At 0315 we left the ship, steering S. The wind drifted us further East than expected and we sighted the Lyndvig fiord after 15 mins., when we steered along the coast to the Blaavand Point. Here Capt. Thyne dived and left formation due to engine trouble. I turned and slowed up to see what had happened to him but lost sight of him. Went dead slow for a time to give him opportunity to pick up, but as he was within gliding distance of the coast, did not waste further time searching, but carried on in V formation of 3 in S. E. direction. The clouds were now at 4000 and it was so difficult keeping one's bearing through holes in them that I dived and came below them opposite the Isle of Fane. Shortly after I sighted railway and having taken careful compass course along this, climbed above the clouds again to avoid observation. After 15 mins., which I calculated should have brought me to a point some two or 3 miles N. of Tondern, I descended below clouds again.

At 0445 saw Tondern some 10 miles to S.W. and steered W. A short while after fairly heavy anti-aircraft fire opened up on us. I was unable to see sheds for some minutes, but eventually three A.A. batteries close together attracted my attention, and near them I discovered the sheds, two large ones and one smaller, one of the larger having the roof partially destroyed and emitting large volumes of dense black smoke. When in position I gave the signal and dived on the remaining large shed, releasing my bombs at 800 to 1000 feet. The first fell short but the second hit the centre of the shed, sending up a quantity of smoke or dust. Whether this burst into flames later I am unable to state, as the whole surroundings were thick with mechanics or soldiers armed with rifles and machine guns, which gave so disconcerting a fire that I dived with full engines to 50 ft. and skimmed over the ground and in a zigzag course to avoid it, and by the time I had got clear was unable to see the sheds on account of thick screen of smoke from the first shed. The clouds were now very low and a general haze made visibility bad. I searched in all directions for the remainder of my flight, but seeing nothing made straight for the prearranged rendezvous at Brede. Here I slowed down to wait for others but after doing a circuit at slow speed and still nothing in sight, decided it inadvisable to wait longer as I had already been in the air nearly two hours and wind had increased; also the clouds were so low and thick as to give all of us, though separated, ample protection from superior forces of hostile craft.

I proceeded in a N.W. direction above the lower clouds, and on descending to pick up bearings, my engine failed to open out and I got to 400 feet before getting a single fire. Then two or three of the cylinders cut in, but I dropped to about 24 ft before getting 1000 revs. which was just enough to keep me in the air. I skimmed along at this height until engine gradually got better, but it was quite 20 mins. before she was doing 1200 again. I followed the coast until sighting Lyndvig Light, when I made out to sea, and after two or 3 minutes saw destroyer. I released the axle pins and dropped the wheels up by sidestepping alternately, and landed ahead of HMS *Violent* at 0630.

I had tried to empty [the] Vickers gun before landing, but after four or five shots it misfired, so did not trouble. The engine was absolutely perfect except for the one unaccountable drop, giving the 1250 revs for long periods. The objective would be particularly easy to find on a clear day as all roads seem to be of a very white nature and show up more distinctly even than railways.

Thyne's engine trouble had led him to return to the fleet; Yeulet was drowned after his aircraft presumably ran out of fuel, and Dawson – along with two of the three pilots from the first flight – landed in Denmark and was interned.

Commander Bonham de Laune Faunce, HMS *Vindictive*
from the private papers of B. de L. Faunce, IWM Reference 3181 87/3/1

Vindictive was a converted Cavendish-class cruiser, commissioned as a carrier right at the end of the war. After nine months, she grounded in the Baltic, requiring extensive repairs, and was reconverted to a cruiser. Having recovered from his amazement at being posted to a carrier (page 15), Faunce made another discovery:

My next surprise was that I was again going to be president of a Gun Room Mess. In the *Neptune*, at least the members were mostly younger than me, but this lot consisted of five RNR midshipmen who had all done a trip to the west coast of South America as apprentices, in a square rigger, and had had since done about two years on the Northern Patrol in the 10th Cruiser Squadron. Then there were a mixed bunch of pilots, some wearing RNAS uniform, and some having changed into RAF. As they all had only one stripe and there was no room for them in the wardroom, they were gun-room officers. Last but by no means least came five Observers all ex-yeomen of signals or PO Telegraphists. They were a grand lot, and if there was any hint of trouble with the others I could rely on them to the back me up.

Some of the pilots were a good lot too. There was Massey Hilton, who I often met later, eventually as a director of Fairey's when we had the first production Swordfish in the *Courageous*. In the wardroom was W. W. Wakefield, the adjutant of the flying contingent, and another useful supporter in times of trouble. We had a rugger match on Boxing day 1919 and I thought he seemed a bit out of the class of the rest of us, and was not surprised to see him captaining England a few years later.

While at Rosyth I had my first flight from Turnhouse with one of our pilots – no seat-belts or harness, but we did a couple of loops.

The *Vindictive* was accident-prone. On our acceptance trials she grounded in the Belfast Lough and we had to dock again briefly for examination and to clear the mud out of the various inlets. Later she repeated the performance up the Baltic, and followed that up with a mutiny. We eventually commissioned, finished trials, and steamed up to Scapa, doing a run on the way through the Minches which was quite exhilarating.

At Scapa which was otherwise deserted, we spent a lot of time steaming round the Flow with men holding up a variety of wind-measuring devices on the launching deck forward of the bridge, and on the landing deck aft. Some aircraft from Hatston flew over the deck to see what sort of turbulence the funnels, mast and bridge produced. They had strict orders not to attempt to land. However, Wakefield, having made several passes over the landing deck in a Sopwith Pup, decided to put her down, and did so with no trouble at all. He climbed out and walked forward to the bridge along the gangway past the funnels, and received a blast from Tomlinson, the Wing Commander, who was furious, and a rebuke from Dasher Grace – when we had anchored Dasher sent for him and stood him a drink in his cabin.

We were still at Scapa when the Armistice was signed and were afraid that we'd missed the surrender of the German Fleet. However, we sailed for Rosyth in time to take part. My action station was in the auxiliary gun control position between the funnels. It was a great thrill to see the German ships appearing out of the mist and heading West between the two long lines of British and Americans. I tried to pick out the ships I had seen just once before, fleetingly, at Jutland: *Koenig* class battleships, and particularly the battle-cruiser *Seydlitz* which I had seen hit on her after turret redoubt by one of our shells. I saw them again when the *Vindictive* went back to Scapa for more working up and trials, when they were bottom up or with only masts or upper works showing [after the Germans had scuttled their High Seas Fleet in June 1919].

William Hawkins, Armourer, HMS *Furious*
IWM Sound archive reference 19

Starting the engine: we had to crouch a bit, and another aspect was the wind from the running propeller. It had to run, and you had to keep clear of it. In those days you didn't have anything to start your engine by. The seaplanes had an air-bottle, but in a lot of cases you had to swing it yourself. I saw one man decapitated.

4
The Interwar Years

Even before World War I ended on 11 November 1918, the Allies had embarked on an unsuccessful campaign of just over a year to support the White Russians against the Bolsheviks, who had taken power during the Russian Revolution of 1917. Two British seaplane carriers were sent up to the Baltic to assist operations.

Work on building proper flat-top aircraft carriers continued, as HMS *Furious* finally lost her remaining gun and emerged from refit in 1920 as a flush-deck carrier with two hangers and, until 1939, no island. In 1916 the uncompleted hull of the Italian liner, *Conte Rosso*, building in the UK, was purchased by the Admiralty to become HMS *Argus*. The first carrier designed from the keel up was HMS *Hermes*, which had been laid down at the start of 1918, at the same time as their lordships took over the hull of a Chilean battleship under construction and began to turn it into HMS *Eagle*.

British experimentation and expertise were not limited to developing Royal Navy carriers; both were also put at the disposal of Japan, with which Britain was at the time in alliance. Japan was already building its first true carrier, *Hosho*, when in 1921 a civilian delegation led by the Sir William Forbes-Sempill – usually known as the Master of Sempill – went to that country and successfully helped it to create a naval air arm. The delegation included Frederick Rutland, who stayed on, working for the Mitsubishi Corporation in both Japan and the USA; he was interned in England after Pearl Harbor, suspected of spying for the Japanese.

The 11,250-ton USS *Langley*, the United States' first aircraft carrier, was also a conversion – from the navy collier, *Jupiter* – commissioned in 1920 and entering service two years later. Like most of those early or experimental carriers, she was a peculiar looking vessel, aesthetically unpleasing and with funnels that folded down. The US Navy's next carriers owed their existence to the first attempt at international arms control.

The development of naval air power was given a major boost by the Washington Naval Treaty that was formulated in 1921–2 and ratified by the USA, Britain, France, Italy and Japan the following year. Germany was never asked to sign up to it, as her navy was already severely limited by the 1919 Treaty of Versailles. The Treaty aimed to avoid another such arms race as that which had taken place in the run up to World War I and concentrated on limiting the size and armament of capital ships – battleships and battlecruisers. Britain and the USA were capped at 525,000 tons, Japan at 315,000 tons and France and Italy at 175,000 tons each. Aircraft carriers were subjected to the same ratio: the USA and the UK were allowed 135,000 tons, Japan 81,000 tons, and France and Italy 160,000. Only two carriers per nation could exceed 27,000 tons each. Carriers under construction or deemed 'experimental' were not included in this figure.

This meant a radical change to naval procurement plans, encouraging the building of aircraft carriers, several of them utilizing hulls that had been laid down for battleships and battlecruisers. Thus the Americans gained *Lexington* and *Saratoga*, both converted from battlecruiser hulls. The British converted *Courageous* and *Glorious* to join their sister *Furious* in 1930 and drew up the plans for *Ark Royal* (the second carrier to be so named), commissioned in 1938. France scrapped four out of five *Normandie*-class battleships under construction leaving Béarn to be completed as a carrier, albeit a rather slow one. Italy commissioned a former passenger liner as *Giuseppe Miraglia*, an experimental aviation carrier, but she had no flight deck, and Mussolini refused to agree to the building of a carrier, believing that Italy itself provided the perfect airstrip for aerial domination of the Mediterranean.

Carrier design reflected the role the ships were expected to play. America and Japan saw themselves as mutual enemies, and any war between them would be fought at long range by carrier groups in the Pacific. Thus the US constructed big carriers capable of operating large wings of aircraft designed to deliver a decisive attack. These could be parked on the flight deck as well as in the hangar to maximize the number carried while keeping the carriers within the displacement tonnage limitations imposed by the Washington Treaty. The British, who wanted their carriers to carry out reconnaissance, anti-submarine warfare and torpedo bombing as part of battlefleet operations, opted for smaller, more heavily armoured ships in which the aircraft had more protection. The development in the 1930s of the dive-bomber led the Royal Navy to specify armoured, rather than just splinter-proof, flight decks for carriers under construction. American flight decks were constructed of wood.

Ship building was only one part of the story. The task of organizing and training the aircrew, developing aircraft capable of carrying out the strategic roles assigned to carriers, and finding the most efficient way of operating those aircraft were addressed with varying degrees of success during the interwar period by those navies that opted for carrier fleets – primarily Japan, Britain and the USA.

In 1918, the Royal Flying Corps and the Royal Naval Air Service had been amalgamated to create a third independent service, the Royal Air Force. It would be twenty years before the Royal Navy regained control of the naval arm, designated the Fleet Air Arm in 1924, and during the intervening years its requirements, particularly in terms of planes fit for purpose, came second to those of the RAF. As a result, the Royal Navy fell behind the USA and Japan, both of whose naval air squadrons were an integral part of their navies. The Royal Navy was forced to accept 'marinized' – modified for operation at sea – versions of RAF aircraft that were not necessarily suitable for carrier work, and multi-purpose aircraft in which compromise left them able to do several things quite well but without superiority in any one field. A prime example of that arrived in 1936 in the form of the Fairey Swordfish, a Torpedo Spotter Reconnaissance biplane that could also carry bombs or depth-charges. It was slow, limited in range, primitive in construction and in certain respects outdated even before the outbreak of a war in which it quite perversely went on to perform miracles and outlast every other naval aircraft in service at the outbreak of hostilities.

The advent of the true aircraft carrier had at last allowed landing on for as long as the flow of air over the flight deck acted as an adequate brake on the slow, lightweight aircraft of the period. But this was now a situation that could not continue as new aircraft were developed – particularly in the USA. Soon carriers would need a more efficient means of halting aircraft than the sandbagged wires that had stopped Ely in 1911. The US Navy opted early on for a run of transverse wires that would catch a hook fitted to the tail of the plane. The sandbags were replaced by friction brakes. Initially, the Royal Navy worked on longitudinal wires, but by 1931 it too used transverse wires, and shortly before World War II, more than a decade after the US Navy, it brought in a crash barrier. This screen of vertical wires, which could be raised and lowered, arrested any aircraft that failed to catch a wire. Hitting the crash barrier was a last resort – it would damage the aircraft and could injure the pilot – but it was infinitely preferable to going into the sea or crashing into aircraft parked forward. The advent of the crash barrier greatly streamlined operations.

Nevertheless, a pilot landing on a carrier had to rely on his own judgement. He had no communications with a control tower, no sophisticated technology to bring him down – and no stable airstrip surrounded by grass in case he overshot or slewed sideways. His runway was a narrow strip of wood or metal which, depending on the weather, could be rolling several degrees and pitching perhaps thirty feet at the stern. His fuel reserves were likely to be low, and diverting to land was a rare luxury even in peacetime.

Early on, the US Navy introduced the Landing Signal Officer (LSO). This was an experienced pilot whose directions helped the landing-on pilot to refine his approach and cut the engine at the right moment. Not until 1937 did the Royal Navy create their equivalent, the Deck Landing Control Officer (DLCO), who came to be known as the 'batsman' because the paddles he used to convey his instructions were shaped like table-tennis bats. Landing on still remained dangerous for aircrew – and also for the DLCO (for whom a net was provided in case he had to jump off the flight deck to save his life). This system was in use until the early 1950s and the arrival of jet aircraft.

Taking off also retained its difficulties. When it came to getting seaplanes airborne from capital ships, the US Navy preferred the catapult to the short turret ramps favoured by the Royal Navy. The new flat-top carriers did not require catapults for anything other than seaplanes. Their decks were sufficiently long; and the new generation of fast US fleet carriers, in particular, generated plenty of wind over the deck. The planes themselves could take off at comparatively slow speed, adding the speed of the ship to their own speed along the deck. The Royal Navy had briefly begun work on catapults in 1916, but it was not until 1922 that catapult development got into its stride, this time with the RAF in charge.

Compressed air provided the power, though experiments with explosive propulsion also took place on both sides of the Atlantic.

A general programme of rearmament among all the major powers accelerated in the later 1930s. Japan's desire for raw materials brought her into conflict with China and created diplomatic tensions with the USA across the Pacific. Germany's 1938 invasion of Czechoslovakia was followed by her attack on Poland in 1939, the match which set off all the explosive alliances signed in the interwar years, one after another.

THE RUSSIAN CAMPAIGN

Lieutenant C. H. Bridge, RAF, HMS *Nairana*
from the papers of C. H. Bridge, IWM Reference 1592

Formerly a merchant navy officer, Bridge joined the RAF and qualified as an RNAS/RAF pilot. Around the end of World War I, as a pilot officer, he was posted to the former Australian ferry *Nairana* which had Fairey Campanias on board and which was one of the two seaplane carriers that participated in the North Russia campaign.

Life was pretty dull at Scapa Flow and when we were ordered to Dundee, it was welcome news for all hands. On arrival Dundee, we were given leave as the ship was in for a refit. When we rejoined, after a nice spell at home, stores of all kind were coming on board but we had no idea what our next commission would be. When we saw bundles of mosquito netting coming on board it was a case of 'we must be for the Mediterranean'. Later on all kinds of sheepskin coats and flying boots made us change our minds and say we must be bound North. North and Russia it turned out to be. Murmansk soon saw us in safely moored alongside. A Russian Battleship [cruiser] was anchored in the inlet named *Askold* and she had five funnels. The Bolsheviks were in possession and it was rumoured that the crew had murdered their officers and thrown their bodies into the furnaces. The British Navy boarded the ship with very little opposition and Captain Wills took command. It was soon Wills of the Packet – of Woodbine. We were soon to leave Murmansk and was working a Monitor along the coast, spotting whilst the Monitor with a single 16" gun [was] shelling different targets, distance 15 miles. We eventually joined up with a squadron to take Archangel. I was ordered away with my seaplane and observer and two 250lb bombs attached, observing and reporting enemy troop movement as our troops were landing. While so doing I made my longest flight in the air ever. I could not say for certain for how long, but I would guess it to be over four hours,

My instructions on setting off were not to drop my bombs unless I was ordered to do so. It so happened that we never received an order to drop the bombs on a target. So when ordered to return to my ship both the observer and I were very concerned having to land with the bombs still attached.

Anyone not having any knowledge of flying would say that if the bombs were safe to take off with why not safe to land with? The difference is that landing is very different from taking off. And much more difficult. Bear in mind landing on water especially if the sea is calm is not unlike landing on a mirror as the water [has] that effect. It makes it difficult for the pilot to judge the distance he is above the water . If he flattens out too soon he could make a heavy bump, rise some 10 feet or so, and then come down with another heavy bump, and with bombs attached they could become detached from the plane and explode. Bearing this in mind I had to plan my landing with care, knowing that I had not been instructed to drop my bombs. I made a very good landing and as we came to rest my Observer, bless him, hugged me and said well done Sir. We then taxied to the ship and it was not long before we were safely lifted on to the deck of our ship.

Archangel was not a very clean looking place: the sidewalks contained wooden planks and a lot of them were in disrepair ... The people were poorly dressed and short of food. The Bolsheviks had searched all the houses before they evacuated the town and took away food. When the Allies arrived we brought relief for there [sic] shortages. Flour and salt particularly. There was no beef to be had and on the mess it was always Corned Beef ... A contingent of Americans arrived and I remember that they soon put up the prices of everything that was for sale. Polar Bear skins and furs of all kind to name a few items. However they were soon in action joining the British and Royal Russians driving the Bolsheviks South.

Bridges was Mentioned in Despatches for his part in the campaign. On the way back to Britain from Russia:

a messenger [came] from the captain of the ship requesting me to report to him on the bridge. This would be the first time that a RAF officer was called to the bridge by the Navy and needless to say was greeted with concern by all in the Officers' Mess, and no less by myself. On arrival on the navigating bridge the captain took me into the chart room. His first question to me was 'Have you a Board of Trade Certificate?' I said 'Yes, First Mate's Certificate'. He then said 'Lieutenant Dalziel has informed me so, and I would like you to take a sight of the sun as the RN watch keeping officers do not agree with the position of the ship as indicated by the Navigating Officer Lieut. Dalziel'. A case of the RN versus the MN ... The captain then gave me his sextant and I then took my observation of the sun and gave the reading of degrees and minutes of the Altitude observed. The captain thanked me and said 'we will now work out your position of the ship'. Sometime late [sic] Lieutenant Dalziel came into the Mess and said 'Order what you would like to drink; the Merchant Navy put one over the Navy today – your sight was in keeping with mine.' That was very edifying to have become so useful to a four ring Captain of the Royal Navy. The next night the captain sent his messenger and invited me to take dinner with him, a very great honour indeed. Needless to say I was delighted and accepted with thanks.

Commander Bonham de Laune Faunce, HMS *Vindictive*
from the private papers of B. de L. Faunce, IWM Reference 3181 87/3/1

In the summer of 1919, while still an aircraft carrier, HMS *Vindictive* joined the North Russia Campaign.

Going up the Baltic was memorable for three things. The sight or smell of pines still brings back the heavenly scent of forests on the offshore breeze when we were still some hours steaming from the coast of Reval. Not so good was finding the officer I was relieving for the middle watch asleep. A look at the Captain's orders and the chart showed that we should have altered course to have kept in the swept channel an hour before, on passing a light ship an hour previously. We had therefore gone some 18 miles into the unswept area. I ordered 'slow' on the engines and called the Captain and Navigator; we retraced our course to the light ship without hitting anything, and headed on for Reval, but before we arrived a more serious incident occurred.

As we approached the anchorage from the West the Navigator mistook the leading marks, being misled, I think, by the fact that some upturned broomstick buoys had been changed. I came on to the bridge to take over as Officer of the Watch entering Harbour just as the pilot realized the error. It took him a moment to get it across to the skipper and by the time the engines had stopped and were starting to go astern, we felt the bows rise and the ship come to a fairly gentle halt. I was sent with a man with a hand-lead to sound all round the ship ... We had gone on to a smooth, gently-sloping gravel bank and, amazingly, no damage was done although we must have been making 15 knots when we hit. There are no tides in the Baltic and we had to get a lot of weight out of her before the ship floated. All the remaining coal, most of the oil, the ammunition, a lot of stores, and some armoured doors and hatches came out into Estonian lighters labelled, I remember, 'Tallinn Sadam Kapten', the first we had heard of the port's new name.

After several days, a westerly wind raised the water level an inch or two and, with the help of the ship's company jumping in unison on the Quarterdeck, a destroyer pulled [us] off. We put everything back before going on to the advanced base at Biorko

There was quite a fleet at Biorko. The 2nd Cruiser Squadron, a big destroyer flotilla, a submarine depot ship and submarines. The anchorage was among lovely pine-clad islands with sand off the Finnish Coast, and it was hot and sunny. It was peaceful too except for an occasional visit from a Russian seaplane which stayed well out in the offing where it sometimes deposited a bomb. The Finns had a German Heinkel seaplane which they operated from a lake separated from our anchorage by a narrow neck of land, and hidden by a thick belt of pines. People were a bit trigger happy with regard to aircraft in those days and so the *Curacoa* used to signal on her bridge semaphore: 'Finnish seaplane up' as it took off, and 'Finnish seaplane down' as it alighted. One afternoon I was on deck and heard the sound of the seaplane's engine and at the same time, the signalman on watch started to read out 'Finnish- seaplane – up'. Just as he got that far, there was a resounding crash and a column of black smoke rose over the pines. With a barely a pause the signalman went on 'Finnish – seaplane – down – full stop – finish Finnish seaplane'.

One afternoon I was on watch when the flagship signalled 'enemy aircraft in sight'. I told the Bugler to sound 'A-A guns at the double'. The Commander and Captain were soon on deck. The former was most put out that an Acting Sub-Lieutenant should have dared to order the gun crews to close up. However, the Skipper approved, but said: 'I think we'll make it action stations'.

THE 1920s

Rear Admiral Jackson R. Tate, USN, Rtd, USS *Langley* (CV-1)
from *Proceedings*, October 1978

At the Washington Naval Conference in the early 1920s, the great naval powers haggled over what they would have in the way of ships and tonnages. The big item was the battleship, then the queen of the fleet. After that came the cruiser, and on down the list. The high-ranking officers in the front seats fought for battleship and cruiser power; in the back sat a junior commander named Kenneth Whiting who kept insisting on being heard for something called the airplane carrier. No one cared much, but he finally got authority for an experimental carrier, and when the United States agreed to scrap her new battle cruisers, he held out to get the first two, the *Lexington* and *Saratoga*, converted to airplane carriers. What Whiting was asking for was ships that would replace the battleship as the backbone of the fleet and would thus change the whole concept of naval warfare.

The first US carrier, however, was a converted navy collier.

No one was sure what the aviators wanted, except that there was to be a deck that planes could land on. The flight deck was to consist of several sections, because a solid deck was deemed unable to withstand the ship's hogging and sagging in a seaway. There would be a catapult on the forward end of the flight deck and some sort of arresting gear to stop the planes. Small items came up from time to time, such as side booms for radio antennas, a net aft to catch any planes that might fly into the stern, and extensions on the bridge under the flight deck to obtain some additional visibility …

Those of us who were attached to the Navy's first carrier were not treated to a life of luxury. The flight officers' quarters were built of wood on top of the wardroom and the old ship's staterooms. They competed with the uptakes from the boilers for space under the flight deck and constituted one of the best fire hazards the Navy ever built.

Whiting and Chevalier [Lieutenant Commander Godfrey De Courcelles 'Chevvy' Chevalier] were involved in almost continuous daily conferences with the Navy Yard officials. Whiting insisted on a large and complete photo lab, because he proposed to take both still and motion pictures of every landing. On the stern, an elaborate pigeonhouse was built with food storage, nesting, training, and trapping areas. (It was later to be rebuilt into the executive officer's quarters.) The radios of those days were very rudimentary, and most cross-country flights carried crates of homing pigeons in case of emergency. The attempt to train pigeons to return to a ship was a great failure, but provided an excellent supply of squab for the mess. To bring the ship to the desired draft, a 10-foot-deep layer of cement was poured into the holds which once had been filled with coal.

The building of the flight deck progressed slowly. There arose new problems daily, such as where to establish stations for control of the flight deck and arresting gear. To provide refuge for the deck crew during landings, outriggers were installed about 3 feet below the flight deck level. Wire netting was installed for the crew to jump into in order to observe and control the gear.

The actual arresting gear had to be designed as well. The British had used fore-and-aft wires strung about a foot apart, 10 inches off the deck and covering the aft 200 feet. These wires converged at the forward end. Friction on the hooks on the landing gear axles provided the retarding element. It had not been very satisfactory. Whiting and Chevalier felt there should be a positive and controlled arresting moment. In a previous experiment on a special deck built on the armored cruiser *Pennsylvania* (ACR-4), Eugene Ely had used cross-deck pennants with sand bags at each end and a hook on the landing gear of the plane. This was successful. Lieutenant Pride, aided by 'Horse' Pennoyer, did most of the work in designing the *Langley*'s landing gear ...

Finally, the decision was reached to commission the ex-*Jupiter* into the USS *Langley* on 20 March 1923. Her acting commanding officer was Commander Whiting, the ship's prospective executive officer. Her future commanding officer was to be Captain Stafford H. R. ('Stiffy') Doyle, a non-aviator who had no idea what the ship was all about, what her mission was, or any of the ideas Whiting and Chevalier were working toward. Though stationed only 25 miles away at Hampton Roads, Doyle did not see fit to attend the commissioning. Even after the commissioning, work progressed very slowly. It was almost six months until the *Langley* was able to leave the yard. Late in the summer came the big day. Following dock trials of the main power plant and the firing of a dead load from her catapult, the new carrier was finally ready to go out for her post-conversion trials. Captain 'Stiffy' Doyle took over, and the ship proceeded down to the Hampton Roads Naval Base, where she was assigned dockage at the merchant ship end of the terminal. The masts were in the up position, and a commission pennant now flew proudly from the main, but no one at the base was yet willing to admit that this unusual and ugly apparition was a warship. Planes of various types were brought down from the air station and hoisted aboard for the training of the crew in plane handling. After loading supplies, the *Langley* finally got under way and proceeded up the Chesapeake Bay to Tangier Sound for tests of the new installations …

Whiting had developed a routine of daily conferences in the wardroom to settle all problems, both major and minor. He had listed a series of tests with smoke pots to examine the flow of air over the flight deck under various conditions of speed and at headings up to 10° off the direction of the wind. Another minor problem was the choice of a bugle call to use for 'flight quarters.' Some argument arose when he selected 'Boots and Saddles,' the old cavalry call to mount horses. The pigeon quartermaster appeared once to protest vociferously against the test firing of the 5-inch/51-caliber guns situated on either side of the stern; the pigeon house was a wooden structure built between the guns and not more than 20 feet away. The gun firing was deferred more or less permanently …

Planes in those days had no brakes or tail wheels; shock absorbers for the main gear and tail skeg consisted of rubber bungees. Engines were started by swinging the prop by hand and using a magneto booster. These proved to be problems on a crowded deck. Plane handling crews were established, with one man on each wing and a man on the tail dolly. The plane captain was the director, and signals had to be devised to direct the crew and pilot. There were no radios, so we had to figure out how to tell the planes to land. The solution worked out was to fly a white flag at the aft end of the flight deck as a signal to land, and a red flag as a signal not to land. It was suggested that a steam jet be placed in the bow to assist the officer of the deck in keeping the ship headed into the wind. The chief engineer objected to this waste of steam, and so the jet was operated, when desired, from the bridge. All of this shows that the problems and growing pains on board the *Langley* were many, but somehow solutions were found …

Finally, on 17 October, Lieutenant Commander Virgil C. ('Squash') Griffin was designated by Whiting to make the first carrier takeoff. This was not so simple as it sounds or as it is today. In the first place, planes in those days had no brakes. In order to allow a plane to turn up to full power and start its deck run, it was necessary to develop a device consisting of a bomb release attached to a wire about 5 feet long. The bomb release was hooked to a ring on the landing gear and the end of the wire to a hold-down fitting on deck. A cord led from the bomb-release trigger to an operator on deck, who could release the plane on signal. Planes at rest sat nose high, and it was necessary to raise the tail 3 to 4 feet at the start of the roll. A trough about 4 feet long was built and mounted on saw horses, and the tail skeg was placed in the trough to keep the plane in flight position. The ship was hauled into the wind laboriously by the winches to the stern anchors, and a plane's propeller was started by hand. After all tests were completed, Griffin turned the Hispano Suiza engine in the

Vought VE-7SF up to its full 150 horsepower and gave the signal to pull the trigger on the bomb-release gadget, which had been given the name 'tension gun.' The released plane rolled down the deck and lifted off easily before it reached the elevator. Griffin flew back to Norfolk.

More days were devoted to practice approaches, especially using the Aeromarine 39-B. Finally, a week later, the *Langley* got under way and proceeded out into Chesapeake Bay for the first landing. It was a cool Monday morning, 26 October 1922. The ship turned into the northeast wind off the 'Tail of the Shoe' shoal inside Cape Henry. Chevalier flew out from the beach in an Aeromarine 39-B and passed along the deck. The arresting gear was all set, and the white flag was flying at the stern.

The idea of having a landing signal officer was not to be thought of until six months later, so Chevalier was entirely on his own. His right wing dropped slightly at the end, but he corrected and made a landing catching the second wire. The fiddle bridges crashed down, and were showered down on the deck along with the pies. The axle hooks held the plane down, and the tail hook stopped her in a very short run, but a high tail rise let the propeller nick the deck. Overall, it was a good landing, and the crew went wild with joy.

No one at the celebration could predict that in less than two weeks 'Chevvy' would be killed in a plane crash …

The winter drew to a close, and the *Langley* headed north again to Norfolk for modification of the ship found necessary by the six months of experience. Before entering the yard, she made a publicity cruise up the coast – much against Whiting's wishes. Landings made at anchor in New York and Boston were a sensation for the press. Captain Doyle went ashore and attended a few Chamber of Commerce meetings. Some of his speeches revealed his utter ignorance of the aims of what was being done and so infuriated Whiting that he went to Washington and convinced a few influential political figures to pass [a] law requiring that all ships directly connected with aviation be commanded by aviators. Few people there realized how far into the future he was looking.

Commander Roy Struben, RN
from the private papers of R. F. C. Struben, IWM Reference 86-60-1

Although observers needed excellent eyesight and proficiency in Morse Code, Struben managed to qualify.

Lee was the well-known nautical instrument maker at the Hard at Portsmouth and together we designed lenses for flying goggles. For some reason it was not then possible to have the shatter-proof eyepiece of goggles ground to correct bad vision. Therefore we devised lenses to be mounted on the outside of standard service goggles, hinged at one side and clipped at the other so I could open them out to wipe off mist, spray or rain when flying. The aircraft of the FAA had open cockpits and goggles were essential against wind and slipstream.

Naval Observers were required to read and send wireless signals in Morse code at twenty words a minute, and the only way to reach that was by daily practice for months, until one ceased to hear the longs and shorts and heard each group as the letter itself. This change would suddenly break through to one after a sufficient time. Thinking that we were not to be tested until the final examination at the seaplane base, most of us postponed extensive training in Morse and concentrated on the more complicated aspects of wireless signals. But, to our consternation, the first test was given before we left the signal school, where several of us failed to pass and were told that we would probably be returned to general service. That weekend was an unhappy one.

But our bacon was saved by a bit of luck, for Ian Elliot happened to meet in his club in London a Captain under whom he had recently served, the formidable Freddy Dreyer, who asked him why he was looking so depressed. When Elliot explain, Freddy snorted 'Nonsense, my boy, I'll soon put that right'. And of course he could not save Elliot without saving the rest of us.

There were no flying accidents at Lee[-on-Solent], though two of the course had a very narrow squeak. Flying Officer Hume-Wright, an experienced RAF officer but new to seaplanes, had heard that one cannot loop an aircraft with floats, but he did not believe it. He did it. But only half way round the loop, for the machine stuck upside down and flew at a steep angle of dive, while the pilot struggled frantically with the controls and the makee-learn Observer, Ginger Dale, and a sombre Scot whose name I forget, clutched in terror at the edge of the open cockpit to hold themselves in.

Hume-Wright tried all the dodges which he had been taught to drag the Fairey IIID out of its suicidal plunge, but the wind on the upturned floats held it in a relentless grip, while the hard glittering waters of the Solent rushed up. At last, in a forlorn hope, the pilot applied the rudder and joystick in precisely the opposite way to the orthodox manner and the aircraft rolled over and flew on safely.

Aviation Instrument Mechanic George J. Campbell, USS *Langley*
Interview with Mike Miller, NATTC PAO, source unknown

I joined the *Langley* in October 1921 before she was commissioned as an aircraft carrier. This made me a plank owner ...

My rate was Aviation Instrument Mechanic, which wasn't too hard a job in those days. Mainly I repaired and calibrated the tachometer, altimeter, the oil and water temperature gauges, the oil pressure gauge, compass, air speed indicator and the bank-turn indicator which was just a gyroscope). There were supposed to be clocks mounted in the dash too, but they were very nice clocks and usually disappeared in short order.

If you think about it, we really didn't know anything at all in those days. For the first year we never landed our airplanes when the ship was moving. All landings were made with the *Langley* at anchor. And we didn't use the Catapult very much in the early days; most of the planes we carried could take off in about one-half the length of the flight deck. We did use the catapult for the seaplanes. The seaplanes were kept in a cradle device and we would attach the cradle to the catapult. The cradle would remain on board when the seaplane was launched.

Landings were different, too. For one thing, the arresting cables weren't hydraulically operated. Where the cables ran down the side of the ship, there were weights made of slotted boiler plate. When the arresting cable was engaged by the plane's tailhook, the cable's bitter end engaged the first weight, and as more cable played out, the second then the third, etc. Each piece was heavier than the next, so that the planes were brought to a stop pretty quickly in the early days. The tails usually broke off. They weren't designed for that sort of stress, you see.

Of course, those weights had to be greased so that they'd slide across each other easily. The seamen had that job, not the most popular aboard as you can imagine.

One of the things they were most concerned about was the plane sliding sideways across the deck. To prevent this they had fore and aft wires installed about 10 inches apart down the flight deck. Now in those days, the wheels on the planes were attached to a common axle which ran between the landing struts. There were no wheel brakes but there were hooks attached to the axle and when the Plane landed, the fore and aft wires would rise out of the deck and engage those hooks. Once a pilot was in, he had no options to leave.

We had a lot of [Curtiss] 'Jennys' attached at first, but as I recall, the pilots didn't like them because they were not responsive enough. Then there were some Chance-Voughts and, oh yes, a TS-1 seaplane. That was flown by a pilot we called our 'attached/detached pilot', Lieutenant Al Williams. He was mainly a good pilot and never stayed aboard very long.

We had a 'barricade' aboard the *Langley* but it doesn't really relate to the barricade you use today made of nylon webbing. Ours was made of channel irons which rose out of the deck about a foot apart. It was used mainly as a wind break but I guess it could have been used as a plane stopper.

I left the *Langley* in October of 1923 for a tour of the Canal Zone. By then the planes were getting bigger and faster with more and more horsepower. When we first started flying abroad, the airplanes had seven cylinders. When I left the ship, they were already up to 18. The planes became too powerful to land them aboard the *Langley* so they would be barged out, catapulted off and would be landed ashore. After leaving the *Langley*, I spent two years in the Canal Zone and then got out of the Navy. I visited friends on her several times afterwards, but it was evident that as a carrier, she was becoming obsolete. The *Saratoga* and *Lexington* had been built – *Langley* just couldn't take those bigger, heavier, and faster planes.

Commander Roy Struben, RN, HMS *Eagle*
from the private papers of R. F. C. Struben, IWM Reference 86-60-1

Struben's anecdote demonstrates that while there were still Royal Navy officers who failed to understand the value of carrier-borne aircraft, there were others in very high places who were not merely enthusiastic but who wanted an understanding based on first-hand experience. The accident sustained by Sir Roger Keyes occurred on 28 October 1925.

As an extreme example of their school of thought – the most extreme of all, let us hope – there was the verdict of a rear admiral, who was one of a number of Rear Admirals and Post Captains attending short courses at various establishments, to be put in the picture about the latest technical developments in the Naval Service. At a lecture given by a Lieutenant Commander, an Observer, on the function of aircraft in co-operation with surface ships, he was somnolent and displayed no interest. Some of his classmates did listen, though others passed humorous notes to one another or threw paper darts ... At the end of the lecture the Observer respectfully asked his pupils to make comments or to question him, but few responded, while the somnolent Admiral merely growled succinctly 'Aeroplanes are no damn good at all'. The lecturer, being vastly junior to his hearers, was in a most delicate position so, disguising his astonishment at the Admiral's belief, he again referred to the tremendous value of aircraft in reconnaissance, pointing out how they could perform at a fraction of the cost in men and materials, the scouting duties of cruisers.

'Nonsense' snarled the old salt. 'You can't see a thing from an aeroplane'.

'Have you had much experience, sir?' enquired the lecturer very deferentially indeed.

'Never been up in an aeroplane in my life, and don't intend to. But I did climb the Rock of Gibraltar one day and I couldn't see a damn thing from the top.'

In that dampening climate of opinion it was a tremendous reinforcement to the morale of those who believed in the vital function of aircraft in the Royal Navy when Admiral Sir Roger Keyes, C-in-C Mediterranean, came out strongly on our side and gave us every encouragement. He had also been amongst the first to realise the possibilities of submarines in their infancy. Sad to tell, the Fleet Air Arm rewarded gallant Roger, our champion, in a manner which nearly lost him to us entirely and in any case might well have weakened his support for our cause. He announced his intention to inspect *Eagle* at sea, giving us a week or two in which to prepare. Ashore at Hal Far aerodrome the officers and men of every flight – of the Blackburn Darts, Fairey IIIDs, Blackburn Spotters, clumsy Bisons and tiny Fairey Flycatcher fighters – tuned their aircraft and equipment to the highest pitch of perfection, while on board the carrier the flight deck parties, salvage parties, lift workers and so on practised their functions assiduously – from the simple task of snatching away chocks from the undercarriage wheels for the take-off to rushing to save the aircraft, on the point of falling over the side after a bad landing, by extinguishing fires and rescuing the crews should they crash on the deck. On the great day the *Eagle*, normally in a most efficient state, was faultless in every department, from her aircraft standing by on the aerodrome to the ship herself, steaming about off Malta.

The first to land on was the Blackburn Spotter piloted by Flying Officer [W. C.] Venmore carrying the Commander-in-Chief himself and his Air Staff Officer, Wing-Commander Bromet. Our Captain, Munro-Kerr, received Admiral Keyes on the flight-deck and escorted him up the ladders stage by stage to the high bridge, whence he was to view the Fleet Air Arm 'doing its stuff'.

Out flew the aeroplanes, flight by flight, landed and were neatly brought up by the arrester wires, unhooked and trundled by many hands up to the lift, to be struck down in a flash into the vast hangar below. All were embarked without a hitch in record time.

Then the Darts took off and disappeared in a steep climb into the blue, to come screaming out of the sun a few minutes later to attack *Eagle* with torpedoes. Meanwhile the Flycatchers, which had been romping round doing wild aerobatics, came tumbling and roaring down to machine gun the decks and superstructure. The fighter pilots were addicted to beards and 'Tramp' Tidd's vast shaggy one fluttered in the slipstream as he hurtled grinning past the bridge. Then the Fairey IIID's and Blackburn Spotters bombed targets while the Bisons lumbered about wind-finding and making enemy reports. In fact a magnificent show was put on by our patron Roger.

At the end of it all, when the other aircraft had flown off to Hal Far, Venmore's Blackburn waited, engine ticking over on the flight deck while the Commander-in-Chief expressed his great satisfaction at the day's display and the fine state of efficiency of all concerned. Leaving us filled to the brim, he and Bromet climbed into the open cockpit behind the pilot and strapped themselves in, while Venmore ran up his engine in a roaring burst and held up his thumb: a few moments later the chocks were whipped away by the two sailors lying flat behind the wheels and away flew the aeroplane with its august passengers.

Eagle was still on her flying-off course, the plume of steam streaming dead down the white centre line, and the Blackburn had not risen more than 200 feet, when Venmore fired a red Very's light and banked steeply to port. Something was amiss and he was manoeuvring to land on again, while all eyes in the ship would be locked on the Blackburn. Tell-tale steam was issuing from the nacelle and the anxious onlookers guessed that the radiator was leaking and the engine seizing up – a hazard always present when flying behind those water-cooled engines. To the horror of all on deck the aircraft went into a spin as it turned, plunged into the sea and was soon submerged up to the tailplane. There seemed little hope for the three men in the wreck. The attendant destroyers had rushed with creaming bow waves to lower their sea boats.

But the two racing whalers, oars flashing furiously, had not yet reached the scene when Venmore popped up for an instant then dived like a cormorant, to reappear with the unconscious Admiral and delivered him to the first whaler, which arrived at that moment, and duck down again for Bromet. To keep himself warm, as he explained, the little pilot pulled an oar in the boat on the way to *Eagle*.

Venmore was rather old for his seniority, having been a schoolmaster for some years before joining the RAF. He was a small man, but by dogged determination he had practised body building exercises until he had fantastic control over his muscles. He used to give displays at ship's concerts, standing on the stage in bathing trunks and swelling up muscles in all parts of his body, until his normally slight figure looked formidable. As a grand finale he would work up his belly muscles until they appeared to be chasing each other round and round under his skin: that always brought the house down. In that crash he had bruised his face terribly against the cockpit and, but for his prodigious muscles, he would have broken his neck, while the Admiral and the wing-commander would have been drowned. The latter, now in 1970 a retired air marshal, to this day attributes the crash to the Admiral who had rashly said to the captain: 'Well, Kerr, you did not provide any thrill today.' The Admiral was so severely shaken up that he had to spend a few days in the naval hospital, but, believing in the principle that the best thing for one's nerve after a bad fall is to mount again and take some fences, he insisted upon going in the air again as soon as he was on his feet. What was more, he ordered Venmore to take him up, to show that he had confidence in him as a pilot.

Rear Admiral George Van Deurs, USN (Ret)
The Covered Wagon Association / USS *Midway* Museum

According to my order file, I only served aboard her for a few hours off Panama, on March 9, 1926. That day I stood in the nets and watched my first carrier landings when the planes returned from Coco-Solo. Beside me another pilot exclaimed, 'Those aren't landings, they are controlled crashes.' I could not have agreed more.

Captain R. Ramsbotham, OBE, RN
from the private papers of R. R. Ramsbotham, IWM Ref 11493

December 1925 – August 1926.
I was really appointed to the 'Warspite' ... but as she was going to become Flagship of the Mediterranean Fleet, a commander (N) was required, [and] I was given the 'Eagle'. I was slightly shocked when I 'bought' her, as her Bridge was on the island on the starboard side of the ship, and going into Harbour, one had to con her from her Flying Bridge, which extended over the flight deck and gave one a view down the centre of the ship. It was a bit lonely out there by oneself. However, I soon got used to it. My Captain was Munro Kerr, a dour Scotsman who had been a Navigator in his time ... After we got to know each other, we got on

fine. We had a large number of exercises whilst I was in her, besides several excitements. We always had a couple of destroyers with us to pick up aircraft if they made a bad landing and flew into the ditch. Once, one aircraft made a bad landing, tried to get away with it, hit the top of the funnel, and somersaulted into the sea. He was picked up, but was somewhat shaken. Another plane flew into the bottom of the island. Of course, he wrote off the plane, but the only damage to him was the loss of the top of his little finger. Just over where the plane hit was a small compartment where quite a lot of officers used to gather to watch the planes land. Needless to say, these 'goofers' abandoned their front row seats ...

Another difficulty in aircraft carriers is that one is always afraid of fire. We had left Yokohama and sailed for Kobe in the Inland Sea of Japan. We were going to play Kobe at soccer on arrival. It was blowing hard during the night, and harder in the morning. The sailors always have a funny party on these occasions to back up their team. They had made a painted canvas horse and had stowed it on the outboard side of the island which was the weather side. The men always had a stand easy at 10.20. I had left the bridge, where I had been talking to the captain, and went down to my cabin. At about 10.15, I heard the alarm signal for fire stations. I rushed up to the bridge to see small lumps of red hot bamboo blowing forwards around the forward end of the island, and straight across and down the lift on to a plane in the lift well, which was down. Luckily, there were some officers in the hangar, standing about and as the red hot bits of canvas and bamboo settled on the fuselage, they managed to put their coats etc. on it. You could see little roundels of fire spreading out on the fuselage, but by the mercy of God, the fuselage did not get really alight. If it had, the wind would have taken the flames through the hangar and set all of the planes alight; the sides of the hangar would have become red hot as we had no drenching system in those days; nobody would have been able to pass outside of the hangar to get to their boats, and even if they had, I doubt if the boats would have floated due to the heavy sea running. And now, why did the canvas horse get alight? Painted canvas is very inflammable and so, of course, is bamboo. It was thought two sailors wanted to smoke before the stand easy, so they got into the canvas horse. By mistake, they set it alight as there was straw in the tail of the horse. After everything was quiet again, I fell every man in on the flying deck and told them what could have happened. I asked them all to give me of the names of the two sailors. Did I get them? No, even though I had made an impassioned speech. Whether the ship's company dealt with them themselves, I don't know. All I do know is we were bloody lucky. A whole ship's company was nearly lost through one cigarette.

Brian de Courcey Ireland, Observer, HMS *Furious*
from the private papers of Stanley Brian de Courcy Ireland, IWM Reference 1739 92/4/1

The Home Fleet Spring Cruises were rather dreaded by the wives, particularly the Carrier wives, and generally unpopular with the Fleet ... The battleships spent much time in harbour, and the Aircraft Carriers much time at sea. And regrettably in those days there were casualties from time to time; it was something that one had to live with.

The 1927 cruise began somewhat inauspiciously. The weather was poor when the flights set out from Gosport to rendezvous with the ship in the Channel, and progressively got worse. When our turn came to land on the ship it was pitching in a heavy swell and the deck rising and falling fifteen or twenty feet. It was somewhat nerve-wracking; on the first approach the deck suddenly began to rise up as if to hit us just as we were crossing the stern; on the second it equally suddenly fell away. As we circled for another attempt Connolly called out over the Voice Pipe: 'If I don't make it this time I'll have to ditch alongside; not enough petrol to return to Gosport.' The T.A.G. and I looked at each other. He mopped his brow: 'Last time I did this I broke my leg,' he remarked gloomily. We got on; and it was only then that I realised that we were the last but one to land. Two days later one of the torpedo bombers spun in directly below us during a practice attack on the fleet, and sank with the crew in it. The practice torpedo broke loose underwater and shot about 30 or 40 feet into the air. And during the cruise there were other casualties.

Well, it was nice to be back home again at the end of March and laden with the spoils of Gib.: crate of oranges, Spanish nougat (made with honey), small barrel of olives.

Radioman 3/c, later Lieutenant, Dale C. Charles, USS *Langley* (CV-1) and USS *Saratoga* (CV-3)
The Covered Wagon Association / USS *Midway* Museum

In 1927 *Langley* went to Seattle to embark the first radial-engined fighter planes, produced by Boeing.

Pilots were trained with them while on a cruise to Panama that year. One plane was lost while attempting to land one day. As it approached and was about to touch down, the ship's stern suddenly sank. The pilot desperately raised his plane's nose, and gunned the motor to clear the stern part of the flight deck of the ship, but his tailhook snagged onto a fore and aft cable. I had been standing in the safety netting when this happened and saw him fly straight into the sea when the cable snapped. We saw nothing but bubbles for a short period of time then the plane surfaced, and behold, there was the Pilot astraddle the back edge of the cockpit. He was later unable to tell how he got there.

In all the time I was aboard the *Langley* I only saw one fatality. In 1928 we went on Manuevers on the way to Pearl Harbor, Hawaii. One scouting plane took a nose dive while taking off. The plane disappeared in front of the ship, and sank. The radio man Bagoria RM1/c came up and was rescued. The pilot was not so fortunate, however, as he went down with the plane and was lost.

In 1927 we covered a large area between the U.S. Coast and the Hawaiian Islands looking for the Dole fliers that were lost at sea. After a long search, no wreckage was ever found. It was reported later that many of them never made it.*

Later in 1929 when I was transferred to the *Saratoga* and served with Admiral Reeves, the Carrier planes theoretically scouted and bombed and strafed the entire Panama Canal on both sides. It wasn't until the raids were completed that the enemy theoretically spotted the planes as they were landing on the *Saratoga*. That event was really the beginning of Carrier planes used for that kind of action. Previously the Navy used Destroyers for scouting purposes and the Carrier planes just flew around to observe the maneuvers.

THE 1930s

Commander Bonham de Laune Faunce, HMS *Glorious*
from the private papers of B. de L. Faunce, IWM Department of Documemts Reference 3181 87/3/1

When the *Glorious* joined the Mediterranean Fleet in 1930, I was transferred to her. She was virtually the same as the *Courageous* but a bit more modern. At Gibraltar at the end of the spring Cruise, we had a new Captain and a new Navigator on the day before we sailed. The Fleet was doing exercises as it steered East and the Captain decided to leave ahead of the rest to give us a clear manoeuvring space for flying aircraft on and off. We had hardly got our fighters and most of our reconnaissance aircraft airborne than we ran into thick fog. The only thing we could do was to turn round and get out of it at high speed. The next units of the fleet were some way astern. We had seen a liner steering East several miles inshore of us and justifiably assumed that she would reduce speed and maintain her course in accordance with the Rule of the Road. Suddenly we heard a siren faintly on the starboard side. We stopped engines, but were making well over 20 knots. The siren sounded again very near, and almost at once we saw the tops of a ship's masts on the starboard bow crossing our track. We rang down for full astern and the engines had just about started to turn when we hit. The ship gave a lurch and came to a stop, and we stopped engines so as to stay locked into the liner which we could now see. The top of our flying-off deck was overlapping the liner's foredeck and people started streaming off her on to us. We had all the 750 passengers and crew aboard.

In the meantime, I had signalled to the Fairey IIIs, which had radio, to try to collect the fighters which had not, and to await orders. They were fairly successful as all except three fighters eventually landed at Malaga. The other three came down on the water and were lost, but the pilots were picked up. The commander reported that our collision bulkhead was holding and that it

---

* In 1927 millionaire businessman James D Dole sponsored an air race from Oakland California to Honolulu – some 2,700 miles. Only two planes completed the distance and three "Dole Fliers" as they were called were lost without trace over the Pacific.

would be safer for us to back out and the Captain of the *Florida* and one of our our officers found that we had holed one hold only and that the bulkheads fore and abaft it seemed to be intact. We put our engines astern and pulled out to an infernal creaking and screaming of torn metal. Two destroyers which were now with us went alongside and made another examination of the *Florida* and came to the conclusion that she was in no danger of sinking. They had secured one each side of her, head to stern, and very slowly went ahead and steered for Malaga. We kept with them a few cables clear, and we arrived early the following morning. When we had disembarked our passengers into lighters, we made for Gibraltar where we arrived with an enormous bunch of bananas hanging from our undercut stem, part of the *Florida*'s cargo.

Before we backed out of the *Florida*, Johnny Johnston, the skipper of one of our destroyers, had a quick look round to see if any one was left on board. He was just going to pass through the first class lounge when he beheld a tiger coming through the other door. He jumped out on deck and slammed his door, and got back on to his own ship as quick as he could. That was his story, anyway.

The collision occurred on 1 April 1931.

Rear Admiral Sir Murray Sueter
from *Hansard*

By then MP for Hertford, Sueter had been instrumental in the setting up of the RNAS. This statement is part of his speech to Parliament on 9 March 1935 during a debate on air force numbers.

Many of the Air Committee went to Weymouth and went on board H.M.S. 'Courageous' and saw these young officers being catapulted off the deck of the aeroplane carrier. It was a wonderful sight to see the way in which they were catapulted off and came back and landed on the carrier within six inches of a line down the centre. I found the Admiral, Sir Alexander Ramsay, taking a great interest in the airmen and doing everything he could to encourage them. That was very different from the old days when I was in the Royal Naval Air Service

Captain Brian de Courcy Ireland, RN, Staff Officer to Admiral Ramsay, HMS *Courageous*, 1935
from the papers of Stanley Brian de Courcey Ireland,
IWM Reference 1739 92/4/1

During the 1930s the development of the steam catapult and accelerator ... speeded up the operation of carrier borne aircraft considerably. Aircraft could be hurled into the air, as it were, in rapid succession; and without the necessity of the Carrier steaming directly into the wind or with such a high wind speed over the deck. They could also on occasion be flown off at anchor.

The latest accelerator had been fitted in the Carrier Flagship and had just completed its trials before the Abyssinian crisis in 1935; when the Admiral decided that he would be accelerated as a passenger, piloted by one of the senior Pilots. He was quite fearless in these matters, and greatly respected and admired in consequence.

There was only one snag: he objected to wearing flying clothing, and his staff always had great difficulty in getting him dressed for the part. In fact this was usually only accomplished by a united effort involving much heaving and lugging accompanied by a running commentary of grumbles, complaints and not a little invective.

The drill for being accelerated added considerably to our tribulations. We had to impress on him that he must face aft, place his crossed forearms on the gun ring, rest his head on his arms and not look up, otherwise the sudden and violent jerk would almost certainly rick his neck. Eventually we got him into the front seat of the after cockpit – normally occupied by the Observer, and were fairly satisfied that he would observe the correct drill. A signal was made to our consort that the Admiral would be paying them an official visit by air shortly, flying his flag, and among other preparations the Bugler was placed to sound off the 'Alert' as the aircraft took off.

The RAF Squadron Leader operating the Accelerator then took up his position, the Pilot revved up his engine, raised his thumb to indicate that he was ready. The Squadron Leader lowered his green flag as an order to the Chief Mechanic who pulled the operating lever.

Nothing happened!

The Squadron Leader raised his red flag, the Pilot throttled back, there was a hurried consultation and the Admiral looked up and registered annoyance. The drill was repeated.

Nothing happened!

The Admiral looked even more annoyed. The drill was repeated a third time.

Nothing happened!

The Admiral stood up and shook his fist at the Squadron Leader. He also said something, and although it most certainly wasn't 'abracadabra' it achieved results. The accelerator operated suddenly and without warning. The Admiral, caught completely unawares, described a perfect parabola and landed head downwards and legs in the air in the rear of the after cockpit. His face made an unwelcome contact with the knobs of the wireless set, and his legs formed what was in a few years' time to become the famous 'V' sign.

The Pilot was of course also unprepared. He had in fact begun to throttle back his engine, when he suddenly found his aircraft being hurtled into the air. For several seconds he battled desperately to keep airborne; and he was in fact within an ace of hitting the water before he gained flying speed and full control.

It was another minute or so before he had gained sufficient height and speed to think about his passenger, and when he did turn round all he saw was a pair of legs. He also became acutely aware that a searchlight was trained on him, 'Verey' pistols were being fired, and the signal for an emergency landing was hoisted. He wasted no time, and after executing one of the tightest turns I have ever seen, came straight in for a landing.

On deck the spectacle of the Admiral's departure created a picture which was to remain vivid in our minds for many a year; the proceedings being added to by the Marine Bugler, who true to the traditions of his Corps sounded off the 'Alert' as he had been ordered to do. The fact that the Admiral was upside down was to his mind immaterial; when Admirals leave the ship officially, you sound the 'Alert'.

The Pilot made a remarkably good landing under the circumstances, came to a stop, and cut his engine as the handling party ran out to seize the wing tips and place the chocks under the wheels.

There was an unexpectant pause: not a sign of the Admiral. The PMO (Senior Doctor) advanced apprehensively and with obvious reluctance; and had just reached the side of the after cockpit when the Admiral emerged – right side up. He was not a pretty sight: his helmet was all on one side, and blood was trickling down his cheeks from several scratches. It was immediately evident however that he was in full possession of his faculties. The PMO, being the nearest, got the full blast, and positively reeled under the impact.

It was a full minute before the Admiral ran out of breath and/or expletives. Having done so he climbed out slowly, stalked across the deck to the island and disappeared into his sea cabin. Shortly afterwards his long-suffering and imperturbable Coxswain was observed to answer his buzzer and enter his cabin with a bowl, towel and other accessories. I took the opportunity to put through a call to his Steward and place an order.

Failing a definite summons it was immediately agreed by everybody – except myself – that I should be the first to beard the presence. 'I can't leave the bridge,' said the Captain (quite untruthfully) 'and you are his senior Staff Officer'.

So that was that, and I waited. In due course the Coxswain emerged. 'He's O.K. Sir,' he whispered 'but a bit wild still;' and I went in. The Admiral was sitting in his chair, his cheeks covered with sticking plaster. He looked up and glared at me.

'I didn't send for you,' he said. 'Get out.'

I stood my ground. 'The Captain asks permission to cancel your visit to *Glorious*, Sir, and to act independently,' I said.

'Tell the Flag Lieutenant to make the necessary signals,' he replied, 'and get out.'

I went to the door, opened it, nodded to the Flag Lieutenant who was outside, and returned with a glass handed me by the Admiral's Steward. 'I told you to get ... what's that?' said the Admiral suspiciously: 'Brandy and soda,' I replied, 'I thought you might like one.' 'The Admiral brightened perceptibly and seized the glass.

'That ... prick-farrier* hasn't been doping this?" he enquired inelegantly.

'No,' I answered, 'he's not been near it.'

The Admiral grunted, swallowed his drink, and regarded me with something approaching favour. 'That was a near run thing, Colonel,' he said. 'What's happening?'

'The Captain is holding an enquiry, Sir, as to what went wrong. I don't think it was the drill on deck; something down below in the works probably. The Pilot made a wonderful recovery, Sir,' I added. 'Would you like to see him?'

'Of course I would,' he said, 'at once. Get hold of him. And, er ...' looking at his empty glass ... 'he could probably do with a drink too. Give my apologies to that Doctor and tell him he can titivate my face later on.' He grinned, and winced as the plasters pulled. 'You ought to have seen his face,' he added.

The horrors of Gas Warfare as practised by the Italians against the Abyssinians had alerted the British Fleet at Alexandria; and the Commander in Chief had issued instructions that all ships were to review their defences against this form of warfare, and to carry out realistic exercises to test their efficiency.

We decided, among other things, to simulate a bombing attack on the Carriers during flying exercises at sea by a squadron using flour bags as gas bombs. Sufficient warning of the attack would be given to enable any aircraft on deck to be flown off or struck below to avoid unnecessary damage. It promised to be an interesting test, but so far as the Staff were concerned there was a snag. The Admiral refused to carry or wear a gas mask. Nothing would induce him to have anything to do with one.

'If you think I am going to wear one of those damned gargoyles,' he said truculently, 'you can think again. Proper Charlie I'd look with that on me face. Mine don't fit anyway; and yer can't see or breathe or eat or smoke when yer get it on,' he added somewhat inconsequentially.

We tried various tactics: setting an example; what the sailors would expect; getting used to what he would have to wear in war; the discomfort he might suffer if a practice gas canister was let off near him. It was to no avail; and there is a point beyond which you cannot go with an Admiral – with safety.

So we all took up our 'Action Stations' in the Admiral's Plot, a small compartment above and behind the Bridge, whence we could direct operations. We donned our gas masks – the Admiral did not. I imagine it must have been the reference to a 'gas canister' that put the idea into the Flag Lieut.'s mind. The Flag Lieut. was a very able and efficient 'Signals' specialist. He also possessed a great sense of humour, too great in fact.

There were times when you could pull the Admiral's leg; there were times when you had to stand up to him, stick to your opinions, and endure the wrath vented on you. In return the Admiral respected you for holding onto your convictions and riding his temporary anger. But there was a point beyond

* Doctor. A 'fang-farrier' was a dentist.

which a wise Staff Officer did not go. The Flag Lieut. was strangely insensitive to this point.

The Flag Lieut. decided in fact, that he would teach the Admiral a lesson. He obtained one of the little gas canisters used in practice, and climbed the ladder on to the 'Monkeys Island' above the Admiral's Plot. This position contained a small binnacle, bearing indicators, and a voice pipe to the Plotting Room below. He removed the cover to the voice pipe, blew down it to sound the whistle in the cover below, waited until someone answered by removing the cover, then after activating the canister popped it down the pipe.

It was the Admiral who had answered. He was bending over the plotting table, and the canister, after trundling down the pipe, hit him on the ear and landed on the table. The scene that followed was perhaps best viewed in retrospect. The Secretary and the SOO2 [Staff Officer Operations 2] seized the Admiral, and opening the square port at the side of the room thrust his head and shoulders out into the slip stream of wind blowing past. I knocked the canister off the table, and opening the door, kicked it out. It landed in a flag locker on the signal deck below, where it continued to exude its foul contents. It was unfortunate that the Signalmen, finding it difficult to read flag signals whilst wearing gas masks, and thinking no one would see them, had removed theirs. There was thus considerable confusion on the flag deck.

The Admiral had by now recovered his voice and was in full flow. The Secretary and SOO2 still had hold of his legs and were holding on grimly; otherwise he would have surely fallen through the port, and I opened up every aperture to clear away the gas. On the Bridge below and forward of the Admiral's Plotting Room the Captain and the Officer of the Watch had been conducting a muffled conversation through their gas masks, when their ears were suddenly assailed by a flow of invective that could only have one origin. Glancing upwards they were astonished and horrified to see the Admiral, head and shoulders protruding dangerously through a square port, his face scarlet, and tears streaming down his cheeks, while above him the Flag Lieut. was leaning over the Monkey Island, a look of consternation and dawning realisation of the enormity of his action on his face.

Sometime later I was sent for by the Admiral, who was recovering in his sea cabin.

'Where is he?' he enquired grimly.

'Gone to his cabin,' I replied, 'trying to make up his mind whether to come and apologise or write a letter.'

'What would you do if you were him?' said the Admiral.

'Come and apologise at once,' I replied.

He nodded. 'You would, Colonel. But I don't want to see him or have a written apology. Tell him, will you?'

Thus did the Flag Lieut. terminate his seagoing career, and find the outlet for his undoubted talents in research appointments ashore.

The Flag Lieutenant is almost certainly W. A. C. Binnie, who did indeed go ashore, to work first in Signals and post war in the Radio Equipment Department before retiring as a Commander in 1946.

AMM 1/C William C. C. Carpenter, USS *Langley* (CV-1)
The Covered Wagon Association / USS *Midway* Museum

As you know, the Airdales* were bunked in the former old Coal Bins that were filled up with about 18 feet of concrete – plus several 18 inch Coastal Howitzers and various sized Naval Deck Guns, or so the Old Timers on the 'Old Tub' said, were in the bottom. Our bunks were three high, and the 'Heads' were about 10 feet from the living compartment. As the Squadron that I was attached to lived in the forward compartment, we were blessed with a Boatswains Mate that was transferred from the old U.S.S. *Maryland*.

To him the lowest forms of life were the Airdales, and he never was one to let us forget it. Which was a mistake on his part, as our whole aim in life was to make him UNHAPPY. His name was McCormike. He was the outfit's Master at Arms. So, if you remember, after inspections of personnel, we would have a below decks inspection. When that happened, McCormike would close off both Heads, and leave us 1 Stool, 2 Urinals, and 2 Wash Basins for 65 Airdales to prepare for inspection. So one payday we had a council of war. It was a Friday night and we had this meeting in the 'Old Crows Nest' which was a dive just across from the Army Navy 'Y' on Broadway, in San Diego. At that time it was a Boot-Leg joint. There were 5 or 6 of us drinking that God awful Rot Gut that you could buy there. Up came Mac's name and what we could do to screw him up. Someone suggested that we wallpaper the Head that was closed completely for inspection. It was the one that was beside the ladder going down to the living quarters. So about midnight the war council broke up and we all went up to the 'Rite Spot Cafe' to get an egg and bacon sandwich, which cost 15 cents, and some coffee we all needed was 5 cents. All plans completed, so we got aboard the old Nickel Snatcher that chugged over to the North Island Dock where the *Langley* was tied up. At that time, we only went out to sea about 10 days a month as it was during the depression and the Government was about broke, and Mrs Hoover said that we Sailors ought to serve for a dollar a year. Boy the crap really hit the fan that summer of '31 over that statement … but to get back to the dirty deed coming up … We borrowed the keys for the Head door by the Ladder. We got about 10 to 12 rolls of that wrapping paper the Navy calls Toilet Tissue. We started wall papering the Head until all the Bulkheads (walls) were covered with paper. We festooned the lamps and all the rods between the stalls and anything else that the paper would stick to. Quietly we replaced the keys back into Mac's pants, locked up the Head, and as far as could be told, the place had not been bothered since myself and the other Captain of the Head had finished painting the place.

---

* US Naval crewman who is either aircrew or a naval rating with the task of supporting flying operations.

The inspection went off as per usual with all the old peace time bull that 'Admiral Tie Tie Butler' could think of. (He got his nickname from his inspections of the enlisted men, by checking the ties in the backs of our pants to see if they were tied in a square knot threaded right side over the left. He was a genuine bastard.) So after the personnel inspection was over, the word was passed to prepare for below decks Inspection. 'Mac' unlocked the chain securing the hatch on the Head, and went below to check on the other one. Back he comes, just in time to greet the inspection party. He throws open the hatch door and immediately swallows his tobacco chaw. The sight of our wall papering was too much for him, and he almost passed out. Admiral Tie Tie's explosion down there was fantastic. It got the whole Squadron restricted to the ship until the culprits were caught. No one would admit it until about 3 P.M. a Yeoman Striker went to the Skipper and told him that he knew who had done it. Lt. Cmdr Pride was our Skipper, and he did not take kindly to what the Yeoman had to say. He told him he did not like Stool Pigeons and to get ready for a transfer in 1 hour.

Then he called Mac in, and chewed him out for his pettiness about locking the Heads off during inspections. But as you recall in those days, 'Boatswains' were not known for their smarts and so the feud simmered on. He went out of his way to make life miserable for the rest of us.

Some time later, out came an order from some 'Flat Head' that we had to have our rates sewn on our sleeves so that the middle of it was on the outside crease of our sleeves. This was so anyone coming up behind the man could tell if he was a 1st, 2nd, or 3rd class petty officer. Boy that was just another petty thing prevailing in the Navy at that time. But the new order became a God Send to us in the Squadron. One night before inspection we got ahold of Mac's inspection uniform, and we created a new rate for him. We sewed Wings on the crossed Anchors. The next day at inspection, he is standing there, no one is talking to him, and he won't talk to us undesirables because we don't act like Battleship Sailors. He never noticed the new rate that he now has. We fall in for inspection, and along comes Lt. CDR Pride. He stops, steps back and looks at Mac's arm, and asks 'when did that rate come out, Mac?' Mac still don't bother to look down at his arm and replies, 'It came from the ships small stores sir'. Pride asks, 'Are you sure'? Then Mac looks down and starts screaming, 'Them S.O.B. Airdales did it to me again.' Pride then suggested to Mac that he try to get along with us, and not to expect to get a transfer back to the regular Navy, period!!! After that Mac really tried hard, and he wound up to be one hell of a good man. Just before Pride was transfered back to Washington, D.C. he got Mac promoted to Chief, and we throwed him a hell of a party plus throwed him in the Bay clothes and all.

Bill Carpenter was one of four seamen detailed to remove not only the offending paper, but also 25 coats of old paint ...

I Just Got Another Wave-Off (Tune: *John Brown's Body*)
from *The Fleet Air Arm Songbook*

This Fleet Air Arm song reflects the gratitude of pilots for the introduction in 1937 of the Landing Signals Officer. A 'wave-off' told the pilot to abort landing and make another attempt.

He gave me a 'Low Dip' and a 'Roger' in the groove,
I have had a 'High' and 'Fast', but what's it going to prove?
The L.S.O. will kill you yet, but what're you going to do?
 'I'll make that bastard jump into the net.'

CHORUS
I just got another wave-off, I just got another wave-off,
I just got another wave-off
But I made that bastard jump into the net.

If the ship is on my wing he says I'm close it seems,
So if I move a foot more out then I'm far too wide abeam.
If he waves me off again I'm ready and I'm set.
I'll make that bastard jump into the net.

Captain Alan 'Alfie' Sutton, CBE, DSC*, then an Observer, 823 Squadron, HMS *Glorious*
IWM Sound Archive Reference 12149

We went off to the Mediterranean, to the *Glorious*, and joined her in 1938, just about the time the Fleet Air Arm was being turned over from the Air Force to the Navy. That was a strange period, because the vast expansion of the Air Force meant that they were calling back their own pilots ... We started to get the first of the Air Branch officers joining the ship and replacing the Air Force officers who were going ... The Air Branch were restricted to air duties, but they were made to carry out a number of ship duties as well. They were specially recruited for the Fleet Air Arm; they wore an A inside the circle of their badge of rank on their sleeves. They were deeply resented, to start with, by the ordinary executive, straightforward naval officer. This appeared to be a dilution of the status of officer, to have these specially recruited officers brought in, who weren't fully seamen; and indeed some people I knew on the ship wouldn't talk to them at all.

It was a peculiar situation: you had these men who were now manning the squadrons both as observers and as pilots, and some old-type naval officers just said they weren't naval officers, they didn't want to know them, didn't like them. You can't live in a ship like that without dissension: it was an unhappy situation ... In fact the *Glorious* in some ways became an unhappy ship, as it hadn't been when I first joined it under [Captain Arthur] Lumley Lyster. Oh, it was alright, an efficient, fine fighting ship. He left, and was relieved by a chap called [Captain Guy] D'Oyly-Hughes [DSO, DSC]. Now D'Oyly-Hughes was a well-known submariner from the First World War. He'd made his name in those early submarines, fighting up in the Sea of Marmora and the Dardanelles against the Turks, and done amazing things … But he was now a senior captain, and he wasn't the same sort of man he'd been when he was a young officer. He was cantankerous and difficult, and he didn't believe that the ship was efficient. He thought the ship was inefficient and he'd better lick her into shape. He had a certain conception about the tactics we were employing in attacks with the main strike weapon we had, which was the Swordfish with the torpedo or bombs, and tried to impose them … when the Squadron personnel knew that to employ his tactic we were going to lose all our lives.

He had a violent temper, furious temper. He also had the unhappy habit of propositioning his young officers' wives. I mean, this was great fun, but it doesn't make for a happy ship. I remember being ashore at a club in Alexandria and one of the young officers' wives came up to me and sat down and said: 'What can I do? The Captain's pestering me the whole time to go to bed with him.'

I said: 'Tell your husband.'

She said: 'Well, I have, and I've also protested to the Captain that I'm going to tell my husband; and he said "Well, tell your husband. Tell him to go to hell. Are you coming to bed with me?".'

I don't know if he was laying the girls or not, but it didn't make for happiness. It's a peculiar thing when you're young men together like that. You have a particular protectiveness to your fellow officers' wives in your unit. Maybe you're trying to lay the loved ones in other units, but if they're in your group you protect them, they're yours … It's the morality of the 1930s, and he was flouting it.

D. J. Clist, HMS *Eagle*
from *Eagle's War*

Unlike present-day aircraft carriers *Eagle* was unique in having an upper deck round which you could walk from stem to stern and so enjoy the benefits of sea breezes and see what was going on – like a Mediterranean cruise! Having taken a walk round the ship it was easy for me to visualise much of what the various dockyard refits had finally achieved. Upon what had been mainly the normal upper deck level of the old battleship had been emplaced, along practically the whole length of the ship, steel plating supported by girders to form the deck of two hangars. There were no gangways from the hangar to below decks; these were from the walk. On the same level as the hangars were the quarterdeck and forecastle. These latter two positions enjoyed an abundance of fresh air; therefore they were very popular for sleeping billets for both officers and men. The peculiar positions in which the hammocks were slung gave one a certain amount of surprise as to their comfort – but not one of those persons would vacate such a billet for one below decks. All the messdecks on the old *Eagle*, except where the artisans, miscellaneous petty officers and senior ratings lived, were immediately below the hangar spaces and thus did not provide very much fresh air in the tropics. These messes stretched the whole width of the ship. One comforting factor was the lack of compartment doors – no knee raising or head ducking but, of course, wartime standards demand numerous doors for safety purposes.

The first time I saw the old *Eagle* was at a place in North China called Wei-hai-wei. This place of course no longer 'exists' so far as the British Navy is concerned, but it is an island situated between the Gulf of Pehida and the Yellow Sea, south of the well-known former Russian base of Port Arthur of 1904 fame, and more recently the Korean war – being only a stone's throw from North Korea itself. The climate there varied to the extreme – heavy snowfalls regularly in winter, but very hot in summer. The China Fleet (as our Far East squadron was known pre-war) used to leave Hong Kong annually when the summer approached and sail for Wei-hai-wei, where, although it was hot, the heat was not so trying as at Hong Kong which is further south and hemmed in by hills.

Part Two

CARRIERS GO TO WAR

1
Life on Board, 1939–1945

Petty Officer Telegraphist Ken Taylor, HMS *Formidable*
IWM Sound Archive Reference 26562

There were a lot of us going to *Formidable* because she was a brand new ship just commissioning ... all standing on the jetty looking up at this. The older sailors ('cause a lot of older sailors don't like going to big ships; it's like being in the barracks – the discipline, the routine, the bugle calls, that sort of thing) saying a few choice words about going to a big ship, but I was excited: it was my first ship. They always sent boys to cruisers and above – they never sent boys to small ships – so that, therefore, you were still under strict control, 'cause they were responsible to your parents for you – you were under age.

Fantastic ship! I looked at this with a bit of trepidation. Would I cope? ... My first ship, and a big carrier, they had a big boys' mess deck: there were fifty boys in the boys' mess deck ... The boys were kept separate: you had your own heads, your own bathroom; and you had two instructors. The boys were a mixture of signalmen, sparkers and seamen, and, basically, apart from working, you were also training ...

One of the first jobs I got – and it frightened the life our of me: the Chief turned round to me and said 'The hydrophones are not working. They've got the hatches to the double-bottom open' – because these carriers were built with a double skin, with a passageway between them – 'I want you to go and check them'.

I couldn't tell him what a hydrophone was, at first.

They gave me a spanner. You go down as low as you can, and you've got these little plates – they can't hardly call them hatches – with about 32 nuts on which the Engine Room department remove, and you go down. People have to know you're down there because you could get shut down there and no one would know, because there's no sort of ventilation where the keel is. I got down there, and I had to have a wandering lead, as we call it: a bit of long lead with a light on the front. It's quite narrow when you think of the ship. There's the keel there, there's the side of the ship, there's metal strengthening, so I could have one foot that side, one foot this. There's all water down here where the keel was, and I saw these objects on either side of the ship; they were, I suppose, about 12" in diameter with some nuts on ... I thought: these have got to be the hydrophones. So I got this spanner and I start undoing the nuts, and water starts coming in. I thought I'd sunk the ship! I did a bit on one, and the water stopped. So I took them off, and the hydrophone has a very sensitive microphone in there, and this is why they were not working: they were full of water. So I put them all back together and tightened all up, and went back up to see the Chief, and said 'They were full of water, Chief.'

They weren't bothered with them, I don't think they ever did work …

EAT …

Cecil P. Wareham, Royal Marines, HMS *Unicorn*
from the private papers of C. P. Wareham, IWM Reference 5546 96/31/1

Traditions in the Navy do not change just because you are in hot temperatures. Even boiled beef and carrots with real potatoes if we were fortunate were always served on a Wednesday whether you were in the Arctic or on the Equator!

Lieutenant Commander Otto C. Romanelli, USN Rtd., USS *Lexington* (CV-16)
from *Blue Ghost Memoirs*

We received mail from home via Fleet Post Office. My mother would bake hard cookies which, many years later, my daughter dubbed the 'one-two' cookies because of the number of chocolate bits in each. The cookies were a welcome treat from home which I shared with my roommates. My roommate Dick also received packages from home. His family owned a candy factory and his packages bore the name of the factory and the contents were labeled as 'chocolate syrup.' In fact, the packages contained a bottle of Haig and Haig Pinch, a fine Scotch.

Our room had a wall safe which was to be used to safeguard classified documents but the only time the safe was locked was when it contained Haig and Haig Pinch. Of course our friends were always on the lookout for 'chocolate syrup,' for that meant a party of 'one-two' cookies and Haig and Haig Pinch.

The 'tip-off' on when we expected action from the enemy came in the morning when we were fed a 'battle breakfast' of steak and eggs. For the rest of the day and maybe the following night the meals consisted of just Spam sandwiches.

Petty Officer Telegraphist Ken Taylor, HMS *Formidable*
IWM Sound Archive Reference 26562

We had to go to Scapa because … we'd got the degaussing cables on, and there's a degaussing range there. Travelling through this range, they could neutralise the magnetic field of the ship. To go up to Scapa Flow, you go round the Pentland Firth … You talk about Cape Horn, you talk about various other places: there's nothing like Pentland Firth in bad weather … We put to sea, and next morning – of course, carriers have a very long roll – and we had a lot of old destroyer sailors on, and they were seasick. Because of the weight of the flight deck and the way it spreads out, once they start rolling, they don't seem to stop. You can get a dead calm sea and they're still doing this for quite a long time. Every boy on the mess deck was seasick except me and old Jacko. The breakfast that morning was sausage and beans, and we had trays and trays and trays of sausage and beans. There was boys lying on the deck, they were in the heads, in the bathroom, groaning and moaning, and me and Jacko sat there and made pigs of ourselves on sausage and beans.

Ronald Vaughn, Division 2, USS *Kitkun Bay* (CVE-71)
from the Ronald Vaughn Papers (#658), Joyner Library

When I first got up, I was feeling a little bit seasick, and by the time we secured battle stations to go to breakfast, I was so sick I couldn't get within smelling distance of the mess hall without wanting to throw up. The second day, I got as far as the top of the ladder going down to the mess hall. The third day, I got to the bottom of the ladder before having to go topside for some fresh air. I had a bad case of what is known as the dry heaves because there was nothing in my stomach to throw up. The fourth day, I finally got through the chow line and got a little food down. That was the medicine I needed, because from that time on I was never seasick again.

S. J. Guise, 825 Squadron, HMS *Vindex*
Communication with the Editor

The 'hero' of the story was John Baker, a gunner on the ship.

Emily was sworn to him by the Irish to be a good egg-laying hen. (We had come in off a convoy; Xmas leave was expected – instead, another convoy). The bird was christened 'Emily' and kept in a crate by the twin 4" gun aft and was scrupulously avoided by the Captain. But fed rum and everything else. The ship's call sign [became] 'cockerel' since this is what the bird turned out to be (red faced gunner). Eventually the bird became too big for the crate and had to be looked after by one of the gun crew. He was returning to the Clyde, and Emily was taken home in a carrier bag. Guns didn't find this very funny. The rest of the ship did: ship's gunner going ashore with bird in bag, alive and crowing. It was rumoured that when killed for the table Emily was too tough to eat. After what it was fed, it most likely was!

DRINK ...

Lieutenant Commander Otto C. Romanelli, USN,
USS *Lexington* (CV-16)
from *Blue Ghost Memoirs*

Joshing with Dick about drinking ashore, I said, 'Should I order us a couple of cool Tom Collins?' As a tease, I picked up the ship's phone and dialed 000, knowing that that number was not listed as being assigned to any compartment on the ship. I said, 'This is Ensign Romanelli in JO Bunkroom number one. Please send up two Tom Collins' on the double!' Dick gave a reluctant laugh at my sense of humor, since he would have to wait for another day to savor a drink.

I went ashore as a passenger on the boat, savoring the relief of responsibility. I traipsed around Norfolk, where there were signs in some neighborhoods that said, 'No dogs or sailors allowed,' not exactly a welcoming greeting on behalf of the natives. I had a couple of Tom Collins' and then returned to the ship.

Along the passageway I passed the Executive Officer, Cdr. Sutcliffe, 'Evening Sir,' 'Hi Rummy,' and he gave me a broad grin, which he had never done before. When I reached the bunkroom, Dick was there and said, 'Boy are you in hot water!'

'What for?'

'Well, your telephone order for the Tom Collins' went out over the bullhorn and was heard loud and clear by the Admiral of the Atlantic fleet in his command ship tied up on the opposite side of the mooring. He called our exec and wanted to know who Ensign Romanelli was. Our exec explained that 000 was an unlisted emergency number which you knew nothing about. He told him it was a boyish prank. Boy, you're going to get it!'

'Yeah, so that's why he smiled.'

Cecil P. Wareham, Royal Marines, HMS *Unicorn*
from the private papers of C. P. Wareham, IWM Reference 5546 96/31/1

With brackish-tasting chlorinated water to drink the crew improved the flavour with Andrews Liver Salts. Taken occasionally, it soothes an upset stomach. Frequent consumption has an inconvenient side effect.

Taking Andrews at sea was a little more risky for us as the mess deck being in the after part of the ship was quite some way from the Heads which, traditionally, were housed in the bows of the ship. The journey was like going on an obstacle race with watertight doors every twenty five feet or so that you had to open, by turning about seven heavy cleats then stepping in the next section, closing the bulkhead door, and so on. We also had to go through a passageway where the casing from the ship's boiler comes up, and the extra heat always expedited the need to want to relieve oneself. If the ship was responding to a heavy sea you could add fifty per cent onto your journey time, and upon arrival, pray (probably the only time we ever prayed) that there was a vacant cubicle.

Jack Needham, Able Seaman, HMS *Indomitable*
IWM Sound Archive Reference 1991 92/27/1

Since leaving Jamaica there had been a series of systematic raids on the wardroom wine stores carried out by some of the thirstier ratings; at this time in the RN of course, beer was taboo for the lower deck, but one of the brighter ratings who had possibly been a cracksman in his civilian days had found a way of getting into the store and this blossomed out into a rather large syndicate of about 12 of us, each raid becoming more daring and the quantities of beer 'removed' getting larger each time until we were filling hammocks with the bottles and tins of it. The store itself was on one of the lower decks and beneath about three watertight doors, so the removal of this amount was criminally hair-raising. One night about 10 of us were passing up crates of the stuff when an officer came down with the inevitable question 'and WHAT are you, mmm?' To which one of the quicker-witted blokes replied 'wardroom working party, sir, getting up supplies.' The officer concerned seemed satisfied with this explanation and obligingly stacked three crates before descending for his rounds of inspection. Everyone's hair was standing on end and beads of guilty perspiration were in great evidence. All crates, hammocks and boxes were taken up to the mess decks in double quick time and watertight hatches clamped down.

On the ship at this time was a 'wind finding party' whose job was to determine the direction of the wind for flying off aircraft. There was a steam driven catapult on the port side near the bows and [this] achieved about 80 miles an hour in a very short distance. The small fighter planes, Grumman Martlets, were placed on four supports on the catapult and whisked off. Anyone who was in the front of this had to run a trifle sharpish. After our alcoholic ruse came to light it was known as the 'beer finding party' and was a seven day guffaw. The small fighter planes were made in the USA and were afterwards called Hellcats [Wildcats]. They were small, compact and very heavy and if they sank on take-off they sank instantly, not giving the pilot much of a chance of getting out, unlike the Stringbags which did sterling service and in fact sank more enemy shipping than any other plane, despite their top speed which was an optimistic 90 with a following wind. But I digress – back to the adventures of the 'beer finding party'. After the recent narrow escape the project was 'rested' for a day or two, but thirsts demanded slaking and operations were resumed. The steel framed doors of this spirit store had a chain across, which would have just about restrained a captive parrot, but this was fastened with a huge brass Admiralty lock which must have weighed a couple of pounds. To the odd rating who, prewar, had engaged in petty crackmanship this chain posed no problems; the only difficulty was to leave the place looking as if it had not been violated. The odd thing which struck us all when matters came to a head, was the fact that the huge quantity of ale which had been appropriated had not been missed. However things were not going to last. One of the more unreliable ABs joined the party and instead of imbibing wisely, slurped down a vast quantity of ale and when we were getting 'fell in; for the morning's ritual of scrubbing he was doing an excellent impression of a straw waving in the wind. The Petty Officer asked him if he was drunk and how and this AB went for him tooth and nail. Then it hit the fan in a big way – a locker search was ordered and several bottles were found. Two of these in my locker. Whether these had been 'planted' or placed there and forgotten I cannot remember but I was 'weighed off' the next day in front of the captain's table. To give this worthy his due, he was a great seamen and a just type of person but when he asked me why I had been one of the beer filching band, I replied quite truthfully that I was thirsty. Several officers present put hands over mouths and the net result was that I was sentenced to 10 days in 'the brig' as I refused to give any names of the others.

Actually this wasn't too bad. I was searched thoroughly, told to dress in canvas duck trousers and led below to a small cell right forward in the bows, where the 'bed' and pillow were made of plywood, not exactly Ritz accommodation but at least I was spared the endless scrubbing of already spotless decks and 'flats' (the name given to endless corridors and spaces which had a corticine covering). My diet consisted of a ship's biscuit and water. These ship's biscuits – for the information of those who never broke a tooth on them – were harder than a Blackpool landlady's heart, so the only possible way to eat these was to dunk them in water, otherwise you were in danger of a major dental refit. The choice of reading matter was either the *Manual of Seamanship* or the *Bible*. Having been a Freethinker for several years, although officially classed 'C of E', I decided to give this tome the benefit of the doubt and read it from cover to cover, which did nothing to convince me but only reinforced my views. Anyone who believed that a whale could swallow Jonah would be capable of swallowing anything and how a kangaroo hopped across from Australia to get into the Ark was never explained. A marine sentry was permanently outside the four cells, which on that ship were usually occupied, as the discipline was the harshest of any ship I ever served on. One day I observed that the door was fastened by the same sort of chain as on the spirit store which had been plundered and an even larger brass lock, but the securing nut on the chain was on my side of the cell. This was only finger tight, so on several occasions in the early hours I would unscrew this and creep up to the mess cupboard and grab a few goodies like corned beef and any leftovers, scurrying back to eat these in the confines of my cramped quarters. One night out of sheer devilment I emerged and tapped the slumbering sentry on the shoulder and asked him if he would be interested in purchasing a battleship. He looked at me with a horrified glance such as would be reserved for a viewing of Marley's ghost and said 'bleedin' 'ell, 'ow did yer gerrout?' But I made no further forays as this would have only landed the bloke in serious trouble. One day one of my 'oppos' flew down and passed an opened tin of baked beans through the gap in the chained door. This was only prior to the 'Jaunty's' rounds of inspection so I had to hang this from the porthole clip by bending back the lid to form a hook. It was a time of suspense as the Jaunty peered round the cell, looking under the plywood pillow from which some occupant had removed some of the nails and of course he found nothing but fresh air.

Part of the punishment was to pick a pound of oakum (thick tarred rope) per day and this had to be done because another pound came every day. An old three-badger put me wise on this some months previously. To do this job with the fingernails alone would soon reduce fingers to ribbons so I had secreted a razor blade in the hem of my canvas ducks and so the job was a pushover as the rope could be painlessly shredded. This punishment was a relic of Nelson's day when the resultant pile of rope fluff was used for sponging out gun barrels. I was allowed out every day for exercise on the flight deck for an hour and the witticisms from the peasantry at large were amusing – in fact it seemed that the 'beer finding party' had occasioned some measure of amusement, even amongst some of the officers, and I detected a quite a few knowing smirks from some of the latter in the Engineering Branch who were a little more human than the dyed in the wool RN fraternity who used to look at lower deck ratings like a blocked-up toilet.

Surgeon Lieutenant Commander E. V. B. Morton, HMS *Battler*, 1945
from the Private Papers of E. V. B. Morton, IWM Reference 1311 87/16/1

'Chiefy' was also a genial and happy alcoholic, in fact he later became one of the few patients I have ever seen with full blown classical acute delirium tremens – with green dragons appearing from under his bunk and all!! ...

[The Principal Medical Officer] and the chief engineer formed an oddly assorted, but inseparable drinking partnership, spending most of the available hours at the wardroom bar drinking and playing shove ha'penny! They made a fascinating if incongruous pair, the genial giant of a P.M.O. and 'Chiefy', small wiry and wrinkled, the one slow and shambling, the other hyperactive and birdlike. The wardroom echoed with triumphal shouts in both Irish brogue and broad Devonshire as they battled over the wooden shove ha'penny board. The other contrasting difference between the two of them was that whereas the engineer would become rapidly more noisy and obviously intoxicated as the gins were consumed, the doctor just never seemed to be affected; he had a remarkable tolerance for alcohol.

Only once in the whole commission did I see him the worse for wear, though it was reported that on one occasion in Cochin he was brought back to the ship in a rick-shaw quite incapable of independent locomotion so that the duty part of the watch had to be turned out in the small hours to carry him up the gangway and to his bunk! On the other hand it was the P.M.O. who without assistance would often put the Chief Engineer to bed! The latter, on one famous occasion after a party in another ship, returned on board in the duty M.F.V. and turned in only to be awoken later that night by the rightful owner of the bunk as not only was 'Chiefy' in the wrong cabin, he was in the wrong ship! Admittedly it was another escort carrier and most of these were very similar in appearance and in general lay out.

AND BE MERRY ...

Cecil P. Wareham, Royal Marines, HMS *Unicorn*
from the private papers of C. P. Wareham, IWM Reference 5546 96/31/1

There were inevitable punch-ups ashore [in Colombo] to relieve the boredom, mainly against the personnel from the French battleship *Richelieu*, Dutch cruiser *Tromp* and American aircraft carrier *Saratoga*. It appeared to be complete madness that these fights could take place and perhaps the next day these ships along with ours would be knocking hell out of the Japanese!

I had never played hockey before but I seemed to take to it very quickly as well as liking the game immensely, and was eventually selected to play for the ship at left back, and alongside me playing right back was Captain H. L. St. J. Fancourt, DSO, RN, the ship's Captain. I felt rather embarrassed at first, but playing on the hard grassless pitches ashore where youth was the prime ingredient, I often had to cover his side of the pitch (he must have been about fifty years* of age) and I believe that he was grateful for this. My confidence soared and although to me he was always the Captain of the ship, I relaxed enough to enjoy each game that I was playing.

Seaman Gunner W. 'Tug' Whymark, HMS *Eagle*
Quoted in *Eagle's War*

There were brief interludes of course when one could relax and 'Jack' always knows how to make the most of them, especially in wartime. In Alexandria it was warm enough for 'hands over the side to bathe' to be popular. We also had boat sailing on which I was particularly keen myself. About once a month I got the chance to be in the crew of the ship's whaler. And usually the start of any day in harbour would be hands to muster for a spell of PT (Physical Training) under the supervision of the ship's PT Instructor (not the most popular man in the ship!) and then double around the flight deck to the music of the Royal Marines band. At times, if you were one of the 4 inch or 6 inch guns' crew you would have to lift a shell up and down above one's head to see how many times one could do it. The shell weighed 100 lbs. In the evenings too the ship's company would play Tombola (from which the modern game Bingo is derived).

Commander Eugene Robert Forsht, USS *Ticonderoga*
Dallas B. Long, Jr., Collection (#636), Joyner Library

When we were getting ready to leave the Fox Pier at San Diego, we were provisioning ship. At that time it was an all hands evolution to get all the provisions aboard; loading the fresh provisions aboard right before we left. We

---

* A veteran of the Battle of Jutland, he was 44, and lived to 103.

were using the bomb dollies to take the stuff from forward bow back to the bomb elevator which carried the provisions down below deck. The crew was running the stuff like an endless chain on the bomb dollies.

Captain Dixie [Kiefer] was well-known for all his friends in Hollywood. There was a rumor that he owned the Colonial Restaurant in Hollywood. He was quite familiar with Hollywood, and I guess a lot of the Hollywood celebrities were familiar to him. Anyway, on this day, two of the big Buick Stationwagons (they were the old wood body top with red hoods) with chauffeurs came down and pulled up to the officer's gangway. Captain Dixie went out to meet them. There were six or eight prominent stars who got out. Dixie took them to the Captain's cabin. I guess they had an afternoon of talking and entertainment. They left around 4:30. I remember Captain Dixie kissed the ladies goodbye and shook hands with the men. If you remember, the Fox Pier did not have any bars or anything. All it had was 12 × 12's at the end of the pier. That was the only thing to keep cars and people from driving or walking right into the water. Captain Dixie was waving goodbye to the two station wagons as they were leaving. He was stepping backward waving goodbye, looking forward, and he fell over the 12 × 12 and right into the drink beside the ship. The OD on the officer's gangway passed the word – 'Captain overboard'. At that time I think about 50 of the crew jumped in after Captain Dixie. Needless to say everybody got out OK. Needless to say all hands were having quite a chuckle over it. The captain and everyone who went to rescue him were covered with most of everything (the debris and everything else from all the ship) in the water. He came up to the OD and grabbed the microphone and passed the word 'All of you have a good laugh on me … I'm going up to have a shower, change clothes and come down and help you provision ship.' He was as good as his word. He came down in his dry kackies and went over to Burns, a First Class Ordnance man who was about the shortest man in the crew. Captain Dixie told him 'to take a rest, I'm going to take your bomb dollie.' Dixie started loading the bomb dollies with fresh provisions aboard. About 11 o'clock that night, we finally finished provisioning ship. Captain Dixie asked if the night rations were ready for those men who had been provisioning ship. The OD informed the Captain that because of the ration money, there wouldn't be any night rations. Captain Dixie informed the OD that 'We are going to have chow, and chow for all hands.' So very shortly the supply officer was down, and the Captain and crew provisioning the ship had steak and eggs.

Lieutenant David Wright, 893 Squadron, HMS *Formidable*
IWM Sound Archive Reference 28498

We dined in the Officers' mess and we had the Wardroom. I've accompanied Noel Coward on the Piano. I was playing in the wardroom and Noel Coward was taking passage, ostensibly to go back to England from Gibraltar. (In fact we turned back so he had to fly home eventually.) As I was just playing … probably *Getting Sentimental Over You* – popular pops of the time – he came into the Wardroom and stood in the corner and started singing to me. When I got to the end, I got off. I used to play mucky songs basically [and] pops of the day. [The piano player]'s never short of beer. There's always a pint on the corner. But I was also one of the world's first DJs. I was very interested in Jazz music, Swing and Jazz, Benny Goodman, Harry James and Count Basie … and I used to collect records when I was in England, but you could get them in Gibraltar too. This is the Swing era … and every Thursday night at half-past six I had a half hour programme throughout the ship's company, 1500–2000 [men], with a microphone in my hands, playing records. I talked over the records. I said: 'Now this next riff is John Kirby on bass.' And I was talking about the music … to entertain the ship's company.'

Singing has long been a tradition in all services, and the following song – of which Wright was one of the two original composers – became the Fleet Air Arm's unofficial anthem. There is no one single version; the song reflects changes in ships, and aircraft have been added over the years. The title refers to the A25 form a pilot had to complete if he pranged his aircraft. The tune is taken from the folk song *Villikins and his Dinah*.

The A25 Song
From *The Fleet Air Arm Songbook*

I'll sing you a song about sailors who fly,
A Formidable Fleet Air Arm pilot am I
I've seized up 'em all – Merlins, Cyclones and Taurus
And many's the time that I've chanted this chorus

CHORUS (between each verse)
Cracking show, I'm alive,
But I've still got to render my A25.

They say in the Air Force a landing's okay,
If the pilot gets out and can still walk away,
But in the Fleet Air Arm the prospects are dim
If the landing's piss poor and the pilot can't swim.

I fly for a living, and not just for fun,
I'm not awfully anxious to hack down the Hun,
And as for deck-landings at night in the dark,
As I told Wings this morning, 'Fuck that for a lark.'

Tail up down the flight deck to do an umbrella
I remember too late to fine pitch the propeller,
So I stamp on the wheel brakes and then get the shits,
As the whole bloody issue goes arse over tits.

When the batsman gives 'Lower' I always go higher,
I drift off to starboard and prang my Seafire,
The boys in the Goofers all think that I'm green,
But I get my commission from Supermarine.

I sat on the booster, awaiting the kick,
Amusing myself by rotating the stick,
Down went the green flag, the engine went 'Cough',
'Cor blimey' said Wings, 'He has tossed himself off.'

As I roar down the flight-deck in my Martlet Mark IV,
Loud in my ears is the Cyclone's sweet roar,
Chuff clank clink, chuff clank clink, chuff clink clink clink,
Away wing on pom pom, away kite in drink.

I thought I was coming in low enough but,
I was fifty feet up when the batsman gave 'Cut',
And loud in my earholes the sweet angels sang,
Float, float, float, float, float, float ... Barrier ... PRANG!

They gave me a Seafire to beat up the Fleet,
I polished off the *Nelson* and *Rodney* a treat,
But then I forgot the high mast on *Formid*,
And a seat in the Goofers was worth fifty quid.

No one in their right mind stream lands after me,
They'll have to go round again sure as can be,
'Cos I've found a way to get on to a carrier,
Bugger the batsman, aim straight for the barrier.

The Moral of the story is quite plain to see,
A Fleet Air Arm Pilot you never should be,
But stay on the shore and get two rings or more,
And go out every night on the piss with a whore.

Willie Lagarde, Div 2&3, S1/c USS *Yorktown*
www.ussyorktown.net

We considered shore duty on one of the recently captured islands the worst possible assignment. The threat of transfer to an island was often used to keep us in line. This usually meant exile until the end of the war. However, like any other duty there were advantages here. These men often had access to fleet stores and provisions as well as beer and sometimes liquor. Whenever we were in a lagoon we usually had a major portion of the fleet with us. If you had a relative or friend on another ship you were allowed to visit and spend the day with him. Darken ship regulations were relaxed and we could leave the hangar deck curtains up at night for movies and other activities and to smoke on the weather decks. This was important to our crew because the dangers of smoking were not fully known and the vast majority of our crew were smokers. Our band of ten or twelve musicians set up nightly on the hangar deck and played the popular music of the era. They really sounded good and brought to mind all the good times past. We were also allowed to swim off the side of the ship but only at special designated times when a couple of our marines with rifles on the gallery deck acted as shark watch and one of our whale boats was in the water.

Geoff Shelton, Seaman, HMS *Vindex*
Communication with the Editor

In the middle of the seamen's messdeck was an office which was used by a Chief Petty Officer. I will not reveal the purpose for which that office was intended, for to do so would identify the Chief concerned – probably to his embarrassment. Now this Chief had what one might say a reputation for the ladies, you get my drift. One day while anchored in The Tail O' the Bank, a young and attractive Wren was escorted to the aforesaid office and introduced to the Chief. The Chief's eyes lit up, the escort departed, she was the ushered into the office and the door firmly closed.

A silence had descended on the mess as this apparition of feminine beauty passed a host of love-starved open-mouthed and boggle-eyed sailors and entered the office. Each matelot indulged in their own flights of fancy as to what was happening. Someone in a loud whisper said, 'Turn off the fresh air motors and we can hear what's going on'. 'Better still' said another, 'when the motor is off we can stick our ears against the air vent 'cos it passes through the office'. As the motor droned to a halt a rush was made to climb onto tables and benches each one having their own listening device as ears were pressed against air vents.

It soon became apparent what type of business the Chief had his mind on, because we heard little innuendoes to test the young lady's reaction followed by leading suggestions, followed by ... The lads took in every word that was uttered and imagined every sound. Safety valves were at dangerous levels as we all endeavoured to suppress the need to spoil their fun, but someone had to give vent to his feelings, there's always one ... He put his mouth to the air vent and yelled, 'You dirty bastard'.

When they came out of the office they both looked rather sheepish. The Wren was blushing heavily as she smoothed down her skirt, while Chiefy gave a guilty smile. They then had to pass through an avenue of grinning matelots.

Cecil P. Wareham, Royal Marines, HMS *Unicorn*
from the private papers of C. P. Wareham, IWM Reference 5546 96/31/1

On one visit [to Colombo] a dance was organised, especially for our ship. We wondered if we would be dancing with the natives – or as someone suggested

'Those with fair 'air takes the ladies parts', to answers of 'Not b***** likely'. Much to our surprise there were ladies present when we arrived at this dance hall, all wearing the same outfits! The Wrens ashore had been detailed to attend and were not very pleased, as they were used to high level social functions with the officers' mess ashore, and to have to dance with the ship's company was degrading ... These were not the mixture of Wrens we had seen back in England or were to see in Australia ...'

Lieutenant Commander (A) E. E. Barringer, RNVR, 835 Squadron, HMS *Nairana*,
from *Alone on a Wide Wide Sea*

It was quite a good admixture of RN, RNVR, and RNVR (A) to which was added the further element of the engineering, electrical and supply officers who had come from the Merchant Navy and were given RNR rank. These officers had had a different training and standards. They operated under a different contract from their naval colleagues, known as the T124X contract. This enabled merchant navy officers to serve aboard RN ships and thus provide much needed skilled personnel to assist in running the ship. The T124X officers had some practices which were strange to the RN officers and even to the RNVR officers who at least tried to emulate their RN colleagues. For example, if an T124X officer had had a night watch, he considered himself perfectly entitled to spend the morning in his bunk, a practice completely unheard of in the Royal Navy. On the whole, the RNVR(A)officers found it easier to get on with the T124X officers than their RN colleagues which was understandable. This fellow feeling was perhaps encouraged a little by Bill Armitage who flattened a drunken and somewhat disputative T124X S/Lt. (E) with a crunching short left ... witnesses swear that it travelled less than six inches but the news travelled a lot further. After that, the RNR (E) T124X officers got on well with their RNVR (A) shipmates: One of them, S/lt: (E), Bob Jolly, was an undisguised admirer of the aircrews and their performance. But, above all, it was the friendship and enthusiasm of Commander (E) Edwardson, RNR, the Chief Engineer who was a Kiwi, and the Chief Electrical Officer, Lt. Cdr. (E) Robbie Bruce, RNR, which we remembered most. They were both a bottle of whisky a day men and nothing delighted them more as their alcohol level increased than to discuss with us the problems of deck landing and lighting and such esoteric matters as the maximum length to which a carrier could be built before it would break its back in a heavy sea! So with normal process of the RNVR gentlemen trying to be officers and sailors and the RNR endeavouring to be officers and gentlemen and the RN officers, assured in all departments, assisting them in their separate endeavours, everyone knitted well together in the wardroom and the *Nairana* became a happy ship.

Surgeon Lieutenant Commander E. V. B. Morton, HMS *Battler*, 1945
from the private papers of E. V. B. Morton, IWM Reference 1311 87/16/1

We sailed from Sydney on 12th January and had a relatively uneventful passage across the Pacific, enjoyed clay pigeon shoots from the after end of the flight deck to Panama, untroubled by either enemy action or weather. We played deck hockey, ostensibly provided to help aircrew 'keep their eye in' and various more formal entertainments were organised in an attempt to keep the ship's company happy. These varied from cinema shows in the now empty hangar deck to a series of lectures from various 'experts', quizzes and a semi serious debate.

The limited supply of films available meant that they soon became all to familiar, but this only added a new dimension to the enjoyment by the sailors who could anticipate events and certain suggestive lines of dialogue – thus adding spice to the barracking! I recall a certain film in which George Sanders as a Scotland Yard officer is showing some glamorous actress round the Black Museum. She indicates some murderer's axe and innocently inquires 'what is this chopper for?' The ship's company always made the most of this – by a crescendo of noise and 'cat calls' all fairly pertinent each time the film was shown.

Quizzes were organised between departments on the same lines as the deck hockey league and we took the 'Poulticers' (Sick Bay team) to the semifinals where we lost. An unexpected interest was shown in a debate organised by the commander at the Captain's suggestion, the motion to be debated being 'That this house approves the introduction of a system of trial marriage'.

Aviation Chief Ordnanceman (Dr) Alvin Kernan, then an air gunner, VT-6, USS *Enterprise*
from *Crossing the Line*

As USS *Enterprise* headed home and the crew looked forwards to 30 days leave, Kernan spent 50 cents on a ticket for a sweepstake known as the 'Anchor Pool', betting on the time when the ship drops anchor or ties up on its return:

With only one chance in 720, I forgot about it as the ship at last in late March came in sight of the coast, rounded Point Hard On, and worked up to a dock on the western end of the Naval Air Station. Looking at the Naval Training Station across the channel, it seemed a lifetime away. The monkey fist sailed out in the air and landed with a clunk on the dock. '1024, first line across' came the announcement over the loudspeaker. I went down to get my seabag since the Airedales were to be transferred to some old buildings in the park at the San Diego Zoo, the other animals having gone somewhere else, when it hit me. I scrabbled to find my ticket, and there it was – '1024!' Few joys have exceeded that moment in my life. To get off ship, to go on leave, and to be rich, all at once. Three hundred dollars was a lot of money in those days, but now I had to move fast to make sure that I found the operators of the pool before they left the ship with all the money, or hid out somewhere aboard until I was locked up in the zoo and couldn't get back. Such guile was not unknown in naval life, and all my suspicions were aroused, but the sailor who ran this pool was an honest man, hunting all over the ship for me, greeting me with real pleasure and counting out the money in old tired tens, fives, twos and ones, a great wad I couldn't get in my wallet.

FOR TOMORROW ...

Willie Lagarde, Div 2&3, S1/c, USS *Yorktown*
www.ussyorktown.net

[It] was sometime in early March 1944 when defective fuses began detonating 5" projectiles as soon as they cleared the gun barrel. This premature explosion would usually kill the entire gun crew. After several men were killed on other ships a check of our inventory of projectiles revealed most of ours were in that particular lot. Sabotage was suspected and it was one of two cases I remember being discussed during the time I was aboard *Yorktown*. The other was when striking material was found inside match boxes next to match heads. I don't know if this is the only reason we were going to Espirito Santo in New Hebrides but that is where we changed out all the fuses in our 5" projectiles.

S. J. Guise, HMS *Vindex*
Communication with the Editor

1.25 am in the middle watch March 1944, Swordfish patrol came in to land on. Missed the wires, crashed into the barrier, took off the undercarriage and crashed on deck with two depth charges still unused on. Aviation leaking, caught fire and the Swordfish went up in flames. The night was shattered by an explosion as the depth charges went up. A hole eight feet by four was blown in the flight deck. Next deck down OD AB Hampton was asleep in the forward recreation space ready for the next watch. A piece of the depth charge hit him in the stomach killing him instantly. By 7 am the wreckage had cooled enough to commit it over the side. 11.15 repairs had been made and normal flying resumed. 2.30 pm March 25th: Colours lowered half mast and OD AB Hampton committed to the deep.

Edward Wilson Whitley, Air Fitter, HMS *Illustrious*
IWM Sound Archive Reference 28496

Whitley survived the bombing of *Illustrious* in 1941.

Next morning we start clearing up, and that was one of the worst parts of the job because there was the smell of the German bombs – they have a particular smell which we got to know very well in Malta – and there was wreckage all over the hangar, and there was also body parts, so that you'd clear something and find something horrible. Then you'd hope somebody [else] would do the next one. I picked up a shoe, and it had a foot in it ...

KEEP YOURSELF CLEAN ...

Willie Lagarde, Div 2&3, S1/c, USS *Yorktown*
www.ussyorktown.net

Fresh water priority was drinking, boilers, cooking and bathing last. When we were 'battle cruising' in Indian country (combat zone) often at high rates of speed there were sometimes water shortages. Shower opportunities were limited and when allowed the rule was 15 seconds to wet down, turn off water to soap down and then 15 seconds to rinse. No one was timing with a stop watch but if anyone was wasting water the other men let him know about it.

Body odor was a fact of life and almost everybody had a can of talcum powder in his locker. Men who used it frequently to hide the body odor were called 'puff dusters.' There were five cold salt water showers down on the fourth deck along with salt water soap that would lather in salt water. These were available for use as often as anybody wanted them. They got the dirt off but left a film of salty residue on your skin that was irritating to heat rash and other ailments. Some of us began beating the system by taking a salt water shower then filling a gallon can from the scuttlebutt (drinking fountain) to wash off the salt. When this was discovered we were threatened to have the drinking water cut off. They actually did this for a short period and put a stop to our little scheme. In retrospect, the gallon of water wasn't critical to water management and shutting off drinking water was only to encourage adherence to the spirit of the regulation. In spite of the water restrictions, which we understood, we were told to keep our bodies as clean as possible to lessen the possibility of infection if we were wounded. Almost everyone had heat rash and some had other conditions like impetigo and acne. One of my gun crew mates had acne so bad when we came into the States in 1944 he didn't go home. Heat was a part of our lives during the Pacific war and we endured it because there was no other way. Also, we were aware whatever hardships we faced, our brothers and friends running up those beach heads had it worse.

This working party may not have been typical but was not unusual. We were loading 50 cal ammunition. We used a lot of it because each of our F6F fighters had six fifty caliber machine guns while the TBM's had two in the wings and one in the turret. Three of us were down in the magazine stacking the wooden boxes as they came down on the bomb elevator. These boxes weighed about sixty pounds and there was only a slight indentation on either end of the box to grab them with the finger tips. When we first went down, the deck in the magazine was spotless. Temperature was probably well over a hundred. We stripped to our skivvy shorts and began stacking the boxes in the bins. Before we were finished we were slipping and sliding in what appeared to be a thin muddy slurry on the deck. We realized that every bit of the moisture came from our bodies and the particulate matter from the boxes. I believe if they had told us to clean it up the Port Chicago mutiny may have been the second in WW2 history. Not really. Thankfully, we didn't have to wash our own clothes as we did in boot camp. Dirty clothes were collected in bags and sent to the laundry on the designated day for your division. There was always some enterprising individual, or individuals who for a monthly stipend would sort the laundry when it was sent back to the sleeping compartment. If you didn't ante up you would have to scrounge for your clothes. It was well worth the buck or two. When we were operating near the Japanese home islands especially Hokkaido, it actually got cold and we were issued jackets and foul weather gear. Kamikaze activity increased but what a pleasure it was to sleep in our bunks and covering with a blanket.

Ronald Vaughn, Division 2, USS *Kitkun Bay*
Ronald Vaughn Papers (#658), Joyner Library

Kitkun Bay was heading for Luzon as part of the invasion task force when she was hit by a Kamikaze on New Year's Day 1945.

When the suicide plane hit us, he knocked out one engine and one set of fresh water evaporators. Because of this, we were unable to make enough fresh water for us to take fresh water showers. Salt water showers were the rule, and usually left the skin sticky until it dried, and then it would cause itching because of the dry skin. This led to the practice by all on board that every time the ship passed through a rain squall the message would be broadcast on the ship's public address system, and all who weren't on watch would grab soap and towel and run up to the flight deck for a shower. It was funny to see the flight deck covered with people taking showers. Most of the time, about the time you were all soaped up, the rain would stop and we would have to dry off without rinsing. This led to the practice of using the outer part of our combat helmets to catch rain water so we could rinse off.

TRY TO GET SOME SLEEP ...

Edward Wilson Whitley, Air Fitter, HMS *Illustrious*, 1940
IWM Sound Archive Reference 28496

Get up to make the dawn range, get the anti-submarine aircraft ranged for patrol, and then you'd perhaps nip away to get some breakfast, and then they would fly all day, and the flying was organised so that the aircrew always had their meals. So it was a long drawn-out business. And you flew until it got dark. And then you did the servicing or roll change or preparing the aircraft for an operation, for example. They occasionally went off to bomb places at night, besides doing the anti-submarine patrols. Once, they went out to attack a convoy and it was a very long day. I was so tired that I put my camp bed underneath an aircraft. It had three anti-submarine bombs on the wing right over my camp bed. There were people fiddling about in the cockpit of my aircraft, and I couldn't be bothered moving. When I woke up in the morning, the aircraft had gone and somebody had done my stint up on the flight deck – because I was in the pin party that leapt on the aircraft and folded the wings when they landed and spread them before they took off.

I'd gone sick because I was so tired, and the MO said 'Why don't you go ashore and get some beer?' I don't know what he thought we did! The Taranto raid was put back because of a hangar fire, which I think may well have been caused by a tired sailor. I think he dropped an armoured fuel hose across the battery in the middle cockpit of a Swordfish, and it started a fire. Yes, we were [tired] but you just got on with it. Obviously, later on they must have realised, because later on there were shifts so that you had enough people to work nights. But during the war this didn't happen.

Willie Lagarde, Div 2&3, S1/c, USS *Yorktown*
www.ussyorktown.net

When we operated in the central Pacific there was no such thing as a good night's sleep. To begin with it was only on every third night that we had the 'night in' where we were off watch from 8 PM until 4 AM. There were forty or more bunks in many sleeping compartments and only a few of them could feel the air from the oscillating fans. These bunks were claimed by the senior petty officers and no one argued about it. If you got in your bunk and actually fell asleep you would soon awaken soaked with sweat. Many of us tried covering with a towel we had wet down with cold water but it would quickly assume room temperature and once again you were sweating. Your bedding became damp with sweat and the fire proof mattress cover kept it from drying out completely during the day. We did have opportunities to air bedding occasionally but we learned if you attempted to sleep in your bunk the only way to keep it from becoming smelly was to leave the cover on. As for myself, once the cold wet towel method failed I looked for other places to sleep about 70 to 80% of the time we were at sea.

Temperature on the flight deck at night was always bearable, even pleasant most of the time, but it rained almost every night, usually it seemed, just about the time you fell asleep. Sleeping under an airplane didn't work, the rain drops would find you. Covered weather decks like the foc'sle and fantail were popular sleeping spots but they were crowded. Wherever you decided to sleep it had to be some place where you could be found in the dark when it was wake up time for your watch. None of the gunnery department people I served with ever got enough sleep. Anytime of day or night if you were able to lay down in a cool spot there was no tossing or turning, you fell asleep almost immediately. 'I gotta get some sleep' was the most uttered phrase in the gunnery department.

The longest hour at night was on the 12–4 a.m. watch when it was your turn with the phones. When control would start calling mounts for a phone check every hour or so invariably someone was sleeping and men on other mounts would holler or try to get over and wake him up before the third or fourth call. Even though I managed to sleep through the GQ gong one morning (I was already on my battle station), reaction of the men to the GQ gong was almost like a reflex reaction or instantaneous as if they had been hit with a jolt of electricity. One moonlit night while standing the 12–4 watch on Mt # 5 40 MM, I had the phones on when we were alerted that bogies were about ninety miles out and closing. Whether or not they knew of our whereabouts or intended to attack we expected GQ to sound shortly. Since I was already on my battle station, for the first time I was able to observe the men on the flight deck react to the gong. The initial sound of the gong and men moving was almost simultaneous. It was reported on one of these nights a man jumped up, ran over the side and was never seen again.

Ronald Vaughn, Division 2, USS *Kitkun Bay*
Ronald Vaughn Papers (#658), Joyner Library

During these routine operations, and after the ship had secured for the night, I would go up on the flight deck before going on watch and watch the stars in the sky and marvel at the wonder of them. When there was no moon present, and all of the ships were running dark, the stars would seem so close you could almost touch them. During these moments to myself, I spent a lot of time talking to God. Also, during these operations, I got in the habit of sleeping somewhere on the flight deck, or catwalk, because it was too hot down in the sleeping compartments. I would tell someone where I would be sleeping so they could wake me to go on watch. I would then angle across the flight deck until I found the lifeline (a chain across the end of the flight deck). I would follow the lifeline by feel until I got to the end which was about 2 feet from the side of the flight deck. It was then just a matter of stepping to the edge and jumping down on the catwalk to my watch station. One night when there was no moon, and I was awakened to go on the midnight to 4 a.m. watch, I got up and angled across the flight deck to where I thought the lifeline was. I started feeling around in front of me for it, but it wasn't there, and it was too dark to see. When I couldn't find it, I thought to myself, 'Maybe I haven't gone far enough,' so I started to take a step forward to see if I could find it. When I started to move, a voice said, 'Don't move,' so I stayed where I was and started feeling for the lifeline again in front and to each side of me. When I couldn't find it the second time, I started to walk forward again, and the voice said again, 'Don't move.' This voice gave me a strange feeling because there was no one else close to me. I once again started feeling for the lifeline, and this time I reached around behind me and felt the end post to the lifeline directly at my back. If I had taken one more forward step, my feet would have hit a curved steel plate, sending my feet out from under me, and putting me in the drink. Needless to say, I got on the right side of the lifeline in one big hurry ...

[In January 1945] we slowly made our way back to Leyte Island. During this cruising time, one of my shipmates who slept a couple of bunks above me started talking in his sleep. I told him about it, and he said, 'The next time I start talking in my sleep, wake me up.' A few nights later, after completing an 8 p.m. to midnight watch, I went below to turn in. When I started to crawl into my bunk, my friend started talking in his sleep. I shook him to wake him up, and he said, 'What's the matter?' I said, 'You were talking in your sleep.' He said, 'I was?', and swung his legs over the side of his bunk. I said 'Yes you were.' He then jumped down from his bunk and went at a fast pace to the passage between the bunks. As he turned the corner, I suddenly realized that he was walking in his sleep. I ran to the corner he had just turned, and he was nowhere in sight. I ran all the way to the fantail looking for him, but couldn't find him. I went back to my bunk wondering who I should tell, and about that time he came back around the corner and crawled back up into his bunk. As soon as he lay down, he opened his eyes and woke up. When I told him what had happened, he was scared to death, but made me promise not to tell anyone because he didn't want to be transferred off the ship. A sleepwalker was not allowed to serve aboard ship for fear of them walking off at night into the water.

COPE WITH THE STRESS ...

Lieutenant Colonel Ronnie Hay, Royal Marines, DSO, DSC*,
Air Coordinator British Pacific Fleet, HMS *Victorious*
IWM Sound Archive Reference 13856

It is worth noting that Admiral Vian was completely in sympathy with Hay's views and, by making it a resigning issue, ensured that British aviators did no more than six-month tours of duty, thus bringing them into line with US aircrews.

I had been doing 18 months non-stop. Fortunately we had the grog in our ward rooms. Poor old Yanks – all they had was coffee. You can't keep going on coffee ... But we could get over our problems by a drink or two ... We had this treatment ... When a chap's in real shock, when he'd been in battle, when his friend has been shot down, he's a blubbering almost shivering mess, so his flight commander would talk to him, take him into the wardroom; squadron commander would talk to him. Finally he'd find himself in front of the big white chief, which is me, and I said: 'Look, son, we've all lost people, and I'm going to give you a little stiff whisky, and I'll give you this one, because you're going to come back for another one.' and I give him a whisky, because he thought I was God in those days. I'd speak kindly to him, told him: 'it's a long passage. You go back and have a drink with your mates, and turn in before midnight and you'll be on duty in the morning.' – They were … It was the only thing, I think, which sustained our aviators, not because they were British or got guts or grit or anything, but they had this means of alleviating the tension. When you're young – nineteen, twenty – as some of these fellows, and you see a fellow shot down in flames … All that is very 'undoing'. Give him half a dozen strong Scotches, and half of it's gone, and by next morning he's eager for battle again. That proved it again and again.

Lieutenant, later Commander, Desmond Wilkey, Observer, 1770 Squadron, HMS *Indefatigable*
IWM Sound Archive Reference 14150

We didn't get any counselling. The occasional officer got twitch, but this was understood and he was sent home, usually. It was treated as a medical state. We had, I think, one pilot and one observer sent home with what we called twitch, which was battle fatigue. But this was why morale had to be kept high. We were very sympathetic to aircrew who got twitch.

PUT UP WITH THE WEATHER …

Commander Eugene Robert Forsht, USS *Ticonderoga*
Dallas B. Long, Jr., Collection (#636), Joyner Library.

Ticonderoga retired from combat on 16 December 1944 in order to refuel. Shortly afterwards she encountered the typhoon that sank three destroyers – tin cans, as Forsht calls them – and cost the US Navy some 800 lives.

We first got notice that we were going to get into bad weather. That was when we first started to oil the two tin cans that were there with us as a plane guard. They were the two that turned over. We watched them, we couldn't do anything about them and we couldn't get oil to them because of the rough seas and we broke our hoses. But at that time when we got notice of the bad weather coming, I drew out all the cable from Supply that I could get and I had ½ inch and ¾ inch cable and clamps and we took all the planes and secured them on the flight deck and hangar deck with cable to struts and from the struts right down to the steel tie-downs on the hangar deck. This took quite a long time. All during the typhoon we went around and tightened whichever cable stretched out. During the worst weather, we lost several planes over the side in the back, and all we ended up with were several sets of landing gear struts. Also on the hangar deck we had a couple which had torn the struts out. However, it ended up that we still had the planes, so we were able to salvage most of the planes with the parts which we could use from other planes which were damaged in combat. Typhoon days I remember we stayed up all night and we always had to darken the ship so that all the side curtains were down and everything was closed. You could look from the bow to the stern of the front of the hangar deck to the after part of the hangar deck and see overhead lights that looked like a snake. We were bending around so bad that you could go on the outside and look down on the expansion joints which were opening up and letting the light out to the outside. That is how much we were going up and down and turning.

Edward Wilson Whitley, Air Fitter, HMS *Illustrious*
IWM Sound Archive Reference 28496

Hit some very rough weather, and in those days all the heads – toilets – were in the forward part of the ship ... and they still had scuttles or portholes, unlike the later ships that never had any. Some of these had been knocked in by the weather and had lumps of timber bracing them. As I sat there, a piece of 4 × 2 [inch timber] whistled over my head. So I spent a lot of time in the ship looking for alternative toilets.

Lieutenant Bruce Vibert, DSC, CD, RCN(R), Pilot, 836 Squadron, HMS *Fencer*
Communication with the Editor

The US-built escort carrier HMS *Fencer* participated in both Atlantic and Arctic convoys.

The Fleet carriers didn't have the chumminess of the escorts. Big carriers had four squadrons coming and going, they didn't get to know one another very well, I think. The ones I know best, of course, the escort carriers, had just one squadron.

Fencer was a comfortable ship. It was noisy because it had almost no wood in it – that's a precaution against fire. If someone dropped a spanner at the forward end of the hangar, and you're sitting in the wardroom on another deck level, you'd still hear it. It rolled in wet grass, as we used to say, which didn't help. I can recall that in the worst of the winter storms we would have to tie ourselves into our bunks really solidly. That class was reckoned to capsize at 54°.

We had rolled to 48 degrees and we had split our hull. I've often wondered since what they did with that hull because, after the war, she became five different merchant ships ... But she was well appointed, being American built ... so we had a comfortable life, two to a cabin, and ... we were well fed and the only problems that arose were when we had to leave the ship.

Can you imagine yourself up at 2000 feet in an open cockpit on days far colder than the ones we've been experiencing? Try. With a wind in your face 2½ hours, with nothing more than a string vest, long johns and the flannel shirt and what we called a 'poopy suit', which was a two-piece garment: rubber cuff, rubber round the neck, a long rubber skirt which you rolled together, and for the men, naturally a little thing there with a cork. Boots were sealed. And that was what was supposed to protect you if you went in the water. It was unpleasant: no use in pretending otherwise. It was worse, or as bad, I think, for the Germans if they came to the surface because ice was everywhere: everything iced up. Then you think about our own small escort ships: iced up, in danger of capsizing because of the weight. We had the comfort, on returning, of going back to a semblance of normality.

Contrast Bruce Vibert's memories of the Arctic with John Maybank's of flying in the Pacific during the Okinawa landings in 1945:

Lieutenant John Maybank, Pilot, 1830 Squadron, HMS *Illustrious*
IWM Sound Archive Reference 27341

It was pretty warm. On a hot day you were sitting in that cockpit which was unpressurised so you could open up the hatch a little bit without getting swept away and let the air in, but that was sometimes a bit uncomfortable too because it was too agitated. You were sweating a lot of the time and I got the most fearsome prickly heat between my thighs and around my shoulders and down my chest. And I had dermatitis on my face which, of course, stayed for years, and it was round the rubber oxygen mask around my face, where the rubber rotted – and, of course, it's not good for you: rotten rubber against your face. But the heat was that intense. They tried to repair it by giving me calamine [lotion] and they put some black stuff in with it – and of course putting that around your testicles between your legs: it smarts like hell. They stopped doing that, obviously, because it was aggravating rather than curing! I had to get out of the tropics for it to go properly.

Sometimes [I would wear] a pair of pyjamas and flying suit because it was so bloody hot. It really was, but not always, and so sometimes I'd be in a pair of blue pants, a shirt then a flying suit. I never wore a uniform. Very rarely did I wear a uniform or a jacket or anything. Too hot. I wore long trousers. But I didn't fly in shorts.

DEAL WITH UNINVITED GUESTS ...

Sub-Lieutenant (A) L. J. Williamson, 797 Squadron
from *A Very Ordinary Naval Airman* (unpublished memoir)

HMS *Khedive* was sent out to the Indian Ocean in January 1945, arriving in Colombo in early February. En route ...

We were sitting on the flight deck of HMS *Khedive* just after sunset, listening to romantic music on our gramophone when someone shouted 'Hey, who threw that?' 'Pack it up!' 'What was that?' Then panic in the lowered lift where some lads had put their bedding out for the night. We soon realised that the ship had been invaded by a swarm of locusts and in the morning there were piles of them, dead and alive, all over the place

October 1945. India. New type. Corsair. Long nose, bags of power. Climb away, check speed.

Zero knots. Not stopped. Land quick. Check check. Pivot head blocked. Length of wire. Dig deep. Remove beetle. OK. Take off. Fly on. Smell smoke. MAYDAY MAYDAY. No transmission. Tears in eyes. Land at Trinco. Radio U.S. [unserviceable] Fire in aircraft. Check check. Short circuits in radio under seat. Oh well, these things do happen.

Surgeon Lieutenant Commander E. V. B. Morton, HMS *Battler*
from the private papers of E. V. B. Morton, IWM Reference 1311 87/16/1

The only unwanted, but permanent fittings were the cockroaches, some of which reached an enormous size (several inches long), with which the ship was infested – and all were utterly fearless, invading every space and department.

TRY NOT TO BE ILL ...

Jack Needham, Able Seaman, HMS *Indomitable*
IWM sound archive Ref. 1991 92/27/1

Following the attack on Diego Suarez in 1942, Needham was taken ill.

For the last few weeks I had been suffering severe stomach pains and was duly dispatched to the Sick Bay with a temperature of 103, not allowed any solid food and felt desperately ill. Now in the RN at that time, anyone who was a Surgeon-Commander or similar rank was always rumoured to be 'a Harley Street specialist' with typical matelot's gift of exaggeration. Considering the vast number of Medical Branch Officers there were in the Navy during the war of 1939–1945 I can only come to the conclusion that Harley Street must have been a much longer street than I had ever imagined. However, I was gently prodded here and there and it was discovered that instead of suspected appendicitis, I had cholecystitis, which is as painful to endure as it is to spell. The officer concerned said 'Right laddie, your gall bladder's rotten, so we will whisk you off to Mombasa Hospital as soon as we get in.'

Surgeon Lieutenant Commander E. V. B. Morton, HMS *Battler*
from the private papers of E. V. B. Morton, IWM Reference 1311 87/16/1

The sick bay was quite palatial and extremely well equipped, including a complete operating theatre and instruments, some of which we were never likely or indeed qualified to use – such as a case containing a complete set of instruments for complex ophthalmic surgery! Indeed there was enough there to equip a small general hospital at home. The sick bay office contained all sorts of modern office fittings including a desk the centre panel of which folded over to reveal a large built-in office typewriter!

Our main physical problem was the unsuitability of such a ship for tropical conditions; ventilation was poor or virtually non-existent, there was of course no air conditioning and many of the air vents had become blocked. The tropic sun just beat down on what was essentially a flat topped tin box with a whole series of small tin boxes inside which naturally gave rise to great heat, high humidity and discomfort within. Sweat rash, prickly heat and a variety of skin troubles were endemic and made up much of the sick bay's work.

AVOID TROUBLE ...

Commander Eugene Robert Forsht, USS *Ticonderoga*
Dallas B. Long, Jr., Collection (#636), Joyner Library

The incident to which Forsht refers probably occurred around 13 December 1944.

I remember the time when the stewards got into the problem of using butcher knives on each other. Captain Dixie had the Marines put all the stewards down in a ward room and had a Marine stationed at each one of the compartment doors. Of course, we all had the word passed about what happened. We watched when Captain Dixie went in there with his .45. He was in there about half an hour. When all the stewards came out they were really scared. We had a very nice steward up in Boy's Town* and we talked with him afterwards about what happened. He explained that Captain Dixie told them that if ever any of them picked up a knife to fight with anybody on the ship or in the Allied Command, he would hang them up on the yardarm for 24 hours, make a hard turn to the starboard and cut them down at sea. With this, we all knew he meant what he said. From then on we all had to cut our own meat in the ward room because the stewards would not pick up a knife to even cut meat.

HMS *Illustrious*, Log
ADM 53/11246

Officers were as capable as anyone of going on a spree and finding themselves in trouble. Nine days after his brand new ship arrived in Alexandria harbour, Captain Boyd recorded:

I have this day had occasion to admonish Lt. (A) William Douglas Morford Royal Navy for his conduct while ashore in uniform 18 October 1940 in
1) Being improperly dressed ashore namely by wearing a taboosh on his head
2) Using insulting language to Captain John Leeper Anketell Macafee, Royal Marines, the Assistant Naval Provost Marshal Alexandria
3) Violently resisting an escort when being brought to HMS *Nile*.

* Accommodation compartment for the Ensigns.

Surgeon Lieutenant Commander E. V. B. Morton, HMS *Battler*
from the private papers of E .V. B. Morton, IWM Reference 1311 87/16/1

Battler's crew included a seaman known as Newfie who was perpetually in trouble.

However the one episode I remember above all others occurred when we went alongside at Woolamaloo to unload our cargo of aircraft. 'Newfie' by this time had had his initial run ashore in Sydney – with its inevitable outcome and he was once again under stoppage of leave. Now, on the dockside close to where we were berthed were some enormous gash bins, there were also the usual motley collection of dockyard mateys and interested locals. In particular I remember quite clearly, a brace of well endowed and over exposed 'young ladies' probably from the fleshpots of Kings Cross (anyone who remembers Sydney in those days will recognise the significance of that). These two were exhibiting themselves and their charms pretty freely and attracting much attention and many comments from the lads on the flight deck.

As one of the working party of men under punishment, Newfie was told off to take some boxes of ship's waste down on to the dockside and ditch them in the gash bins. Guess what? Despite the watchful eye of the duty P.O. Newfie somehow managed to find the time and adequate cover to not only became acquainted, but intimately acquainted with not one, but as he later informed me with both these ladies of 'easy virtue' and return on board before anybody missed him.

The reason that I know all this is because Newfie told me himself when he presented at the Sick Bay some four or five days later, describing his complaint with that 'Jack Speak' euphemism that old sailors will remember 'I'm squeezin' up Doc.'

Willie Lagarde, Div 2&3, S1/c, USS *Yorktown*
www.ussyorktown.net

Our boss was a Storekeeper 1/c who we called 'Keys' because of the many keys he carried. He had access to every store room and to all the goodies to be had at that time, including the beer. He treated us very well and we all liked him.

Three of us were carrying 50lb sacks of flour from one of the dry storerooms to the bake shop when Chico, from a small town in Colorado, noticed a book hidden among the sacks in the storeroom. In the book was an envelope with pictures of bare breasted native women. After hiding the envelope in his locker he put the book back where he found it. Most of us never saw any of these island women but those who did have contact with them were warned; taking pictures of their naked boobs was strictly forbidden and anyone found guilty of this crime would be punished by a thousand lashes, keel hauling, walking the plank or hanging. Well maybe not that bad but the word was out, take no pictures!!!

When we were stacking the last three sacks in the fourth deck compartment under the bake shop two men came down and one of them had the book in his hand. Trouble ahead. The man with the book was a powerfully built BM 1/c who was also a big shot in the 'third deck clique.' Men in this group were usually senior petty officers who had access to any of the privileges available during those days and could provide them to each other. They lived better than the rest of us and could be identified by their pressed dungarees. Actually, we didn't begrudge nor were we envious of their status or any of their privileges. We felt for men with their rating and seniority in the Navy, this is how it should be.

Keys, who was a member of the clique, must have tipped off the BM his stash was probably discovered. I was one step up on the ladder when he confronted Chico asking if he took the envelope.

When Chico denied having seen it, he began threatening him with disciplinary action. I told Chico not to worry he wouldn't dare make a complaint to anybody. Without even looking at me he said; 'you keep out of this you loud mouthed bastard.' I don't know what got into me but I said, 'who are you calling a bastard'. Had I the option, I would have taken back those words and did just what he said. Too late now, the die has been cast, the Rubicon crossed and I'm in serious trouble.

This will be classic boy against man and not just an ordinary man but a Neanderthal. He looked at me seemingly in disbelief that a lowly seaman would have the gall to say anything to a big shot like him. He put the book down on a table, faced me and said; 'you heard it.' Forced to shit or get off the pot and knowing I'm probably in for ass kicking I hit him in the mouth. He grabbed me around the neck and was hitting me on top of the head when a lieutenant who had been in the bake shop above and who was probably a clique member also, came down the ladder and broke up the fight. When I stepped back the BM was bleeding from a cut on his lip. Wiping the blood with a baker's apron he told me, 'this ain't over, you'll get yours'. The officer must have been aware of the situation because ordinarily if a lowly seaman hit a BM 1/c that would be brig time at least. Nothing was done and the next day I must admit I was proud when I saw his fat swollen lip especially since Keys spread the word throughout the clique and I didn't have a mark on me. I sensed I had Keys' support.

Needless to say, the pictures disappeared over the side, after another quick peek of course. Whenever he saw me he had a little comment to make about my impending doom but I gave no thought to his promised retaliation until a payday shortly before pulling into San Francisco a year or so later. He was at the pay table and the last to count the money. When he handed it to me he said; 'I'll be seeing you soon superman.' Exact words; I'll never forget them.

I was at a bar with a friend a couple of days later when I saw him walk in with a BM2/c and hoped he wouldn't see us. No such luck, he saw me and pointed us out to his partner before walking over. I told my friend Russell I had big trouble coming and if he didn't want to get involved he best leave now. 'I'm with you Willie'. Good old Russ, what a friend. As always, my tailor-made uniform I had only worn a few times was a major concern of mine, especially in the first hour or two of a liberty. I turned on the stool to face him and had my back against the bar to get good leverage because I figured when he swung or reached for me my only chance would be to shove him back with my foot hopefully knocking him down and taking it from there. Russ should be able to handle his friend. So, what happens? He tells the bartender to give us a drink, shakes hands and leaves. Hallelujah! The Lord takes care of his children.

AND KEEP IN TOUCH WITH THE FAMILY BACK HOME

Frederick George 'Pat' Oikle, Seaman, HMS *Activity*
IWM Sound Archive Reference 17529

It was forbidden to write anything to friends and family back home that gave information likely to be of use to an enemy, but Oikle found a cunning way to communicate with his fiancée:

'Is there any chance you could tell me where you are?' And I said 'Well, yeah,' and devised a method. After the letter I would put blocks of kisses. One of them was longitude, the other was latitude, and she could look at a map and know where I was at any given time.

2
1939

When war broke out in September 1939 (1940 for Italy and 1941 for the USA and Japan) the carrier strength of the main navies, by tonnage, stood as follows:

Great Britain		Japan		USA	
HMS *Furious*	22,450	IJN *Hosho*	7,470	USS *Lexington*	43,055
HMS *Courageous*	22,500	IJN *Akagi*	26,900	USS *Saratoga*	37,681
HMS *Glorious*	22,500	IJN *Kaga*	26,900	USS *Ranger*	14,575
HMS *Ark Royal*	22,000	IJN *Ryujo*	10,600	USS *Yorktown*	19,875
HMS *Eagle*	26,800	IJN *Soryo*	15,900	USS *Enterprise*	19,875
HMS *Hermes*	13,700	IJN *Hiryu*	17,300	USS *Hornet*	19,875
HMS *Argus*	15,750	IJN *Shokaku*	25,675	USS *Wasp*	14,700
		IJN *Zuikaku*	25,675		
France				**(Germany**	**Nil)**
Béarn	22,146			**(Italy**	**Nil)**

As hostilities began, nobody really foresaw the pivotal role that the aircraft carrier would play. In World War I the weapon had been too underdeveloped to do much more than advertise its potential, and though major naval exercises gave grounds for optimism, the crises and conflicts of the interwar years had provided no opportunities to test it in combat against a determined enemy. How effective would carriers be against German submarines and heavily armoured raiders? How vulnerable would they prove? 1939 was not encouraging.

At the beginning of the war the Royal Navy aircraft carriers operating with the Home Fleet and the Channel Fleet – *Ark Royal* and *Furious* in the North-Western Approaches, *Hermes* and *Courageous* in the South-Western Approaches – were primarily used in hunter-killer groups to sink U-boats which, though few and far-between at this time, were already highly active against merchant shipping. The risks to which this policy exposed the carriers was underlined within the first three weeks when both *Ark Royal* and *Courageous* were attacked by German submarines on 14 and 17 September respectively. The former was lucky on that occasion: the torpedo tracks were spotted in time for the carrier to turn, and *U-39* was subsequently sunk by the destroyers, the first Allied success against the U-boats. *Courageous*, however, was torpedoed by Kapitänleutnant Otto Schuart's *U-29*, with heavy loss of life. She had been caught at her most vulnerable moment: turning into the wind ready to fly off her aircraft to support SS *Kafiristan*, which had radioed that she was under submarine attack. As a result, carriers were withdrawn from anti-submarine work.

Hermes was sent to the Caribbean before departing for the Indian Ocean, and after providing air cover during the operation to rescue the submarine HMS *Spearfish*, *Ark Royal* was ordered to the Chilean port of Montevideo where the German pocket battleship, *Admiral Graf Spee*, had taken shelter; *Furious* was occupied searching for raiders in the Atlantic. Following her recommissioning out of the Reserve Fleet, HMS *Argus* patrolled the Gulf of Lyons. While it was widely anticipated that Italy would enter the war on the German side, and the Mediterranean Fleet was in a state of readiness at Alexandria, HMS *Glorious* patrolled in the Gulf of Aden and HMS *Eagle*, based at Colombo, was sent to patrol the Indian Ocean; both were looking for German raiders.

Captain Michael 'Pinkie' Haworth, DSC*, CBE, 823 Squadron, HMS *Glorious*

from the private papers of M. G. Haworth, IWM Department of Documents Reference 3320 95/5/1

In September 1939 I was serving as an Observer in HMS *Glorious* an Aircraft Carrier which was based in Alexandria in Egypt ... The Mediterranean Fleet was normally based on Malta but in those days of tension with Italy it was decided the whole fleet would transfer to Alexandria so as to be less vulnerable to Mussolini's bombers ... Peacetime life in the Eastern Mediterranean was agreeable. We went to sea from time to time and carried out exercises or visits to foreign ports. When we were in Alexandria it was a very pleasant place where we could play various games: golf, tennis, cricket, very good bathing facilities, and attractive cosmopolitan society which boasted rather more sophisticated forms of amusements like restaurants, than would be the case in our normal base at Malta. This agreeable experience could not be expected to go on ...

Captain Alan 'Alfie' Sutton, CBE, DSC, Observer, 823 Squadron, HMS *Glorious*

IWM Sound Archive Reference 12149

But as HMS *Glorious* patrolled the Gulf of Aden, Sutton's pre-war doubts about his captain increased:

D'Oyly-Hughes said that if we encountered a raider, he was going to engage her with gunfire. This scared us stiff. The ship had a number of guns, but they were basically anti-aircraft guns. He wasn't going to use his aircraft, which is the main striking force, and hold off on the enemy and sink her with aircraft ... And we young officers began to think that this chap was absolutely round the bend. He went on with various sorts of things like that, that made us believe that he had become really unbalanced. He had a rather fierce quarrel with his senior air officer, [Cdr] Guy Willoughby, but most of all he loathed the senior observer on board, a chap called Slessor* who was, in fact, the

---

* Lieutenant Commander E. H. P. (Paul) Slessor.

114

Operations Officer on board the ship. So you had a captain whose ideas of war scared his officers and who was quarrelling with his senior staff, and luckily for me I was taken out of the ship and brought home to join a squadron at home.

By the end of the year, *Glorious*'s aircraft had been flown off to Malta and Sutton had been posted to the brand new HMS *Illustrious*, which would enter service the following year. Here he found a very different style of captain.

We mustered back home a number of fully-trained night-flying crews from a number of the carriers and were formed into [squadrons]. My squadron was 819 squadron ... A whole group of us were ordered to the Admiralty to meet our new Captain, Denis Boyd, and he gave us a pep talk, said how pleased he was to meet us all ...

Guy Beresford Kerr Griffiths, 803 Squadron, HMS *Ark Royal*
IWM Sound Archive Reference 16641*

Having volunteeed as a replacement at the very last minute, Griffiths was only briefed about this operation after take-off in the Skua in the afternoon of 12 September.

My observer told me we were looking for the *Fanad Head* which had sent out an SOS** saying they were being attacked by a submarine. So we went to Rockall – that was a data point – and we then went out on what we called a search patrol. One went north-east, one went north and I went north-west. The one who arrived first on the target was Lt Thurston who attacked the submarine when it was underneath the stern protecting itself from being spotted ... The next person was Lt. Cdr Campbell, the commanding officer, who arrived on the scene a few moments later after doing his square search. Seeing two people in the seawater he thought they'd been abandoned by their submarine crew but in fact they were the pilot [Thurston] and the observer [Petty Officer James Simpson] of the shot down Skua which had crashed – blown up – in flames from its own bombs when attacking the target. At the time, [pilots] had to attack not as a dive bomber but in a shallow dive ... which is dangerous when you're doing it at low level ... Thurston swam to get help for his observer, and he passed out from his burns, and the German apparently dived into the sea (he was aboard the captured *Fanad Head*) and saved his life, pulled him up and grabbed the rope, hung on until his fellow German on board joined him and helped him ... My observer said: 'There's a merchant ship over there; let's go and have a look at it, and it was the *Fanad Head*, the same merchant ship which had [been boarded by] the German crew ...

The safe height to bomb at was several hundred feet, but we were already at about 20ft searching for this particular target to check the name and port of

* In the original interview, the sequence of events is out of order; here, paragraphs are re-ordered chronologically.
** Ships attacked by submarines usually tried to send out SSS rather than SOS.

registry. You had to go right down; only then did we see the submarine crash diving so there was no time to get to a safe height, so I was obliged to bomb at near enough zero. I just stall-turned and came back on the submarine and he disappeared under the nose of my aircraft, and with that I pointed the thing straight at the target and then pulled out, and at that moment there was a terrific crash. Apparently, according to the Germans – who saw me in their periscope, I went up with part of my tail missing and then went straight back into the sea, and they said 'your aircraft was 50ft long and you didn't stop in three times that, so you went down 150ft at least.' So I didn't know very much about it, except that I was fighting to get out, but the engine had been ripped out through the sinking wreckage of the engine and was sucked out. I eventually came to the surface. My right hand was a bit damaged and I didn't know at the time that my watch had been driven into my wrist. But outside that I didn't do any [more damage] and thank goodness I had my Mae West on. But the Germans told me later when they showed me my Mae West that there wasn't anything left of it. It was just an empty bag: it had all been ripped open – but my belief was such that I believed I was being supported. It was a mile and a half swim in the winter.

The Observer, PO George Vincent McKay, went down with the Skua.

I climbed up the apparently rope ladder which was hanging there and pulled myself up, and only then did I discover on board there was Thurston, unconscious from his burns, and two Germans, one a petty officer and one a seaman, who were getting the records of the ship but who in the interval had tried to resuscitate Lt Thurston. So, at that time the Germans called out [from the submarine] and said: 'look, we've got some Swordfish attacking us at the moment. Look out. Get over to the sea, we're going to put a torpedo in her. Get rid of those chaps.' So we were ordered into the water and we had to swim for our lives … and the attacking aircraft literally arrived as we were crash diving.

Thurston and Kerr-Griffiths found themselves on board U-30.

The Germans … treated us extremely well … The captain was Kpt Lt. Lempe [Fritz Julius Lemp] and he was a great figure of a man with a red beard, and his No. 1 (First Officer) was a bearded giant of a man. They had a great sense of humour and like all submariners we found they were exactly like our own people: couldn't do enough. The crew all volunteered – with so few things, they only had one change of pyjamas; after they just slept in their clothes, and they all volunteered, one by one, to give Thurston their pyjamas … He was burnt to a cinder. His wounds were so bad that he was soaked up – so they volunteered, every one of them to supply him with pyjamas and a change every few hours. We then went back to Wilhelmshafen, which took us two weeks.

The attack on the submarine had damaged U-30's engine; it gave out in the Skaggarak and for a time they drifted in a German minefield. When they arrived at Wilhelmshafen, Lemp went to his prisoners and said:

'We'll have a pleasant party.' So he got some schnapps out and he said 'Wishing you a short prisoner of war time, and we'll drink to the end of the war.' There was nothing about who's going to win or anything. And just at that moment three SS officers arrived on board and knocked the drinks clean out of Lemp's hands, ordered him to stop drinking with the enemy and said they'd be reported – and that was that.

Thurston was taken to hospital; Griffiths to a POW camp. Unlike Lemp, both survived the war.

Lieutenant Commander G. R. Grandage, DSO, RNR, then Assistant Navigation Officer, HMS *Courageous*
from the private papers of G. R. Grandage, IWM Reference 473 87/16/1

An RNVR officer at the start of war, Grandage was appointed to *Courageous* as Assistant Navigation Officer at the end of July 1939.

On the evening of Sept 18, we received a report that a German submarine had been sighted. It was a good way off so we increased to maximum speed and three aircraft were flown off. I was officer of the watch on the bridge just after 8.00 p.m. when we were struck by two torpedoes on the port side amidships. From my position I would say that the second torpedo went through the hole of the first one and well into the ship and exploded.

The ship heeled over at once and in a very short time it was obvious that there was little hope of saving her. Those of us on the bridge remained for about ten minutes with the captain, Macaig-Jones, who quietly said 'Anyone who wants to go, can go.' We climbed out of the bridge, the captain coming last, and started scrambling down the ship's side. I paused a bit to take off some clothes and shoes. At this time I would say the ship was about 50° over.

As she took the final plunge I found myself in the sea and being sucked down with the ship. There is no telling how far I went down or how long it took but I know it was quite dark before I found myself being shot up to the surface without any effort of my own. I had a few seconds on the surface and saw the captain quite close and then went under again in a whirlpool. He was never seen again. Three times I went under. I managed to keep calm as I knew it was no use struggling against that suction. The third time up I found a calm sea and it seemed so quiet. The sea was strewn with wreckage of all kinds and over all a thick layer of fuel oil giving off a smell that was almost choking.

A merchant ship, *Dido*, was about two miles away and turned towards us and lowered their lifeboats to pick up survivors. About 300 of us were picked up in this way and at about midnight four destroyers came alongside and took us off. We arrived back in Devonport three day later. In the meantime the Germans had broadcast the sinking but Joan [his wife] had to wait another 2 days before I was able to phone her.

The ship sank in 18 minutes, and 518 men were lost.

3
1940

In April, the Norwegian campaign began. The European land war was approaching the end of that phase known as the Phoney War, with the Battle of France only a month away, but Germany and the Allies had a longstanding strategic interest in Norway. It was through Norwegian ports that vital exports of Swedish iron ore would be exported to Germany, and Norway's coastline could provide the Germans with useful naval bases. Both sides had drawn up plans. The Allied operations began with the mining of the Norwegian coast on 8 May, coinciding with the German seaborne invasion.

Ark Royal had been in the Mediterranean; *Glorious* had refitted at Malta: both carriers were recalled to take part in the Norwegian campaign along with *Furious*, and on 12 May *Glorious* sailed for Norway with 701 Squadron (Walrus) and 64 Squadron RAF (Hurricanes). *Furious* carried the Gladiators of 263 Squadron RAF. They met up with *Ark Royal*, and for the very first time three carriers were deployed in a single operation. The flying off of 64 Squadron's Hurricanes, which was delayed until 26 May, was another historic moment – fast, powerful monoplanes had never flown off a Royal Navy carrier before.

But already the campaign appeared to be a disaster. This was a desperate period for the Allies, coming at the same time as the retreat that ended on the beaches of Dunkirk. The evacuation of some 25,000 troops from Norway was ordered: Operation 'Alphabet'. *Glorious* was given the task of re-embarking the squadrons that had been doing outstanding service at Bardufoss. At the same time, relations between Captain D'Oyly Hughes and his officers had broken down. He had quarrelled violently with the Commander Flying, J. B. Heath, and relieved him of his command. Worse, not only was *Glorious* sailing independently of the fleet with just two destroyers for escort, her captain had not ordered any patrols to be flown by the carrier's own Swordfish of 823 Squadron. On 8 June, *Glorious* became the first – and last – fleet carrier to be sunk by the guns of a capital ship.* The dead included her commanding officer.** Although the Allied campaign had failed, ten German destroyers had been sunk and *Gneisenau* and *Lützow* had been damaged. Germany's submarines, however, remained at large.

With the fall of France in June and the entry into the war of Italy, it was left to the Royal Navy to take full charge of the defence of the Western Mediterranean. The Eastern Mediterranean was well covered by the Mediterranean Fleet based at Malta and Alexandria, and a new fleet, known as Force H, was established in June

---

* At the Battle for Leyte Gulf, q.v. the USS *Gambier Bay* was sunk by surface ships, but she was a small escort carrier neither built nor equipped to take on a whole battlefleet.
** For the full story, see John Winton's *Carrier Glorious*.

at Gibraltar under the able command of Admiral Sir James Somerville. The composition of the fleet changed during the nine months of the fleet's existence – the first flagship, HMS *Hood* was relieved in August by *Renown*, but *Ark Royal* remained at its heart. Working in both the Atlantic and the Western Mediterranean, Force H acted against German raiders, and defended Malta-bound convoys.

Its first action, however, was against the French Fleet, which in June 1940 was perhaps the French Government's only bargaining counter during its Armistice negotiation with the Germans. The British wished at all costs to prevent the fleet falling into German hands and being made operational. The final terms of the Franco-German Armistice Commission allowed the warships at Toulon to be effectively mothballed, but there remained a significant number of naval vessels at Alexandria, and Mers el-Kebir/Oran. The British ultimatum, sent via Admiral James Somerville, commanding Force H from Gibraltar, asked the French to choose between continuing the fight, sailing their ships to Britain and handing them over to the Royal Navy, demilitarising them in a colonial port in the Caribbean, or letting the neutral USA look after them. Failing that, the Royal Navy would sink them. Admiral Gensoul was apparently not made aware of the demilitarization option, the negotiations broke down, and Operation 'Catapult' went into action, causing huge loss of life among the French sailors.

Two carriers had been lost, but two new ones, *Illustrious* and *Formidable*, were on their way, and not before time. With Italy now in the war, the conflict swiftly extended into the Mediterranean and North Africa. The naval base at Malta became absolutely vital if control of the Mediterranean were to be maintained. The Italian Navy was both newer than and superior in size to Cunningham's Mediterranean Fleet, and Malta was within reach of the Italian Air Force.

As early as 1935 the Royal Navy had drawn up plans for an attack on the Italian naval base at Taranto, and on the night of 11/12 November a revised version of the plan, codenamed Operation 'Judgement', was put into action. *Illustrious* had arrived in the Mediterranean, and it had been intended that she and *Eagle* should launch a Trafalgar Day attack, but a fire on *Illustrious* and damage to *Eagle* put back the date and ruled out *Eagle*. In the event, only 21 Swordfish were available, five of them from *Eagle*, split into two waves. Ten were equipped with bombs and flares to illuminate the targets, the rest with torpedoes. For the loss of two aircraft, the attack crippled three of the six Italian battleships. The brilliance of the operation opened all eyes to the effectiveness of naval air warfare and the importance of the aircraft carrier; particularly impressed were the Japanese delegation that happened to be present at Taranto at the time.

The Fairey Swordfish biplane remained the backbone of the Fleet Air Arm. Although outdated – the USA would enter the war with fast, powerful monoplanes – it had a number of virtues. Its nickname 'Stringbag' is often thought to derive from the web of tensioning wires that held it together, but, allegedly at any rate, the name arrived after someone went home on leave and described how his aircraft could carry anything and everything: bombs, depth-charges, torpedoes, etc. His wife likened it to her string bag, which expanded to accommodate any amount of shopping.

Despite its importance, Malta had not been adequately supplied with aircraft for its own defence. It became the task of the Royal Navy not only to rectify the immediate deficiency but thereafter to resupply the island with (primarily) Hurricanes, after combat losses and damage threatened its survival. RAF crews and pilots were brought from Britain by the old HMS *Argus*, which was then escorted by Force H until she was close enough for the aircraft, guided by navy Skuas, to fly off and land on Malta. These were dangerous operations. Nonetheless, the first, code-named 'Hurry', was extremely successful. The second, 'White', was a disaster because the Hurricanes were flown off with insufficient fuel.

Wing Commander Patrick Geraint 'Jamie' Jameson, then Flight Commander, 46 Squadron, RAF
IWM Sound Archive Reference 1034

During the Norway campaign two RAF Squadrons, No. 46 (Hurricanes) and No. 263 (Gladiators) had been operating out of Bardufoss in Northern Norway. If the pilots were to escape with their aircraft, they would have to land on HMS *Glorious*, but they had no hooks with which to engage the arrester wires. This was critical for the Hurricanes which were far more powerful than the Gladiators.

However, since we had come out, [Squadron Leader] 'Bing' Cross flew out to the *Glorious* in a Walrus [seaplane]. The captain promised that he would put on every ounce of steam he could make so that we should have a reasonable chance of getting the Hurricanes down. We calculated that he could, at a pinch, get 28 knots out of her, and we decided that would probably be enough. I took off in a rather ropy Hurricane which had bullet holes all over it. We had been told, when I took off [for] my flight, that, if we could not land on the *Glorious*, we should have to try to land on the *Ark Royal* nearby. The *Ark Royal* had a longer deck – but her deck would not take the Hurricane wingspan.*

The captain of the *Glorious* kept his word. When we saw the carrier, it was going flat out, steam pouring out of every rivet hole. While we were waiting for the signal to land, one of our sergeant pilots went down and made a perfect landing. When I tackled him about it later he said he had had engine trouble, but I suspect he really wanted to be the first chap to land a Hurricane on the carrier. As we came into land, the ship's company, drawn up behind the safety net, gave us all a terrific cheer. It was the first time in history that such planes had been flown onto a carrier, and the admiral in the *Ark Royal* sent us a congratulatory message.

When the rest of the Squadron came on the only damage caused was to

---

* The deck was wide enough for landing, but because Hurricanes could not fold their wings they could not use *Ark Royal*'s deck lifts and so would be left cluttering up the flight deck.

break three Hurricane tailwheels; the Fleet Air Arm had three new tailwheels ready next morning, but unfortunately we never needed them.

I went to my cabin for a long sleep, but some hours later I was awakened and told that two German cruisers were coming upon us. Out of range of our own armament they opened fire and the second salvo set our Hurricanes in the top hangar on fire. All our work had gone for nothing.

One of our escorting destroyers charged in on one of the cruisers hoping to do a torpedo attack, but before it could get within range it was blown out of the water.

It was a new experience to stand on the *Glorious* and see the flashes of the German cruisers' guns, miles away. After each flash we waited for a moment or two, then there was a terrific explosion as another salvo of shells hit the ship, Finally we were given the order to abandon ship, and after swimming a quarter of a mile I climbed onto a Carly float. I found that Bing Cross was already aboard, with 26 sailors and one airman. By this time our carrier was just a mess of smoke and flames, and we never even saw it sink because of the smoke pall. We climbed onto the float about 6-o-clock in the evening, and I shall never forget the sight of our second destroyer firing and firing until she was sunk. They were brave men aboard that ship.

As I said, there were 29 of us aboard that float. There were only 10 left by morning. It was bitterly cold; 19 died during the night from exposure. Curiously enough, the three of us who were RAF men all came off safely. During that day, three more died, leaving only seven of us. We never gave up the belief that we would be rescued. Bing had a brilliant idea. We were sitting round the edge of the float, with our feet in the water, and he suggested that with my pocket knife we should cut the bottom trellis out of the float and rest it on the top. It took a long time to cut it out, passing the knife around from hand to hand, but we managed it and were able to get some sleep. For three days we floated without food or water, and then we saw a trawler coming up. To see that it was flying the Norwegian flag gave me the sweetest moment of my life ...We found it was escaping from the Germans, and we were surprised when they told us we were only 120 miles from the Lofoten islands.

It would be impossible to exaggerate the kindness of the Norwegian crew. They gave us their bunks and provided us with every comfort. I went down into the stokehold and slept on the catwalk round the engine. They put some old clothes on the catwalk, and I think it was the most comfortable bed I ever had.

Heinkels later circled the ship at mast height, and we were afraid that we should have to start all over again. When the first one flew off we expected he would come back and bomb us, but he didn't. I think the Norwegian flag saved us again ... Two more of the party died on the trawler, and though the ship eventually landed 30 survivors from the *Glorious* only five of our little raft party were left, and one of these died in hospital.

Two or three days afterwards, when we came into a Scottish hospital, the feeling came back to my feet. They were swollen white with the immersion in the water, and I remember that, when I touched the skin, my finger made a little hole as though it had gone into a soft pudding. My feet gave me agony, and the hospital tried all sorts of oils with which to massage them; but they gave me no relief until a dear old lady who owned some stables nearby bought along a bottle of stuff called Mermaid Oil. It said on the bottle *For use in stables, kennels and piggeries*. But I didn't care: the oil certainly did my feet good. My DFC came through while we were still in hospital, and we had a grand party that night.

Ernest Blackwell, RN, Warrant Telegraphist, HMS *Glorious*
ADM1/19406

Blackwell's formal account of the sinking was written after his return from POW camp Stalag XB.

During the night 7/8th June 1940, in a position somewhere off Narvik, *Glorious* flew on RAF Aeroplanes from Norway.

An aircraft general purpose W/T set was rigged on the Compass Platform to enable a RAF Wing Commander to transmit advice and information to pilots when landing on.

All aircraft were taken on safely.

On completion of the above operation, at about 0300, *Glorious*, *Ardent* and *Acasta* were detached. The signal ordering this, I believe, also detailed our route.

To the best of my knowledge we proceeded without our usual air cover.

I spent the afternoon in the D/F office, situate[d] at the after end of the Flag Deck. Passing the chart house on my way to tea, at about 1615, the Captain stopped me and asked 'On which wave do we make an enemy report, Mr Blackwell?'. The Captain often asked such questions and I had no idea of the real situation as I replied '253 Kc/s, Sir, but knowing this area would suggest H/F as well.' (*Glorious* had left Narvik zone and had shifted to Home waves at 1300) As I finished speaking, Action Stations sounded, and the Captain thrust a message into my hand saying 'Then make this quickly, both waves.'

On my way to the Remote Control W/T office, 'Away 82– Squadron'* was sounded, and at the same time I heard the first salvo, but felt no impact.

Entering the R.C.O. I called to the two operators already there to switch on Main and Second Office W/T Sets. Handed the original signal to the 253 Kc/s operator for transmission and told the H/F operator to carry on calling while I made a copy of the signal for him.

The message was self-evident, reporting two *Deutschland* class battleships.

A voice pipe order to switch on the beacon came from the Plot. Mr Clark having arrived in the R.C.O. now took over and I left to attend to the beacon,

---

* 823 Squadron (Swordfish), commanding officer Lieutenant Commander C. J. T. Stephens, RN.

the set being new to the ship and requiring a little experience in handling. Passing through the Compass Platform I heard the Captain order 'Tell the Destroyers to make smoke.'

Impact somewhere – seemed to be aft. Beacon operating satisfactorily, I returned to R.C.O., noticing en route that destroyers had commenced making smoke and *Glorious* was altering course to Port.

Arrived RCO to hear that main W/T aerial had been carried away.

Left for main office. Casualties in flight deck lobby and in passage outside main office. Believe brought in from Flight Deck and Starboard Upper Galley.

Gunfire from enemy constant.

Connected Main W/T to Second Office and Second Office to 4H aerial. Made my way to flight deck to estimate extent of damage to aerial. The after W/T [wireless telegraphy] mast in Starboard side had been shot away.

Huge hole in Flight Deck with two or three Swordfish blazing at its edge. The upper hangar appeared to be on fire. A gusty wind seemed to be breaking up the smoke screen into isolated patches. Could see *Ardent* and *Acasta* through the screen and they appeared to be going in to attack. Splashes all round them.

Glorious shook, and I heard someone shout: 'below water line'. Abandon ship was piped.

Went to Plot to see signal officer. Captain in the wheelhouse speaking on Engine Room Telephone. I heard him say 'Give her all you've got, chief.' He then called 'Cancel abandon ship.'

I repeated this into the SDO and RCO and continued to Plot.

In Plot the signal officer told me there had been no answer to our Enemy Reports. I suggested that we tried to get through on Narvik waves, either by shifting frequencies on the main set, or by using aircraft general purpose sets, one of which was fitted in RCO and one in Main Office.

He favoured the latter method and by voice pipe ordered RCO to get on Narvik reconnaissance, whilst I went to Main office to put the set there on Narvik H/F.

Glorious now had an obvious list to starboard.

Standing near Plot/Coding office voice pipe I heard someone in the Plot shout, 'One destroyer has gone.'

Heard and felt a heavy crash, apparently somewhere below main office. Valve in main transmitter broken and machine stopped. Still trying to get through on GP set.

Abandon ship piped again. Tried to get into communication with RCO and Plot by voice pipe, buzzer and telephone. No reply from either place on any system.

List to Starboard increasing. Articles sliding over.

Sent Coder to ascertain if T.S. [Transmitting Station] just forward of main office was still manned. Returned to say abandoned.

All confidential books and matter collected, placed in steel chests and transported by Main Office personnel along cross passage to Port side.

Awkward journey owing to the now big list, but considered safer that making for the side nearest the sea. Noticed Port forward TS and 2nd W/T office had been abandoned. This part of the ship seemed deserted. Passages very hot and much fire extinguisher chemical around. Enemy still firing. Steel chests thrown overboard. I went over the side and stood on rubbing strake [a pencil query has suggested he means Bilge Keel]. Cutter aft, manned to capacity, hanging at extent of falls, but several feet from water. Someone in it shouting for an axe. I saw no other boats or floats.

Men forward, edging aft, pushed me until I reached a break in the rubbing streak [strake], where I fell into the water.

Glorious well over to starboard, disappeared through clouds of smoke and steam. I saw one destroyer still engaging the enemy. She withdrew, came quite near where I was swimming and then returned to the attack. Smoke drifted across and my next impression of the enemy, now ceased firing, making away. I did not see them stop to pick up any survivors.

My seeming detachment from any particular action station is due to being a passenger, my relief, Mr R R Clark, joining *Glorious* at Scapa Flow and taking over the duties of Warrant Telegraphist of the ship on 6th June 1940. Circumstances kept me employed in my own department and I had little chance of observing much which went on outside it.

More than 1,500 men died in the three ships; there were less than 80 survivors, taking into account those who were picked up alive but died soon afterwards.

Seaman Gunner W. 'Tug' Whymark, HMS *Eagle*
quoted in *Eagle's War*

After a refit in Singapore, the elderly HMS *Eagle* had joined the Mediterranean Fleet as its only carrier.

I can remember that once Italy had declared war our patrols became more interesting and we spent more time at first degree readiness instead of the previous second degree of readiness. When we closed up at our battle stations I was stationed at the forward 4 inch HA gun and we were constantly in action in those early months. The Italian bombers nearly always came over at very high level, and during the first attacks were fired off some 750 plus rounds of 4 inch in defence of the ship. *Eagle* was kept very active at the start and periods in harbour at Alexandria long enough for leave were rare. Even when, later on, we were in harbour more, there were only limited facilities ashore there. During these periods our aircraft were put ashore and kept in action supporting the troops in the desert.

As the Mediterranean war hotted up so we spent more time at Suda Bay in Crete and carried out many air raids against the enemy in North Africa, Tripoli, Benghazi and the like, also against the islands of Leros and Rhodes, as well as escorting troop convoys to Greece. Several times we caught the enemy unawares, as I understand it from those who went up in the Swordfish on these raids, but once or twice we got caught and spanked.

Heavy units of the Italian Navy did not show themselves too much after Calabria, and when they did sail seemed to always keep close to land, Taranto and so on. On the first occasion they were visible through binoculars and gun sights I believe. Our heavy units straddled them several times and got a hit. After that we didn't see them at all. Instead we used to send our Swordfish off with torpedoes to try and stop them but they seldom scored any hits.

On one occasion I can recall us steaming for Malta from the direction of the Crete area and there was a gas alert. The ship was closed up at action stations at this time and respirators were ordered to be worn, so someone was expecting the worst! However, within a short time a gas 'all clear' was sounded. I do not really know at this distance in time what had caused the original alert; neither side actually used gas. At the time we ratings believed that what sparked the alarm was that it was a very warm morning as the weather was perfect and the breeze almost motionless. The fumes from the collective ships' smoke, or from a smokescreen being laid, lay heavy on the sea and someone mistook it for gas. I suppose a toxic smell could have resulted and hung around but in all my years at sea I never experienced a similar alert at all.

As the air attacks increased so we got counter-measures. Anti-aircraft cruisers joined the fleet, but better was RDF on some ships. It gave us much more advantage as the range and height of the enemy aircraft were known accurately and it gave more time to open fire. Extra guns were placed wherever possible, close-range weapons for use against low-flying aircraft like torpedo bombers of which the Italians had many. Several of these were placed around *Eagle*'s flight deck, in fact these twin Lewis guns were my night and harbour action station. It proved hair-raising sometimes during night raids. A pitch black night in Alexandria harbour with all hell let loose overhead. And there we were, heroes all, with just a tin helmet for protection against the Regia Aeronautica, or, more lethal, the rain of shrapnel from our own guns ashore coming back down! We opened fire through a seeming maze of other people's tracers which were tracking hostile low flying aircraft, if they existed. I think it was anyone's guess where all these rounds of ammo went but I doubt if they troubled the Italian airmen very much as they preferred high or medium bombing.

At sea we had some Sea Gladiator fighters and very active they were too. All the pilots were volunteers and were magnificent. *Eagle* always seemed a prime target, unmistakable I suppose, and an easy choice to pick from high up. Anyway we were bombed by enemy aircraft all round the clock when we put to sea. I can recall one very near miss which exploded close off our bows. Thick black smoke and powdery soot emitted from the explosion and blackened parts of our guns and the bridge area as well as all our personnel closed up in these areas. But it did us no great harm; in fact lots of the lads thought it hilarious and we all hoped the Italians manufactured all their bombs like that one!

The fleet was very active now all the time and extra manning of warships to see to all the new equipment was necessary. Replacement crew members were beginning to arrive in Alexandria after long hazardous convoy journeys around the Cape. *Eagle* received many new members which were by now mostly HO (Hostilities Only) ratings, but very determined lads and marvellous really. You found out why later. One particular AB from London I later palled up with was always hell-bent on going into action. I said to him eventually, with the wisdom of a regular, 'You are too keen!' He replied, 'Well, it's like this, before I left Blighty I lost my wife and child in an air raid.' I never questioned his motives again.

Admiral Sir Ian Easton, then a pilot, 803 Squadron, HMS *Ark Royal*
IWM Sound Archive Reference 10644

The first operations we carried out once we joined Force H was the attack on the French at Mers-el-Kebir. That was a singularly horrific operation. Of course, we didn't know too much about the political and strategic background to it. I don't think that there's any doubt that the generality of feeling was one of considerable sickness that we found ourselves in this position. But, of course, initially we didn't expect the French to do anything but accept one or other of our terms, because the terms were very generous. I mean, they were that they could either sail the whole of the Fleet to Martinique or Guadeloupe and be interned there for the war in French territory, or they could join us, which seemed to us to be the sensible answer – or they could sink their ships where they were; and if they weren't prepared to accept any of these alternatives, then we would have to open fire on them. The terms of the ultimatum were taken in by our Captain who had been the Naval Attaché in Paris just before he joined us as Captain of the *Ark Royal*, and we waited for a very long time, past the time when the ultimatum had expired, and we went on waiting. After a while we sowed magnetic mines in the entrance to the harbour, and very shortly after that, if I remember rightly, the French cruiser *Strasbourg*, with two destroyers, broke clear of the port. If I remember rightly, one of the destroyers went ahead and blew up on a magnetic mine. She [*Strasbourg*] followed in the path and got through … We detached the *Renown* or the *Repulse* – one of our faster battlecruisers – to try to bring her to action, but although it pursued it to the east for a considerable while, it was unsuccessful, and we then opened fire.

I was flying a Skua on fighter patrol over the fleet at that time, and we were ordered into Oran to protect some [Swordfish] we sent in to do some torpedo bombing, and it was a very sickening sight to see these huge chunks of the jetty going up in the air, and vast explosions and flames leaping out of the French ships – our allies of the morning before. Anyway, I got a Dewoitine on my tail, a French Dewoitine fighter, that attacked me, but either his gun jammed or he didn't open fire, because although I couldn't get him off my tail, we weren't hit.

We came from that to Gibraltar, and it was a day or two later we went in again and we sank the *Dunkerque*. The *Dunkerque* had been damaged, but she hadn't been sunk; she was still okay. She was attacked by torpedo bombers and torpedoed … we simply provided fighter protection for the Swordfish. There was a rather sickening episode in the second attack on Mers-el-Kebir when the *Dunkerque* was torpedoed, because one of the torpedoes hit a liberty boat which was approaching the *Dunkerque* and a very large number of French seamen were in the water, and one of our Swordfish pilots, in the mess after the attack, was boasting that he had machine-gunned the French sailors in the water. I was very pro-French at that time, and I remember having a flaming row with him. It wasn't just I; I think that everyone in the mess was disgusted with him, and he very quickly realised that this was not a boast that he'd better persist in because people were on the whole very sickened by it. He was a short-service entry into the Fleet Air Arm. He had in fact been flying for Franco during the Spanish Civil War: he was a very buccaneer type chap; he was a very good pilot. He was a brave man, I think, but he had a very big gap in his moral armament.

We came back to England, and 803 equipped with Fulmars and we then joined HMS *Formidable*, and *Formidable* was part of the fleet that went down to West Africa to try and take Dakar.

Edward Wilson Whitley, Air Fitter, HMS *Illustrious*
IWM Sound Archive Reference 28496

Along with a friend, Whitley joined *Illustrious* in 1940 and was involved in her flying trials and working up around Bermuda.

We were both 18 and we went out from Glasgow dock into a pub called *The Caradoc* – and we'd never been in a dockyard pub before. We fled back to the ship, and we went to sea eventually. I'd been told to ballast the aircraft for the trials … and when we started it up, and I was putting the starting handle in its holder in the back cockpit, the pilot said: 'Get in.' I said: 'Please, sir, the C/O said …' But he said: 'Get in.'

Fortunately there was still a harness in the aircraft, so I have the distinction of being a passenger in the first aircraft that ever landed on the ship – a Swordfish, one of our own Squadron, 819 Squadron.

Illustrious's hangar was armour-plated. Armour plate on the flight deck, armour-plate fore and aft, and the bulkheads on the ship's side; it was divided into three by fire screens, and it was quite difficult because you didn't have much space, and, in fact, if you lost an aircraft it was a relief because it meant you had room to fiddle the things around. [Of] the last three that went into the hangar, two of them were pushed out on rails into the corners of the hangars. Of course the hangar surface was steel; parts of it were hot because [of] the machinery spaces and so-on underneath it. The stores were overhead, and a lot of aircraft spares were lashed in the deckhead. You really were working in very close confines – and noisy, hot – but when we had to sleep there at sea …

we used to sleep on camp beds. Occasionally we used to think 'this is a hard camp bed' – and then you'd realise you'd fallen off it.

Planes had to be manoeuvred to get out. We used to call it 'hangar drafts', and it was all done by hand at that stage – we didn't have tractors ... So you pushed them all and they went up on the lift, and you pushed them down to the after-end of the flight deck when they were flying. We had seamen in the squadron. They were on the guns, I think, and they would help, but you didn't want too much help because, if people didn't know what they were doing, they could damage the aircraft. It didn't matter with modern metal aircraft; but the fabric aircraft, it was quite easy to damage them, and you sometimes wished you weren't getting any help.

The aircrew were mainly peacetime naval officers. There were some ex-Air Force officers among them because of transfer, and when you're starting a new service you need both fliers and maintainers. So quite a lot of transferring took place. There was quite a big gulf between our Navy personnel and the officers in those days, but they knew how much work we were doing, because they would sometimes come up to the hangar with some lime juice.

Lieutenant, later Captain, Alan 'Alfie' Sutton, CBE, DSC, Observer, 819 Squadron, HMS *Illustrious*
IWM Sound Archive Reference 12149

In November, HMS *Illustrious* showed the aircraft carrier's true potential for the first time.

Up to that time, the *Eagle*, the old First World One battleship converted to an aircraft carrier with a flat deck put on top of her, had been pounding along trying to provide cover for the fleet. She had, I think, a dozen Swordfish on board, and three fighters – Sea Gladiators – which they'd pinched from a store in Malta, and they had been up trying to spoil the aiming of the Italian bombers which were coming over in droves, and had no effect really, but they were there: they gave a certain element of protection and disturbance to the enemy.

Then we arrived. A modern carrier with RADAR ... and fairly modern fighters ... We had Fulmars, and the impact of this on the fleet was quite incredible. They saw, first of all, first one Italian aircraft shot down, then an Italian reconnaissance aircraft shot down. Another Italian bomber shot down ... You could feel the whole fleet cheering, you couldn't actually hear it ... She was the heart of the defence of the fleet with her modern facilities. They had voice communications from the aircraft to the ship and back, which hadn't happened in the early part of the war. With the *Glorious*, if we put up a fighter patrol, the patrol was put up on a patrol line and just stayed there. They couldn't communicate with the ship: there was no way of talking.

The newly arrived carrier was about to write one of the great chapters in naval aviation history – Taranto.

Above: Eugene B. Ely flies his Curtiss pusher from USS *Birmingham* in Hampton Roads, Virginia, during the afternoon of 14 November 1910. USS *Roe*, serving as plane guard, is visible in the background. (US Naval History and Heritage Command [USNHHC])

Below: Seconds after this photograph was taken on 7 August 1917 aboard HMS *Furious*, Squadron Leader Dunning's plane had crashed into the sea, killing him. (Getty)

Top left: HMS *Engadine*, a passenger ferry converted to a seaplane carrier, was the vessel in which both Lieutenant Erskine Childers and Flight Lieutenant F. J. Rutland served during World War I. (CPL)

Top right: USS *Langley*, the US Navy's first carrier, was a converted collier, and her flat top (typical of the first true carriers) earned her the nickname 'The Old Covered Wagon'. In this early image, *c*.1922, an Aeromarine 39-B is landing on. (USNHHC)

Middle left: A seaplane in the hangar of HMS *Ark Royal*, commissioned in 1914. Aircraft were hoisted on to the deck by steam cranes. (CPL)

Middle right: HMS *Furious* still in World War I dazzle paint, and with a landing-on deck aft as well as a flying off deck. Note the large crash barrier behind the funnel. (USNHHC)

Below left: Lieutenant Charles Bridge, who flew with the RNAS during the 1919 Russian campaign, is seen here in his uniform as an officer in the Ellerman Lines. (Courtesy Mrs A. Proffitt)

Below right: Commissioned only seven years after USS *Langley*, USS *Lexington* looks far more modern with her offset island. (USNHHC)

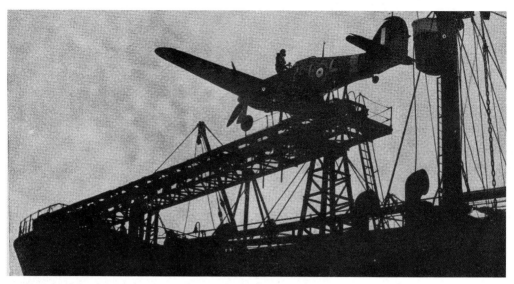

Top left: A Hurricane on the catapult of a Catapult Armed Merchantman, possibly during early trials in the River Mersey in 1941.

Top right: Commander Alan Swanton, who participated in the mission to sink *Bismarck*. (Courtesy Henry S. Swanton)

Middle left: On 24 May 1941 aboard HMS *Victorious*, crews wait for the order to take off and attack *Bismarck*. (CPL)

Below left: Swordfish landing on HMS *Illustrious*, date unknown. (CPL)

Below: Three carriers in line during Operation 'Pedestal': HMS *Victorious* with her Sea Hurricanes, *Indomitable* and *Eagle*. (CPL)

Top left: A unique moment as a B-25 bomber successfully flies off USS *Hornet* to attack Japan as part of the Doolittle raid. (USNHHC)

Middle left: Fire breaks out on USS *Yorktown* after she was hit by Japanese dive-bombers at the Battle of Midway, 4 June 1942. (USNHHC)

Below: 'Down a bit!' DLCO Jack Thomas signals to a Swordfish pilot of V Flight, 836 Squadron, as he comes in to land on the grain carrier MACship *Empire MacKendrick*. (Courtesy Jack Thomas)

Top left: Sub-Lieutenant Ralph Cocklin's 45th deck landing on the escort carrier HMS *Tracker* ended with a badly buckled Swordfish for the maintenance crew to repair. (Courtesy Ralph Cocklin)

Middle left: Swimming was fun, provided there was a shark-guard on duty; climbing back on board was rather more demanding. (Courtesy Willie Lagarde)

Below left: Sub-Lieutenant Jack Thomas by the propeller of his Fairey Swordfish at RNAS *Maydown*, HQ of the MACship wing. The photographer told him, 'When you are killed, this photograph will be released to the press for your obituary.' (Courtesy Jack Thomas)

Below: Swordfish pilot, Lieutenant Bruce Vibert, DSC, in 'battle dress' as a sub-lieutenant (A) on HMS *Fencer* 1944/5. (Courtesy Bruce Vibert)

Top left: Wearing sunglasses, Surgeon Lieutenant. Commander Eric Morton relaxes on HMS *Battler* en route from Cochin to Suez, November 1944. (Courtesy Mrs Morton)

Middle left: Action on 40mm guns, USS *Yorktown*, during the Truk raids. (Courtesy Willie Lagarde)

Below left: Crew fight to save USS *Saratoga* after a kamikaze attack on 21 February 1945. (CPL)

Commander George Going, DSO, OBE, 819 Squadron, HMS *Illustrious*
Fleet Air Arm Reference C7/4

Going almost missed the Taranto raid on two accounts, the first being when the engine of his Swordfish cut out during a dawn anti-submarine patrol with an inexperienced pilot:

'I told him to point the aircraft in the direction of the fleet and glide down. When the aircraft struck the water I was thrown out – the easiest ditching I have ever made. We got the life raft inflated and I swam over and lit a flame float. This was seen by the *Gloucester* which steamed over and picked us up. I knew, because of the shortage of aircrew, we were wanted aboard the *Illustrious* so I went to the Captain and asked if we could be flown back in his ship's Walrus amphibian. Captain More obtained permission so all three of us crowded into the Walrus piloted by Lieut.'Tubby' Lane. It was a most illuminating experience. I had never catapulted before and of course the Walrus had no arrester hook.

Edward Wilson Whitley, Air Fitter, HMS *Illustrious*
IWM Sound Archive Reference 28496

We were not told a great deal, for security in the war, and the first I knew about the raid on Taranto was: we had a blackboard in the corner of the forward end of the hangar where the aircraft loads and so on were listed when there was any operation, and it was headed 'Blitz on Taranto' with a list of the aircraft. *Eagle* should have been at sea for that operation, but she had mechanical problems, so some of *Eagle*'s aircraft were in the ship at the same time. And all the aircraft were prepared for the operation. In my case, I think about four of the six aircraft I was supervising then were going, and another job I had was [this]: the torpedoes had an air tail which controlled the angle of their drop, and this was attached to some drum control gear – behind the air gunner's cockpit – which was a shaft with a weight on it. Two spools of 21½ feet of cables were on this thing, and they went down and were tied to the end of the air tail. One of my jobs was to wind all these, which I did by hand .

And then, when everything was ready, some of the planes that were flying went into the sea with water in the petrol ... Nobody knew which of the planes had been refuelled at which of the filling points, so we had no option but to drain them all. To drain them all you had to take off the armament, which was already on them, and the torpedoes, because you want to get at the drain-plugs which were beneath the fuel tanks. You also had to lift the aircraft into flying or rigging position so that all the fuel would go out, refill them through chamois leathers, which is a long and tedious business, and then put back all the panels and the armament for the raid ...The aircrew were helping, which I felt was a bit hard on them as they were going to be flying all night.

Eventually we got them all ready, and 815 and some of *Eagle*'s aircraft did the first wave … Then we got all our aircraft on the flight deck, and our aircraft were taking off until we got to the last two. They both moved forward together to the Deck Officer's signal, and they met, and Clifford and Going's aircraft was on the centre line. The aircraft Morford was flying [was] an aircraft with a centreline tank instead of a torpedo. Anyway, the Swordfish had a slot on the top wing, which was metal, and it made an enormous hole in the bottom wing of Clifford and Going's aircraft, and Haggis-Russell said 'which aircraft can go, and which can't?' I said: 'That one can and that one can't.' Morford flew off and Clifford and Going also disappeared up the flight deck saying 'Let's go and ask the Captain if we can go after them.' I thought they must be mad … So we pushed the aircraft down in the hangar, had a quick look inside the hole – and the wing structures, the spars and bracing tubes and the bracing wires are all okay, so we push all the broken ribs back into the wing, dobe on an enormous fabric patch, and take the aircraft back to the flight deck. Off they went after the rest.

Then we all sat back and never expected to see any aircraft coming back, or at least not many of them.

Captain D. G. Goodwin, DSC, OBE, Observer, 824 Squadron, HMS *Eagle*
Fleet Air Arm Museum Reference C7/15

We were transferred in Alexandria harbour before *Illustrious* sailed, without a clue as to what was going on, except that it must be something big.

In those days flying over the sea in a single-engined aircraft, particularly at night, tended to be a rather lonely occupation, and the psychology of confidence in one's companions and equipment was an important factor. I only mention this so as to emphasise how very grateful I personally felt in being able to fly that night in my own aircraft from *Eagle* and with my own pilot. He and I had been flying together for nearly two years – Captain 'Olly' Patch RM whose guts and imperturbability considerably outweighed his tiny stature. He was the tiniest Marine that I ever met. I know that if I had not been with him I would have been much more frightened that night than I was, which is saying quite something.

The pre-flight briefing in *Illustrious* was first class. We took off on the first wave without incident, formed up – we were leading a sub-flight – and set off. Then on the climb to passage height we hit thick cloud and lost formation – or they lost us. Anyway, that was one of the few nasty moments of the trip. It certainly felt lonely, and I well remember thinking what Charlies we would look if all the others had turned back, or lost their way, and we hit Taranto on our own.

We found Taranto alright, and when we got nearly over it there was not a doubt that our other aircraft had also arrived – the fireworks display of shells and searchlights was a lovely sight. We were one of the few aircraft carrying bombs and not torpedoes, so we had to fly right over the outer harbour before diving on the inner one where our cruiser targets were berthed, while most of our companions were diving into the main defences to let go their fish. I reckon they had the far worse job, what with the barrage and all that tracery.

As was usual in the Swordfish of those days, on a long trip requiring extra fuel, we had to carry a huge petrol tank, strapped onto the observer's normal seat like a monstrous growth, while the observer squashed himself with all his navigating instruments into the air gunner's seat. One was thus separated from one's pilot by this monstrosity, which was maddening because in those days we did not have proper intercom, only Gosport Tubes which always got bunged up with fluff. It did not normally matter because one was quite used to tapping the pilot on the shoulder even over the open cockpit and communicating in sign language. But not, of course, on that night. 'Olly' Patch was blinded by the fireworks down below and could not at first see our target, and I well remember being unable to make him hear and slapping the fuel tank futilely with my hand, mad with frustration, trying to get his attention. Anyway, he saw them alright, dived and let go. We pulled out just above the ship's masts and got out of it at roof top height.

Commander George Going, DSO, OBE, 819 Squadron, HMS *Illustrious*
Fleet Air Arm Museum Reference C7/4

The rest of the afternoon was spent getting ready for the raid which we all knew was going to be a really big show and which none of us wanted to miss. Then just as we were taxiing, the wing of Sam Morford's Swordfish sat on top of ours. Everybody got in an awful flap and thought our aircraft was badly damaged but Lieutenant Clifford disagreed. He was an absolute genius about aeroplanes and said it could be repaired in ten minutes. I went to Captain Boyd and asked permission to make a late start on the raid. He passed me on to Admiral Lyster who listened to me and said 'Well you're flying the bloody aircraft – off you go.'

Half an hour after the other members of the squadrons, they flew off, and 25 miles from Taranto they saw 819 squadron amid the barrage.

It made navigation really easy. It was the finest flying display I have ever seen. We thought we would go in over land which would be the way the Italians would not expect us. We flew hard over the top of the harbour – it was a lovely moonlit night – and nobody knew we were there. When we dropped our bombs at a cruiser neither of us could see if they went off. I was all for going round again but Lieutenant Clifford would have none of this. By then the fireworks display had become a little awe-inspiring. 15 years later I learned that our bombs went right through the fo'csle of the cruiser and just stuck in the mud. They did not go off because they were semi armour piercing and the Italians did not have armour on their decks.

Captain K. Williamson, RN, then a Lieutenant Commander commanding 815 Squadron
Fleet Air Arm Museum Reference C7/13

After taking off from *Illustrious* we passed through a layer of cloud and the bomber aircraft became detached. They proceeded independently to Taranto arriving there shortly before the main body. We were still about eight miles short of the target when the bombers went in. There suddenly appeared ahead the most magnificent firework display I have ever seen. The whole area was full of red and blue bullets. We had to fly low for about three and a half miles through these bullets. They appeared to approach very slowly until they were just short of the aircraft, then they suddenly accelerated and whistled past.

All the torpedo aircraft reached the battle fleet and all, skimming over the water, dropped their torpedoes from heights varying between 30 and 15 feet above the surface. Just about then, the short-range anti-aircraft fire was intense, and every bullet has to come to rest sooner or later. I often wonder how many finished up in the town and dockyard.

In the meantime, the bombers and flare droppers were bombing ships in the inner harbour, the three cruisers to seaward of the battleships, a seaplane base and some oil storage tanks. Half an hour later, 819 Squadron appeared on the scene and repeated the performance. In all, 11 torpedoes were dropped … I doubt if any of the aircraft were under fire for more than five or six minutes, yet in that short space of time half the Italian battle fleet had been put out of action for many months.

About 20 seconds after I dropped my torpedo at the *Cavour* Class battleship, I ran into a lot of flak from a nearby destroyer and crashed in the harbour. I eventually surfaced and swam to a floating dock, hotly pursued by armour piercing and incendiary bullets. I climbed onto the dock and was immediately set upon by about six Italians, and I feel I enjoy the dubious distinction of being the first British Naval Officer to be captured by Italian dockyard maties. These creatures proceeded to strip me naked, and for a moment I feared I was to suffer a fate worse than death, but I was spared that. After the raid was over I was taken to the destroyer *Fulmina*, which I joined in my birthday suit. The Italian officers were rather ashamed and gave me and my Observer, Lieutenant Scarlett, who was also captured on the dock, some clothes and a glass of brandy. Later on, one of the Italians rather shyly asked me if they were treating us as we would treat them. I said 'yes', but Lieut. Scarlett, who was more of a realist, said: 'we generally give them some beer'. Beer was provided.

The following morning we were allowed to see the local newspaper, which stated that no damage had been sustained by the Italian fleet … It appears that on the morning of November 11th the Italian battleships had been intended to carry out some sea exercises, and all their anti-torpedo nets had been removed. The sailing was postponed for 24 hours at the last moment, and the

Port Admiral said the nets were to be replaced. This the Commander-In-Chief refused to do because he considered it to be a waste of time …

Lieutenant Commander John 'Tweeny' Neale, DSC, Observer, 815 Squadron, HMS *Illustrious*
Fleet Air Arm Museum Reference C7-17

Neale flew in aircraft 4C piloted by Sub-Lieutenant 'Spike' Sparke.

Our morale was very high. We had a wonderful briefing about Taranto. I reckon I knew more about the Harbour at the time that the harbour master himself. We flew off in the dark at 2030 at 170 miles range – a long way in those days. My navigator's cockpit was full with an overload petrol tank, so I sat in the air gunner's seat. It was so windy that we put our charts under sheets of perspex on our chartboards and slid them under the Lewis gun.

We all realized that this was one of those nights when we had more than the usual chance of being knocked down, and I – like most of the others – wore my best uniform. If you were going to be a prisoner of war, you might as well be properly dressed. Our form of attack was to stagger up to our ceiling of about 9000 feet and make the final approach throttled back to deceive the sound locators, diving very steeply in the last run in to give us some speed.

We were all used by now to being shot at, but this barrage was quite fantastic – a complete ring of fire round the great harbour with all calibre weapons firing inward over their fleet in a solid flat cone. It was reported, I believe, that shore batteries alone fired 13,000 rounds. My pilot flew magnificently. I remember passing him the course for home before we got too involved, and he set this on his compass in case anything happened to me. Then I could only help with advice now and then about ship positions and ranges of targets. We flew at an average height of about 15 feet passing under most of the gunfire – marvelling all the time that they could not hit us, although the run across was nearly 2 miles each way.

I remember there was quite a lot of moon, and with the masses of tracer and with our own flares dropped by specially detailed aircraft it was all very much lit up. We ran to within half a mile of the *Cavour* battleship, dropped our torpedo and spun round for the return. I remember timing the torpedo's run with my stopwatch. The little explosion I saw after 110 seconds was most disappointing and it was not until afterwards we realized that with the new magnetic pistol on the warhead, the torpedo was running too deeply to show much result.

Sparke and I were the first ones back to the ship, and I can remember great surprise when all the aircraft but one were eventually flying around and landing back on. I thought that we would have been the only ones to come away from that lot alive. Also, I can remember feeling thankful to the Italians for leaving the light on in one of the lighthouses on the heel of Italy. It helped my navigation considerably on the way home.

Captain Alan 'Alfie' Sutton, CBE, DSC, then an Observer, 819 Squadron, HMS *Illustrious*
Fleet Air Arm Museum Reference C7-17

I was in the second striking force which took off at 9. 30 pm., 50 minutes after the first. We sighted the lighthouse on the tip of the heel of Italy, Santa Maria Di Leuca, on the way to the Gulf, and fixed ourselves on it, and then held off to the west. But we were detected – the enemy had a very good sound locating gear, though he had not got effective radar in those days. Anti-aircraft guns hopefully opened fire as we passed along 15 miles offshore. Then we were about 60 miles off Taranto, we saw the place – a great greenish coloured cone of anti-aircraft fire and searchlights, for the Italians were still keeping things going after the first attack had retired.

We made to the North West of the town, crossed the coast at about 9000 feet, and then crossed and re-crossed the coastline to put off the anti-aircraft guns which had started to get uncomfortably accurate as we approached the harbour. The noise of the breaking waves on the beach tends to confuse the sound location if you do that.

The harbour by then was dark. There were shore based searchlights probing for us, and plenty of guns firing. The flare droppers had been released before we crossed the coast, and our own leader, Lieut. Cdr. Hale ordered flares to be dropped and then started his dive. At this moment the dive bombers should have run in to bomb the cruisers in the inner Harbour, to attract fire, but we had not got enough aircraft in the ship to provide bombers, so there was nothing to draw the Italians' attention from us. As we went down, the Italians had put up an intense box barrage for us to fly through. In a box barrage all of the guns are fired so that the shells burst in an imaginary box which is placed ahead of the aircraft. The rest of the leader's sub-flight of three followed him down, and then over we went and down in that screaming whistling torpedo dive – down, down.

The aircraft ahead of us had been hit. We saw an orange flash of flame and he spun away out of control. All the close range weapons had opened pouring stuff out, right next to our dropping position. We pulled out a bit to starboard. Tracer and incendiaries and a horrible thing we called 'flaming onions' came streaming up at us. We came down a bit too short. We found ourselves down over the cruisers, pulled out … over the mass of the cruisers and down to our dropping height on the other side. The cruisers saw us and opened fire. We could see the tracer streaming along past us, seeming to float along.

My pilot, Torrens-Spence, called out 'The one to port is too close. What is that ahead?'

'Dead ahead is *Littorio*.'

'Right.'

We had been in too close to one of the old *Cavour* class battleships to attack her, but were now motoring in over the water towards one of their fine new *Littorio*s – something like our *King George V* class battleships, only a bit larger.

She saw us, and opened fire. The flash of her close range weapons stabbed after us, as first one, then another along her length opened up. We were coming in on her beam, and we were at an incredible mass of crossfire from the cruisers and battleships and shore batteries.

No worries about clear range of guns for the Italians. They just fired everything they had except the 15 inch, and I could see the shots from the battleships bursting among the cruisers and merchant ships. The place stank of cordite and incendiaries, and was wreathed in smoke.

Torrens-Spence fired the torpedo. It did not come off. The magnetic release had failed. He finally released at 700 yards, by which time that *Littorio* battleship just about extended over the whole horizon, and we seemed to be looking down the muzzles of the close range guns.

A steep turn to starboard, straightened out and smack! We hit the water. We're down. But we weren't. We had hit with the wheels only, and Torrens-Spence took us through the balloon barrage, flying between the floats, and out of that incredible cauldron of fire. Suddenly everything was quiet. No one was firing at us. We set course for the gap between the forts out of the moon path, and got away really low down ...

Edward Wilson Whitley, Air Fitter, HMS *Illustrious*
IWM Sound Archive Reference 28496

'Sammy' Morford came back first because his tank on the torpedo rack had fallen off ... and then the rest of them started coming back. We couldn't believe it: we got them all back, except two,* and then of course we began to find out what had happened, and it was very exciting, particularly when we got back to Alexandria and there were headlines in the paper.

The way that you handled the aircraft in those days is: they landed on, the barrier went up, and you wanted the aircrew out of the aircraft so you could fold them [the aircraft wings] and get them down. So they [the aircrew] used to disappear into the dark, and you really didn't get anything [by way of news]. It's dark and there's a howling gale, and all you're interested in is making sure that they get out before the wings chop their heads off.

Operation 'White', official reports
ADM 116/4190

'White' was one of several difficult operations to keep Malta supplied with vital aircraft.

RAF Station Kalafrana, Malta
17th November, 1940
Report on Hurricane Forced Landing
Operation White

* The second crew were killed.

Sir,

I have the honour to submit the following report on the above.

On the 17th. inst. at 06.15 hours following instructions I took off from HMS *Argus* in Hurricane V. 7413 in Yellow Section led by Sergeant Pilot Knowall. I had normal full fuel of 90 gallons. The flight consisting of Red and Yellow Sections was led by Skua aircraft. At Galita the lead was taken over by a Sunderland. During the flight the air-speed was generally 150 mph. At approximately 08.50 hrs on checking my petrol I found I had just over 10 gallons left in the reserve tank. I had already emptied my main tanks. Yellow Section was then flying at 2000 feet, and Yellow 1 signalled that he also was short of petrol. His signals appeared to indicate that he anticipated making a parachute descent and he throttled right back so that it was impossible to keep in formation, and I went ahead following above Red Section. Two or three minutes afterwards I saw a Hurricane diving steeply towards the area and a parachutist following. I communicated this fact to Red Leader but received no reply. I could not risk going down to him (Red Section were flying approximately 1000 feet) as I had anticipated having to jump myself. Apparently Knowall's descent was seen as the Sunderland turned and flew in the direction of the crash. At approximately 09:00 hours my engine began to cough and I prepared myself for the jump. When the engine stopped altogether I released my safety panel and jumped. During my descent the Sunderland flew past me, and apparently sighted me. On entering the sea took the necessary precautions and with the aid of my lifejacket kept myself floating until I was picked up by the Sunderland. I cannot state position of the aircraft when I jumped, but particulars can be obtained from the pilot of the Sunderland No.'T'.

I have the honour to be,
Sir,
Your obedient servant,

[signed] R. A. Spyer.
Sergeant Pilot
Number 228 Squadron, Royal Air Force

The Director of Naval Air Division generally agreed with the findings of the Board of Inquiry, which compared the figures for the successful Operation 'Hurry' with those of Operation 'White'. There were few differences in terms of flying off distance, influence of wind direction, actual distance flown and height flown. But ...

3. There was, however, a very big difference in the two operations in that operation 'Hurry' the Hurricanes had 2 speed air screws whereas in 'White' they had constant speed air screws. It would appear that the Air Ministry supplied *Argus* with the same information on both occasions (Air Ministry's memo S 65336/ D.W.O. of October 23. 1940 ...

4. The pilots do not appear to have been warned that Hurricanes with constant speed air-screws are most economical at 1800 revs, but knew that the most

comfortable speed was 2200 revs. Figures given by the Ministry of Aircraft Production show that this increase in revolutions would decrease the maximum range by 10% (not 15% as given by Board of Inquiry). By flying at 2000 ft instead of 10,000 ft a 10% reduction in range would be caused, thus giving a total reduction of 20% after having taken departure. … the Hurricanes in the White operation were the tropical type with larger radiators and constant speed air screw. No allowance had been made for this in the General Information sent from the Air Ministry to HMS *Argus*.

David Musk Beattie, HMS *Ark Royal*
from *The Log of a Naval Airman*, Fleet Air Arm Museum

DIARY

ENSA* arrived and we went to Theatre Royal – bloody awful. They also came aboard and gave a show on the flight-deck. We got 'em tight afterwards – it's a good thing the Lord Chamberlain** didn't hear their show that night at Theatre Royal.

DEC. 9th. Training cruise in Western Med. and Atlantic.
DEC 11th. Hard work. Buckled rather a lot of kites, but all O.K. soon except two more Fulmars, one of which went into the drink (no juice) and other hit crash barrier when going well. They've only about four left now. Appleby had a collision and spun in from 150 feet – I found Pussy Grant's body, that's all. Spain and Ceuta looked grand from 2,000 feet – hope photos are O.K. After Appleby had gone young F……….. was so shaken that he hit the crash barrier when air-borne. The torpedo came off and whistled up the deck until Lamb straddled it and brought it to a standstill. Old G. Fausett accidentally dropped a runner torpedo from 5,000 feet. Did it go down! F.O.H.*** was with us on this dummy attack and kept sending weird messages, as he was handling the W/T. He's a game old bird – he did everything that Stringbags and Skuas will do except an A/S patrol …
DEC 18TH … Afternoon – suspicions realised – we are putting to sea again, probably with *Resolution*. Does this mean we are going to escort her to the U.K.? *Resolution* didn't come – so that means East, and more bombing.
DEC. 21ST Yes, we're going East. As Admiral Somerville says, it's Force H v. the Wop Navy. There are 3 Wop battle waggons at sea in the West Med. or Tyrrhenian, so I've got a torpedo on my kite and shall not get my clothes off tonight.
DEC 22ND. Stood by all night armed with torpedo. We rendezvoused 6 hours steaming East of Galite. Had just lost the destroyer *Hyperion* by mine. Tony and McWilliam whilst on recco. met and attacked a Cant seaplane – and took it

---

* Entertainments National Service Association, which was succeeded by the perhaps better known Combined Services Entertainment.
** The government-appointed censor.
*** Admiral Somerville, Flag Officer Force H.

on the lam (*sic*). Visibility is closing down a bit (lunchtime). Took torpedo off at 17.00 – released at last. Shadower seen and chased off by fighters just before sunset.

DEC. 23RD. Did Security Patrol this forenoon. Nothing sighted. Pat and Jeff had to make an emergency landing. Blowing at 26 knots – hope we'll make Gib. before the 25th.

24TH. We have started getting ready for Christmas. The 'tree' is now being rigged on the Quarter Deck. The sun coming up this morning shewed up the coast from Gib. through Malaga to Almeria – and the pink colour of the snow on the Sierra Nevada was very beautiful. We made Gib. by 12.00 and we are all thrilled to know there is NO MAIL. I got a parcel of Brian's wedding cake and also a telegram from Home – but there is no mail proper. I always thought that *Ark Royals* AT WAR were pretty impressive, but you've got to see them at Christmas Eve-ing to see them at their best.

Strewth! What a party!

25TH. Up with the lark – Divisions – then Carol Service. Then we had our presents off the Christmas Tree, and heard that a raider was out and *Berwick* was within range and doing her stuff. Grabbed a quick lunch – had the afternoon and we put to sea at 14.00. Pretty bloody! Heard *Berwick* had been in action with a *Hipper* class cruiser and had lost her in the thick weather. *Bonaventure* then had a crack, but lost touch. *Furious* there, too – but weather too bad for flying. Had a big party in the Wardroom: Johnnie had a marvellous time with a toy train.

DEC 26TH. Standing by with a torpedo on the kite. Rumoured that another P.B. [Pocket Battleship] raider is off the Western Isles.

4
1941

The Battle of the Atlantic was raging, and German U-boats inflicted unsustainable damage on Allied convoys in the Atlantic. There were no carriers to spare to help the convoy escorts, and land based air-cover from Canada and Britain left a great hole – the Atlantic Gap – in which merchant ships had little protection from submarines, surface raiders and long-range Focke-Wulf Condor aircraft, which operated out of occupied France and which, as well as bombing ships, passed information about convoys to the U-boat packs.

Things were about to change, albeit slowly, with the first of the CAM ships. Just as the first aircraft carriers were hasty conversions of warships, so the Catapult Aircraft Merchantmen were converted merchant ships fitted with a catapult. Mark I Hurricanes were catapulted off if – and only if – an enemy aircraft was spotted; they did not fly routine patrols because there was no possibility of landing on the CAM ship at the end of a mission. In some cases the landing gear was removed to save weight and, therefore, improve fuel consumption. The pilot would have to ditch or bail out close to the convoy and hope to be picked up – the aircraft was expendable. For the ships, there was no protection from submarines, and in fact the first CAM, *Michael E*, was torpedoed on 2 June, less than a week after leaving with her first convoy. Rudimentary as this stop-gap measure was, CAMs enjoyed some success, with eight enemy aircraft destroyed and one damaged during their service. The first Condor was shot down by HMS *Maplin* in August 1941. Responsibility for CAM ships lay with the RAF's Merchant Ship Fighter Unit at Speke, near Liverpool.

An even more significant arrival was that of HMS *Audacity* which was commissioned in June and carried out her first operation in September. Originally a captured Norddeutscher Lloyd passenger-cargo vessel, she had been converted to the Royal Navy's very first escort carrier. Unlike the CAMs, she had a flight deck, and significantly 802 Squadron was equipped with eight Grumman Wildcats from America. For the first time the Navy had a modern, high-performance fighter that was specifically built for carrier work. *Audacity*'s life was short, but her contribution was significant because she shot down seven Condors and attacked *U-131*, which was then sunk by the destroyers.

For the Allies in the Mediterranean, 1941 dawned dawned brightly. The damage inflicted on the Regia Marina at Taranto had made the Italian high command more protective of its navy and had given the British an opportunity to supply Wavell's army, now fighting the Italians in North Africa. Farther east, the Greek army was driving the Italian invasion forces back into Albania. Unfortunately, those very successes forced the Germans to divert significant resources to the

Mediterranean to prop up their ally and take the fight to the British and the Greeks. Luftwaffe squadrons equipped with Stukas were deployed to Sicily and lost little time in repaying *Illustrious* for the Taranto raid.

Illustrious was patched up sufficiently to limp in great secrecy to the USA for repairs, and her newly commissioned sister *Formidable* took her place. Taking *Formidable* through the Strait of Gibraltar was too dangerous, so she was routed via Cape Town and the Red Sea. Hardly had she arrived than her aircraft played a vital role in the Battle of Matapan. Although Matapan was primarily a night action for the big guns of Cunningham's Mediterranean Fleet, and *Formidable* was kept safely out of it, her Swordfish, Albacores and Fulmars performed vital reconnaissance work. Moreover, by torpedoing *Pola*, they brought the Italian cruisers back into the path of the British fleet after Admiral Iachino ordered his cruisers to support the crippled ship. A major threat posed by the Italian Navy's surface fleet was all but neutralized.

Despite the scuttling of the German pocket battleship *Graf Spee* the previous year, danger from the Germany Navy had not been neutralized. German surface ships in harbour, such as *Tirpitz*, were tying up Royal Navy resources; others, like *Scharnhorst* and *Gneisenau* were opportunistically sinking merchant ships in the Atlantic, and *Bismarck*, in company with *Prince Eugen*, was set to join them. On 24 May, in the Battle of the Denmark Strait, the two ships were brought to battle by HMS *Prince of Wales* and HMS *Hood*. The former was damaged; the second was sunk by *Bismarck*, leaving just three survivors. Damage to *Bismarck* was slight, but her commander had to make for the Occupied French port of St Nazaire to repair and refuel. Every available Royal Navy resource was immediately thrown into the hunt for *Bismarck*, including the brand new carrier *Victorious*, whose squadrons were extremely inexperienced. That same evening her Swordfish attacked and though they obtained hits, their torpedoes failed to inflict any visible damage. *Bismarck*'s guns and their crews were incapable of dealing with such slow aircraft, and the Swordfish all returned safely. With the *Bismarck* too fast for the pursuing British battleships, Force H at Gibraltar was ordered to slow the German raider down. On 26 May, *Ark Royal's* Swordfish went into action. A torpedo seriously damaged *Bismarck*'s rudder, and she was sunk by surface ships the following morning.

In June, Hitler abandoned his pact with Stalin and attacked the Soviet Union. Escorted Allied convoys began to pass through the Arctic with supplies for the Russians, but in 1941 they had no carriers with them to provide air cover or A/S patrols, and suffered accordingly.

Although the USA was not officially involved in the war, and many Americans inside and outside politics wanted it to stay that way, considerable assistance was being given, and in March the Lend-Lease Act came into force. One effect of this was to allow the British to obtain modern US carrier aircraft such as the Wildcat, and, later on, US-built escort carriers for convoy defence. The US Navy was already extending convoy protection to Allied ships in its waters through the deployment of warships, including USS *Yorktown*.

The last two months of 1941 were disastrous for the Royal Navy. Hardly had the new HMS *Indomitable* been completed than on 3 November she suffered extensive damage during her working up period in the Caribbean and had to join *Illustrious*, which was still at Norfolk Navy Yard completing repairs and modifications. Less than a fortnight later *Ark Royal* fell victim to *U-81* (one of the German submarines operating in the Mediterranean), and in December Cunningham's two battleships at Alexandria were put out of action for months by Italian special forces. That, however, occurred a week after carrier-based Japanese aircraft attacked Pearl Harbor. The USA entered the war, turning an essentially European conflict into a world war. The saving grace was that the US Navy's carriers, which were the primary target of the Japanese raiders, were not at Pearl, and – crucially – US naval air power remained inact.

The US naval squadrons had depended on biplane fighters until the introduction of a small number of Brewster F2A-1 monoplanes in 1940. These were unsatisfactory and were superseded that same year by the Grumman F4F-4, better known as the Wildcat. From autumn 1941, Wildcats were produced with folding wings. Before the Franco-German Armistice, France had placed an order for Wildcats; this was taken over by Britain, and the Wildcat entered service with the Fleet Air Arm too. The Royal Navy named it the Martlet, but crews tended to prefer the US name, and in 1944 it officially reverted to Wildcat.

MEDITERRANEAN

CPO Richard Griffin, RN, 815 Squadron, HMS *Illustrious*
www.maritimequest.com

In January 1941 we embarked on the carrier for what was to be the last time I was on board. As always we read orders of the day. There was a message from the C-in-C commenting that units of the German air force had been sent to air fields in Sicily, and we might expect rather more activity than hitherto. We arrived off Pantelleria. Things started to hot up, and the ship's tannoy system kept us informed of events as they unfolded. The cruiser *Bonaventure* engaged enemy units to the westward. The destroyer *Gallant* struck a mine and her bows were blown off.

I remember standing in the well deck, a grey sea surging past. There seemed to be an eerie still air over the ship. I have often thought about that since ... Fear? Premonition? I know I had a very strange feeling.

Suddenly the fleet came under heavy air attack mainly directed at *Illustrious* by squadrons of Stuka dive bombers. All the guns of the fleet opened fire. Two seaplanes launched a torpedo attack, a diversionary feint. The tannoy told us that large numbers of aircraft were in the air over Sicily. The ship was all closed up at action stations and then all the ships guns opened up. The steel box of the hangar was like a huge sound box.

My action station, as with all maintenance crews, was in the hangar with the aircraft, which by the way were all heavily armed, and loaded with torpedoes ready for an attack on the Italian Fleet.

Illustrious was armed with 16 4.5 dual purpose guns, and 8 6-barrelled 2lb quick firing AA weapons. The ship kept jumping and shaking. Several large bombs hit the ship aft, and the after hangar was on fire. The noise was indescribable. In my baptism of fire, all that sticks in my mind are impressions. I was standing more or less in the centre of the hangar. A chap came down from the flight deck; his rubber suit was full of holes with blood leaking from all of them. I helped carry him down to the casualty station in the washroom flats. The surgeons were busy. Blood washed from side to side with the sway of the ship. I returned to my action station in the hangar. The ship continued to rock and sway.

I looked up with fear and apprehension. Then there was an almighty flash as a 1,000lb bomb pierced the 4 inch armoured deck and exploded. I was only aware of a great wind, and bits of aircraft, debris, all blowing out to the forward lift shaft of 300 tons, which was also blown out. There were dead and wounded all around. My overalls were blown off and I had small wounds to the back of my head and shoulder. I was probably 10–15 feet away from the bomb when it exploded. Luck I survived? I prefer the thought of someone looking out for me. The hangar by then was burning all over. The ship's commander came and said, 'come on lads close the armoured doors.' The overhead sprays then flooded the hangar.

The ship started to sink by the stern, and everyone had to blow up lifebelts. Then came a spot of humour in all that chaos. Poor old Corporal Gater came through a side door white as a sheet saying 'I wish I hadn't bloody joined.' The battering carried on for six to seven hours. There were many wounded piled up. The aft surgeons station had been destroyed, and the forward station was unable to cope quickly with so many casualties.

Captain Boyd finally steered with the engines into Malta. The ship was quiet at last. The next morning we cleared lower deck, and a roll call was taken. An announcement on the tannoy ordered in case of further attacks on the ship, all hands other than gun crews etc. should go over the side, and into the big caves in the hillside. No sooner said than over the enemy came again, so over the side we went!

That same day all air maintenance ratings were dispersed. The surviving 815 and 819 squadron people shipped on the cruiser *Orion* back to Alexandria there to reform as 815, and where we operated an RAF command for the next two years.

There were three aircraft in the air when *Illustrious* was damaged, but there were some spares at Dakahlia, some were sent from the UK, and we were soon fully operational. My last memory of *Illustrious* was clearing lower deck and lining the ship's side to pay a last salute to the destroyer carrying our dead to sea for burial. Lines of white ensigns lay row upon row. The crew were at attention, as we were.

Words are still inadequate.

Edward Wilson Whitley, Air Fitter, HMS *Illustrious*
IWM Sound Archive Reference 28496

The action stations alarm sounded. We usually got plenty of warning because up to that stage we'd been bombed by the Italians from high level and we didn't worry much about it. One piece of shrapnel had actually landed on the flight deck, and so we found out that shrapnel is hot. But on this day I thought I had enough time to get a coffee from the deck-space underneath the flight deck on the way down to the hangar. I had just got there and got one in my hand when all the noise started. So the canteen closed very quickly and my coffee floated away. I was now on Two Deck, underneath the flight deck. I started going down from Two to Three to Four deck, down to the hangar, but this meant going down ladders which were open to the ship's side, and there were a lot of near-misses and shrapnel and water flying around there. Straight ahead of me was the Sick Bay. The doors were open so I thought I'd go in there for a bit. And I arrived in the Sick Bay, and the noise of the ship's guns – the 4.5s and the short range guns were all firing away – tremendous noise. The scuttles had not been closed in the Sick Bay, and the curtains were horizontal, and bottles were flying around. Then I heard a Stuka pulling out of its dive; I'd never heard one before, but I knew what it was.

And then the ship was hit, and it felt as if she'd been lifted out of the water and dropped back in again. You knew, although you'd never experienced it before, you knew from all the noise that the ship had been hit; and you thought: oh dear! Then it happened four or five times again, and you got a bit worried. Then things went quiet, and a couple of sailors came down – three of them came down from the flight deck, and the petty officer had a nick in his chin, which was bleeding, and I remember him saying: 'Never mind about me, go and get the others.'

I thought to myself: I must get to my action station, which was in the hangar. So down I go one deck from the Sick Bay, forward into the hangar access. There's some smoke from a fire forward, and some people say, 'Oh, Leading Hand: how about going to put the fire out?' I think it's more important to go to the hangar. So I enter the hangar, and to my surprise the armoured doors had been closed, except for a gap, and the hangar was empty except one sailor lying on his stomach with a submarine sweater on, and all I could see was some Swordfish in the hangar, two or three of them, with torpedoes on – and all I could see after that was fire.

We'd been taught how to deal with the hangar sprays systems, so you pull a lever which shuts off the ventilation. You then pulled the chain, which either started the pumps down below or told the engineers to start them. Then you wound open a great wheel and the water starts pouring into the hangar.

Before this, I've gone to the chap who is dead, and he was very, very big, so I left him where he was. I've also been completely surprised to find that the forward lift was bent ... Anyway, down comes the water, so you know that's alright, and oddly enough, the next thing you think about is: where's my particular chum. He was called Wilf Jones, so I decided to go up to the flight deck, and as my head comes level with the flight deck, right in front of me is the torso of a man, no clothes, all burnt like a cooked chicken, and, looking down the flight deck, the after lift is on its end in the well, the smoke pouring out of it. There's a hole on the centreline in the middle of the flight deck, and you think: Oh my God. The awful thing is, it's a nice day and you look at the blue sea, and then you see all the other ships disappearing, so you think you'd better stay where you are.

I ran a hose down the flight deck to this hole at the after end – well, it was the midships, actually – and I noticed the S2 pom-pom had taken a direct hit, and saw bits of wreckage. Nothing came out of this hose, and then some gunners came out of the forward gun turrets, hollering for ammunition because the bomb which had gone through the centreline of the flight deck had gone down through the hangar deck and stopped the ammunition supply to the forward guns. Either that, or the bomb which had hit forward and ad bent the lift. We started carting 4.5" shells from aft to forward. That became rather hard work. And eventually there was another raid ...

In between times, the Tannoy ... started working, which was marvellous, really, because you knew what was going on then. The ship was out of control, on fire, steaming around in circles in sight of Pantellaria. Fortunately, there wasn't much on Pantellaria to do us any harm.

I went down to my messdeck to get some cigarettes, and I got a tin of 50 cigarettes, and, incidentally, by the end of the day they'd all gone – I hadn't smoked them all! I had a quick look at my girlfriend's photo and wondered whether I'd see her again, and then went up looking for Wilf Jones. I found in the starboard passageway – and *Illustrious* always had a slight list to starboard – there was masses of water there. Of course, what had happened was that the covers round the drains in the hangar were blocked with wreckage, and the water was running out of the hangar access doors down into the decks below. Although I'd done the drill, I'd never told anyone I'd put these sprays on – although the people in Damage Control headquarters must have known. So we end up pumping water for a while, and then I go back on the flight deck looking for Wilf Jones, when the second raid comes, and I am completely unscathed at this time. I start baling out from the flight deck, and only get down one deck. I'm outside the spud locker when the air raid starts. Rather stupidly I though that if I throw myself flat on the deck I'll be alright. It was not a very wise thing to do, and of course it was wet, so all that happened to me that terrible day was, I got wet.

Then we were told to go and sit somewhere down in the ship, and they brought some bully-beef sandwiches. We were sitting down there, and we must have been over an engine room hatch, and somebody came out of the hatch, popped his head up and said: 'What's been happening?' They must have heard all this noise, and felt the ship shaking and so on, but what's been happening?

We'd been blessing the firm who made the ship because she was standing it so well. Eventually we managed to get into Malta with a tug, and we offload all the wounded people away to hospital. Then we just sort of fall asleep; didn't even bother with hammocks or camp-beds. I remember sleeping on one of the stools on the mess deck.

Captain (later Admiral Sir) Denis Boyd, HMS *Illustrious*
from Miscellaneous Documents, IWM Reference 11842 Misc 223 (3208)

HMS *Illustrious*
3 March 1941

My dear old E J
Your very kind letter of 16th January has just arrived. I knew how you would feel it and longed to be able to assure you that all the team you knew were still alive. I not only could not but dared not say anything until we left Malta and got to Alex as our expectation of life was not very high. But as you know we all survived and live to fight again. How the buzz about Bill started I have no idea as he was more full of life than anyone! My chief sorrows were Lt. Gregory whom you may remember was very sweet to Elizabeth. He was hit on the spine by a bomb splinter and fell down saying 'I think something has hit me'. He then turned very grey and asked for morphia knowing he was dying. Keevil gave him a shot and then he had to be moved as a fierce fire was raging under the quarter deck where he was lying. A marine picked him up and his back was heard to break. He was I think already dead. Cuddington, Ex-England and Navy rugger our Master at Arms was blown to bits in the hangar where a bomb exploded. He was a golden man.

Clifford, a Lieut and pilot who had done very well at Taranto, was wounded in the first attack and then devoted himself to the other wounded. After the third attack he was never seen again. Either he was blown overboard or disintegrated. He was a pattern of gallantry and gentility and one of the best three-quarter* we have had for a long time.

One young marine, Mainsty ... was killed by a bomb which did not wound him but just blasted him. The other officer casualties you would not know unless you remember Mr Anstice [Anstis] our gunner. He was blown to bits by a bomb which hit the pom-pom just in front of the bridge. He and all the crew were in an awful mess but were clearly killed instantly. I ordered them to be thrown overboard as they were awful sights. Arms legs heads and trunks going over the side were awful to see but were better there than lying about on the deck where they chilled the stomachs of others. Analysing ones feelings afterwards I felt no sorrow at the time as my feelings were that the dead had perhaps the easier job. Nor was I afraid. It was all so terrific and ones responsibility so great that I had no uncomfortable feelings other than intense

* A position in the sport of Rugby.

sorrow for the ship as I never expected her to be of any use to us again. I was on the wing bridge watching the bombs come down and I saw both lifts fly into the air like leaves. An amazing sight.

Fear came later when I realised we must have more attacks before reaching Malta. I then felt utterly sick for a while and trembled from head to foot. I went down to my sea cabin, took a good hold of myself offered up a prayer that I'd do my stuff and then went back and was waggling the engines to steer her for the next 8 hours and through 2 more attacks without any particular feeling other than an unsatisfied desire for food. From breakfast until 2pm when we secured I only had cocoa and a biscuit which Lloyd the Padre brought me. Our real strain came with the repeat attack at Malta. On one occasion I was ashore not 20 yards from a cave shelter and the ship was 100 yards away. On the warning I walked to the gangway saying to myself after all there is nothing I can do and when I got to the gangway I stopped, feeling utterly cowardly and bloody nearly ran for the shelter. However I climbed slowly and reluctantly up the gangway and then felt alright. The others were the same I think. I allowed no one on board (there were wonderful shelters) except the gun crews and supply parties. Some of these failed to turn up and we manned the guns with four Commanders, 6 Lt Cdrs, 2 Paymasters Sowman and Westmacott, 4 P.O.s and 6 first class able seamen. [Lt] 'Rosy' Baker and I went to the Air Defence position on the top bridge where we directed the guns onto the targets until the attack developed and then we just watched. However if you have seen [Gunnery Officer?] Bill [Ackworth?] you will have heard as stirring a yarn as ever was spun. I sent Bill home because we did learn a lot and I wanted the powers that be to learn what we learnt. To say I was indifferent to the fact that Bella had had a baby would be a ruddy lie but Bella must never know that I thought of that first! He was splendid and deserved a little thought of that kind. I think my worst job was to see people suffering from strain. It was horrible and some got it badly. [Commander E] Tamplin the Chief, a fat cheerful self indulgent bachelor, went ashore and just couldn't come back so I sent him to the hospital. [Ralph] Duckworth [Torpedo Officer] who was badly blasted cried at the least excuse and yet stuck it and was always there though I think useless. Men I thought tough were no good at all in fact the only good ones were the team and a few sailors and engineers of the quiet nice type. Martin whose funny little wife vamped old N.R. was the senior engineer and he was the supreme man of the whole show and he was quite delighted when owing to the Chief cracking he was left with the whole responsibility.

The senior gunner went to the hospital to see the wounded and collapsed staying there! Others in varying degrees were looking like death but they stuck it well. I think I saved them all from going really potty by abandoning ship for three days after the Sunday attacks. It was a ghastly thing to do but I had to do it and as usual got away with it as during those 3 days we were not attacked. Had I not done so half of us would have been lunies [sic] and in any case we would not have saved the ship. On the Thursday they all came back gladly and were able to produce the goods for our awful passage to Alex. I have often had to bear responsibility but never anything to equal this. To them the three days were a rest, to me they were just hell but I knew I was right …

Captain Michael 'Pinkie' Haworth, 826 Squadron, HMS *Formidable*
from the private papers of M. G. Haworth, IWM Reference 3320 95/5/1

HMS *Formidable* succeeded *Illustrious* as the main carrier in the Mediterranean Fleet and booked her own place in naval history through her contribution to the Battle of Cape Matapan.

On 27 March we received urgent orders to re-embark in the *Formidable*, which we accordingly did with a sort of a crash drill which became more perfected the more we did it during our time there. And it transpired that the Commander in Chief was quietly playing golf in Alexandria when a messenger came out to him with the information that Intelligence reported that the Italian Fleet was putting to sea with the intention of interrupting our convoys in support of the British army in Greece. Emulating the true Drake tradition, the Commander-in-Chief finished his game of golf, not before he had instructed his messenger to make arrangements for the fleet to be immediately ready to proceed that evening. He then went back on board as if nothing had happened in order to mislead any enemy agent with which Alexandria was alleged to be teeming, in case they realised that something untoward was happening. Well then we waited until the evening reconnaissance, flown regularly by the Italian Air force at about five o'clock, had gone over Alexandria Harbour and reported all ships to be still there, and then quietly slipped and made our way towards the Aegean.

The dawn search was flown off on the morning of the 28th, and most of us who were not engaged on it were assembled into the Ops room to hear what might be toward. Reports of ships started coming in and there was a slightly confused situation because our own cruisers were steaming towards a rendezvous with the rest of the fleet, coming down from the Aegean, and the Italians, little known to us until then, were coming towards the same rendezvous without them knowing it! So it was a slightly confused situation, not improved by the general belief that the Fleet Air Arm always made a nonsense of these things, and our own cruisers were rather sceptical. However a report came in which, from the call sign, was obviously originated by an experienced Observer called Pancho Paine, and certainly in our own Ops room we had no doubt that this must have been correct. Pancho, from his time on the carriers, was considered to be a good looker (because lookers was the expression used for observers in the trade), except that no one could ever have mistaken Pancho for an Adonis!

Well our cruisers soon found themselves briskly engaged with the enemy's and rather out gunned by them and withdrew towards the battlefleet as fast as they could come. Inconclusive engagement ensued from which they retired from under cover of smoke, and then the Italian battleship called the *Vittorio Veneto* came on the scene. Also, but more importantly, outgunning the cruisers who found themselves practically straddled by heavy 15 inch shells, one hit of which would have crippled any one of them. So they were extremely glad to fall back on the battle fleet. Meanwhile the Italian Admiral somehow became aware of the fact that he was heading straight into an outnumbering force of three battleships. So he turned tail, broke off the action and made off to the westwards towards his home port of Taranto. By this time the Commander-in Chief had decided to adopt the classic ploy, laid down in the Naval Tactical Manual, of trying to reduce the speed of a retiring enemy fleet by air attack and then bring him to action. A striking force of six Albacores armed with torpedoes was accordingly ranged, and I was the observer in one of these. We took off at about 10 o-clock and soon were in contact, visual contact at any rate, with the said *Vittorio Veneto*. Luckily we were accompanied by two Fulmar fighters, because when we were manoeuvring to get into position for an attack, a couple of enemy aircraft hove into sight, which were promptly dispatched, I am glad to say, by the fighters. I suppose this could be described as another occasion when my Guardian Angel was looking after me. Anyway we delivered the torpedo attack according to a set piece which we had rehearsed many a time in peacetime where aircraft come in from different sectors making it difficult for the battleship to avoid all of them. In fact the battleship did succeed in avoiding all of them although we were quite convinced that we must have scored a hit, which is perfectly normal under the circumstances. I was feeling not very efficient that day because last thing before we took off, the pilot gave me a camera so that we could take a close up of the enemy battleship, and I clean forgot the thing in the rear seat in the excitement of seeing whether we were shot down or not. Anyway we got back and landed on the *Formidable*. The aircraft was refuelled and the aircrew refuelled themselves with lunch in the officers mess. We took off again at 2.00 to go and look for the missing battleship. Of course it had to be yours truly whose pilot sighted it first!

For the next 4 hours we shadowed this ... with me making reports, about position course and speed, which was a slightly complicated exercise because I had a long range tank instead of an air gunner, so I had to write out my reports and then encrypt them with a funny machine we had which I don't suppose provided more than a couple of hours security at the most, put them on the radio and then transmit them. Under modern conditions of course we would have been shot down in 5 minutes by a heat seeking homing missile, but, as it was, apart from another enemy reconnaissance aircraft that sort of gave us a friendly nudge about halfway through this performance, we were left absolutely untroubled. I could see the battleship firing ack ack guns sometimes, but I never saw anything exploding anywhere near us.

After about an hour I noticed that the battleship emitted smoke rings from the funnels, and turned round in a complete circle and appeared to stop for a few minutes before gathering speed and continuing to the westward at very much reduced speed. This of course was coinciding with the second attack delivered by five aircraft from the *Formidable*. The leader made a most gallant and determined attack on the enemy which was reported by the Italian C in C with a great admiration for his courage, but he was shot down and all the crew were lost. I don't think it was his torpedo, but one of the torpedoes of that force did score a hit and it did in fact reduce the speed of the battleship. Eventually it managed to find enough power to proceed to the westward at 19 knots.

The Italian Admiral evidently appreciated that the next act in the Fleet Air Arm show would be a dusk attack, so he gathered all his smaller ships round him, like a hen gathering her chicks, and before I left the scene there were concentric circles of cruisers on the inside and destroyers on the outside which would provide him with the best protection he could expect.

Meanwhile I had been rattling off my reports, nine or ten of which were actually received, decrypted and understood in the carrier. Looking back on that time, I sometimes think when I am in company with a rather garrulous crowd of people and can't get myself heard, that, during that afternoon, for three or four halcyon hours there must have been a telegraphist in every ship in the fleet on reconnaissance wave, listening to my every transmission.

Meanwhile the flagship had catapulted its amphibian aircraft off to take over the shadowing, and I was able to tell my doubting pilot, Ferret Ellis, that we could now go back and land on the carrier in the last of the daylight while we still had a few drops of petrol left, which we accordingly did. At this stage I must pay tribute to Ferret for his extraordinarily intelligent and helpful team work with me in spotting the battleship in the the first instance and then feeding helpful information down the voice pipe to me as to what heading it was following and when it was altering course and speed. We landed on and were led up a proverbial red carpet up to the Admiral's bridge to be given a pat on the head for a useful piece of reconnaissance. Ferret and I having been debriefed were told to turn in early. We would be needed for a dawn reconnaissance next morning.

Meanwhile the dusk strike had gone in. It consisted of eight from the *Formidable* joined by two ex-*Illustrious* Swordfish which happened to be in Crete, and they joined in the fray. The chances of their carrying out a set piece attack were reduced almost to nothing by the skilful tactics of the Italians who laid a thick smoke screen as the aircraft came into attack. Lucky me, I was recovering from my own quite fatiguing exertions during the day and was scoffing supper in the Officers Mess while all of this was going on, and cannot give an eye witness account of the confusing situation facing the pilots as they intrepidly pressed home their attacks. 53 years after the event I was chatting the other day with the pilot of one of the Swordfish from Crete, who had not succeeded in forming up with the main attacking force, and indeed only managed to arrive on the scene by use of his initiative and the sniff of battle in a warhorse's nostrils. He told me how he looked down on the scene, searching for a gap among the milling formations of warships in which he could let down to torpedo dropping height. He found one and fired at a ship which he recognised as the cruiser *Pola*. That ship was hit, but whether by his tin fish or another fired at about the same time, it was impossible in the fog of war to determine. Anyway all the pilots who penetrated that unnerving pall of smoke with cruisers and destroyers milling about in it to screen their battleship, deserved a medal, but in fact none was shot down. They all landed in Crete for the night to avoid the fleet falling further behind the retreating enemy by having to turn into wind for night deck landings.

By a twist in the fortunes of war, which had not favoured the British Fleet so far, the torpedo which hit the *Pola* exploded in the machinery space in which the electric power for the whole ship was generated. By an amazing lack of attention to damage control in the ship's design, there was no alternative supply and most importantly the fuel pumps to the engines had stopped, so did the engines, and the ship lay dead in the water. When the penny dropped on the Italian Commander in Chief that he was short of a ship, he ordered the cruiser admiral to take his remaining two cruisers back to the scene of the night attack to look for it and to take it in tow. In the advancing British Fleet one or two ships were fitted with an elementary radar which was enough to give notice that they were bearing down on an unsuspecting enemy, which was immediately reported to the flagship.

The battleships were accordingly deployed into line of battle. The carrier was told to get the hell out of it, and not to mince matters, the two Italian cruisers were virtually blown out of the water. The after-turret of the carrier was manned by Royal Marines who, observing the engagement decided to write a new page in the annals of their gallant corps by being the first gun crew to be involved in battle. So they let off a *feu de joie* which could be little else with their small calibre AA guns at a rapidly increasing range. It so happened that their turret was located just above the cabin where the author of this account was getting some sleep preparatory for next morning's patrol. When the clatter subsided he went back to sleep and so missed the stirring events of the night when ships from two fleets sought out each other and in the ensuing engagement two further Italian destroyers were sunk and the ill-fated *Pola* was polished off at 1.30 in the morning.

The only three Albacores left on board the carrier took off at dawn to fly to the limit of their endurance to the westward to try and locate the retreating battleship which had managed to avoid being involved in the night action. Ferret soon sighted groups of rafts to which despondent sailors were clinging, and I duly reported their position. They were slap in the path of our advancing destroyers who accordingly fished some of them out of the water, but whilst doing so they were sitting ducks to either submarine or air attack. The C in C ordered them to abandon their humanitarian effort. However he did cause a signal to be sent to the Italian Naval Headquarters reporting the position of the survivors and assuring safe conduct to any ships that were sent to rescue them. In this way several hundred more were saved. During the rest of my patrol nothing more was sighted and we landed back on the carrier to refuel the aircraft and the crew as quickly as possible for a second time in 24 hours.

The next search to the west was again fruitless. For the only time in my experience I was briefed that the fleet might alter course without signal during my patrol and it would be prudent to turn round and come back with time in hand to look around if it wasn't in its forecast position. This was not as callous as it sounds since the carrier was fitted with a radio beacon on which an aircraft could home from a range of at least 100 miles ... We did actually home in on that beacon for 100 miles and landed on at 2.30 PM. Meanwhile the aircraft that were engaged on a previous evening's dusk striking had returned to the ship. The Admiral had decided to call off the hunt and the fleet set course for Alexandria.

Later that afternoon a determined enemy air attack was delivered, obviously aimed at the carrier, which suffered no worse than near misses (albeit frightening enough). Thanks to an umbrella of AA barrage, violent evasive action and the engagement of our own Fulmar fighters, the fleet returned to Alex the following evening without damage to any of the ships ...

My own spoil of victory was the award of the Distinguished Service Cross, in the phraseology of the *London Gazette* 'for bravery and enterprise in the battle of Matapan'. In the sober fact, the plaudit in my case was quite unmerited since I had only done what any observer was trained for: 'to make early, accurate and constant reports of the enemy's position, composition and disposition.' I don't suppose more than one in 100 of us had the opportunity to do so in war, and my good fortune was to have had the chance and kept my cool when it came along, but you can forget the bravery and the enterprise

Following a heavy German spring offensive against Crete, the Allied army found itself facing a situation not unlike that at Dunkirk. C-in-C Mediterranean Admiral Cunningham sent the Fleet to rescue the troops, dismissing army concerns that he might lose too many ships with the remark: 'It takes three years to build a ship, it takes three centuries to build a tradition.'

During May our light forces, cruisers and destroyers, were actively employed covering the evacuation of our ill fated expeditionary force from Greece to Crete, and suffered casualties from air attack which had become more deadly with the deployment of a specialist anti-shipping squadron of Stukas. On 20th May the Germans launched their famous airborne assault on Crete in such strength that our unfortunate ground forces were forced to make their second evacuation in a month, this time to Egypt. On the 25th *Formidable* and two battleships sailed from Alexandria to provide a diversion from the operations to re-embark our soldiers from the beaches on the south side of the island. We delivered a bombing attack with Albacores, backed up by strafing Fulmars, at dawn on the 26th on the enemy airfield on the island of Scarpanto. Whatever damage it inflicted, it had the effect of stirring up the hornet's nest of enemy aircraft which caught us during our withdrawal that afternoon. This time our luck had run out; I felt two judders and thumps as enemy dive bombers pulled out of their streaming dives, but luckily they had not inflicted mortal damage, and the ship was able to return to Harbour. One bomb pierced the forward overhanging end of the flight deck and exploded against the ship's side as it came through, and the other took out one of the after-turrets. Casualties were comparatively light, but the material damage was a heavy enough to necessitate a voyage to the U.S. for repairs.

We were very lucky to have got off with a casualty list of about 30 compared with other ships which suffered appallingly. One, a cruiser, I think it was the *Ajax*, had embarked a large number of troops which were huddled below decks, and it was struck by a bomb which exploded among them causing carnage too appalling to contemplate. She limped back to harbour where the flagship sent out the most doom-laden a message I have ever experienced: 'all sail-makers in the fleet report forthwith on board *Ajax*'. One of the attributes of a sail maker is that he is trained to make a shroud.

ATLANTIC

Commander James Andrew Stewart-Moore, RN, 810 Squadron, HMS *Ark Royal*
© *The Times* and 22.05.1991/nisyndication.com/terms
and
Commander F. A. Swanton, DSO, DSC, RN, 810 Squadron, HMS *Ark Royal*
from the papers of Commander F. A. Swanton, IWM Reference 2077 92/5/1

HMS *Hood* had been sunk on 24 May at approximately 0603 hours.

Swanton

Well bugger me! Or words to that effect. The whole ship had an air of ... Well, I wasn't completely sure what. It was a strange mixture of incredulity, anger and loss. The *Hood* been sunk. The Krauts had quite literally blown her out of the water. One lucky shot, an exploding magazine, and the pride of the Royal Navy had sunk to the bottom of the icy North Atlantic. We had been told that all 1500 hands were lost, although we later heard that three had been saved. We had been recalled at about 0230 on 24 May, 1941, on what should have been the start of a long weekend alongside. It was now shortly after breakfast, and we were steaming at speed, with the rest of Force H to intercept and destroy the Bismarck ... With *Sheffield* and *Renown* in company, we made our way northward with all possible haste.

Victorious, meanwhile, had sailed from Scapa Flow. As usual the weather around Iceland was unpleasant in the extreme. There was solid cloud some 1000 feet up, and it was blowing a gale. As she struggled to close the gap, 825 Squadron were readied for a strike. Shortly before midnight, Eugene Esmonde led his squadron of nine Swordfish into the attack. The squadron was new to carrier operations, but after a few setbacks, they found their target and moved in. Gerry told me later that 'Duke' Norfolk, an old classmate of his, had been flying with Percy Gick, who, as Senior Pilot, led the second wave. 'Duke' it seems, had a camera which was about the size of a large bucket, and immediately after they had dropped their torpedo he shouted to Percy to keep the aircraft steady while he 'took some snaps'. 825 only scored one hit, but the combined effect of the torpedo and previous gun attacks reduced *Bismarck*'s speed to 28 knots, and cut off her forward fuel tanks.

Ark continued to close from the south, but still had a good 24 hours to go before we came within range. More bad news was to follow. Despite the valiant attempts of Fulmars from *Victorious* 800 Squadron to maintain contact, *Bismarck* slipped away somewhere to the south or south east of the Home Fleet. The search was stepped up. Ships were being pulled in from all over the place. We soon came to realise that the Admiralty weren't going to let Adolf get away with sinking *Hood*. Captain Vian in *Cossack* had arrived with his squadron of destroyers, *Ramillies* was pulled out of convoy duties, *Rodney* was recalled from Norfolk, Virginia, where she was going for a refit, and even *London* was sailed from South Africa to join the hunt.

Bismarck remained undetected for a whole day, until we finally heard that an RAF Catalina Flying Boat, operating from Ireland, had found her. Something that wasn't widely known at that time was that the co-pilot was an American Exchange [Officer]. Nothing exceptional about that – apart from the fact that the Yanks had yet to join in the war.

Stewart-Moore

The weather was not helpful. There was a Force 8 gale blowing from the West and the *Ark Royal*'s stern was rising and falling 50ft or more as she rode over the waves. This made landing and taking off, particularly with torpedoes, quite hazardous; it also made handling the aircraft on deck heavy and slow work: 20 men pushing a Swordfish laboriously uphill might suddenly find themselves breaking into a canter as the ship topped a swell and the aircraft rolled happily forward down an ever-steepening slope.

The next step in the flying programme had to be flying off enough Swordfish to keep the enemy ships under observation. Then the aircraft of the dawn search had to be recovered and stowed below. Only then could the striking force be ranged on deck and prepared for action. So it was not until about midday that I took off with 14 Swordfish and plenty of hope.

Swanton

Now came our turn. The weather was getting worse, but we were so wound up about the whole thing that we didn't really feel it. *Ark* had reduced speed several times as she pounded into the waves, but the range was closing fast. On the 26th it happened. A pair of Stringbags up on Surface Search reported contact. A Striking Force was prepared, and, at 0450, 15 Swordfish took off. Our

'Boss', James Stewart-Moore, was leading. We were split into six flights for the attack. I was the 'boss' number three. Gerry had been really disappointed when we went, because it was decided that only the Flight Leaders would take Observers, due to the long range.

They say that bad luck runs in threes. If *Hood* been one, losing *Bismarck* for a day had been two, then this strike was definitely number three. The weather was still against us. The ship slowed to eight knots for the launch, but even so, there was still a good 40 knots of wind over the deck, and it was rising and falling by more than 55 feet.

Stewart-Moore

We had been assured during the briefing that there were NO British ships in the area, so we could make full use of any available cloud-cover to achieve surprise. This was a great help, as it meant we did not have to identify the ships before we started our attack. Further, in view of the uncertainties, I was told to attack whichever ship we found first – the cruiser or the battleship. It all seemed straightforward.

The aircraft next to mine in the leading sub-flight carried one of the first airborne radar sets – A.S.V. – and it was manned by a young sub-lieutenant, Lithgow, and an even younger midshipmen, Cooper. The latter's duties included navigation, radar operation, wireless operator and general look-out. After we had been going for a while, I saw Cooper waving to me (we had no means of communication between aircraft other than hand-signals – our wireless sets were intended for long distance work only). He then semaphored to me that he had a radar contact about 20 miles away to starboard, so we turned the squadron to see what he had found. The position of the contact did not, of course, correspond to either of those already reported, and as there were said to be no British ships in the area, it had to [be] German. After a while we saw the ship and recognized it as a cruiser, and decided to attack. We approached it above the clouds getting an occasional glimpse as we ran in, and dived down through the clouds to drop our torpedoes.

Swanton

After almost an hour of flight, the first aircraft moved in for the kill. One after another, torpedoes fell away from the bellies of the Swordfish. It was only after eleven weapons had been dropped that the pilots began to realise that something had gone horribly wrong. Their target was not firing back at them! It was the wrong bloody ship.

Stewart-Moore

The aircraft of the squadron kept well together, as we all disappeared from view through the clouds, and everything looked promising. As soon as we came out into the clear weather, my pilot, Hunter, called to me down the voice pipe, 'it's the *Sheffield*'. I was watching the stern for other aircraft and turned round to realise that something awful was happening. Hunter pulled out and waved his wings, and did everything possible to attract the attention of the other pilots, but only two got the idea that something was wrong. The rest continued their dive flattened out for the run in close above the surface, and dropped their torpedoes. They carried out the attack very well, while we watched from above, horrified, and praying for a miracle. Unusually, the miracle department was paying attention to incoming prayers, and the miracle was provided at once. Without any apparent reason, all the torpedoes except one or two, blew up within half a minute of striking the water. It was a surprising sight.

Swanton

Just after 1400 that afternoon, C in C Home Fleet, in an effort to maintain contact, had ordered *Sheffield* to detach from Force H and shadow *Bismarck* at a closer range. Too late for the attack brief, the striking force had gone in unaware. Lady Luck however was smiling on *Sheffield* at that date. For the first time, a new design of magnetic detonator was being used. Six of the eleven torpedoes exploded on impact with the sea, and *Sheffield* manoeuvred to avoid the remainder.

Stewart-Moore

Hunter and I gathered up the aircraft and headed back to the *Ark Royal*, leaving *Sheffield* none the worse, though I think everybody's nerves were a bit on edge. About 10 minutes after we left the *Sheffield*, Cooper again came to life. He had got another contact about 10 miles away, so we headed off to see what was there. We were more cautious this time and found that we were approaching what seemed to be three large destroyers. They could only have been German coming out from France to meet the *Bismarck*; it seemed highly improbable that they were British. The uncertainty was resolved by the leading ship making the British identification signal to us by light; I replied with the appropriate answer and turned back again towards the *Ark*. We had hardly got settled down on our new course when my Telegraphist Petty Officer R. H. McColl handed me a message. It was a marked with the top priority 'Operational – Most Immediate' and read 'Look out for *Sheffield* which is in your vicinity'. I thought of plenty of rude replies but none of these are seemed helpful, except perhaps a reference to 1 Kings, Chap. 10:7 'Behold, the half was not told me'. I did not send it.

When we reached the *Ark* we were told to drop the remaining torpedoes and land on, so we took the aircraft away and made a careful run into the wind at slow speed and dropped our last three torpedoes, to give them every chance of a successful run. 'Bang, bang, bang". All three exploded without fail as soon as they had run off their safety range, so we went back and landed without incident.

Swanton

Having counted them out, I counted them all back in again, as one does! The debrief was animated, but lessons were learnt, and another force prepared.

Stewart-Moore

When I reported for debriefing, I was met with profuse apologies: it seemed that the Admiral had told the *Sheffield* to go and shadow the *Bismarck* but had not instructed the signalman to inform the *Ark Royal* that she was being detached. The *Ark Royal* was playing happily with her aircraft problems a few miles from the other ships, and did not notice the *Sheffield*'s disappearance for some time. When it was noticed that she had gone, and whither, everyone expected the worst, which duly happened. The signal sent to me should have had absolute priority, but it had been held up by other traffic for over half an hour. Still, no harm had been done, except that a great deal of time had been lost.

I told the debriefing officers about the peculiar behaviour of the torpedoes, but they seemed uninterested; they were concentrating on the possibility of getting another strike away before dark, so I went to look for the Torpedo Officer, Portlock, and found him drinking tea in the wardroom. I told him about my misgivings, and we concluded that the fault must lie in the firing mechanism of the torpedoes.

Put simply, there were two different sorts of firing pistols: the old-fashioned one relied on the torpedo colliding with its target and the force of the collision working a simple system of levers to set off the charge. The second, new sort, depended on a sudden change in the direction of the magnetic field surrounded the torpedo and the charge was set off by a galvanometer and an electrical circuit. The disadvantage of the old fashioned pistol was that the torpedo exploded beside the ship and most of the force of the charge was vented into the atmosphere. When the new pistols were used the torpedo was set to to run about 4ft. under the target, and the rapid change in the magnetic field occurred as the torpedo passed under the centre line of the target ship. This meant that the force of the explosion could not escape harmlessly upwards but had to force its way through the ship's bottom, causing considerable damage.

We had used the magnetic pistols in the attack on the *Sheffield* and both Portlock and I guessed that it was the torpedo trying to keep its depth in the very heavy swell and steering alternatively [alternately] upwards and downwards, changing its attitude to the earth's magnetic field rapidly and suddenly, which caused the galvanometer to set off the pistols.

We found the Commander (Flying), Commander H. Traill, preoccupied with getting the next striking force ranged on deck and ready to go. We approached him with due deference and suggested that we should revert to the old type of pistols. It was immediately clear that he did not want to be bothered by the technicalities. However, we persisted, and eventually he agreed to take us to the Captain (Maund) for a decision. Captain Maund was no more welcoming, but required less convincing. He decided to ask the Admiral [Lumley Lyster]. The Admiral, who had qualified as a torpedo specialist in his early days, replied at once that we should revert to the old fashioned contact pistols, although he realised that changing the pistols would cause even further delay in getting the next flight away …

Swanton

Gerry came with me this time. Tim Coode, the CO of 818, was leading with our boss as deputy. We launched at 1910. In those waters, at that time of year, it is still light, although the cloud base had fallen to below 1000 feet. This time we had been instructed to find *Sheffield* and depart from her position. We flew in formation until we found her – most of the way there in cloud, always an 'interesting' pastime!

Stewart-Moore

All went well until we left the *Sheffield*, when we ran into a bank of heavy cloud, which proved to be much thicker than we had expected. We flew blind in it for a while, a hair-raising business, but eventually all the aircraft became separated and the squadron completely lost its formation. I do not know what happened to the other 12 aircraft; we got clear of the cloud accompanied as we had been all day by Lithgow and Cooper, and found ourselves in clear weather about 10 miles on the port bow of the *Bismarck*.

Swanton

Then we saw *Bismarck*. In a 4 ship formation behind Stewart-Moore, we descended to 100 feet. There she was, half a mile away, big black and menacing. She had guns all over her, and they all seemed to be stabbing red flame in our direction.

Stewart-Moore

As we turned towards her an aircraft from another sub-flight appeared and joined us, and the three of us flew in to make a rather forlorn attack. Success in torpedo attacks depended on the aircraft being able to put down enough torpedoes in a short interval to make it impossible for the ships to avoid them all. With only three torpedoes in the race, evasion was much easier. The run-in was alarming. We had the *Bismarck*'s undivided attention for at least 5 minutes. The shells we could see seemed to fill the sky; those we couldn't see did not bother us so much, but there were many more of them. Half a league onwards? – When you took account of the *Bismarck*'s speed and the strong head wind against us, our flying machines were not covering the intervening distance much faster that Lord Cardigan's horses.

Swanton

I levelled, 100 feet, 100 knots, heading for her amidships. Gerry, just behind me, was shouting his head off with the usual sort of Observer's rubbish. I pushed the 'tit', the torpedo fell away and the aircraft seemed to jump into the air. Then it all went sour. There was a series of flashes, and flak ripped through the underside of the fuselage. 'Christ!' I yelled, 'just look at this lot.' *Bismarck* had put her main armament on a flat trajectory, and was firing ahead of us. The shells were hitting the sea in front, but were pushing up 100ft mountains of water. We continued low and fast until we were out of range, then Jerry told me the heading for home, and that 'Flash' Seager, our TAG, had been hit, but would be alright. It was then that Gerry spotted the dark stain on the shoulder of my flying overalls. 'No problem,' I lied, 'I'm perfectly OK,' but I did add that it would be nice to get back to the ship. On the way back, I formatted on 'Scruffy' who had a radar, while Jock Moffat joined on the other side.

Stewart-Moore

At last we dropped the torpedoes and turned away at maximum speed – almost 100 knots – and raced for the horizon, dodging like snipe as we went. At last the pilot asked me could we not ease down yet, and I agreed. We were only about 150ft above the sea and the three aircraft were fairly close together, when there was a terrific crash directly below us, as four or five heavy shells struck the water and exploded. It was a remarkable shot. I did not have to tell the pilot to open up again as we were already going like the proverbial bat. We were about 10 miles from the *Bismarck* and the pilot of one aircraft (Swanton) was hit in his sit-upon [buttocks] by a lump of shell, which was fortunately slowed down by his spring-steel seat. He was the only casualty in a long day's flying; he landed on the *Ark* safely and then retired to the Sick Bay to have the lump of steel removed. (In fact, the wound was to his shoulder.)

Swanton

I was glad to have Gerry with me that day. He told *Ark* what was going on, and requested an Emergency Landing. 20 minutes later we arrived on deck. It was a bit of a controlled crash, but I was able to walk away from it!

Stewart-Moore

Our attack was probably the first. It was followed during the next 20 minutes by four or five similar attacks by one, two or three aircraft. When all the aircraft had attacked, the Strike Leader, Lt. Cdr. Coode, signalled to the *Ark Royal* that the attack had been completed and that he thought there had been no hits. Certainly, when last seen, the *Bismarck* seemed none the worse.

So we all landed on the *Ark Royal* and the air crews gathered in the operations room for debriefing. It seemed to be a sorry tale of small ineffectual attacks. However, one pilot who attacked alone believed he scored a hit amidships on the starboard side, and right at the end, the leader of the two aircraft who were last to attack, (Lieut. Godfrey Fawcett) thought he might have scored a hit right aft on the battleship, but the splash of the explosion seemed very muffled, so the signal sent to our ships was amended to one or possibly two hits.

The air crews hung around in the operations room for a while, talking about the possibility of carrying out a night attack, or hoping for better conditions in the dawn, and generally exchanging experiences, when a signal from the *Sheffield* came up the pipe saying that the *Bismarck* was now steering north-west. This was unexpected; if it was true, the *Bismarck* was now steering back towards the pursuing British battleships, but it was possible that there was some mistake.

After a few minutes a second signal was received, this time from the shadowing Swordfish, saying that the *Bismarck* was steering north at only six knots. This raised the level of conversation considerably: it meant that she had suffered a serious injury which might only be temporary, but could be very difficult to repair. Further signals over the next half hour indicated that the *Bismarck* was still compelled to steer away from France and that her speed was much reduced. Shortly Admiral Somerville signalled that we were to rely on a dawn attack. We heard with great relief the pipe in the *Ark Royal* 'there will be no more flying tonight'.

Our two battleships came into action early in the morning and by 10 o-clock they, with the help of the German scuttling charges, succeeded in sinking this remarkable ship.

We learned from survivors from the *Bismarck* that the last torpedo had indeed caused irreparable damage. It struck the *Bismarck*'s rudder when the ship was turning under full helm. The explosion occurred under the ship's counter, which prevented the force of the explosion from escaping upwards. It could not go forward because of the ship's hull, it could not escape to port or astern as these directions were blanked by the angle of the rudder. The full force of the explosion was taken by the relatively weak rudder mounting and the floor of the steering compartment in the counter. The result was a firmly jammed rudder and great rent in the ship's plating which let the sea in and out so freely that repairs were quite impossible. The only thing that *Bismarck* and could do was to go round in circles of varying diameter. It was in this condition that she was found by the *King George V* and *Sheffield* at dawn next day.

To add to the German discomfiture during the night, the destroyers which we had been surprised to meet earlier in the day, arrived in sight of the *Bismarck* at dusk. They kept her in sight all night, carrying out attacks by torpedoes and guns from time to time, and keeping her crew awake and sleepless until the battleships turned up.

Swanton

The next morning I woke up in Sick Bay, just before midday. Gerry was at my side. He came with good tidings. *Cossack* and and the rest of the destroyers had harried *Bismarck* all night, firing over a dozen torpedoes at her. The Polish destroyer *Piorun* had to be restrained from ramming her a couple of times as well. We had put up another Striking Force at first light, this time with 810's CO in the lead, but *Bismarck* had been finished off with a final torpedo by *Dorsetshire* at 1040, just as they got there. The aircraft were arriving back as we spoke.

As for 4C, our Swordfish, Gerry said that he had stopped counting holes when he reached 200! She never flew again, being cannibalised for spares. What is more, she had less than 40 hours on the clock.

We reached the Gib. again on the 29th, and were welcomed back by the pipes of the Black Watch. The whole of the Rock was there to greet us, and the harbour was full of boats of all sizes, all flying flags and shouting. To cap it all, that night the *Sheffield* held an RPC (request pleasure of your company) for us. What a splendid chaps they were, forgiving us for our previous sins.

Lieutenant David Wright, 804 Squadron, HMS *Maplin*
IWM Sound Archive Reference 2849817*

Before joining the Catapult Armed Merchantman *Maplin*, Wright had to learn how to be catapulted, and his first lesson came at HMS *Daedalus*, the shore base at Lee on Solent, which had a standard piston catapult. He deserves particular recognition as an original author of one of the Fleet Air Arm's (many) racy songs.

I had, I think, two launches on that catapult, just to get the feel of getting airborne quickly. And it didn't really matter, then, if you bounced away on the grass ... When you get back to the ship, there aren't any wheels to bounce mid-Atlantic: we took the wheels off, to save weight.

First of all, sit in the cockpit, and then there's a Launching Officer whom you can see down to your left. He's got a blue flag, and when he waves it ... it means start up your engine to full revs, so you push your throttle open wide, tighten the screws, as it were, so it won't come back with the G-force, put each elbow in your stomach, one hand on the stick, one hand on the throttle, put your head back. Then wave your arm up and down! That means you're ready. The launcher presses the button. So you go, and you get a right wallop in the back, and then you fly. That's all.

So I had that training, and then was sent to Speke where the RAF had their Merchant Ship Fighter Unit, where again there was a catapult on a grass aerodrome so, again, if you bounced the wheels it didn't matter – but they were rockets, actual rockets, and that was a big blast. I can remember going one flight, one launch only. That was all they gave you. And I remember I was told: don't watch anyone else launch or it'll put you off, but when I got out of the taxi or whatever it was at the aerodrome, I was walking to the mess to have lunch, and one was launched. Bloody Hell! all the smoke and noise and thunder: it was off-putting: you know, all that power being released to get the aeroplane up. My launch was in the afternoon, but I really ought not to have witnessed that or heard one.

When you get to the rocket catapult, it's the same, except it's a bigger wallop and you black out. What it does is, it drains the blood from the back of the eye, I think, so you black out – but it's only temporary: one and a half seconds, maybe. So when you get your vision back, you're flying. And you don't hear any noise, you're ahead of the sound, and you don't see any of the flame and smoke coming out of the back, so it's all behind you.

---

* The order of the first four paragraphs has been altered for the sake of continuity.

I did about 3 convoys ... We'd escort a convoy going outbound from England if it were going, say, to America, half way across the Atlantic, then meet an inbound convoy to escort it back again. It didn't matter after a certain longitude because then it became out of reach of the Focke Wulf Condors which were based at Bordeaux.

The only time I shit myself ... I was once sitting in the cockpit. The routine was, we never flew at night, never launched at night. There was no point: you couldn't see the enemy, so it was just day. During the day we took turns sitting in the cockpit, two hours, so that we were ready to go at a moment's notice, warming the engine up every twenty minutes so the engine was warm ... In the ship there would be two aeroplanes, one on the catapult, but ... another one abaft the mainmast in reach of the crane, so if the first was fired off it could crane the second aeroplane onto the catapult ... Sometimes there were two pilots crewing the ship, sometimes three. If, for instance, there was a launch, one pilot is gone anyway, so you've only two pilots left, and two pilots can take it in turns, two hours apiece through daylight hours sitting in the cockpit.

Well, my first panic was on duty sitting in the cockpit. There was no signalling but verbal signalling and the launching officer who is making gesticulations at you: Start up; there's a panic on. And I'm preparing then, and going through the routine for a launch ... when the launching officer crosses his arms, which means Shut down. So I closed down, and it turned out – I didn't know it at the time – that it was probably a Hudson of Coastal Command ranging out in the Atlantic. A friendly aeroplane, in other words. If I'd been fired off, I'd probably have shot the Hudson down. You're so geared-up: it's an enemy plane. You can't think: Shall I make sure it's an enemy? But, anyway, that happened often, a friendly aircraft was shot down very often.

And so you go through all the routine of securing the aeroplane, taking out the pins and things – and it was found that the main locking pin in the trolly on which the aeroplane was mounted was still in. If I had been fired off, the aeroplane couldn't have gone anywhere, but fifteen rockets would have gone, and I'd have been cremated!

The other time, we were within ... the Western Approaches and an enemy aircraft was detected again, and Benji Marcus was my Number Two. He was on the bridge. And it was a question of usual routine: full revs with the engine, lock everything, elbows in stomach, head back, and was launched. But suddenly in my earphones Benji Marcus shouting: 'Break away! Break away!' He'd recognised that the aeroplane wasn't a German at all, it was a Southern Eire [Republic of Ireland], which was a neutral country, a mail plane or something. And I was launched in the Western Approaches and I had a full tank of petrol and the wheels back on, so Benji gave me a course to steer, says to me: 'you have plenty of fuel.' I flew to Eglinton in Northern Ireland and landed. So I never fulfilled the function of a catafighter.

We'd an officers' cabin. Actually, we shared a cabin, and I shared with Benji ... Our function was only in daylight hours, so at night we could read magazines, write letters, do what we wanted … We were in the cockpit by dawn, and we were in the cockpit until dusk, so I can only … say it was boring; it was damned boring. I wrote letters. I've always had a turn for doggerel stuff, and I know it was sitting there that I composed … It's rude. We were rude then. When you're a lad of twenty … all your testosterone is going. And so I composed poetry:

I sat on the squirter (We called it the squirter, the catapult), awaiting the kick
Passing the time by caressing my stick
Down went the blue flag; the thing gave a cough.
Cor, fuck me, cried Benji, he's tossed himself off.

It's awfully rude is that, but that's what we were like at that age. And so we were very relaxed. We were an irresponsible lot; we were like playboys. Who else was given an aeroplane to fly, an expensive piece of machinery? It was glamorous, and our uniform in the Navy was more glamorous than the RAF. An RAF officer didn't have a uniform with gold braid … we wore our wings on the sleeve. The birds, popsies, they figured large in our thoughts.

Usually, if a convoy was going to America, that was two or three days out from Belfast or Liverpool or Glasgow, and then we diverted to meet an incoming convoy two or three days coming back. My last convoy was to Gibraltar.

Captain Eric 'Winkle' Brown, CBE, DSC, AFC, RN, 802 Squadron, HMS *Audacity*
IWM Sound Archive Reference 2488

HMS *Audacity* sailed outbound for Gibraltar on 13 September 1941, escorting Convoy OG74, and 802 squadron, flying the Grumman Wildcat, made its first kill: a Focke-Wulf Condor. Her homeward run with HG74 was uneventful; but it was at the end of the following month, with the escort of OG76 and then HG76 that she showed the value – and the vulnerability – of the escort carrier.

The ship itself was an ex-German merchant ship, an ex-banana boat on the Caribbean run, and it was captured in St. Domingo by the cruiser *Dunedin* and eventually brought back to the UK. All they did was literally slice the top off the ship, put a flight deck on it – a very small flight deck – and it really was a merchant ship with a steel deck on it, and a few RN crew. The main bulk of the crew were in fact Merchant Navy seamen. It was an extremely pleasant ship from a pilot's point of view as regards living accommodation because there were six double staterooms and two singles, and the captain insisted that these be given to the pilots. So we lived rather in style: we had beds instead of bunks, and we had square ports instead of portholes (which we infuriated some of the merchant seaman by calling 'windows'); and altogether, from that aspect, it was quite pleasant.

Of course, it was a difficult ship to fly from because the flight deck was only 420 feet long, which is extremely small, and the flight deck beam was only 60 feet, so you were flying from really a very small mini-carrier. The other thing I should say about it was: it only had two arrestor wires, so it required pretty accurate flying to get on. It had these two wires, but there was then a further wire immediately before the barrier. We had a crash barrier in case you missed the wires, but if you caught this third wire (which was always named the 'For Christ's Sake' wire because if you went into this wire you were given very severe retardation which possibly could break the aircraft) if you did pull the wire out to most of its full length, the barrier then collapsed – they were interconnected, so the barrier collapsed and you ran over the barrier, so you could be saved by this third wire.

It had no aircraft hangar as such, so all the aircraft were up on the flight deck, and this made it a very tough business for the maintenance personnel who had to do everything on the flight deck.

Like most pilots who flew it, Brown was enthusiastic about the Grumman Wildcat.

It was a magnificent aircraft for its day. The FAA had really suffered badly from inadequate aircraft ... and when the war came it caught us with aircraft that were really considerably inferior to those of the enemy, and this was probably at its worst in the fighter area. And then suddenly came these Wildcats from America under the lease-lend arrangement, and they were a total revelation to us because they had been designed from scratch for aircraft carrier operations and they were rugged ... they had innovation in the fact that they had what was called the sting-hook: an arrester hook which came out of the tail of the aircraft as opposed to being under [the] belly of the aircraft. This made it much more simple to catch an arrester wire than with the belly type. Also, they were armed with .5 machine guns, which at that time were non existent in this country – we were all using .303, so we were quite heavily armed – and you could also re-cock these in the event of a jam, which again was an innovative feature. They had an extremely reliable radial engine, and they also had excellent ditching qualities, which ... on a naval aircraft was very, very necessary. So altogether they were extremely popular and very effective.

Primarily we did two things. We did anti-submarine patrols, which wasn't really a fighter's job, but that's what we did because these were the only type of aircraft we had. We did a dawn patrol around the convoy first thing, just to see the area was clear of U-boats, and we did one last thing at night, dusk patrol ... During the day we were at immediate readiness for take off against the Focke-Wulf Condor aircraft, which were raiders, really, against convoys, but in the main, of course, they were providing information for the U-boat wolf-packs which were frequenting the Atlantic. So they were very dangerous aircraft from our point of view. They were also very heavily armed – extremely heavily armed – so they were not an easy target to fight against ...

The first time, we spotted two of these. My section leader was the one who caught sight of them first. He called and he assigned one to me and he went off to take the other, I chased mine, and we knew the weakness of the Condor was that it had a rather weak tail unit; that is to say, on landing, for example, if you made a heavy landing you could actually snap the fuselage near the tail, so that was a weak point we knew about from intelligence reports. We'd already had one success with a section firing at the tail unit and breaking it off, so this is the point we tended to aim for at first, but I found this difficult in the sense that when I was flying against this particular Condor, he was flying below a patch of low cloud base, just below it, and therefore you had to come in very flat, and you had no chance to break away above him – you had to break away below – which is, of course, the more desirable way to go. But with the visibility, etc., I was only getting in a one or a two second burst at a time. But on one of these bursts I did set one of his inner engines on fire (of course, a four-engined aircraft) and he popped up into the cloud, so I thought I had lost him completely. It was a fairly thin layer of cloud, possibly 400 feet, so I went above it and hopefully just thought that I might see him – he might pop through it. But he didn't, and I was just milling around generally, hoping that something would happen, when I saw a wingtip come out of the cloud. He was obviously just turning, and on that basis [I] thought I would reverse course with him. But I didn't get it quite right, because eventually when he did emerge I found I was actually head on to him. It was the only chance I was going to get, so I came down fairly flat because I'd realised that the top gun he had – it was a cannon, actually – couldn't be depressed beyond a certain elevation, and if you kept very flat he probably wouldn't be able to fire at you. So I came in, and the main risk at that stage is that you have a relatively high closing speed and there is a great risk of collision. You've got a very, very short firing time, but, after all, we had .5-inch machine guns, which is quite a heavy armament. I just blasted away as I came in, and for the two or three seconds I could actually see the cockpit glass of the nose of the aircraft shattering before I pulled away, and then it just spiralled away down into to the sea. So my guess is, both pilots were killed. We were in the Bay of Biscay, I suppose six or eight hundred miles due West of Brest, roughly.

That success, which rose to four Condors shot down, was tarnished by the loss of the Squadron's CO, Lieutenant Commander J. M. Wintour. On 14 December, *Audacity* was attached to the 2nd Support Group for the homeward-bound Convoy HG76.

On the way back I had another one, and this time I had more time to set myself up with him. He couldn't escape into cloud as easily, so ... having found the head-on attack successful (we discussed that in the squadron after that particular attack, and we decided it was a technique we would try and latch on to, because it was one way of avoiding too many guns being brought to bear on you ...), I set up the head-on attack from the word 'go' and it went the same way as the first ...

When you see the other aircraft, the adrenaline flows a bit. You realise that you are committed to something that may end up with yourself being killed or wounded, but it's survival, so you've got to go for it, and I think you realise this, but, once you've started in, all that is blotted out of your mind …

You inevitably think of the people who have lost their lives. Inevitably, I think, not immediately … Immediately it happens you are filled with elation that you've won the contest, but … maybe in the evening, you sit and reflect, and you think that that's some mother's son, or some child's father – and you think of these things, but you have to put them in the back of your mind, because if you conduct a war on the basis of emotion, you're never going to get anywhere.

In the evening in particular it was quite common to catch U-boats on the surface, and all we could do … we could attack with our guns, but we weren't really going to sink a submarine with .5 machine guns, but at least we made them keep their heads down; it usually caused them to dive, but the main thing we were doing [was] reporting all this back to the convoy commodore who was directing the whole thing, and he could then direct his anti-submarine destroyers or corvettes to the scene, knowing that he'd had a positive sighting. In fact in that convoy, where the commodore was the famous Captain Walker, we had tremendous success: a considerable number of U-boats were sunk. We had set out from Gibraltar and I think we had been out only about two days when the first attacks started, and it was quite obvious that we had a pack of U-boats concentrated against us. There was a lot of activity both in the air and on the surface, and Walker's escorts had a very, very busy time indeed. We had quite a lot of fighting, and in fact we lost one of our Wildcats to a U-boat. One of the Wildcats spotted a U-boat in the surface [*U-131*] and attacked it, and the U-boat shot it down …

We were stepping up anti-submarine patrols, and I was on the very last anti-submarine patrol that evening [21 December] with my section leader, and we left it rather late in fact because they wanted to leave us up as long as possible, and we were kept up much later than one normally was accustomed to. When we came back it really was dusk, and the ship was heaving a bit, not too bad but we had to land on in the evening and it was really half light by this time. In fact the batsman who waved us on was standing with a couple of torches as opposed to the normal paddles he would have had … About not much more than 30–40 minutes after that, I was sitting having some coffee in the wardroom when the explosion hit. What had happened was a torpedo had been fired at us and struck the rudder; we'd a single rudder and we only had … a top speed of 14 knots.

Now the aircraft carrier had in fact left the convoy, and the strategic reason for this was that we had five lanes of ships in the convoy, and normally the *Audacity*, at night, was stuck right in the middle of them, so that she had maximum protection round her. If any torpedoes were fired [they] wouldn't hit the carrier (because this was the main daylight protection for the convoy).

But ... the convoy was so slow, and there were so many U-boats around, that a decision was made that night that the *Audacity* should leave the convoy and zig-zag by herself. Not too far away, but at her full 14 knots. Now the convoy was only about a 10-knot convoy, so it made that little bit of difference. And it was while we were doing this zig-zag that this random torpedo was fired at us and took off the rudder. Well, of course, when we lost our rudder we had no control on the zig-zag whatsoever, so the captain took the hurried decision to heave-to while we assessed the situation. And of course he had warned the Commodore what had happened: the escorts were rushing towards us. But while we were stopped absolutely stark in the water, suddenly we could see on the port side a U-boat surfacing. You could see it because it was dark – but the phosphorescence! it was covered in phosphorescence. A tremendous glow as this thing rose up; it was eerie. And we could actually see the U-boat commander on the conning tower; we could see his hat. So they were as close as that when they came up. It was the *U-751*, Commandant (as we later found out) Bigalk. And there was this tremendous hiatus while we stood looking at each other. Then someone's nerve cracked, and they opened fire with their 20mm cannon, which is like using a peashooter against this thing. It was the catalyst for what happened after, because this fellow opened fire against it, and four seconds later we had four torpedoes rushing towards us. You could see them quite clearly. They left quite a noticeable trace in the water. All four struck us, and the complete bows of the ship fell off. It literally just vanished; about a third of the ship just seemed to disappear, and as it did the real chaos started because the Captain, quite sensibly, when we had been stopped, had assembled the entire crew (apart from those that were at specific stations such as the Engine Room) on the flight deck, all wearing our Mae Wests, or equivalents which the Merchant Navy had. So there were about 400 people up there on the flight deck. And when the bows fell off, some of them went with that, but the worst thing that happened was, immediately the bows went, the ship filled very, very steeply, nose down, and the Martlets at the back – I think at that time we had risen from six in the earlier voyage to eight on board – they all broke their moorings. They were all held down by steel hawsers, but they all broke those ... and rushed down the flight deck. And of course they just scattered people right, left and centre. A lot of them were hit by the machines or swept off the side of the ship. I saw them coming, like many others, and I just jumped over the side – we are talking about a jump of ... at least fifty feet ... It was that or get wiped off. I think many people were killed in the jump. A lot of people jumped on top of the people in the water already ... usually means both get killed in the end. I think we lost well over a third of the crew.

She continued to go nose down, and of course sank pretty rapidly. We were all striking out like mad in case we were sucked under – that was the great worry ... I managed to contact my section leader because we both jumped together. First of all we were swimming together because we saw corvettes coming towards us, and they began picking up people ... We were just unfortunate that where we were wasn't the first area they came to, and they [had] picked up a huge number of people when suddenly they made off ... We tied ourselves together along with about 20 seamen who were also in the water.

Now, we were wearing Mae Wests, and they were wearing this sort of rubber tyre with tapes over it. We didn't know it 'til later that the reason the corvettes had taken off was that they had had an ASDIC ping, so there was a submarine still in the area and they could not afford, overladen as they were with people, to be attacked ... Well, the twenty-two of us, roughly, were actually in the water for six hours before they did come back, and by that time the twenty seamen who were not equipped with Mae Wests, just their rubber tube-things, had all gone. They had got exhausted and fallen forwards, face down in the water and just drowned.

Three torpedoes hit the ship, causing aviation fuel to explode in its forward storage tanks. Some 72 men lost their lives.

Jack Needham, Able Seaman, HMS *Indomitable*
from the private papers of J. E. Needham, IWM Reference 1991 92/27

Indomitable was begun as the fourth of the *Illustrious* class but was modified during construction so that armour was sacrificed in favour of greater aircraft capacity. Completed in October 1941, she ran aground on 3 November.

We left soon afterwards for Kingston, Jamaica and on reaching the approach to the port the pilot came out to guide us through the reef strewn channel, but for some unfathomable reason was sent back. We proceeded up the channel at a good rate of knots when CRASH – we had run on to a reef and the ship stopped almost dead. When 23,000 tons stops dead, something has to go. In this case it was the bows of the ship which were turned up like a sheet of cardboard with the impact. Those of us in the mess deck were flung with great force on to the nearest bulkhead as if by a giant's hand. What was described as 'panic stations' was the order of the day. It was rumoured that when a ship's boat was lowered to survey the damage, that ran aground too. The entire crew of the ship was mustered on the stern of the flight deck and commanded to jump up and down in unison in a frantic endeavour to get the bows off the reef, but without result. It took several tugs to free us. Three days afterwards we left for Norfolk, Virginia, where we were to go into dry dock for repairs.

Our initial reception in America was frankly not very inspiring. All over the walls of the dry dock in huge letters were slogans like 'go back, Limeys' and 'keep USA out of the Limey war' and the berthing party went down the gangway to be met by a fusillade of large stones which were hurled by white and black dock workers alike. These were returned at the people in question with equal vigour. We were each given a dockyard pass – I still have a mine, which is dated with my birthday, November 13, but this was 1941. Also to adjust to the cost of living we were given 2/6d (!) extra. It was an easy matter to 'blue' a week's pay in just buying a slap up meal ashore. Runs ashore were pretty uneventful apart from the odd punch up, but it was obvious that we were about as popular there as a pork chop in a synagogue. I was by this time uprated to Able-Seamen and a small increase in pay was welcome. This was the first time any of us had heard Glenn Miller who came alive over the ship's radio. Whenever I hear *Chattanooga Choo Choo* now that tune immediately transports me back through time, as it was in a dime a dance establishment we heard this tune.

Soon after our arrival in America the Japs attacked Pearl Harbour. I have never seen the mood of people change so quickly as it did that day. Complete strangers would come up to us in the street and offered to buy us a meal or as the RN put it 'Big Eats' and several cans of Budweiser as well. This sudden display of generosity was on occasions embarrassing as, if we had just clobbered back a big meal, refusal was taken the wrong way at times until an explanation was given. But by and large I found the Americans quite a good lot and no one could call them mean. In fact on more than one occasion I was invited up to various houses where the occupants appeared fascinated by my Yorkshire accent which is of a brand you can cut with a bread knife. Our repairs were done in record time and we were soon back in Jamaica, this time without incident. Jamaica at that time was a sailor's paradise: rum ashore was 4s 3d a pint so with a bottle of Coke you could view the world in a rosy hue for 5/-.

John E. Greenbacker, USS *Yorktown*
John E. Greenbacker Oral History Interview (#OH0150) Joyner Library

Well, carriers were not considered number one ... I went to the *Yorktown*. We were very fortunate in that the Navy was expanding. Generally, ensigns would get the job of being assistant this and assistant that. I was given the job of assistant navigator, which generally didn't go to someone who had less than two years or more of service. So, I had very good jobs: first year as assistant navigator and then as the ship's secretary.

Then, the Navy didn't believe in aircraft carriers. There were some influential people who saw that. I remember going over to Hayword Smith, over in the *Colorado*, telling me, 'You ought to be over here in the real Navy.'

The surface Navy was obsessed with the Battle of Jutland ... When I went to the *Yorktown*, two of the four squadrons were biplanes. On reflection here in recent years, I think we have to thank Roosevelt for expanding the Navy as he did. We did not get monoplane fighters until May of 1941.* That was roughly six months before the war started. Suppose we had to go out and fight the Japanese Zeros with what would have amounted to modified World War I type

---

* The first US Navy carrier monoplane fighter was the Brewster F2A-1, a handful of which entered service in June 1940 in small numbers.

aircraft? Furthermore, Roosevelt was always misleading people to get his way. The *Yorktown* they called the WPA ship. It was built down at Newport News and it was not built with a Navy appropriation. It was built under the Works Progress Administration. He got three carriers built down there: the *Yorktown*, the *Enterprise*, and the *Hornet*. We were fortunate that we had those ships and the new aircraft, because there was no way that we could delay getting out there and facing the Japanese ... Also, we were out there in the Pacific and then we were brought around to the Atlantic to conduct Mr. Roosevelt's 'Secret War' which he did by extending out the neutrality zone, and supposedly, we were on 'neutrality patrol'. Actually, in the fall of 1941, we participated in an escort. The Fifth Canadian Armored Division was coming up, being rotated home, so this was a troop convoy. We went out to MOMP, the mid-ocean meeting point which was sort of south of Iceland, and here came this pitiful looking set of escorts that the British had, half a dozen little small things. But we had a battleship, two cruisers, an aircraft carrier, about a dozen destroyers and we brought them back to Halifax and we didn't have any contact with [submarines].

Captain William D. Owen, then a 'Passed Midshipman', USS *Yorktown* (CV-5)
William D. Owen Oral History Interview (#OH0103) Joyner Library

During the summer, we made anti-submarine hold-down patrols for the British from Bermuda to the Azores, to the Canary Islands, and to Trinidad and back up. It was a rectangular patrol. There was not much wind and it was very hot. When it started to get cool, they sent us to Argentia, Newfoundland, at the end of August. We arrived in a snowstorm. It was quite a change. Our duties then were to escort the troop transports from Canada over to the Iceland area where the British Navy took over. Then we would escort dependent women and children back to Canada.

After making one of those crossings, we came down to Portland, Maine, for Thanksgiving, and then down to Norfolk, Virginia, in the first week of December to get some newfangled guns called twenty-millimeters on board. Four of us had gone to Annapolis for the weekend to visit girlfriends. On Sunday afternoon we were listening to a Redskins football game when we were told, 'Everybody return to the ship.' Pearl Harbor had been bombed.

We got together by phone, got our wheels, and got back to Norfolk. Shortly thereafter, we sailed. We loaded a large number of recruits from the Naval training station who had put in only about half of their training time. You could recognize them because the seats of their trousers were dirty. Some of them didn't know how to use soap yet.

We went around through the Canal and unloaded a very large amount of wartime equipment that we had loaded on board at Norfolk. Then we went on up to San Diego, arriving there around New Year's Day, 1942

PACIFIC

Lieutenant Commander Abe Zenji, Imperial Japanese Navy, IJN *Akagi*
from *The Emperor's Sea Eagle*

The Japanese fleet that supported the attack on Pearl Harbor comprised six carriers, two battleships and three cruisers plus smaller vessels. In his first mission, Abe led the squadron's 2nd Division flying Type 99 dive-bombers. Since 2 December, the Japanese pilots who carried out the attack had been under the impression that Japan and the USA were at war. At the time of the attack, the Japanese commanders were told that there were no US carriers at Pearl, but that the battleships were an important target.

Just before sunrise on 7 December (local time in Hawaii), our task force arrived at a position some 220 miles north of Oahu. Roughly three hours before, a bugle call sounded on *Akagi* with the command, 'Wake up and take your stations!' All were supposed to run (not walk at normal speed) to their positions in the ship, some men going to the right down the narrow passages, some to the left, and others racing up and down the ladders. Preparing the sixty-three aircraft of our two strike groups and the eight fighters for the patrols over our carriers, the deck crews lifted the first wave group topside and finished preparing the dive-bombers and fighters of the second wave. On the flight deck, all was busy as crews performed last minute checks, tests, and engine warm-up. Even in the pre-dawn darkness above decks, we could tell that the weather was stormy. Upon completing engine warm-up, we brought up the aircraft of the second wave strike to the hangar via the elevators, while simultaneously spotting the first wave aircraft in flying order, starting from the aft end of the flight deck.

I donned new underwear specially prepared for this particular day. Putting a picture of my family in a pocket of my new uniform, I slipped into my flying suit and left my cabin. After visiting the ship's Shinto shrine, I entered the pilots' waiting room. A staff officer from the Information Department came in during breakfast while everyone devoured the morning's riposte [repast] of rice balls, relating warship status in the Pearl Harbor anchorage, adding that the Americans did not seem to maintain a very strict watch there. I was rather disappointed to hear that the locations of aircraft carriers were yet unknown.

Before long, the order sounded, 'Fall in first wave attacking pilots!' and the aircrews boarded quickly upon receiving instructions from Commander Fuchida Mitsuo, overall commander of the first attack wave. In unison, the six aircraft carriers altered their southerly course, turning east into the wind, and with that, the first wave aircraft commenced takeoff. A Type Zero carrier fighter piloted by Lieutenant Commander Itaya Shigeru was the lead aircraft from *Akagi*.

Seeing Itaya's 'Zero' fighter drop sharply just after passing the forward end of the flight deck frightened me, but the aircraft regained altitude immediately. (This 'dip' was due to the shorter take-off distance owing to the extra division of nine Type 97 attack bombers aft.) Eight more fighters took off immediately after Itaya, one after the other every few seconds. I watched this from the take-off and landing control tower on *Akagi*'s island, which was much higher than the flight deck.

Next in order, fifteen Type 97s of the horizontal bombing unit rolled slowly down the deck. Standing up in the observer's seat, Commander Fuchida wore a 'rising sun flag' headband over his flight helmet. Still on board the ship, of course, the second wave pilots and aircrews all watched and saw him off, waving their caps and lifting up prayers, while others cheered and prayed from the flight deck.

Captain Mitsuo Fuchida, IJN *Akagi*
from *Midway*

One hour and forty minutes after leaving the carriers I knew that we should be nearing our goal. Small openings in the thick cloud cover afforded occasional glimpses of the ocean, as I strained my eyes for the first sight of land. Suddenly a long white line of breaking surf appeared directly beneath my plane. It was the northern shore of Oahu.

Veering right toward the west coast of the island, we could see that the sky over Pearl Harbor was clear. Presently the harbour itself became visible across the central Oahu plain, a film of morning mist hovering over it. I peered intently through my binoculars at the ships riding peacefully at anchor. One by one I counted them. Yes, the battleships were there all right, eight of them. But our last lingering hope of finding any carriers present was now gone. Not one was to be seen.

It was 0749 when I ordered my wireless operator to send the command, 'Attack!' He immediately began tapping out the pre-arranged code signal: 'TO, TO, TO.' Leading the whole group, Lieutenant Commander Murata's torpedo bombers headed downward to launch their torpedoes, while Lieutenant Commander Itaya's fighters raced forward to sweep enemy fighters from the air. Takahashi's dive-bomber group had climbed for altitude and was out of sight. My bombers, meanwhile, made a circuit toward Barbers Point to keep pace with the attack schedule. No enemy fighters were in the air, nor were there any gun flashes from the ground. The effectiveness of our attack was now certain, and a message, 'Surprise attack successful!' was accordingly sent to *Akagi* at 0753. The message was received by the carrier and duly relayed to the homeland, but as I was astounded to learn later, the message from my plane was also heard directly by Nagato in Hiroshima Bay and by the General Staff in Tokyo.

The attack was opened with the first bomb falling on Wheeler Field, followed shortly by dive-bombing attacks upon Hickam Field and the bases at Ford Island. Fearful that smoke from these attacks might obscure his targets, Lieutenant Commander Murata cut short his group's approach toward the battleships anchored east of Ford Island and released torpedoes. A series of white waterspouts soon rose in the harbour.

Lieutenant Commander Itaya's fighters, meanwhile, had full command of the air over Pearl Harbor. About four enemy fighters which took off were promptly shot down. By 0800 there were no enemy planes in the air, and our fighters began strafing the airfields.

My level-bombing group had entered on its bombing run toward the battleships moored to the east of Ford Island. On reaching an altitude of 3,000 metres, I had the sighting bomber take position in front of my plane. As we closed in, enemy anti-aircraft fire began to concentrate on us. Dark grey puffs burst all around. Most of them came from ships' batteries, but land batteries were also active. Suddenly my plane bounced as if struck by a club. When I looked back to see what had happened, the wireless operator said: 'The fuselage is holed and the rudder wire damaged.' We were fortunate that the plane was still under control for it was imperative to fly a steady course as we approached the target. Now it was nearly time for 'Ready to release,' and I concentrated my attention on the lead plane to note the instant his bomb was dropped. Suddenly a cloud came between the bomb sight and the target, and just as I was thinking that we had already overshot, the lead plane banked slightly and turned right toward Honolulu. We had missed the release point because of the cloud and would have to try again.

While my group circled for another attempt, others made their runs, some trying as many as three before succeeding. We were about to begin our second bombing run when there was a colossal explosion in battleship row. A huge column of dark, red smoke rose to 1,000 metres. It must have been the explosion of a ship's powder magazine. The shock wave was felt even in my plane, several miles away from the harbour.

We began our run and met with fierce anti-aircraft concentrations. This time the lead bomber was successful, and the other planes of the group followed suit promptly upon seeing the leader's bombs fall. I immediately lay flat on the cockpit floor and slid open a peephole cover in order to observe the fall of bombs. I watched four bombs plummet toward the earth. The target – two battleships moored side by side – lay ahead. The bombs became smaller and smaller and finally disappeared. I held my breath until two tiny puffs of smoke flashed suddenly on the ship to the left, and I shouted, 'Two hits!' When an armour-piercing bomb with a time fuse hits the target, the result is almost unnoticeable from a great altitude. On the other hand, those which miss are quite obvious because they leave concentric waves to ripple out from the point of contact, and I saw two of these below. I presumed that it was battleship *Maryland* we had hit.*

As the bombers completed their runs they headed north to return to the carriers. Pearl Harbor and the air bases had been pretty well wrecked by the

---

* USS *Arizona*.

fierce strafings and bombings. The imposing naval array of an hour before was gone. Anti-aircraft fire had become greatly intensified, but in my continued observations I saw no enemy fighter planes. Our command of the air was unchallenged.

Suddenly, at 0854, I overheard Lieutenant Commander Shigekazu Shimazaki, flight commander of *Zuikaku* and commander of the second wave, ordering his 170 planes to the attack. The second wave had taken off from the carriers at 0715, one hour and fifteen minutes after the first, and was now over the target. My plane did not withdraw with the first attack wave, but continued to fly over the island so that I could observe results achieved by both assaults. Furthermore, it was planned that my plane would remain until the last to serve as guide back to the carriers for any straggling fighters, since these carried no homing devices ...

Lieutenant Commander Abe Zenji, Imperial Japanese Navy, IJN *Akagi*
from *The Emperor's Sea Eagle*

Arriving over Pearl Harbor, I ordered my men to assault and then released my division for the attack and commenced the descent, picking up speed into the target area. I could see the battleships moored in pairs along the Ford Island's east shore, which meant that the first wave torpedo attack could not have been effective against the ships moored inboard. While hurriedly weighing the decision of whether to attack the battleships, I lost sight of Lieutenant Chihaya's division flying in front, but I could see indistinct, black anti-aircraft bursts, flashes of bursting shells, and tracers flying all around us.

Despite all this, I led the aircraft of my division, following at intervals of 100 meters between aircraft, searching for the best position to dive in. At 2,500 meters altitude just before reaching Ford Island, I banked to port and rushed in from the very best position. I set my sights on the biggest ship anchored at [the] right-end. [According to Japanese records, this was the light cruiser *Raleigh* (CL-7), north-west of Ford Island.] Tracers shooting skyward from the harbor below caught my sight again and again. '800, 600 ... !' Saito shouted out the altitude through the voice tube. 'Yo-i!' With the target growing larger in the sight, I pulled the release at instant of his cry, 'Te!' Pulling the control lever which returned the dive brakes to their normal position, I grew giddy for a few seconds, but flew past the harbor, leveled out at 30 meters altitude, and headed toward Barbers Point on Oahu's south-west shore, where I saw neither friendly nor hostile aircraft. As I flew out toward the sea, I thought to myself, 'I am still alive!"

Aviation Chief Ordnanceman (Dr) Alvin Kernan, VT-6, USS *Enterprise* (CV-6)
from *Crossing the Line*

Nobody returning to Pearl Harbor after the attack forgot the sight that met his eyes:

The smell came first as we moved slowly through the nets guarding the channel, of fuel oil, burned paint and canvas, hot steel. Fires were still burning everywhere, and a heavy cloud of smoke hung over everything that had looked so bright and lively a week earlier. It was eerie, the huge ship moving painstakingly slowly through what was always a narrow channel into the harbor, made now much narrower by a battleship half on the mud on the port side, its stern sticking well out into the channel. The *Nevada* had managed to get under way during the attack but was hit again by torpedoes going out of the channel where she could not maneuver. The captain, realizing that his ship sunk in the channel would block the entire fleet, beached her on the Ewa side, leaving just enough room for the big carriers and their escorts, which was all that was left of the Pacific Fleet, to maneuver around him at painfully slow speed ... It was on the port side, however, that the real devastation was visible, beginning with wrecked hangars and seaplanes on the tip of Ford Island. There, one after another – broken in two, turned over, canted crazily, under water with only the upper masts showing, burned, smoking and smoldering – was the long row of battleships, two by two, that everyone thought of as the main force of the Pacific Fleet and of the U.S. Navy. But in a violent way the attack had underlined that the day of the battleship was long gone, that it had been replaced by aircraft carriers like the one that was now picking her way daintily, almost disdainfully, down the harbor past the smoking hulks of the old navy devastated by planes from other foreign aircraft carriers

5
1942

By the end of 1942 the Royal Navy had been all but forced out of the Indian Ocean. Sailing without air cover in December 1941 because of damage to *Indomitable*, the battleships *Prince of Wales* and *Repulse* became early victims of the Japanese. The Eastern Fleet had retreated from Singapore to Java, to Trincomalee and thence to Addu Atoll in the Maldives. A Japanese fleet that included six carriers and four battleships carried out a raid into the Indian Ocean in the spring of 1942 that cost the Royal Navy heavily: the old carrier HMS *Hermes* and the cruisers *Dorsetshire* and *Cornwall* were among the casualties. The Royal Navy retreated to Mombasa on the East African coast, leaving command of the Indian Ocean to the Japanese.

The island of Madagascar remained in Vichy French hands. Amid fears that it could soon be taken over by the Japanese (with grave implications for the Mombasa base and supply lines routed via the Cape for the Allied North Africa campaign) Operation 'Ironclad' was undertaken in May. The force included the battleship HMS *Ramillies* and the twin carriers *Illustrious* and *Indomitable* with their Alabacores, Wildcats and Swordfish aircraft. The attack commenced at Diego Suarez [Antsiranana], with the honours going to the destroyer HMS *Anthony*, which managed to disembark a party of marines close to the main gun battery in order to put it out of action. Despite Vichy resistance and a torpedo attack by two Japanese midget submarines that disabled *Ramillies* and sank a British tanker, the successful assault led to a gradual push south through the island, which capitulated late in the year.

The importance of the Cape route, up the east coat of Africa and through the Suez Canal to Alexandria, had increased as the conflict in the Mediterranean became increasingly hot. The need to keep Malta supplied with fuel, food and aircraft was constant, but convoys, whether arriving from the east or the west, were heavily targeted by Axis air power and submarines. The island's survival in weeks was frequently reckoned in single figures. In June, Operation 'Harpoon' managed to bring just enough supplies to keep Malta going on starvation rations until perhaps late August. The next convoy, 'Vigorous', which came from the east escorted by Vian's cruiser squadron but without a carrier to provide air defence, was forced to turn back. Every effort had to be made to bring supplies into Grand Harbour during August. The operation was named 'Pedestal'.

Never before had a convoy of merchant ships been given so much protection: four carriers (*Eagle*, *Victorious*, *Furious* and *Indomitable*) and two battleships (*Nelson* and *Rodney*) in addition to numerous cruisers and destroyers, not to mention submarines, corvettes, minesweepers and oilers, which would have to refuel ships at sea. Central to the convoy was the US tanker *Ohio*, the largest in the world at the time, which had been requisitioned and put under a British crew. The convoy reached the Mediterranean on 10 August and passed into legend as the most ferociously contested convoy of the war. Casualties among men and ships were high; one carrier was sunk and two heavily damaged, but – crucially – the haemorrhaging wreck of *Ohio* arrived in Grand Harbour sandwiched between two gallant destroyers.

Elsewhere, the tide was slowly turning in favour of the Allies. In North Africa, the First Battle of El Alamein in July stopped an Axis offensive, while in October-November the Second Battle of El Alamein defeated the Italian and German armies. This was followed in November by Operation 'Torch', the large-scale Allied invasion of North African coastal territory in Vichy French hands. As a result of that Allied success, German forces moved into areas of previously unoccupied France but were thwarted in one aim – that of seizing the French Navy immobilized at Toulon. French commanders either scuttled or, in the case of certain submarines, ran for Allied or neutral ports. Hitler's 1941 repudiation of his non-aggression pact with the Soviet Union and his invasion of that country had opened a second front, and in September 1942 the Germans were halted at the strategic city of Stalingrad. The siege turned into months of nightmare for both sides, with massive casualties that the Soviets were better able to absorb than were the Germans.

The Japanese continued their rapid advance, taking Malaya and the Philippines. February saw the capitulation of Singapore, the Battle of the Java Sea (in which USS *Langley*, now used for aircraft transportation, was sunk along with the planes she was carrying for the defence of Java) and an opportunistic bombing raid on Darwin, Australia.

However, on 1 February the US Navy showed its teeth with successful carrier strikes on Japanese bases in the Marshalls and Gilberts. One task force including USS *Enterprise* rendezvoused with another that included USS *Yorktown*, and, after the successful disembarkation of 5,000 troops at Pago Pago, the two forces headed for the Marshalls and Gilberts, where *Enterprise*'s targets were Wotje, Taroa and Kwajalein. En route on 28 January, *Enterprise* became the first capital ship to refuel at night while underway.

A more famous carrier strike was being planned, one which had no actual strategic value but provided a boost to Allied morale, particularly in a USA still reeling from the shock of Pearl Harbor. On 18 April a force of sixteen B-25B bombers led by Lieutenant Colonel James Doolittle took off from USS *Hornet* around 700 miles from Tokyo, each carrying four 500lb bombs and a crew of five, and hit targets in major Japanese cities. The Doolitle raid served to disabuse Japanese people of their belief that their country was invulnerable to attack and showed how far the US was capable of projecting its power.

The first major naval battle of the Pacific war came early in May when the Japanese sent two fleets – one to cover, one to invade – towards Port Moresby, Papua New Guinea, in order to establish a base from which to attack northern Australia and prevent its use as an Allied base. An additional accompanying force was ordered to occupy Tulagi in the Solomons. Jeopardizing his planning for the more important invasion of Midway, Admiral Yamamoto released two valuable fleet carriers, *Zuikaku* and *Shokaku*, and one light carrier, *Shoho*, for the Port Moresby operation, which was to be carried out by the Japanese 4th Fleet under Vice Admiral Inoue. The invasion force with all its troop transports and *Shoho*, left Rabaul and sailed south, passing to the west of the Solomons, while the carrier force left Truk on 1 May and sailed east of the islands. The carriers had embarked Val dive-bombers, Kate torpedo bombers and Zero and Claude fighters.* However, US cryptographers had broken the Japanese Naval Code, and for the first time Admiral Chester Nimitz had been able to plan on the basis of knowing the enemy's intentions. All four US carriers were despatched to the area (though *Hornet* and *Enterprise*, back at Pearl Harbor after flying off the Doolittle raiders, were too far away to arrive in time). It fell to *Yorktown* (Task Force 17) and *Lexington* (Task Force 11) to rendezvous with the joint US-Australian Task Force 14. On 3 May, Task Force 17 retaliated against the Japanese invasion of Tulagi; three days later the task forces merged, but early the following morning Rear Admiral Fletcher sent a task group to make sure the Japanese invasion fleet did not take advantage of the likely carrier battle in order to sneak into Port Moresby unopposed. It was a justifiable decision, but it left the carriers short on protection.

The Battle of the Coral Sea was the first naval battle in which neither surface fleet could actually see the other's ships (sometimes colloquially referred to as a *no see 'um*), and a great deal of time was spent in vain attempts to locate them. Incorrect or garbled messages left commanders confused about what was going on and where, but on the morning of 7 May the battle began, with the fleets just over 200 miles apart. The air power was almost identical, with US squadrons equipped with Douglas Dauntless dive-bombers, Douglas Devastator torpedo bombers and Grumman Wildcat fighters. Although the US carrier aircraft were superior to those of the British, they were in most respects inferior in performance to the Japanese planes.

Shoho, however, became the first victim, attacked and sunk off Misima Island by aircraft from both carriers during the morning before she could fly off all her aircraft. Squadron Commander, later Admiral, Robert E. Dixon gleefully radioed: 'Scratch one flattop! Dixon to carrier: Scratch one flattop.' Two Dauntlesses from *Lexington* and one from *Yorktown* were lost in the operation. In the afternoon the Japanese invasion force prudently withdrew in preparation for the carrier engagement. In the event, the Japanese attacks on the US carriers were successfully intercepted. As darkness closed in, tired and confused Japanese pilots came close to landing on the US carriers. The following morning, *Yorktown's* bombers flew off, allowed the fighters to catch them up, and went for the *Shokaku*. *Lexington's* bombers arrived half an hour later, and the badly damaged Japanese carrier had to withdraw. Japanese aircraft, however, successfully got

* Val was the Allied codename of the Aichi D3A Type 99, Kate the codename of the Nakajima B5N Type 97, Zero the codename of the Mitsubishi A6M2, and Claude that of the Mitsubishi A5M, ancestor of the Zero.

through to the Americans, starting fires on *Lexington* which appeared to be successfully contained and causing serious damage to *Yorktown*. The battle was over by lunchtime; in the afternoon, a fatal explosion occurred on the wounded *Lexington* when a sparking commutator ignited vapour from leaking fuel. Had the Japanese set a stronger carrier force, the result of the battle would have been very different. Instead, they had divided their forces, spreading their power too thinly, and, to make matters worse, they did not grasp the significance of the unexpected and unwelcome arrival of the US carrier forces. Japanese expansion had been checked for the first time.

Japan continued to plan the attack on Midway, still unaware that their code had been cracked. A diversionary attack would be carried out in the north, on the Aleutian Islands off Alaska; the overwhelming assault and invasion forces would concentrate on Midway, whose central position between Japan and the US west coast made it the most important American base after Pearl Harbor itself. Four carriers, *Akagi*, *Kaga*, *Soryu* and *Hiryu*, would launch air attacks to knock out Midway's defences before the arrival of the main battlefleet with its heavy guns. A third fleet would disembark troops to take over the island and create a Japanese base. News of the invasion would lure out the carriers of Nimitz's fleet, which would be overwhelmed by the enemy's strength. Yamamoto had expected to have six carriers, but the two survivors of Coral Sea were still being repaired.

Nimitz confronted similar problems. With *Saratoga* under repair, *Lexington* sunk, *Wasp* in the Mediterranean and *Yorktown* dragging herself back into Pearl on 27 May with an estimated three months of repairs ahead of her, he had only two carriers available. Forty eight hours later he had three, when a superhuman dockyard effort sent out a patched-up but operational *Yorktown*, which embarked the remnants of her carrier air group and some of *Saratoga's*. Rear Admiral Fletcher's Task Force 17 with *Yorktown* and Rear Admiral Spruance's Task Force 16 with *Enterprise* and *Hornet* were in the vicinity of Midway even before the Japanese carriers arrived.

The Japanese air attack on Midway at dawn on 4 June outclassed the base's air and gun defences, but a second strike was requested to finish the task prior to any invasion. As the aircraft were returning, the presence of the US carrier fleet was reported. For the Japanese it was a race against time to fly on, refuel and fly off their bombers and torpedo bombers while fighters engaged the first wave of Devastators flown off *Yorktown*, *Enterprise* and *Hornet* from 0700. This was an unequal combat: the Devastators were no match for the Zeros and took terrible losses; the Wildcat fighters sent to help them could do little. Their sacrifice did, however, delay the Japanese preparations long enough for the Dauntless dive-bombers to catch the carriers turning into the wind with their flight decks full of fully fuelled and fully-loaded aircraft. More by luck than judgement, *Enterprise's* Bombing Squadron Six (VB-6) and Scouting Squadron Six (VS-6) arrived at precisely the same time as *Yorktown's* Bombing Squadron Three (VB-3) and caught the Japanese by surprise. Two Japanese carriers went down that afternoon; *Akagi* sank the following morning. The only carrier still operational, *Hiryu*, launched an attack on *Yorktown*; seven of her bombers got through and brought the American carrier to a halt. Sterling work by the crew got *Yorktown* underway again, but a second torpedo attack blew a hole in her port side and she began to list so badly that the order to abandon ship was given. Later a salvage party returned, but hopes of saving her ended when she was opportunistically torpedoed by a Japanese submarine.

The might of American economic power was starting to be felt: more and more ships were leaving US yards for the war effort, and among the increasing numbers of highly trained men becoming available were aircrew to replace the heavy losses at Coral Sea and Midway. By contrast, not only was the Japanese carrier fleet broken, it had lost the flower of its aircrews and did not have the capacity to replace them quickly. New US aircraft such as the Hellcat and the Avenger were becoming available to both US and British carrier pilots; the Helldiver was being tested.

On 24 August, US and Japanese carrier groups met again in the battle of the Eastern Solomons. The Japanese had sent their carrier fleet from Truk to cover troop landings on Guadacanal, and to dislodge the US force that had established an airbase there. *Enterprise*, *Saratoga* and *Wasp* were despatched to the Solomons to counter this, but a faulty report that the enemy had not left Truk led to *Wasp* being sent to refuel. *Saratoga* was damaged, and the Japanese lost their light carrier *Ryujo*.

Success in the Pacific must have seemed relatively academic to most of the crews of the Allied merchantmen that made up the Atlantic and Arctic convoys and which were the focus of the U-boat campaign. Along with the cracking of the German 'Enigma' code, Radar and High Frequency Direction Finding (HF/DF, or 'Huff-Duff' as it was colloquially known), were improving the capability of the escorting corvettes and destroyers to detect the U-boats. In addition, the captains of these hunter-killer groups were honing their skills all the time. Nevertheless, Allied merchant ship losses increased substantially in 1942 – the handful of Catapult Armed Merchantmen could not provide anything like the air cover so desperately needed on every convoy. The Home Fleet, including HMS *Victorious*, provided only distant support for the Russian Convoy, PQ17, which was devastated by German attacks. In the latter part of the year, the first US-built escort carriers were handed over to the Royal Navy under the Lend-Lease agreement. Unfortunately, during what remained of 1942 they were busy giving air protection or doing other duties during the Operation 'Torch' landings in French North Africa.

ATLANTIC

Sub-Lieutenant (A) Philip Blakey, RNVR, 836 Squadron
Communication with the Editor

Earlier in the war there were so few carriers that a first line squadron was very lucky to get any seatime in such. After training I took passage to Jamaica to join a new-formed 836 Squadron as a pilot and later flew to Floyd Bennet Field, New York, to bring home HMS *Biter*, an escort carrier converted in Brooklyn Navy yard for the Americans. This flight included a forced landing in Cuba to add spice to the trip.

836 Squadron left the ship on their return to the UK, and MS *Biter* was then used in the Mediterranean to ferry aircraft rather than as an escort carrier, to the despair of 811 Squadron, who expressed their feeling in the following song, well known in the Air Branch and sung to the tune of *The Road to the Isles*. Other NAS squadrons substituted their own numbers and the carrier that they longed to see in the Clyde.

> There's a squadron going rotten, for it's waiting for the war
> And the war is waiting for the Adm'raltee.
> Eight Eleven's simply heaven if you want to stay ashore,
> For we never, ever, ever go to sea.
>
> Chorus:
> From Lee-on-Solent to Arbroath and Machrihanish you may pass;
> You may search the bars and brothels far and wide;
> For we've flown until we've grown a pair of wings upon our arse
> But we'll never see the *Biter* in the Clyde.
> (From *The Fleet Air Arm Songbook*)

Not until March 1943 did 811 (by then amalgamated with 812 Squadron) at last see *Biter* in the Clyde.

INDIAN OCEAN

Jack Needham Able Seaman, HMS *Indomitable*
from the private papers of J. E. Needham

Indomitable's repairs were swiftly completed and by January 1942 she was back in action. In May she participated in the attack on Diego Suarez.

Force H, of which we formed a part, was now about to invade the island of Madagascar at a place called Diego Suarez. Some wit said he thought that was the name of a Spanish dockyard matey. Apparently this place had been used as a refuelling depot by the Vichy French to supply Axis submarines and had to be subjected to a thorough 'softening up' pasting from the air, which was duly done by our carrier and others for about 24 hours. The next day we dropped leaflets, one of which I still have, which depicted the Union Jack and the French flag and was headed 'Camerades de l'air' and the gist of which was that 'we come to you as friends'. After seeing the amount of hardware which fell, we found this unconvincing, to put it mildly.

On the 8th of May we proceeded towards the harbour and it was then we had one of the narrowest escapes of the war. At a few minutes before 8.00 AM just as the lookouts were changing over binoculars, two cotton-thin streaks were seen approaching – torpedoes doing about 40 knots. This must rank as one of the most chilling sights ever. One lookout yelled 'torpedo tracks to port!' – The Captain yanked on the siren and we turned abruptly, although at the time it seemed an age and one of the torpedoes actually touched our P. V. chains, which sent it leaping into the air, the contra-rotating propeller making a hell of a din. It fell harmlessly into the sea, whilst the other missed by about 6 feet. The enemy's timing was spot on and the firing was apparently done from a two-man submarine, which was dealt with in no uncertain fashion.

Albert H. Jones, Stoker, HMS *Illustrious*
from *No Easy Choices*

A survivor of the 1941 bombing attack, Jones was still on *Illustrious* at the time of the Diego Suarez attack.

The fleet massed for the invasion of Madagascar left Durban in two convoys. A slow convoy consisting of special landing ships, supply transports, a tanker and a hospital ship escorted by the heavy cruiser *Devonshire*, three destroyers, and the 1401 minesweeping flotilla sailed on April 25. A fast convoy with the assault troops under the overall command of Admiral Syfret left on the 28th. This was escorted by us, the cruiser *Hermione*, six destroyers, and the battleship *Ramilles*. On May 3 we were joined by *Indomitable* and two more destroyers from the Eastern Fleet.

By the evening of the fourth, the two convoys rendezvoused 95 miles west of Cape Amber on the northern tip of the island. Down in the engine room we knew little of what was going on except what we were told. The next morning in the early hours the attack would take place and it seemed that the Vichy French defenders were mostly colonial troops with white officers and therefore would offer little resistance. That they did. When our forces stormed ashore at 04:30 hours, the enemy were literally caught napping.

At first light our Swordfish dropped leaflets on the Antsirane Peninsula across from Diego Suarez urging them to surrender without bloodshed. We then sank the armed merchant cruiser *Bougainville* and the submarine *Beveziers* and damaged the sloop *d'Entrecasteaux*. Meanwhile our fighters which were now Grumman Martlets replacing the old Fulmars flew cover over the beaches. Sea Hurricanes from the *Indom* attacked the airfield and caught the French aircraft in their hangars and burnt them out.

After a couple of days our troops had advanced a long way but ran up against a strong defensive line at the southern end of the Antsirane Peninsula but couldn't get naval support because the entrance to the bay was guarded by batteries of large guns at Oranjia Pass. The destroyer *Anthony* was given the job of sneaking into the harbour with 50 Royal Marines from the *Ramilles*. *Anthony* slipped past the French batteries and was noticed by the enemy gunners too late. When they opened fire their shells missed the destroyer who replied with her own 4.7 in guns and successfully landed the marines ashore ... The batteries consisted of 18-inch guns in fixed mountings, that is unable to turn or elevate. These two guns were positioned such that they covered the mouth of the bay and anything else that came into their line of sight would be blown to hell. Not knowing exactly what was going on with the *Anthony*, the *Ramilles* and *Devonshire* opened up on the French guns with their 15 and 8-inch guns. Meanwhile, negotiations were being made for the enemy's surrender and the bombardment was soon called off but not before the French had been given a good shaking up. Soon after the enemy forces there and at Diego Suarez capitulated, a mere three days since the first landings had taken place. The breeches from the huge guns guarding Oranjia Pass were later noticed to have been removed and hidden somewhere on the island. Apparently the Vichy French had no intention of us making use of them. I don't think they were ever found either. Our minesweepers arrived shortly afterwards and swept a safe channel into the bay where our victorious fleet then sailed led by *Ramilles*.

Diego Suarez was a big open harbour with no boom defence to prevent enemy submarines from entering. When the operation ended most of our destroyers and anti-submarine vessels left, leaving the fleet virtually unprotected against an underwater attack.

While *Illustrious* lay at anchor I was put on the motor boats as part of the cutter's crew. The cutter which was the smallest of the ship's boats was about twenty or so feet in length and powered by an in-board six cylinder engine. Used for a variety of jobs including liberty men ashore and running errands for provisions and odd jobs the lads referred to it as the 'gash boat' ... The cutter ... was required for the job of surveying for a boom defence. Our crew including myself, the coxswain, bow and stern sheetman, and the survey party of an officer and two others loaded up one morning with all the instruments and a day's provisions and we set out for the harbour entrance. The weather was beautiful and the bleached white sand of the beach looked really enticing like a tropical resort by the sea. As we ran the boat ashore and pulled it up on the beach one of the seamen, Harry Metcalfe and myself were ordered to stay behind to guard the boat until they returned. As there was nothing really much we could do during the long hours we had to wait we decided to take turns having a swim in the turquoise water. All the time we kept an eye out for any stray shark that might venture close in hoping for a free snack on one of our legs ...

Our vulnerability without a boom defence or anti-submarine vessels was made evident on May 30 when two Jap midget subs entered the bay and destroyed the tanker *British Loyalty* (6,993 tons). *Ramilles* was also badly damaged by a torpedo which blew a thirty foot hole in her port side for'ard of 'A' turret ... it's a wonder they didn't go after us, a carrier. The poor old *Ramilles* was crippled and it took until the beginning of June for her to be patched up enough to limp to Durban for more extensive repairs. *Illustrious* would now take more serious precautions in which even the cutter would play an important role.

In response to the torpedoing of *Ramilles* and the risk that the Japs might have other plans with frogmen and limpet mines from their midget submarines, it was decided to do boat patrols around the ship during the night hours while at anchor. Starting somewhere around 20:00 hours we loaded up the old 'gash boat' with rifles, grenades, and Lanchester submachine guns plus an officer and PO with the regular boat's crew to patrol around the ship, constantly shining an Aldis lamp on the waterline looking for tell-tale bubbles or any undue movement which might suggest a frogman. Never more than a few yards from the ship's side we kept up a slow, methodical search chugging along being challenged by a sentry stationed fore and aft on the ship for two hours non-stop before being relieved for two hours rest. Then we were on again armed to the teeth ready to lob a pineapple at anything that looked suspicious and give them a burst. As boring as the task was it was still a tense time for everyone knowing that the Japs had submarines in the area. I remember that the water in the bay was very calm making it easier for us to detect any little waves, indicating trouble.

MEDITERRANEAN

Gordon Wallace, Observer, HMS *Indomitable*
from *Carrier Observer*
and
Oliver James Barritt, Stoker, Royal Marines, HMS *Eagle*
IWM Sound Archive Reference 9176

HMS *Indomitable* had been at Freetown in August when she was ordered to rendezvous with *Victorious* and *Eagle* ready for Operation 'Pedestal'. On the 9th, the convoy passed the Strait of Gibraltar.

10 AUGUST – DAY ONE

Wallace
Night and fog cloaked our entry into the Mediterranean. In the early morning the fog cleared, the sun blazed down, the sea was a brilliant blue cut through by the whiteness of the wakes from the serried rows of ships as we caught up with the convoy and took a station in the middle, *Victorious* ahead, *Eagle* astern and *Furious* in a position off the port quarter.

Barritt
About midnight we finished oiling – or should have done, but we hadn't, so they cut the hose with an axe like they do. I mean they won't waste a second. If it's finish at 12-o-clock midnight, it's 12-o-clock midnight. Of course the pumps were still going on the oiler, pumping the oil all along the beautiful white waist of the old *Eagle*, and the commander, very dapper, comes nipping along the waist.

Next minute he's Torvill and Dean, skating along the waist flat on his back in the oil, and we move out into the Bay where we pick up this massive convoy ...

Wallace

Day one, 10 August, 1942, was a teasing of the nerves, a flexing of muscles, and apprehensive scanning of cloudless skies. Four Hurricanes were ranged on our deck all day at immediate readiness, their engines warmed up at intervals, propellers yellow painted spin flashing in the sun like the shields of the Greeks at Troy. The warriors sat, not in their tents like Achilles, but in their cramped, hot cockpits, canopies slung back, helmet off, hair blowing in the wind, waiting ... For all of us with no role to play it was a great innovation to have the officer commanding our Marines, Major Pym, situated in the fighter direction room from whence he made intermittent broadcasts over the Tannoy describing what was happening around us. This was appreciated by all aboard, particularly by those stationed below decks.

That night I took my safari bed up into the passageway just behind the Quarterdeck and slept fitfully with my clothes on and my Mae West close at hand. I had to be up early as I was to be duty officer in the operations room.

11 AUGUST – DAY TWO

I was pleased to have some small role to play on Day Two, 11 August, a day that we knew would bring us within range of enemy aircraft. I had a shower and changed into my white shirt and shorts for the occasion. After a quick breakfast I hurried up to the island to report to a bleary eyed 'Lofty' Logan and got on with my first job of the day. He dashed to brew up his very special Blue Mountain coffee which he had purchased when we were in Jamaica. The next job was to chalk up the cruiser and aircraft details on the blackboard. An 827 Albacore took off for the dawn A/S patrol, followed at 0630 by four Hurricanes of 880 to carry out the first of the day's 1½ hour combat air patrols at 20,000 feet. *Eagle* also flew off a section of Hurricanes and I watched them all climb into a cloudless sky until they were out of sight. The convoy was now south of Ibiza and only some 350 miles from Sardinia. It seemed surprising that nothing had happened to disturb the peaceful scene ...

When the carriers, with their attendant cruisers, manoeuvred into [the] wind I went out on to the island brow to watch 'Butch' Judd fly off with his section to take over from Brian Fiddes who landed on his section at 0800. As the planes were being taken down the lift for refuelling, Major Pym's voice boomed from the Tannoy to report an enemy aircraft on the radar screen. This proved to be a long range reconnaissance Ju 88 flying at 23,000 feet. This remarkable multi-role aircraft was capable of climbing higher and diving faster than a Hurricane. As it was to happen all too often during the battle our fighters had failed to catch it and there were many frustrated pilots. 'Dickie' Cork, leading the next patrol, had more success, making an attack on another Ju 88 at 15,000 feet and setting fire to its starboard engine before he had to break off. When he came into the OPS room he was complaining bitterly about the poor performance of the Sea Hurricane above 20,000 feet. 800 squadron took over the patrols until lunchtime.

At midday I went outside again to watch *Furious*, out on our port quarter, flying off the first of the 41 RAF Spitfires on that long one way trip to Malta. The first group had just formed up and were climbing away to the east when at 1315 the air was suddenly wrenched with a series of explosions. I looked around quickly to see smoke pouring out of *Eagle* ...

Barritt

We proceeded to sea in the beautiful sunshine, *Eagle* laying behind *Nelson* and *Rodney* at the back when they decided to fly off our cover patrol, which consisted of four Hurricanes: Impatient Virgin, No Orchids For Miss Blandish, I forget the other two, but Lieutenant Commander King-Joyce, who was killed later as a test pilot, flew the Impatient Virgin. A great pilot, great ace. We turned out the wind to starboard towards Algiers and the submarine must have come right under the screen and laid beneath ... I wasn't on the flight deck then; I had been told to go down the boiler room and pump oil from A to B and we had just got down there and the four forward torpedoes hit. That'd be about twenty to twelve: dinner-time, or just after twelve. Pandemonium down there. Every single light went out. Within minutes, everybody screaming, and laying in the bilges, and the first thing I thought is: this is how you die, how you watch them in the films. Water rushing in everywhere, plates all fell out into the bilges. And, by luck more than judgement, I had a torch tied with a bit of cod line* round my waist, but in the panic I had forgotten all about it, and as I was fighting to get out of the bilges it must have banged on something and come on. It was the only torch on in there, only light there was. Lt. Wilkinson, Chief Engineer down there (later engineer, the *Amethyst*) took my torch and told us all to get up the ladders, but that was easier said than done because the ladders, instead of going away from you, went up over you so you had to climb up the backside. When you got up the top, you had a job to get up the hatch. Well I think it took seven ladders. But I saw a marine killed when the hatch was blown down and cut him in half as he was going through it.

I went back down the passage and up the air intakes and came out on the island, and right up on the funnels. And the *Eagle* was gone in seven minutes. Seemed like seven years to me ... I saw Pincher Martin and Dickie Bird, a stoker from Peterborough. The Carley floats, they lay on ramps so they slid off. But the carrier had gone over so they slid onboard, didn't go out ... I knew them two couldn't swim and they jumped on this Carley float, and it went straight down the flight deck at the angle, a terrific angle. They sat on it – two great big fat stokers! – and they took off the flight deck and landed perfect on the water and sat there in the Carley float. I saw another man undressing, a stoker, and his shoes and socks in pairs like he did below his hammock, and the ship's sinking. It's ever so funny when you see it. I saw another messmate of mine go back to get his money out of his locker, and he's still with it now

* Fishing line suitable for catching cod.

185

because he never did get up. We were in the water, nearly, but he went back to the mess deck to get his money.

We swam around ... Captain Macintosh shouted to us: 'Come on lads!' He's got his gold braid cap on. He's just behind us, covered in oil fuel – we all were – and then a destroyer rushed in, dropped depth charges, and that was terrifying. Blew a lot of the lads to bits. But they said the submarine was under where the *Eagle* had gone down, didn't bother about the crews. 1200 men swimming about there. They just dropped depth charges. I'd only got my pants on and when I got picked up by the *Lookout* destroyer, I hadn't got pants really, I'd got tapes hanging down. The shockwaves had cut all me pants and made red lines down m' thighs. One lad I went to see in hospital later in Gibraltar, he had his backside blown right off; they were going to put a silver plated bottom on him. Not very nice being in the water when depth charges were banging off. Everyone was suffering from shock ... And you don't realise until later.*

A most amazing thing ... Little lad, 18 year old stoker, not above eight stone, all spots, you'd felt sorry for him if you could see him, stoker Milligan. When he got picked up by the *Lookout*, and he couldn't swim a stroke, he dived off that destroyer seven times to save men. Never got a mention in dispatches, nothing. Seven times, until the officer said: 'he's not to go off again, it's taking more time to get him back in.'

Wallace

Eagle had four Hurricanes airborne, one landed on our deck and the remainder on *Victorious*. As soon as our own Hurricanes had landed, Cdr (F) ordered the flight deck to be cleared to bring on one of the RAF Spitfires which had developed engine trouble. I don't know why he decided to attempt what seemed to everyone to be an impossible feat; no hook, no deck landing experience and a full load of fuel. I would have baled out and taken the chance of being picked up. Lieutenant Commander Martin Pares took up his batsman's position, the barrier was raised and the ship moved into wind at maximum speed. Every vantage point was crammed with an audience holding its breath as the pilot made two alarming approaches from well astern (the pilot's view from the Spitfire was far from ideal for deck landing), both of them too fast and too low. On the third he came in fast but well centred and touched down comfortably past the round-down to rush headlong into the barrier below me. Apart from the propeller there was remarkably little damage and the very brave pilot climbed out unhurt. The aircraft was pulled free of the barrier cables, trundled down the deck and pushed over the stern into the sea. In other times 880 Squadron fitters would have lost no time in fitting it with a hook.

We were now south of Majorca and still no sign of an enemy air attack – when it did come we were going to miss the 16 Hurricanes which had gone down with *Eagle*. The Fulmars from *Victorious* were now taking a bigger share

---

* However, many of the injuries may well have been caused by the underwater explosion of *Eagle*'s boilers.

of the air patrols and one of them landed on *Indom* in mid afternoon. The pilot came up into the OPS room. 'Hello,' I said cheerfully. He looked at me, frowned and looked around the room – 'My God!' he said 'wrong bloody ship!'

12 AUGUST – DAY THREE, AFTERNOON

Wallace

With all our planes back on board there was a frenzied activity on the flight deck to move them on to the lifts and reposition their replacements: aircrew, dentists and pay branch officers and portly commanders lent a hand at pushing them, and soon order came out of chaos. I turned my attention back to watching the serene progress of the convoy. In an eye's blink a black painted fighter flew down past our port side at eye level and high speed, and no more than 200 yards away. Since my schooldays aircraft recognition had been part of my life and I saw it to be a Reggiane RE 2001, one of the best looking fighters of its day. I was too surprised to open fire and most others thought it was a Hurricane until it dropped two small bombs on *Victorious* which was then on our port quarter. The bombs bounced off her armoured deck and exploded in the sea. I failed to see a second Reggiane whose bombs missed the carrier. It was a brave attempt – with a larger force and better bombs it would have wreaked havoc on any flight deck full of aircraft.

LATER THAT AFTERNOON

Everywhere I looked, SM79s were coming in low through the smoke of the barrage. We boosted off four Hurricanes and continued to land on planes – there was intense activity to get them down before and live – as the first of the Italian Stukas was already diving steeply before releasing its bomb and streaking out at sea level amidst a hail of tracer. Another flew past so close that I could see its pilots and air gunner, and right behind it, one of our Hurricanes. Both pom-pom batteries on my side fired but their tracer seemed to pass closer to our Hurricane than the Stuka. It was the only occasion on which I saw one of our fighters in action and I remember the savage delight I felt when the Stuka started to burn and finally splashed into the sea near *Victorious*. It was the most exciting moment ...

Just before 1900 the destroyer *Foresight* was a hit by a torpedo and then, after the gunfire had begun to fade, I caught sight of a closely bunched formation of 12 Stukas at about 10,000 feet almost directly above us with not a shot being fired at them. I got up and ran on to the flight deck shouting and waving my arms wildly but to no avail. The first Stuka peeled off and I had my first head on view of its sinister cranked wing heading straight towards us with others following behind. I felt disembodied and without fear, unable to move – not that there was anywhere to move to.

Looking like beer barrels, the 1100 pound bombs seemed to float down towards us as though in some dimly remembered dream. The ship shuddered and the dream expanded into a huge sheet of flame which rose up ahead of the island and engulfed it. There was an enormous explosion just ahead of me and then several behind me which seemed to lift the ship several feet. A wall of water rose alongside to some 100 feet then cascaded down on top of me, washing me into the catwalk. For a moment there was a strange silence such as occurs at the end of a great performance, it could have been the final moments of *Gotterdammerung* as flames and smoke billowed near the for'd lift and behind the aft lift.

The ship began listing to port and was moving in a slow circle to starboard. I am told that the list never exceeded 10° but it seemed more at the time and I felt the first knot of fear in my stomach, thinking we were doomed and expecting at any minute another enemy air attack as we were now a sitting target, unable to operate aircraft, or even land on all those we still had in the air. The flight deck was a confusion of people and a snakepit of hoses. Tom Troubridge appeared up on the flying bridge, like Zeus, bellowing at the human ants below. I helped to haul hoses along the slanting deck towards the fire at the stern, passing groups of wounded being helped along the deck. I avoided a direct look at them but a glance told me that most had been burnt, their bare skin stained ludicrously with gentian violet ...

At this point my memory fails me. The bomb had hit abaft the after lift and had made it impossible to use the cabins in that area and another bomb had exploded near to the port side of the ship, completely destroying the wardroom. There was an all pervading smell of smoke and burnt flesh and, of course, nothing to eat – not that I felt like it. Somehow I was allocated a cabin amidships on the starboard side and did not enquire whose it was but slept soundly in a comfortable bunk, without taking my clothes off.

13 AUGUST – DAY FOUR

I awoke as usual to action stations with a feeling that it had all been a dream. I was in a strange cabin and there was still that sickening smell. The sight of the wardroom dispelled any dream: where the side wall had once been was strung a long green tarpaulin and the splintered remains of a door. Breakfast was available, although everyone seemed to be speaking in hushed tones and it was difficult to stop ones eye wandering to the spots of blood on the remaining walls although a remarkable cleaning up had somehow been achieved through the night. All six aircrew in the wardroom had been killed including my cabin mate 'Willie' Protheroe and 'Boy' Cunliffe-Owen. There were many other missing faces. Of those of our fighters still airborne when we were put out of action we learnt that Brian Fiddes had been shot down by our own flak, one of the Martlets had ditched short of fuel (both pilots being picked up by destroyers), whilst the remainder had landed safely on *Victorious* ... We suffered 44 men killed and 59 wounded.

Later that morning all at the ship's company, apart from those on duty, attended the burial at sea which took place on the port side for'd of the island. By the end of the service and with the playing of the 'Last Post' I could hardly swallow for the lump in my throat. The words 'burial at sea' were just words until this moment; the reality was harrowing. I was only a few feet away from the incongruous wooden chute canted down over the side. The first few white canvas covered parcels, Willy's no bigger than a small case, slid down the bleached wood to disappear with a distant splash. On and on until I could no longer see for tears. All that was left of shy, gentle Willie was a pipe and a few photographs in my album.

Lieutenant David Wright, 893 Squadron, HMS *Formidable*
IWM Sound Archive Reference 28498

Following his experience on a CAM-ship, Wright was posted to HMS *Formidable* and participated in Operation 'Torch', which began on 8 November and was commanded from Gibraltar by General Eisenhower.

We invaded the underbelly of Occupied Europe. America's now with us, of course, and the first invasion in North Africa ... this was the first time our war had gone on the offensive ... My ship, *Formidable*, was allocated the part on the North Africa coast around Oran and Algiers. It was decided – we were invading a French-owned part of the world – that if the French had thought this was a British invasion, they would fight, but if they thought it was an American invasion they would accept America rather than Britain. Still today, France and Britain are not friends. So when we came to do this invasion we painted all our aeroplanes under American colours ... a white star was painted. So I flew an American aircraft in American colours, and it worked.

There were two squadrons of Wildcats – we never used to call them Martlets – and there was a squadron of Seafires – they couldn't fold the wings, so they had to be stuck on deck, and they were put on outriggers hanging over the sea, and then there was a squadron of Albacores, which were the torpedo aeroplanes. Our function as fighters was either to escort the Albacores who were on a torpedo mission against U-boats or the Italian Navy, or umbrellas over the fleet to protect the fleet from enemy aircraft – fighters or bombers – which were coming in, or to cover the actual landings, the troops who were doing the dirty work of landing ... Additionally to that, perhaps, a little of what they called anti-submarine patrol, where we ranged far away looking for U-boats, not that we could have done much about them. Bullets from the wing of a fighter aeroplane wouldn't damage a U-boat, but the radio could soon fetch a destroyer up.

PACIFIC

Jack Stout, USS *Saratoga*
Jack Stout Collection (AFC/2001/001/3526), Veterans History Project, American Folklife Center, Library of Congress

Saratoga was operating around Hawaii when she was spotted by a Japanese submarine.

USS *Saratoga* 11 Jan 42

I was the gun captain on the port barrel. And the gun captains, they wore headsets. The big one. A big helmet. So a light flashed and it was a destroyer trying to tell us that the torpedo was coming our way. And about that time somebody on the crows' nest said, *torpedo coming. Port beam*. I said, repeat. They said *torpedo coming on the port beam* and I just told the guys to hunker down and hang on ... Well, it hit right square in the middle. I guess it was the worst place to hit. It seemed like it shook – it seemed like it shook two or three feet or more ... Actually, we lifted over to the left about five or six degrees and then it hit what we called a peak tank and that threw in water on the right side and we never did lose any speed. We just kept making 18 knots.

We pulled into Hawaii and just for a few days and then we went on to Birmington, Washington shipyard. Oh, we was there for quite a while. It seemed like it was maybe June or July before we got back into the city.

Lieutenant Commander William Hollingsworth, commanding Bombing Squadron 6, USS *Enterprise*
from his Official Report, dated 2 February

During the 1 February attacks on the Gilbert and Marshall islands, Hollingsworth's squadron hit Taroa Island. The pilots flew the Douglas SBD Dauntless, affectionately known as the 'Slow But Deadly', dive-bomber.

FLIGHT LEADER'S REPORT OF ATTACK ON MALOELAP
AT 1030, 1 FEBRUARY, 1942, BY NINE SBD'S.

1. At 0930, nine SBD's which had landed at 0900 after having taken part in the Group's dawn attack on Kwajalein, were launched for an attack on Taroa Island, Maloelap Atoll. This group under my command was composed of seven planes of Bombing Squadron Six and two planes of Scouting Squadron Six. Each plane was armed with one 500lb, and two 100lb bombs, and a full load of fixed and flexible machine gun ammunition.

At the time of launching the ship was about ninety-five miles from the objective. Emergency departure was taken and rendezvous was effected en route. Flying in three – three plane sections the group climbed, using 90 to 100 per cent power until an up sun position about thirty miles to the southeast of Taroa Island at 19,000 feet altitude was reached at 1032. At this time, and from this point, a high speed nose down approach was commenced, directly towards Taroa Island, the group remaining closed up in a modified division 'V' formation (one wing section high and one wing section low) for mutual defense against enemy fighter aircraft which were reported to be quite plentiful in the vicinity of the target. When about six miles from the target, the sections were released and when almost at the dive point the individual planes of each section were placed in an opened out ABC formation in a generally north to northwest direction. Flaps were opened and a vertical dive made from

13,000 feet altitude directly over the flying field at Taroa. No fighter opposition and no enemy A.A. fire was encountered prior to the attack. The island showed no signs of having been previously bombarded. The hangars and builds were new, uncamouflaged, and undamaged, and the planes were lined up in neat rows all set to receive the bombs of my group. About twelve 2-engine bombers were parked in a single row on the edge of the N-S runway, five fighters were parked in front of the north hangar, and six fighters were parked at the south end of the N-S runway. Two bombers were parked to the northeast of the runways, and were well separated – a most unsatisfactory target from my point of view, and I feel it was very thoughtless and inconsiderate of the Japs to park these planes so far away from the rest of the group. The remainder of the Japanese Air Armada was in the air – or in the hangars (I hope). The attack was practically unopposed and was practically a complete success.

2. The first section leader dropped a ripple salvo of two 100lb and one 500lb bombs aiming at planes parked on the field. His bombs destroyed two large bombers and set two others afire, there being little doubt that the last two were ruined; three small VF planes were also seen to catch afire from these bombs. The second plane dropped a five hundred pound bomb on the southern-most of two hangars near the field, making a direct hit. The hangar must have contained gasoline as it went up in flames very high after the bomb explosion; the hangar was apparently a total loss. This plane then headed for Ollot Island where the pilot attacked what appeared to be radio towers and an administration building or barracks and a small radio station or power house. He dropped two one hundred pound bombs in salvo, hitting one corner of the large building and the small house; one corner of the large building was blown off and the small house was demolished. The third plane dropped one 500lb bomb and two 100lb bombs at the northern hangar, hitting about twenty feet in front of the hangar. Three VF planes in front of the hangar were demolished.

The second section leader dropped one 100lb bomb at the planes parked on the field from 9,000 feet. This bomb hit alongside a large VB plane which was demolished, and two VF planes were seen to catch on fire. He then dropped a 500lb bomb on an oil storage tank to the southeast of the hangars, making a direct hit and setting it on fire. He then headed for Ollot Island and dropped a 100lb bomb on an anti-aircraft gun emplacement there. The bomb explosion was followed by a series of explosions of white smoke, possibly indicating that ammunition was exploding afterward. The second plane of this section dropped all his bombs in the initial dive, but was unable to note where they hit due to pulling out fairly low. The third plane dropped all his bombs on a T-shaped building that was apparently a barracks or administration building, making a direct hit. The building was opened about half way down the stem of the T. These two planes then strafed a small boat seen proceeding toward a pier on Ollot. The third plane was attacked by a fighter just after pulling out of the strafing run. He did not have time to announce the fact over the radio and was forced to take evasive action by himself. The fighter did not push his attack home, but seemed willing to display the maneuverability of his plane and fire outside of gun range. The pilot of the bomber was able then to evade him and eventually make a safe getaway and return to the ship alone without any bullet holes in his plane from the fighter.

The third section leader dropped his 500lb bomb on the southern hangar making a direct hit. This was the second direct hit with 500 lb bombs on this hangar. He then dropped his two 100lb bombs in salvo at the planes parked on the field. They hit in the middle of the NE–SW runway in the vicinity of the planes but no damage to the planes was apparent. The second plane of this section dropped all his bombs in ripple salvo in the dive, aiming at the northern hangar, but was unable to observe the drops because of pulling out low. No bombs were seen to hit the northern hangar, however, and the point of impact of his bombs is doubtful. The third plane also dropped at the northern hangar, but his bombs all dropped between the two hangars doing no damage apparent from the air. Planes retired to the northward, and when the section leader was about six miles north of the field a fighter dove on him. He took evasive action and escaped with no bullet holes in his plane. Here again the fighter pilot seemed content to display the greater maneuverability of his plane and did not drive home his attack.

3. Throughout the attack no anti-aircraft fire was encountered, except machine gun fire after the first section planes entered their dive. All sections dived through the machine gun fire, but only one small hole in the right aileron of the second section leader's plane was found. A.A. fire from several guns on Taroa and from four or five guns on Ollot Island was observed after the attack. This fire was rather sporadic and inaccurate at first, each gun apparently trying to select its own target. When the flight leader was about five miles on his retiring course, however, the batteries appeared to concentrate on his section and the fire became fairly accurate. The all planes dove for the water, the fire again became very ineffective and ceased when the planes were about eight miles away retiring. The planes had inadvertently put themselves in a position to be enfiladed while joining up on the flight leader. This was soon remedied, however, and no one was hit by the A.A. fire. Seven planes returned together, the two had been attacked by fighters returning singly and joining the group just prior to landing aboard.

Captain Ted W. Lawson, USAAF
from *Thirty Seconds Over Tokyo*

Lawson had joined the army and qualified as a pilot before the USA entered the war. As a First Lieutenant he volunteered for a special operation and, still without knowing what was involved, had to learn short take-offs in a B-25 bomber. Then in late March the crews were ordered to fly to Sacramento and on to a coastal airfield at Alameda. Note that Lawson uses the term 'ship' to refer to both aircraft and warships.

As I put the flaps down for the landing, we all let out a yell at the same time, and I guess we all got the same empty feeling in the stomach that I did. An American aircraft carrier was underneath us. Three of our B-25's were already on its deck.

'Damn! ain't she small,' somebody said in the interphone.

We landed on the field and taxied over to the side where Doolittle and York were beckoning to us. I rolled back my the window and looked down.

'Is everything OK?' Doolittle asked.

I said everything was.

'Taxi off the field and park at the edge of the *Hornet*'s wharf. They'll take care of you there,' Doolittle said.

As soon as I did, the Navy boys jumped all over us. They had drained out all our gas, except a few gallons. One of the boys got in, after our crew got out. An army 'donkey' hooked the Ruptured Duck's main gear and towed it down the pier. We walked down after it and then watched the claws of a big crane reach down and pick up our ship as if it weighed 10 pounds. The crane swung it slowly up on the deck of the *Hornet*.

We were standing there, watching this, when Lieutenant Miller came up to me and said, 'don't tell the Navy boys anything. They don't know where you're going.' I nodded and kept looking at the *Hornet*. I can't describe the feeling I got, standing there, looking up at her sides. Maybe the thing I felt was just plain patriotism. All I know is that it was a fine feeling to know that she was there and ready to help us ...

A day after *Hornet* sailed, Doolittle informed them that they were going to Japan to bomb major cities. There could be no returning to the carrier: they would have to fly to the Chinese coast, hope to avoid the Japanese in the occupied areas, and trust to luck, ingenuity and Chinese help to escape. On 18 April the bombers took off.

Doolittle warmed and idled his engine, and now we got a vivid demonstration of one of our classroom lectures on how to get a 25,000-pound bomber off half the deck of a carrier. A Navy man stood at the bow of the ship, and off to the left, with a checkered flag in his hand. He gave Doolittle, who was at the controls, the signal to begin racing his engine again. He did it by swinging the flag in a circle and making it to go faster and faster. Doolittle gave his engines more and more throttle until I was afraid that he'd burn them up. The waves crashed heavily at the bow and sprayed the deck.

Then I saw that the man with the flag was waiting, timing the dipping of the ship so that Doolittle's plane would get the benefit of a rising deck for its take off. The man gave a new signal. Navy boys pulled the blocks from under Doolittle's wheels. Another signal and Doolittle released his brakes and the bomber moved forward. With full flaps, motors at full throttle and his left wing far out over the port side of the *Hornet*, Doolittle's plane wobbled and then lunged slowly into the teeth of a gale that swept down the deck. His left wheel stuck on the white line as if it were a track. His right wing, which had barely cleared the wall of the island as he taxied and was guided up to the starting line, extended nearly to the edge of the starboard side. We watched him like hawks, wondering what the wind would do to him, and whether we could get off in that little run toward the bow. If he couldn't, we couldn't.

Doolittle picked up more speed and held to his line, and, just as the *Hornet* lifted itself up on the top of a wave and cut through it at full speed, Doolittle's plane took off. He had yards to spare. He hung his ship almost straight up on its props, until we could see the whole top of his B-25. Then he levelled off and I watched him come around in a tight circle and shoot low over our heads – straight down the line painted on the deck. The *Hornet* was giving him his bearings. Admiral Halsey had headed it for the heart of Tokyo.

The engines of three other ships were warming up, and the thump and hiss of the turbulent sea made additional noise. But loud and clear above are those sounds I could hear – the hoarse cheers of every Navy man on the ship. They made the *Hornet* fairly shudder – and I've never heard anything like it before or since.

Travis Hoover went off second and nearly crashed. Brick Holstrom was third; Bob Gray, fourth; Davey Jones, fifth; Dean Hallmark, sixth, and I was the seventh.

I was on the line now, my eyes glued on the man with the flag. He gave me the signal to put my flaps down. I reached down and drew the flap lever back and down. I checked the electrical instrument that indicates whether the flaps are working. They were. I could feel the plane quaking with the strain of having a flat surface of the flaps thrust against the Gale and the blast from the props. I got a sudden fear that they might blow off and cripple us, so I pulled up the flaps again, and I guess the Navy man understood. He let it go and began giving me the signal to rev my engines.

I liked the way they sounded long before he did. There had been a moment, earlier, when I had an agonising fear that something was wrong with the left engine. It wouldn't start at first. But I had gotten it going, good. Now after 15 seconds of watching the man with the flag spinning his arm faster and faster, I began to worry again. He must know his stuff, I had tried to tell myself, but when, for God's sake, would he let me go? ... After 30 blood sweating seconds the Navy man was satisfied with the sound of my engines. Our wheel blocks were jerked out, and when I released the brakes we quivered forward, the wind grabbing at to the wings. We rumbled dangerously close to the edge, but I braked in time, got the left wheel back on the white line and picked up speed. The *Hornet*'s deck bucked wildly. A sheet of spray rushed back at us. I never felt the take off. One moment the end of the *Hornet*'s flight deck was rushing at us alarmingly fast; the next split second I glanced down hurriedly at what had been a white line, and it was water. There was no drop nor any surge into the air I just went off at deck level and pulled out in front of the great ship that had done its best to plant us in Japan's front yard.

After hitting their targets, the planes set course for the Chinese mainland as planned. A following wind assisted most of them to crash-land in China; one diverted to Vladivostok, and Lawson ditched his plane in the sea. Badly injured, he reached land and eventually returned home minus his teeth and one leg. Eleven of the men died or were killed by the Japanese. Doolittle was among the survivors.

THE BATTLE OF THE CORAL SEA

Midshipman, later Captain, William D. Owen, USS *Yorktown*
William D. Owen Oral History Interview (#OH0103) Joyner Library*

USS *Yorktown* and Midshipman Owen had arrived at San Diego at New Year.

Ten days later, we took her out loaded with fighter aircraft for the defense of Samoa. They were loaded by barge and taken off by barge. They weren't flown, because there were no aviators to do it except the regular ship's [TF 17] squadrons.

After unloading the aircraft in Samoa, we joined the Pacific Fleet and conducted the first offensive of the Pacific, when we bombarded the Marshall and Gilbert islands. That was on President Roosevelt's birthday, January 31. Afterwards, we came back into Pearl Harbor. It was our first time in Pearl Harbor since the Japanese attack, and we saw the debacle. Even then, there was lots of oil still floating around under the pier. We stayed there for about a week.

Around the tenth of February, we departed for the Coral Sea. We were down there for quite a while patrolling south of New Guinea, conducting raids on ports and airfields around Salamaua and Lae. Then we got involved in the Battle of the Coral Sea, which was the first one in naval history where the ships themselves were never really engaged. They never saw each other. The exchange was all done by naval aircraft. My battle station was up in the anti-aircraft director, the one aft of the stack. We were lucky to get out of that in one piece. We got one bomb down the forward elevator that raised it a foot or so and another one off the port quarter that put a big gaping hole in the fuel tanks. One went through the catwalk on the starboard side forward. This was the battle where the *Lexington* got hit so badly that it sunk, mostly because the gasoline system caught on fire. We didn't know too much in those days about damage control, but we learned later on through incidents such as this ... we were being attacked by dive bombers. We had our fighter squadrons out to protect us but a lot of their planes were still able to get through. I was in the gunnery department. I was up there seeing it all. It was an all-day affair. There were about three or four different attacks. We had one bomb go down on the main deck just underneath where my battle station was. It was a twelve-inch armored projectile and it was deflected down to the armored deck underneath the soda fountain area and blew up down there.

* Some of the paragraphs from Captain Owen's narrative have been re-ordered for continuity.

Another one of my duties on board the *Yorktown* was treasurer of the ship's services. In those days, the supply department had not yet taken over the administration of the laundry, the barbershop, cobbler shop, soda fountain, and that sort of thing. I had a little office in a space on the laundry deck. That was also where the battle station was for the repair party to fight fires and explosions. The bomb that went down through the superstructure exploded right underneath this repair party. The officer in charge received a Medal of Honor for his work of gasping through the last minute work of turning on the water and directing the fire fighting.

We had a bomb to go off right on the main deck aft of the stack where there were two 1.1 quad mounts. One was stacked above the other almost. I looked down after the bomb went off and the officer in charge of the mount was the only one left standing. As for the rest of them, all I could see were rib cages or the lower half of their torsos. They were just cut in two. There were probably about twenty people in that spot, another thirty or forty up forward, and a few here and there and around. We probably had around seventy-five killed at the Coral Sea.

One interesting incident happened in the dark of the night. Two airplanes were flying around wanting to come aboard. We didn't know what carrier they were from. We noticed that their amber lights were a different color than ours. We thought they might be left over from the *Lexington*. Of course, it was darkened ship and the airplanes were dark except for those little faint lights. Suddenly, we realized that they were Japanese planes trying to find a place to land. They were mistaken, too. We opened up fire with everything we had and they disappeared in a hurry. I don't know where they went. Night carrier landings at that time in the war were unheard of. If they had been ours, we would have gotten them on board one way or another; we could always have lit it up.

Masatake Okuyima and Jiro Horikoshi, IJN
quoted in *The Longest Battle*

Our aircraft soon fell victim to the delusions and 'mirages' brought on by exhaustion. Several times the pilots, despairing of their position over the sea 'sighted' a friendly aircraft carrier. Finally, a carrier was sighted, and the remaining eighteen bombers switched on their signal and blinker lights as they swung into their approach and landing pattern.

As the lead aircraft, with its flaps down and speed lowered, drifted toward the carrier deck to land, the pilot discovered the great ship ahead was an American carrier! Apparently the Americans also had erred in identification, for even as the bomber dropped near the carrier deck, not a single enemy gun fired. The Japanese pilot frantically opened his throttle, and at full speed, swung away from the vessel followed by his astonished men.

Our aircrews were disgusted. They had flown for gruelling hours over the sea, bucked thunder squalls and, finally, had lost all trace of their positions relative to their own carriers. When finally they did sight the coveted American warship, cruising unsuspecting beneath eighteen bombers, they were without bombs or torpedoes.

Only eighteen out of the twenty-seven planes that had flown out that afternoon made it back. All the dead were veteran pilots, and could not be easily replaced by the Japanese.

Captain William D. Owen, USS *Yorktown*
William D. Owen Oral History Interview (#OH0103) Joyner Library*

After it was over, we retreated during the night to the southeast and then went on to anchorage in Tongatabu, the capital island of the Tonga Islands. It was owned by the British at the time. We refueled from A.L. number one – A.L. #1. It looked like a wooden hulled ship from the Civil War. We took off the next day for Pearl Harbor. When we got in to Pearl Harbor, we did the unconventional thing of re-gassing, re-fueling, re-arming, re-supplying, and welding all at the same time while in drydock. We needed to get out to Midway. Through the great success in breaking the Japanese code, we had the intelligence that the Japanese were en route. That was a great piece of work. I think we were in there for about two days and then off we went. Normally, you weren't able to re-gas, re-arm, re-supply, and weld at the same time; however, we got out of there in one piece.

THE BATTLE OF MIDWAY

Commander Mitsuo Fuchida, IJN *Akagi*
from *Midway*

The leader of *Akagi*'s air group at Pearl Harbor was suffering from appendicitis, leaving him a helpless spectator of the battle.

Preparations for a counter-strike against the enemy had continued on board our four carriers throughout the enemy torpedo attacks. One after another, planes were hoisted from the hangar and quickly arranged on the flight deck. There was no time to lose. At 1020 Admiral Nagumo gave the order to launch when ready. On *Akagi*'s flight deck all planes were in position with engines warming up. The big ship began turning into the wind. Within five minutes all her planes would be launched. Five minutes! Who would have dreamed that the tide of battle would shift completely in that brief interval of time?

Visibility was good. Clouds were gathering at about 3,000 metres, however, and though there were occasional breaks, they afforded good concealment for approaching enemy planes. At 1024 the order to start launching came from the

---

* Some of the paragraphs from Captain Owen's narrative have been re-ordered for continuity.

bridge by voice-tube. The Air Officer flapped a white flag, and the first Zero fighters gathered speed and whizzed off the deck. At that instant a lookout screamed: 'Hell-divers!' I looked up to see three black enemy planes plummeting toward our ship. Some of our own machine guns managed to fire a few frantic bursts at them, but it was too late. The plump silhouettes of the American Dauntless dive bombers quickly grew larger, and then a number of black objects suddenly floated eerily from their wings. Bombs! Down they came straight toward me! I fell intuitively to the deck and crawled behind a command post mantelet. The terrifying scream of the dive bombers reached me first, followed by the crashing explosion of a direct hit. There was a blinding flash and then a second explosion, much louder than the first. I was shaken by a weird blast of warm air. There was still another shock, but less severe, apparently a near-miss. Then followed a startling quiet as the barking of guns suddenly ceased. I got up and looked at the sky. The enemy planes were already gone from sight.

The attackers had got in unimpeded because our fighters which had engaged the preceding wave of torpedo planes only a few moments earlier, had not yet had time to regain altitude. Consequently, it may be said that the American dive bombers' success was made possible by the earlier martyrdom of their torpedo planes. Also, our carriers had no time to evade because clouds hid the enemy's approach until he dived down to the attack. We had been caught flatfooted in the most vulnerable condition possible – decks loaded with planes armed and fuelled for an attack. Looking about, I was horrified at the destruction that had been wrought in a matter of seconds. There was a huge hole in the flight deck just behind the amidship elevator. The elevator itself, twisted like molten glass, was drooping into the hangar. Deck plates reeled upward in grotesque configurations. Planes stood tail up, belching livid flame and jet-black smoke. Reluctant tears streamed down my cheeks as I watched the fires spread, and I was terrified at the prospect of induced explosions which would surely doom the ship. I heard Masuda yelling, 'Inside! Get inside! Everybody who isn't working! Get inside!' Unable to help, I staggered down a ladder and into the ready room. It was already jammed with badly injured victims from the hangar deck. A new explosion was followed quickly by several more, each causing the bridge structure to tremble. Smoke from the burning hangar gushed through passageways, and into the bridge and ready room, forcing us to seek other refuge. Climbing back to the bridge I could see that *Kaga* and *Soryu* had also been hit and were giving off heavy columns of black smoke. The scene was horrible to behold.

Akagi had taken two direct hits, one on the after rim of the amidship elevator, the other on the rear guard on the port side of the flight deck. Normally, neither would have been fatal to the giant carrier, but induced explosions of fuel and munitions devastated whole sections of the ship, shaking the bridge and filling the air with deadly splinters. As fire spread among the planes lined up wing to wing on the after flight deck, their torpedoes began to explode, making it impossible to bring the fires under control. The entire hangar area was a blazing inferno, and the flames moved swiftly toward the bridge.

Because of the spreading fire, our general loss of combat efficiency, and especially the severance of external communication facilities, Nagumo's Chief of Staff, Rear Admiral Kusaka, urged that the Flag be transferred at once to the light cruiser *Nagara*. Admiral Nagumo gave only a half-hearted nod, but Kusaka patiently continued his entreaty: 'Sir, most of our ships are still intact. You must command them.' The situation demanded immediate action, but Admiral Nagumo was reluctant to leave his beloved flagship. Most of all he was loath to leave behind the officers and men of *Akagi*, with whom he had shared every joy and sorrow of war. With tears in his eyes, Captain Aoki spoke up: 'Admiral, I will take care of the ship. Please, we all implore you, shift your flag to *Nagara* and resume command of the Force.' At this moment Lieutenant Commander Nishibayashi, the Flag Secretary, came up and reported to Kusaka: 'All passages below are on fire, Sir. The only means of escape is by rope from the forward window of the bridge down to the deck, then by the outboard passage to the anchor deck. *Nagara*'s boat will come alongside the anchor deck port, and you can reach it by rope ladder.'

Kusaka made a final plea to Admiral Nagumo to leave the doomed ship. At last convinced that there was no possibility of maintaining command from *Akagi*, Nagumo bade the Captain good-bye and climbed from the bridge window with the aid of Nishibayashi. The Chief of Staff and other staff and headquarters officers followed. The time was 1046.

On the bridge there remained only Captain Aoki, his Navigator, the Air Officer, a few ratings, and myself. Aoki was trying desperately to get in touch with the engine room. The Chief Navigator was struggling to see if anything could be done to regain rudder control. The others were gathered on the anchor deck fighting the raging fire as best they could. But the unchecked flames were already licking at the bridge. Hammock mantelets around the bridge structure were beginning to burn. The Air Officer looked back at me and said, 'Fuchida, we won't be able to stay on the bridge much longer. You'd better get to the anchor deck before it is too late.' In my condition this was no easy task. Helped by some sailors, I managed to get out of the bridge window and slid down the already smouldering rope to the gun deck. There I was still ten feet above the flight deck. The connecting monkey ladder was red hot, as was the iron plate on which I stood. There was nothing to do but jump, which I did. At the same moment another explosion occurred in the hangar, and the resultant blast sent me sprawling. Luckily the deck on which I landed was not yet afire, for the force of the fall knocked me out momentarily. Returning to consciousness, I struggled to rise to my feet, but both my ankles were broken.

Capt. William D. Owen, USS *Yorktown*
William D. Owen Oral History Interview (#OH0103) Joyner Library

We were with the *Enterprise*. The *Yorktown* and the *Enterprise* were the only two carriers available at that time. We had a number of cruisers, one of which was the *Pensacola*. We were a couple of hundred miles southwest of Midway when an engagement started that was another one of those *no see 'ums*. We couldn't see the surface ships at all. The attacker forces passed in midair almost, but not in sight of each other. While we were bombing and torpedoing them, we were getting the same thing.

A Japanese Val came down and let its bomb go. I could see all four vanes behind the bomb and I knew it was coming right at me. Fortunately, the ship was in a hard port turn and it passed overhead about fifteen to twenty feet. In my innocence, I emptied a string of forty-five caliber pistol shots into the plane. It did crash right behind me, but I think it wasn't my pistol shooting that did it!

Shortly thereafter, we had a bomb go down the stack about fifteen feet away. It exploded on the protective grates – armored plating with slots in them – that are put in there for the fires to go through. It blew all the fires out in the boilers.

We finally got back up to eighteen knots of speed when we had a coordinated torpedo plane attack. A coordinated attack means they come in at right angles to each other so that whichever way the ship turns, one of the group is going to get you broadside. Two torpedoes hit us midship portside. During our preparations, we had taken every thirty-caliber machine gun available and welded them to stanchions along the whole outside of the ship on the flight deck. They were manned by plane-handling crews or anybody else who was available. When those torpedoes hit, the explosion lifted some of those gunners a good twenty feet into the air. I don't know whether they landed on deck or went overboard. That was at portside midship, which was on the opposite side of the ship from where I was. That brought us to a halt! The ship started flooding. We were keeling over probably somewhere between 25 and 30 degrees. It was difficult to stand up, particularly with the gas and grease and oil running out of the planes that were still on board, both on the hangar deck and the flight deck.

My little office was in one of those expanded wire cages that could be locked up, because I had a safe in there. There was about ten thousand dollars in cash in the safe, because we had been out for quite a while and I had had no chance to deposit it. During the course of the battle, a piece of bomb fragment hit the knob on the safe and I couldn't unlock it. I didn't have time to get anybody out there to do it because I had my regular job on board ship to do, too. I was responsible for getting the division ready to go: re-armed, re-supplied, and re-provisioned. When we got to Midway, the ship was sunk, and all that money went down with it. There were also a couple of vehicles that belonged to the ship's service department. They were tied up in the overhead and they went down with the ship, too. For three or four years after that, I got letters from the Navy Department, wanting to know about the money and equipment.

Not too long thereafter, we got the word to abandon ship. I was a member of the 3rd Division, and my job was to help get everybody off. I went down to my station, which was on the starboard quarter. That was the high side, because we had keeled over to port. One destroyer came alongside and practically tied up. She was getting quite a bit of damage to her superstructure due to the rocking. We got all of the wounded off. We practically hand carried them across. All of a sudden we found that there were just three or four of us left, so we decided that we'd better get off. We could see destroyers circling around a mile or two away. I stripped down, leaving my skivvy shorts on. I had a life jacket. In those days they had pockets, so I put my wallet in one. I threw my forty-five overboard and went down the knotted line, dropping the last ten or so feet into the water. All the planking and other stuff that had been available to float on in the water had already been pushed over aside for other people. I had thrown one of those new tightly-wrapped aviation tires from the aviation supply room into the water. I caught up with it and pushed it for about a couple of hundred yards before it proceeded to sink. I thought, What futility! The water was warm and I didn't see any sharks around, but I was covered in oil. I was about to get to a destroyer when it decided to get out of there because of a suspected sonar contact. Finally, I got picked up about another half a mile further down by the destroyer *Balch* ... probably an hour or so of swimming.

When we got back to Pearl Harbor after the ship went down, it seemed like every company we had done business with sent us duplicate bills, even though we had paid them. I had only my memory to go on, but we had paid everything before we left. I guess they had been worried about whether we were going to come back.

Captain Eliot Buckmaster, commanding USS *Yorktown*
BBC Reference 4852, dated 23 September, 1943, IWM Sound Archive Reference 2591

The *Yorktown* joined up with other carriers in attacking Jap forces. Our air group immediately hit one carrier with torpedoes and bombs. Later it was reported that the carrier sank. About this time our fighters intercepted a large group of the enemy dive bombers and fighters. Then all the sky was filled with falling Japanese bombers. The anti aircraft fire of the supporting ships and the *Yorktown* was magnificent. Our gunners chopped the enemy planes apart. Every single dive bomber that came towards us was blown to bits but two or three managed to make hits on us before being destroyed. By this time our engines had stopped but through superhuman efforts our engineers got our boilers operating. But a swarm of the enemy torpedo planes appeared. We avoided several torpedoes but two dropped close aboard. We could not escape. The ship listed heavily. Soon it was impossible to stand on deck. I felt that the ship would capsize very soon. Reluctantly I gave the order: abandon ship. The courage displayed by the officers and crew throughout the engagement is beyond my powers of expression. When I got aboard one of the rescue ships I believed the *Yorktown* was stricken beyond repair. Later on, however, I returned with a small salvage party. With the help of the destroyer *Hammann*, we were able to right the ship 2°. We felt sure she would live. Then suddenly four torpedoes fired from an enemy submarine outside our destroyer screen were sighted. We were heavily hit and the destroyer *Hammann* alongside was sunk. As our destroyers were attacking the enemy submarine, our crew was transferred to a small tug [*Vireo*] to await the arrival of salvage tugs at daybreak. However, next day from a companion ship I saw the *Yorktown* slowly sink beneath the waves. Yes, the *Yorktown* went down and the Japanese lost four aircraft carriers in that engagement and many of their best aviators. In the *Yorktown*'s four short years she destroyed more Japanese planes and ships than any other single United States ship. And tonight the *Yorktown* rests on the bottom of the Pacific, but her name will be remembered as long as America continues to breed generations of freedom loving fighting men – for ever ...

John E. Greenbacker, USS *Yorktown*
John E. Greenbacker Oral History Interview (#OH0150) Joyner Library

When the torpedo planes came in, I had to admire our fighter pilots. They hadn't refueled. They took off and turned and came in on the port side ... We were shooting and they were close to our line of fire. So, I had to admire our pilots for having that kind of determination. We got hit by two torpedoes. Of the dozen or so that came in, only two of them got hits.

Ernie Davis was a genius at getting the air defense organized, and that's why we survived the Coral Sea. He said that our gunnery wasn't as effective, but I think we were fighting against pilots that came very close to having the kamikaze attitude. You know, if you expect to go home and see your family, when that fire starts getting heavy, you drop the torpedo and turn away. They flew right by the ship. The ones that hit us actually flew right by. The pilot was waving his fist at us.

I really didn't have time to reflect on anything. I think our experience in the Coral Sea probably gave us a little more self confidence than we deserved to have. I think we were calmer about it, because we'd been through something like that before. Of course, it was just momentary. This attack came in and then we became dead in the water. The fact that we could only get up to twenty knots rather than thirty knots had a considerable impact on the fact that they got the hits they did with the torpedoes. The first lieutenant called up to the bridge and said, 'Tell the captain that I can't do anything to take the list off the ship.' People have written articles criticizing that, but ... There was no way that we could get power to the pumps. We didn't have the portable equipment that we have [now] and we didn't have the cables, electric cables, that plugged into the bulkhead and had power. They had that later on in the war. There wasn't anything he could do. They hit the forward distribution board. It flooded and killed everybody there … So, there wasn't anything could be done, and, of course, the ship capsized with everybody aboard. One of the things that they did learn from that battle was to disembark or abandon ship the people they didn't need for damage control. That's something that they did later in the war. They would have a partial abandon of ship, all the air group for example or people with the guns, but the damage control people stayed on board and tried to work on the thing.

Everyone abandoned. We didn't have any left. As a matter of fact, we hadn't even practised abandoning ship, because Captain Buckmaster thought it was bad for morale to even think about abandoning ship. People didn't know … For example, my roommate went down there in the boat and his battle station was in a motor launch. They went down there and sat in the boat and wondered where the crane operator was. There was no way that under 'abandoned ship' we could have done anything except go down those lines. They hadn't taught the people how to abandon ship by going down those knotted lines, and some of the people that slid down got burns on their hands, and the knots ripped up the strings on their lifejackets.

Ernie Davis was damaged that week when we abandoned the second time. For some reason he got in the water and the underwater explosions gave him a lot of intestinal damage. I didn't want to get wet, so I was one of the last off. I went down to the quarter deck. Up in the racks, underneath the flight deck, were spare rafts and I went up there and got one of those two-man life rafts. Inflated it, put it in the water, and got ready to go down, but by the time I got down there, some other people had gotten it and were paddling away. I was afraid that I had too much. I had my binoculars and my pistol and a flight jacket that I had picked up on the flight deck. (Actually, it had fifteen hundred dollars of Fighting Forty-Two's money in it. Had I known that, I could have stuck it in my shirt.) They panicked also, but I got to the raft and I put all my stuff in it and was pushing it along. Then the destroyer nearby started sounding its alarm; there was an air attack coming in and they wanted to recall their boat. So, I left the life raft and went over and climbed in the motor whale boat. Then, once I was aboard the ship, somebody had brought the binoculars and the pistol, but not the flight jacket … The pilot had said 'Look outside the ready room because I've got my flight jacket there and it's got Fighting Forty-Two's welfare money in it.' I said, 'Sorry, I tried to get it. It didn't make it.'

6
1943

Set against the previous torrid twelve months, 1943 was a quieter year for the aircraft carriers, and the tide turned irreversibly in favour of the Allies. German forces in Stalingrad surrendered in February, and that same month the Japanese evacuated their troops from Guadalcanal. The Allies met at Casablanca and resolved a new strategy: a campaign to take Rabaul. One force would approach via New Guinea, a second via the Solomon Islands. Later in the year they adopted the 'leap-frogging' tactic – advances which simply avoided the heavily defended Japanese islands. US carrier losses had left only one US carrier operating in the South Pacific, USS *Saratoga*, part of Admiral Halsey's Third Fleet, and the US asked Britain to loan them a carrier while the new *Essex* class was commissioning. HMS *Victorious* was chosen as she was due to refit at the Norfolk Navy Yard, temporarily renamed USS *Robin* and re-equipped with Avengers in place of their Fairey Albacore biplanes. During the invasion of New Georgia, *Victorious* provided air defence while *Saratoga* took care of air strikes. Both navies learned from one another, and *Victorious* returned home with ice cream makers and cold drink dispensers.

Atlantic convoys were finally benefiting from the arrival of escort carriers, including USS *Bogue*, HMS *Biter* and HMS *Archer*. These joined the hunter-killer groups of corvettes and destroyers, finally closing the Atlantic Gap that had allowed the U-boats so much freedom. 'Black May', as that month became known, saw a ferocious assault on the U-boats that left so many sunk or damaged that Grossadmiral Dönitz temporarily recalled them from the North Atlantic convoy routes. It was on these small carriers, and the many escorts and MACs which followed, that the Fairey Swordfish, obsolete aboard the fleet carriers, acquired a new lease of life. Its slow speed was ideal for convoy work; it could take off and land on the smaller flight decks of the escorts, even in poor conditions; it carried a variety of weapons from depth-charges to rockets; it was easily repairable; and the crews had confidence in it. While no use as a fighter, it could call up fighter protection from the Wildcats to deal with German aircraft such as the Condor. CAM ships continued to operate their Hurricanes.

The U-boat focus switched to the UK–Gibraltar route, where again the escorts were active. Within the Mediterranean, Allied warships still found warm work, but the convoys were getting to Malta and North Africa with far less difficulty. In July, the liberation of Europe began when Operation 'Husky' saw Allied troops land on Sicily, a campaign that involved more than 2,500 Allied warships, including HMS *Indomitable* and HMS *Formidable*. In September the Italian Government requested an armistice and joined the Allies as co-belligerents. German forces immediately moved to seize as much of their former ally's territory as they could, and Allied landings took place at Salerno, with air cover provided by *Formidable* and *Illustrious*.

ATLANTIC

Flying Officer J. A. Stewart, DFC, RAF, MV *Empire Darwin*
Courtesy RAF Millom Aviation and Military Museum

R.A.F. Stn. Speke.

To:- Headquarters, Fighter Command
Headquarters, No. 9 Group (for G.I.O.)
Date:- 4th August 1943
Ref:- SPK/S.388/INT.

INTELLIGENCE FORM F.
PERSONAL COMBAT REPORT

All times D.B.S.T.
A. Date:- 28th July 1943.
B. Unit:- M.S.F.U. [Merchant Ship Fighter Unit]
C. Type & Mark of Aircraft:- Hurricane Mk.I.
D. Time Attack was Delivered:- 19.45.
E. Place:- 43°03'N 16°06'W
F. Weather:- Vis. 15miles 2/10 cloud on horizon increasing to 6/10 at 10,000.
G. Our Casualties Aircraft:- One Hurricane Mk.I. Cat. E.
H. Our Casualties Personnel:- Nil.
J. Enemy Casualties in Air Combat:- One F.W.200 probably destroyed.

I left Gibraltar 23rd July on aboard CAM Ship *Empire Darwin* in convoy bound for U.K. at 19.30hrs on 28th July 1943 enemy activity was reported and I was ordered to readiness. At 19.38hrs I was signalled to land and immediately made visual contact.

I recognised it as a F.W.200 flying at 1,000ft and gave chase, he was flying N. but turned and flew south for a minute the[n] proceeded eastward and reducing height to about 200ft. I had no difficulty overtaking at 6¼ boost, 2600revs and approximately 250m.p.h. and made my attack on the port quarter out of sun. My attack was delivered from 40° to 15°, opening fire at 300yrds and closing to almost point blank. I aimed at the cockpit giving 1½ to 1 ring deflection and gave a five second burst. I could see strikes in the sea round the nose, then a vivid white flash from near the turret, return fire was very heavy and uncomfortably close, but I could not see any strikes on my aircraft. Having broken away to port I repeated the attack but my guns ceased firing after about ½ second. However I kept making dummy attacks but gave up when I saw I was drawing well away from the convoy, and returned.

I last saw him flying eastward towards a bunk of cloud about 10 miles away. On my return to the convoy I started circling at 1000ft. but reception on the R.T. had broken down. As I reached the port side of the convoy I observed the escorts opening fire at another F.W.200 which was making a bombing run from W. to E. at height of about 8000ft. I saw two near misses on H.M.S. *Scylla* and started climbing, I caught up with at 7000ft. and made a few dummy attacks, then followed him until he disappeared into cloud about twenty miles from the convoy. Having once more returned to the convoy I gave the appropriate signal to indicate that I was bailing out, about climbing to 4,500ft about three miles ahead I cleared the aircraft successfully and everything functioned perfectly. I was in the water for about 15mins. before being picked up by H.M.S. *Leith* where I received every consideration including a hot bath and a glass of whisky.

The ships officer's also referred to the fact that they had seen the flash from the enemy aircraft.

Claims:- One F.W.200 probably destroyed.
J A Stewart F/O.

Sub-Lieutenant (A) Jack Thomas, MV *Alexia*
Communication with the Editor

836 Squadron of the Fleet Air arm was unique. Based at HMS *Shrike*, Royal Naval Air Station Maydown, Northern Ireland, it served the fleet of 19 MAC ships, or Merchant Aircraft Carriers; grainships and tankers under Merchant Navy control, fitted out like small escort carriers with a flight deck, bridge and arrester wires.

It was the largest Squadron in the world, with 450 aircrew, 400 maintenance personnel and 23 flights of three or four Swordfish aircraft; 83 planes in all. Amazingly its Commanding Officer only held the rank of Lieutenant Commander. Smaller than the average escort carrier, the main problem with these vessels was their comparatively slow speed – about 12 knots. This meant that the only aircraft capable of operating from them was the Fairey Swordfish and when the Mark III version appeared with a large radar dome between the legs of the undercarriage, they needed to be fitted with a fine-pitch propellor, which provided extra power for take-off together with RATOG. This Rocket Assisted Take-off Gear gave a valuable extra boost, particularly in low wind conditions.

I was a pilot in J Flight operating from the MV *Alexia*, a tanker, for a time, and later became a Deck Landing Control Officer, or 'Batsman' with V Flight on board a grainship, the MV *Empire Mackendrick*. As we were serving under the Red Ensign, to make it legal all officers signed on as 'Supernumerary Deck Officers' in the Merchant Navy and the ratings took out articles with the Master. By painting out the words 'Royal Navy' on the side of the aircraft and substituting them with 'Merchant Navy' we found out later we might have been arraigned as pirates – operating offensively from a merchant vessel without 'Letters of Marque'.

Frederick George 'Pat' Oikle, Seaman, HMS *Activity*
IWM Sound Archive Reference 17529

Oikle had left a reserve occupation to join the Navy. After training, he was posted to HMS *Activity*, which at the the start of 1943 was acting as a Deck Landing Training Carrier.

Anyway, I was on the carrier and my first job was to go into the Firth of Clyde and train pilots to land on the aircraft carrier. Previous to this they had been landing on a dummy flight deck, on land at a place called Machrihanish, and when they thought the officers were trained they said: 'Right, you're going to land on an aircraft carrier.' Well, they came out and landed but not a lot made a good landing. I was the messenger for what is known as the batsman ... I had occasion to go up in one of the aircraft as a passenger and fly on and so it gave me the experience of what the pilot looked at, what he could see when he landed. And [the carrier] was just like a matchbox! And, believe me, I can't blame them for the things they did – I mean, they panicked. Some of them came towards us, and we had a big net on the port side that we could jump into and roll down against the bulkhead to get out of the way of the aircraft, and, well, it came towards us, went over the side; they overshot the arrestor wires and went over the forward end. The only part of the flight deck that was not damaged was the bit in front of the bridge, 'cos they couldn't get at it. They even landed on the deck, the arrestor hook caught the arrester wire, but they must have panicked and tried to take off again, and just got pulled back. Some of them made good landings, and went on to do good things, no doubt.

HMS *Activity* continued in this role for most of the year, then went in for refit.

Ralph Cocklin, Lieutenant (A), RNZNVR, 836 Squadron, HMS *Tracker*
Communication with the Editor

While 811 Squadron was still waiting to 'see the *Biter* in the Clyde', HMS *Tracker* was already in business.

816 RN Air Squadron of which I was a member was embarked on HMS *Tracker*. This was an escort carrier which was attached to the 2nd Escort Group of six Bird Class Sloops to form an Air Support Group to patrol the 'Gap' as an anti-U-boat force. The Group was under the command of Captain J.Walker, CB, DSO***. The squadron was made up of 12 Swordfish bombers and 6 Seafire fighters.

On 5th November 1943 with my crew of Observer Jack Durban and Telegraphist Air Gunner Jock Liddell I took off for an A/S patrol of 60 to 100 miles from the Group.

Towards the end of the patrol of 2 and ½hrs Jack suggested we fire off a couple of Verey [sic] cartridges to celebrate Guy Fawkes Day. We were still debating the wisdom or otherwise of the proposal when the engine gave a loud bang and we started to lose height and speed. I fired my load of 8 rocket projectiles and told the others to jettison anything moveable. Jack sent out a Mayday signal and we slowly regained some of the lost altitude and headed for the carrier. Several times the engine cut and we lost 20 to 30 feet. Each time I coaxed the aircraft back up to 200ft and eventually reached *Tracker*, which was already heading into wind ready for us to land on immediately. I approached on the high side to allow for loss of engine power and landed successfully.

It turned out that the rocker box arms on two cylinders had broken, thus reducing power by over 20%.

Two days later I was flying the now repaired aircraft but I did not know that a special torsion spanner required to complete the repair was not available on board the ship so the repair was less than satisfactory.

This time we completed our patrol, but while waiting to land on the engine started cutting again. The escorts were hunting a U-boat, probably one which had fired a couple of torpedoes at the carrier the previous night. Fortunately for us, they exploded about one to two hundred yards short of their target possibly due to the stormy conditions.

I slid alongside one of the escorts and prepared to ditch. We were below mast head height when Jack called through that *Tracker* was swinging into wind and I could attempt a landing. I flew the aircraft laboriously back to 200ft carried out a cautious approach on the high side. The engine was belching fire and smoke – a fearsome sight to those on deck. The engine coughed two or three times, but as we crossed the rounddown at the end of the flight deck we were at the correct height for a landing. When I opened the throttle to taxi forward there was a dead silence, but the wonderful old Pegasus engine had got us safely home. I had saved the Admiralty about ten thousand pounds sterling but I think my TAG never really forgave me for depriving him of a chance of membership of the Goldfish Club by saving himself by his Mae West.

Cocklin's Swordfish was a rather more amenable aircraft for such an emergency than Adlam's more powerful Wildcat.

MEDITERRANEAN

Hank Adlam, Pilot, 890 Squadron, HMS *Illustrious*
from *On and Off the Flight Deck*

The invasion of Italy began in September at Salerno. HMS *Illustrious* and HMS *Formidable* provided protection for the four escort carriers that in turn gave air cover for the amphibious landings.

For the Seafire to land on the small deck of an Escort Carrier, even under ideal conditions, calls for considerable skill and experience on the part of the pilot. But at Salerno, the wind conditions were no better than a zephyr breeze and almost a dead calm, conditions entirely to have been expected at that time of year. Thus the Seafires had to operate with a total wind speed over the deck of only sixteen knots, being the maximum speed of the Escort Carriers, whereas they needed a total wind speed over the deck of at least twenty-eight knots. These were desperately difficult landing conditions for the Seafire pilots; conditions which surely should have been anticipated at the outset when the whole Salerno operation was being planned by Rear Admiral Vian who, despite never having flown an aircraft or having served in an Aircraft Carrier, had been put in charge of this, the first multi Carrier Fleet of the Royal Navy.

After two days the four Escort Carriers had virtually run out of Seafires, no less than forty-eight of which had been written off as the pilots attempted to land in those windless conditions. The situation was made worse by the limited sea space available for the Carriers so close to shore; this limitation must have created a frantic situation with so many crashes occurring while other Seafires were waiting to land on. How many of the Seafire pilots were killed or seriously hurt in this fiasco does not seem to be recorded. Nevertheless, in spite of the appalling crash rate, many sorties were flown in that short period from the five small Carriers. It was a courageous performance by the Seafire pilots under dreadful conditions. Unfortunately, another ten Seafires were shot down by German fighter-bombers largely due to the lack of radar in the Escort Carriers preventing the Seafires reaching an advantageous combat position.

Meantime, further out at sea, the second task force of two Fleet Carriers, HMS *Illustrious* and HMS *Formidable* were stationed with the secondary purpose of providing air cover over the Escort Carriers. Their complement of fighter aircraft for this task was thirty Wildcats and fifteen Seafires and these aircraft flew about four hundred sorties on patrol over the Escort Carriers and the beach head. On the second day, *Formidable* sent some of her Seafires to join in with the crashes taking place on the Escort Carriers. When there were no more Seafires, the Wildcats from *Illustrious* and *Formidable* were sent to land on the Escort Carriers to take over the task of patrolling the beach head. It was no problem for the Wildcats to operate continuously from these small Carriers. Moreover, since the Wildcats could patrol for a full two hours and more, the Carriers needed to turn into wind only half as frequently as for the Seafires ...

My personal part in the Salerno operation was very minor as just another Wildcat pilot flying twice-daily patrols from HMS *Illustrious* to cover the air space over the Escort Carriers plus a small part of the beachhead. We chased about the sky after the faster German bombers none of which seemed bothered to attack our Escort Carriers. It seemed that the Germans were aware of our difficulties and were content to let the Seafires write themselves off, at a high rate each day. The Germans seem to have thought, 'Why bother to attack the Escort Carriers when they are doing such a good job in writing off the Seafires and their pilots for us.' At the end of the second day, when the supply of Seafires was exhausted, our two squadrons of Wildcats were ordered to land on the Escort Carriers and continue patrol operations over the beach head from there. My squadron flew off early on that third morning and formed up ready to land on whichever of the four Escort Carriers indicated that it was ready to take us. The first flight with the CO had landed on and, while there was some sort of delay on the flight deck, we were told to orbit and patrol overhead at 5,000 feet.

It was an intensely hot day with the sea glassy like a millpond and, looking down, I could see the Isle of Capri like a jewel sitting on a bright blue cushion. I was idly thinking of Gracie Fields, whom I believed still lived on the Island, and of her cheerful songs, when there was a kind of hiccup from the engine which then began to run roughly. I looked down at my instruments to find that the engine temperature gauge showed at red and the oil pressure was just about nil. I certainly didn't want to ditch again. The mirror-like surface of the calm sea would make ditching difficult and this was a further factor which encouraged me to attempt a landing on a deck. I was still getting some power from the engine and I reckoned to land on whichever deck would take me. I pressed transmit on the R/T and in a voice cracking with anxiety called out 'Mayday, mayday, this is Red Two and I require immediate landing.' I squeaked this message out twice more. Down below one of the Carriers was already turning into wind preparing to take our flight on board anyway and, when I saw this, I made up my mind definitely to go for a landing on it.

Meantime, I was getting very little power out of the engine and by now was down to about three thousand feet. I was ahead of the ship and more or less on the downwind leg calculating that I had sufficient height to circle round to position myself reasonably well for the final approach. I glanced quickly round; no other aircraft near me or in the circuit, they were all keeping clear. I decided to assume that there would be no power at all from the engine should I need it, so I closed the throttle completely to concentrate on an engineless landing. I would have to come in very high on the final approach and might have to do an old-fashioned side-slip to get down. Also I must remember how very little wind speed there would be over the flight deck, sixteen knots no more and therefore the deck would appear to be rushing at me twice as fast on my final approach.

All this had gone through my mind but now, at some two thousand feet, I selected wheels down, half flap, hook out, straps very tight and hood locked open. I had already put the prop into fine pitch as soon as the engine had started running rough. There was no going back now; the decision to attempt a deck-landing instead of ditching was made. If I missed the deck, it would not be possible to ditch safely as the wheels would catapult the Wildcat on to its back as soon as they touched the sea and, whether I could swim or not, I would be drowned. Meantime, over the R/T from the Carrier, which was now into wind, I had received the affirmative to land.

I was turning on to the final approach, prop still rotating, speed at eighty-five knots, selecting full flap now, very high up astern of the Carrier with the batsman frantically signalling me to 'come down'. Everything was happening very fast. Yes, I was too high; would fly straight over the crash barrier at this rate; side slip down to port, red Very light from the DLCO platform, meaning

'Abort landing, go round again'. A second red light with the batsman waving me off furiously. Straightening up from the side-slip, speed eighty knots. Oh dear Lord, I had overdone it, I was now slightly lower than I should be and I might not quite make it to the deck. I opened the throttle for the first time but only a brief response from the engine for a second before it expired, then I was over the deck to stall and thump down catching the first arrestor wire. Somehow, I was down and safe.

The propeller had jarred itself to a halt as soon as the aircraft landed and I lay back in the cockpit gasping with relief as the handlers pushed me forward. As they did so, a furious batsman jumped on to my port wing and harangued me for not taking his 'wave-off'. I looked at him; I didn't know the man; I said nothing but gave him a couple of fingers sign and so he jumped off again. As usual, the flight deck was all activity preparing for Jack and the rest of the Flight to land. The Tannoy blared out, 'Pilot to report immediately to Lt Cdr 'F' and the Captain on the Bridge.' That's me, I thought and, without any hurry, I undid my straps to climb slowly out of the cockpit then made my way across the deck to the Island and up to the Bridge. I was confronted by the Lt Cdr 'F', red-faced with anger and, a few feet behind him, the Captain also with a boot-face. 'You stupid man,' the Lt Cdr 'F' shouted at me, 'you deliberately disobeyed a clear instruction not to land; you were likely to crash on to the deck and put the Carrier out of action; you were even more likely to have killed people on the deck park; and don't tell me that you had no engine power because I heard it. You are a menace and I personally shall see to it that you are court-martialled.' The Captain nodded his agreement.

I waited a little before I said anything; not because I was frightened of them but because I needed to contain my anger and to be sure of giving them a quiet, composed answer. I knew that I had just completed an astonishing feat of airmanship; a forced landing without engine on the deck of a small Carrier in conditions of nil wind, could be regarded as nothing less. I was not prepared to be brow-beaten by these two non-flyers. I replied, 'Sir, you were aware that I was in a forced landing situation from my Mayday call, you gave me the affirmative to land; by the time of my final approach I had no engine power available. I suggest you wait for the report of the Air Engineer Officer, who is now examining the engine, to confirm that the engine had no power.' The Captain interrupted the confrontation immediately and agreed that the Engineer's report must be obtained before anything further was said.

Investigation revealed a broken oil pipe in the engine.

Lieutenant David Wright, 893 Squadron, HMS *Formidable*
IWM Sound Archive Reference 28498

Having survived 24 catapult launches from HMS *Maplin*, Wright was posted to 893 Squadron which, following the Italian Armistice, was also covering the Salerno landings.

On one of these patrols I had my flight section tucked tightly in. We'd just taken off to do a 2 hour umbrella off Malta, I think it was – between Malta and Gibraltar. We'd taken off *Formidable* and were relieving another flight from 888 Squadron who were finishing and were coming in to land. We four, three in echelon and one in the box, were climbing whilst the other four were descending. We were climbing off the carrier to go out, and they were coming down to prepare to land. The wing man, and my wing man, Jack Cole, collided within ten feet of my shoulder. All I was aware of was a flash, and then I saw them both going down. Peter Lang, he went straight in … and Jack Cole, he got out of the aeroplane but his parachute roman-candled – it didn't open out – and he hit the sea – decelerated a bit but not fully, and he was taken into Gibraltar with a broken back. He died in Gibraltar, and he was the only married member of the squadron.

PACIFIC

Aviation Chief Ordnanceman (Dr) Alvin Kernan, then an air gunner, VT-6, USS *Enterprise*
from *Crossing the Line*

Unlike the simultaneous army landings on nearby Makin, the invasion of Tarawa during November 1943 was a bloody affair for the US Marines, and the Japanese were sending bombers down from the Marshall Islands to look for the US fleet. To oppose this, the first carrier-based night-fighter operations were planned. When Japanese 'Betty' medium bombers were picked up on the radar, two fighters plus Kernan's Avenger were launched. His pilot was Lieutenant Commander John Phillips, while in the crew tunnel sat Hazen Rand, who operated the primitive new radar set and who would be hit in the foot during the engagement. Flying the fighters were the famous pilots Butch O'Hare and Ensign Warren Skon.

I unlatched the armor plate below me and crawled down in the bucketing plane to sit on the green aluminum bench beside Rand. A pale, thin-faced man anyway, his face in the ghoulish green light of the radar screen was now a skull. A single bullet had come through the plane just forward of the armor on the floor where his foot was braced while he peered into the radar scope, and it had torn off the side of his shoe and foot. It wasn't a mortal wound, unless he bled to death, but it was sure a painful mess. I called Phillips on the intercom. 'Shall I give him an injection of morphine?' (We carried Syrettes in the medical kit.) The answer shocked me. 'No, we will need the radar again.' The logic was obvious, though I didn't think Rand was going to do much more work that night.

I took the opportunity of being in the tunnel to change the ammunition can for the turret gun, a terrible job hunched over in close quarters, the plane rising and falling rapidly, trying to shove a long can weighing about a hundred pounds one minute and ten the next up into a narrow slot. Each time I would get it nearly up to where the retaining latch could catch it, the plane would suddenly rise, and the can and I would go down to the deck or be flung against one of the bulkheads, trying all the time not to step on Rand, sitting there with his teeth gritted tight, or slip in his blood. Finally the ammo can clicked into place and I jumped back into the turret, glad to get out of the confined tunnel, dark and bloody. We had by this time lost the Japanese planes, but a lone Betty drifted under our tail and I got off a few rounds. Phillips, true to form, began searching again. In my heart I wasn't as sure I wanted to find them as he was. The radar was our only chance, but Rand picked up no blips in any direction. He was making heavy going of it by that time and not functioning well, though trying gamely. We were now circling at some distance from the carrier, and I became increasingly disoriented. The second of the two Bettys that had crashed was burning in a long smear of gasoline on the water, and as we turned in the pitch black, I thought the ocean was the sky and the light from the burning plane another plane turning in, in a long curve for a run on us. I called out on the intercom that it was attacking and requested permission – even here this was still the battleship navy – to begin firing. Phillips, using his instruments, put me right side up again. The ship's radar could see both us and the fighters, and the fighter director officer was trying to move us together. At this point Phillips – at O'Hare's request – turned on our running lights, and the fighters, all lighted up themselves like Christmas trees, slid suddenly in, coming down across our tail from below and aft, O'Hare on our starboard side wing one or two hundred feet away, somewhat below, Skon on the port, bright blue in the flare of their exhausts, six guns jutting out of their wings, quite scary. Canopy back, goggles up, yellow Mae West, khaki shirt, and helmet, seated aggressively forward, riding the plane hard, looking like the tough Medal of Honor recipient, American Ace he was, Butch O'Hare's face was sharply illuminated by his canopy light for one brief last moment ...

Looking to my right, I saw a long black cigar shape climb up from below and aft of Skon and swing into formation above us on our starboard side, behind and slightly above O'Hare. Realizing his fatal mistake, he began firing. 'Butch, this is Phil. There's a Jap on your tail. Kernan, open fire.' The intercom went dead as I began shooting back at the Betty, firing by our tail between Skon and O'Hare. The air was filled with gunfire. A long burst nearly emptied my ammunition can at the Betty to our rear, which, as the tracers arced toward him, broke away across our group to disappear in the darkness behind Skon.

Rand, in pain but staring hard out of the tunnel window, had a good view of the exchange of fire, but he missed O'Hare's plane slipping under us, just forward of Skon, and away in the dark. I thought I saw O'Hare reappear off to port, for the briefest glimpse, and then he was gone. Something whitish gray appeared above the water, his parachute or the splash of the plane going in. Skon slid away instantly to follow O'Hare, and then returned to join up on us again when he could not find him ... Phillips took us down to drag the surface for another long half-hour before giving up and making our way about 2100 back to the *Enterprise*. Skon landed first without any trouble. But for us the evening was by no means over. We still had to make a landing on an unlighted carrier deck at night. If it had been done before, it was certainly not standard procedure, and Phillips, despite having a thousand hours as an instrument instructor, had never done it, even in practice. We homed on the white wake that marked the ship in the water, but there was no light anywhere on deck except the fluorescent wands of the landing signal officer standing on the end of the flight deck. We came in too high, and just as Phillips was about to cut the engine the landing signal officer waved us off. Full throttle, nearly stalling out, wheels, flaps, and hook down, we hung for a moment above the deck, neither rising nor falling. In the bright blue light of the exhausts I saw the huge, dark shape of the carrier's island structure just a few feet off our starboard wing, the parked planes on the deck just a few feet below, the men standing there looking up at us. We hung there for an eternity, then picked up speed all at once and flew away to go around again.

The *Enterprise* captain, Matt Gardner, must have known we would never make it with the cumbersome plane in the dark, the pilot tensed to the snapping point, so he courageously turned on the shaded lights that marked out the flight deck for the crucial moment. They could only be seen from low and aft by a plane approaching for a landing, so they didn't reveal the ship very much for very long to a submarine or the Bettys still flying about. This time it worked. We dropped heavily on the deck. The corpsmen took Rand away, Phillips disappeared to talk to the admiral, and I, still crouched on the turret seat, straightened out my legs with great pain and made my way to the head just below the flight deck, where I stood and pissed for what seemed like five minutes. Where did it all come from, on and on, emptying all the accumulated fear and tension out with the water that had built up in the longest three hours of my life, before or since.

Really messy firefights don't sort themselves out in the mind clearly, either sooner or later, and heavy feelings of responsibility and guilt lurk around all combat deaths. Without doubt I had fired at the trailing Japanese plane that tried to join up on us, and he had fired at everything in his range, including O'Hare and us, but had I, blasting away, hit the group commander as well? Like the cigar-shaped Betty sliding out of the darkness to our rear, guilt felt still for my mother's death slid across my mind. No one else on the flight had any doubts about what had happened, though we all saw the action from different angles. But my question would shortly be voiced openly in an unpleasant way by a newspaperman.

My first encounter with media arrogance came before I was even out of the head. He came charging in and while I was still standing at the urinal trough asked, 'What happened? Where were they? How many? Where is O'Hare? How many did you shoot down?' The tone was hoarsely aggressive, and I discovered that I felt that the night flight was a complicated and deeply personal thing. I certainly didn't feel like talking about it to anyone as abrasive and unpleasant as this man. He bored right in, though, and began to try to construct the scandal he wanted. 'How far away from O'Hare were you when he was hit? Were you shooting too?' And then, there it was: 'Did you hit him?'

Letting me know that he was somehow an official who had a right to news and that anything of interest belonged to the public, especially his newspaper, he played on my doubts and shock to try to get some sudden, unconsidered remark that could be gotten by the censor and turned into sensational fare for his readers. If he had come at me with more sympathy I might have tried to tell him how mixed-up it all was, but his bullying got my back up, and I walked away shouting, 'Get the hell away from me.'

He went off muttering about reporting me to the officers, as if I had broken some kind of rule by not telling his newspaper all, but he never came back.

Lieutenant Commander Otto C. Romanelli, USN Rtd., USS *Lexington* (CV-16)
from *Blue Ghost Memoirs*

On 4 December 1943, USS *Lexington* participated in air strikes on Roi Island, Kwajalein and Wotje Atolls, where many Japanese aircraft were based. Flying the new Hellcat gave the US pilots combat superiority, but at midnight the carrier was hit by a Kate bomber.

At that time, my Battle Station was in the Gunnery Control Center, an open area in the island structure above the Navigation Bridge; I was monitoring 'Bogey' reports coming from CIC (Combat Information Center). Many 'Bogeys' were all around and above us. We kept shifting our fire control directors and guns onto the most threatening, closer-in targets. As targets advanced to within range, our 5-inch anti-aircraft battery opened fire with a 'BOOM, BOOM, BOOM' that awakened feelings of both excitement and danger. As the targets got closer, the 40-mm battery opened fire with a sharp 'SPLAT, SPLAT, SPLAT,' which heightened the trepidation. Further in, the 20-mm battery opened up with a frantic 'RAT, TAT, TAT' and it was time to hold one's breath and say a few prayers.

For some time we went through a number of these firing sequences and we were fortunate to escape damage; the feelings of danger eased as time wore on. However, eventually there appeared a Kate, armed with a torpedo, undeterred by our firepower. The torpedo hit and exploded with a dull THUD. The deck beneath our feet started shaking from side to side and up and down in a sort of spiral motion like a giant shudder.

'MY GOD, WE ARE HIT!!! We failed to shoot down that Kate!'

There were pangs of remorse that our team failed to protect the other shipmates who were relying on us. There was smoke from the fantail. The ship was going around in circles and we couldn't straighten it out. We were sitting ducks with all those flares glaring down on us. We wondered if Kate's brothers would now come in to finish us off.

What would it be like to have to abandon ship?

Make sure your life jacket is secure.

But wait ...

'This is your Captain speaking ... leave the worrying to me. I got you in here and I'm going to get you out. I'm counting on every man to do his job and I will pull us through.'

Good old Felix! Fear and trepidation were dispelled by a determination to do our best and see the thing through! The task group was ordered to circle the *Lexington* in the opposite direction to protect her from further attack.

The torpedo had sheared off the outboard starboard propeller, jammed the inboard propeller shaft and had incapacitated the steering gear, locking the rudder at 30 degrees left. That was why we were going around in a circle and couldn't straighten out. Through the sound-powered (voice-powered) telephone system, the crew stationed in the steering gear compartment reported the extent of the damage. The only hope of straightening the rudder was a small, manually-operated hydraulic pump that had been installed by a prescient engineering officer as an alternative for just such an emergency.

Meanwhile, the compartment above the steering gear compartment was flooding and the compartment atmosphere was being poisoned with escaping Freon gas. Breathing was very difficult and the crew requested permission to abandon their station. The Captain said that he would leave the decision up to the crew, trusting their judgment between duty and personal safety. But he said he wanted them to report to him first if they decided to abandon their station. The crew decided in favor of duty and remained on station long enough to complete their mission; they were then rescued and rushed to sick bay.

Captain Edward Steichen, who was onboard on a photography mission, later remarked to Captain Stump what a wonderful act of trust and leadership it was for him to leave the decision to the crew. He asked what Stump would have done if the crew had decided otherwise. The reply was, 'Then I would have had no choice but to order them to stay.'

7
1944

The entry into active service of increasing numbers of escort carriers and MAC ships hamstrung the U-boats in the Atlantic and Arctic and caused losses vastly disproportionate to their successes. It was not that the carrier-borne aircraft sank dozens upon dozens of them – they sank comparatively few – but their very presence disrupted the submarines, and they could call up the escort sloops to attack them. In addition, they shot down the Luftwaffe's Ju 88s and Condors that were the eyes and ears of the U-boats. Convoy protection was a team effort. The escort carriers consisted primarily of British-built, Royal Navy ships such as HMS *Activity*; US-built, RN-operated ships typified by HMS *Fencer*; and US-built, US-operated carriers including USS *Bogue*. MAC ships were not strong enough for Arctic weather conditions – conditions that caused serious problems for the British-built escort carriers with their steel decks.

1944 saw a final series of Fleet Air Arm operations to sink *Tirpitz* and release Allied naval units for other theatres. The battleship had been repaired after the midget submarine attack of September 1943 and was preparing to put to sea from her anchorage in Altenfjord when the first operation, codenamed 'Tungsten' took place, involving HMS *Victorious* and HMS *Furious*, together with the Escort carriers HMS *Emperor*, HMS *Fencer*, HMS *Pursuer* and HMS *Searcher*. Six direct hits were scored by the first wave of Barracudas, eight by the second – despite the smokescreen going up. However, *Tirpitz*'s thick armour protected her from serious harm. Heavy defences and lookout were thereafter maintained and Operation 'Mascot' in July resulted in a single near-miss, then, despite the smokescreen, two hits were recorded on the 24th. During August Operations 'Goodwood I', 'II', 'III' and 'IV' were carried out, and during the last of these the Barracudas obtained two hits. One 1,600lb bomb penetrated the armoured deck and would have sunk the battleship if it had exploded. But *Tirpitz* never moved again and the RAF was able to finish her off using Lancasters carrying the 'Tallboy' bomb designed by Barnes Wallace (of 'Dambusters' fame).

The Allies in the Mediterranean now concentrated on driving German forces out of the South of France, Italy and Greece, with escort carriers providing air cover. Some of the Royal Navy carriers transferred to service in the Indian Ocean or prepared for a move to the Far East where the carrier war was entering a decisive stage. They would form the largest carrier task force that the Royal Navy had ever assembled, though it would find itself dwarfed by the carrier groups of a US Navy that, since the previous autumn, had been on all-out offensive against the Japanese.

Early in 1944, US carrier groups successfully targeted air bases on Wotje, Kwajalein and Maleoelap and ships at the naval base of Truk. Then the US turned its attention to the key islands of Guam, Saipan and Tinian in the Marianas – islands that would bring mainland Japan into range of their heavy bombers. To counter the American invasion the Japanese assembled their most powerful force, including the carriers *Shokaku*, *Zuikaku*, *Junyo*, *Hiyo*, *Taiho* (Vice Admiral Ozawa's flagship), *Ryujo*, *Chiyoda*, *Chitose* and *Zuiho*. Against them, Admiral Spruance's Fifth Fleet comprised Task Force 58: five task groups with 15 fleet and light fleet carriers divided between four of them. These four groups also included cruisers, light cruisers and destroyers, while seven battleships and four cruisers made up a fifth task group. What those statistics fail to show, however, is the vast gulf in training, experience and technology of the US pilots and their Hellcats over the Japanese Zeros.

However, Spruance did not hold all the aces. Although warned by submarine of the approach of the Japanese fleet, he had little information about its progress. He decided not to send Task Force 58, under Vice Admiral Mark Mitscher, in search of them, knowing that Ozawa might be setting a trap for him that would leave Vice Admiral Turner's Joint Expeditionary Force unprotected. Early on 19 June carrier-based aircraft fought with Japanese land-based planes but, after shooting down more than 30, were recalled to take on the Japanese carrier-launched planes. The result was carnage as US pilots shot the enemy out of the sky. After a pilot allegedly referred to the action as being like a turkey shoot; the Battle of the Philippine Sea came to be known as the 'Great Marianas Turkey Shoot'. During late afternoon the following day, Mitscher sent more than 200 bombers, dive-bombers and fighters to attack the enemy. Japanese aircraft losses were such that that their few remaining carriers would be incapable of returning to strength. Midway had halted the hitherto unstoppable Japanese advance in 1944; now the Battle of the Philippine Sea arguably sealed the US victory.

The next major US goal was the liberation of the Philippines, commencing with a landing at Leyte Gulf. The invasion force comprised Seventh Fleet under the command of Vice Admiral Kinkaid: more than 700 ships, including three Task Forces, each of six escort carriers, plus their destroyer protection, designed to attack land targets, defend themselves and and to bomb Japanese submarines. Protection against the Japanese fleet was assigned to Halsey's Third Fleet. This was actually the renamed Fifth Fleet, now rotationally under Halsey's overall command, comprising Task Force 38 commanded by Mitscher and subdivided into four powerful Task Groups.

Against this, Japan prepared to throw one fleet carrier and three escort carriers with less than 120 aircraft between them. However, the IJN still included 9 battleships and 20 cruisers. Its plan was for Ozawa's small carrier force to lure away the US Third Fleet with all its fleet and light carriers while the battleships and cruisers, divided into two fleets, would attack the landings from different directions: Rear Admiral Kurita via the San Bernardino Strait and the island of Samar; the Central Force of Rear Admiral Nishimura via the Surigao Strait.

On 22 October Halsey sent TG38.1 and TG38.4 back to the base at Ulithi to reprovision. The following day, two scouting US submarines sighted and caused serious damage to Kurita's Centre Force. The weaker of Halsey's absent task groups was recalled, but the stronger, 38.1, was not recalled until the 24th. As Kurita pressed on, Ozawa launched an attack on Halsey's TG38.3. Halsey accepted the bait and sailed out of the San Bernardino Strait, without telling Kinkaid that his fleet was now entirely unprotected. Nevertheless, during the battle of the Surigao Strait, Seventh Fleet comprehensively defeated Nishimura's ships and also saw off another force commanded by Vice Admiral Shima. The weight of Kurita's fleet, spearheaded by the battleship *Yamato*, fell on the three CVE Task Forces, known by their Task Force call signs as Taffy One, Taffy Two and Taffy Three. The small carriers and their destroyers and destroyer escorts pulled off the unthinkable and forced Kurita to give up the engagement.

Meanwhile, Halsey's three available Task Groups were off the island of Luzon and heading for Ozawa's carriers, which they located just after 0700 on 24th. At the Battle of Engaño the fleet carrier *Zuikaku*, Ozawa's flagship, and two of the three light carriers were sunk; the third was put out of action. At 1000 a message from Nimitz was received demanding to know where Task Force 34 was. (Halsey had created TF34 from within TF38). Halsey duly turned round, but too late to intercept Kurita's battleships and heavy cruisers, which were able to escape.

As far as carriers were concerned, the IJN was finished, but until the end of the war the US Navy would have to contend with suicide attacks by land-based aircraft such as the new 'Judy'.

NORTH SEA AND ARCTIC

HMS *Victorious*, Operation 'Tungsten'
ADM1 15806

From the Commanding Officer, HMS *Victorious*, 5 April 1944, to the Vice Admiral Second in Command, Home Fleet ...

3. Cold weather on the Northward trip caused me considerable anxiety regarding the serviceability of the aircraft necessarily parked on deck. *Victorious'* flight deck is very wet in any weather, and the spray and speed were freezing on the deck, and it is yet to be proved that the Barracuda and Corsair types can stand North Atlantic winter conditions on deck with wings folded, not only as regards condition of the planes and flaps but on account of the immense amount of delicate 'guts' that are exposed to the elements with wings folded. I am no aviator, but it looks thoroughly unseamanlike to me. However, thanks to the reduced number deliberately carried on board, it was generally possible to park them with wings spread, the only prudent course to meet winter and Atlantic conditions.

In order to obviate starting difficulties with the exposed Corsairs, engines were started and run up every 2 hours. All these and other special measures taken succeeded in ensuring full serviceability at zero hour.

4. As will be seen from the Air Narrative, the complicated process of warming-up and ranging had to be gone through before launching the 1st strike, owing to the plain fact that *Victorious* was carrying more aircraft than she was designed to operate. The same difficulties arose in arming-up with mixed loads: in many cases the bombing-up party had to chase their aircraft through the hangar, up one lift and along the flight deck, owing to changes in the elaborate bombing-up procedure caused by last-minute unforeseen servicing requirements. These matters are typical examples of how overcrowding, particularly if two types of aircraft have to be handled, reacts on the timely execution of a programme ...

Signed Michael M Denny
Captain

Report by 52 T.B.R. Wing Leader:

1. The Second Striking Force consisted of 19 Barracudas of 52 T.B.R. Wing. Between 0525 and 0535 all aircraft took off, with the exception of one which developed starting trouble and was struck down. The squadron was formed up at between 50 and 200 feet when the wing took departure at 0537 on a course of 150 degrees.

2. At this stage the information was good although difficulty was experienced in keeping formation in line astern at so low a height. Nevertheless, when the wing was put into 'Vic' formation all the difficulties in keeping good formation disappeared.

3. A smoke float was dropped at intervals of a minute for 3 minutes after departure to give to the escorting fighters some indication of the course taken by the Second Strike.

4. The weather was fine, sea slight, swell nil. Cloud over target less than 1/10 at about 15,000 feet.

5. Initial approach from 10,000 feet was made with the T.B.R. Wing in a shallow double 'Vic' which, as no fighters were seen, was altered to two double columns when flak was encountered to facilitate evasion. The approach was continued so as to bring the target on the port bow, the starboard column being manoeuvred slightly back and up so as to keep the leader's column roughly between it and to the target.

6. Speed from crossing the coast was 165 knots (true) for about 12 miles. This height was slowly reduced to increase the speed to 195 knots (true). After forming columns, this was increased two about 210 knots (true) and the final attack dive was commenced to from between 7,500 and 7,000 feet.

Hellcats went down to attack heavy gun positions when these opened fire and Wildcats attacked the *Tirpitz* herself, immediately prior to the main attack. The final dive was carried out in quick succession, port column diving first. The whole attack occupied about 1 minute.

8. Medium dive bombing except aircraft carrying 1600 15 A.P. bombs which

carried out steep glide bombing. Mean height of release and angle of dive are as follows: Aircraft carrying 1,600lb A.P. bomb – 3000 feet – 45 degs, remainder slightly under 3000 feet – 50 to 60 degs.

9. Considerable close range flak mostly in the form of a box barrage round the target. *Tirpitz* had ceased firing by the time the last aircraft dived. Fire with close range weapons was opened much too early.

10. One Barracuda was hit whilst over the target. It is believed that this aircraft carried out it's [sic] attack in spite of this as it made it's [sic]get away with the remainder and was seen diving vertically on to the mountainside in flames.

11. A large round smoke screen had been laid from generators all round the target area and from the *Tirpitz* herself. This was visible 40 miles away. It did not interfere with bombing but must have hampered close range weapons considerably.

12. Unquestionably strafing attacks by fighters and the use of powerful blast bombs by the first few aircraft are of the utmost value in ensuring the safe arrival of the armour piercing bombs carried by the latter half of the attacking forces.

13. After clearing the coast on a course of 335 degs N, two destroyers were sighted and later the fleet itself.

We landed on without mishap.

Signed
Lt Cdr (A) V. Rance, RN.

Report by Fighter Wing Leader:

Eleven Corsairs were ranged; took off; formed up and took departure with the First Strike without difficulty. By the time that height was reached the sun was well up and on the port bow but cross cover was easily given by flying at 11,000 feet on the down sun side of the Strike. In spite of the excellent visibility aircraft below were difficult to see against the 9/10 snow covered ground, owing to the slow speed of the Strike, compared to that of the escort, the force was fairly loose and some difficulty might have been experienced in identifying friend from foe if enemy fighters had once got into the beehive.

Long range tanks were jettisoned between Alta and Lang Fiords after one hours and five minutes flying.

2. The *Admiral von Tirpitz* was sighted when about 5' SW. When the Strike went down Corsairs swept up to Talvik and back to a point 5' SW of the target at 10,000. When the target was first sighted, she was beginning to make smoke and during that sweep smoke procedures came into action all round Kaa Fiord. Bomb strikes were seen on the target by some fighters and a large tanker was seen to be on fire amidships.

3. Corsairs swept North to the entrance of Lang Fiord and round [Rafsbotn] where two destroyers were getting under way; then South over the airfield where no activity was observed; round the southern end of Kaa Fiord and

across the the centre of Lang Fiord. Flak experienced all round Kaa Fiord was accurate for height but astern. No fire was observed from the two destroyers, which with a large tanker were lying at the head of Lang Fiord. A medium sized cargo vessel was lying stopped half way down the fiord.

4. At 0600, about 30 minutes after the attack, course was set to return to that base. Over Oxfiord [Oksfjord], about 9000 good two way communication was established with the ship and it was reported that the whole target area was obscured by smoke. The smoke was high enough to cover the ridge stretching from 400 370 to the SW and extended from the head of the fjord to the entrance where it was spreading into Alten Fiord and dissipating.

4. All aircraft landed on by [illegible]. Longest sortie was two hours and thirty minutes. Least fuel remaining 60 Imperial gallons, this aircraft had made the whole flight with undercarriage fairings open.

Signed F. R. A. Turnbull
Lieutenant Commander (Acting) R N

Sergeant S. H. Brown, RAF, HMS *Activity*
from his diary, Fleet Air Arm Museum

The escort carrier HMS *Activity* had spent most of 1943 as a deck landing training carrier, but in 1944 she became a convoy escort, initially in the Atlantic (see later in the chapter). In March, along with HMS *Tracker*, she escorted Arctic Convoy JW/RA58 from Loch Ewe to Murmansk. The convoy included the cruiser USS *Milwaukee*, which was being handed over to the Soviet Navy. The two escort carriers brought down six German aircraft, and four U-boats were sunk: U-961 by HMS *Starling*, *U-355* by HMS *Beagle* and HMS *Tracker*, U-360 by HMS *Keppel* and U-288 by aircraft from both *Tracker* and *Activity*. Distant cover was provided by the Home Fleet, including its carriers, which was engaged on Operation 'Tungsten' against *Tirpitz*. (In the interests of readability, some punctuation has been added to Brown's diary entries.)

29th	Joined a convoy of 55 ships – speed 10 knots, leather sea boots and Duffel coats issued. It must be cold where we're going. *Tracker* and sloops and destroyers. *Howe, Anson, Vic, Furious* and 4 escort carriers 100 miles in rear – bait for *Tirpitz*.
30th	This morning one of our fighters shot down a Ju 88. He was giving subs our position; nice work.
31st	Our fighters got two Fw 200s – HMS *Tracker*, who is also with us, also got one. One of the *Tracker*'s machines crashed landing-on and caused a nasty fire – pilot killed but fire rapidly got under control. We have Killer Walker's escort group with us again – they got a U-boat today.
April 1st	Another Jerry shot down today – a B&V 138 – one of our fighters went over the side landing on – pilot picked up frozen but

otherwise O.K. He thawed out O.K.

April 2nd	Our fighters shot down another Ju 88 today. *Tracker*'s Avengers damaged a U-boat. It is getting very cold now with plenty of snow.
April 3rd	Estimated 12 U-boats round convoy; more depth charges than that going off all day long. With the help of *Tracker* we got one U-boat; the others were unsuccessful with their attacks – no ships lost.
April 4th	Arrived at Kola Bay, Russia, this morning, the first Russian convoy to get through undamaged.
April 5th	Still in Kola Bay – looks very picturesque – plenty of snow about, pretty cold.
April 6th	Still in Kola Bay, hope to leave tomorrow.
April 7th	Left Harbour this morning and joined up with convoy on our way back, not sorry to leave Joe's country – too desolate in this part.
April 8th	We expected trouble today but things were very quiet.
April 9th	Day began with 22° of frost – talk about cold – carried out usual patrols – machines smeared with de-icing paste* to prevent ice forming on wings.
April 10th	Still very cold – wind goes through you on the flight deck.
April 11th	Jerry not having much luck with his U-boats – tried releasing mines ahead of the convoy hoping we would run into them but we safely avoided them. We left convoy at 8 p.m. this evening and steamed in on our own – one of the escorts, HMS *Onslow*, had three tin fish fired at her but safely avoided them.
12th April	All quiet today.
13th April	Arrived back at Scapa Flow.

Frederick George 'Pat' Oikle, Seaman, HMS *Activity*
IWM Sound Archive Reference 17529

Pat Oikle was also on that convoy, as the Batsman's Assistant.

I was on the flight deck crew. I had to take messages from the bridge and give them to the batsman. We had no radio ... And they were flying low through the ships of the convoy and swooping over the ships, firing at us. Of course, we were taller than most of them so they could get at us. We sustained quite a bit of damage but we eventually got into Kola Inlet which is ... at the bottom of the river. The convoy went into Murmansk. We had a couple of shore outings – we were allowed to go ashore, but very hostile, very hostile. All army. I don't think I saw a civilian while I was there ... I had an incident where I'm walking across the snow, and I went round this building and there is a chap in front of me shoving a bayonet at me, and it couldn't have been any more than a couple of inches from me and he shouted something, I've no idea what it was, so I left.

---

* De-icing paste was one of several de-icing compounds made by the British company Kilfrost which still specialises in such products.

I think generally speaking they didn't want us ashore … We took an American cruiser up there for them, the *Milwaukee*, to give to them, so we should have been described as friends.

We stocked up with aviation fuel, water, stores … And within 48 hours we set sail again, and about eight days out we met up with another convoy. We were going to Russia again. No respite at all. I can't remember anyone that came off a Russian convoy and within hours [was] back on another one. But two days out the weather worsened and there was no chance of us flying any aircraft off because the temperature dropped dramatically and we had a time when we were chipping the ice off the flight deck. It got just slightly better, and they decided they were going to fly aircraft off … The aircraft stooging round was still there, even on the second convoy … I got a message from the bridge to give to one of the pilots, and I spoke to the batsman about it, and it was my job to convey any messages to the pilots as well. He said: 'On your way'. I suppose, looking back, it's silly now – it was very cold, it was a heck of a job getting the aircraft ranged up ready to go, and I possibly wasn't thinking as straight as I should have been, and instead of going under the wing I decided to go out and go through the middle, which I did. And as I was passing the airscrews – they were turning, obviously, warming up ready to take off, I felt something hit my arm, and I thought: 'that's stupid' … There were nets all round the aircraft flight deck and that's where the flight deck crew used to stay when they weren't manoeuvring aircraft on deck. And I just thought someone had thrown something at me. I gave the message and went back, and the batsman, when I got back, said: 'That was close!', and I said: ' What was?' And he said: 'The airscrew'. I said: ' O my God, that was close – I didn't realise.'

I had walked into an airscrew. At the time I couldn't feel my arm, and things were going on. Sick Bay was always working pretty hard. I carried on … I had a big watch coat – that's a big black coat that goes right down to the ankles for warmth. And [my arm] started swelling up. So I said to the batsman 'My arm: I can't feel it. I think I've done something to it. I don't know what.' He said: 'Well, get a replacement and get down to sick bay'. So I went down, and by the time I got down there I could feel it: it was like a tennis ball. There was trouble going on and nobody could look at me. Other people were a lot worse than me, through different incidents, and I thought well, I might as well go back and I said: 'It's no good down there, I'm in the way' so we carried on. The aircraft never did get off. They couldn't get them off, couldn't fly them because the ice was forming again and they wouldn't have been able to keep on a straight line on the flight deck to take-off off, so they were shut down … The batsman went back and I went below again, and it swelled up again but I never got to sick bay to get it treated. But it went down and I don't think I have had a problem with it since. I realise the air screw was turning in a clockwise direction which threw me off. If it had been turning in the opposite direction, I've been told since, I would have been dragged on to it. So I was very lucky.

Lieutenant Bruce Vibert, DSC, CD, RCN(R), HMS *Fencer*
Communication with the Editor

For the second convoy, RA 59, the new, American-built carrier, HMS *Fencer* replaced *Tracker* as *Activity's* consort.

The object was to go to the Arctic with two carriers and escort vessels, to collect the merchant ships which had scattered across the Arctic over the months for one reason or another – damage, engine failure and so on. There were several of them in Murmansk and we had been sent up to collect them. On top of this we had also been sent to collect a gentleman called Admiral Levchenko. Now Admiral Levchenko and his staff came aboard us; we were bringing them back to England to pick up the *Royal Sovereign*, the old battleship, which we were giving to them. And the crew were scattered among the convoy. So there we were in Murmansk, not enjoying it – actually we were north of Murmansk and at Kola Inlet – a horrible place, I may say.

I can remember walking the flight deck when we were in Kola at anchor. While taking the air on the flight deck, Captain Bentinck called over to me and we walked up and down for a time and I can always remember him saying: 'you know, we're going to be fighting these people one of these days.' He was referring to the Russians. We weren't treated well while in Russia. The aircrew were allowed on shore provided we kept in crocodile. We were watched over by soldiers with guns. They were very suspicious of us; they thought we were all spies.

Eventually we sailed, and as expected we were picked up shortly after sailing by a German aircraft. Bear in mind we were in easy reach of German airfields and warship anchorages. We were attacked, I think it was by 12 boats, and, this being April–May, night was only half light: it didn't get dark: we had proper day and half light, and there were snow storms and ice. So we flew round the clock because we, being American-built, had a wooden flight deck with steam vents running transversely which helped us keep the snow clear. The other carrier – British built, steel deck – couldn't cope with the amount of snow on deck, and said: sorry, got to stop flying, so we took over their job as well. So we worked for 3½ days round the clock.

We were then 12 aircraft, Swordfish with Wildcats, round the clock, up and down, up and down, keeping them down. Soon as we passed over them they popped up again. They kept on driving at us and I think one of the reasons why they kept on popping up so soon was because they were desperate. I do believe they were a different bunch from those who were in the North Atlantic. They weren't battle savvy, they were in constricted waters, they knew the country was in trouble, they were desperate people, and how they would get out onto that U-boat casing and bang away! and I may tell you they are master craftsmen with guns: their reputation with Ack Ack is well deserved. I guess that the crews were very different from those in the early days in the Atlantic; they had probably been in battleships or cruisers or something like that beforehand. We know that, of course, they were conscripted. They were young and inexperienced but they were very daring, very dashing.

I said three and a half days, and that's exactly what [the U-boats] did. They clung to us until we were not all that far north of the Shetlands. We sank three of them. Now the one I dealt with – well, it was a pair, but I got one with the rocket. Bear in mind that the convoy is hugging the ice barrier, making it difficult for our escorts with ASDIC. So our escorts are not picking things up. We took off from the carrier for a patrol and in no time, call from the back: got a contact, such and such a bearing. I did exactly what I was told (the captain of an aircraft in the Navy is the Observer in the back): *Climb into cloud, and if you turn 90 degrees to port and dive, the boat'll be right in front of you*. I did exactly that: dived, and there wasn't one: there was a couple. They were having a little chit chat. The furthest one was facing where we were coming from, obviously saw what was happening, and by the time I fired [my rockets] it was half submerged.

Now the rocket is interesting. The thing is, that one should be in a thirty degree dive, one should have a bit of altitude and one should then aim *short* of the target, but *ahead* of it. Now on entry into the water, the rocket – and these are sixty-pound, armour piercing, remember, and you are releasing them in pairs – levels out and it actually gives it the best strike angle. But I am told by those who have seen it that whether you do it that way or directly onto the boat, it's curtains. It's such a remarkable thing. I carried out that attack, 30 degrees, range about 1000 yards. At the time, no evidence that it worked. But RT Intercept later told that it had been sunk. I personally did not know until six or seven months afterwards. I did a third, that was a rocket business, but from too much of an angle and I felt sure they would have glanced off.

The submarine was *U-674*.

We now come to an interesting chap in our squadron called Cooper. He's the only F.A.A. man to have sunk 2 U-boats without any help, and he did it by disobeying orders, as so often happens, with depth charges. On one of these attacks after landing they picked an unexploded 20mm shell out of the mainframe and threw it overboard. I've often wondered: did he catch it as it reached the top of its trajectory and was about to fall? After all, it's only made of insubstantial stuff, this aeroplane, and certainly things would pass through without doing any harm.

One cheeky blighter must have seen that I wasn't watching properly, that I hadn't swung the nose of my aircraft. I was at 1500 feet or something. He must have seen me and though *oh, he can't see me; I'll have a go at him*. The first thing I knew I was *bang bang* to the right of me, *bang bang* to the left, *bang bang* up there – probably underneath as well – and I thought: this is a very bad thing. And the first time you get this sort of thing happen to you one feels insulted. Anyhow, I got the heck out of it, pretty smartly, following orders which were these: If you're only carrying depth charges, don't go for a U-boat on the surface, particularly in the late years because by then they had the whole bandstand stuck on the backside to fire at you. You wait. You call up for a fighter and then you go and do something. I waited. Before the fighter arrived the U-boat dived and I was too late to catch him.

This is a feature that explains why our naval aircraft only managed just over 30 boats worldwide in the Second World War. Because the aircraft involved were almost invariably the Swordfish. It was too slow. Coming from downwind of the target, it takes you all day to get up to it. It gives him a lot of time to line up on you. So we were told, you call up a fighter and carry out a combined attack, which in theory works well – if you have the right aircraft – and in fact the Americans showed that it did work very well because they did it on the New York–Gibraltar run. Eight of their escort carriers, including names like *Bogue*, *Guadalcanal*, sank 32 boats by the combined attack method using the Avenger and the Wildcat. We had the Swordfish and the Wildcat. The difference in approach speeds was such that to get it right was almost impossible.

To the best of my knowledge that particular convoy was the only time when the Russians ever got a close look at the West and its carrier operations. Afterwards they had to build their own *Kiev* class and learn for themselves. They were interested, definitely, in what we were doing. We had to keep sentries standing outside some of our spaces, because they were very curious as to what was inside.

Although we were flying day and night each of us had one of their staff to look after. I was given the political officer. I don't know why. He had, I think, been to Moscow University and he knew his Dickens. As I say, we were flying all the time and you can imagine 12 Swordfish for three and a half days round the clock makes a lot of flying so we didn't have much time to join these fellows. They, when the bar was open, would be there. Now spiritous stuff is very cheap, or was, aboard a warship, and they enjoyed it and they understood the stuff and they used it. We, incidentally, at sea, never drank unless one was absolutely certain that the following morning one would be safely in port. Anyhow, we got our own back. I can recall going ashore in Gourock, in the Clyde, with some of these Russian gentlemen and we took them to – I think the name of the lady was Two-Ton Tessie O-Shea or something like that, who ran a hotel bar overlooking the Tail of the Bank* which is in Gourock, and we plied these gentlemen with our good beer. My last memory of them is of a 15cwt truck outside, with tailboard up and a row of faces hanging over the back. Anyway, they got the *Royal Sovereign* and we were told that they had difficulty manoeuvring her under the Forth Bridge, which didn't surprise me.

Geoff Shelton, Seaman, HMS *Vindex*
Communication with the Editor

Shelton was part of Convoy JW 59, which escorted the former HMS *Royal Sovereign* from Scapa Flow to Russia in August 1944.

* Assembly area for convoys in World War II.

Looking out over the grey waters one could see other ships preparing for sea, and the sound of many cables being hauled through the hawse pipes heralded the news that another operation was about to begin, though why so many ships? This suggested that something bigger than a hunt for U-boats in the Atlantic was about to take place.

After an hour at sea the noise in the mess deck abruptly ceased as the tannoy came to life. 'This is your Captain speaking'. Then he went on to inform us that in the early hours of the morning we would be meeting up with a convoy and escorting it to the north Russian port of Murmansk. Shipmates who had prior experience of these convoys fell silent and turned pale. One particular old sailor kept on saying, 'Well it won't be as bad as the Malta ones.' For my part I had no experience of either but from listening into the discussions taking place I soon realised that it may not be too healthy. But as the conversation went on each story became a little more embellished, well I hope it was embellished. But whether it was or it wasn't, my initial apprehension was quickly replaced by fear.

My eavesdropping was interrupted by a messenger, 'Anyone here named Shelton?' he said.

'Yes, that's me,' I replied.

'You're wanted in the Master at Arms office.' Somehow the fact that the master at arms wanted to see me overrode the fear that I had so recently acquired of the Russian convoy ahead. Why does one always feel guilty when authority desires, nay demands, your presence? The Master wasn't there but the Jaunty, Regulating Petty Officer Sandy Lane, was.

'Shelton,' he said 'I'm going to elevate you'.

'Me, Sir,' I meekly replied. Teenage or ordinary seaman always called anyone wearing a peaked cap 'Sir'. 'Are you making me up to Able Seaman?'

'No,' he said.

'Surely, Sir, not a Leading Seaman.' I asked. My mind was already racing ahead of my tongue. I could already see myself attired as an Admiral before this trip was through. I was grinning at my own thoughts when he brought me down to earth.

'I said that I was elevating you, I didn't say I was promoting you. The masthead lookout has reported sick so you are his replacement. Report to the stores and get yourself a kitted out with cold weather gear.'

I don't know why I said 'Thank you, Sir' but there was no sincerity in my weakened voice.

Down into the stores they gave me a fur lined leather hat with muffs that came down over my ears. I received a heavy canvas coat lined with sheepskin, a pair of fur lined gauntlets and a pair of leather sea boots.

Back in the mess they all thought it was hilarious, but the bit that niggled me was the fact that in the mess there was another lad of similar age to me but shorter and with a quite an athletic figure. He used to prance around wearing simulated leopard skin trunks, doing his keep-fit exercises. An old boy in the next mess (any one over 30 was old) had kept looking at this lad and giving him a wink. At the time I was too naive to know the meaning of this behaviour but with hindsight (maybe that's the wrong word) – but in retrospect I now recognise that the look would have been classed as a leering lustful one. But I digress, this fit young man, as soon as he heard the Skipper's speech, reported sick and he was the masthead lookout I had to replace.

I turned in early as I was due to keep the first watch at 0400, but I didn't sleep, just lay there thinking about what the lads had been saying and dwelling on what might lay ahead. Occasionally one's thoughts were interrupted by a rat running along the deckhead girders just above your hammock. I guess survival was a mutual interest we both shared.

Just before 0400 my hammock was shaken and a voice in a loud whisper said, 'come on Joey, time to turn out.' I don't know why they all called me Joey, but somehow the name stuck. I swung out down to the deck and quietly put on all my new gear. The mess deck was quiet except for a cacophony of snores coming from within many hammocks. The emergency lights were dim but nevertheless showed the chrysalis-shaped Micks [hammocks] swinging in gentle unison as the old ship rolled from side to side.

I reported to the Gunnery Office to pick up some binoculars and then made my way to the upper deck. The sky was a collection of angry black clouds forever changing shape as strong winds scattered them over the ocean. To get to the mast one had to go over the flight deck, then clamber up and over the side of the bridge before making the ascent. The Skipper was on the bridge. In fact I can never remember him not being there. With him was the Navigating Officer, a young Subby, the Yeoman and a messenger. No one spoke and the only sound was the regular and monotonous thump of the engines, the wind whistling through the aerials and the noise of the waves crashing into the bows.

The mast was of geodetic construction with the iron ladder going up the centre. And a small square hole at the top opened out onto a platform. Towards the stern were the radar aerials, and extending about 9 foot forrard was the lookout position. A narrow ledge about 9 inches wide meant you had to walk crabwise with stanchions coming up to your knees. In rough weather this was a precarious manoeuvre. Arriving at your post there was the canvas baffle about 4 foot high to protect you from the elements. I might add that it wasn't very successful. Behind was a construction of sheet metal which was intended to protect us from strafing aircraft.

There was always two of us on duty at the same time, and even then we were only allowed to do one hour up and one down, and then, in a 4 hour watch, we would do the second hour. In the winter in the Arctic one hour was more than enough. In our one hour off we would go to the galley and get a fanny full of Kye [a container of hot chocolate] which we would then distribute to all the lookout and gunnery crews.

Visibility was bad and except on a moonlit night you could rarely see the other ships, but we knew that we would be meeting up with the merchant ships in the middle of the night, but up the stick we, unlike those who had the benefit of radar, did not know if the meeting had taken place, but then as the dawn was breaking we could identify ghostly shapes running parallel to us on either side. When it became lighter we could see the entire convoy. There were 34 merchant ships within a circle of destroyers, corvettes and frigates which like protective sheepdogs were constantly scurrying to and fro.

From my perch up top it looked as though the entire ocean was covered in ships. I had such a panoramic view it nearly took your breath away, and then suddenly astern of one of the merchant ships I saw a periscope and then another and another. I yelled down the voice pipe to the bridge only to be assured that what I could see was the masts of 12 Russian P. T. boats that were manned by Russian sailors and had come over from the USA and were being delivered under our escort to Murmansk.

Lieutenant Nigel Matthews, 828 Squadron, HMS *Implacable*
Communication with the Editor

Completion of *Implacable* had been delayed; her sister, *Indefatigable* was already in service by the time Matthews joined the brand new carrier in the September of 1944.

I flew as an Observer in Fairey Barracudas, torpedo x bombers – God help us all! –and then in Grumman Avengers. Barracudas were really horrendous aircraft. They were supposed to be UK's answer to American naval aviation aircraft, but in fact the Americans had built some marvellous aircraft for carrier operations including: Avengers, Helldivers, Corsairs and Hellcats. All were great aeroplanes because they were rugged, and, moreover, when landing on, you could see out of the front, which you couldn't in aircraft that had an inline engine such as the Barracuda had. But we started life on *Implacable* with these Barracudas, which were intended to be highly versatile. They had flaps which went down for landing and up for dive brakes, so you could control the speed of the dive, and to be fair, they were very good at that. Their wings folded, they had a Rolls Royce engine, and, unlike the Swordfish, they had an enclosed cockpit. On the debit side, they had a weak undercarriage and they looked like nothing on earth; they weren't a lovely aircraft like the Spitfire/Seafire.

In late October 1944 we carried out one final operational sortie before *Implacable* joined the fleet in the Pacific, and it took place off Norway's Lofoten Islands. On the 28th we sank a merchant ship, the *Karmøy*, at Lødingen, and, as we turned away, soldiers on the end of the breakwater opened fire with automatic anti-aircraft guns and hit us. Fortunately, although they damaged the starboard wing and I was hit in the backside by shell fragments, mine was one of the Barras that survived. We landed back on the carrier and I had a few weeks leave.

The pilot was [Commander] Alan Swanton, DSO, DSC*, of *Bismarck* fame.

Peter MacDonald Scott, 1840 Squadron, HMS *Indefatigable*
IWM Sound Archive reference 11244

Operation 'Goodwood' was yet another attack on *Tirpitz*, at the end of August 1944 when Scott was a newly-trained pilot.

The main fleet ships ... went up to Norway as part of a Russian convoy really. It was more or less a strike force in disguise. There were three aircraft carriers up there: the *Furious*, the *Indefatigable* and the [*Formidable*], but that would have represented over 150 aircraft altogether – a mixed bag of fighters, fighter-bombers and torpedo bombers. I think there were Barracudas, which were the principal torpedo bomber; there were Fireflies which were to deal with the ground attack side. The Hellcat was supposed to play a dual role as fighter cover and also dive-bombers, and so we were all fitted with five hundred pound bombs and long range tanks because it was quite a long way in off the coast. I suppose the flight inward from the ships to the target was something in the order of ¾ hour, so that ¾ hour had to be multiplied there and back, add the time over target, so that the whole operational flight was something in the order of three hours, so additional tanks were required – drop tanks, which were disposed of before you crossed the coast. They carried about another 150 gallons of fuel.

Being in the land of the midnight sun more or less we had to get up at 4.00 a.m. or 3.30, and we had our breakfast and we were airborne by about five, and this is broad daylight of course. It took about 15–20 minutes to get all the aircraft off the decks of the three ships and they formed up as a fairly large formation, with the torpedo bombers below and ourselves about 2,000 feet above, I suppose. And then we flew over the coast, climbing all the way once we had crossed the coast we climbed – we had to of course because it was [a] very mountainous area and we still wanted to get as much radar cover as possible. So we went in very low over the sea, and we climbed up – there was snow on those beautiful mountains. It looked absolutely splendid. And, I suppose, when we got to the target area things began to hot up a lot rapidly after that. There weren't any aircraft opposition, at least not that I remember, but the anti-aircraft fire was extremely concentrated, as indeed it could be in a fjord which is a bit like an amphitheatre, really, and of course the Germans had always used this business of smoke screens so that the target would be completely obliterated ... And these screens were activated usually as soon as they had the first radar information that aircraft were on their way, so that there was a lot of smoke in this fjord at the time we got there, and then it was our job to dive-bomb ... Very difficult to tell if you were making strikes or not. You were usually reliant on other observers, in other aircraft, to tell what the result was, but then, having finished that, you are off dealing with any targets you might find on route – seaplanes, there were smaller ships, there were destroyers, there were radar stations...

We joined up again with our own squadron people so it was up to the C/O to find something interesting. We did find some seaplanes which were destroyed and we then dealt with a radar station. My C/O, I might add, was a go-getter type of person and he decided that the best way of dealing with a radar station was to lower the arrestor hook on the aircraft and try and remove the aerials, which indeed we succeeded in doing but it was an extremely dangerous thing to do, not something that would normally be recommended. An aircraft weighing eight tons and travelling at that speed could reasonably take aerials away – you just look them and there is nothing much to stop it ...

I don't think dive bombing a big ship like that [was a wise tactic] especially in that location because she had so much ground-based aircraft defences, of course, and she also had at the mouth of the fjord a flak cruiser sitting there, which also meant that your escape route out was taken care of as well, so that the anti-aircraft fire was extremely heavy. This operation was repeated five times over the next four days, and the losses [of] aircraft were really mounting up: in my squadron alone there were three chaps shot down including the C/O himself, who was killed, and as we were not a very big squadron in the first instance three people out of 12 is quite a substantial loss ... I only went once, but that was only due respect to any new boy. All the regulars did all four.

[The Hellcat] was a marvellous aeroplane. We had all flown Wildcats a lot, and the Hellcat, I suppose you could say, was a 2× Wildcat. It was about twice the size, twice the power, a very robust aeroplane ideal for deck landing purposes. A marvellous gun platform and quite capable of being a fighter-bomber, and a dive bomber and an aeroplane capable of firing rockets and all sorts of things, so it was an excellent aeroplane, very user friendly, we might say. She wasn't designed as a dive-bomber – she was a fighter pure and simple, but she happened to be a very robust fighter so she was quite capable of carrying bombs. We didn't have dive brakes or anything else of that nature, which meant that dive-bombing was [at] very much higher speeds, and nor did we have tailor made bomb sights either. [We attacked at] 45°–50°, not much more than that. The speed build up was so great. You can't use flaps because they were not structurally designed to cope with that sort of situation, so the chances were that at the end of the bombing run you were doing anything up to 360 to 400 knots. The aeroplane is buffeting rather heavily at that point, so it's quite a job to get her out of the dive, and there was only one exit to this particular fjord ... It was quite a hair raising experience. There was a lot of tracer mixed up with the flak ... The big ship itself was also very heavily armed and they were using everything other than main armament. Quite a Dante's inferno. Tracer is a great dissuader. You see these things, balls of fire, coming in your general direction, and you always think they're going to get too close.

ATLANTIC

Frederick George 'Pat' Oikle, Seaman, HMS *Activity*
IWM Sound Archive Reference 17529

One day we eventually went back into Greenock – we used to go out for five days and come back at the weekend. Well, this weekend we didn't go back out, we went into dock and the dockers came on board. They ... took all the aviation fuel out of the tankers and filled it with diesel, then they put a big hose on the flight deck backwards and forwards, and it was attached to a cable – hawser. Anyway, we left and we went out into the Atlantic and we met up with a flotilla of the sloops. They were captained by a chap called Captain Walker. He was known as 'Killer' Walker because of the exploits ...

Anyway, we went out in the Atlantic and we positioned ourselves in one of the convoy lanes, and it wasn't long before a submarine was round. You can pick them up on ASDIC but they dropped a few depth-charges and it went. The convoy came through and we would meet up with it and travel for a day with it and then we'd return somewhere in mid-Atlantic or at least deep water. And we still didn't know what we were there for, but it wasn't long before we found out. Captain Walker and his sloops were due to go back to refuel because we had been out for a few weeks, but instead of going back in they came astern of us and we fed the hose out to them and we fuelled them. We did this in darkness, each night we'd refuel a couple. Well the U-boats, knowing he used to come out on a regular basis, and go back on a regular basis, they had got carte blanche because the only escorts that the convoys had, when he had to go back and refuel, were the escorts that were with the convoys, and on the Atlantic convoys, the ones from America, they didn't have an awful lot of escorts. He didn't go back in, he stayed out. They must have got careless because he sunk quite a few, and we kept on refuelling him overnight and we stayed out, I think it was, three months, and in one 24-hour period alone he sank three U-boats.

Eventually we came back into port, and he was stationed in Gladstone dock in Liverpool here, and he came back to a welcome and he was in the papers' headlines, and we just crept back into Greenock, and not a word to be said to us! Anyway they fixed us up with our aviation fuel again and took the hose off. That made us ready for the next convoy

Lieutenant (A), later Commander, E. E. Barringer, 835 Squadron, HMS *Nairana*
from *Alone On A Wide Wide Sea*, from the papers of E. E. Barringer, IWM Reference 732

Nairana was another of the British-built escort carriers that became available during 1944. She made a fine addition to 'Killer' Walker's escort group.

Captain Taylor was a capable and considerate man who worked well with his officers, particularly his Commander (Flying) and had the good sense to listen and to respect his advice ... an attribute which was regrettably rare in carrier captains who had been reared in the battlefleet tradition ... It was Commander F.'s responsibility to operate the aircraft and determine when and what the aircraft should do. It was thus essential that Commander (Flying) was always on the bridge when aircraft were being operated. As flying was in progress most of the day and night, Commander (F) could spend little time in his cabin and sleep was very limited. Often, during the convoy operations in February, March and April 1944, Edgar Bibby would sometimes go for two weeks without taking off his uniform. But Edgar Bibby was a great leader. He never asked anyone to do what he was not prepared to do himself. He often flew in the Swordfish to try new techniques and he led the first Swordfish aircraft to take off and land on the *Nairana* while she lay at anchor in Greenock on 22nd January 1944 when, with Johnny Hunt, Bob Selley and Teddy Elliott, he flew the Flag Officer, Carrier Training, Admiral Lumley Lyster and his staff to Renfrew after their inspection of HMS *Nairana* and its squadron.

There were several modifications which required action and which Edgar Bibby wanted to carry out quickly without going through the labyrinthine routine of Admiralty approval. A simple example was the question of camouflage for aircraft, particularly the Sea Hurricanes. It was obviously advantageous for them to be able to close on their targets without being spotted until the last possible moment. Naval camouflage had always been designed to merge with the sea but the green colour was very visible against the clouds and often revealed the approach of the fighters and enabled enemy aircraft to take evasive action. After getting the approval of the Hurricane pilots, Edgar Bibby went ahead without reference to the Admiralty and had the Sea Hurricanes painted white. While it would obviously be difficult to prove, the later successes of the 835 [Squadron] Sea Hurricanes could perhaps in some measure be attributable to his foresight. This was typical of many of the unofficial changes which Edgar Bibby made to improve the efficiency of the carrier and the operation of its aircraft.

Sergeant S. H. Brown, RAF, HMS *Activity*
from his diary, Fleet Air Arm Museum
(Editor's note: once again, some punctuation has been added for clarity.)

Saturday 29th Jan 1944
3-0 AM Left for unknown destination in company with aircraft carrier HMS *Nairana* and 2nd Escort Group comprising sloops HMS *Wildgoose*, *Starling*, *Wren*, *Magpie* and *Woodpecker*. Fairly heavy swell running, but felt no sign of seasickness yet. We did no flying today – had a quiet night except for rolling of ship.

Sunday 30th Jan

Weather increasing, sea quite rough – still unable to do any flying, shipped a heavy sea as I was walking up the flight deck this morning – got wet through – had to change all my clothes, managed to peck at my dinner, but tummy didn't feel too happy; wasn't actually sick though. I must be a better sailor than I thought I was. I stood aft this evening watching a school of dolphins swimming around the ship. It was nice to look around and see our escort of sloops all around us – gives one a comforting sort of feeling – crack lot of sloops here, too – have quite a number of U-boats to their credit.

Monday 31st Jan

Ship rolled rather badly in the night – didn't get much sleep – lovely morning, though, sunny and fairly calm – quite nice to be on the flight deck this morning – we haven't done any flying yet. About 12-o-clock noon today one of our escorts, *Wildgoose*, I think, contacted a U-boat and sank it with depth charges, skipper broadcast the news over the loudspeakers. Nice work (*U-592*). Wind freshened and sea got quite rough about tea time – weather still bad for flying – some of the fellows a bit under the weather with sea sickness – still OK myself as yet – mustn't shout too soon though.

Tuesday 1st Feb

Lovely morning again – managed to get off a couple of patrols this morning – ship seems to roll very badly, one of the machines returning from patrol crashed on landing due to ship rolling – nobody hurt, but gave us plenty of work getting it off the flight deck, have only just finished work 10:15pm – feeling pretty tired – shan't need much rocking tonight, but I expect I shall get plenty, she is rolling enough.

Thursday 3rd Feb

It's been a lovely day again today – sunny and quite warm like a summer's day – haven't done any flying today, and nothing exciting happened – I spent most of the day basking in the sun on the flight deck – we are now heading south so may get a few nice sunny days – some of the officers not on duty were indulging in a game of deck hockey this evening, and then some of the lads had a go. I thought to myself, I wonder what Jerry would think if he popped a periscope above the water and saw them playing games in the middle of the Atlantic with a war on. We must be a good way across – we have put our clocks back two hours ...

Sunday 8th Feb

We woke up this morning to find ourselves surrounded by ships – we are right in the middle of the convoy stooging along at seven knots. When you look at the ships they look as though they are at anchor, they are moving so slowly. Don't like the idea of being in the middle of this lot – about eighty ships – am afraid they will attract too much attention from Jerry, but so far today no excitement.

Wednesday 9th Feb
2:30 A.M. Have only just finished work – have been very busy today – have just heard that *Wildgoose* and *Magpie*, part of our escort, have just sunk another U-boat. Kill No. 2. Am just going to turn in – am feeling pretty tired. (*U-762*)
9 A.M. we are still in the middle of the convoy – we got off a patrol this morning, aircraft made an attack on a U-boat but result of attack unknown – it is pretty foggy – heard a lot of depth charges going off this morning and the skipper has just informed us that *Wildgoose* and *Starling* have sunk another U-boat – there are supposed to be four stalking the convoy, so that leaves two. Nice work – we have rubbed out two today – that makes kill No. 3 (*U-238*).

The time is now 6.30 P.M. Good news – the skipper has just informed us that *Starling* and *Magpie* have just sunk another U-boat – the third today and fourth of the trip – great work – kill No. 4 (*U-424*)

Saturday 12th Feb
We are now proceeding up the Clyde estuary – you can tell we are getting near Scotland by the weather, drizzling with rain and quite cold. Safely anchored at Greenock at 12-o'clock noon. So that's that.

Wednesday 23rd Feb
6.0 A.M. Have just left for unknown destination believed to be Gibraltar in company with HMS *Nairana* and half a dozen sloops names unknown and convoy of 49 merchantmen – sea very calm – we are stooging along at six or seven knots – have carried out the usual flying patrols.

Sat 26th Feb
Wind freshened to nearly gale force, sea rough, ship rolling badly – we are unable to do any flying owing to weather – no excitement – no sea-sickness.

Sunday 27th Feb
Sea still very rough – ship rolled badly during the night – have been unable to do any flying – nothing exciting happened – wind seems to be dropping a bit.

Monday 28th Feb
Sea still very rough – we flew off a couple of patrols this morning – one Wildcat crashed when landing on deck and went over the side into the sea – the pilot was picked up by one of our escort – a French corvette – he was none the worse except for a wet shirt and a shaking – caused a flutter of excitement for a while – otherwise things very quiet except for rolling of ship – we were told today we are on our way to Gib. Hope we get a chance to go ashore there.

Tuesday 29th Feb
Had a very bad night last night – ship rolled very badly, up to 35° – very nice day today though ship still rolling pretty badly – got off a few patrols today – have just turned in 1-0 A.M. – had a spot of bad luck this evening – machine crashed on deck, landing on – gave us a lot of work getting it off the flight deck

– bit difficult working in the dark: daren't show any lights for fear of attracting attention from the U-boats. Still stooging along with convoy, haven't lost any ships yet.

Sunday 5th March

Have just heard that *Nairana* – the other carrier – had a bit of bad luck last night – they had a crash during night flying and the air gunner and observed both killed, and pilot injured – buried the two dead at sea today – we are expecting to make Gib tomorrow …

Tuesday 7th March

Arrived at Gib yesterday evening, quite an impressive sight as you steam into Gib harbour, and what a lovely day – blue skies and sunshine. It looked lovely ashore after dark with all the lights twinkling like a seaside resort in peacetime – there is no blackout here, and when the moon came up it looked lovely.

Wednesday 8th March

Glorious day again today – it was lovely to be up on deck in the sun – I went ashore yesterday evening and sent off a cable home, and had a wander round – plenty of fruit here, bananas, oranges, lemons, figs etc and grapes, but all very dear. It was wonderful after dark to see all the shops blazing with lights, no blinds drawn – it was a taste of what it will be like when the war is over.

On her return trip, *Activity* escorted Convoy MKF.29, which was bringing back troops in preparation for the D-Day landings. With them was the battleship HMS *Warspite*, which was returning to the UK for repair after sustaining major damage.

Thursday 9th March

We set off for home at 6 a.m. this morning – we have taken five German prisoners on board, part of a U-boat crew sunk recently – there are four officers and one rating – they were all led aboard blindfolded last night. We are bringing back a convoy of 19 ships all big liners loaded with troops and we have as escort the battleship *Warspite*, the cruiser *Glasgow* and the anti-aircraft cruiser [HMCS] *Prince Robert* about 6 sloops and ourselves and *Nairana* – quite a formidable escort for only 19 ships, but the convoy is very important and very valuable – we are steaming at 12–14 knots which is a welcome change from the six knot convoys – we should be home in 6 or seven days all being well.

Sunday 12th March

Had a spot of bad luck this evening – one machine went over the side [during] night flying – the crew of three had to swim for it – we stood by in the dark while one of the escorts searched and found them – they were lucky enough to get away with bruises and a shaking.

Wednesday 15th March

Arrived this evening about 7-o'clock – a very quiet and unexciting trip.

Lieutenant Bruce Vibert, DSC, CD, RCN(R), Pilot, 836 Squadron,
HMS *Fencer*, 10 February 1944, Atlantic
Communication with the Editor

There were two carriers escorting convoy ON223, ourselves – *Fencer* – and *Striker*. The latter was providing anti-submarine patrols on that day and we were on fighter standby. We had both one fighter and one Swordfish on the deck, and the crew of the Swordfish were walking around, and suddenly there was a shout and we all looked and there was a conning tower popping up between the two carriers. A white cap appears on the conning tower, takes a look round and rapidly bobs down. Down goes the conning tower, during which time the crew had jumped into the Swordfish and the two blokes had started the aircraft up. To cut a long story short within about seven minutes that boat was sunk.The Swordfish took off, did a tight climbing turn to port, went astern the convoy, saw this thing coming up again and sank it. From records in Germany I now know that that boat had been damaged earlier, and the damage had made it necessary to surface. It must have been an awful shock for him to pop up there and find himself in the middle of the convoy. The fact that he had to come up again shows how desperate the situation must have been for them.

And that is the only U-boat sunk by our naval aircraft on the North Atlantic without anybody else's help. The rest were with, for example, a fighter, such as one from *Archer* which was the first aircraft to use rockets anywhere, and that was *U-752*. The Swordfish pilot was Harry Horrocks and the carrier was HMS *Archer*.

MEDITERRANEAN

Lieutenant Commander (A) H. D. B. Eadon, RNVR,
809 Naval Air Squadron, HMS *Stalker*
from the private papers of H. C. Jefferson, 12959

Eadon's letter refers to Charles Edmond Hugh Jefferson, HMS *Stalker*, shot down on 28 August 1944 during the landings in South of France.

I did want to get something definite about Hugh before I wrote. We all felt up to last week, when we had almost definite confirmation of his death, that there was just that vague hope that he might have survived and be returning to us. But now I fear not as I say, with the circumstantial evidence and knowing the district where he crashed, I am afraid there can be no doubt. The letter we had in the squadron said he had been buried in the cemetery at St Remy.

It is always very hard to express one's feelings when one loses a great friend, and he was a great friend to all of us. To me, as his squadron Commander, he was the most loyal, likeable and, in every way, fine man you could ever wish to meet. I had recently made him a flight commander and I always knew that any job I gave him would be done as well as humanly possible. Both on the ground and in the air he was a very thorough man. Now he has left us we all feel his loss very much indeed ...

PACIFIC

Willie Lagarde, Div 2&3, S1/c, USS *Yorktown*
www.ussyorktown.net

Yorktown was part of Task Group 58, a constituent of Fifth Fleet. During the early weeks of 1944 the Fleet carried out attacks on Papua, the Marshall Islands and the major Japanese stronghold of Truk in the Caroline Islands.

The carrier task force was divided into two to four groups only rarely coming within sight of each other. Each group was formed around at least one large carrier and usually another or a smaller CVL. It was spread out over three to five miles. Knowing we would be the target of choice for any enemy counterattack we always liked to see another large carrier with whom to share the honor. There were only ten battleships fast enough to operate with us and because of their firepower we hoped for at least one.

The AA cruisers were also reassuring. Some of them could fire fourteen five inch guns at an incoming attack. That's compared to ten for the battleships, eight to starboard and twelve to port for us, eight for the light and heavy cruisers and five for most of the destroyers. The sight of those AA cruisers opening up on a target was awesome. They could put out over 200 five inch rounds a minute and would almost disappear in the gun flash. Two of these ships were sunk early in the war with a loss of 846 men. We felt fairly secure with two battleships in our group as we headed out for another raid. Rumor had come down it was going to be a 'big one.' After we were out a few days the captain told us we were going to Truk. We were very apprehensive about this raid because of all we had heard about Truk. At the time it was known as the Japanese Pearl Harbor and had never been attacked before. When our captain spoke to us over the PA system describing Truk and what we expected to find there he closed with, 'We are going to give those little yellow bastards their own Pearl Harbor to remember'. I often think, in this day and time that statement would probably have cost Capt. Ralph Jennings his command if not his career. But this was in the days before our country became a victim of PC insanity and there were no overly sensitive ears on our ships therefore no complaints of harassment or discrimination. The Japs prided themselves on never surrendering and fighting to the death so as one of our admirals put it, we're here 'to kill Japs.' More on Truk later. Sometime in the Truk raid time frame, while standing gun watch on the blackest night I have ever experienced I heard a crashing roar somewhere off the port quarter. Other gun mounts were calling in saying they heard it and were wondering what could it be. We found out at daybreak, *Washington* and *Indiana* were no longer with us. They collided in that black night [1 February 1944] and the fast carrier task forces were down to eight battleships for the next few months.

I was on Mt. 5 40MM for these two events; it was sometime in early 1944 and we were on our battle stations. For this attack I was assigned to the handing room a half deck lower than the gun mount and entered from the gun tub through a door about 2'×3'. 40MM ammunition came to us in heavy galvanized cans each containing sixteen rounds in four clips. In addition to the ammunition in the handling room, cans were placed all around the outer edge of [the] gun tub deck. Ammunition from these cans was used first. My job was to keep ready ammunition available to the loaders. Most men in a gun crew could only look at an incoming attack if for one reason or another their gun wasn't firing. Also, after the firing began a change in time perception turned seconds into minutes. It has been said events happened in slow motion. All of the action described in this event from the time our gun stopped firing until the Jap plane crashed into the sea actually took place in less than a minute. So it was for this particular attack. Mt 5 had stopped firing and the only reason I can offer is the plane was too low for our director operator to bring the gun to bear on him. Mt 7 just aft and lower than us was still firing as were all the other 20's and 40's on the starboard side with the exception of Mt. 3 (although I am not sure) which was on the forward end of the island structure and higher than we were. I had the opportunity to watch the one remaining plane of a torpedo attack flying through a hail of flak. I have seen footage of this plane many times in films and documentaries. A single engine plane with the torpedo carried externally, flying through a stream of tracers. I had remembered being told, perhaps in boot camp, if you knew a torpedo was about to hit your ship to flex your knees to absorb the shock. I don't know how important that was but I was still new enough at the game not to question. I estimated it was too late to stop him now and a torpedo hit was inevitable. I moved to the port side of the gun mount, flexed my knees waiting for the hit. The next thing I saw was this plane, still carrying the torpedo, flying over the flight deck just forward of the island structure almost eye level with me. He had a small fire behind the canopy. The pilot was slumped over and the man in the back was looking us over, the last sight he would ever see before he died seconds later. If I had known him I could have recognized him. There was much speculation on why the torpedo wasn't released, the pilot had to be alive to pull the plane up over our flight deck. Another example of *Yorktown* luck? It had to be, he had us cold. Did our God trump his God? After all he went through was it just a mechanical malfunction that denied him a seat of honor among all the dead samurai? I have often thought, had he been a kamikaze, our ship may have survived a torpedo exploding at hangar deck level, but many, perhaps hundreds of our crew would have died …

One of our fighters returning from a strike couldn't get his flaps down and would be the last to land. We had witnessed many crashes of all kinds from our battle station but no one could remember a plane attempting to land without flaps. I doubt if the flight deck crews had either. I was the only one in the gun crew that bothered to watch this one, everyone thinking this shouldn't be much of a problem. Having seen hundreds of landings and knowing what a good approach looked like, I sensed early on he was coming in much too fast, he was in trouble and maybe the ship as well. He caught the sixth or seventh cable and hardly slowed down. As he pulled the cable out to the maximum he hit Mt. 7 gun house, breaking off a wing. Half the plane from the cockpit on back broke off and stayed hooked to the cable as the rest of it spun around and continued to disintegrate. When it finally stopped I could look down on the pilot and see what appeared to be a slight trickle of blood on his neck. He stepped out of the cockpit and calmly walked away from the wreck. Footage of this crash has been shown in the movies 'Fighting Lady' and 'Midway' as well as the TV series, 'Victory at Sea.' In one of the still frames taken from this footage I can be seen watching the action from Mt. 5.

Among the pilots who carried out the raid was Lieutenant James D. Ramage, USN, Executive Officer of Bombing Squadron 10 aboard *Enterprise*.

Lieutenant, later Rear Admiral, James D. Ramage, USN, VB-10, USS *Enterprise*
http://www.cv6.org/1944/truk/default.htm

Admiral Raymond Spruance's big drive through the Central Pacific started on 29 January 1944 with carrier air attacks on the Marshall Islands. His Fifth Fleet seized the key island of Kwajalein, and by early February his powerful force was at anchor in its new base at Majuro in the eastern Marshalls. On 11 February, LT Lou Bangs and I were tossing a medicine ball with a circle of naval aviators on the flight deck of *Enterprise*. It was clear that something was up because ships' boats were churning around the lagoon. We obviously were getting underway fairly soon. Powerful Task Force 58, with six heavy and six light carriers, was impressive, particularly when compared to a scant year before when the Big E had been the only fleet carrier in the South Pacific. Our air group commander, CDR William R. 'Killer' Kane, came up to our circle and beckoned to Lou and me to join him on the bow of the flight deck.

'We're going to hit Truk,' he said.

All I could say was, 'Wow!'

My gunner, ARM 1/c Dave Cawley, says that he specifically remembered how tense and concerned we all were as we contemplated hitting Truk: the Japanese 'Pearl Harbor' of the Pacific. He fully expected a significant portion of their fleet to tangle with us. 'For the previous two years of the war, the very thought of approaching Truk seemed fatal.' Operation Hailstone, the attack on Truk, was to cover the seizure of Eniwetok in the western Marshalls. Truk had a magnificent harbor and contained four airfields. Carrier aircraft alone would take on this large land-based air defense. The atoll was the major Japanese fleet base in the Pacific and was the anchorage of the Japanese Combined Fleet.

There is always an apprehension of the unknown, and we knew so little about Truk. There were no current maps of the atoll. We were more at ease when LT Denius ('Denius the Genius'), the intelligence officer from RADM Reeve's staff, gave us the estimated enemy order of battle. We could expect up to 200 enemy fighters plus other aircraft. I thought, 'Hell, this wasn't bad! We had almost 300 F6Fs in Task Force 58.' We did not know then that Admiral Koga, Admiral Yama[mo]to's successor, felt uneasy when the Americans began the assault on Eniwetok and withdrew his fleet to the Palaus in the western Carolines. I went to bed on the night of 15 February thinking of the great carrier battle that would occur on the 16th.

Not so ...

Cawley remembers:

'The morning of 16 February was clear, cool and beautiful as we launched from *Enterprise*. We approached from the east, and action started as we were at about 12,000 feet, nearly over the center of the lagoon. Our targets were in the anchorage adjacent to Dublon Island. Unlike most of the islands we had seen and attacked, which were low, flat atolls, the Truk Islands were volcanic with quite high peaks. Just before we reached the roll-in, we were in quite heavy AA, diving very close to a steep hill or peak on Dublon.'

Our launch point was only 80 miles from the outer cays of the atoll. The course to Dublon anchorage was 250 degrees magnetic. Prior to launch, we received the unwelcome news that most of the Japanese fleet had left but that there were plenty of ship targets that remained. Also, our F6Fs were having a field day with the Zeros. It was up to us to do our job. As we passed over the outer cay, a green-brown Zero zoomed by on a parallel course to starboard. No guts! I could see heavy AA coming up from the anchorage area and surrounding islands when 'whoosh,' I saw a horrendous mushroom cloud rising from the roadstead. Someone had blown up an ammo ship. The fireball that resulted went up 300 feet. As I looked over the targets, I picked out the biggest ship of a group of about a dozen. She was a tanker at anchor.

In answer to my signal, wingmen LT(jg) Bill Schaefer and LT(jg) Oliver Hubbard began to fall back. We did not roll in from an echelon because we liked to keep our defensive 'V' as long as possible. I split my dive flaps and settled my pipper on a position just forward of the bridge. I manually released my 1,000lb. GP bomb at 2,000 feet and turned left on pullout to see the results. The tanker was covered with smoke and water splashes. I could not count the hits; one had detached the stern from the ship and she was definitely going down by the stern. The tanker was empty and hence hard to sink.

After pullout, the second division was attacked by four Zeros and a Rufe seaplane fighter. ARM 2/c Honea, gunner for ENS Bob Wilson, shot down one Zero and damaged a second.

We had a second strike that afternoon. By that time, the shipping was pretty well beaten up. We found the 13,000-ton *Hoyo Maru*, hit her on the centerline just forward of the stern and set her afire. Bangs division scored two hits on the aviation stores ship *Kiyozumi Maru*, likewise leaving her on fire and sinking ...

'I remember a Japanese cruiser (*Katori*) up to the north of Truk lagoon,' states Cawley. 'I'm sure I watched it on the clear calm sea as a TBF attacked with four 500-lb. bombs. They were dropped in a row with two missing, one hit and one (exploding) close aboard. There was considerable smoke from AA, fires and bombs.'

When I sighted the cruiser, she was low in the water and barely moving. Since we were without bombs and ammo, I opened up on guard channel, saying 'Any strike leader from 51-Bobcat, there is a damaged Japanese cruiser just to the north of the lagoon. Come sink it.' Immediately on guard channel came back, 'Bobcat leader, this is Bald Eagle (Mitscher). Cancel your last. Do not, repeat do not, sink that ship. Acknowledge.'

I was stunned! I later found out that ADM Spruance wanted to move his surface ships up for target practice on the cripple. I guess the battleships had to participate in some way!

In the summer of 1943, LCDR Bill Martin shifted from commanding officer of Scouting Squadron Ten to command Torpedo Squadron Ten. Martin was convinced that the carriers should do more in night attack. The TBF Avenger offered a platform to prove his ideas. He took his case to RADM Reeves, who recommended to Mitscher that VT-10 be scheduled for a night strike against Japanese shipping remaining in Truk lagoon on the night of 16–17 February.

At 0410, twelve TBF-1Cs catapulted from *Enterprise* for a night masthead-level bombing attack on shipping. LT Van Eason, VT-10's exec, led the strike. It was planned that individual runs would be accomplished by radar; the bomb release point would be determined by the pilot, assisted by radar. Radar reception was hindered by the many coral islets in the lagoon. Also, many of the ships were anchored close to larger islands which caused merged radar echoes. Most pilots searched for 30 minutes before they identified their targets. The aircraft carried four 500-lb. bombs with a four second delay fusing and released their bombs at 250 feet.

Shore batteries put up heavy but inaccurate fire. Ships did not open fire until the attacking planes were within 400 yards. One aircraft, flown by LT(jg) J. Nicholas, did not return from the attack. The cause of his loss is unknown. Damage assessment indicated that 13 of the 48 bombs dropped sunk two oilers and six cargo ships, with six additional cargo ships damaged. This first night strike effort was certainly a success, and was a payoff to Martin for the special training he had insisted on giving VT-10 prior to its deployment. He states, 'VT-10 specialized in night radar search and attack and specifically requested this mission. I believe that this was the first time our carrier forces launched a night, minimum-altitude bombing strike.'

A second, mopping-up strike took place next day.

THE BATTLE OF THE PHILIPPINE SEA

Lieutenant Commander Abe Zenji, Imperial Japanese Navy, IJN *Junyo*
from *The Emperor's Sea Eagle, Abe Zenji*

The Japanese fleet detected Admiral Spruance's task forces early on the morning of 19 June, but the aircraft sent against them in the Battle of the Philippine Sea suffered more than 50% losses and achieved nothing. The Grumman Hellcats now flown by US pilots outclassed the Japanese planes; too many of the Japanese pilots and observers were inexperienced. Lieutenant Abe was flying a modern Suisei, but these new aircraft were in very short supply.

My bomber group from the 2nd Carrier Division led off the Second Stage Attack [Raid IV]. At 1115, the following units totaling fifty aircraft took off; one division of dive-bombers from *Junyo*, two divisions from *Hiyo* (totaling twenty-seven Type 99 dive-bombers), led by twenty escort fighters and three Tenzan level-bombers. The attack force leader was Lieutenant Miyauchi Yasunori of *Hiyo*. Some minutes later, I departed with my lead division of nine Suisei, taking off later so as not to overrun the slower Type 99s. A second wave of eighteen aircraft, consisting of four Zero fighters, ten lighter-bombers and four Tenzan, departed from the 1st Carrier Division at 11.20. I heard later that this latter group returned without finding anything, most probably owing to the crews' poor navigational abilities. Adding insult to injury, the returning formation broke up, with the result that eight fighter bombers and one Tenzan became lost and failed to return.

Having departed earlier, the Miyauchi group arrived at the supposed target area but no enemy fleet units appeared below. Having flown nearly 400 miles, there was now insufficient fuel to make the return flight to *Hiyo*. Accordingly, Miyauchi opted for a forced landing on Guam. However, just prior to landing, thirty F6F 'Hellcats' swooped down from the clouds and attacked Miyauchi from the rear, shooting down fourteen fighters, nine dive-bombers and three Tenzan.

Meanwhile, prior to takeoff, I was standing by on board *Junyo* wearing a flight suit over my summer uniform. I carried nothing but a Navy-issue pistol in my trouser pocket and a pocket watch suspended around my neck. My division officer, Lieutenant Kuga Junichi walked up and reported, 'Commander, the crews are waiting in line.' Though I felt it was a bit early to man the aircraft, I still stood in front of the line where my men then saluted me. I said nothing, as my excellent divisional officer and Ensign Nakajima had given all the necessary last-minute instructions to my men already. Rear Admiral Jyojima's 2nd Carrier Division staff instructed me to fly on to Guam after attacking the enemy task force, to refuel there, and thence return to *Junyo* on the following day at a position which would be revealed to us at that time.

Four days previous, U.S. forces assaulted Saipan on 15 June, which meant that our forces (and certainly our airfields on Guam) were now under threat and accordingly, had lost a substantial portion of their counterattacking potential. Only 120 miles separated Saipan and Guam; in the air on a clear day one can see the islands from a distance of fifty kilometers. Being somewhat accustomed to U.S. practices, we should have expected the Americans to begin softening up our positions on Guam even before commencing the Saipan landings. Consequently, I was rather uneasy regarding our orders to land on Guam, much less on Saipan.

Despite these concerns and misgivings, at 1145 I lifted away from *Junyo*, leading nine Suisei dive-bombers and our accompanying escort of six Zero fighters under Lieutenant Takasawa Kenkichi. I had not held a control stick in my hand for forty days, and even on 10 May while in Suonada I flew for less than an hour. My ears were ringing, possibly from engine noise, and I could not hear Nakajima's voice coming through the voice tube very clearly. Neither did he seem to understand my words at all. I seemed a bit unsteady on my legs and had an uneasy feeling as if I was simply riding in an aircraft flown by somebody else. Never had I experienced that kind of feeling since becoming a pilot. (I did not realize, but I was sick at that point.) Other planes and crews might have been unsteady, too. And just then CPO Kosemoto Kunio, piloting my second plane, and Lieutenant Iwai Kiyomi, my third Shotai-cho, turned back because their landing gear failed to retract, both aircraft aborting to Yap. Then, escort pilot CPO Manabe Shigenobu aborted due to engine trouble and returned to *Junyo*. Predictably, the strain placed on both men and machines of having not flown for forty days had begun to take its toll.

Flying just south of east and climbing up to 6,000 meters attitude, I put on my oxygen mask and breathed deeply. An hour later, Nakajima informed me through the voice tube that our little force had shrunk still further as Ensign Tani Hiroshi's Suisei and three Zeroes were no longer there. I was deeply puzzled; had they dropped out because of engine trouble, or had they crashed into the sea due to hallucinations from oxygen starvation? My force in view was down to only six Suisei and two fighters.

Continuing to fly for another hour, we arrived at the point where we expected to encounter the American fleet but I could not see anything owing to a hazy layer in the atmosphere at low altitude. Perhaps my own my eyesight was failing. I inhaled more oxygen, and started a search of the surrounding area within an eighty mile radius, using our initial position as center point – this eighty miles being equivalent to four hours steaming for the U.S. fleet. However, strain though I might, I could not find anything below still hoping that the eighty miles might compensate for either navigation error on our part or movement by the enemy.

With no targets, at 1340 I finally gave [up] on the attack and focused instead on the flight ahead, shaping a course of 45° to Guam. At length, seeing Guam, dimly in my mind through the haze at about two o'clock low, I descended gradually keeping 'three eyes open' to the surrounding expanse of sky. When the altimeter read 4,000 meters, Ensign Nakajima shouted, 'A big crowd of the enemy in our left front, Commander!' Just at that time, to the left underside of the engine cowling, I confirmed the presence of a U.S. Task Force, all with the helms turned hard to port, cleaving glistening white wakes into the blue water below. There were over twenty enemy vessels in a ring formation with four aircraft carriers at the center [TG 58.2 with carriers *Bunker Hill*, *Wasp*, *Cabot* (CVL28) and *Monterey* (CVL26)]. I gave the attack order and increased speed. The Americans must have noticed us much earlier, as Grumman fighters were already climbing up to intercept us. We were in a very unsatisfactory position to deploy for the attack and had found the enemy almost too late. Now there was not a moment to lose. Lost seconds would mean certain death for all of us.

I careered seaward in my attack dive through a heavy barrage of anti-aircraft fire. Even though my dive angle was far too shallow, I elected to release anyway, dropping a bomb into one of the big aircraft carriers in the center. Incredibly, after flying past the enemy ships I found no one following me as I escaped from the hemisphere of anti-aircraft bursts. Nakajima later reported to me that he saw two fireballs in our rear as we dashed away from the target area.

While circling to collect what was left of my group, four aircraft approached, and I had already noticed that there was something peculiar about their silhouette. They were Grummans! I adjusted the propeller pitch, pushed my throttle to the stop and raced away from them. Fortunately, scattered clouds lay here and there at about 800 meters altitude. Opposing these single seated fighters, we certainly stood no chance, even with one-to-one odds. I still hoped to keep out of sight, but all too soon the small patches of clouds gave way to blue sky. 'There's a Grumman, up and to the left rear, Commander!' shouted Nakajima. I again pushed the throttle forward, escaping into the nearest cloud. These Hellcat pilots were really tenacious, following us with a division of four aircraft. While fretting about our fuel situation, I heard Nakajima again, 'Grummans! Grummans!' While I scrambled to configure our evasive maneuvers so as to close on Guam, poor Nakajima was soon hoarse from screaming out his warnings. In turn, I was becoming disoriented in this fitful game of 'Hellcat hide-and-seek', which by now had lasted for the better part of an hour. With daylight beginning to fail, I, had no idea when our engine might stop and prompt me to dive into the sea crying 'Long reign the Emperor!' Thankfully, when I came out of clouds there were no Grummans to harass us this time.

I remember looking around and thinking, 'Oh good, I've shaken off the Grummans now,' when a land mass came into view for a fleeting moment. It was a small island, and I could barely make out what appeared to be a runway in the center of the island. I descended to 100 meters, all the time flying closer and closer to the island. Then I saw another aircraft wagging its wings to identify itself as a friendly, flying east along the island's south coast. Although it was nearly sunset, it was just light enough for personnel on the ground to identify a red hinomaru on an approaching aircraft. If there were Japanese troops present perhaps they would wave handkerchiefs. Though I felt very anxious and apprehensive over the prospect of landing, I had almost no fuel left. So, while flying a circular pattern over the northeast end of the island, I throttled back the engine and pushed my nose down toward the runway. The landing gear came down and locked without any problem; perhaps I could make a satisfactory landing. Just as I was on final approach, it felt as if someone had thrown pebbles and hit my flight helmet. 'Oh, no! I've landed in the middle of the enemy!' A hoarse Nakajima croaked 'Grummans above and to the rear, Sir!'

Hardly waiting for the aircraft to roll to a stop, Nakajima sprang from his rear seat and fled toward the woods on the right. Looking back, I thought that I saw a second Hellcat crashing. Yanking the voice tube from my flight helmet, I ripped loose my parachute harness and lap belt, and at last crawled out from the cockpit. A third Grumman flew away overhead, his engine roaring. I waited for the machine-gun fire from the fourth fighter as I lay on my face having run five or so meters into the bushes. This must have been the four plane division that had followed me so tenaciously earlier in the afternoon. After finishing their strafing runs, the four Grummans reversed course, dove in from the opposite direction, each aircraft appearing to drop a small bomb on my lone Suisei. Satisfied that they probably destroyed my aircraft, they turned back toward their home base and flew out of sight.

Lieutenant Abe had landed on the island of Rota and became part of the garrison until its surrender in September, after which he became a prisoner-of-war on Guam until repatriation in 1946.

The overwhelming US air combat victory in the Marianas threatened to turn sour in its immediate aftermath.

Lieutenant Commander Otto C. Romanelli, USN, Rtd, USS *Lexington* (CV-16)
from *Blue Ghost Memoirs*

By mid-afternoon Spruance received a sighting report of the location of the enemy fleet and it became obvious (by the count of downed enemy planes) that the Japanese forces had 'shot their load.' By joint agreement between Admiral Spruance and Admiral Mitscher, it was decided to 'go get the surface ships,' Of course our pilots cheered ...

Our strike found the enemy fleet at dusk and immediately started bombing runs. Our planes sank one first-line carrier and two oilers and shot down 65 carrier planes. Another first-line carrier was severely damaged and three escort carriers slightly damaged. Having expended all their bombs and torpedoes in the fading light, our planes started straggling back to their carriers in small groups, cutting back on their throttles to conserve gas. The carriers had started steaming west at 22 knots to shorten the return distance for the aircraft. But there was also the additional problem of finding their home carriers in absolute darkness, provided their fuel lasted long enough. Very few of the pilots had experienced landing at night. Contemplating the desperate plight of the returning pilots, those of us on the carriers felt a lump in our throats. This included Admiral Mitscher, who had ordered that the strike take place in late afternoon, knowing that the return would be in total darkness. His compassion elicited a startling order to all carriers:

'Turn on the lights!!!'

He had made a painful decision in ordering his beloved pilots to fly off at maximum distance and return in unaccustomed blackness; that was his duty. Now, listening to radio reports of planes lost and ditching into the sea, his heart spoke:

'Turn on the lights!!!'

And the rest of us on board ship felt the tightness in our throats relax. We were doing the only thing that could be done to lead our 'kid brothers' home, at the risk of exposing our ships to any submarines or bombers in the area. But landing operations were extremely chaotic because of crashes, tail hooks not catching and planes landing on 'sister' carriers. Radio signals from ditched aircraft were recorded on the charts; that night and in the following days, rescue ships and float planes searched the reported downings. Approximately half of the pilots and crews from the ditched planes were rescued.

THE BATTLES FOR LEYTE

Lieutenant, now Dr, Doy Duncan, Pilot VC-20, USS *Kadashan Bay*, Taffy Two
from *Abandoned at Leyte*

Duncan was flying a Wildcat from an escort carrier that formed part of Task Force Two, known as 'Taffy Two.'

The Escort Carrier Group was situated east of Samar Island about midway up the side. Each day we would get our assignments, sometimes flying combat air patrols over our own group, and sometimes protecting the invasion fleet or being available for anything else that needed to be done. We would simply circle and make sure no Japanese planes came into the area to disturb the invasion force. When our troops ran into an area where the Japanese ground forces had concentrated, we would get a call to go down and clean them out. That was a little more exciting than circling around and around.

One time we were called on to attack some heavily occupied trenches at the edge of a village. In order to make sure we didn't shoot our own troops, soldiers on the front lines would put down smoke bombs at the front edge of our line to let us know exactly where they were. Anything beyond that line we could attack. That was the first time I felt sure I had killed somebody. Coming down in a run, I saw a blink, blink, blink from a road alongside a trench, and I knew it was a machine gun firing. I kicked a little bit of rudder and fired away. If I didn't hit him, I figured I scared him to death.

We did not want to kill Filipinos if we could help it. One pilot accidentally dropped a five-hundred-pound bomb right in the middle of a village. From above, it looked like a pebble in a lake the way those huts went down from the center. It pretty well flattened the village. We found out later that all the Filipinos friendly to us had moved back into the hills, so I feel in my own mind that the pilot at least didn't kill any friendly Filipinos.

Zachery Z. Zink, USS *Kadashan Bay*, Taffy Two
Communication with the Editor

Abruptly the role of the three escort carrier groups with their destroyers and destroyer escorts changed from supporting the landings to taking on Kurita's powerful fleet after Halsey took the entire Third Fleet to chase Ozawa's decoy carriers.

My general quarters station was on the aft on the bridge. That morning we were called to general quarters. Our squadron flew off on their general missions. When general quarters was over we returned to our regular station; in just a few minutes general quarters was sounded again. Captain Hunter came on the speaker and said for all pilots to report to the squadron on the double and for all torpedo men to report to their station and arm all torpedoes.

I heard then that VC-20 pilot En's Jensen had spotted the Jap fleet, and reported it to Taffy 2. He was the first to report the sighting. After it was all over I heard that a pilot had spotted it after Jenson and reported to Taffy 3. He got the credit, Taffy 3 was the flag with all the big brass.

Things really got popping: all planes got armed with torpedoes, booms, and every thing we had. We only had 7 torpedoes; they were the first to go. We were not supposed to be in situations like this.

We launched and landed planes all morning. Armed, fueled and sent them back, not only our planes but planes from other ships, it was a busy time. Commander Dale flew off the ship three times. The second time his plane was all shot up. Oil flying out the motor, his turret gunner (Walker) was wounded by shrapnel and taken to sick bay on a stretcher. CMM Dale's plane was so shot up they put it on the catapult and shot it off into the ocean. Dale got into another plane and took off for his third strike. When he did not come back we feared he got shot down. But later we learned he landed on the invasion beach and flew back the next day.

Then I really got worried: a Jap Cruiser with its big guns appeared on the skyline. Taffy 2 sent two destroyers out to intercept it. The Japs shot several salvoes in our direction, none came close to any of our ships, and the ship disappeared from the skyline. This was a pleasant surprise. We then learned the Jap fleet had retreated north. This was a big surprise to all of us. They had all the big guns and the speed, we were no match for them. The CVEs [had] only 1 five-inch on the fantail, the rest of our guns were 20s and 40s anti-aircraft guns. Our escorts were destroyers, their largest guns were 5 inch. No match for the Jap's battlecruisers and cruisers. Our top speed was 20 knots, if that, and theirs were 35 knots. No way we could get away. They could have wiped us out and gone in and wiped out the invasion ships of Leyte.

It is my belief that air planes from Taffy 2, Taffy 1 and the planes that got off of Taffy 3 were responsible for the Jap retreat. There must have been 100 planes attacking the Jap fleet all through the Battle, some just made dummy runs on them, just to make them turn out of formation. It is hard to believe how many pilots risked their lives to stop the Jap fleet. During the battle a young pilot came up on the bridge, he was white as a sheet. He told me this was his first combat. When he was in training they told him to never strafe a battleship or cruiser. His first combat instructions were to go down and strafe a battleship.

Lieutenant, now Dr, Doy Duncan, Pilot, VC-20, USS *Kadashan Bay*
from *Abandoned at Leyte*

My fighter group had to sit on the deck for a while because we were to be the second wave to go out to meet the Japanese fleet. While we waited, we had our radios turned on so we could listen to the battle communications. We heard cries of 'Mayday, Mayday,' which couldn't help but to shake us up a little.

In a coordinated attack, the torpedo planes came in at about eight thousand to ten thousand feet. We (the fighter planes) would do a thatch and weave over the torpedo planes to give them protection. We escorted the torpedo planes until they got to a certain point. Then we led in, blazing away, to try to get the Japanese gunners' attention. We fired nothing but .50-caliber bullets. We had two machine guns on each wing. Meanwhile, the torpedo planes with five-hundred-pound bombs were right behind us. We were supposed to distract the Japanese gunners while other torpedo planes came in at water level. Our goal was to get the Japs' attention so we could get the guys with the torpedoes in close ...

On my first run against Kurita's fleet – to put it bluntly – I was scared. But once I started shooting, I overcame it. We thinned out a little bit so they couldn't concentrate on any one clump of us, and we began shooting. Every fifth round was a tracer. You could see it. It looked almost like the Fourth of July with all the red tracers floating back up toward us as they bounced off the deck of the battleship. And we knew that for every one we saw, there were four we didn't see. The *Yamato* had a tremendous amount of firepower. I don't believe we did the *Yamato* any particular damage on the first attack, at least not much. We went back up, regrouped, and went at him again. That time I was really concentrating on shooting at it. All of a sudden, I noticed I was too low. As I jerked back on the stick, I looked at the altimeter. It read two hundred feet. We were supposed to pull out at about one thousand feet. I had had no intention of getting that close to it because, of course, it was very dangerous. However, since we went in as straight down as we could, shooting at us was much more difficult.

As I pulled out of that near disaster I saw clouds at about three or four thousand feet. I ducked into one of them to try to get out of the Japs' gun sights for a moment. When I came out the other side of the cloud, I got quite a scare. There were planes coming out of that little cloud from all directions. There is no telling how close we came to each other inside it. We gathered and went down for another run. A boy from our squadron named Andy Anderson got a torpedo into the *Yamato*. We came back around, reorganized, and came at it a third time. That time I didn't let myself get quite so low on my strafing run. I came down from approximately twelve thousand feet. I couldn't believe the amount of ack-ack. It was so thick, it looked like you could get out and walk on it. It looked as though it would be impossible for a plane to come down through it and not get hit. I was somewhat amazed at how few planes were hit after going through that.

On that third run just as I pulled out, I looked back over my shoulder and saw the *Yamato* take two torpedoes in rapid succession. It looked like it was going to turn upside down. It is my understanding that it had eight watertight compartments, and any four of them could be punctured and it would stay afloat. Those torpedoes I saw might not have punctured even three of them. They could have hit pretty much in the same place.

Forced to ditch after his Wildcat was hit, Duncan spent some sixty hours in the water before being rescued, hidden on Samar Island and brought back to health by Philippino guerrillas who had already saved a second pilot from *Kadashan Bay*. He returned to his carrier on 24 November to find that he had been reported dead.

Ronald Vaughn, Division 2, USS *Kitkun Bay*, Taffy Three
Ronald Vaughn Papers (#658) Joyner Library

The *Casablanca*-class *Kitkun Bay* was one of the six escort carriers of Rear Admiral Clifton Sprague's Taffy Three.

The third day, after securing from our early morning call to battle stations, and while the crew was beginning to eat breakfast, battle stations was again sounded, and when we got to our battle stations, we found ourselves under attack by units of the Japanese fleet. My work station at this time was in the scullery (where the dishes were washed). When battle stations was sounded, I got so excited that I forgot to turn off the dishwashing machine and one of the cooks had to do it. I hit the ladder going topside at full speed, and when I got topside I saw shells splashing around the ships in my group. The attacking group consisted of two Battleships four heavy Cruisers , and ten Destroyers. We immediately turned into the wind to launch aircraft, but by doing so we were headed toward the Japanese ships instead of away from them. As soon as our fighters and bombers were airborne, we turned the other way and ran for our lives. The Japanese were shooting from about 20 miles away, and the biggest gun we had on board would only reach 5.5 miles.

For the next two and a half hours we were chased by the Japanese ships. Most of our Destroyer escort had left us to go and attack the Japanese ships, while some stayed to help us lay [a] smoke screen. All the ships in the task force were laying thick black smoke as fast as they could to make range finding more difficult. In spite of this, hits were being scored on the ships in my task group. The ship which normally sailed behind my ship in formation (*Gambier Bay*) took repeated shell hits, and eventually took enough hits so that she could no longer maintain steam. As she fell back, our Destroyers went back to pick up survivors, and had to engage Japanese ships first. Every ship in my task group took shell hits from the Japanese ships except mine. The reason we didn't take any shell hits was because our Captain was smart enough to chase salvos. If a salvo landed on the Starboard side, he would order the helmsman to turn hard to Starboard. The next salvo would then land either astern or on our Port side. When this happened, the helmsman was ordered to put the ship hard to Port causing the next salvo to land to Starboard or ahead of us.

The closest they came to my ship was when a salvo landed about 20' off our fantail. The resulting concussion was so violent that I thought we had been hit. During this time, the Japanese ships had closed to within range of our 5" gun, and we began to return the shell fire, scoring several hits of our own. The planes from my ship accounted for 2 Cruisers sunk and a Battleship dead in the water from 5 bomb hits and 2 torpedo hits. As the Japanese ships closed in, we found ourselves heading in a direction that would run us aground in another hour. We could, in fact, see the land ahead of us. About this time, the Japanese ships suddenly turned and headed away from us. As we turned away from the approaching land, our radar picked up a flight of enemy planes but lost them shortly after. We began landing operations for the aircraft from our task group, and it was suddenly discovered that the Japanese planes were intermingled with our own planes. As our planes scattered to get out of the way of our anti-aircraft fire, each of the Japanese pilots picked a Carrier out of the task group and headed for it in a suicide mission. The plane that chose my ship was coming in over the stern section of the ship and headed for the middle of the flight deck. Our anti-aircraft fire was hitting the plane from both sides as he made his dive. The only guns that could fire were the last twin mount 40mms on each side of the ship (Port and Starboard). In other words, only 4 guns were firing because the rest of the guns had been shut down by an automatic cut-off that kept them from firing across the flight deck. At about 500 feet, the plane suddenly buckled in the middle and exploded. This knocked him off course, and he narrowly missed the ship, taking about 25 feet of the Port catwalk and one man with him.

Another Carrier [USS *St. Lo*] wasn't so lucky. The plane that chose her for his target hit in the middle of the flight deck and set their aviation gasoline on fire. As the fire spread, the bombs on their aircraft began to explode, as well as the powder magazines for the flight deck anti-aircraft guns. As the men abandoned ship, the explosions on board sent pieces of steel weighing several hundred pounds each into the water, killing several hundred men.

As night began to fall, we were ordered back into position guarding the troop and supply ships for the invasion. The next day, my entire task group was ordered to proceed to Pearl Harbor for temporary repairs.

Verner Carlsen, SHIP'S CHAPLAIN, USS *Gambier Bay*
USS *Gambier Bay* Association / Judith Hoefs

I was in the ward room eating breakfast on the morning of Oct. 25 after we had secured from General Quarters when General Quarters sounded again. I grabbed my helmet and raced to the bridge where my battle station had been assigned by the Captain. I was to give a running account of what I observed for the men below decks over the PA system. I remember seeing the first geyser like eruption as an eerie pink color. Then another came closer of another color. It seemed at the time that all hell broke loose as we felt the ship shudder. I am not sure how my description of what was transpiring came across to the men below decks. I do know that some of them, including Al Hartin, who was one of my roommates, said my battle description changed from an account of what was happening to prayers, and that the voice ceased in the middle of prayers. I do remember that Gunnery Officer Stringer finally told me I could just as well hang up the mike because the line was dead. I have since often hoped that some of those prayers may have reached the wounded and dying in different parts of the ship and given them some kind of comfort in a time of dire need.

The order to abandon ship was given.

When I hit the water I kept going down, down, down and finally rose to the surface. All around me were men coming down the ropes, or swimming away from the ship. I saw a number of rafts in the water already with several men aboard them. I took off rapidly for one of them.

I remember that Buzz Borries had taken his place at the head of the raft and stayed there kind of keeping control during those 42 hours. The spam pieces and malted milk balls were doled out at his direction. The water kegs had popped their bungs when the rafts hit the water and they filled with salt water. The lack of water to drink was a desperate situation.

Homer Smith, Radio Operator, USS *Kadashan Bay*, Taffy Two
Communication with the Editor

We were aware through reports on our radios that Taffy 3 to the northwest and nearest to the entrance to San Bernardino, was in serious trouble from enemy gunfire. By 0800 all our carriers were launching planes repeatedly to attack the Japanese fleet and their land-based plane cover. Fighter planes protected the torpedo planes by strafing the ships to divert antiaircraft fire. At 8:40, our circle, Taffy 2, was straddled by yellow and green waterspouts 200 feet high from enemy cruiser fire attempting to determine the range for their 8-inch shells. Soon larger water spouts told us that a battleship was testing for its 14-inch guns. Our captain would steer the ship toward the last water spout assuming that the gunners would not repeat the aim that missed. Around 0900 the Japanese ships were so close to us that we could see the pagoda topmasts from our signal bridge. They knew where we were because that morning their land-based scouting planes had appeared long enough to spot us before our fighter planes could shoot them down.

Our Taffy 2's Admiral Stump ordered our three destroyers to take a position in column about five miles to our rear and be ready to attack any light enemy forces coming ahead of an enemy cruiser or battleship.

Our fighter and bomber planes and planes from the other five carriers in Taffy 2 had been in the initial strike at the Jap Fleet attacking Taffy 3 for about an hour. Now they were called in to protect us, Taffy 2. We had already turned toward the Japanese coming at us three times to launch and land planes into the wind. Now we had to do it again. We and the *Ommaney Bay* were the slowest of the six carriers in our Taffy 2 with 16 knots top speed compared to 28 knots by the pursuers. We both had poor engines, frequently in dock for new rings and other repairs. Being slower, we didn't get protected by the big smoke screen as well as the others were and the enemy could find us easier. But when our planes were in the air, they were as deadly against the enemy as those of the other carriers.

In the Communications shack, all messages on the radio, normally in code, were now in plain language. I was taking down the transmissions on a yellow pad, trying to sort out who was reporting and keeping our Captain informed on the progress of the battle. Others were doing the same. One plane scouting the enemy at 0937 told us that a battleship was on our tail, but fortunately this target faded from our screen to the relief of all hands. We heard from Taffy 3 that the *Gambier Bay*, CVE 73, a carrier twin to ours, trailing and out of the smoke screen, takes a hit on the flight deck, loses its power, and is put out of operation by enemy guns. My notes which I still have, read that it was smoking and drifting back through the Japanese Fleet. The carrier is hit about once a minute, then sinks about 0900, flaming brightly with gasoline and strafing members of their crew in the water. With ammunition exploding and with a Japanese cruiser firing at her from 2,000 yards away, I'm sure that I was not the only one recording the message who mentally substituted the *Gambier Bay*'s fate with our own possibility as soon as the Japanese fleet reached us.

A friend of mine from Harvard days was a communication officer on the *Gambier Bay*. I was sure he was lost so I was glad to run into him at Pearl Harbor much later. Somehow he had been picked up after his ship sank.

Reports from Taffy 3 told of its other carriers being hit as well as the sinking of the *Gambier Bay*. Later their *Saint Lo* was also sunk by a suicide plane. You can read in the books on the battle – how two of their destroyer escorts, the *Hoel* and the *Johnston* were sunk in almost a suicide battle defending them from the Japanese fleet. To the south, Taffy 1 was under attack by suicide planes, a new Japanese desperation tactic that was later to put us out of action. We sent some of our fighters to ward off Taffy 1's land-based enemy planes even though we needed all we could put up to harass the ships approaching us. While Taffy 1 had the full complement of six squadrons, many were out helping other ships in the task force or refueling on muddy landing strips ashore.

More than 1,000 men were lost from the three escort carrier groups.

Commander Eugene Robert Forsht, USS *Ticonderoga*
Dallas B. Long, Jr., Collection (#636) Joyner Library

After her trials and working-up period, the new *Essex*-class carrier went into action for the first time on 5 November, joining the other carriers in the continuing support of the Leyte invasion and facing the Kamikaze threat.

Just where and what was I doing on November 5, 1944?

I remember it very well as we had nine F-6-F-5's on the flight deck ready for combat air control. I remember very well that we had two who couldn't get their engines started, so I ran back to the flight deck to get the last one started. An Ensign Crow had some problems and got it flooded. We did get it started and he was the last plane off. As I ran back to the flight deck control, Boatswain Alexander who was the Assistant on the flight deck for launching aircraft and respotting aircraft, came out and tackled me. Just about that time, I happened to look up – there was a Jap plane going over. Needless to say there were splinters flying on both sides of us where the deck was peppered with machine gun bullets. However, thanks to Boatswain Alexander, I never even got a splinter. That was my experience of baptism under fire.

8
1945

During 1945, Arctic convoys continued to run, mostly unscathed, while a few U-boats remained in the Atlantic until ordered to return and surrender. However, the final year of the naval war focussed on supporting Allied landings on Japanese-occupied territories and trying to fend off increasing numbers of deadly Japanese kamikaze attacks.

The US fleet sailed from Leyte to Luzon on 30 December 1944 to cover the landings that began on 9 January. TF38 then went north, through the South China Sea, to attack shipping and land-based targets in Japanese-held areas along the Chinese coast before heading for Formosa and Okinawa, where a kamikazi attack caused serious damage to the Fleet Carrier USS *Ticonderoga*. February saw the capture of the small but strategic island of Iwo Jima, close to Japan itself.

On its way to join up with the US Navy, aircraft from the four carriers of the British Pacific Fleet carried out difficult but successful attacks on vital Japanese oil installations around Sumatra, which were inaccessible to other forms of attack. Losses were not inconsiderable, and later it was learned that the Japanese had beheaded a number of aircrew whom they had taken prisoner. The British joined the US Fleet at Manus in early March, and despite the opposition of Admiral King, the two fleets cooperated to good effect. The British carriers were initially stationed off the Sakishima Islands with the task of preventing Japanese supplies and reinforcements reaching Okinawa, where massive landings (Operation 'Iceberg') began the following month, heavily opposed both on land and in the air – many carriers took kamikaze hits including USS *Essex* and USS *San Jacinto*. The British carriers with their steel decks fared somewhat better than the Americans, although *Illustrious* was sufficiently badly damaged to have to retire. Okinawa fell in late June, by which time nearly 2,000 kamikaze attacks had been launched against Allied ships. The death toll on both sides and among the civilian population was vast, approaching a quarter of a million.

The war in Europe ended on 8 May with the unconditional surrender of Germany. The Pacific conflict continued after the fall of Okinawa, with US and British carriers bombarding the Japanese mainland and launching air strikes from the carriers. On 6 August, the first atomic bomb was dropped, on Hiroshima, by a Superfortress based on Tinian; on the 9th, a second bomb hit Nagasaki; Japan surrendered on the 15th.

For the carriers, the war was not entirely over: some of the Japanese-held islands were surrendered after Japan's capitulation. In addition they had the task of helping to liberate and repatriate thousands of prisoners-of-war, many of whom were in terrible condition.

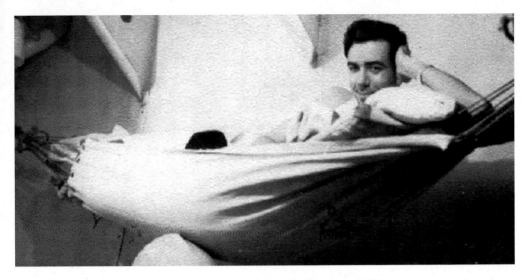

Above: Sleeping arrangements for Omar Fowler, HMS *Illustrious*, 1948, were not much different to those in Nelson's day. (Courtesy Omar Fowler)

Below left: The US Navy's first African-American aviator, Jesse Leroy Brown, in 1949. He was killed in Korea in 1950. (USNHHC)

Below right: Aviation Electronicsman 1/c Jim Stephens, Airman, on USS *Essex* off Korea. (Courtesy Jim Stephens)

Above: Rescue for downed Firefly crew Sub-Lieutenant Neil MacMillan, RAN, and CPO Phil Hancox, RAN. (Original painting by David Marshall, courtesy of the artist)

Below left: Private 1/c Clinton Cox, USMC, poses proudly aboard USS *Coral Sea*, 1955. (Courtesy William Cox)

Below right: Commander David 'Shorty' Hamilton strikes a martial attitude by his Sea Vixen. (Courtesy David Hamilton)

Above: The Deck Landing Mirror Sight fitted to HMS *Albion* greatly improved the safety of deck landings. (CPL)

Right: A gift for Prince Charles from HMS *Eagle* during the Queen's visit in 1959. (Courtesy David Hamilton)

Above: Anglo-American co-operation. The USS *Independence* is refuelled at sea by the Royal Fleet Auxiliary tanker *Tidereach*. (USNHHC)

Left: Defence Minister Mr Bansi Lal shaking hands with the Commander of 300 Squadron, Vinod Pasricha, aboard INS *Vikrant* (ex-HMS *Hercules*) in the presence of Admiral Schunker. (Courtesy Rear Admiral Pasricha)

Above: A street party on the flight deck of HMS *Invincible* in 1981 to celebrate the wedding of HRH Prince Charles and Lady Diana Spencer. (Courtesy Mark Bennet)

Below left: Harrier pilot Commander Tim Gedge days before deploying to the Falklands. (Courtesy Commander Tim Gedge)

Below right: Lieutenant Barry 'Skull' W. Hull on the flight deck of USS *Saratoga* as she passes through the Suez Canal on her way to the Gulf. (Courtesy Barry W. Bull)

Above: Commander Mark Fox, USN, gets ready to launch in his Hornet. (US Navy)

Left: HMS *Illustrious*, USS *Harry S. Truman* and USS *Dwight D. Eisenhower* during Operation 'Bold Step', 2007. (Jay C. Pugh USN)

Top right: Command Master Chief Kathleen A. Hansen cuts a slice of her golf-themed birthday cake on USS *Ronald Reagan*. (Courtesy Kathleen A. Hansen)

Below right: The Royal Navy's Commander Henry Mitchell, left, on exchange with the US Navy, being briefed in the ready room of Strike Fighter Squadron (VFA) 11 before flying from the *Nimitz*-class aircraft carrier USS *Harry S. Truman* in 2007. (Matthew D. Williams, USN)

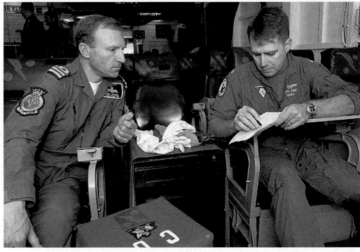

Above: ITS *Giuseppe Garibaldi* and USS *Harry S. Truman* during 'Majestic Eagle 2004', an exercise in the Mediterranean. (Josh Kinter USN)

Below: MEDEVAC. A medical team from *Cavour* stabilises a young Haitian accident victim during the flight to the carrier. (Marina Militare)

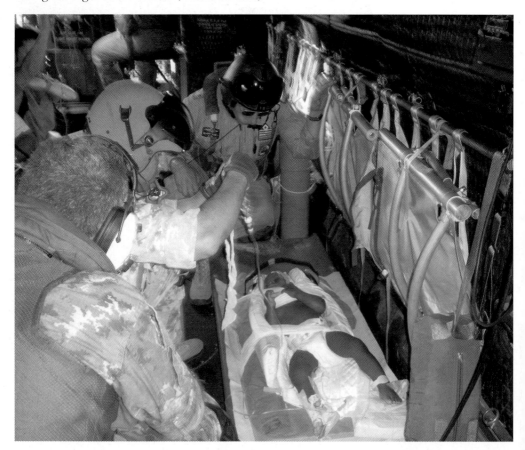

Geoff Shelton, Seaman, HMS *Vindex*
Communication with the Editor

It's an ill wind that does not do somebody some good, and how true that is.

On the 11th January 1945 Convoy RA63 left Kola Inlet to return home. We experienced no problems with enemy aircraft or U-Boats, but when we were somewhere north east of the Faroes we were hit by a storm. It was not just a storm, it was a gale in fact it was more than a gale – it was horrendous. There were no lookouts closed up, there was no manning the guns. These positions were just not accessible and the only people on the upper deck were the Skipper and two others …

Now we get to the best part. Imagine a mess deck two hours into the middle watch, the hammocks are swinging in unison in the dim lights of the emergency lamps. The water can still be heard sloshing about from side to side. The gale force wind tended to stifle the snores and the grunts emanating from the hammocks. The duty watch fully clothed but unable to carry out their duties played cards in the dim light. A furtive figure swung down the hatch. 'Quick' he said. 'The barrels in the Rum Locker have burst open and the Officer of the Watch has ordered that it be pumped overboard in case of fire'. A look of horror spread over their faces, they were in shock. We had survived thus far everything that the enemy and the elements had thrown at us but this, it was too much. I have never seen so many men at one time so near to tears, and then suddenly it changed, for they leapt to their feet and grabbed any object they could lay their hands on that would hold a liquid, and then they acquired any cloth that would assist in mopping up this liquid gold. The Officer of the Watch was surprised that so many were desirous of protecting their ship and especially the thoroughness with which they were kneeling down with filthy swabs soaking up the rum and with it the dirt and grime of many years standing, not to mention the accumulation of flakes of red lead and other coloured paints.

Retiring to the mess deck with fannies* full of contaminated rum, they proceeded to filter through clean handkerchiefs. When we dropped the hook in the Faroes there was no ship as happy as H.M.S. *Vindex*.

Sub-Lieutenant (A) Jack Thomas, LSO, *Empire Mackendrick*
Communication with the Editor

Despite the arrival of the true escort carriers, the MAC ships continued to operate as convoy escorts in the Atlantic.

With the short, narrow flight decks it was necessary for a pilot landing on to obey the mandatory signals of the Batsman who was guiding him down and

---

* Metal mess kettles or cooking containers – named, with black humour, after a young girl, Fanny Adams, who was savagely killed and dismembered in 1867, at the same time as tinned mutton was issued to the Royal Navy. Sailors claimed that parts of her remains had got into the tins. She is also commemorated in the phrases 'Sweet Fanny Adams' and the euphemistic abbreviaton F.A.

except in really rough weather conditions landings were fairly straightforward. The big problem was getting airborne in light wind situations and here the Ratog [Rocket Assisted Take-Off Gear] was a godsend. The Swordfish would be ranged aft on the flight deck as far as possible. The pilot ran up the engine to full throttle, held on the brakes: the Batsman waved away the chocks, signalled with a green flag to begin the take-off run and at a predetermined point more or less level with the bridge, the pilot pressed a button and with a dramatic burst of flame the rockets fired and the plane was literally hoisted into the air. That is, if all went to plan!

It was 14th March 1945, a day of flat calm in mid Atlantic. Swordfish NR 931 was ranged ready for take-off. The Pilot, S/Lt. Alan Spencer with his Observer, S/Lt. Jim Milroy followed my instructions and trundled off down the deck. At the appropriate point he pressed the button. Nothing happened! The aircraft wallowed off the deck sinking towards the sea. A few hundred yards ahead and to port of the bows it finally stalled and fell into the Atlantic with a big splash. The Master went full astern and turned the ship to avoid hitting the aircraft which was floating tail-up as the ship came close alongside. I rushed to the port side of the flight deck and shouted: 'Are your depthcharges fused!?' If they had been and the aircraft had sunk close to the side of the ship there could have been a rather nasty explosion possibly blowing a hole in the carrier. Alan, by now struggling out of the pilot's cockpit to reach the aircraft's dinghy which had self-inflated, just shook his head. Jim in the rear cockpit which was still clear of the water, partly by stepping on Alan's shoulder and driving him underwater, climbed into the dinghy first – without even getting his feet wet. They were both picked up by the rescue ship in a few minutes.

Jim always maintained that his action merely proved the superior intelligence of an Observer over a Pilot.

Sub-Lieutenant (A) Stanley Brand, RNVR, 836 NAS, MV *Empire MacColl* from *Achtung! Swordfish!*

During early 1945 irreparable damage to three of *Empire MacColl's* four Swordfish gave Brand the idea of building one operational aircraft out of the remains of the three so that the MAC ship – the only carrier escort in the convoy – had two serviceable aircraft. The task took place during the typically rough weather of the North Atlantic in winter.

Starting work on Queenie One, we put a strop around the mast with a block and tackle on it. Then, with the aid of a ladder and a long pole, we pushed the strop up the mast as high as it would go. The rope through the block was fastened to the lifting eye provided on the upper mainplane centre-section of all Swordfish for lifting a seaplane version aboard a ship. The strain was taken, enabling Q1 to be slewed around until she was pointing to the side of the bridge. We then fastened a block and tackle between the tail wheel and a stanchion in a gun sponson on the port side of the ship. With many steadying hands on the wingtips of Q1 we able to lift her with the two blocks sufficiently to remove her damaged port wings, port wheel, wheel struts and oleo leg (all for scrap), and to remove the starboard undercarriage complete for salvage. The damaged propeller was scrapped and the splined propeller shaft was padded with a cushion made out of a bundle of sacks. By repetitive juggling of the ropes through the two blocks, the aircraft was lifted into position with the propeller shaft resting against the side of the bridge structure. In this position there was no danger of the ship's rolling causing damage to the engine by allowing the aircraft to move back and forth with the shaft acting as a battering-ram on the bridgework.

The good starboard wing was then supported on trestle jacks at a low level and an undamaged pair of port wings was manhandled from Q2, and placed beside Q1 on more trestle jacks and adjusted for height to be level with the wings on the starboard side. After much jiggery-pokery, letting-out and heaving-in of the two tackles, and grunting and groaning of the hands on the wings, the latter were eventually bolted into place, the locking pins inserted and locked home with the retaining clips. From our previous experience, these clips were closely examined independently by Bill, Johnnie and myself, without collusion or discussion! Q3 was divested of her propeller, complete undercarriage and tail plane, and these were all fitted to the hybrid Q1. We didn't re-number her Q1-2-3 as one wag suggested.

The fitters and riggers then demonstrated their professional pride by asking all supernumerary hands to get to hell out of their way to let them check over everything without hindrance or interference. My rigger, with a wry smile, said, 'Leave us to it. After all it is your life which concerns us'. I knew then that he would not have made such a joke if there was the slightest doubt in his mind, about the feasibility of the action we had taken.

The new Swordfish emerged in just 30 hours. The only question remaining was: would it fly? Bill Thomson insisted that he was going to come with me, in spite of my protests that it was foolish to expose both of us to risk, because I would not be going out of sight of the convoy, and it was the only time he ever pulled rank – he had two weeks' seniority over me. Our Flight Commander, Lieutenant Bruce Frame, agreed that Bill should go with me on the grounds that if all was in order, then nothing was lost but if there was a problem, then two minds were better than one.

Ranged right aft with the whole deck stretching ahead of me seemed strange but I went through all my drill meticulously, giving Bats the requisite thumbs-up and the ship started to turn into wind. Bats wound me up to full throttle and as soon as the steam jet blew straight down the deck he sent me off. My tail came up unusually fast, before I was level with the bridge but it was too late to abort. The nose was so heavy that I was afraid the propeller would foul the deck and I wound back the tail-trim wheel to take some of the pressure off the joystick, which I was heaving back into my stomach. I went over the bow and in spite of putting one foot on the instrument panel to give force to my joystick leverage, my wheels touched the crests of several waves. I shouted to Bill to hold tight for ditching as I couldn't gain height and she was terribly nose-heavy. He replied 'Don't ditch! I'm going aft'.

A few moments later some of the adverse trim eased a little so that I dared glance behind me, to see Bill getting astride the fuselage where the TAG's Vickers machine gun was supposed to be. As it improved further I was able to claw a little bit of height until I was about Macship deck height of thirty-two feet, and again I glanced around to see Bill astride the fuselage out at the tailplane with a handhole cut into the leading edge of the tail-fin, to which he was clinging like grim death until he saw my head turn whereupon be let go with one hand long enough to give me a quick thumbs-up, illuminated by his familiar grin, with white teeth accentuated by his black beard, something I was getting used to seeing under conditions of adversity. All this time I was flying at full throttle and any attempt to reduce power and speed would cause the nose to drop and lose the height, which had been gained at the risk of Bill's life. The concern for our safety on the part of our colleagues made them focus many pairs of binoculars upon us, especially after we dropped over the bow and paddled our feet upon the water 'like an obese swan weary at the end of the mating season' as one friend put it. Realising what was wrong and that I needed an emergency return, especially seeing Bill acting as he did, the Skipper of our ship kept into wind while I got round an unorthodox circuit and made my pass at the deck at full throttle with hook down but tail up high. Bats could do nothing except give me 'steady as you go' and then 'Cut' as I came over the round down. Whether the barrier should be up or down under these circumstances was a topic of indecisive conversation for some time afterwards, but my preference would be for it to be up. As there was no way I could go round again I would much rather have wire hawsers wrapped around my propeller and wings than ditch immediately in front of an 8000 ton marine steamroller with a 3,300 horsepower bacon-slicer fitted underneath it.

We caught the fourth wire because fortuitously I came over the stern with the ship horizontal but with the bow rising giving me an uphill run. It was sheer luck that things went well. I had no reserve of power to avoid a rising stern, and if I had hit the rounddown or caught an earlier wire, Bill could have been catapulted to his death. Once again Maydown dismissed Bill's action as being self-preservation and hence unworthy of recognition or commendation except that his 'flimsy' (the written assessment of an officer given every six months) drew attention to 'his prompt and well-considered response to emergency'.

On a previous flight, when he and Brand served on the Macship MV *Alexia*, Thompson had climbed out on the aircraft wing to lash down a malfunctioning locking handle that could have led to the wing folding up in flight. Although comparable to the heroism of an RAF pilot who received the VC, Thomson's bravery went without reward.

Sub-Lieutenant (A) Jack Thomas, 836 Squadron
from *The Lonely Sky and the Sea*

With the end of the European war on 8 May, 836 Squadron was disbanded. Their MAC ships slowly returned to merchant service and their anachronistic Swordfish were consigned to the emotional memories of those who had crewed and serviced them.

Swordfish – LS 384 (The Dingbat)

Where are you now,
you broken down old rattletrap?
you canvas, wire, wood and steel contraption?
Your engine was a teased-out, coughing,
living scrapyard:
but it always staggered on,
flogging the cold Atlantic air
with a nicked propeller.

Each time we trundled down the deck
I thought we'd never make it;
yet, somehow, improbably,
you'd clamber up the law of gravity
and balance at five hundred feet,
five knots above the stall;
carting on your creaking wings
a load of flares, depth-charges, rockets that
would break the back of any like-sized plane.
Over the hungry, grey Atlantic you wove
a melting network of Vipers, Adders, Crocodiles and Lizards
reptilian tracks that kept the U-Boats down.
(They were afraid of you inside their cold grey shells
pulling in their tortoise-head periscopes
when you went rumbling by.)
I can remember still,
(and I have the marks to prove it!)
the draughty discomfort of your cockpit.
On the knuckles of my left hand
is a small white scar.
A sharp projection by the throttle
bit it regularly,
and shredded my gloves.
On long patrols, left heel jammed
beneath the rudder bar
right knee hard up against the stick,

you'd draw a bee-line.
(Look, no hands!)
who wants an autopilot anyway?

Landing on, flogged into attitude
by the batsman's magic arms,
you'd thump on to the clanging deck
with all the grace
of a stalling pterodactyl;
and yank the snatching wire
out to full-twanging stretch,
dripping black oil over your dirty chops
as, engine-stopped, wings-folded,
you were un-born
into the steel womb of the hangar.

Where are you now, you Stringbag,
rag-bag, battered, lovely monstrosity?
I know!
In a Yorkshire field I left you,
knee-deep in buttercups beside a hawthorn hedge.
left there to rot you were, when they had done with you
and I was sent to fly a
streamlined, perspex-lidded,
electronic can.
But you've been spared the shame of
Ploughshare-beaten swords;
while many a newer aeroplane
has metamorphosed
into saucepans on a kitchen stove,
you are your own memorial:
A skeletal reminder ...
A rusting, rotting relic in the bindweed and the nettles.
Yet only a degree more weathered
than you ever were.
Ready for resurrection, and for tearing off,
shedding, shredding vegetation as you go:
bouncing across the pasture, and heaving up
at stalling speed
into the teeth of a north-west gale.

George Center, USS *Ticonderoga*
Dallas B. Long, Jr., Collection (#636) Joyner Library

On 21 January the Fleet Carrier USS *Ticonderoga*, part of TF38, attacked airfields on Formosa. Shortly after noon, a kamikaze hit the carrier, and, as the crew fought to save their ship a second plane managed to get through.

Someone called Primary Fly on the intercom and asked 'what is the best way out of here?' The response was 'Port side Aft'. That advice looked good from the island, but actually directed us precisely into an oven. By now the smoke was so thick that visibility was about one foot. It was really scary, when we were turning back from the third route attempted for departure, I had difficulty finding the relative cool of the ready room. Successful egress was finally accomplished by forming a human chain of those of us remaining by grasping the belt of the preceding person. I led a chain of about five midships and aft (the chain kept getting longer) and ultimately reaching the starboard catwalk, and fresh air forward of the No 3 elevator. It has been said that the gas masks were no good for smoke – but they certainly saved us.

Thereafter we helped tend the wounded and manned the twin 3 caliber guns in rear of SB2Cs, but were unable to bear upon 2nd K due to folded wings as it approached from broad on the starboard beam. It struck the island.

When the fires were out and the port list was being taken off, it was good to see the last of the bombs and torpedoes being safely returned and secured within the magazines. Although there was about five inches of water remaining (from fighting fires) in my stateroom area, I finally got to sleep that night in my own (lower) bunk – with my hand dangling over the side to know that the water was not rising.

One contributing reason for this catastrophe was that Task Force 38 was positioned entirely too close to the SE coast of Formosa (approximately 40 miles). The *Ticonderoga* was the closest major carrier. We were so close that our strike aircraft had to make a large climbing orbit after rendezvous to clear the mountains (12000ft) and approach target area.

Lieutenant Colonel Ronnie Hay, Royal Marines, DSO, DSC*, Air Coordinator, British Pacific Fleet, HMS *Victorious*
IWM Sound Archive Reference 13856

In December 1944 Ronnie Hay had been appointed to the newly created post of Air Coordinator, with the rank of lieutenant colonel. Victorious was sent to the Far East, and on 24 January carried out Operation 'Meridian I' against the Pladjoe refinery, near Palembang on Sumatra. The strike force crippled oil production and set the oil storage facility on fire, as well as destroying Japanese aircraft on the ground and in the air. 'Meridian II' took place on 29 January, this time against the Soengi Gerong refinery, again near Palembang. The squadrons involved were 820, 1830, 1833, 1834, 1836, 1839, 1844 , 849, 854, 857, 887, 894 and 1770.

Here was this prime source of oil in south east Sumatra still intact, so they said 'well the only thing to do is to do it the proper way, with a daylight raid by the poor old Fleet Air Arm'. We had done one or two of those horrid things earlier on, like the *Tirpitz* ... We had Avengers and we had Corsairs and Hellcats and they all had endurance of 6 hours. 5 hours, easy; with long range tanks, more ... You can go a long way in 5 hours as opposed to 1 hour 50 that the Seafires had got ...

As a daylight raid with four carriers, we had something like 160 aircraft of which, say, 80 or 90 of them were bombers, and each bomber with, I think, 4000 pounds of bombs, and 80 fighters, and I was put in charge of the whole lot. That's where I got my interest in seeing that this is put in the right perspective in the history, because it is the first time that the Navy had sought to destroy a strategic target which was quite inaccessible – except for the B-29s who had proved ineffective – and so we did two strikes. There were two refineries and we did Pladjoe one day and a few days later we did Soengi Gerong ... And I was taking photographs at the same time as telling the chaps which piece of plant was still active and which bit wasn't. It was a bit difficult with all that smoke about. We lost a fair number of people, I suppose five per cent, but the results proved dramatic. The thing was put out of action. It showed that naval air power, or the Navy, shall we put it more broadly, was able to strike where no one else could in those days...

I shot down four Japanese fighters during the two days I was in that particular business, and I think we lost about 20 aircraft one way or another. Piece of cake. You only had to look at a Japanese and he burst into flames. When I say that, I mean to say you just point yourself generally at him, pressed the button, and he immediately blew up. They had no self-sealing tanks. They were made mostly of wood or maybe bits of tin with wood round them. One squirt and they'd blow up. I was very pleased because it saved ammunition. I never had any trouble fighting the Japanese. We could outclimb them. The first time ... in the whole war, except when I was doing ramrods* in Spitfires over France, I was totally in command of the air, not just all of the air that was there, all our own friendly air, but there was no aeroplane could touch me. I could outclimb, I could outfly. The Corsair was an absolutely marvellous aeroplane. I could outmanoeuvre a great number; I could certainly outdive all the Japanese, and I'd got armour plated glass and self-sealing tanks.

**Lieutenant, later Commander, Desmond Wilkey, Observer,
1770 Squadron, HMS *Indefatigable***
IWM Sound Archive Reference 14150

We were the Admiral's ship, and [Admiral] Vian joined us. He was going out there as the Admiral commanding aircraft carriers, and he was a tough cookie, if you like. Our first memory of Vian is him having all the squadrons lined up in front of the bridge – I think it was pouring with rain. He stood in the shade of the bridge, not getting wet, while he talked to us.

---

* Fighter/bomber missions to destroy ground targets.

Vian was a man who just didn't like being in harbour, didn't like not being on operations … But, on the other hand, Vian did one thing that made sure all the aircrews were loyal to him, and in fact we revered him. A plane was shot down when we did some operations against Sumatra not more than 10 or fifteen miles from the coast. It was too dangerous to send a destroyer in to pick up the aircrew so he took the fleet in to pick up the aircrew, and after that, as far as the aircrew were concerned, Vian could do no wrong. He could bully he us as much as he liked, as long as he looked after us when we came down in the drink.

We wanted to do our job. We were trained. But the Americans said they didn't want us until we had put out the oil fields of Sumatra at Pangkalan Brandan and Palembang, so we had very good models of these. Our job was to … strafe certain key buildings, pump house. We were told if we could put the pump house out of action the whole thing would be out of action for months. So we had to identify that. We had an excellent model of it. The problem was we had to fly off and climb to about 1500 feet to cross a range of mountains, and Palembang was about 100 miles in from where the fleet was. So, if the Japs had many fighters there, we were going to come under quite savage attack on the way in as well as during the attack.

Anyway, we practised this and in fact I very well remember that the exercise that we did was an absolute shambles. It didn't go very well. We didn't form up very well, and we were thinking: I hope it goes a lot better than this on the day. In fact it did. And on 4th January we did the attack on Pangkalan Brandon which was the first of the oil fields. It was called Operation Lentil, and this was the second time we had trouble with barrage balloons because the whole oil field was protected by barrage balloons. On the way in, the Flight Commander in charge off the attack, Major Ronnie Hay, a Royal Marine, who directed the attack from about 20,000 feet, told us to take on the barrage balloons and shoot them down, so the Avengers would have a free run. And we shot down as many of them as we could but they're not easy to shoot down, actually. You see, you puncture the thing and then they don't float down so you don't really know you have got rid of them until they go down. We fired our rockets at this pumping station but as navigators we were too busy looking out for Jap fighters, and in fact our plane was attacked by a Jap fighter. The attack wasn't pressed home that much because we had a lot of high level cover who came down and had a dogfight with them. We lost a fair number of the crews. The Avengers lost a few crews and we lost one crew, a chap called Danny Levitt, our senior pilot, and that was very sad.

We had eight rockets. They had sixty-pound war heads – they had quite a bomb up on the front of them – which would blow up and wreck machinery in a pumping station. They were a new weapon. They were particularly efficacious against submarines because they used a solid warhead which pierced the submarine's casing, but they were also very good on ground attack … They added another dimension to the capability of the Firefly, which was then a very good ground attack fighter as well as long range reconnaissance.

Frederick George 'Pat' Oikle, HMS *Activity*

IWM Sound Archive Reference 17529

Oikle remained with HMS *Activity* after she was converted from an escort carrier into an aircraft ferry, taking replacement planes out to the Indian Ocean and the Far East

Going through [Suez] with a ship that size ... the bow wave is pretty hefty if you're going too quickly. Alongside the banks were what they used to call bumboats, native rowing boats and so on, and as our bow wave washed out, it washed them over the banks of the canal and onto the sand. We got through and I think we moored up in the Bitter Lakes, and it was a matter of getting that far before it got dark. We had search lights on even then. We carried on and we were in a theatre of war near Burma, Java and Sumatra ... The incident that happened next to me was – we weren't even allowed to tell our own ship mates what was happening – but apparently Met men were placed on little islands around the area, with a view that they would radio the weather back, and nobody knew which of those little islands were occupied by the Japanese. They used to relieve one another, and the job to get them there was [done] with a rowing boat, no engines, and we weren't allowed to carry guns, so you had a choice of weapons ... Every one that did this volunteered to do it, because, I suppose it was pretty dangerous. I was young and innocent and thought: well I'll have a go at this; so I did. And you were basically allowed to choose whatever weapon you wanted, so long as it was quiet, and I chose a knife, a beautiful knife, double bladed – blade must have been a good 8 inches long, beautifully balanced. You could have a garotte, like a cheese cutter ... it was serrated so it acted more quickly. One chap had a crossbow.

I seem to remember doing three of those ... There was always three of us to do the job, no more because that's five people in a small boat, pitch black and we had quite a way to go because the ship couldn't come inshore. It took a few hours overnight. [On] two of them we got back alright; the third one ... We had always said to one another: if one of us is killed the rest of us can do nothing, but if it's a wound we'll try and get you back ... We were just approaching the boats and we hadn't heard a thing, we didn't know there was anybody on the island, we had done the job ... They were in, and I was pushing it off, and I can't remember hearing a bang, but I felt something on the leg and next thing I remember was waking up in Sick Bay, and a chap sitting by my side, and he said ' Oh, you're with us again.'

Lieutenant Colonel Ronnie Hay, Royal Marines, DSO, DSC*, Air Coordinator, British Pacific Fleet, HMS *Victorious*

IWM Sound Archive Reference 13856

When ships arrived out the Far East, they all had people on board with UK rates of pay. The sailors that were shore-based in the Far East all got Local Overseas

Allowance which was quite a considerable increase in their rate of pay. On the other hand, they also acted as a pool to replace casualties, sickness and so forth for the ships' companies that were out in the area. So that when you got your draft ship in the Far East from HMS *Bherunda*, shall we say, which was a nice convenient air station to be on, and drafted to HMS *Victorious*, for duties at sea, what happened? You immediately suffered a catastrophic drop in pay. You lost your Local Overseas Allowance. So poor sailors, there was a dreadful general discontent about this. By being forced to give up their soft-perch, battle-free area in Ceylon, to go in these noisy, hot, overheated aircraft carriers or frigates, they suffered this reduction in their pay. And after all they had all got wives and things ... To be forced to take a reduction in pay to go and fight the Japanese ... There was very nearly a mutiny out there. Everyone was on the sailors' side. It was grossly unfair.

Commander Desmond Wilkey, Observer, 1770 Squadron, HMS *Indefatigable*
IWM Sound Archive Reference 14150

We were ready to go to the Pacific and help the Americans. Now it's a matter of record that the Americans didn't want us out there. Admiral King refused the offer of of a British Pacific Fleet and was forced by Roosevelt to take them, and they didn't want us, they wanted us to attack Borneo, they didn't mind what we attacked as long as we didn't join up with them, but in fact Roosevelt said: 'No you will use this offer – this is a good fleet and you will use them', so the terms were that we should under no circumstances have logistic support from the Americans, we would take our own logistical support, and we did our very best to take our own logistical support but in the point of fact the Americans were very good to us – they knew this was nonsense. They could support us and we had to prove to them that we were worth supporting. So after a short spell in Australia ... We went to a place called Manus which was the rear base. There we picked up our oilers and fleet train and then we went to Ulithi. Now this was a big shock. This was when we realised what small fry we were. We went into Ulithi; we were directed to an anchorage in a part of the atoll, and the rest of it was taken up with four large carrier fleets. There were about 30 carriers there, American, compared with our four, and we then realised, if we hadn't realised it before, the Americans were in the big time, and we really had to prove ourselves to them. We were up there for Operation Iceberg, the invasion of Okinawa and we were allocated the task of seeing that the Japanese didn't stage any planes into Okinawa or attack the American invasion fleet from the south west, from Formosa. There were some islands called Ishigakijima. There were three airports there and it was our job for every two days out of four to go in, to strafe them, to bomb them, to strafe the radar stations there, to strafe all the facilities there to make sure those airports were not used by staging planes.

The Fireflies were used for escort to the Avenger bombers, for combat air patrols and 'Jap' patrols. These were very low, about 30 miles from the fleet, and you flew up and down about 20 miles in the direction you expected attack, so that if the Japanese kamikaze bombers came in low you would give the fleet an early warning. And this was monumentally boring and monumentally tiring. You had to look: after all, you were protection for the fleet, but on the other hand you're just flying up and down, up and down, looking out. All you could see was the destroyer which was out there as the picket.

The other job we were occasionally given is what's called Dumbo CAP. Now Dumbos are the submarines that were placed throughout the Pacific at strategic points to pick up ditching aircrew, and they always had a couple [of] aircraft flying over the top of them to make sure the Japs didn't bomb them, and they were long, long exercises. And I think the Americans began to be glad they had a fleet there. But they weren't really pleased they had a fleet off there until the kamikazes started attacking their fleet ... A kamikaze attack on an American carrier is a horrendous affair. The *Franklin* was burnt down to the waterline, and eventually the Japanese found us and *Indefatigable* was the first to be attacked.

And I was asleep. I got up, and we briefed the crew for take-off. One of our crew was on the front of the carrier ready for take off to do one of these jobs like Jap patrol. I had flown late the previous night and I was still getting up and shaving. There was a bang and this kamikaze hit the base of the island. It killed a Canadian doctor we were very fond of, it blew the bugler down the steps and he broke his legs. It killed about two or three more people and put the operation room out of action, but it didn't put the flight deck out of action. Within half an hour we had our barrier back in use and we were landing on planes. The American liaison officers we had with us were astonished at this: they thought this was the greatest thing since sliced bread.

Lieutenant Colonel Ronnie Hay, Royal Marines, DSO, DSC*,
Air Coordinator, British Pacific Fleet, HMS *Victorious*
IWM Sound Archive Reference 13856

When you're on deck with a full deckload of aircraft, all fully armed and full of fuel, long range tanks, of course, you're turning into wind, and the kamikazes want to catch you with a full deckload fly off ... We couldn't hear because with the engines all running it makes quite a noise ... But you could see what's going on because suddenly [there's] a bloody black ball in the sky: anti-aircraft devices, and I looked across, and I saw *Indomitable* being hit. *Indomitable* was only about six cables away, and I was in *Victorious*. And when you're strapped in ... I was right on the outside edge. Ship was turning in, hard over to port, and the whole aircraft leans – it was going to starboard ... So I looked down, and there was the sea underneath me.

Lieutenant Nigel Matthews, Observer, 828 Squadron, HMS *Implacable*
Communication with the Editor

HMS *Implacable* arrived in the Pacific in June 1945, and the accident took place on 14 June.

Before we went out to the Pacific we converted to Avengers at Fern near Tain, Scotland.

On the way to the Pacific we put into Ceylon [Sri Lanka] and there we upgraded from Avenger Is to Avenger IIs, which we initially thought was jolly good news. They looked virtually the same, but they had a better radio set and a bigger and better engine. But in upgrading the engine Grumman didn't get things quite right, and inexplicably we lost a couple of crews who just disappeared on perfectly straightforward exercises performed on passage between Ceylon and Perth, Western Australia. This caused a lot of head-scratching as to why this was happening. Then some pilots reported that they had lost power when they were in the landing circuit, and a couple of aircraft actually ditched. I think we lost one crew and the other chaps all got out. The problems were ultimately ascribed [to] a fault with the spark plugs.

I would not say that we were frightened during this episode, but there was a bit of stress, and, as with everything else, you have to get used to things; there's under-confidence at first. As you get better, it does not cause any drama: you come to terms with it quite quickly – particularly if you're in your twenties and you've got a job to do and that job is flying the aeroplanes well.

Anyway, the pilots were briefed that, on take off, they should just check the revs as they went past the carrier's island, and if they weren't getting full revs they should abort the take off. We were doing the last operation before we finally joined the BPF. They sent us from Sydney, Australia [east coast] to Manus island to do one operation, over two days, on Truk atoll. By that time, the Japanese, who had been there in force, had fallen back because of the imminence of the American invasion of their Homeland. So there were minimal defences and we just used it as a practice. The first strike took place at dawn, when we were, I suppose, 40–60 miles west of the atoll. We had a flight deck full of Seafires, Fireflies and Avengers with 3500lb bombs. It was a very hot, humid, tropical morning; there was hardly a breath of wind, and the ship was having some difficulty in finding enough wind across the deck to launch the strike, but there were pockets of light wind generally on the edges of tropical rainstorms which you could actually see in the area. Eventually the ship found enough wind, and we were flagged off. I was in the leading Avenger with the CO, Lt. Cdr F. A. Swanton, as I was the Senior Observer. As we went past the Island the CO decided he wasn't getting full revs so he chopped the engine. Calculations had indicated that there would be enough deck space left to stop the aircraft before falling off the end but, because of the rain, we never quite made it; we skidded and toppled off the front of the carrier – which was steaming flat out at 30 knots.

One of the great features of the Avengers was that they were very nice to ditch (if you had to do it). Unlike the Barracuda, which would plunge to the bottom of the sea like a dart, the Avenger would 'waffle down', wings level. If they didn't have the power and were about to stall they didn't go into some terrible sort of spin.

I suppose we were doing about 70 knots, not enough to maintain flying speed, but too much to stop. So we waffled down and sat on the water with the wheels up – the pilot had managed to raise the undercarriage. We fell into the water about 200 yards ahead of *Implacable*, and we started getting out, which was a well-practised drill, but we'd all forgotten, of course, that here was *Implacable* charging up behind at 30 knots.

She hit the aeroplane and broke it in half. The starboard wing went down the starboard side – and the rest, with the three of us, went down the port side. The pilot, who was anchored to his seat by his dinghy and parachute on his bum, went down a fair way and swallowed quite a lot of the Pacific, but when the air gunner, CPO C. Ward, and I got out we were alright because we took our dinghies with us. However, we lost the dinghies in the collision but we were very relieved to see the pilot bob up a few yards away from us. After about 20 minutes we were picked up by HMS *Terpsichore*.

The most interesting aspect of this story (apart from the fact we all got out) is that as the ship went past us – and I can remember it well! – I heard a most sinister rumbling noise, a sort of room-room-room, and I deduced that this must be the ship's screws. I thought I'd be very fortunate to get away alive, but in fact, as *Implac*'s island passed us shortly afterwards – we were bumping along the side – the noise died away, and we floated off into the wake. The engines had been virtually stopped, before they reached us.

Years later I was at the Ministry of Defence, Admiralty, London, in a job in which I used to get copies of all aircraft accident reports [A25]. About 5 or 6 years after the war I saw one about an Attacker that had gone in ahead of *Eagle*. The pilot never got out of the aeroplane – the ship smashed it. The 'experts' said: 'Well, no chance. Ship couldn't possibly stop.' So I wrote a memo that effectively said: 'Well, actually, you're wrong, chaps, because it is possible to virtually stop the engines.' And the entire hierarchy of the air engineering world fell on my head and said it was quite impossible.

All I can say is that I wouldn't be here now if it hadn't been for Commander [E] D. S. Holt Wilson, D.S.O., R.N. He had been in *Penelope*, a light cruiser, when she was known as *Miss Pepperpot* (because she got so badly bombed in the Mediterranean), and he perfected a procedure so that when an emergency occurred a buzzer, operated from the bridge, sounded in the engine room. This indicated that everything was to be done to stop the engines because an aircraft had gone in ahead of the ship. And all I can say is, he did it in our case. If the ship's going flat out, there's a most tremendous inertia built up, and they actually have to let in a certain amount of steam into the steam turbine anyway. It's a fine judgement and a very risky business, because if you don't get it right you're running the risk of stripping the turbine blades and thereby depriving the ship of movement.

After the Truk operation we attacked the Japanese mainland and I think that lasted about three or four days before *Implacable* went back to Sydney. The other carriers had all been through the business of Okinawa and Iwo Jima where some of them had been bombed ... There were a number of kamikaze attacks around us but they didn't hit the ship. We were operating with the Americans as part of their fleet and we did about three or four attacks on the Japanese mainland and on the Inland Sea against shipping, but the only one I recall as being of any consequence was an attack on an airfield just before the war ended. We lost a couple of aircraft on that raid.

Long before one came close to the Pacific Fleet, which was a very large, you began to hear the voice radios going, and radio silence (which had to a much greater degree, but not totally, applied to the British carrier force) simply didn't apply to the Americans at all. They talked all the time about what was happening and who was going where, and I think the enemy could have picked up a tremendous amount of information. But presumably the USN must have thought it didn't matter very much because the Japanese were clearly on the defensive. At that late time I don't believe any attackers got through to hit the fleet.

American aviators, in my opinion, are absolutely first class. They had, again in my opinion, better aircraft than we did. Our Seafire was a lovely aeroplane; it was a very good fighter but it was not designed as a carrier-borne aeroplane and it had a very weak undercarriage. In spite of this it performed well in the Pacific. The Firefly wasn't bad at all. It was more rugged and it was built for carrier work, but we were always happy to have American aircraft.

Ronald Vaughn, Division 2, USS *Kitkun Bay*
Ronald Vaughn Papers (#658) Joyner Library

The sailing was routine until we started through the straits between the islands. At that time, the Japanese once again began using the suicide planes to attack the convoys. The convoy just ahead of us was hit several times, and a small carrier like mine was sunk just two days before D-Day on Luzon. As we approached Luzon, we were called to battle stations because our radar had picked up a flight of approaching enemy planes, but some of them got through our Combat Air Patrol. As the planes came in, we began a very heavy barrage of anti-aircraft fire, but one of the planes had singled us out for his target, and although we had an almost solid wall of anti-aircraft fire he was able to penetrate and hit the ship on the Port side right at the water line. At the same tine the Cruiser on our Starboard quarter fired an anti-aircraft shell into the Starboard catwalk of the ship. The suicide plane killed one man in the engine room, and the anti-aircraft shell killed 16 men topside. When the suicide plane went through the side of the ship, she began to take water rapidly, and to list heavily to Port. When this happened, the skipper ordered everyone on the Port side to move to the Starboard side. Shortly after this, it seemed as if the ship was going down, so everyone was ordered to abandon ship, except for a small group of men who volunteered to stay behind to see if they could save the ship. As I was starting to my abandon ship station, two medical corpsmen came carrying a stretcher with a severely wounded man. They asked for help to get the stretcher to the fantail so they could attend to more wounded. After several minutes of struggling down the ladder, we finally reached the fantail. When we did, one of the ship's doctors was there to examine the wounded man. After examination, he pronounced him dead. An officer who had helped get the stretcher to the fantail got the man's wallet and asked if anyone had a flashlight. I said that I did, and we went just inside a hatch off the fantail to look at the man's I.D, and find out who he was. As we shut the hatch, the sight that greeted us was an eerie one. The passageways were dark except for a couple of emergency lanterns that had been blown loose from the bulkhead and were swinging back and forth by their electrical cords. It was a typical scene from a war movie. The hatch we went into was reasonably close to my sleeping compartment, and I had a very strong urge to try to get to my locker to salvage my picture album – I wasn't worried about the rest of my stuff, but I didn't want to lose my pictures. However, my better judgement got the best of me and I decided nor to try it.

While we were moving the wounded man down from the flight deck, a Destroyer had maneuvered in under our Starboard catwalk. A line was secured, and the men from my ship began jumping across to the Destroyer. I helped transfer the body of the dead man from my ship to the Destroyer, and then I jumped across. After the Destroyer had taken as many men as she could, we cast off the line and began moving to catch up with the rest of the convoy. The Destroyer sailors were showing the men from my ship where they could sleep for the rest of the night, because darkness had fallen while this was happening. Being extremely tired from the excitement of the last few hours, I lay down and went to sleep. About daybreak the next morning, we were awakened by the five-inch guns on the Destroyer firing very rapidly. We later learned that they had shot down another Japanese plane.

The ship-fitters who had stayed aboard the *Kitkun Bay* had managed to keep the ship afloat and to restore power to most of the ship. About mid-morning of the next day the Destroyer was ordered to return us to the ship so we could take her to Leyte for repairs. As we were sailing back to the ship, we were all topside getting some fresh air, and one of the crew members from my ship sat down on the stretcher holding the canvas wrapped body of the dead man from my ship. When someone told him what he was sitting on, he jumped like he had been shot and left the area in a big hurry …

When we got to Leyte Island, they had frogmen come out and weld a patch on the side of the ship so they could pump the water out of the engine room and machine shop that were flooded. When the patch was in place, pumping operations were begun. When the pumping was about ¾ finished, they suddenly abandoned the engine room, and ordered all personnel to stay away from the mess hall and galley area. The reason was that they had found two 500 pound bombs in the engine room. One of the bombs was inside one of the boilers broken in two. They immediately called for a bomb removal team from Leyte Island to come and defuse the bombs so they could be disposed of.

Mark A. Hardisty, AOM1/c, USS *Hancock* (CV-19)
by courtesy of Jim Verdolini, *The Vanishing Generation*

I was a turret gunner. Coast of Japan. This particular instance. We were after the remaining Jap fleet. The ones able to go out and attack our invasion forces. There was a Jap cruiser, a heavy cruiser, the *Aoba*, and it was in the Kobe harbor, surrounded by anti aircraft guns. Our intention was to sink it to get rid of it, so it wouldn't be a hazard to the invasion force. My pilot Lt. D. Temple was the section leader. So we had the privilege of going down first. We were carrying four 500# bombs, and my pilot always loved to get a hit. In fact, the results of his hits, he was awarded the Navy Cross. In our dive shortly after releasing the bombs, we were hit by a large caliber anti aircraft shell. Which took a tremendous hit into the starboard wing, a hole you could walk through. It put the plane out of control. We were too low to bail out, when we leveled off ...

I had one hell of a pilot. He was able to horse that plane out to the waters edge, there we crashed into the sea. We were so close to shore, that small arms fire was able to even fire out at us. Thank God, I was able to get out of the turret, got the raft out, my pilot he got into the raft. But my radioman Janskow, trapped down in the bilge. We had some very trying moments there till he popped to the surface. We all three got in the raft. As I said, they were firing at us from the shore but it was an offshore wind. If you have ever been in a raft when the winds blowing it scoots the raft across the water. Of course we paddled like hell, and this radioman of mine, a big husky fella, when he got on the paddles you would think we had an outboard motor on the damn thing. Because away we went out to sea, getting out of range of anything in the way of firing. O.K. We sweated it out, and kept paddling to get further out to sea, but the current was taking us down the coast. And as we looked down the coast we could see that the land jutted out ...

This was a pre-dawn flight, so we hit em very early in the morning. We spent the day paddling that raft but knowing that the current was going to take us into land that night. None of us said it, we didn't have to say it to each other. We knew we weren't going to be taken alive, we were all armed, guns, knives things like that. But, there was no hooperah about taking the damn thing. We were just going to do what we had to do. But, all day long, we sweated out, but just at dusk over the horizon came a puff of smoke. And I thought well, maybe it is a Jap ship; if it is, we would probably have surrendered to that, knowing the civilians would eat us alive. But, I fired up the 30 caliber revolver I had with tracer ammunition, and sure enough they saw it. Well, in they came, and Oh God what a wonderful, wonderful thing it was. It was a destroyer, American destroyer. The U.S.S. *Benham*.

Derek Morten, DSC, Pilot, HMS *Formidable*
Communication with the Editor

Formidable was launching strikes against Japan itself, on the east coast, north of Tokyo.

I was leading the second flight of a two-flight operation – 1841 Squadron, flight 1842 – our leader Lt (A) from 1842 had returned to the carrier with engine trouble – in his absence I took over. Now I quote from my log-book: 'Led attack on Matsushima and south of Yonezawa. Hit in petrol system over Yonezawa and forced to ditch off Kin Kizan. Picked up by USS Peto.' In fact I had petrol in the bottom of the cockpit, and being aware of the fire risk I at once dropped my belly tank, and realising that my flying time was very limited I headed out to sea. The petrol fumes were almost overpowering, even with a full supply of oxygen through my mouth, and by the time I ditched I was quite drowsy. So drowsy in fact that I got out to the wing tip and realised that I had left my life-raft in the plane. Luckily the plane floated long enough for me to go back, get the life-raft and get into it, scarcely getting wet other than my feet.

I estimated that the plane floated for between one and two minutes. I think it was about four and a half hours before the submarine surfaced nearby.

Incidentally, had I landed back on the carrier, it would have been my 100th deck landing.

I was flying a Corsair, and I never flew anything else operationally. The Royal Navy had me, and many others, carry out all our training in the USA, and, as a result, I never at any stage flew a British-built aircraft. My opinion of the Corsair? A truly magnificent aircraft for the work we were doing. Rugged enough to stand up to a hammering and to heavy deck landings; longer ranged than the Seafire, good fire-power, capable of carrying a 1000lb bomb, and having good speed. Although I never flew one, the Grumman Hellcat seemed to me to be the only possible all-round rival. Admittedly the Corsair did have deck landing problems (particularly the early models) but I remember that our squadron did 500 deck landings without even a burst tyre. My record was one burst tyre and one barrier.

One episode to stress the ruggedness of the Corsair: 28 July 1945, as part of escort duties, my wing man (Sub Lieutenant (A) E. Humphries) and I strafed a small coastal vessel in the Inland Sea. We were flying very low, in line astern, and the vessel blew up in Humphries' face. After a couple of minutes, Humphries' voice came over the R/T: 'I am in trouble, she's very rough over 140'. I rejoined Humphries and we headed slowly back to the fleet – about 20 minutes flying time, from memory. After landing on, his aircraft was found to have: a very large lump of timber stuck in it and destroying the two bottom cylinders, no oil pressure, and other minor damage. It was dumped over the side at once. Humphries was not injured. I feel sure that no other aircraft would have kept flying on long enough to get him back to the carrier.

Frederick George 'Pat' Oikle, Seaman, HMS *Activity*
IWM Sound Archive Reference 17529

After the Japanese surrender, the carrier put into Singapore, where Oikle, now a coxwain, had to take his Commander (F) to visit American ships.

Believe me, it opened my eyes. I'd get to the gangway and their equivalent of the officer of the watch would get the messenger to take me to their canteen where I'd stay until I was piped to go back again, and they'd fix one up with a meal, and theirs was absolutely out of this world. Ice cream! We never saw ice cream! And I'd go back and I'd get [my mates] green with envy when I told them what it was like. Did it a few times ...

We had tied up in the harbour in Singapore, and I was piped to the gangway and the officer of the watch said 'Oh, there is a vehicle down there.' It was a small pickup, and what they had done, they had got all the sweet out of the canteen and loaded it, and he said 'I want you to take that to Changi jail.'
Well, Japs had only just surrendered so they were still in pockets all over the island ... I said 'where is Changi jail then?' And he pointed: 'Well, somewhere in that direction.' I started off. The Indian infantry were there as well – they were the people rounding up the Japs – and the Ghurkas. I asked a couple of questions, and it took me about 3 hours to get there, and basically it's round the corner. But when I got there, the main gates were open so I drove in and inmates were wandering around. They were like zombies, shuffling around, terrible state, and I shouted: 'Here are some sweets for you.' And nobody came near me. So I went to the back of the vehicle, got a couple of handfuls and I threw them to a group that was standing quite close to me. And they picked them up, went mad over them. The vehicle was emptied in less than no time.

World War II ended with aircraft carriers helping to transport home the thousands of Allied prisoners-of-war liberated from Japanese POW camps. During the war, carriers had put themselves at the heart of the major navies. Many ships had been sunk; many aircraft had come down; losses had been high on both sides. But the aircraft carrier had fully justified the faith of men such as Whiting and Rutland, and the vision of Ader.

Part Three

POST-WAR TO VIETNAM

1
Innovations and Expansion

The end of World War II left the British and the US with surplus carriers. Lease-Lend escorts went back to the USA, orders were cancelled and some ships were mothballed or sold off over the years to friendly nations. This allowed France to regain her naval aviation arm and other navies to gain their first carrier.

No navy rivalled the USA in terms of the size of its carrier fleet, but the US administration temporarily fell out of love with naval air power in the new Cold War situation. In 1947 the United States Army Air Force became the United States Air Force, and the new Secretary of State for Defence, Louis A. Johnson, put his faith in long-range strategic bombing using nuclear or heavy conventional bombs, stating: 'There's no reason for having a Navy and Marine Corps. General Bradley tells me that amphibious operations are a thing of the past. We'll never have any more amphibious operations. That does away with the Marine Corps. And the Air Force can do anything the Navy can do nowadays, so that does away with the Navy.' A new class of supercarrier was cancelled days after the first keel was laid, but almost immediately afterwards the outbreak of the Korean War signalled that amphibious operations had not been consigned to history, and in 1951 USS *Forrestal*, first of the supercarriers, was ordered.

On December 1945 a de Havilland Vampire landed on HMS *Ocean*, becoming the first jet to land on a carrier deck. The following July, the US Navy began trials of their first carrier jet the XFD-1, later designated the McDonnell FH-1 Phantom. Jets were faster, bigger and heavier than their piston-engined counterparts, exacerbating the problems of take-off, landing and aircraft handling on a conventional flight deck. By the mid-fifties many of those difficulties had been solved by the introduction of the steam catapult, the angled flight deck and the mirror landing system – all British innovations. The modern aircraft carrier had arrived, and the final triumph was the commissioning of the first nuclear powered ship, USS *Enterprise*, in 1961.

Some of the Royal Navy's famous World War II carriers lingered on, but the smaller and more economical Light Fleet Carriers that came in to service around the end of World War II were deployed for the Korean War and the Suez crisis of 1956. A much-delayed HMS *Ark Royal* was completed in 1955 as the world's first carrier to be constructed with an angled flight deck, and HMS *Hermes*, another wartime order, was finally commissioned in 1959. Plans for a new class of modern aircraft carriers were scrapped by the Government in 1966.

Jets did not entirely eliminate propeller-driven types, which were in front line service in the Vietnam War, and, even after piston-engine planes were dispensed with, turboprop aircraft were, and still are, used in specialized roles. But by April

1956 a Vought Crusader F8U-1 had become the first supersonic jet to be catapulted from a US carrier.

Viable rotary wing aircraft had been developed before World War II, but only afterwards did helicopters come into their own aboard carriers. They provided an anti-submarine warfare platform, acted as plane-guard to rescue aircrew and other personnel from the water, and could be embarked on most ships, not just carriers.

Captain Eric 'Winkle' Brown, CBE, DSC, AFC, RN, HMS *Ocean*
from *Wings On My Sleeve*

Brown was closely involved with work on jet fighters and was to become the world's foremost test pilot.

On 2nd December [1945] I went back to Ford, did just one brief ten-minute session of ADDLS [Aerodrome Dummy Deck Landings], and put my Vampire on ice in the hangar. I was desperately keen to beat the Americans at being the first to operate jets from carriers. I did not want to risk delay by damaging the machine on the airfield. I just could not wait.

I took off early on the 3rd, partly because I had a certain amount of fuel to burn off before I could get down to the right weight for landing on, partly because the plane was still a prototype and did not even have a compass. I took my own private wrist compass with me, but it was not the most reliable instrument in the world, and I had to find the ship in the Channel.

Because of my early take-off I missed a signal from the ship telling me to remain at Ford because the weather was too bad for a landing. The Captain – again Captain Caspar John – was actually just announcing over the ship's loudspeakers that I had been told to remain at Ford when I burst like a banshee on to the scene and screamed round the Ocean.

Caspar John was a very experienced carrier trials captain. He knew me, he knew the aircraft, he knew the ship. He very quickly weighed up the situation and ordered 'Land on'. This was a big moment for the Navy. If things went well today we should have moved into the jet age, the first navy to do it.

I was very conscious of all this as I prepared to make my landing. Coming round the ship I could see that she had a fair amount of movement on her. I realized that when I made my approach I should have to decide very quickly and very early on whether I was going to carry on or go round again, because at this stage in jet-engine development my Goblin engine was very slow in accelerating. This was the thing I had to watch most.

I settled down on to my final approach to the deck, and immediately realized that the ship was moving much more violently than I had thought before, pitching and rolling. But my Vampire was so steady in her approach descent and the batsman was giving me such a steady signal that it never even crossed my mind that I might have to go round again. I came straight in and made a very gentle landing, although camera shots showed that the pitching stern had hit my tail booms just before I touched down.

I refuelled and went straight on with the trials. The shortness of our take-off run astonished all the goofers on the island. We soared past them at captain's eye-level, twenty feet up …

On the fourth landing we had some trouble when the very large landing flaps struck the arrester wires.

We had succeeded, we had arrived – but the Vampire never went into squadron service with the Navy.* There were two reasons for this. First was the dangerously slow acceleration pick-up of her jet engine. The Vampire was in all other respects a perfect deck-landing plane, but we felt that at this stage no jet could be trusted entirely in an emergency requiring a sudden increase of speed. When a piston-engined machine was opened up suddenly on a wave-off the wings got an immediate increase in lift from the slipstream of the propeller. With a pure jet there was, of course, none of this. A pilot relied on getting his extra lift entirely by increasing the aircraft speed. The early jet engine's acceleration response was very sluggish as the Germans had already found out.

And there was another important snag. We decided that the Vampire's fuel capacity was too low for carrier work. Its radius of action would be far too limited for the long and uncertain hauls over the sea which naval flying often entailed, especially with the possibility of having to circle the ship and make several approaches to the deck before finally getting down.

Ensign, later Commander, Tex Atkinson
from *From The Cockpit*

The Panther was the US Navy's second carrier jet, and the fastest of the series, the F9F-5, had a top speed of 604mph (972kph). The following illustrates the problems of landing a jet on a conventional, straight flight deck. It must be remembered that the pilot had only half the length of the flight deck, the area forward of the barrier being used for parking and take-off.

Ken and Sober were both flying F9F straight-wing Panthers from the deck of the *Princeton* during carrier qualifications off San Francisco. Ken was on the starboard cat and had received the catapult officer's signal for a full power turn-up, just as Frank Soberski was over the ramp of the carrier and received a cut for landing. A VF-191 Panther being used that day by a photo pilot was behind Ken, waiting to pull onto the starboard catapult as soon as Ken was launched. Behind the photo pilot's plane was Scotty Jones in another F9, also waiting his turn.

Sober cut power and his jet touched down in good position to catch number three wire. But the F9's hook bounced and stayed in the up position too long, because the hold-down tension on the tail hook was not working properly. The hook continued to bounce and stay up all the way past number

* It did not go into front line service.

nine wire, Sober's last chance for an arrested landing before hitting the barricade. At high speed, Frank Soberski's F9F went through the barrier of steel and nylon straps that stretched across the *Princeton*'s flight deck. The barricade installed was one designed for the F7F, a higher twin-engine propeller aircraft; it had little effect on the low, slick Panther.

Ken Wallace had applied full power to his jet engine, checked all of his cockpit gauges and was ready for a cat shot. He turned to his right to receive the launch signal from the catapult officer. Ken said there was not a soul in sight. Everyone forward on the flight deck had disappeared into the catwalks. Ken kept full power on his F9 for a long moment, because he was afraid the catapult might still fire; then he cut power when he became aware of an aircraft sliding toward him.

Frank Soberski's Panther struck the two F9Fs waiting to launch behind Ken Wallace. Scotty Jones' F9 wound up without a tail section, then Sober's Panther bounced off the photo plane leaving his starboard wing on the flight deck. Soberski, still strapped into the cockpit of what was left of his aircraft, continued sliding up the flight deck towards the launching catapult. The nose of Soberski's jet came within feet of Ken's cockpit, but the two aircraft never touched. Soberski's F9 wound up hanging on the round down at the bow of the carrier, with Frank staring into green water. No one was seriously injured and thus ended Frank Soberski's second lucky break.

THE STEAM CATAPULTS

Lieutenant Commander Keith Wake, Flight Deck Engineer,
HMS *Victorious*, June 1959 to April 1961
Communication with the Editor

A British development and perhaps the star performer of the flight deck engineers' armoury. These simple and effective machines replaced their compressed air/hydraulic lumbering predecessors. The steam catapult re-introduced the hot air railway technology of the Victorian era. The one ton of steam expended for each launch gave acceleration over all but about the last 6 feet of the 145 foot launch way.

Twin slotted cylinders under the deck each had a piston connected to the other and to a single tow shuttle on deck. The cylinder sealing strips were opened then closed by the connection arm, allowing the expanding steam from storage accumulators to drive the pistons forward. Near the end of the power stroke a tapered nose cone on each piston entered a water filled retardation tank stopping the pistons in a few feet. The shock could be felt throughout the ship. Then the shuttle and pistons were reeled aft by an under deck recovery wire and readied for the next launch while the steam accumulator was re-charged. 'The boiler room gulped' and converted another ton of water to steam, the unseen 'stokers' below did their stuff and their mates, the badgers on deck, looked for the next aircraft to launch.

The catapult officer I was lucky enough to work with was a most competent and very cool engineer with a notice on his cabin door reading 'Gone to Launch'.

Once the aircraft was loaded on the catapult the flight deck officer [himself an aviator] would exchange final checks with the pilot, wind it up to full power, check the air space clear and signal 'go' to the Petty Officer Engineering Mechanic in his Howdah. Button pressed – the catapult end speed relative to the ship would be perfectly achieved! Add to this the natural wind plus the ship's speed and you're flying.

There were hot and humid days in the tropics when the aircraft would dip out of sight of the deck, carve twin wakes in the sea with their jet streams and slowly climb into cooler air. At the other end of the team those boiler turbo blowers were also fighting for air to burn the fuel, to make the steam, to charge the catapults to get the next skilled aviator airborne. Sometimes the 'stokers' and the aircrew met but they always admired the others' work. But you need good 'grunt' from aircraft and catapult. Deck wind speed, you need, of course, but above 45 knots wind speed work on deck becomes difficult.

Captain Eric 'Winkle' Brown, CBE, DSC, AFC, RN
from *Wings On My Sleeve*

The new steam catapult was first trialled in HMS *Perseus*, which then sailed for the USA to demonstrate it to the US Navy during February 1952. Brown was to fly a Grumman F9F Panther.

On the day set for the trials the carrier was alive with VIP American brass and officials. To everyone's chagrin a five-knot tail wind was blowing over the flight deck – instead of the ten-knot head wind which had been hoped for. A huddle of frustration gathered. The Americans shook their heads firmly at the idea that a jet could be shot off with the ship tied up and a tail wind blowing over the catapult. But Commander Mitchell, the inventor of the catapult, was there – a man with whom I had worked closely many times on catapult trials in Britain. Without a flicker of emotion he said, 'Of course we'll launch. These are just the sort of conditions this catapult likes.' The Americans protested. The risk was unjustifiable. Then the *Perseus'* Engineer Commander spoke out of the awkward silence. 'We'll risk the British pilot if you'll risk the aircraft.'

There was a hush. I had not been consulted, of course, but the gauntlet was down now. The Americans agreed. So I, the innocent in this drama, climbed into my cockpit and was flung off at 4.3 'g' at a speed of 126 knots through a maze of dockyard cranes and workshop chimneys.

We had proved our British invention. Trials continued into the next day, when the awkward tail winds increased. Eventually I was shot off at 4.5 'g' and 132 knots – and thanks to the new machinery it was the smoothest catapult ride I had ever had. In fact a launch from this steam catapult was so smooth that for a second one imagined it had misfired. In contrast to the ordinary catapult, which starts with a fierce kick up to the 'g' level, the new one took one gently up to 'g' then held it until the plane was airborne. Afterwards we went to sea and continued trials in Chesapeake Bay, with the aircraft loaded up to maximum weight. There were no hitches.

Commander David 'Shorty' Hamilton, RN
Communication with the Editor

Hamilton carried out deck landing trials with the second of that trinity of post-war British advances, the angled deck, consigning Soberski's type of accident (see page 318) to history.

In 1951 Captain [later Rear Admiral] D. R. F. Campbell, Royal Navy, thought of the Angled Deck, which turned out to be the most revolutionary improvement to carrier operations ever. A simple idea, like most successful inventions. The front end of the flight deck was pivoted to the left so that the landing area was angled about eight degrees to the direction the ship was steaming. The benefits were immense – a pilot missing the wires could open the throttle and take off again to attempt another landing. Carrier jet aircraft, which were just being introduced, did not have to face hitting a metal wire barrier, which, as the pilot of a jet had no engine ahead of him, could have been fatal. The whole deck area to the right of the flying deck could be used for parking, even abreast of the island. Also, aircraft could be launched off the starboard catapult at the same time as landings were taking place.

The US Navy recognising the potential, and with their usual 'get up and go' attitude immediately modified the USS *Antietam*, an *Essex* class wartime carrier. In Britain it was suggested that HMS *Ark Royal*, which was building, could be fitted with an angled deck and, in the meantime, HMS *Triumph* had an angle painted on her deck so that some trials could take place immediately These were 'touch-and-go' approaches as the arrestor wires were not usable, being installed for straight deck landings. These trials were satisfactory but the Admiralty, amazingly, decided that angled decks would not be introduced until the next generation of carriers were built—possibly one of the most stupid decisions ever made by My Lord Commissioners, especially when this 'next generation' was cancelled in the 1966 Defence White Paper. However, in 1953 the US Navy kindly sailed the *Antietam* to the UK, and RN aircraft conducted landings while she was in the English Channel. The success of these trials was such that the Admiralty changed its mind. HMS *Centaur* had the arrestor wires moved and other minor modifications to suit the new direction of landing, and of course, to do things as cheaply as possible, an angle was painted on the straight flight deck.

Such was the slowness of action, it was not until May 1954 that I did some deck landing trials on the ship in a piston-engined Hawker Sea Fury XI, three years after the idea was mooted. I was unable to get any briefing on what to expect or diagrams or photographs of the deck, so got airborne and rendezvoused south of RNAS *Ford*, Sussex. I carried out a normal pass over the ship and could see the big yellow centre line painted at an indeterminate angle [no one said what the degree was]. Turning on finals I was picked up by the Landing Signal Officer [LSO] who gave me a 'roger' indicating a correct approach path. I flew a normal curved landing pattern, essential as one could not see directly ahead due to the large engine in front. Arriving over the flight deck, at what I guessed was the correct angle, still receiving the 'roger', I was given the 'cut', closed the throttle and caught a wire. Just as I was thinking 'a piece of cake' and had nearly come to a halt there was a clunk as the port wheel fell into the catwalk.

I climbed out of the aircraft and went up to Flying Control [Flyco] situated in a balcony on the port side of the island, overlooking the deck. I then, in a few terse words, pointed out that once lined up on the approach the centre line could no longer be seen and there was absolutely nothing to indicate to the pilot the right direction. If a proper angled deck had been built one would have had the left hand edge of the deck to line up on. I suggested that a white line be painted, on the port side of the deck, parallel to the yellow centre line, so that the pilot could see this throughout his approach. When this was duly done I did seven more landings with great ease.

Later on in the year I carried out my first jet angled deck landings on HMS *Albion*, which were much easier because the flight deck was properly marked and in the Hawker Sea Hawk, like all our jets, the pilot sat in the nose with a clear view of what was ahead. The whole procedure, whilst still needing maximum concentration, was far less stressful both on the pilot and the aeroplane.

The whole matter of operating aircraft efficiently from carriers took a giant step forward, especially at night. Up to that time very little night flying was done, due to the inherent dangers, and I recall I was only involved in a small number of night landings by 814 squadron, in Fairey Fireflies. During my career I was able to do 117 angled night deck landings without incident, and without missing a wire. This in itself shows how much easier the operation was. I think it is true to say that jet flight deck operations without the angled deck would have been very difficult. It is also true that none of our smaller carriers ever had full angled decks, they varied between five and a half and six and a half degrees, a 'full' angle was around 8 degrees. However, a great deal of extra night flying was able to be done with these ships, enabling round the clock flying operations if needed. The only down side I can think of was the use of the small area (caused by the angling of the landing deck, port side right aft) for parking aircraft, or stores, even when aircrew were doing night deck landings. In our smaller carriers with big aeroplanes there was very little margin for error. Aircrew were lost when wing tips struck the obstacles.

Lieutenant Commander Keith Wake, Flight Deck Engineer, HMS *Victorious*, June 1959 to April 1961
Communication with the Editor

With batsmen giving way to mirror landing sights and then projector sights, arresting wire numbers had been reduced from ten [in the light fleet carriers in Korea] to only four in the modernised *Victorious*; the target wire was no. 2 counting from aft. The angled landing deck allowed aircraft to land with the full power they needed if they missed all wires and were to stay airborne to go round again.

It needed extra heavy arresting gear. The former steel wire rope barriers as 'long stops' to protect the deck park for'rd were no longer needed. Pilot safety also precluded their use. Vertical nylon strip emergency barriers could be erected in the event of arresting hook failure but were seldom required.

A serious problem arose with Scimitar aircraft. It was found that an aircraft's own tail skid could so damage the arresting gear centre span that the aircraft's hook could sever the weakened rope. Prior to this discovery a total of four broken wires in one or more strands would condemn the rope. The centre span would be quickly removed and the rest of that flight would have three ropes only available.

In daylight flying, once the arresting gear had been re-set the rope could be safely checked from the deck edge. At night, even with the landing intervals increased to three minutes, the duty flight deck engineer needed a good hand torch to inspect the reset wire and to be seen by flyco as still on or definitely clear of the landing area – no light, land on!

The tail skid damaged wire and the hook problem was soon solved by the visiting Royal Corps of Naval Constructors officer. He ordered the fitting of additional bowspring supports under each deckspan. This proved immediately successful.

Commander David 'Shorty' Hamilton, RN
Communication with the Editor

The Royal Naval inhabitants of the Naval Air Stations based in the south western area of England were wont to frequent the numerous country hostelries in their leisure hours. These country pubs were often equipped with a skittle alley which could have been in use for a couple of hundred years. Each had its own quirks but they were all were nine skittle [pin] alleys. Skittles were set, by hand, in a standard size diamond pattern., and there was sufficient space for the small wooden ball to go between the skittles and out the back without knocking any over. A player was allowed three balls a 'turn' and if he knocked all the skittles over in one hit they were reset and he was given an extra ball. If however he rolled one through the pack without hitting anything a loud cheer would go up from the spectators: BOLTER!!!!! and the player would give a sheepish grin as he knew that he now had to buy his team members another round of beer or scrumpy. With the advent of the angled deck it was natural for a deck landing aircraft which missed all the wires to be called a 'bolter'. US Navy and US Marine Corps aviators on exchange, who participated in these games, took the expression back to their carriers.

The term has crossed the English Channel and is also used by the French.

Admiral Stanley Arthur, USN, USS *Coral Sea*, 1978–9
Communication with the Editor

When you're a pilot with a carrier based squadron, you're not too concerned with the workings of the ship. You want steam to the catapults, a steady deck, ample wind over the deck, from the right direction, and the right coordinates for the launch position. What it takes to provide these basic needs is the ship's problem. As simple as these demands are, achieving them takes an amazing amount of training and coordination among the many departments aboard the ship. When 'Flight Quarters' is sounded, the ship takes on a very distinct transformation. The alignment of the propulsion plant is modified to provide additional redundancy, the bridge team is structured to ensure that the helmsman can steer a steady course without excessive rudder swings, and the team can determine a course that will bring the wind directly down the axis of the ship (for launch) and then slide it over so the wind comes down the angle deck (for recovery).

Once the ship is ready to launch and recover airplanes, those on deck have their tie down chains removed and they become very vulnerable to sliding around if the ship takes an unexpected roll. Steering a steady course minimizes this problem. In light wind conditions, when the carrier must make most of the wind, over the deck, with its own speed, getting the wind down the angle deck often requires more turning to the ship to accomplish this. At night, this becomes more critical as you don't want the aircraft continually correcting for a wind direction that is not down the centerline of the landing area.

As one might expect, there is always an opportunity for a difference of opinion between the pilot's view and the ship's view and thus the Captain of the Carrier (who always has an extensive background as a carrier pilot) becomes the final judge of what is 'good enough'.

My entire operational carrier flying was from WWII era *Essex* class carriers of various conversions. When I was selected to command USS *Coral Sea* (CV-43) I was awed by her size. She was from the class of carriers that were developed at the end of WWII and was significantly larger than the *Essex* class. I had had 7 landings on her, several years before, during a Saturday morning for some of us checking out in LTV A-7 Corsairs. I thought what a treat to have a big deck like this to land on. The Air Wing that was assigned to *Coral Sea* had just finished a cruise on USS *Enterprise*, our first nuclear powered carrier and she was much larger than *Coral Sea*. One night, after a pretty sorry bit of night qualifications, the Air Wing Commander (CAG) and I were discussing the issue.

He remarked: 'you know, the pilots are a little spooked, because they've been used to the larger deck of *Enterprise*'. I replied: 'tell your pilots that the Captain has never landed on a deck larger than this one.' Things got better.

MEATBALLS AND AUTOPILOTS

Commander David 'Shorty' Hamilton RN, HMS *Albion*
Communication with the Editor

The flying I did from HMS *Albion* involved trials with another British naval invention, the Deck Landing Mirror Sight.

In broad terms the bats system was used when aircraft had an approach speed below 100 knots; as they increased to 120 knots and more, the reaction time that the two humans needed became marginal. By happy coincidence at about the same time as the Angled Deck appeared came the invention of the Deck Landing Mirror Sight, by Lieutenant Commander [later Rear Admiral] H. C. Nick Goodhart, both an Engineer Officer and a Pilot. By placing a large, slightly concave, mirror facing astern on a platform on the port catwalk of the flight deck and shining a strong spotlight at it from farther down, the pilot, sitting in the nose of a jet, had a good view of it and the deck. Keeping the spot on the mirror in line with a bar of green lights, sited on each side, ensured that the aircraft flew down a glide slope on to the deck and arrestor wires. The glide slope could be adjusted by changing the mirror settings, to suit the 'pilot's eye/distance to hook' measurement, which varied with different types of aircraft. If the approach was too high the 'meatball', as it was called, was higher than the bars, and if too low it would be below them. A person monitoring the landing could switch on two large red lights if he was unhappy with the approach, indicating to the pilot to abort and try again ...

It was so easy to assimilate that after very little practice I did some shipborne trials on HMS *Illustrious*, the trials and training carrier – which incidentally had a straight deck! I remember the original mirror was long and thin and looked if it had been taken from an old-fashioned wardrobe, distinctly Heath Robinson.* I then conducted more trials in HMS *Albion*, a smaller carrier – in all, 35 deck landings. Going from bats to mirror was the same quantum leap as piston to jet aircraft. The combination of the mirror AND the angled deck was a whole new ball game, reducing pilot stress and training time, accidents and fatalities, speeding up deck operations and generally boosting aircrew confidence and morale. Night operations became a considerably less dangerous operation, both for the aircrew and the deck teams. As the system was adopted by most navies it made cross operating between different sizes and nationalities of ships a breeze.

* A noted British cartoonist, famous for cartoons depicting extraordinary contraptions based around ropes and pulleys to perform basic tasks.

**Lieutenant Commander, later Rear Admiral, Peter B. Booth, USN,
VF-102 (Diamondbacks), USS *America*, 1968**
from *True Faith and Allegiance*

The Diamondbacks were equipped with the latest F4J Phantoms.

Our Phantoms were really slick airplanes. They were about a thousand-pounds heavier than our early models back in 1961, but crammed with the latest state-of-the-art gadgetry including automatic throttles (euphemistically called 'approach power compensator system,' (don't you love it!), leading-edge droops in the stabilator to help the airplane rotate quicker on cat shots, electronics on top of electronics, drooped ailerons to fly slower on approach, a revolutionary radar and alas, the capability to land hands off on the carrier!

I've been scared a few times coming back to land on board ship, but none gets the heart rate up more than a fully-automatic (mode I) night-carrier landing to a trap totally untouched by either hand. It went like this: While hundreds of miles from the ship, you engaged the autopilot and 'coupled' the airplane to an airborne E2C or ship system. That system then flew the airplane like a drone. All you had to do was drop the gear, flaps and hook and hit a few buttons. It's the weirdest flying I've ever done. There you are, in an absolute black hole at 1,200 feet and ten-miles astern of the ship with the stick pumping furiously, the rudders pulsating and both throttles jumping to and fro! What makes most guys not like the system, is that for the average carrier pilot, it flies a better carrier pass than he can. This was true at least most of the time and this little caveat is what got the heart rate on the occasional high end.

REDUCING THE AVGAS HAZARD

Rear Admiral Euan McLean, HMS *Ocean*
Communication with the Editor

My unforgettable mentor in that ship was Commander John Francis Tucker, DSC, from Dundee, who had joined the Navy as an artificer, was commissioned and had spent a hard war entirely at sea. He was of unrivalled experience and he remains my hero. I was No. 2 Flight Deck Engineer when he decided to inspect an aviation gasoline (avgas) tank. While aviators will rightly tell you that the introduction of the angled deck, the mirror sight and the steam catapult, all British inventions, transformed their lives, for me an equally significant advance was the introduction of Sir Frank Whittle's jet engine. It heralded the end of avgas and the many problems which went with it. This high-octane, heavily leaded fuel represented a constant source of danger to both pilots and ship. The ship reeked of it and we spent much of our time in a fuel danger state. So toxic were its fumes that men spent no more than three months in the avgas party and were often inebriated and sickened by its fumes. To counter its ill effects they were given extra rations of milk.

Imagine half a dozen large road tankers filled with avgas tipped on end and for safety all completely immersed in fresh water in a large structural tank. The ship had three such tanks. So that Commander Tucker could carry out his inspection, we opened the manhole door at the top of one avgas tank and he descended wearing a primitive breathing apparatus. To avoid sparks everything associated with avgas had to meet stringent safety rules. Spanners, nuts, overall buttons were of brass. Footwear was gym shoes, and torches met mining industry standards. The access ladder was not built in to the tank but was wooden and had been brought down from the forecastle by a couple of stoker mechanics. I had failed to check it. As I watched his descent, Commander Tucker fell from the ladder and landed on his back in the pool of avgas which lay in the curved bottom of the tank. He picked himself up, inspected the tank and ascended soaked in avgas. He changed into clean overalls in the operating compartment which lay above the tanks and left. An hour later he sent for me and asked, 'Were you trying to kill me?' 'No, sir', I replied. In a calm and deliberate Scots voice he said, 'Not only were there two rungs missing from that ladder, they were con-sec-u-tive.' An early lesson in self control.

Other tales concerning avgas suggest that we were indeed a lucky ship. I recall an avgas leak in harbour in the hangar – so deep that we used rubber squeegees to sweep it down the hangar drains, and the soles came off my gym shoes when the fuel dissolved their adhesive. On another occasion we badly burned half the port after-side of the ship as we lay alongside in Kure, Japan, while embarking avgas from a *Wave* Class tanker which in turn lay alongside us and miraculously, because of wind direction, did not itself go on fire. Avgas had spilled into the sea and been ignited by a Japanese welder who, understandably, was unable to read our gangway warning notice (which unfortunately was in Chinese!). We lost several aircraft which were burned on deck.

A final tale – avgas was raised to the flight deck by pressurizing individual tanks with air at a pressure of about twice the average household water pressure. A non-return valve between air and fuel systems failed and the whole of the extensive air ring main flooded with fuel. This was discovered by a coppersmith who intended to cool a red hot copper pipe on which he had been working by using air from the ring main. There was no handle on the air cock so he was obliged to put down the hot pipe first. On opening the air cock a jet of avgas shot across his workshop. He was white when he reported the problem, which took several days to clear.

Lieutenant Commander R. J. 'Jock' McCandless, DSC, Flight Deck Officer, HMS *Hermes*, 1960–1
IWM Sound Archive Reference 27344

It was the first of the light fleet carriers to fly the heavy jets like the Scimitar or the Vixen, and they're very big aircraft for the size of the deck that we had available for them. And they're not only big, they're very heavy compared to the equipment we had to work with them. For example, a fully loaded Vixen was much heavier than the tractor that was supposed to be pulling it ... but there is a very big difference between moving an airliner on level ground compared with moving an aircraft across a moving deck, particularly if the deck has had a fuel spilled on it ... We had these tractors which were very good: they were four-wheel drive, four-wheel steer, quite heavy and they could move the aircraft very easily on a level, flat, dry deck. But the aircraft we were flying were Scimitars and Vixens, and if there was one fault the Scimitar had, it was spewing fuel. Almost every time it was refuelled it would spew out fuel. Every time it was launched, without fail it would spew out fuel ... So if the aircraft was being moved across an area where fuel had been spilt before it was cleared up, the tractor's wheels would skid, the aircraft wheels would move sideways – and if the ship was rolling or tilting in a turn, both tractor and aircraft could move sideways, and the number of occasions when we nearly had a tractor and aircraft going over the side was really quite amazing.

First thing I found out when I went on board is that here is a beautifully painted ship. Nice clean flight deck with white lines and green paint and grey paint and all looking absolutely smashing. I went and inspected the flight deck, and when I was walking I thought 'this paint feels loose'. I started looking at the paint and then I got the captain of the flight deck – senior rating – and I said 'I think there is something wrong with the paint on the flight deck. Better have an inspection over the whole deck and see what we can find.' So we found some areas where the paint was indeed not sticking to the steel. So I dug up a piece of this ... About a square yard came off in my hand, as it were. So I broke a bit off of this, about a square foot and went off into the dockyard at Portsmouth to find the paint shop. I found the senior civil servant in the paint shop, and he said: 'What can I do to help?' I laid this piece of paint on the desk and I said: 'That's the flight deck of HMS *Hermes*.' He looked at this, absolutely bloody horrified ... here was the full paint ... best part of half inch thick, but not sticking to the deck. He picked it up and smelt it, and he said 'My God', and he looked so bloody miserable. Anyway, I said: 'Can I leave this to you, and let us know what you're going to do about it?' So he said 'Yes.' So I went back to the ship and I said to Commander Air: 'This is the situation ...'

And then, about a week later, the executive officer of the ship, second in command, stopped me and started to give me the most enormous blast about the fact that the paint was wrong and he said: 'You realise, of course, that you are adversely affecting the main armament of the ship because the aircraft will not be able to fly.' I said: 'I know perfectly well; that's why I made the complaint.' He said: 'You didn't tell me.' I said: 'I told Commander Air – he's my immediate superior.' He humphed and umphed, and I suppose he went off and had a go at Commander Air, I don't know – but, God, was he cross. But, of course, you see, you couldn't afford to have a jet blasting across paint like that because it would just have picked it off and blown it all over the place, and severely injured anyone it hit.

Lieutenant Peter Taylor, 824 Squadron, HMS *Centaur*
Communication with the Editor

At the time, the *Centaur* was coming to the end of its life, and as well as a squadron of Westland Whirlwinds it had embarked squadrons of Supermarine Scimitars and de Havilland Sea Vixens. These were both modern aircraft and fairly heavy, and probably not really suitable to be operating from such a small, slow carrier. My impression of operating in the Gulf was that it was all very dodgy. Fixed wing aircraft have an optimum take off speed which is a combination of wind over the flight deck, the power from the engines and the speed of the catapult. With heat and no wind the *Centaur* would shake itself (and us!) to bits trying to get to its maximum speed. Fixed wing aircraft have very little 'needless' parts, which meant that taking everything into account they would be thrown off with very little fuel. My impression is that they just about managed to scream across the desert and frighten a few goats before hurrying back to 'mother,' as your parent carrier is always called.

Wind is the naval aviator's friend. For a helicopter to remain stationary relative to the sea it has to fly into wind at the speed of the wind. This takes less power than hovering when there is no wind. Similarly, the heavier the helicopter the more power is required to maintain a hover. Out in the Far East, and particularly in the Persian Gulf, it is both hot and often devoid of wind. This has a dramatic effect on the performance, and typically endurance (in a typical ASW sortie profile) would be less than half that in a temperate zone. To try and squeeze more endurance, the Whirlwind was stripped of all 'needless' parts in order to reduce the weight. We therefore flew with no doors or windows; the tail fairing was removed as were the landing lights – and other odds and ends.

All engines lose efficiency the higher the ambient air temperature. I flew in the Whirlwind Mk 7 on *Centaur*. This helicopter was the first in the world with dipping sonar, but also happened to be a pretty unreliable aircraft. It did, however, give you a few seconds warning of engine failure by issuing a discreet cough! To operate in the anti-submarine warfare role (ASW) the helicopter has to hover stationary over the sonar which is lowered into the water. If the sonar (ball) dragged at all it would, of course, be useless at detecting submarines.

Lieutenant Commander P. H. 'Jan' Stuart, 824 Squadron, HMS *Ark Royal*
Communication with the Editor

January 1961 saw us leaving the warm and welcoming Mediterranean for quite a different environment. This was to the Davis Strait, inside the Arctic Circle north-east of Canada between Baffin Island and Greenland. The object of going to this cold and forbidding place was to find out how the low temperatures would affect helicopters. For instance, would the rotor blades become covered in ice and cause the aircraft to crash? The temperatures were in the region of –14C, which was not as low as we wanted, but it did show up one serious defect. In the event of a ditching, the escape drill from the cabin of the helicopter under water was to push out the window and crawl through the hole. The perspex window was held in place by a thick rubber strip, which was easily pushed out in temperate regions, but here in the arctic the rubber went hard and would not budge. We therefore adopted the practice of flying with the large cabin door locked open. This gave us a wonderful view of the pack ice but made it too cold for us to operate the sonar equipment until we were provided with electrically heated flying suits. Even so I would not have wanted to crash into the sea in that area.

Anonymous
A helicopter is an assembly of forty thousand loose pieces, flying more or less in formation.

2
Accidents

All the improvements in technology undoubtedly saved lives and improved operational effectiveness, but aircraft carriers and cockpits remained dangerous places.

Lieutenant Commander, later Captain, George Hunt, DSO*, DSC*, First Lieutenant, HMS *Triumph*
Communication with the Editor

One day while I was in *Triumph* we were fuelling our attendant destroyer by means of a hosepipe between the two ships steaming at about 80 feet apart. This is quite normal but does require good judgement! Jackstay transfers at sea between ships is a convenient way of moving stores, personnel or oil fuel, but it requires about six to eight stalwart chaps to man the 'in haul' or other various ropes required to do the job. On one occasion we had got to the stage of completing the refuelling of our attendant destroyer and we had eight Royal Marines leaning back on the 'in haul', rather like a tug-of-war.

At a given signal the Captain of Royal Marines orders: 'Let go!' and that should have been that. Unfortunately, one of the Royal Marines, who was closest to edge of the flight deck, failed to let go at the same time as his mates, and he got whipped over the side and into the water between the two ships.

Now, as it happened, in accordance with the rules we had a helicopter sitting on stand-by at the after end of the flight deck. By good fortune, the pilot sitting in the cockpit saw it all happen and revved up his engine and took off. Furthermore, it so happened that his helicopter had a sproule net,* so without further ado he hovered over the Royal Marine, lowered his net and scooped him into it, rather like scooping the net under a rather nice trout or salmon. Having got the chap in the net he returned to the flight deck and gently lowered a rather wet Royal Marine to the deck. All that was splendid stuff, and the pilot did very well, but the Royal Marine sprang to his feet, marched up to the Captain of Royal Marines, slammed to a halt and a splendid salute and said in an incredibly English public schoolboy accent, 'I say, Sir, I'm most frightfully sorry!' The point is that it so happened he was what was called a 'CW** Candidate' – in other words he had already been singled out as being of officer material and so, after exams etc., would probably be made an officer.

* Helicopter rescue net named after its inventor Lieutenant Commander John 'Sprocket' Sproule.
** Commissions and Warrants

Patrick M. Lynch, USS *Forrestal*, 1958–60
Communication with the Editor

I started learning the hot suit procedure and volunteered, which made the others in the crew wonder if I had all of my senses. Jobs like that always festinated [fascinated] me for some unexplained reason, and besides I was big enough to wear the hot suit.

It was made completely of asbestos, similar to a jump suit, but had a hood with a hard hat sewn in and a glass face-plate. To get the gloves on one had to pull them with your teeth. A K-Bar knife was attached to the front of the suit. It was used to break the pilot's grip on the ejection seat (using the handle not the blade) and for cutting the safety harness the pilots wore. The hot suit man was stationed at the edge of the landing area during landings and in the event of a crash on deck was responsible, with his partner who was on the opposite side of the landing area in the catwalk, to rescue the pilot and/or crew. During my time in the hot suit, which spanned 6 months or so, there were about a dozen 'crashes', some not too bad and two very bad. Most of the time it was just a matter of assisting the pilot out of the cockpit and on occasion prying his hand loose from the stick or seat arms. On occasion I think they were just finishing up a short prayer. I'm sure the experience of crashing on deck was a lot more harrowing than being on deck watching it. The most apprehensive time was during night operations when you could not actually see the plane until it was next to you . All I could see was the landing and wing lights. Standing at the edge of the landing area I always had company. The Flight Deck Officer would stand right in front of me (so I could block the wind for him, which was around 30 knots or so) and direct the plane to it's 'parking place' after landing. We always worked out a 'get out of here plan' in the event of a crash or something coming loose from the plane during landing. The words 'the plane in the grove has hung rockets' always raised the hair on the back of my neck since the 5-inch rockets carried in a pod of 19 tended to come flying out if they did not fire correctly. I had a theory that standing still was the better option then running. If I stood still, the loose object had to hit the 2 square feet I was occupying. If I ran I stood a chance of running in front of the object. The theory worked well, since I never got hit, but a few times at night, watching the sparks as a piece of something bounced down the deck, made me wonder.

The good part of the hot suit assignment was: when we were not flying, the hot suit man had no duties. We just lounged around smoking and drinking coffee. Also when wearing the red shirt with 'Hot Suit' on it there were no lines to wait in. We went to the head of the chow line or any other line, so there was a real benefit to the job.

Omar Fowler, naval airman, HMS *Illustrious*, 1948
Communication with the Editor

On the night of Sunday 24th October 1948, I was duty watch and stuck on board, while many of my young mates went off for a night out in Weymouth.

For some reason a strong feeling of foreboding came over me, like a heavy dark weight pressing down on me. I could not understand or explain the feeling, which persisted all that evening.

I had always been a bit 'arty' and often drew cartoons and sketched aircraft and ships. On this particular night I sat down and drew a sketch of the sea and a looming black figure, with outstretched arms, rising out of the sea; it was very macabre.

After finishing my duties for the night, I jumped into my hammock and tried to sleep. My sleep was fitful, with moving figures and raised voices disturbing my sleep. Finally, came the dawn. It was then that I discovered the terrible event that had occurred the previous night.

The HMS *Illustrious*, 'liberty boat', a pinnace under the command of a Midshipman and crammed with sailors returning from their run ashore, had hit rough weather and heavy seas in Portland Harbour. It had overturned and 29 sailors were missing, feared drowned. The majority of them were young Naval Airmen, many only seventeen and some eighteen. The tragedy hit the newspaper headlines the following day. Many of my friends I would never see again. It was something that you might expect in war, but it was a tragedy in peacetime and took many young lives.

Frank Skull, L.M.(E), HMS *Indomitable*
Communication with the Editor

Although jet aircraft were being tested on other carriers, in the 29 months I was on *Indomitable*, May 1950 to September 1952, all the aircraft in use had piston engines and propellers ... Unfortunately on one of our cruises an aircraft handler walked into a propeller with fatal results. In the time-honoured way, an auction sale of his kit was held one evening on the foc'sle, many of the items being bought and handed back for resale many times. In this way a considerable sum was raised for his next of kin.

Lieutenant Commander P. H. (Jan) Stuart, RN, 849 Squadron, HMS *Albion*
Communication with the Editor

The flight deck of an aircraft carrier is an excruciatingly noisy place when operating aircraft, and no one in his right mind would venture there without ear defenders. This noise is spasmodic, reaching its highest levels during the launch and recovery of aircraft, especially those with jet engines. Less intense but permanent is the roar of the forced air ventilation throughout the ship. On a still summer night with the ship at anchor, in Plymouth Sound for example, this roar can be heard half a mile away.

There is a contrasting quiet which cannot be measured like noise, with decibel meters, but there are different levels of quiet as between an empty cinema and a graveyard. In an aircraft carrier a deep, almost painful, quiet can be experienced when there is a sudden power failure and the ventilation fans stop. This does not happen very often, but it is a fact of life and when it occurs you suddenly find that you are shouting at your neighbour with whom you thought you were having a normal conversation a few seconds earlier.

There is yet another quiet, happily not experienced by many people, but it came to me in the darkness of the Moray Firth on the night of 21st May 1957. I was an Observer in C Flight of 849 Squadron operating from HMS *Albion*, flying the magnificent Douglas AD-4W Skyraider. My pilot was David Burke, and we were briefed for a shipping reconnaissance. Normally we would take off under our own power, but this time we were placed on the catapult. David wound the elastic up to full power and with a gentle surge the catapult fired and we were airborne – for all of 2 seconds! Suddenly the exciting roar of the 2700HP radial engine stopped and there was silence, black, impenetrable, inky silence. David was muttering to himself in the driving seat, but I was far too busy to listen because I was checking that my waterproof packet of cigarettes and matches were handy in the pocket of my immersion suit. Ditching is one thing, ditching in the dark is another, but ditching without fags and matches is something else and unacceptable. All was in place and I was ready for the splash when the quiet was shattered by the splendid sound of the Wright Cyclone as it burst into life and resumed its rightful place in the scheme of things. We had not touched the water and David wasted no time in hauling the aircraft round and putting it back on deck.

Lieutenant Commander William A. Ettles, HMS *Bulwark*, July 1957
Communication with the Editor

I joined the ship in the south of England, and we were operating off Cornwall with *Culdrose* as guard and safety. The Met Office, however, made things difficult by producing thick fog. The Captain (Percy Gick, who flew a Swordfish against the *Bismarck*) called the S. Met Office and asked, 'Where's the weather better?'

Commander Alun Meredith (Welsh Rugby International) answered without consulting charts or anything else: 'Off the north coast of Ireland.'

'Right,' said the Captain, 'We'll go!'

So we blinded up the Irish Sea in thick fog, scaring off hordes of trawlers, and, if a gap appeared, firing off the Gannet and fetching it back at the next gap.

Meantime another problem arose. As you will know, empty fuel tanks are a dangerous weapon, so the custom was that, when empty, they were filled with seawater. Unhappily, some **** had opened the sea-cocks too early, and let water into non-empty tanks, so that the fighters were filled with a mixture of fuel and salt water, on which they do not fly well. Each one had to be stripped, cleaned out and refuelled with the correct fluid. Since this was liable to take a lot of time, the Captain decided to anchor in Bangor Bay, prior to proceeding to Short & Harlands in Belfast and tying up in their yard, where an airstrip would allow the Gannet to fly. Meantime, just for exercise, the Gannet would do a catapult take-off at anchor.

The catapult was duly set up, the Gannet attached and the crew boarded. The catapult revved up, but, just before the green flag ordered 'Fire' a hold-back strop broke and the Gannet trundled gently along the deck and fell off the front end. Very quickly, three heads appeared and we saw the crew surface. The Captain picked himself off the deck, where he had collapsed in laughter, and ordered, 'Send a boat.' Believe it or not, the boats were all ashore! The crew were finally fished out by two holidaymakers in a dinghy, and – adding insult to injury – one of them was the son of a Group Captain R.A.F. *The Daily Mirror* had it on the front page. It was funny then, but, had it happened at sea, the crew might well have been killed by the ship.

CPO Bev Sanders, 815 Squadron, HMS *Ark Royal*
Communication with the Editor

I was on the old *Ark Royal* with 815 (Westland Wessex) anti-submarine squadron and we had just arrived off Singapore straight from UK.

It was decided that all the tool boxes and personal kit would be placed in cargo nets and, using the cargo hooks, flown from ship to Sembawang airfield. Having arrived on deck early, my case went in the first net, which was then attached to the CO's aircraft. A gentle lift to test the hook was carried out and then the chopper flew sideways clear of the deck and took station on the rear port quarter of the ship. Hardly had the chopper taken station than we saw the net parting company with the chopper and descending into the sea. Bearing in mind that the *Ark* was still steaming forward at about 20 knots we soon lost sight of what still remained afloat. Although divers from the safety chopper tried to recover some cases, the majority had disappeared to the sea bed – yours truly's included along with the CO's.

I subsequently discovered that I was missing my Post Office savings book and wrote to the PO in London asking for a claim form. There were two questions on the form that came back from the Post Office that still bring a smile to people's faces when I tell this story:
1) Where did you lose the book? I gave the lat/long from the ship's log.
2) What attempts have you done to find it? It is now in about 60ft of shark infested sea and I wasn't going there for the contents of that book for anyone. There must have been some wry smiles and lots of chin stroking back in London when they read my claim form!! Eventually we got replacements for the kit lost and I got a new POSB pass book.

By the way, the CO only had his flying overalls, Bonedome and headset and a pair of gym shoes when he signed in to the officer's mess at Nee Soon, which didn't go down well with those pukka army types.

And the hook? Well that was found to have a inherent fault extending back to when the remote release was fitted during the aircraft's manufacture, so Westland's had egg on their face as well as us.

Commander Pran Parashar, Indian Navy, CDR (Air), INS *Vikrant*
Communication with the Editor

We used to have lot of Fire Warning lights coming on in Sea Hawks. On one such occasion flying off Singapore, one Sea Hawk was diverted to Changi airfield. *Vikrant* was to take part in exercises with the Fleet en route to Mumbai. To retrieve the aircraft from Changi, the ship would have to go to the Naval Dockyard. The aircraft would have to be towed from Changi to the Naval Dockyard. For it, the permission of the Police and their assistance would have been needed. It could have taken anything up to four days. Accompanied by the Air Engineer Officer, we flew to Changi in a Chopper. A creek was adjoining the airport. We investigated the chances of ferrying the Seahawk by sea. For that we would have needed an LCT and a crane capable of lifting the aircraft.

Changi had a mobile crane that could go up to the creek, but the aircraft was too heavy for this crane. Realising that we always allow a safety factor in the design of the cranes etc, I managed to persuade the Air Force authorities to try it at my written undertaking. Contacted the Army. They too very readily agreed to provide a LCT. We towed the aircraft to the creek and tried to lift it. The crane *could* do it but with the warning bell ringing. I took the risk and accomplished to bring the aircraft back to the ship. I wonder if any one even noticed it. I consider it one of my major achievements. A lot of money and embarrassment was saved. *Vikrant* joined the Fleet Exercises ...

Sub-Lieutenant, later Lieutenant, Bill Hart, 890 Squadron, HMS *Ark Royal*, 1963
Communication with the Editor

In August 1963, Hart and his pilot, Lieutenant David Dunbar Dempsey, spent a short period shore based in Malaya at China Rock. He was about to chalk up the first of a record two successful ejections from a Sea Vixen, a jet fighter with a shocking reputation for killing aircrew.

Well, about the middle of the week we had a visit from a Malayan Police patrol; they informed us that we had to make sure our 'compound' was securely closed after dark, the reason given being that a pair of tigers had been seen in the area. The next morning the Houseboy arrived with news that a woman and a small child had been taken from the village during the night. Needless to say, we took security very seriously from then on. After the squadron finished with the Range we went back to Changi and I rejoined 890 at Tengah, where I had an Air Interception sortie ashore on the 26th prior to our attempted re-embarkation on the 29th.

Here the fun begins. We were briefed to fly north-east out across the South China Sea – in the process passing close to the Range. Then we were to carry out some mutual low-level intercepts with another Vixen, finally heading back to the circuit for visual recovery to the *Ark*. All went well for about ten minutes as we ventured farther out over the South China Sea – as I recall about 150 miles off shore – at which point we had realised we were having a fuel transfer problem. Let me explain at this point: no aircraft had permission to land on with fuel in any drop tank. For a variety of safety reasons, it was strictly forbidden. This was where our problem began to surface, despite both of us having the required system knowledge we could not achieve a transfer of fuel from the drop tanks, which was the first fuel to be used operationally.

Dave tried all the options; we had *Pilots Notes* open at the relevant pages, but got nowhere, and then we started to experience flameouts to add to our problems. We abandoned our part in the Air to Air Interceptions, and I gave Dave a heading for Changi, the nearest base at that point. We declared an emergency using the standard international radio procedure (a 'PAN PAN PAN' call). We were then at about 2,000 feet and a long way out, at least 150 miles, and on one engine! We also could not establish which fuel booster pumps were operating correctly, so we began a 'cruise climb' at the correct 'Range and endurance speed' – slowly we climbed and achieved a relight on the engine at which point the other engine flamed out. We had to lose height in order to get to relight speed so down we went. This process happened several times, each time we successfully relit the dead engine, but it meant as we approached the coast in the China Rock area we were back below 3,000 feet with no chance of even gliding to Changi.

In short, it was impossible to diagnose the cause of our fuel starvation problem and as we neared the Range both engines flamed out and it was impossible to achieve the speed for a relight, so Dave pulled into a turn, I transmitted a *Mayday* call with absolutely correct position information, which was acknowledged by the ship. We had already discussed the routine for our ejection so Dave levelled on a parallel heading to the shore, to use the onshore breeze to our advantage, and I jettisoned my hatch (more about that later) and then pulled the seat handle at 1,800 feet and about 250 knots – Dave followed immediately so we found ourselves at about 1,500 feet some forty yards apart and drifting to shore.

Pilots Notes and Emergency Procedures always detail how to trim an aircraft about to be abandoned, usually to ensure the crash will be in a safe place. I told Dave about the village so he trimmed the aircraft to go to the right after we ejected, as we were flying north north-east along the coast at the ejection point. As we watched from our parachutes it went the other way and once it got to roughly a heading of west it straightened out and went inland at 90 degrees to the beach. It was amazing to see the treetops being cut off as it gouged its way in a slow descent followed by an enormous fireball and then a large plume of black smoke as it hit a very large tree some half mile inland and exploded. We heard the explosion but were then more intent on the final part of our descents.

Below lay the bay to the north of China Rock, and we drifted towards the headland, which had a large sandy spit. Dave said he would aim for a landing in the middle of the spit. Since I was slightly higher, I opted to try for the top of the beach but ended up crashing through a rainforest canopy, hitting the ground and then being wrenched back up to about twenty feet off the ground as the tree which I had gone through regained its normal shape.

Dave had made his target area but sadly there was one rock, about the size of a soccer ball, right at ground zero – and as he landed he pitched forward and gave the rock a resounding head butt and collected a broken nose despite having his face visor down as recommended. Meanwhile I was doing an impression of an oversized marionette, which was quite painful as my harness had ridden up when I hit the ground. In fact the webbing of the harness had ridden right over the quick release buckle preventing me from using it, and as I was suspended too high for Dave to assist me I had to use the aircrew knife to cut myself down. I had to cut each parachute line – there are an awful lot – so it was quite some time before I had cut enough for the canopy to slide free of the top of the tree. When it did I fell and landed very awkwardly. It was now approaching sunset and, having told Dave about the local tiger problem, we decided to inflate our dinghies and have them ready for a swift paddle out to sea if required.

It was also decided to activate my SARBE, the radio beacon and walkie talkie device fitted in each Mae West. Within minutes we heard an aircraft approaching from the north-east – it was a Shackleton, so we fired a flare, but the aircraft continued on to the south-west. Later we discovered that the SARBE aerial was defective and nothing was being transmitted for the search aircraft to home in on. We also learned later that the Shackleton was on a routine approach pattern to Changi.

Darkness arrives very rapidly in equatorial locations; being aware of this, we had already decided on our plan of action and it had of course gone completely dark at this point. Survival chances are always better with planning and practice, so our third string is what saved the day. The first string was the SARBE, the second was the flares fired at the Shackleton and our third, and successful string, was a huge tree on the edge of the beach, which having at some time been killed by a lightning strike, was actually a huge collection of dry timber. We gathered a pile of small branches at the base and ignited it using a flare – in a flash, literally, it was a huge inferno and was sighted by a Wessex of 815 Squadron, which was some 15 to 20 miles offshore at the time. Within minutes we heard the sound of the chopper, which was being flown by Lt Cdr John Kelly, the Squadron CO.

Now at this point the beach was illuminated for about a hundred yards either side of our position by the blazing tree. As we looked to the northern end we both thought that we could see two pairs of yellowish eyes peering from the undergrowth. Not a word was said as we instantly sprinted to our dinghies and began to paddle seawards. At this point the Wessex arrived and, with it hovering with the wheel about two feet above the water, we were hauled rapidly into the cabin by the winch men. As I was half in and half out the winch man tapped me on the head and pointed over my shoulder – where we saw two adult tigers approaching the point where we had been hauled out of our dinghies.

There are many 'ifs' and 'buts' in this tale, but one I often think about is the one that goes – What if I had not been to the Range and thus been unaware of the presence of the tigers along the coastal strip. Or what if there had been no dead tree. Anyway we survived and I was told some time later that it was the first night helicopter rescue; mind you John Kelly did have the entire area lit by the blazing tree which made the night hover more of a daytime exercise.

Within days of our arrival back on board we were put in front of the mandatory Board of Inquiry – should more correctly be called the 'Inquisition'. We didn't need to consult each other as we both knew that we had done everything by the book and that something odd had happened to the aircraft fuel system. However, the Board tried to make it look as if we had mishandled the fuel system which we strenuously denied …

Commander Pran Parashar, Commander (Air), INS *Vikrant*.
Communication with the Editor

We were doing the squadron training also en route to Singapore. During night operations, one Alizé suddenly disappeared from the radar and lost touch with the ship. Much to our relief, we received a message from Colombo airfield that one of our aircraft had landed there without lights and blown all tyres on landing. We obtained the clearance from Colombo to send a relief aircraft with spare wheels and an engineer. I was to do so myself. On arrival at the Colombo airfield when on finals, all the airport runway lights were switched off and I was instructed to circle the airfield whilst they obtained instruction from the higher authorities. I circled the airport for almost two hours and was finally told to return to the ship. It was all very mysterious. We had been trying to obtain the clearance from Colombo airport every two hours. We had one Alizé aircraft ready to take off with spare wheels and a volunteer Engineer Officer. We could not afford to leave the aircraft or our officers ashore. Nor hang around.

We received the clearance around 0700 in the morning and straight away took off for Colombo. When we landed, included in the reception committee was the Chief of the Ceylon Navy. He happened to know me. There were also two representatives of the Indian High Commission. It transpired a very high Chinese dignitary was visiting Ceylon. The name of our pilot was Lieutenant Grewal. It was construed that we were trying to land a 'lieutenant general' under a surreptitious name. The Alizé crew of three officers had been interrogated all night without any meal. None of us had any money. Surprisingly, the representatives of the Indian High Commission also claimed that they had no money. As it happened, the Chief of the Ceylon Navy would not think of me trying to find a way to pay for their breakfast. He was most apologetic for the whole fiasco.

AO-3 Michael W. Gentry, VA-145 1968–72, USS *Enterprise*
Communication with the Editor

When the fire aboard the *Enterprise* started I was in the ready room. As the alarms sounded we could see on the monitor the rushing around on the flight deck and could feel the explosions. Since the flights were no longer going on, I was still sitting with a headset on that was used by the flight boss to let me know about each aircraft, so I could relay the info to the pilots as their aircraft were ready and spotted. A Chaplain came in the ready room and motioned for me to come with him. We were going down the passage way when an Ordnance Chief, Duebner, asked me where I was going, and not to go to the flight deck because there were people getting killed up there. The Chaplin had gotten me to help him record the names of the dead as they brought them to the hangar deck. Evidently there has to be verification of the dead by more than one person. The only real memory of any of those was a Lieutenant that had been gotten from a McDonnell F-4 Phantom. The only things left on his body was a huge collar around his neck, which at one time had been his helmet, and most of his boots. The sights were terrible, but the smell is what I remember most.

Vice Admiral Vinod Pasricha, INS *Vikrant*, 1976
Communication with the Editor

At the time of the incident, which he has written in the third-person, the Vice Admiral was the *Vikrant*'s Lieutenant Commander (F). Peter Debrass retired as a Rear Admiral, and Captain Ram Tahiliani retired as an Admiral, having served as the Indian Navy's Chief of Naval Staff.

'Right. Let's man aircraft'. With that the four pilots went off to the flight deck to strap up into their Sea Hawks. As the carrier turned into [the] wind, Lieutenant Commander (Flying), affectionately called 'Little (f)', blared over the flight deck broadcast, 'Stand clear of jet pipes and intakes. Standby to start up the Hawks. Five, four, three, two, one, start up'. All four starter cartridges fired simultaneously, and a moment later the engines started revving up. Preflight checks were completed and R/T checked out. The search and rescue helicopter was ordered to get airborne and with all ready for the launch, Little (f) switched on the amber light, thereby permitting aircraft movement on the flight deck.

Being the leader, Peter's aircraft moved straight onto the catapult. Little (f) flicked the control light to green and Peter started his launch procedure. All systems go, Peter gave the hand signal to the FDO who, after a last minute check-up, dropped his green flag and waited a micro-second for the catapult to fire. As all eyes watched from Flyco, Little (f) saw that something was amiss. The sequence had somehow gone awry as the hold-back parted and simultaneously the bridle dropped down and the Sea Hawk started moving even before the catapult had fired. A second later, the shuttle shot forward but to what use? The aircraft and bridle had already disengaged.

'Brakes, brakes, brakes', came the reflex R/T call from Little (f). David McKenzie and his colleagues heard this urgent message, but on Peter's headset it came only as a crackle.

'Something seems wrong' thought Peter, 'but since there is no signal from the FDO, all must be well'. Years of training to not throttle back on launch unless specifically signalled had its effect. The FDO noticed the bridle falling but could not figure out why. In that split second before he put his hands up to cross his flags, the Sea Hawk had overtaken him. He ran behind the aircraft, but was no longer in Peter's field of vision and so the Sea Hawk majestically plunged into the sea.

Captain Ram Tahiliani, in command of INS *Vikrant*, was sitting on the Captain's chair on the bridge. Having himself commanded 300 Squadron and been Little (f), his reactions were copy-book and instantaneous. 'Starboard 30. Stop both engines', followed immediately by 'Full astern both engines'. Both these orders are given only in a serious emergency. But the momentum of the carrier with its 20,000 tons displacement takes time for the speed to reduce and thus *Vikrant* sailed over the Seahawk.

The Martin Baker ejection seat of the Seahawk sends the pilot into the air along with the seat and his parachute. For this 'chute to deploy, the aircraft must have a forward speed of at least 90 knots. As Peter fell off the deck, he realized that the aircraft did not have the necessary speed to permit him to eject, and there was little that he could do to prevent his going straight into the sea.

'Should I eject underwater?' came the immediate thought. Theoretically it was possible, but Peter also knew that in practice no one had ever tried it. For an underwater ejection to be successful, the aircraft would have to first sink for seven seconds to at least thirty feet below the water surface, so that when separation between the parachute and the pilot occurs, both are still below the surface of the water.

'Thousand one, thousand two ... thousand six, thousand seven', as Peter counted it occurred to him that the propeller noise had died down, so the carrier must have crossed over. With that he pulled the blind. Bang! The ejection seat fired. What Peter didn't appreciate was that the carrier was still very much on top of him. It was only that the propellers had stopped and were now beginning to go full astern and thus there was little noise. Also, because of this reverse thrust, he was pushed away and thrown away from the ship's side rather than being pulled into the propellers.

The rescue helicopter, call sign 'Jumbo', was at its station, flying just clear of the carrier abreast the catapult. Strapped in this helicopter was the aircrewman diver, ready to jump into the water to reach the ditched pilot and hoist him up by a winch into the Jumbo. The pilot of this [Aérospatiale] Alouette, Lieutenant Timky Randhawa, was to later recall, 'I saw the Seahawk plunge into the water at an attitude of 45 degrees just twenty yards ahead of the ship. Immediately after hitting the water it started sinking very fast. It was almost fully underwater when the ship hit the starboard wing of the aircraft. Immediately after that I observed glass pieces flying out of the water to the port of the ship. At this stage I dropped a marine marker to mark the position and asked the aircrewman diver to stand by to jump. But thereafter, there were just no signs of the pilot or the aircraft.'

Action alarm was sounded on board the ship and it was fully ready to deal with the emergency. The doctor, medical and rescue teams and look-outs were all alerted, with everyone on the flight deck searching the water, but Peter was nowhere in sight. Suddenly Jumbo called out 'Flyco, I see a Mae West on the starboard side a little away from the ship. Am proceeding to investigate.' This inflatable life jacket, aptly named after Ms Mae West, is bright orange in colour and is invariably the first object to be sighted during any search. Timky had done well, and soon his elated call came over the R/T, 'It's Peter all right and he has given me a thumbs-up signal.' Relief all over, and in less than a minute, Jumbo had landed back on deck with Peter safe and sound. The entire chain of events had taken less than a hundred seconds. All was well and Peter was back with the squadron.

'After I pulled the blind, the next thing that I became aware of was that I was scraping against the ship's side. I tried to push with my hands and kick with my feet to clear the ship. However, I felt I could not get away as there was a lot of turbulence in the water. I released my parachute, which was dragging me down, and inflated my Mae West whilst still underwater. Suddenly I found I was thrown away from the ship's side. When I surfaced I was well clear of the ship and was immediately picked up by Jumbo and brought back on board.' ... If Peter had time to make his R/T call on that fateful day, he would definitely have said, 'Leader *Re*-born ...'

3
Asian Conflict and Cold War

If anyone had imagined that the end of World War II would usher in a new period of peace they were soon disillusioned. Once again aircraft carriers were called in to fly reconnaissance and surveillance missions, provide Combat Air Patrol, support amphibious landings, troop movements and ground offensives, and destroy strategic targets in a whole series of conflicts.

THE FIRST INDO-CHINA WAR

After the defeat of Japan, the French had been returned to their status as the colonial power in Indo-China. A communist movement led by Ho Chi Minh declared independence, and a major boost to its ambitions came when Mao Zedong's communist forces came to power in China, changing the balance of power in the region. The French attempted to hold Vietnam, with French carriers supporting the ground troops and disrupting enemy communications, but following defeat at Dien Bien Phu in 1954 they assisted with the evacuation. Vietnam was partitioned.

Vice Admiral Roger Vercken, 12-F Squadron, Marine Française,
Arromanches
from *Au Delà du Pont d'Envol*

The French carrier *Arromanches*, purchased from Britain just after the war and commanded by Capitaine de Vaisseau Charles-Edouard Lahaye, arrived off Vietnam on 8 November to support French land forces in the north of the country. Lieutenant de Vaisseau Vercken commanded Squadron 12-F, equipped with Grumman Hellcats and known by its call-sign 'Numa'; Lieutenant de Vaisseau Hervio commanded the Curtis Helldiver Squadron 9F, known by its call sign as 'Spartacus'. GATAC (Groupement Aérien Tactique – Tactical Air Command) had the call sign 'Torricelli'. On 15 October, the carrier's catapult had broken.

The catapult on which Engineering Officer Gerard and his team had worked continuously was finally ready on 4 November. After numerous checks and dummy runs, it was time to launch the first aircraft – one with a pilot on board. I volunteered myself as a guinea pig. I wasn't superstitious, I had full confidence in Gerard who had personally and conscientiously overseen the work, and I knew I was not taking much of a risk. But, to put on a show for the goofers, I turned up to my aircraft in swimming trunks, goggles and flippers. The whole crew enjoyed the joke apart from our esteemed engineer, who had worked day and night and who thought I was casting aspersions on his competence. However, I wasn't averse to showing Lahaye that my 'algebraic inflexibility' was not, on occasion, devoid of humour. Having left goggles and flippers with the crew chief and got my flying kit back on, I started the engine and the catapulting went off without a hitch ...

Operation Lorraine had hardly ended than we all returned to the Thailand road where Na San, now turned into a veritable fortress and nicknamed 'Versailles', stood out as a large ochre stain in the jungle. [General Raoul] Salan had decided to await the offensive of [General Vo Nguyen] Giap's troops there and, to use an expression current at the time, go and smash the Viets. A fleet of [Douglas DC-3] Dakotas shuttled in daily, bringing tonnes of supplies and munitions as well as reinforcements for the troops, and raising a distinctive cloud of dust which could be seen from far off and which formed an unmistakable landmark for the pilots.

We resumed our attack-reconnaissance patrols over different sectors of the deep gorge cut into the landscape by the Black River, searching for an invisible enemy. Flying at low altitude, we followed meandering courses, which GATAC elegantly nicknamed 'Beatrice' or 'Madeleine'. We enjoyed the exhilaration of climbing out of deep ravines in empty valleys, emerging unexpectedly over Ban Mo or Ta Khoa. For us the names of these lost villages, long forgotten, were charged with adventure. Peering into the sun we hoped every time to surprise a Viet column making a detour along a track, or behind a ridge. But we made too much noise, and, anyhow, the enemy had the nights to move around undisturbed save by the high level drone of 8F's Privateers.

Returning after our epic excursions, we would go down to the briefing room to report on our missions. A midshipman from the Photo-Intelligence Service was waiting for us, with the gloomy air of a civil servant. Still elated from the flight, my head full of impressions and landscapes, I thought to interest him by narrating the catalogue of my wanderings. But after two minutes he cut me short.

'Okay! Now then! You saw nobody? You didn't attack anything? Result: Nil!' And he ticked a box on his form.

Pardon me! Nil? I had an overwhelming desire to attack him! Mind you, for him this campaign must have been unimaginably tedious.

Little by little our area of operation shifted to the south-west of the Black River, along the RP 41, which became its backbone. This 'Route Provinciale' split off from the RC6 on the outskirts of Hoa Binh, crossing the river, climbed the cliffs and then threaded its way north-west across the hills toward San La and, well beyond, towards a village with an even more bizarre name than the rest: Dien Bien Phu. On the way it took in many villages, such as Moc Chau and Yen Chua, as well as the entrenched camp at Na San. The free passage of that road, or at least certain stretches of it, had for a long time been hotly fought over by our troops and the Viet. But, with a battle at Na Sang imminent, it was a priority to stop the enemy from using it.

The faithful Criquets* tirelessly circled the region, reporting the slightest hint of suspicious movement and marking it with smoke flares to show us the precise position to attack. We also had to take into account the enemy flak which, thus far, had given us little cause for concern. It was fortunately small calibre – 7.7mm – and, even if a few aircraft had returned with holes in the fuselage, wings or flaps, there had not been any major damage. The pilots had not even realised it while they were flying. That's how Kerhaos-Hermine was hit by a bullet that went through his half-full belly tank, and continued his operation as though nothing had happened. It was noticed only after he was back on board.

Over this period, the mixed patrols set up by Charles-Edouard turned out to be worthwhile. While the Hellcat attacked the target with the machine-gun or with a rocket, the Helldiver flew high, spotting the flak firing and, if necessary, bombing the position. Taking account of the terrain, we dived time and again at a low angle to achieve the greatest accuracy possible. But the act of operating at low level further increased the pilots' chances of being shot at by the Viets. We also carried light cluster-bombs with built-in parachutes which could be dropped in flight without the aircraft being hit by the shrapnel. Instantaneously arrested by the parachute, the bomb actually fell vertically from the release point while the aircraft continued on its flight. Now and again we were tasked with cutting the RP41 ...

Since 22 November we had been called in every day to the area immediately around the entrenched camp, maintaining a presence in the zone through continuous patrols. On the 24th in the mixed patrol that I was leading, the Helldiver piloted by Hervio had good old Father Gendront, the *Arromanches'* chaplain, in the back seat. Even he was keen to understand what it was that we did. The plan was in no way altered. At Na San, we were put under the orders of a Criquet which had us attacking several targets, in support of our forces. I offered our passenger a low-level return along the Black River valley as far as Hoa Binh. He was delighted by this sightseeing trip. However, when were back on board he was taken with a fit of religion and charity and whispered to me in confidence 'I hope we haven't killed too many people.'

The Vietnamese were gradually tightening their grip around Na San, but Salan was determined to fight. GATAC had set up a PC [Command Post] annexe of Torricelli, nicknamed 'Torri Vert', coordinating missions between, on the one hand, the Criquets and, on the other, the B-26s, Bearcats and ourselves. At night, 8Fs Privateers took over.

From 25 to 30 November, 9F and 12F carried out more than 80 sorties, either as close support for our troops or on attack and bombing missions in a radius of 50 kilometres around Na San. The attack on the entrenched camp

* Morane Saulnier MS 500.

became imminent. On the night of 30 November / 1 December an opening attack was unleashed against two pressure points around the perimeter and repulsed by Colonel Gilles's commandos. Ten of my aircraft were in action at Na San on the 1st. Giap launched the grand offensive in the evening. Savage hand-to-hand fighting took place amid an avalanche of gunfure, but the 12 battalions at Na San halted three Vietnamese divisions. In the morning of December 2, the latter disengaged, leaving hundreds of corpses on the ground, and continuing to be harassed from the air. General Salan had gained some breathing space; but the lesson would not be lost on Giap.

Méchanicien Jacques Dauvergne, Marine Française, *Dixmude*
Communication with the Editor

The former US-built Lend-Lease escort carrier HMS *Biter* was sold to the French Navy shortly after World War II, when the French had no operational aircraft carrier, the old *Béarn* being too expensive to refit.

Now to our mission in Indochina, a country equally magnificent, but at that time it was at war. We arrived at Saigon by sailing up the river; we stayed in there for a while; the town was very quiet, the hinterland being more dangerous. During this period we were busy sprucing up the ship as usual (in particular painting, polishing the brass, etc.).

One particular day, the evening before we sailed to go back to towards Tonkin, the cleaning department decided to spread rat poison throughout the ship, because when in port there are always rats who get aboard via the hawsers. We had had such an invasion and they were running about everywhere. As an aside, when we hung our hammocks nearly at ceiling height, the rats were wandering some 50 centimetres from our heads; in fact, one morning I found myself with a large hole in the the sole of my right foot. The rats nibbled the wound by slow degrees so that you felt nothing. I went to sickbay to get myself patched up.

It was unfortunate if you had leather bags because they ate them.

We had put down electric traps to catch the rats because it is a custom in the navy when you catch a rat you turn up, with the rat, at the galley and you are entitled to an extra measure of wine.

To return to the rat poison: that was liberally scattered everywhere. The weather was warm and humid in that region, the fans were indispensable and running at their usual speed, so the powder was stirred up in the messes, and we, the ship's company, were affected by the poison. Three-quarters of the crew were confined to bed – or rather hammocks – and so the next today it was impossible to sail. One day, after welding work on a bulkhead, a fire broke out – it was nothing other than the nests that the rats had made in our stuff. The two events followed one another.

A few days after the crew was back on its feet, we sailed for Tonkin. Our task was to repatriate the population of Tonkin in North Vietnam to Saigon, South

Vietnam. In order to do this we went as far as the bay of Along. And there we waited for other small ships, because we could not go to the quay at Haiphong, the depth of the water not being sufficient for the *Dixmude*.

At the time of that embarkation we took some 2,000 civilians comprising women and children and prisoners. We had to feed everyone (rice in particular) treat the sick, deliver pregnant women who in that country don't need doctors. It was not the norm for a young man like myself to see all this at 19 years old. It took us four days to get down to Saigon, and if I remember correctly we had to make a dozen round trips. We were not the only ones involved in this work. American ships were doing the same job. When our mission was over the *Dixmude* set off to return to France, and that was practically the end of the Indochina war for France (1954).

THE KOREAN WAR

Almost contemporaneous with the First Indo-China War came the Korean War. Following the Japanese defeat, Korea had been divided at the 38th Parallel as a prelude to a full solution. The communist North was backed by the Soviet Union; the South by the USA. On 25 June 1950, after a long period of minor clashes, Soviet-equipped North Korean troops crossed the border. The recently formed United Nations condemned the North Korean aggression, and a wide coalition of some fifteen nations was formed to end it. Troops under General MacArthur drove back the Communists to the Parallel, then crossed into North Korea. When the UN advance into the North brought troops close to the border with the People's Republic of China, the latter became a belligerent on the North Korean side.

The conflict was land-based, with aircraft carriers from the USA, Britain and Australia (the three largest providers of military forces) flying missions against shore-based targets to disrupt the movement of enemy combatants and supplies and cover amphibious landings and advances. Most of the aerial combat took place between land-based aircraft, but some carrier-based aircraft engaged in dogfights with the formidable MiG-15s. The conflict, which cost a huge number of lives, concluded in 1953 with the status-quo restored.

Ken Sheale, HMS *Triumph*, 1950
Communication with the Editor

A group of RN vessels, including HMS *Triumph*, headed to the northern tip of Kyushu, Japan's main island, to visit Ominato Bay. Rumour reached the lower deck that the bay was being prospected as a possible Fleet Anchorage. At the time of arrival I was at my usual post in the forward machinery space as throttle watchkeeper operating the Starboard main engine. The Port main engine was in the after machinery space operated by another Leading Stoker.

When 'Hands for entering harbour' was piped, Commander (E) appeared and took over the high chair usually reserved for the Chief of the Watch. From there he could monitor the operation of both machinery spaces as we had repeaters of the Port engine located to one side of the throttle platform. I can visualise him now although I regret that I can no longer remember his name.

Usually, coming to anchor meant Stop followed by Slow Astern as the anchor cable was laid out, possibly a couple more orders before a final Stop, Finished with Main Engines. On this occasion the orders kept coming and I could hear the clang of the Port engine repeaters on my right playing a similar tune. After about ten minutes of this, Commander (E) climbed off the chair and disappeared in the direction of the air lock. He reappeared a few minutes later and said to the Chief, 'Silly buggers up top think they are playing billiards. Trying to go in off *Green Ranger*.' (The Fleet Oiler attached to the Far East Fleet). I don't know if it was wind or currents or a combination but it took nearly an hour to come to anchor.

Commander William H. Koenig, VF-32 Squadron, USS *Leyte*, CV-32
from *On Jesse's Wing*, available in full on
www.vf32.info/articles/on_jesse_wing.pdf by permission of the Author

Koenig shared a cabin with Ensign Jesse Leroy Brown who, despite bitter racial prejudice in some quarters, had became the first African American to qualify as a US Navy pilot.

We arrived at the French Riviera July 3rd and would stay through July 14th, what a treat. Cannes beach in the summer time is a mecca for sun worshippers, and the ensigns in the VF-32 bunkroom (Boys Town) were hustling their slowpoke shipmates so they could make the first boat ashore. One of those waiting, called to the laggards, 'Get a move on so that we can lie in the sun and get black as ...' Lee Nelson, Jesse's close friend, described the moment as a short period of silence broken by Jesse saying, 'Don't wait for me. I'll catch the next boat. Besides, I've got a head start.'

The war in Korea had begun just before our Cannes visit. On August 15th, the *Leyte* was ordered to return to Norfolk at high speed and prepare for emergency duty with UN forces in Korea ...

We had one night's shore leave in San Diego; Tom Hudner and I took advantage of it. We had just seated ourselves in a cocktail lounge at one of the better hotels when in came our VF-32 ensigns. After we exchanged greetings, they headed for the more active part of the lounge – only to leave a few minutes later, walking out as a tight knit group, and in passing said, 'They wouldn't serve Jesse.' Tom and I joined the exodus. We were offended to the point of anger, but Jesse wasn't. It was nothing new to him ...

At one point in our transit to Sasebo, our squadron duty officer was notified by *Leyte*'s Supply Department that hard hats (correct term: anti-buffet helmets) were available for non-jet aviators, but not all sizes were in stock. We F4U pilots were still wearing cloth helmets. The line formed quickly at the issue room. Jesse and I each came away with a white hard hat. Back in our room, eager to see his image in jet age gear, Jesse put his helmet on and looked into the mirror. Bobby and I heard him comment, 'All I see is a white helmet, white teeth and eyeballs showing through ...'

Leyte joined Seventh Fleet October 9th, 1950. We flew missions the next day over the port of Wonsan. After our division had been on station as TARCAP for an hour, we were released to look for targets of opportunity. Some of the islands in the harbor had mobile shore batteries located in caves. This artillery was giving our minesweepers a lot of trouble. Jesse got a good look at one of the tunnel openings and fired a HVAR [High-Velocity Aircraft Rocket]. Viewed later, his gun camera film showed a good hit. I found a large truck, partially concealed, and fired a HVAR from a close and slightly flat position. My film showed a hit, and it also showed me flying through the mud and debris. Because of my transgression I was directed to land aboard last so Repair Eight Crash Crew could hose down my plane ...

November 27th our division was assigned to reconnoiter the area from Manpo-Jin to Linchang. The flak briefing for the route starting point was the usual, heavy automatic weapons fire, radar controlled, to 20,000 feet. Target weather was overcast, tops at 15,000 feet and base at 2,000'. We pushed over at 17,000' and passing through 12,000 feet I heard a distinctive thump that caused my memory to jump back to destroyer days – sounded just like the 5"/38 AA common round exploding. The fabric on the rudder of Jesse's plane was shredded and the letter 'K' was half gone. 'Three's taking departure,' he said, as we eased to the right and steepened our dive. The road of our search area divided and paralleled a ridgeline for twenty miles near the end of the route. We would split, and again rendezvous at what showed on the chart to be a prominent hill at the end of our route. I finished my segment and after orbiting the hill for five minutes, I asked my leader for his position. He replied that he was anchored at the agreed-upon hill. We were orbiting two nearly identical hills a few miles apart but only one of them showed on the chart. As I slid smoothly into place on his wing, Jesse raised his goggles and smiling at me shook his head, – there it was – white helmet, white teeth, and eye balls!

December 4th we were a six-plane flight assigned road recce and on-call close air support in the Yudamni area near the Reservoir. Our LSO, George Hudson, was flying as Dick Cevoli's wingman, Tom [Hudner] was on Jesse's wing, and I had a floating section with Ralph McQueen on my wing. It was approaching mid afternoon and we had just entered the route. I was moving the section to a perch position and as we crossed behind Jesse and Tom, I noticed a thin stream of vapor from the underside of Jesse's aircraft. The Corsair's automatic fuel transfer system sometimes didn't shut off when the main cell reached full. I called to him to check the fuel transfer. Immediately he responded, 'I'm losing power; I'm going down.' Sadly, it wasn't a fuel transfer problem. Jesse made the best of a most unfavorable situation; low altitude, slow airspeed, and snow covered rocky terrain for a landing site. Tom stayed on his wing calling air speed and the two important emergency landing items, shoulder harness locked and canopy locked open. Jesse hit the ground hard and the aircraft buckled at the cockpit trapping him.

In a short time Tom went down to help him. Making the simulated carrier landing approach we practice when ashore (FCLP), he landed wheels up close to Jesse. VMO-6 rescue helicopter pilot Charlie Ward arrived about an hour after Jesse went down. He and Tom worked feverishly but were unable to extricate Jesse from his plane. Darkness comes early in December, at 4,000 feet MSL [mean sea level] and 40°-36' North latitude. Ward's helo was not instrument equipped to fly at night, so of necessity they departed while it was still light enough for him to navigate the mountainous terrain. We stayed with Jesse until it was dark. Dick Cevoli and George Hudson were carrier night qualified so they returned to the ship. Ralph McQueen and I diverted to Yonpo, the former North Korean airfield now operated by the Marines, where we spent the night.

Tom arrived at Yonpo the next morning just as Ralph and I was [sic] about to man aircraft. We had only a few minutes to talk. He described Jesse's condition when he left him, and I asked Tom about his landing and his condition.

Leyte was replenishing that day; so her stragglers were being recovered by *Philippine Sea*, Commander Task Force 77 flagship. Within a few hours after we landed, an officer from CTF 77 staff sought me out. 'We thought you, as the leader of the *Leyte* flight, would like to read this,' he said, and handed me a clipboard with an impending Public Affairs Office press release. The opening line read, 'A Dramatic Rescue of Navy's first Black Aviator and his shipmate who saved him.'

My first thought was for Jesse's wife Daisy. How dreadful it would be if she believed that Jesse had survived a crash landing in enemy territory and had been rescued, when in fact she would soon receive a telegram from the Department of the Navy which will read, 'The Secretary of the Navy regrets to inform you — .' Returning the clipboard to the bearer I said with emphasis, 'This is wrong! He's dead; they couldn't get him out!' The press release was cancelled.

Hudner had set fire to the two aircraft and given his friend a warrior's funeral. He could have been court-martialled for deliberately crash-landing in enemy territory; instead, he received the Congressional Medal of Honour for 'conspicuous gallantry and intrepidity ... Lt (J.G.) Hudner's exceptionally valiant action and selfless devotion to a shipmate sustain and enhance the highest traditions of the U.S. Naval Service'.

Ken Sheale, HMS *Triumph*
Communication with the Editor

By sheer chance I came across a site dealing with *Triumph*'s role in the Korean War and read a reference to a Firefly that crash-landed on the deck on 29 August 1950. One blade of the propeller broke off, went through the window of the Operations Room and fatally injured the C/O of 800 Squadron, Cdr I. M. McLachlan. When I read that I was shocked that I could not remember anything about it, probably because I don't remember a funeral service. It brought home the fact that the various departments had very little contact with each other. I knew very little about the day-to-day work of the seaman branch and the FAA handlers and mechanics were in a different part of the ship and virtually unknown.

Mechanic 3rd Class Jack Campbell, VA923 Squadron, USS *Bonne Homme Richard*
Communication with the Editor

We crossed the International Date Line on May 23rd· 1951 and on the morning of May 31st we joined Task Force 77 and prepared to launch our first strike.

I will never forget that first morning. The ship's P.A. blared out General Quarters at 4:00 a.m. I climbed up on the wing of my plane and slid down in the seat. I turned the engine over, it caught on the first prime and, spraying exhaust to the winds, it purred at any RPM I moved to. I glanced about me, just able to see the fleet that surrounded me in the dim light. I'll be damned if it didn't look like every ship in the Navy was here. I made out the USS *Boxer* launching their planes and a slew of destroyers and supply ships surrounding us. My pilot jumped up on the wing and we switched places, he sinking down into the seat I'd been warming for him. Our first strike was on its way as I watched the exhaust flashes from departing planes speckle the pre-dawn sky. The thought passed my mind that I would have been here in WWII if the damn Navy hadn't screwed me out of it.

It took us all a few days to mesh with the routine the ship's company had set up, to move our planes about the deck during the launch and landing sequences. The ordnance people would arm your plane with bombs or rockets prior to the strike, and ship's personnel would hand you a hose to gas up your plane.

The Task Force had two carriers working together, with another carrier in Yokosuka, Japan, doing liberty and taking on supplies. Every 30 days one carrier would be relieved to do the same. My only job onboard this ship was my plane. When it wasn't in the air, it was with me until it was officially secured for the night. After breakfast I went to the plane, fired it up until I was satisfied enough to certify it for flight. Then I would check with the Chief to see if it was going on a strike. Some days, depending on weather or circumstance, the plane was static. Most days that meant I had the day off, unless they needed me to work tune-ups on the hangar deck. I always asked my pilot how long the mission was so I could gage my time off for personal tasks. It was a seven-day war, and you grabbed the time to pamper yourself wherever you could – just one thing, though: if you were not there when your plane hit the deck, it was your ass, big time!

A few weeks into our cruise, our squadron executive officer informed me that from now on my plane would be available to the Air Group Commander whenever he chose to fly it on a strike. Seems he was checked out on all the aircraft onboard including the Panther Jets, which he flew most of the time. 'Congratulations,' he says: 'the Plane Captain to the Air Group Commander rates full time flight pay.' Wow, I'm thinking, up until now I only got flight pay if I went as 'observer' on a strike, now I get it whether I fly or not. I was brought back to earth when I found out Commander Funk likes to have me sitting in the 'observer compartment' when he flies my plane. I think he wanted somebody in that seat in case he got shot down, then he'd have company; I was going to earn that flight pay and see the war. Though he only flew my plane a few times a week, it didn't mean I could goof off the rest of the time. Depending on the type of strike and how many aircraft it required, other pilots flew my plane. Though we had stopped being 'aircrew' and getting flight pay when we got the new aircraft, I felt lucky as hell to still be getting it full time.

Well, with my new window on the war, I started attending Mass and Confession more often, among other things. I also started stashing survivor gear in the plane and little items that might come in handy in case we got shot down.

'Pilots, man your planes' rang out a few days later, and I climbed in behind the Commander and waited for the last jet to be catapulted, before we led the 'Skyraiders' off the deck. We were in and out of the clouds all the way to the target, but broke clear just as we dived towards the rail yard. We led the way for five other planes, and dropped a 500lb. bomb into the crowed rail yard. Pulling up in a tight turn, I was able to get a good look at the resulting damage, as flak tracers tried to find our range. The five other planes following our run made accurate strikes, leading to fire and explosions intense enough for the Commander to call off another run at the target.

We had just formed up when I hear the Commander say, 'We'll make a 20mm gun run, north to south for targets of opportunity' I always hated going down on the deck, for the following reasons: ground fire has a better shot at you; tall trees, electrical wires, and any dude with a gun can ruin your day. And the biggy: any box car that blows up in front of you is kind of like trying to dodge a hand-grenade in your shower. We did some more damage, and then formed up for the ride home.

It was dusk when we landed, and after I fueled and secured my plane. I went below for some hot chow, and ran into my bunkie, who proceeded to lay some bad news on me. It seems Delbert Krebs was killed during the pre-dawn launch. He was hit by a whirling propeller and killed instantly. My plane was already in the air, so the news was late in coming.

Delbert was a plane captain like me, and part of our job is scooting under and around spinning props, it's what we do. His demise was a little more personal with me than most of the guys. Delbert was illiterate, and I early on volunteered to write his letters and read his mail to him. I will miss Delbert; he was what we called 'a good old boy.' He had a good heart and loved being a part of this squadron. He often told me how proud his parents were of him; I'm sure they were.

After 30 days on station we were relieved by the USS *Princeton* and headed for Yokosuka, Japan, for R&R and needed supplies ... It had been five years since I had seen Japan, and I was really anxious to check out the changes the post war had brought.

R&R was either liberty in Yokosuka or three days up in the mountains at a resort hotel the US had taken over after the war. We had a draw to see who went where. My best buddy and I both got the hotel trip. At the resort we could do any damn thing we wanted 'within reason', no formations or curfews, just softball, fishing, horseback riding and all the good chow you wanted, every thing was free. Wherever you were on the grounds, just raise your hand and you had a beer in it; boy what a winner!

Well, Commander Funk showed me one hell of a lot of North Korea at the Navy's expense, and he got us through it without a scratch.

Sub-Lieutenant Brian Ellis, 802 Naval Air Squadron, HMS *Ocean*
from his interview with Rowland White

On 9 August 1952 four Sea Fury FB. Mk 11s landed back on HMS *Ocean* after a successful engagement against eight MiG jet fighters in which one of the MiGs was shot down. It earned Commander Peter 'Hoagy' Carmichael, the flight commander, the DSC. The combat took place inland between Pyongyang and Chinnampo.

Carl Haines, Hoagy's No. 2, who had extremely good eyesight, reported 8 bogies. Carl saved us. He saw something move against a pale daylight moon which gives you an idea of how sharp he was. If you want somebody who needs a lot of credit, there's the first guy. So we immediately got into pretty fair battle formation. There was about 400 yards between us and we started rubbernecking, looking for these things. I think almost simultaneously as I got my head round I saw something out there getting very close, very fast and a stream of tracer went past. So I called 'break', which was the second positive thing the flight did. 'Break' without 'left' or 'right' meant you did a scissors, you went in towards each other, which almost instantaneously put us head on to a group of MiGs. They were the first ones that shot through. We got rid of our drop tanks – one of mine wouldn't go so I fought the rest of the engagement with about 30 gallons of fuel on one side, but that didn't seem to be too much of a worry at the time. We continued hard turning. Hoagy and Carl – I didn't see what they were up to – but I think they just stayed in pretty tight turns. Briefly we rolled out head-on to the next group of MiGs as they approached, got a few shots off and, as they shot past we did another very tight turn to try keep them in sight. The MiGs were rather disorganized. What they should have done is left a couple of pairs above us to come in and pick us off at the appropriate time. They seemed to be very uncoordinated. They were coming at us four at a time. It all happened very, very quickly. And I can understand why there are so many disputes about aerial combat. As we did another hard turn one shot past me. It had obviously almost got on my tail, but hadn't. We had done a hard break and this MiG came round on the outside of the turn with its airbrakes out. I just rolled and to my amazement I was actually getting closer to this guy. And that was when I started rattling stuff in. It was like World War Two footage, you know, bits were flying off the damn thing. It didn't blow up or anything like that. It didn't spin in, but a little later I saw one go away very much slower towards the North with two others in company. They clearly had not worked out how to do it. They had no answer to our defensive tactics.

I don't think anybody else actually had a stern attack on anybody. They all said, 'Oh we hit them when they were coming head on'. Over the years I have come to doubt this. The chances of getting an effective burst in with head-on closing speeds approaching 800–900mph are remote. What we thought were hits head-on were more likely to have been flashes and smoke from the MiG's armament as they fired at us. You just can't get a steady bead on them at that speed. You have collisions head-on, but you stand very little chance of shooting anyone down that way.

The quartet shot down one MiG and badly damaged two others. In an interview shortly afterwards, Carmichael stated that the kill was a team effort.

Ensign later Commander, Tex Atkinson
from *From The Cockpit*

Frank's third escape from death was the most frightening of all. It came months later. Frank and Pat Murphy were flying F9Fs [Grumman F9F Panthers] on a low-level mission near Wonsan Harbor, when several 50-caliber bullets struck Soberski's Panther. One of the shells penetrated Sober's windshield and fragments from the explosion shattered into Frank's face and blinded him. Pat Murphy quickly joined on Frank's wing and gave constant instructions so that Sober could keep his F9 under control. The flight was too far north to consider making it to a friendly landing strip, thus landing back aboard the carrier [USS *Princeton*] blind and bleeding, ditching in freezing ocean water, or ejecting for a parachute drop into those same cold waters were Frank's only choices.

Pat Murphy was an experienced Blue Angel jet pilot, who had joined VF-191 with the rest of the Blue's team shortly after the beginning of the Korean War. Pat assured Sober that he could guide him to a safe landing aboard the carrier. Frank says that while he was sitting bloody and blinded in the cockpit of an F9F listening to Murphy's verbal reassurances, he was remembering an old joke about a Chicago attorney pleading with his client in a soft reassuring voice, saying 'Trust Me!' But Frank pushed the thought aside. He had little choice but to have faith that Pat Murphy and the Landing Signal Officer aboard the *Princeton* would guide him to a safe landing.

The LSO waiting on the *Princeton* that day was Mabry Blaylock. When he received word that a jet was coming in with a blinded pilot, he called another LSO, George Parker, for assistance. He told George that the mike at the fantail was not working properly and that he would like to have both a mike and paddles to work the jet aboard.

George dashed to the office of the Air Boss high in the island structure of the *Princeton*. From there he had a good view of the entire operation and could communicate with both the pilot and with Mabry Blaylock. He told Mabry to drop the screen behind the LSO platform so he could see the signals of the paddles. George then proceeded to give voice instructions that could be heard by both Frank Soberski and Mabry Blaylock. Mabry then gave paddle signals to reinforce the communication.

George Parker still remembers well the day Soberski landed blind. He says that he appreciates the credit that has been given him through the years, but that the truth of the matter is that Pat Murphy flew Soberski to the ramp of the carrier in such good shape that about all the LSO had to do was signal a cut ...

Commander David 'Shorty' Hamilton
Communication with the Editor

During the war in Korea our carriers worked continuously, supporting the armies ashore. During one launch of Fairey Fireflies, Peter Reynolds was mis-loaded on to the catapult. Pushed back, he was again loaded off-centre. By the time he was loaded correctly all the other aircraft were airborne. In a mad rush to catch up he forgot to put his flaps to the take-off setting and was shot off with a full load of bombs. He fell off the end of the flight deck, and, reappearing in a cloud of spray, made like a speedboat into the distance as the Firefly slowly, slowly staggered into the air. On returning from the sortie and landing, a message came over the Tannoy: Lieutenant Reynolds report at the Compass Platform. There the Captain, Charles Evans, addressed him. 'Reynolds, for some days I have been severely constipated – thank you very much for curing me.'

Aviation Electronicsman 1/c Jim Stephens, Airman, USS *Essex*
Communication with the Editor

In March 1952 I was awarded my Combat Aircrew Wings. In June a team was formed, comprised of a Pilot and another aircrewman and myself. The Pilot was Lt. J. C. Norton. Then there was Aviation Electronics Technician First Class Benjamin Killingsworth, and finally, myself (Aviation Electronicsman). In July of that year, my team with three other teams boarded the USS *Essex* (CV-9) for our first Korean tour ...

As we approached the Equator, the ship received orders to proceed to the Philippine Islands for replenishment and then to participate in what was named 'The China Parade'. At that time, Communist China was threatening to invade two small Nationalist Chinese Islands named Quemoy and Matsu. We participated in a show of strength along the China coast for several days. We then proceeded to the Sea of Japan for operations with Task Force 77 against North Korea. We commenced operations about 1 August. My first flight was an ASW flight around the Task Force. My next flight was a combat mission over North Korea. Our bomb load consisted of ten 250-lb bombs and six 'Tiny Tim' rockets. Our mission was to destroy any troop or supply convoys or to destroy supply trains, or any other targets of opportunity. These missions were always scheduled as night missions and were given the title 'Heckler' missions. This first mission was fun for me and (it seemed) like the Fourth of July. Imagine a night mission with flack bursts all around you and tracer bullets flying everywhere.

My aircraft was a dive bomber. The [Douglas] Skyraider was a well built aircraft. All of us aviators who flew in it loved it. It was a large, powerful aircraft that could carry an unheard of amount of ordnance for a plane with only a single engine. (It could carry as much ordnance as the old WWII four engine B-17 bomber.) It was loud, dirty and uncomfortable and loved very much by all who flew in it. I was proud to be a crew member of that aircraft. We would dive from eight or nine thousand feet down to about one thousand feet before releasing our bombs and then rapidly climb back to a safe altitude. This Skyraider version was equipped with Radar, Electronic Countermeasures equipment, and High Altitude Bombing gear. It was designed to carry a Searchlight and Sonobuoy dispenser for AntiSubmarine warfare.

The aircraft could carry a 2000lb bomb under the fuselage, two 500lb bombs under each wing stub, and six 250lb bombs under each outer wing. Also, depending on the mission, it carried flare dispensers, Rocket pods, or Napalm. In jest, the aircraft was titled 'The Flying Dumptruck.' It was winterized with de-icer boots on the wings and a propeller especially for use in the Korean winters.

On 8 August at approximately 4 a.m. we were thrown from the starboard catapult of the *Essex*. We climbed to about 10,000 feet and proceeded inbound to the Northeast coast of Korea in search of trains, truck convoys, or even bridges to destroy. After about 15 minutes of search, we found a North Korean supply convoy of trucks. We dove on the convoy and destroyed several of the trucks. While on a diving rocket attack on the remainder of the convoy, the aircraft was hit with shrapnel from a 37mm cannon shell burst. The shrapnel apparently cut an oil line, causing our engine (the only one) to catch fire. The pilot was able to gain enough altitude before the engine seized and quit, that he was able to get us out over the water, near a small Island named Yang-do. There, he was able to ditch the plane. I was so excited that I never felt the jolt of the crash. Upon impact with the water, the plane disintegrated, according to a pilot flying overhead at the time. The aircraft apparently broke into several pieces and sank rapidly. The pilot was the first out, then my crewmate. My shoulder harness was fouled and I had difficulty getting out. The plane was probably 20 or 30 feet underwater before I was able to extricate myself. Thank goodness I was trained for this. I popped to the surface and we three got our life rafts from our seat packs and inflated them and tied them together. We hoped the *Essex* would send a helicopter to pick us up, but decided that it was too far away. We drifted for a few hours, and then saw a ship's small boat coming toward us. The crew of the boat was firing rifles toward us, which caused us great concern. Upon coming alongside the rafts, they indicated they were shooting at the sharks all around us. They took us into the boat and proceeded to the USS *Ozbourn* (DD-846), a Destroyer from the Task Force. We stayed aboard the *Ozbourn* until about 4pm. We were then transferred via highline back to the USS *Essex*. It was nice to be home.

Air Artificer William 'Glynn' Thomas, HMS *Glory*
from the papers of William G. Thomas, IWM

Saturday 30th November 1952

Dear Mum
Just a short line to let you know how I am.

We left Japan Friday morning for our second operational tour, and have been very busy since, although things are quiet as regards alarms etc. Some people think the war will soon be over out here, I HOPE SO.

We hit a gale when we left Japan, I've never seen it as rough anywhere. The old ship was rolling and pitching all over the place. I have a small tin of *special* sea-sick pills, and they had never been used, but I thought I *had* to have one and I felt much better, though I left my dinner in the oven until tea time. The captain gave everyone (except those needed to make the ship go) the day off; and I'm sure that most of them would have been useless anyway. So I went to bed and when I woke up at teatime I felt fine. It was so bad that waves were coming over the flight deck which is fifty feet above the water line. But we suffered no damage and the weather is fine now ...

The big Xmas pudding has been made on the ship, it weighs some hundreds of pounds!! I hope the sea is calm on Xmas Day so as we can enjoy it ... I find I'm on duty on Xmas Eve, so I'm clear from noon Christmas day... All my love Glyn

Thurs 11/12/52 [At Kure, Japan]
I have plenty of Naval special winter clothing, especially a big hooded waterproof coat lined throughout in thick sheepskin, it has *metal* catches to keep it closed. Then I wear that old school scarf (The one Mai knitted red and black) that goes round my neck twice, *then* a big fur and leather cap that leaves only the front of my face (bearded of course) and we wear special light waterproof laced boots. So you can see I wear enough. But I need it all, that wind cuts like a knife if it gets in anywhere. Actually, at sea, we can wear any article of clothing, you see some queer rigs: golf jackets and thigh boots!! ...

there aren't any Yanks, consequently the prices are easier for us. But a bottle of beer costs us 190 yen, which is roughly 4/–; still very expensive. Mind you, it's worth it, Japanese drink is cheap, and their whisky is 4/– a half bottle but we never risk it; we'd rather a bottle of English beer.

Sub-Lieutenant Neil MacMillan, RAN, HMAS *Sydney*, 1951
from *Flying Stations*

Sydney's CAG was participating in Operation 'Strangle', designed to cut off the North Korean supply lines.

At 1500 on Friday 26 October 1951, 26 Flight, consisting of five Fireflies, was catapulted off HMAS *Sydney* to attack a railway tunnel, north-east of Chaeryong. On approaching the target the flight split into two sections; 26 Leader and 2 were going to attack from the north. The first section went in, made their attack and pulled away. At this time my section leader and I commenced a steep diving turn to port, preparatory to running in on the target. We were to carry out a low-level run, endeavouring to place our bombs, fused for a 25-second delay, into the mouth of the tunnel.

On the run-in I was positioned about 300 yards (275m) astern, and just below my section leader, who was strafing the tunnel entrance as an anti-flak precaution. It was just prior to releasing my bombs that I saw what I thought to be ammunition links from my leader's aircraft passing over my canopy. This was later ascertained to have been tracer from a flak position situated near the entrance to the tunnel. At no time during this period had I felt any hits on my aircraft.

After releasing my bombs I pulled away and at the same time my observer, [CPO] Observer 1 Hancox, informed me that we had been hit. The port nacelle tank was streaming fuel, while the starboard wing had two six-inch (15-cm) holes in it, one through the gun-bay, and the other through the roundel. I immediately informed my section leader of the damage and asked him to come and check my aircraft for any further signs of hits. As I did this, I smelt burning in the cockpit and, on checking instruments, found the oil pressure to be reading zero.

At this time my altitude was 1000 feet (300m), so I immediately switched off the engine and fuel and told my leader that I was carrying out a forced landing, there being quite a few flat paddy-fields in the area. I had to abandon the field I had first chosen due to high tension lines across my approach path. I chose another and we jettisoned our canopies.

I failed to jettison my nacelle tanks. The approach and landing were quite satisfactory, the aircraft coming to rest at the intersection of two large ditches in the western corner of the field. The time of landing was 1555. The nacelle tanks remained on the aircraft and the radio was still working. However, not knowing what enemy concentrations were in the area, my observer and I cleared the aircraft at once. (It was later pointed out at FEAF [Far East Air Forces] HQ that enemy troops had been ordered to shoot at the cockpits of forced-down aircraft for the very purpose of preventing the survivors from using the radio.)

We moved about 50 yards (45m) along the ditch running east-west. I carried my parachute while Observer Hancox brought the Owen submachine gun and his navigation bag and maps. On settling into the ditch we placed out our yellow fluorescent panels to signal to the remainder of the flight, now acting as RESCAP [Rescue Combat Air Patrol], that we were both uninjured.

Having done this, we took stock of what we had and where we were. Between us we had: one .38 revolver and 50 rounds; one .45 automatic and 40 rounds; one Owen SMG and two magazines, each of 28 rounds; two 'X' packs; three emergency rations (tins); special rations (tins); one pair of binoculars; and 50 cigarettes. We were both warmly clothed and wearing heavy boots.

As for our position: approximately 200 yards (185m) to the north-west was a small group of houses. Two of the inhabitants, wearing white robes, were peering at the aircraft through a picket fence. Assuming them to be civilians we did not worry about them. To the west was a knoll about 200 feet (60m) high, about a mile (1.6km) distant, from which concentrated automatic fire was engaging the RESCAP all the time we were down.

About five minutes after landing, one of the aircraft from 26 Flight fired a green Verey cartridge, letting us know that help was on the way. This cheered us up no end. By this time the Fireflies had been joined by four Sea Furies [from HMAS *Sydney*] and a flight of Meteors from [RAAF] 77 Squadron.

We then noticed several men situated on the knoll to the west, looking in the direction of the aircraft. Through the binoculars we identified them as enemy troops. However they disappeared over the other side of the hill and we did not see them again.

Forty-five minutes after landing, the Air Group Commander (LCDR Mike FELL, later VADM Sir Michael Fell KCB DSO DSC*) flew low over our position and dropped a message in a container, which landed about 25 feet (8m) from the edge of the ditch. The Air Group Commander's aircraft was hit during this run and subsequently returned to a friendly airfield. The message was a very welcome one, stating that the ETA of the rescue helicopter was 1730.

From that time, until about 1720, Hancox and I kept a lookout for signs of enemy activity and awaited the arrival of the helicopter. At 1720 we heard two bursts of machine gun fire nearby. Looking over the edge of the ditch we saw a Chinese soldier about 100 yards (90 m) away, who immediately starting waving his arms and shouting, no doubt calling us to surrender. At that moment Observer Hancox saw the helicopter coming, so I opened fire on the soldier with the Owen gun. He very smartly dived into the ditch that ran at right angles to ours. I then placed a red panel alongside the yellow, pointing to the enemy. (This is the Air Group's signal meaning that we were being fired on from the direction indicated). At once, two Furies dived and strafed the area.

By this time the helicopter was on its way down, while the air crewman in it was firing his submachine gun at the enemy troops. The helicopter landed some 20 feet (6m) from our position alongside the ditch. I fired several rounds at the enemy position as Hancox climbed aboard, and I then followed him – at the rush. As we were taking off one of the enemy stood up to fire at the helicopter, whereupon he was shot by Air Crewman Gooding.

The trip to Kimpo was uneventful, except that the last 30 minutes were flown in darkness.

I should like, here, to praise the helicopter crew for their devotion to duty in travelling 120 miles (193km) to effect the rescue, knowing full well that they could not return to a friendly base before nightfall.

The Dragonfly helicopter that effected the rescue returned the crew to *Sydney* the following day. The helicopter pilot, CPO Arlene Babbit, USN, received both the Commonwealth Distinguished Service Medal and the United States Navy Cross, making him the only Allied serviceman in Korea to be decorated by two countries for the same action.

Seaman Photographer Jack Reynolds, USS *Oriskany*
Communication with the Editor

On 6 March 1953, during a hectic period of strikes on land-based targets, Lieutenant E. L. Kummer aborted his mission and returned to the carrier. He had jettisoned all bombs except one, which refused to go, and was allowed to land on. The bomb came loose and exploded, causing sixteen casualties, two of them fatal.

I was the photographer who was given the task of developing the gun camera film in a Houston machine, that confirmed the downed aircraft and the kills. When the bomb blew up I was the duty photographer in the photo lab. I grabbed a camera and walked out of the lab to see what was going on. I walked into the hangar deck and into about ½–1 inch of jet fuel. Shrapnel had pierced fuel tanks on the hangar deck.

Saw nothing there. I came back out of the hangar deck and climbed the ladder to the flight deck and walked out on the flight deck and looking aft, saw the F4U [A-4] with the hot suit men working to get the pilot out of the aircraft. Also they had spread foam on and around the plane. Walking aft on the flight deck, I walked over to the port side and took a picture of a Marine in a gun tub that I think had lost an arm in the explosion. Continuing aft toward the F4U I continued taking pictures of the hot suit and the ordnance men unloading the F4U's machine-guns in case the plane caught on fire. I then walked over to the starboard side and, looking down to the catwalk, saw corpsmen working on a man. Took pictures of him laying there with something covering his forehead.

By this time there was nothing else to photograph and I was probably out of film, so I returned to the lab to develop the film. When I came out of the darkroom I learned that the man on the catwalk was John [Photographer Airman Thomas L.] McGraw. He received the Bronze Star because he was the first photographer to take a picture of the actual missile that killed him. Later I was assigned the task of going through his locker to send his personnel effects to his mother. John and I and another photographer rotated duty as follows: one day as duty photographer, one day off and one day taking movies of the plane's tail hook catching the arresting gear. So either I had been doing what John was doing the day before or I was scheduled to do it the next day. My wife back in Atlanta heard about a photographer being killed on the *Oriskany* but did not hear that it was not me until we got back to Japan and I called her.

SUEZ

In 1956 President Nasser of Egypt announced the nationalization of the Suez Canal after Britain and the USA decided not to go ahead with their agreement to finance the building of the dam on the Nile at Aswan. This response was seen by Britain and France as a serious threat to their oil supplies. On 29 October, at the Anglo-French behest, Israel attacked Egypt, thus offering an excuse for France and Britain to seize the Canal on 5–6 November. But then, condemned by the USA and the United Nations, the two Allies were obliged to pull out.

Commander David 'Shorty' Hamilton, Flight Deck Officer, HMS *Albion*
Communication with the Editor

In 1956 HMS *Albion* was part of the task force in the eastern Mediterranean assembled, with French forces, to persuade the Egyptians not to nationalise the Suez Canal. Flying operations meant that the flight deck was a hive of activity day and night.

However I had an understanding Commander (Air) and co-operative Squadron COs so was able to fit in 9 sorties in Sea Hawks over the period of operations. During the first one, on Combat Air Patrol, while scanning the area, I suddenly wondered what year it was – there, flying nearby, was a flight of four Chance-Vought Corsairs, in their standard dark blue paint, straight out of World War Two. I then realised that they must be from the French carriers, *Arromanches* or *Lafayette*.

[Operation] Musketeer was a world first in that the military forces, when hostilities started, were all air lifted into action by helicopter. Later there were seaborne landings. A friend of mine, in 45 Commando, Royal Marines, spent about a minute on the beach before he was wounded and air lifted straight back to a carrier. Some Westland Wyverns were patrolling the beachhead, under the orders of a Forward Air Controller, and were told to strafe 'enemy forces' and were given the map reference of the beach. The flight leader queried the position three times and each time was told to carry out the order. My friend was one who copped a 20mm round, which hit him side on, smashed his right elbow and then cut a shallow [but hot] groove across the small of his back. He was lucky on one count—a couple of inches further forward and he would have been cut in half. There were about 25 casualties all told. That 'friendly' fire again!!

Lieutenant Commander P. H. (Jan) Stuart, RN, C Flight, 849 Squadron, HMS *Albion*, November 1956
Communication with the Editor

Paratroopers had gone ashore and captured the airfield at Gamil but, alas, all was not well because the wily locals had put something nasty in the water supply. A cry for help went out from the Paras, and *Albion* was quick to respond. The initial plan was to fill the long-range drop-tanks of our four Douglas AD-4W Skyraiders with fresh water and fly it ashore, but despite the tanks being new and unused the Medical Officer declared them contaminated and unfit for carrying water.

Something else had to be done, and the ship's welfare committee hit on the brilliant and generous idea of sending canned beer to the soldiers. A quick check showed that if one of the two observers was left out of the crew the Skyraider could carry 1,000 cans. At 1015 on 6th November the Flight Commander, Lieutenant Commander Derek Fuller, executed a free take-off in WV 178 with only me in the back with my feet up against the beer crates to stop them sliding about as we headed into Gamil. I was not trained for this but I managed! Handing the cargo over to the squaddies was one of the sweetest things I have ever done.

We had started something new here because the Paras were soon thirsty again, and looking to HMS *Albion* and C Flight for succour. *Albion*, however, had done them proud and any more beer would have to be paid for, which the soldiers were happy to do. *Albion* did not carry unlimited supplies of the stuff, and a deal was arranged with the NAAFI Manager at RAF Akrotiri, Cyprus, to supply it. C Flight would undertake the transport task.

All 4 Skyraiders of C Flight took off from *Albion* at 1200 noon on 25th November and to allow maximum space for the beer I was the only Observer on the trip. We were at Akrotiri in an hour, loaded about 5,000 cans of beer and some mail and were on our way back to the ship at 1405, heading south. To get the best radar picture for navigation we had flown up at 9,000 feet and planned to do the same on the homeward journey. About 20 minutes out of Akrotiri, at 8,000 ft and climbing, we received a message from the NAAFI manager to warn us that the beer cans were pressurised and they could explode if we went above 5,000 feet – what a mess that would have made! We split the difference and continued on our way at 6,500 feet, landing on board at 1455.

THE COLD WAR

Rear Admiral D. J. Treacher, Commanding Officer, HMS *Eagle*, 1968–70
ADM 330/91

The Cold War between the Soviet Bloc and NATO included much intelligence work, by spies, aircraft and warships. Large naval exercises attracted particular interest on the part of the enemy, and Soviet intelligence-gathering vessels played regular cat-and-mouse games with patrolling NATO ships.

My experience in *Eagle* started virtually from sea trials when I took over after a DED* period with AGIs** in relatively constant attendance, but not very close company. As soon as the ship started her work up in the Moray Firth and the South Western approaches we had AGIs in close attendance. They invariably closed the ship on the starboard bow, very often when we were not flying and caused us on a number of occasions to alter course. In the Moray Firth area in *Eagle* in particular, which has a great many other systems other than aviation – four twin turrets, six Seacat systems, plus the best radar set in the fleet – we had to try to get on with these exercises, which also constrained my movements, almost as much as if I was flying. I did not want to alter course before these AGIs; as it was, he came in and took up his position and turned quite happily without my giving way to him and having to make international signals to him periodically that he was getting into danger. This pattern went on for the whole of the work up – we ran into a certain amount of trouble with CBs [Confidential Books], but we got modifications to the instructions about what you can operate with AGIs. After this single exercise in which the *Eagle* took part we were constantly shadowed, with the exception of a major part of 'Peacekeeper', where again they fell back on AGIs. In [Exercise] 'Peacekeeper' the *Eagle* task group was screened by the Standing Naval Force Atlantic and we also had an American missile ship locked on Circle 4. It would have been highly embarrassing to have had the Russian warship lock on to that system, but we went from AGI to AGI and only on one occasion did an AGI embarrass me to the point of forcing me to alter my course in a three ships RAS at night. It shows that they are required to gather a certain amount of information, and in this case for altering course. I had agreed with the Standing Naval Force that when we were doing three-ship RAS we would try not to alter course for other shipping, keeping the others clear.

One *Tjerke Haddest* made a 360 degree turn and came right back into my screen a mile and a half ahead of me; I had hoisted two red balls but he forced me to alter course and presumably ticked off his bit in the book. That was the only one that I would have classed as a harassing. I then went on to [Exercise] 'Deepen Furrow' where I was never not shadowed. Relations were friendly to the point where I was given a 'good morning' by light. They appeared to be well up on manoeuvering signals and occasionally hoisted international flags to indicate which way they were turning, but never embarrassed me to the point where I thought that a close quarters situation would develop. There was always a chance that a close quarters situation might develop but they always altered and settled down to somewhere between 1 to 1½ miles. They usually turned at ½ mile, perhaps a mile – I was never faced with having to take

* Docking and Essential Defects – period of repair rather than a refit.
** NATO abbreviation for a Soviet Auxiliary General Intelligence vessel – a spy ship.

avoiding action. The pattern went on through [Exercise] RANULAR, and then I had a short period when I was operating off Toulon when I was not shadowed.

Summing up, my own experience is that they will approach on the starboard side so that if you are not a hampered vessel they put you in the position where you think you may have to give way. If you gave way on every occasion I don't think you would ever complete the exercise. You always expect them to turn, unlike a merchant ship, on to the flying course, but in my experience they always left you in doubt until the last minute.

Getting too close, however, sometimes had unfortunate consequences:

Captain G. V. P. Crowden, OBE, RN, HMS *Ark Royal*, 1970
Previously published in the *Journal of Naval Engineering*, December 1971

From first light it had been a normal flying day for the fixed-wing operation of Phantoms, Buccaneers and Gannets, and regular flights for the Sea King helicopters. At one period, when not required for SAR duties, the Wessex helicopter had done a 'milk run' with fresh bread, rolls, mail and papers to the frigate in company. This frigate would be the plane guard for the evening's night flying. A spectator to the day's activities had been the SAM *Kotlin*, the uninvited but ever present Russian observer.

After a dog-watch break, a fresh flight deck crew was ready, the night flying air crews were briefed and the aircraft manned. All the ship required was the Captain's permission to alter course into wind and to increase speed. The first Phantom was ready to load on the steam catapult. Below decks the ship's company, some with work finished for the day or off watch for a period, was relaxing, perhaps watching closed-circuit TV, writing letters, chatting or sleeping. In the wardroom the majority of officers had finished their evening meal, although some late arrivals were about to get their coffee.

Unconsciously each man on board noted the alteration of course and the increased tempo of the main engines as they were adjusted to the higher rpm. The reverberations of the first Phantom's engines on 'repeat 2' permeated the ship's ventilation systems and departed as the aircraft left the flight deck. The ship shuddered as the catapult pistons were retarded at the end of the launch stroke. Everything was set for some good night flying; there was enough wind, not much swell and sufficient visibility to see the horizon and the clear navigation lights of the plane guard in station on the port quarter. However, before the night was over the airborne Phantom was to be diverted ashore.

The noise of the second night launch never came. Instead, the vibration aft changed suddenly and it became clear that the ship was no longer steaming ahead but was actually working up to a fast full-astern! Had the first Phantom ditched ahead of the ship? No one below could tell. Inquiring glances were answered by the strident call of the alarm rattler for Emergency Stations. Clearly something serious had happened.

Messdecks emptied and passageways filled as everyone not on watch made his way to his emergency station where he would report and remain ready. The two hangars and the night deck were thronged with Fleet Air Arm officers and ratings and others with no direct responsibility for ship safety and damage control.

Quick contact with the controlling engine room showed that the Engineer Officer of the Watch had been informed from the bridge that the *Kotlin* had been hit despite the full-astern. All engines were set to 'stop' and fortunately no power had been lost. The effects of the impact would soon be established by the damage control teams and reported to Damage Control Headquarters – HQ1. HQ1, in turn, would pass the damage reports to the Captain on the bridge.

In this instance, the collision could have caused damage and extensive flooding in the forward section of the ship. The first task of the damage control parties was, therefore, to achieve the highest state of water-tight integrity – DC State 1 – as quickly as possible by closing doors and hatches, and isolating ventilation systems where they penetrated decks and bulkheads below the waterline. Simultaneously a check of every man on board was started to determine if anyone was missing or had become a casualty. The ship's motor boats were also prepared to search for survivors in the water.

As only No. 1 DC Section reported damage to HQ1, Nos. 2, 3 and 4 Sections were reverted to normal and were fallen out along with everyone else not concerned with any rescue arrangements.

The ship had been holed in the Boatswain's Store and there was a 3ft × 4ft hole in the half-inch steel stem contour plate. Fortunately the hole was about 4 feet above the water-line and very little water had entered the ship. The 'Shipwright Officer' inspected the damage and assessed the repairs required for restoring water-tightness and hull strength. Clearly the hole would require some hours of outside repair work in daylight. The immediate action was therefore to seal off the damage to the stem as quickly as possible. This would enable the ship to get under way again without risk of flooding from the bow wave.

The position of the hole made the construction of a 'cement box' possible and, in addition, a small 'cofferdam' or water-tight bulkhead would be built. The box would have forward and after panels, about 30 inches apart, made out of 2-inch tongued and grooved planks. The undamaged shell plating and the deck plating – with a convenient steel breast hook – would make up to two sides, the bottom and the top. While the more jagged edges of the hole were burned away with oxy-acetylene by some artificers, other artificers and engineering mechanics were selecting, marking and cutting the timber shores which would be wedged into the ship's structure to support the tongued and grooved planks. When the forward timber bulkhead was in position, it was 'dogged' together with steel clenches to prevent any movement of the timber in a sea-way which might crack the cement seal. After the second bulkhead was similarly secured, the cement was handed down in buckets.

Unknown to the 'Mate Between Decks', the newly painted ship's company heads made an admirable mixing area. Tins of hard fast-setting damage control cement were piled in one alcove and two or three hardboard 'mixing pads' were elsewhere. Each mix was stirred and prodded professionally by a 'stoker' with a shovel. (Yes – we still have a use for shovels!) Granulated cork was added to the mix to give it body and in the cement box extra reinforcement was given by adding short lengths of angle iron. This was to be no normal cement box since it would have to take the pressure of the ship thrusting its way through the water when operating aircraft and in a month's time it would have to withstand the stresses of a full-power trial, which was to be followed shortly afterwards, by a winter passage through the Bay of Biscay.

About 6 hours after the collision the cofferdam plate was welded in position and a temporary plate had been secured over the hole used for filling the cement box. The ship was then ready to get under way again at speeds up to 12 knots. To finish the job, the artificers fitted 4in. × 4in. vertical and breast shores to stiffen the cofferdam and the area above the cement box ...

The entanglement with SAM *Kotlin* will long be remembered by the Royal Navy and by most people everywhere as it was an international incident. The MEA(H)s [Marine Engineering Artificers (Hull)] and engineering mechanics of *Ark Royal* will remember it but not with any special feeling. They met the situation as a professional team and, with no fuss, they devised a very strong and highly successful repair from baulks of timber, nails, steel plate and cement. In fact, they took their 8 hours' work through the night as being 'all in a day's work'.

Captain, later Rear Admiral, Peter B. Booth, USN, USS *Forrestal*
from *True Faith and Allegiance*

ASW was an ongoing part of the Cold War, and NATO exercises were designed to maximize capability.

Both our carriers were in the Med with the 6th Fleet participating in a very-large, multi-national exercise code-named National Week. The name of the game of this particular NA war game was, 'Don't get sunk by submarines,' so both of us were doing max knots and really-random courses to prevent that unwanted 'through-the-periscope' photo signifying a hit by a sub. Well, the *Kennedy* was 'sunk' by an unknown sub and ordered out of action ...

At the exercise debrief on board *Kennedy*, the fleet arrayed through the anchorage, Jerry and I sat side by side on his hangar deck while the Italian lieutenant commander sub CO, proudly showed his carrier picture from the podium and described how he had sunk the *Kennedy*. Jerry just went under the seat in mortification. Everyone applauded for a job well done, the sub skipper took his bows and we all returned to our ships.

A month-or-so later, I received a large, crystal-clear photo of *Forrestal* taken through the periscope of an Italian submarine dated the same day Jerry and

Kennedy were ordered to the sidelines. It was with heavy heart that I copied the picture and sent it to Jerry with some opportune forwarding remarks of endearment. C'est la vie. Sorry about that Jerry.

VIETNAM

After the French withdrew from Vietnam, the USA began sending aid directly to South Vietnam, concerned that if the country fell to the communists the whole of the region would go the same way – the domino theory. As communist insurgency, supported by infiltrating North Vietnamese communists, increased in the South, the number of US military advisors rose to around 12,000 by 1962. War broke out in 1964 following an incident in the Gulf of Tonkin; the US launched a retaliatory strike against North Vietnamese coastal targets from the carriers USS *Ticonderoga* and USS *Constellation*. For three and a half years from March 1965, Operation 'Rolling Thunder' saw bombing attacks against the North, targeting supply lines and troop movements.

At the same time, increasing numbers of ground troops were sent to South Vietnam until a total of half a million was reached in 1967. US air attacks were conducted from carriers and, in the case of the US Air Force, bases in Thailand. The carriers were assigned primarily coastal targets and operated from a position east of Da Nang known as 'Yankee Station'; ships on the station were said to be 'on the line'. There was considerable frustration on the part of US military commanders because for most of the war they were forbidden from carrying out attacks on North Vietnamese ports and other strategic military targets. This stemmed partly from the administration's desire not to provoke the Soviet Union and China, both of which were arming the North Vietnamese with weaponry that included Surface to Air (SAM) missiles and MiG fighters.

Early in 1968 the North Vietnamese launched the Tet Offensive in South Vietnam, taking large numbers of towns and villages. It took a massive US operation to regain control, and General Westmoreland declared that 200,000 additional troops would be needed to defeat the Vietcong. News of the massacre of civilians at My Lai in 1968, coupled with US combat losses and the leaking of secret documents, strengthened anti-war sentiment in the US. To encourage a peace process, the recently elected President Richard M. Nixon reduced ground forces in 1969, and inconclusive peace talks began in Paris in 1970. In 1972 the North Vietnamese attacked the South in the 'Easter Offensive', leading to the US authorizing Operation 'Linebacker', in which four, rather than two carriers were deployed 'on the line'. USN as well as USAF strikes were now launched in great numbers against the North, including attacks on previously forbidden targets.

Following renewed negotiations, the US withdrawal from Vietnam took place in 1973. Two years later, following the attack on Saigon by North Vietnamese forces, all remaining US civilians and marines, plus many South Vietnamese, were evacuated as the city fell.

PO Third Class Christopher Earl Egbert, Seaman Robert P. Graham II, and Airmen Bob Malanga and Tom Blackman, USS *Forrestal*
Communications with the Editor

The catastrophic fire that broke out on *Forrestal* on 29 July 1967 was caused when a power surge fired one of four Zuni rockets mounted under the wing of an F-4 Phantom. The rocket hit a fuel tank on an A-4 Skyhawk and, although it failed to explode, it ignited leaking aviation fuel. The resulting fire set off a 1,000lb bomb and, as fire and shrapnel spread over the flight deck, more bombs exploded.

Graham
Of course, we were at Yankee Station, launching planes on the day of the fire. I had been assigned the 0400–0800 watch in the port steering gears. During this time, we launched our first sortie of the day. A few minutes before 0800, I was relieved by James Blaskis, a fellow quartermaster and friend from Cleveland, Ohio. As was normal after that watch, I had breakfast at the mess decks and reported to my regular duty station, the secondary conning station.

Blackman
I was a 21-year-old airmen, in the Flight Deck Crash Crew, CVA-59. Half of our crew worked launches, and the other half handled recovery operations. At the time I was handling recoveries, my job was to hook up tow bars to the incoming planes, so they could be moved by tractors, while other planes landed. On the launches at around 10:30 a.m., there was a call for an 'Alfa Launch', which meant almost every plane on the ship that was flyable would launch.

Malanga was dealing with a helicopter that had developed a fault:

Malanga
The tow team arrived, hooked us up to a tractor, I jumped in the back of the helicopter and off we went. We were then backed in and parked right behind the island. When we stopped I was jumping out of the helo so I could take a look at the engine. However, when I got out I looked across the deck and saw a fire under and around an A-4 that was piloted by the later Senator John McCain. I then heard General Quarters sounded with the words 'Fire on the Flight deck'. When that is sounded everyone aboard ship has their assigned duty. I looked around for a minute, because my assigned station was in the hangar deck, and I was looking for the best way to get there.

Blackman
I was leaning against the front of an F-4 Phantom; out of the corner of my eye I caught a glimpse of a smoke trail coming from the starboard side aft, traveling across deck toward the port side aft, directly at a group of A-4 Skyhawks. That's when all hell broke loose: this smoke trail, I found out later, was a misfired missile. It hit the 'Belly Tank' on one of the A-4s, and then it was a chain reaction. The initial hit dislodged a bomb, or bombs, from the parked planes. Pilots of these planes were trying to get out, as there was a huge fire caused by

the first hit. Among all the chaos, I noticed a pilot had jumped from his plane and injured himself when he hit the deck. There was another sailor over top of him trying to assist, I ran toward them to help. As we took off the pilot's helmet, we looked around and saw a bomb, laying on the deck not far from us. We both decided to head for the island and, hopefully, safety. As we picked the pilot up and began running, a bomb exploded, knocking both of us down, as well as the pilot. As I picked myself up, I knew I was injured. I made it to the island, and as I entered a hatchway an officer told someone to get to sick bay, I asked who, and he said you, talking about me. I started down the ladders to sick bay, about five decks below. As I got to sick bay level, I felt myself getting weak; as I struggled down the passageway, I remember asking for help, then I passed out.

Egbert

I was in the VA-65 AMS Shop located on the port side, aft, of hangar bay two, right behind the hangar bay doors, when the first notice of a fire on the flight deck was announced over the ship's public address system. Shortly thereafter, the General Quarters, 'All Hands Man Your Battle Stations' order was given. My General Quarters Station happened to be the VA-65 AMS Shop. The AMS Shop was located just forward of the liquid oxygen plant ...

I was inside the compartment when the first 1,000-pound bomb exploded. The hole blown in the flight deck was about 20 yards aft of the compartment. It blew a hole through the flight deck, down through the hangar deck and three decks below that. The explosion shook the compartment so violently that the many layers of gray Navy paint were vibrated off the bulkhead and overhead. I found myself standing there covered in small paint chips.

Graham

As I made my way aft, I could see what looked to be haze or smoke ahead of me. A column of men was running my way shouting, 'Forward-down! Forward-down!' Even though I knew that the North Vietnamese didn't have weapons that could reach our carrier, I was beginning to believe that the ship was actually under attack. I ducked into an access that allowed me to take a ladder down to the hangar level, where I came out somewhere near the port side and forward end of bay number two. It was the beginning of pandemonium there. Men were running every which way heading to their battle stations, but the most memorable sight was the ordnance men who were beginning to jettison bombs and missiles off of the starboard elevator that was at hangar level. The noise was immense.

I found my way across the bay to the series of ladders that would lead back up to the flight deck level and on up to the bridge. Already, by the time that I was able to go up a level or two, I was encountering wounded men who had been taken into the shelter of these spaces. As I passed the flight deck, I began to get a sense of the severity of what was going on, but I continued on toward my battle station. A hose was running up the ladders and the smell of smoke was intense. I remember wondering with some fear, what I would do if the bridge were on fire? Where would I go if my GQ station were unmannable?

Malanga

I saw the fire crews dragging hoses toward the fire. One of the hoses they were dragging got caught on an aircraft wheel. I ran over to free it. As I grabbed the hose the first explosion went off and threw me into the catwalk. I felt I was hit by a giant fist. I landed in the catwalk netting next to a few other shipmates. One of them was badly injured. Myself and another grabbed our injured shipmate and made our way towards the island. We wanted to get between it and the explosions to get this injured crewman down to sick bay. It was really chaotic, but we managed to do just that.

Afterwards I made my way down to the hangar deck where my GQ station was. Shortly thereafter we were removing ordnance (bombs and missiles) from the aircraft and throwing them overboard. If we couldn't remove a bomb for some reason we pushed the entire aircraft overboard. Some of us were then assigned to relieve the fire fighting crews on the flight deck. I remember walking on the flight deck, past body parts, and the soles of my shoes were melting off. We got to one of the hose crews and took over. We were standing over a gaping hole about fifteen feet wide, caused by an exploded bomb, and began pouring water into the hole. I guess we were there about 30 minutes and I turn to see someone coming towards the hole with a ladder. He was also wearing oxygen gear. He places the ladder into the hole and climbs down. About ten minutes later he comes back up. At the same time we were being relieved so I went over and helped him pull up the ladder.

As we both were walking away I asked what he was doing. He told me that from below deck they spotted a 1,000-lb bomb just below the hole entrance, and he went down to disarm it. When things are happening all around you, you don't have time to think or be scared. However, at that moment his words sent a chill down my spine.

Graham

I made my way through the interior navigation room to the starboard side of the bridge. I donned my helmet and stood by for further instructions. My recollection is that I manned a sound-powered phone that connected various navigation sites throughout the ship. Unlike sea detail coming into an anchorage, there was no one on the open bridge, and the only sailors on line were those in the steering gears and someone at an engineering location. I probably rotated duty, keeping a dead reckoning plot on the navigator's chart, relieving the quartermaster of the watch and whatever other chores were necessary over that period of hours while the fire was being fought.

At one point, Captain Beling had everyone on the bridge team moved to the forward and starboard side of the bridge. He personally remained near his chair and command station where he coordinated the damage control efforts. At the peak of explosions and fire, the Navigator, Commander Howard, put his arms over my back and head in a protective way and told us that we may be going to lose the ship. During this time the fire advanced to the port quarter and had found its way deep into the ship, all the way to the aft steering gears. I was no longer on the phones, but one of my watchmates was in communication with Jim Blaskis, my earlier replacement. A bomb had exploded down through the access trunk that led to the gears. Either the electrician or machinist mate had been evacuating the gears when the blast occurred. He was killed and the other had a limb seriously wounded. The threaded mechanism of the watertight door had also been damaged with the blast and prevented the door from being fully closed. Smoke and noxious fumes began entering the space, and it was cut off by fire from the rest of the ship. Jim gave what aid he could to stop the bleeding of the other sailor. Eventually he was overcome by the lack of oxygen and he suffocated. The process was not quick and we were in voice contact over the period of time. It was a tough position for Jim to face and he agonized in his final minutes of life. It was hard to be brave under the circumstances and the rest of us were totally helpless to aid him in any material way.

Egbert

Not being able to help by staying in the compartment, I, along with the other shipmates, left the compartment and entered the number two hangar bay, port side, just forward of the number three hangar bay door.

As we were crouched behind the metal partition, the sprinkler system came on in the number three hangar bay. Simultaneously, the hangar bay door closed off the number three hangar bay.

Not long after this, the elevator came down to the hangar bay and an officer asked for volunteers to go up to the flight deck. I, along with several other sailors, got on the elevator and went to the flight deck.

After reaching the flight deck, I went towards the fantail. As I reached the port side of the island, I found the body of Gerald A. Wehde lying on the flight deck. Gerald Wehde was from VA-65. The top of his head was blown off and most of the bones in his body were broken. I removed his watch, wallet, and other personal affects and then helped put him into a body bag. His property was later turned over to a squadron Chief Petty Officer.

I then assisted in removing other bodies from the flight deck. We had to put water on the ones that were burnt to cool the bodies down because they were too hot to touch with our bare hands. Sometimes we had to use makeshift scrapers to get the burnt bodies removed from the hot steel flight deck.

Egbert

While on the flight deck, we were provided some sea rations to eat. I think these were from the 1940s. At one point late in the day, we were instructed to go to an officers mess hall located forward to get something to eat. As I was walking down the catwalk leading to the mess hall, I found lying at my feet someone's nose. I picked it up and threw it over the side into the sea. Whoever it belonged to didn't need it now. After having to deal with charred bodies, what does the Navy feed us, none other than barbecued beef sandwiches.

The dead sailors were placed in the number one hangar bay behind a tall partition. You could not see them but you could not help smelling them every time you had to walk through the hangar bay.

Blackman

When I awoke I was in a rack in the sick bay area, along with quite a few others. I was there for a few hours when a corpsman came to take x-rays; as I stood up for the x-rays, I passed out again. I found out later I had a piece of shrapnel go through my right foot, and a piece lodge in the rear of my left knee cap, also severing a major artery to my lower leg. With this I had blood loss resulting in my passing out every time I tried to stand. Later I was taken into an operating room and had the shrapnel removed from my left leg, had the artery repaired, and had the wounds to my leg and foot sewed up.

Graham

So it was on July 29, 1967. I stood the 0400 quartermaster watch in the port gears during our first set of flight operations and was relieved by Jim Blaskis at 0800 before the second set of flight ops began. Whether through an arbitrary set of circumstances or an eternal plan, the disaster occurred on Jim's watch and I survived the unfortunate inevitabilities.

Lieutenant Commander, later Rear Admiral, Peter B. Booth, USN, VF-102 (Diamondbacks), USS *America*, 1968
from *True Faith and Allegiance*

Our euphoria for the war was at a high warble for we were bombing everything in sight including some targets with minimal military value. When we were not bombing or doing 'night reccee' over the beach, we were providing air cover for the ship in the Gulf of Tonkin in the direction of Haiphong. These CAP hops were a study in contrast, for we would sit in air-conditioned comfort at 20,000 feet, 25-or-so miles from Haiphong harbor, get refueled a couple of times to keep our fuel nearly full (combat package) and watch all the foreign ships heading in to unload their war-making wares into North Vietnam. You didn't have to be a Ph.D. to realize that the next night we'd be trying to ferret out these same supplies wending their way southward by bicycle and WBLC (water-borne logistic craft – really sampams).

One day on our first line period, we lost our skipper, Commander Gene Wilbur and his RIO, Lieutenant Bernie Rupinski. His wingman, Lieutenant Emory Brown, saw the MiG close behind Gene and called for his leader to 'break hard right,' but got no response. Emory fired a Sparrow missile at the homeward-bound enemy, but to no avail. Bernie, we think, went down with the airplane and Gene became a long-term POW. Sad day, for both fliers were respected and liked within the squadron.

That first line period we flew mostly at night. In fact, our normal flight operations were from 1800–0600, for 40 straight days. We really got comfortable around the boat at night, which is a statement few naval aviators get a chance to make. Usually returning to the ship at night generates at least an order of magnitude increase in resting pulse rate (defined as 70 to 140).

A typical-night hop for us had one machine loaded with a bunch of magnesium flares in pods (18 total) and the other with 6,500-pound bombs. No matter what our mission, we always carried a minimum of two heat-seeking Sidewinders and two radar-guided Sparrow missiles. We would launch, take on 3,000 pounds of fuel from one of our friendly airborne tankers, go feet dry over the beach and 'look for targets of opportunity.' When the weather was good we could usually make out bends in the rivers or a bridge on our radar. Out would go a covey of flares at about 5,000 feet and #2 would lay some bombs at whatever WBLCs or bridge he could see. Invariably, there would be a visual snake or two of colorful 37mm tracer fire. Usually, the only thing that could get us into trouble was leaving our external lights on …

One night my good friend and fellow maintenance officer in our sister squadron, VF-33, Lieutenant Commander Zeke Burns, was shot down (we were airborne nearby) by a SAM and he and his pilot shelled out [ejected]. They were about 30 miles inland so a[n] SAR rescue helo was dispatched to attempt a pickup. There then ensued one of naval aviation's incredible stories of survival, guts and determination on the part of a lot of folks that night, because the area that Zeke landed in was infested with Vietnamese troops. Using a handheld radio, they vectored in the pilot of the rescue helo, Lieutenant Clyde Lassen. Braving gunfire from all directions, Zeke and his pilot were picked up and deposited on a destroyer with but five-minutes of fuel left in the rescue helo. Clyde's Medal of Honor citation is an awesome litany of five guys in a rickety old helo on an overland trip, low on fuel and hundreds of folks on the ground trying to kill them. It was just another chapter in the heroism repeated thousands of times each day in this eight-year war. As those who knew him would expect, Zeke was in the air the next day! …

The Diamondbacks were blessed with seven, spring-loaded-to-the-go-position lieutenant commanders in addition to the CO and XO, both full commanders. Day by day and night by night we did our best in the air and about the ship. Hard work, good spirits, teamwork and honest leadership were common traits. We were pros and good at our chosen profession and proud of it. But we had glimmers of disappointment in the way the war was being fought. We wanted to go north; we wanted to hit the ships in Haiphong harbor; we wanted to go into the Laos sanctuaries just 100 miles to the west. The bosses would have none of it and, even if they had wanted to, it would have made no difference, for unbeknownst to us, the war was being minutely manipulated out of a big white house at 1600 Pennsylvania Avenue in Washington, D.C. by an unknown covey of gratuitous advisors and a political president in way over his head.

The politics of the war, in our case in that summer of 1968, dictated that we were prohibited from attacking the enemy's underbelly up north. Earlier and later in the war, the action in the north in and around Hanoi was far more intense than we were to experience simply because the northern targets were more lucrative and therefore more heavily defended with gobs of Soviet supplied AAA and SAMs. But, even in our case, the available targets were subject to micro manipulations from inside the Washington beltway. The list of allowable targets was heavily skewed to the restrictive side of the ledger.

Lieutenant, later Admiral, Stanley Arthur, USN, VA-164 (Ghost Riders), USS *Hancock*

Communication with the Editor

On 6 April 1972, I launched from USS *Hancock*, leading a two ship section of A-4Fs. My wingman was LCdr Jeff Miles. This was at the time that the North was attacking south across the DMZ [De-Militarized Zone]. Our mission was to proceed to the DMZ and provide SAM Suppression for any units that might be operating close to the DMZ.

My wingman and I each had two Shrike anti-radiation missiles. We proceeded to the DMZ and set up a race-track pattern on a north/south axis. This kept one of us always pointed towards the SAM sites that were to the North of us. The weather was not ideal for this mission. We were in and out of multiple cloud decks, a real no-no for dealing with SAMs since it was always better to visually acquire them soon after lift-off. In view of the criticality of providing cover for units operating in support of the guys on the ground, I elected to keep us on station. Jeff was a very experienced combat pilot and both of us had prior experience with SAMs.

It didn't take long before we became targets of interest for the SAMs. Lucky for us, they were not using a multiple launch profile. We'd get the warnings from our EW gear and whoever was in the North-heading leg would be cleared to launch a Shrike against the site, forcing them to shut down. We continued to play this cat and mouse game until we were both 'Winchester' (no more missiles). They had us well located as we saw at least four missiles zip by.

Cleared off station, we proceeded East to get feet wet and out of the SAM envelope. We then took a Northeast vector to return to *Hancock*. Shortly after taking up the new heading, we heard an emergency call on guard about an A-7 hit by a SAM several miles north of the DMZ. The aircraft had made it 'feet wet' before the pilot, from VA-195 Squadron, ejected. We were not far from the location. We commenced a descent and headed for the pilot's location to help until the RESCAP package arrived. We got overhead the pilot only to find SAMs being fired out over the water. They were firing them on a flat, low trajectory. I had never seen this before and they were not tracking us very well. We seen 3 or so of the SAMs and then the RESCAP package arrived. We departed in time to meet the tail end of our recovery period aboard *Hancock*.

This was one of those missions that didn't seem to be destined for much excitement, but I'd never seen as many SAMs fired against a single section of A/C.

NP 402 was my plane when I was XO and it had an elephant painted on it, because on one of my missions the controlling FAC gave me credit for the destruction of a 'heavy mover' on one of the logistic lines to South Vietnam. We later found out what the heavy mover really was ...

PO3 Noel Burkitt, USS *Midway* (CVA-41), Vietnam
Communication with the Editor

Burkitt was a Machinist's Mate when he joined the carrier.

1971 ... I have been thru the Detroit riots, seen the Detroit Tigers win the pennant, cruised Woodward Ave. I've toured Europe and been to the Caribbean. Grew up in an upper middle class family. I had a good life. I was ready for the world (or so I thought).

Then at 17 years old I received my draft notice. In 24 hours my life changed. My girlfriend broke up with me that same day, said she could not bear to wait for me not knowing if I was alive or dead. My parents were not happy at all. All my friends started growing distant. I enlisted in the navy and after 5 months of training and school, I received orders to the USS *Ranger* CVA- 61. 2 days later I volunteered to go aboard the USS *Midway* CVA-41 which was headed to Vietnam.

April 16, 1972 ... We left the carrier pier in San Diego with protesters on the pier, and as we pulled under the Golden Gate bridge more protesters poured gallons of paint and trash on the flight deck. We picked up another 2 squadrons in Hawaii, stopped in the Philippines. And arrived 'on the line'. Vietnam, April 30, 1972.

During all this time, there is drill after drill after drill, 24 hours a day. Crash drills, fire drills, collision drills, man overboard drills, take offs and landings and of course General Quarters. Did I mention that there are even more drills (engineering type)? During all this you still have to stand your watch, man unrep parties and do the normal maintenance work. So it is possible to go 20 hours a day or more. This is what it is like 'on the line', day after day.

The engine room where I worked was cramped and the temperature ranged from 120 degrees to 180 degrees depending on where you were in the space.

During our 11 month cruise, we were up in North Vietnam, bombing Hanoi, protecting the marines on the northern border and bombing the Ho Chi Min trail. We constantly had air warfare with Russian and Chinese fighters. On the surface we had to deal with Chinese junks and Russian trawlers. I also was there when a riot took the USS *Kitty Hawk* off the line and back to America. Plane crashes and storms. There was a lot of segregation and tension, and this was when I started to drink. I did not like alcohol, but I learned to like it in no time.

Watches on ship varied. They could be 4 hours on and 8 off, or 6 on and 6 off, or even 4 on 12 off if there were enough people. I stood watch as a 'Throttle man in #4 engine room'. It was hot, dirty and loud down there. A normal day would be 0600 wake, breakfast, 0700 quarters, 0730 duty station, 1200 lunch, 1300 duty station, 1600 off; if it was your turn for shift you go do it, if not you can do what you want – unless, of course, there was a drill.

General Art Bloomer, US Marines, then a Lieutenant Colonel, USS *Midway*
University Archives, Emporia State University

With the war finally recognized as unwinnable, all that was left was evacuation. On 30 April 1975, Bloomer, a distinguished aviator, wrote home to his wife Susie:

At about 6:30 a.m. yesterday it started to happen. A Vietnamese Army pilot had flown a CH-47 Chinook helo to the USS *Blue Ridge* with his family. The *Blue Ridge* is a small ship with just a small landing area and was the Communications Control ship for this operation. It was BGen Carey's flagship. Gen Carey was in charge of the Ground Support Forces who occupied the landing zones while the helos picked up the evacuees. Gen Carey spent about 14 hours on the ground in Saigon during the evacuation. After the landing on *Blue Ridge* a Marine pilot then flew the Chinook to *Midway*. At 0830 the highest ranking Vietnamese official flew aboard *Midway* in his helo with several of his General officers. That was Nuyen Cao Ky. Off and on for the remainder of the day until about 3:00 p.m. small Vietnamese helos flew out to *Midway* and landed. Most of them were just pilots who had picked up their families and came on out. At 3:00 we got the official word to execute the evacuation plan and all of the USAF big helos lifted off to bring them out of Saigon. It originally was supposed to be a single lift to bring out just Americans but it turned out to be a mass exodus of multi lift. The helos from *Midway* made 6 lifts and brought out about 1800 people. In the meantime several Air America helos took refuge on our decks. Even though we began transferring the evacuees to other shipping capable of handling large numbers of people by smaller helos, we still had over 1200 evacuees on board of all nationalities mostly Vietnamese, during the night. Now all of that may sound exciting but it was nothing compared to today. We were only supposed to have a maximum of 500 on board because of our limited facilities, sanitation, food, etc. Several Marine helos almost out of fuel had to make unscheduled landings on *Midway* when they couldn't get back to the USS *Hancock*. This resulted in a very confused situation at times, at night with USAF helo pilots making their first night carrier landings with very overloaded helos, some with as many as 90 people on board. We were refueling helos while still running to get them off so others could land before running out of gas. All in all it was a fantastically well executed operation. We lost two Marine helicopters. One crashed just after taking off from the USS *Hancock* and everyone was rescued. Another UH1E

[UH-1E] (small one) ran out of gas and ditched beside a destroyer with no injuries. A Marine helo was shot down with a missile in Saigon but repaired and flown out. Some helicopter pilots flew for 19 straight hours and 150 of the Marines Ground Support Forces did not get lifted out of Saigon until early today at about 06:30 a.m. The US Ambassador came out at about 04:00 a.m. The last USAF helos completed their lifts at 04:30 having started at 3:00 p.m. the afternoon before. Some of the Marine Ground Support Forces were lifted out by the USAF helos from *Midway* and spent what little bit was left of the night on our hangar deck. There were people scattered all over and instead of 500 maximum we had over 1200 which I think were very well managed considering the circumstances.

Today was the really exciting day. Thinking that our main job was over we initially, this morning, concerned ourselves with how to get the 1200 people transferred to other ships equipped to handle them. But, the mass exodus of UHIE helos from the Vietnamese Air Force began in earnest. They were all flying their families out. The weather turned worse today with rain which complicated their problem of finding the ship. It wasn't bad as long as only one UHIE (Huey) came out at a time. But soon they started coming in twos, threes, 6, & 7s. Most were low on fuel, scared to death and grossly overloaded. One guy came in with 4 people in the front seat, where only two belong, and 50 people, mostly small kids in the back.

The biggest thrill of all though was an L-19, a small single engine plane, that came out and kept circling the ship when the deck was completely packed with helos. He did not speak English and his radio was VHF instead of UHF which complicated speaking to him. He made several low passes trying to throw a note overboard and finally got one on the deck. He said he was a major and had his wife and 5 kids on board. This is a 2 place airplane! We found out from a Vietnamese who talked to him on the radio that he had 1 hour of fuel remaining so Capt Chambers (the ships Capt) made a very gutsy decision and decided to let him try and land on the carrier. This is an airplane without a hook! But first to clear the landing area took 30 minutes to tow all the big helos forward on the catapults. Then by heading into the wind and steaming the ship at 25 knots we gave him a headwind of 30 knots. He had about 400 feet to stop safely in and made a beautiful landing, stopping the plane on the deck with brakes.

Later on some really hairy things happened but miraculously we recovered all the helos who tried to land on our deck. There was a flight of 25 who all tried to land at the same time. In that group we had to push 3 helos over the side into the water to make room for the last three.

It's dark now and we have resumed the transferring to other ships. At one time we were just holding our own. About as many Vietnamese were flying out here trying to land as were flying off to other personnel transportation ships. But now at midnight we are down to about 400. We have 45 Vietnamese UHIEs on the deck plus 3 CH-47 Chinooks plus our own ships 3 SH-3G plus the 10

USAF CH/HH-53 Jolly Greens whose blades do not fold making parking a difficult task.

Assuming we get everybody off early tomorrow, we'll head for Utapao Thailand so the Air Force can fly their big ones off and we can turn around and go back to the Philippines ...

THE INDO-PAKISTANI WAR 1971

Rear Admiral S. Ramsagar, Indian Navy, INS *Vikrant*
First published in *Quarter Deck*

The independence and partition of India in 1947 created the state of Pakistan, which not only comprised territory to the north-west of India, bordering Afghanistan, but also a separate eastern wing created by the division of Bengal along religious lines. During 1971, Bangladesh began a struggle for independence, which was supported by India, and on 3 December a pre-emptive strike by Pakistan aircraft against India led to a declaration of war. At this time INS *Vikrant* was undergoing refit and the engineers won a race against time to make her operational.

The Cobra squadron, INAS 310 under the command of late Cdr Ravi Dhir (who earned his VrC [Vir Chakra] during the war) with me as his Senior Pilot and late Lt Cdr S P Ghosh (also a VrC awardee in the war) as senior Observer of the squadron, flew the squadron from Cochin INS *Garuda* to Chennai 'Meenambakkam' airfield ...

As soon as the engineering department managed to flash up the unserviceable second boiler the carrier could give sustained speed of 18 knots for the [Sea] Hawk squadron also to embark and so they too started flying from the carrier ...

In the mean time *Vikrant* was quietly moved to Port Blair in [the] Andaman Islands and finally positioned in Port Cornwallis Lagoon. On third December evening, we heard on radio that [the] Pakistan Air Force struck many of our airfields. *Vikrant* had just received orders to sail and strike enemy airfields in East Pakistan at the earliest. The briefing by the erstwhile Commander (Air), Cdr Parashar (fondly called by the aircrew as 'The Superman'), spoke just one sentence: 'Gentlemen this is it.'

On the morning of 4th, the Hawks struck Dhaka airfield and the harbour. They faced no air opposition but heavy anti-aircraft ground fire. The Alizé, being slower anti- submarine and reconnaissance aircraft, flew through out the night of 3rd and 4th December providing the carrier force in depth anti-submarine surveillance and early warning of enemy ships.

On the first day of War, NHQ directed that only those ships which were of Pakistani origin should be sunk. This resulted in the Alizé aircraft flying low over the merchant ships, establishing their identity before attacking them. All the ships seen by our squadron had many women and children, all waving white flags from the open decks. It was suspected that on the first few days many Pakistani civilian officials with their families left East Pakistan with all their gold and money.

Only when we received clearance to fire at the ships that were coming out or heading towards East Pakistan the Alizé came into their own in the war as the Hawker Hunters were not cleared for night operations. The good old Alizé had to do night strikes on enemy targets. We carried out night strikes using 500 pound bombs; we could see tracers coming all the way up to our aircraft and just missing us. We confirmed that the attacks by Hawks during day rendered havoc in the harbour and there was just no enemy fighter opposition.

As there was no enemy air opposition, Captain Swaraj Prakash, cleared yours truly to fly over and inspect the beaches for amphibious landing operations. INS *Magar* and the landing craft recently acquired from Russia were to do this operation. I flew low over the whole length of the beach south of Chitagong and found it totally deserted, so I continued my reconnaissance sortie over the road leading to Chitagong. The road was strewn with abandoned vehicles and people running helter-skelter. As there were no suitable targets to bomb, I continued on to Chitagong. There we saw people looting every house of all its articles. Just then we sighted a wireless station with large transmission towers and a Govt. office. We successfully bombed the wireless station with our 500lb bombs but left the Govt. building as it had a red cross on it. Later we learnt from the Mukti Bhahini this act of ours saved many innocent Bangladeshis in the hospital but successfully destroyed the enemy hiding in the wireless station. My report helped [the] Navy to change the landing operations to directly proceed to Chitagong town. With the help of Bangladeshi fishing vessels guiding our amphibious force, the Navy landed the Ghurkas, for a heroes' welcome by the locals.

As we had no knowledge of the goings on at the Western end of East Pakistan, I was launched to fly all the way up the Mutha-Mulla river to the Ports of Chelna and Khulna during daylight hours. On reaching Khulna, I noticed that there were five merchant vessels anchored in line in the river. I carried out a daylight rocket attack on one of the ships. Immediately there was heavy anti-aircraft fire from a gunboat, and as my mission was to recce and report on the state of the harbours, I pressed on to Chelna and found the harbor deserted. After reading my report, Admiral Sri Harilal Sarma, FOCEF appreciated that the ships in Khulna were the evacuating merchant ships for the Pakistani troops and so launched Cdr Ravi Dhir and me that same night with five 500lb bombs each. There was very heavy ack-ack fire from shore, with tracers just missing us. We successfully bombed the ships. Our attack was so effective that the ships that were fit to sail cut their anchor chains and sailed out towards the mouth of the river to sea.

Two days later, I was launched to check the situation at the Khulna and Cheina harbours. I sighted at the mouth of the river, a Naval Tug towing two very long boats camouflaged with branches all over. On closer examination, it was noticed that the boats contained troops who were being ferried to the

Eastern sector to Dhaka or Chitagong. Immediately I attacked the naval vessel with my rockets. We saw that the tug was still firing its focsl'e gun. As we had expended our rockets we decided to strike with depth charges. For a good depth charge attack, the strike had to be done practically skimming over the target. My crew, Lt Bhagwat and Lt Pawar, both valiantly agreed for the low level strike to prevent the Pakistan forces escaping to safer areas.

After our successful depth charge attack, the enemy hoisted a white flag and turned the vessels on to the beach and abandoned them. Our aircraft was hit by a spray of 20mm bullets right along the centerline all the way to the rear. Lucky for us the crew sits with the pilot on the left of centre, the navigator on the right and the rear radar operator also sits on the right of the centerline. So all the direct hits on the aircraft missed us by inches but the aircraft lost electrical power, hydraulics and the radome was hit causing a small fire – still the aircraft was able to fly back to the carrier at slow speed. We had to lower the undercarriage and the hook by gravity.

As we were long overdue and the Carrier was unable to contact us on radio, *Vikrant* launched young Lt Mohanan … to look for us. By then we were in visual range and could inform the ship on VHF operating on battery that we were coming in directly for landing. The ship suggested that we use the 'Net' for our landing but I refused as I knew that once the aircraft uses the net she would sustain greater damage. I successfully did the night landing and saved the aircraft …

The Cobra Squadron during the war earned five Vir Chakras and one Mention-in-dispatches. The wonderful Alizé aircraft performed all its tasks excellently under the able guidance of the valiant Cobra squadron's crew. So ended the saga of wonderful aircraft, Breguet Alizé 1050. She is no more operational in the service except in museums. May God bless the soul of the designer of this aeroplane.

4
All in a Day's Work ... and Play

Peter Taylor, 824 Squadron, 1961–2, HMS *Centaur*
Communication with the Editor

I have no complaints about the flying clothing and safety equipment except perhaps the persistent rumour that the shark repellent fitted on our mae wests actually attracted sharks.

Herman Doernbach, EM2, USS *Coral Sea*
Communication with the Editor

As I recall, back in 1951 or 1952 we were on our way to Guantanamo after coming out of the Portsmouth yard. This story commenced on a Saturday evening.

I was on watch on No. 3 switch board when it was reported that a bearing on 3A generator exciter was running hot. It was determined by a conference of knowledgeable snipes that the bearing would have to be pulled, rebabbitted, scraped and reinstalled that night because all the ships machinery will have to be functioning once we entered Guantanamo for training.

I along with Harold 'Goldy' Goldsberry, EM1, and 3 Machinist Mates were then ordered to commence working on this by our Engineering Officer until the job was complete. 'Any questions?' the officer asked. Goldy who was placed in charge replied, 'If we are to work thru' the night I want a chow chit as these men will be hungry come midnight.' The officer wrote out the chit and work commenced. Come midnight we all proceeded to the after galley for our rations. (You have to picture this scene): the galley was filled with cooks, friends, etc., who were writing home, shooting the breeze etc. The cooks had steaks on the grill and all in all it looked like we were going to be well fed. Goldy knocked on the fence gate and was greeted by a disturbed cook who asked what the f*** we wanted. After looking at the chit he threw it on the deck and said we did not rate chow. We then proceeded back to the job, Goldy called the Engineering Officer of the watch and told him about the food situation. The officer called the galley, after a while telling us that there was nothing he could do about it and to go back to work.

Goldy was hot, he said: 'Come with me.'

Off to officers' country we went, finding Cdr Buckley's (Chief Engineer) cabin, we knocked on the door. After a while Cdr Buckley opened the door; standing in his pajamas, he wanted to know what was going on. After being told the situation he put his hat with the scrambled eggs on and marched to the after galley with us. Knocking on the fence gate he was greeted with a short abbreviated whaaaaaa and was saluted by the cook. 'Why was this chit by the engineering department not honored?' Cdr Buckley asked. 'We were told by Cdr Stanley that if they were not on the watch list they were not to be fed,' said the cook. 'Go and get his ass up here on the double,' Cdr Buckley told the cook. 'But sir ...' 'Did you hear me sailor?' Yes, Sir,' and off he went. After talking to us about the job and asking questions Cdr Buckley saw Cdr Stanley (Supply Officer) approaching and really tore into him about honoring engineering requests. Did you ever see two commanders in their pajamas with their scrambled egg hats on standing nose to nose raising their voices? Well, it was not long before Cdr Stanley told the cook to feed us. We watched as the cook went to the refrigerator took out a big baloney and was ready to slice some horse c— to make some sandwiches when Goldy yelled that we wanted what they were eating. The cook said we did not rate that. 'Do we have to get Cdr Buckley up here again?' said Goldy. 'Oh hell, how do you want your steaks?' asked the cook.

Sub Lieutenant Antony Wilson, HMAS *Melbourne*, 1968
Communication with the Editor

On the 5th May 1969 the ship left Sydney for the far East and the temperatures and humidity in all the machinery spaces soared. Together with the heat and climbing up and down vertical ladders, I soon learned to take salt tablets and lime juice. I should explain that HMAS *Melbourne* was not designed to operate in the tropics, rather for Arctic convoys, as it was first laid down in WW2 as HMS *Majestic*. There was an absolute nightmare of steam heating pipes everywhere, which were never required the whole time it was in commission.

While I was still doing all this engine room training, the disaster of 3rd June happened. At 3.15 a.m. we had sliced through an American destroyer and the front half had sunk taking with it 74 American lives. My emergency station was the 'after machinery space' where I was watch-keeping on a rather ugly turbo generator. Being so new to the whole Navy organisation I was having a lot of trouble distinguishing a practice emergency from the real thing, and it was not until I came off watch at 8.00 a.m. for breakfast that I got the full picture. 'Why are these American sailors in our mess drinking our beer at 8.00 a.m.?' I remember the two Chaplains being very busy.

The ship then sailed for Singapore and immediately went into dry dock. All the crew were billeted on shore as there was no water or sewerage in the dry dock. I remember having my own room with a large mosquito-netted bed and ceiling fan. If you left your shoes outside the room at night, some servant would clean them. I could take more of this. Sadly, the dockyard in Singapore soon put a temporary patch on our bow, and we were off back to Sydney.

Once back in Sydney we went straight back into dry dock to have a completely new bow fitted. The dockyard concerned still had the pattern as it was only four years earlier that the *Melbourne* had sliced through the HMAS *Voyager*. Since there was nothing to further my training while in dry dock, I was given leave for three weeks. Upon my return the ship was still in dry dock; however, with the repairs completed the dockyard union decided to highjack the *Melbourne* by not allowing her to leave the dry dock until their pay demands were satisfied. Consequently, there was further delay, but, because I lived on board rather than local, I used the time to complete all my sketches, and was learning now the job of a Petty Officer Stoker: steaming the ship's boilers. When it was finally decided that the dockyard management staff would secretly flood the dock and open the gates very early one morning, we had the task of starting up all the steam and other machinery as the water level rose so that the ship could escape under her own steam, rather than rely on tugs which were also on strike. It was quite exciting, and the local Sydney newspapers had headlines like 'NAVY ACTS – HOSTAGE FLAGSHIP OUT TODAY'.

By October I was watchkeeping on the ships boilers ... I was also given a 'part of ship' to look after. Being the most junior engineer, this was the so called 'Double Bottoms Department', so named because most of the fuel and ballast water was stored in tanks located between the outer and inner skin of the ship... The most exciting task for the 'double bottoms engineering officer' is the RAS or Refuelling At Sea exercise. While steaming at about 20 knots, an escort, typically a destroyer, would come alongside the *Melbourne* to receive fuel. A 6-inch hose would be sent across and we would start our massive transfer fuel pumps and in half an hour give the other ship enough fuel. My station at that time is in the Engineering Office in the centre of the ship where I was in telephone communication with each stoker stationed at the various tanks. Even more exciting is when we are receiving fuel from a tanker. In this situation every 5 minutes I have to telephone each stoker who is stationed at the top of each tank with a dip tape so as to know when we are full, so to inform the Captain when to stop pumping etc., and I vividly remember during a RAS one stoker informing me that he had lost the dip tape and so had no idea of how much fuel we were taking. It was not unknown for a tank to overflow if too full and the black oil to flood into adjacent sailors' kit lockers.

Private First Class Clinton 'Tuffy' McKay Cox, USMC, USS *Coral Sea*, 1955
Communication with the Editor shortly before his death

I was standing my post in a military manner that day in 1956 aboard the USS *Coral Sea*. Post Number One was a special weapons post where the technicians worked with their nuclear bombs. That is why I was there, to make sure no unauthorized persons could enter this space, steal the bombs, blow up the ship, or for that matter, the whole world ... I heard a commotion through the open hatch to my left. Navy officers were coming towards me. There were lieutenants, lieutenant commanders, commanders, and the Captain of the USS *Coral Sea*. Behind them followed Admiral Pirie, Commander of Carrier Division Six. A commander blurted out, 'The Admiral wants to inspect the Special Weapons.' There I stood, with at least fifteen officers in front of me. I stammered out, 'Sir, only persons with cards can pass through this hatch.' 'Private, the Admiral wants to inspect the Special Weapons,' the commander said raising his voice. I stammered, 'Sir, only persons that have a card can pass through this hatch according to my orders.' Then the Captain stepped forward and said, 'Private, I will take full responsibility for the Admiral.' And I replied to him, 'Sir, he must have a card.' The Captain turned and huddled with his junior officers. After conferring with them for a few moments, the Captain returned and looked me straight in the face and said, 'You want a card? I'll get you a card.'

While the Captain was conferring with his junior officers, I tried to call the Corporal of the Guard to have him report to my post. He was nowhere to be found. Sergeant Lee, the Sergeant of the Guard, happened by. As he made his way through the officers that were assembled, his large brown eyes getting wider, he said, with hurried voice, 'Private Cox, what's going on here?' Replying to him I said, 'Following orders, sir.' 'What do you mean Private Cox?' 'Sir, my orders say that no one is to go inside the special weapons post unless they have a card, and they want to go in, but don't have cards.'

About that time, a Navy lieutenant came through the hatch to my right. He had, as I remember, three cards with him. One of the cards was for the Admiral that was now standing face to face with me. I took the card that he had just been given, without asking him to identify himself, [and] let the Admiral pass through the hatch. Two other officers passed through the hatch after giving me their cards. The rest of the officers had to wait outside. They just milled about glaring at me. Sergeant Lee seemed to calm himself as the crisis seemed to be over. He tried to locate Lieutenant Horne using my telephone but was not successful. About twenty minutes passed. I just stood there, not saying a word but thinking that I was in big trouble. The hatch swung open and the Admiral came through the hatch. He looked happy. The Captain looked happy. The commander following them looked happy. Everyone seemed happy except for me.

Jimmie Stewart, EM2, USS *Forrestal*
Communication with the Editor

In a little less than a year after reporting for duty and being assigned to the Lighting Shop I took the exam to be elevated to the rate of EM2 (Electrician's Mate 2nd Class). When I returned to the shop after completing the test the Chief Petty Officer in charge of the shop, Chief Mayer, asked how I thought I'd done with the test. Before we get into my response let me tell you a little bit about Chief Mayer.

Chief Mayer didn't particularly like anyone taller than him. Chief Mayer stood about 5'4"; therefore, just about everybody was taller than him. The Chief also had a very cocky attitude. But, when you stopped to really look at the man you had to respect him. The Chief had served in the 2nd World War, the Korean Conflict, the Berlin Wall Crisis, the Cuban Crisis and now we were entering the Vietnam era. Then you had to consider the fact that he was a Chief Petty Officer. In the Navy you only advanced by passing an exam designed to determine how proficient you are in your field of expertise. You literally compete for your position against thousands of other sailors for openings that may be very few in number. You really had to respect the man for what he had done.

Well anyway let's get back to how I responded. I turned around and in a tone of voice that I thought the Chief would understand (you know: when in Rome) I replied: 'Come on, Chief; that test required 3 hours of my life that I can't afford to waste. I passed it'.

Well, you could hear a pin drop. When I looked around I realized that everybody was looking at me. Or maybe they were glaring at me. I quickly rationalized that my response did not go over that well, so now I was about to enter the Ice Age.

It takes about 90 days before the results of the test are posted. For me it was a long 90 days but it finally came. When it was announced that the results were available I went as fast as he could to see what they were. When I arrived I noticed that just about everybody from this shop was crowding around to see the scores. I thought that was strange since I was the only one in this shop that took the test. As I struggled to see the results one of my shipmates looked back and said:

'How does it feel to be 2nd Class, Stewart?'

I felt a huge weight lifted off my shoulders. I didn't have to go through the retaliation I would have earned by failing the test. But what I didn't realize was, I wasn't quite out of the woods yet. A few days went by and I was summoned to the Lighting Shop to meet with Chief Mayer. The Chief informed me that he was assigning me to the position of 'Educational Petty Officer'.

Talk about retaliation. This was a pencil-pushing paper job … Needless to say, I was not a happy camper at this point in time. That night when I climbed into my rack I was fuming. I tossed, I turned, I mumbled expletives. And then, I thought, this is exactly how they want me to respond.

The next morning I went to the shop and asked the Chief if I could speak to him about an idea I had. The Chief listened as I requested that I be given the use of an empty void not far from the shop two days a week for one hour each day. Most of the shop personnel were not lucky enough attend Class 'A' School so I wanted to give them a course in Electrical Theory. The Chief just looked at me never saying a word. I continued: 'Come on Chief: you gave me a job; let me do something with it.' The Chief said he would think about it.

A week went by, then two weeks. I approached the Chief and asked him if he had made a decision. The Chief replied: 'What was it you wanted?' I explained it again. The Chief reluctantly said OK, but he didn't seem to have much faith in the effort being successful. And so the first seagoing Electrical Theory School in the U.S. Navy was created.

John S. Gill, Ordnanceman, V2 Division, USS *Essex*
Communication with the Editor

1968 was my first year in the Navy. I was stationed aboard the USS *Essex* in V-2 division (ordnance), the last V-2, now combined in V division. On the 22 of October 1968 the USS *Essex* was charged with recovering the Apollo 7, the first manned Apollo [space mission].

At 7 in the morning there was a bit of fog, so we couldn't see the capsule come down, even though it was less then 2 miles from the ship.

As the *Essex* pulled up along side the capsule, a crane was run out on the port aircraft elevator. The capsule was hoisted up and placed on a rolling carrier. When it was brought in to the hangar bay the crew was allowed to view it. We could even stick our heads in the capsule.

The astronauts' cake was assembled in the bomb assembly space in a secure area on the 9th deck. The 900lb. cake had butter cream icing and the emblems were made of hard sugar. Since it was a classified area, ordnance personal had to be there 24/7. Every time the chefs would make a mistake they would scrape it off and redo the area. If one of the 3 emblems cracked it was replaced. The bunch of us from Ordnance were sick of icing and sugar by the time the cake was finished. The only things that were not eatable on the cake were the model of the USS *Essex* and the space capsule.

The cake was loaded on to the number 1 bomb elevator and I shut the hatch. Then set the elevator to go to the hangar bay. We all rushed from the 9th deck to the hangar, I sat on the deck with my back against a tow motor to watch the ceremony, and the astronauts Walter M. Schirra (commander), Donn F. Eisele (pilot), and R. Walter Cunningham (LM pilot) cut the cake.

AO-3 Michael W. Gentry, VA-145, 1968–72, USS *Enterprise*
Communication with the Editor

As a mess cook, we supply all items to the galley. At some time during our deployment we received several hundred cases of Girl Scout Cookies. We would send up several cases and these would be opened and set on the mess line for the crew. As it turned out, since these were not a part of regular supplies there was no real inventory kept.

There were three things that I really wanted before returning to NAS Whidbey Island. A Navy leather flight jacket, a pair of flight boots, and a parachute bag. I found with a commodity like Girl Scout Cookies and fresh milk, not powered stuff, you could get just about anything you wanted. The flight jacket I got, and still have, I swapped my peacoat to a pilot for his girl friend. The others were gotten by trading to the parachute riggers and ships supply for cookies and fresh milk.

Captain, later Rear Admiral, Peter B. Booth, USN, USS *Forrestal*
from *True Faith and Allegiance*

Booth took command of *Forrestal* in 1977 when she was undergoing a nine-month refit.

Early on, we had what I considered to be an unacceptably high unauthorized absentee (UA) rate – folks that just didn't show up for work and left his shipmates to do his work and stand his watches. I got the idea of calling the parents of each one to see if they knew the whereabouts of their son, from my friend Jerry Tuttle, the innovative skipper of the *Kennedy*, another large-deck carrier. Parceling out the names, a few of the senior guys, including myself, started calling one night. I was looking for Johnny Jones and got a little girl on the phone in Jackson, Tennessee. I asked, 'if Johnny was there?'

She said, 'Who's this?'

I said, 'Captain Booth, Johnny's captain on the *Forrestal*.'

Excusing herself, she returned to the phone with, 'Johnny says to tell you he's not home.' Johnny not withstanding, let me tell you that we managed to solve the problems of many of our wayward shipmates and, in most cases, help them back to the ship.

Severing ties with our home base in Norfolk, we steamed ignominiously down to Mayport to join the U.S.S. *Saratoga* in sunny Florida, ignominious only in the sense that instead of a bunch of airplanes, we had about 1,000 cars on board so that our crew would not have to make their way back to Norfolk and then drive south for 15 hours. Super idea on someone's part.

Pat Lynch, PO3, USS *Forrestal* 1958–60
Communication with the Editor

When I reported aboard *Forrestal* I ran into a friend from boot camp. One of the things we did in the little spare time we had was to play guitars and try to learn the latest rock and roll songs. R&R was just starting and Elvis and the Everly Brothers were popular. As soon as my boot camp friend saw me he introduced two other V-1 guys who wanted to form a band but didn't play that well. We spent a lot of off duty hours learning from each other and after a few months both of them passed me in ability and we started playing at USO clubs in the Norfolk/Portsmouth area. I took up the bass, the other two played guitars, we picked up a drummer and did a lot of Elvis's music. I did the singing for a while until we found a really good singer and a sax player. One unique feature was four of us were white and the singer and sax player were black. None of us realized that it was not popular to mix races like that in the late 50s.

I don't think I ever thought about it until we tried to play at a club in Jacksonville, Florida. When I arrived with one of the black guys to set up they would not let him in the front door. One thing led to another, somebody shoved someone and both of us ended up in jail. The good times, however, came in Europe. While on a Med. Cruise we made port in Naples, Italy, Nice, France, Barcelona, Spain, Piraeus and several other places and in each we had a chance to play in local clubs. We did PR work for the Navy during the day (orphanages, civic affairs etc.) and clubs at night. Europe was ready for rock and roll. We played with the Bob Hope Show during one of his Christmas Shows on board *Forrestal* and probably would have been reasonably successful if we stayed together, but sadly we went our separate ways as each of us got discharged.

Lieutenant Commander P. H. 'Jan' Stuart, HMS *Ark Royal*, 1960
Communication with the Editor

I have no idea what was going on at the time but it may have had something to do with the looming emergency in Kuwait where General Kassem of Iraq was massing his troops on the Kuwait border, threatening to seize their oilfields. Whatever it was, we were required to get to Plymouth fast, so dear old *Ark Royal* crossed the Atlantic at high speed. On arrival at Plymouth it was discovered that she had sprung 7 leaks at various places in her hull, none of them structurally serious. One leak, however, had caused flooding in the wardroom tobacco store where there were thousands of pounds worth of cigarettes, cigars and tobacco. Some of this had naturally been contaminated by salt water and would have to be written off. The store functioned as a bonded warehouse because no duty had been paid on the contents and therefore it was necessary for the Customs and Excise officers to come on board and satisfy themselves as to the damage before they could issue a certificate for it all to be written off. They did this but insisted that ALL the contents of the store would have to be destroyed. This didn't make a lot of sense to us because many of the cigarettes were in airtight/waterproof tins of 50. These were mostly the quality items, and the largest proportion was for use at cocktail parties in foreign ports and were gaily coloured. There were pink ones, green ones, blue ones and yellow ones, all with gold coloured tips. Right at the top of the range were the Balkan Sobranies, black with gold tips. The water could not possibly have got into these tins, but the Customs & Excise people were adamant that the lot had to be destroyed. We were at anchor in Plymouth Sound at the time and I was put in charge of a small party of Royal Marines on the quarter deck, each armed with a marlin spike. As each crate of cigarettes was brought up from below they had to take the tins out one by one, make a hole top and bottom and throw the mangled tin over the side into the sea. It took all day to get rid of them and it was sacrilege to those of us who were smokers.

Rear Admiral Euan McLean, HMS *Ocean*
Communication with the Editor

Then there was the morning that I was called by Marine W, a Northcountryman, who invited me, 'Sir, coom and have a look at Lieutenant X.' There, stark naked, face upwards on his shoulder-level bunk in the cabin next to mine, lay my brother officer. I exaggerate. He was not stark naked. He was wearing a perfectly tied black bow tie. And it was not round his neck!

HUMANITARIAN MISSIONS AND SHOWING THE FLAG

Lieutenant Peter Taylor, 824 Squadron, HMS *Centaur*, 1961
Communication with the Editor

We were quietly meandering our way through the Mediterranean when we were diverted to Mombasa, Kenya, to assist with flood relief duties. The aircraft were stripped of the sonar equipment, and four were detached to Malindi (about 100 miles north of Mombasa). There was a grass airfield there where we set up our operations. Kenya was still at that time a member of our empire. We set about flying sacks of maize to four or five villages which were cut off by flood water. Each aircraft could carry about four bags – and with a pilot only, they flew all day, every day as I recall. All the heavy work – humping maize, refuelling from fuel drums, etc., was carried out by inmates of the local prison. The ops staff (a couple of Observers) did all the admin and scheduling, and, armed with the population of each village, planned the drops and briefed the pilots.

There was some surprise therefore when we became aware that the natives were restless, and complaining about unfair allocations. It transpired that the CO (who shall be nameless) only knew his way to one village (Kakoneni) and so flew there every time – ignoring the briefed destination.

I flew into Kakoneni with the 'boss' as we had got word that the village chief had to get to hospital. This was therefore a genuine casualty evacuation (CASEVAC), another feature of the range of activities in a helicopter squadron. We flew in to quite a reception – as they were obviously pleased to see the white man in great iron bird who called several times a day to shower them with maize. They were not so happy to see me because I was replacing two bags of maize. There was no sign of the chief – not unexpected because we had no way to communicate with them and so I hopped out and tried to sort things out.

The chief lived in his hut some way from where we were and so I borrowed a bicycle and rode through the jungle on my errand of mercy. I was in flying clothing of course and I think I even kept my bone dome on as I worried how I was to recognise the chief's hut. I like to think I said something like 'big chief Queen Elizabeth has sent big iron bird to take little chief to white man's witch doctor' but suspect I exchanged a few words and much gesticulation. Anyhow, I got the chief and bundled him into the helicopter but he seemed to prefer lying on the floor rather than sitting on the seat. We later learned two things. The chief got to the hospital and had the boil on his bum lanced, and the fact is, in all probability the maize we conscientiously spread around the countryside was mainly turned into alcohol. We may not have done much feeding of the population but we stayed in the best hotel in Malindi and I suspect it was only the British stiff upper lip that stopped us complaining about the large number of occasions that lobster featured on the menu.

Lieutenant, later Commander, Brian Swan, HMAS *Melbourne*
Communication with the Editor

I was recalled to the ship on Christmas day 1974 to get the ship underway to assist Darwin after cyclone Tracy. The ship was then at 48 hours' notice for sea and was well into a self-maintenance period. We worked all night; parts were retrieved from the Garden Island workshops, and the engine/boiler rooms were reassembled, and steam was raised in the wee small hours of the 26 December 1974. We could have sailed at 1000 or so but had to wait for the hatch race to Hobart to clear the harbour. We sailed at 1300 and were about 250 men short. As a lieutenant I took the place of a Petty Officer and steamed the boilers. Other officers were in a great variety of positions to make it all go. When we got to Townsville a ferry, overloaded to billy-oh, came out to us, much to our great relief. At last we could sleep!

On our approach to Darwin a group of officers were flown by helo to meet with Captain E. E. Johnston, the Naval Officer in charge North Australia, and the Police Chief together with the Mayor of Darwin. During the conference the Police Chief explained that there was some looting going on and packs of dogs were hunting for something to eat. He wanted the sailors to come ashore armed. Rear Admiral D. C.Wells was the Fleet Commander and he said: 'We are here to help the people of Darwin. If there is a law and order issue that is for the Police to deal with. Sailors will not be armed.'

Daily we put about 1,000 men in the field. I was the works manager looking after over 400 tradesmen. Other sailors were assigned to the suburb of Nightcliffe, where every home had a fridge and freezer filled with rotting food as there was no electricity. Each house's rotting food was placed in a hole in their front garden. My tradespeople were busy restoring the sewerage system by hooking up portable generators to sewerage pumps; a team had to right a trawler which was on the slipway and had been blown over. (This was a most important task as the Navy patrol boats, one of which had been sunk (HMAS *Arrow*), had to be slipped so that the Northern approaches to Australia could be patrolled.) The slipping and unslipping was done using a bulldozer instead of the slipway winch, which was electric and therefore useless.

A vehicle carrying a radioactive source for the hospital had been damaged and we didn't know exactly what the state of the radioactive source was. We despatched a team, suitably attired, to render the situation safe.

The Northern Research Fisheries deep freezers had 60 tons of prawns in them and, with no power, they were rotting. We hooked up a portable generator, refroze them, then got a fork lift and put them on to a tip truck. They were dumped in a swamp.

A priority was to prepare accommodation for the civilian workmen coming from all over Australia. We had a team working to get the caravan park back on line. The big hotel in town (I forget its name) had its air conditioning machinery in the basement which had been flooded. We pumped out the water, removed the huge 50HP motors and go them up to street level. Then a helicopter lifted then on to the roof of the hotel where the motors were disassembled and dried out in the sun. We reversed the process to get them back down to the street. After a lot of work by the electrical department, the air conditioning was working.

We reroofed the leprosarium, repaired the brewery, made houses safe and some watertight. After 17 days of working from 0600 to 1800 each day, and with the arrival of a great many civilian tradespeople from all over the country, we withdrew.

Lieutenant Commander, later Captain, George Hunt, DSO*, DSC, HMS *Triumph*
Communication with the Editor

George Hunt had been posted to HMS *Triumph* as First Lieutenant in 1946.

Circa July 1946 we took Admiral Sir Bruce Fraser, First Sea Lord, to Russia to receive the Order of Suvorov. As we approached Kronstadt one of the minesweepers which were sweeping us in hit a mine and was damaged. Lucky it was the minesweeper and not us! While we were there the Russians challenged us to soccer and beat us 6–2. However we were well entertained in the Officers' Club and the sailors were also well looked after. However, before Sir Bruce left the ship to go up to Moscow to receive the decoration he said, 'When I get back I will be giving a dinner party, for the local Russian naval Senior Officer, on the quarterdeck!'

This entailed a mammoth job as the tables in the wardroom had been put in while the ship was being built. So now we had to saw the tables to pieces small enough to get them up ladders and through hatches before reassembling them on the quarterdeck. This was achieved in time for Sir Bruce's return, and the dinner was duly held at which some of the Russians burst into song. Not to be outdone, Sir Bruce, who was of course a Scot, suggested/detailed/asked/ ordered me to do a sword dance! He knew I was a Highland dancer as he had seen me performing several years ago, and so I did what I was told and got a 'well done' from Sir Bruce. (Music by a Royal

Marine band violinist sounding just like the bagpipes: amazing.) It impressed the Russians.

Lieutenant Commander R. J. McCandless, DSC, 810 Squadron, HMS *Albion*, 1955–6
IWM Sound Archive Reference 27344

During 1955–6, HMS *Albion* was on a world tour, and cocktail parties would be held on the flight deck for visiting dignitaries.

Then towards the end of the cocktail party we used to have the Beating Retreat and Sunset, and the Marine guard and band would parade. And the drill was: the Marine guard and band would form up on the aircraft lift down on hangar level, and they would bring the whole lot up with the band playing and everyone going full belt, and of course the whole of the cocktail party guests would muster round the after lift and watch this going on. Then the guard would march up and down and the band would play everything and at the end they would have the Sunset ceremony with the flag being lowered while they played the evening hymn.

Lieutenant. Commander P. H. 'Jan' Stuart, 324 Squadron, HMS *Ark Royal*, 1960–1
Communication with the Editor

I was not sorry to leave this place and head south to our next port of call, New York. What a run around we had been given, from the balmy Mediterranean way up to the frozen and desolate north and now south to the teeming and busy metropolis of New York. Whether it was the Foreign Office in London or the British Ambassador to the USA, somebody had decreed that we should promote British trade with a mini-exhibition in the upper hangar of HMS *Ark Royal*. 824 Squadron was given the task of reproducing a typical English country pub, and, boy, did we go to town. We built the framework of timber and made the walls of hardboard which our tame squadron artist embellished with superb country scenes of cattle grazing, a foxhunt in full cry and in the distance a church; it was a masterpiece. We had a complete bar with barrels of beer, the traditional type with wooden taps, and some of the modern pressurised metal ones with decorated bar pulls. Bottles of spirits adorned the side of the bar complete with optics and there were glasses of all types including pint pots with handles. On one end of the bar there was a complete Stilton cheese already scooped and doused with port, and wrapped in a white cloth. All aircraft had been moved up to the flight deck and so the hangar was empty, giving plenty of room for features by the other squadrons. There was a bakery turning out bread and cakes, a miniature bowling green and a magic roundabout for the children driven by one of the small tractors normally used for moving aircraft around the flight deck and hangars. The smell from the bakery reminded me of my days as a schoolboy when I used to hang around the bakery in the small North Devon village where we lived. The New York newspapers gave our exhibition a glowing write-up, and one rich character wanted to buy our 'pub', lock stock and barrels ...

Commander David Hamilton, Senior Pilot, 894 Squadron, HMS *Eagle*
Communication with the Editor

On 29th April 1959 HMS *Eagle* was visited by HM Queen Elizabeth accompanied by Prince Charles, aged 11. She had expressed a desire for this private day and I am sure it was a welcome relief from the endless official engagements, crowds of people, press and minders. She had a tour of the ship, meeting many of the crew, an air group firepower demonstration, aerobatics and flypast. Prince Charles was presented with a miniature rum tub and had a helicopter flight. She ended her walk at the Wardroom where some of us were presented to her. While this was happening Prince Charles was entertained in the Wardroom Anteroom by some of the officers. He was asked if he would like a drink and replied, 'Yes, please, a gin and tonic.'

Part Four

FROM THE FALKLANDS INTO THE FUTURE

1
Harriers, Helos and Hornets

In 1973 the first of three new aircraft carriers had finally been ordered for the Royal Navy, but for political reasons they were defined as 'through deck cruisers'. Initially the vessels were designed to carry only missiles and helicopters, enabling the Royal Navy to fulfil its primary Cold War role of ASW and marking the end of fixed-wing flying by the Fleet Air Arm. However, a prototype Hawker P.1127 Vertical/Short Take Off And Landing (VSTOL) aircraft had been tested on *Ark Royal*, and this was to become the RAF's Harrier Jump Jet. In 1975 the Ministry of Defence placed an order for a marine version for the Royal Navy – the Sea Harrier, sometimes abbreviated to (and pronounced) SHAR.

Modification to the specification of the new ships was made, including the fitting of a 'ski-ramp', an upward-curved extension at the front of the 170-metre flight deck. This was the brainwave of Lieutenant Commander D. R.Taylor, RN, who mathematically calculated the most efficient angle needed to optimise the benefits of such a device, specifically for the Harrier VSTOL. Imparting an upward component to the aircraft as it accelerated over the bow enabled a greater payload to be carried. It would not be suitable for carriers with CTOL [Conventional Take-Off and Landing] aircraft, as it would not be safe for aircraft 'boltering'. (World War II pilots had anticipated the ski-ramp by timing their take-offs to coincide with the upward pitch of the bow, and in rough seas all launches were arranged, where possible, so that the carrier's bows were rising when the aircraft left the deck, both from catapult and running take-offs.

The lead ship of the 20,500-tonne class, the largest in the world to be powered by gas turbines, *Invincible* entered service in 1980, followed by *Illustrious* in 1982 and the slightly larger *Ark Royal* in 1985. Including the air wing, the carriers each had a complement of just over 1,000, with provision for accommodating Royal Marines, too. However, in 1981 – to reduce the defence budget – the British government proposed to sell both *Invincible* and the Royal Navy's only other aircraft carrier, the elderly HMS *Hermes*, to Australia and India respectively. Then, just as the outbreak of the Korean War had derailed US ideas of dispensing with aircraft carriers, so the outbreak of the Falklands War in 1982 abruptly reminded the British government that the Royal Navy required two carriers in commission. Australia offered to withdraw from the purchase of HMS *Invincible* (and that signalled the end of aircraft carrier operations for the Royal Australian Navy) and in 1986 India went ahead with purchase of HMS *Hermes*, renaming her INS *Viraat*. Still in service in 2010, she is the world's oldest carrier in commission.

Without two carrier decks in the South Atlantic, it would have been impossible for the Royal Navy to provide the level of Task Force protection, land strikes and air cover for the amphibious landings that were essential for the liberation of the Falkland Islands in 1982. Operating aircraft from the nearest base, Ascension Island, would have required an 8,000-mile round-trip, necessitating several periods of in-flight refuelling. This was actually achieved by an RAF Vulcan with a mission to bomb the airfield at Port Stanley, but it was a huge logistical operation, not a template for daily CAP routines in a war zone.

The US built upon its renewed faith in large carriers and ever more powerful fixed-wing, CTOL, supersonic carrier jets. Fifty percent longer than the Royal Navy's *Invincible* class, and with a complement approaching 6,000, including the air wing, USS *Nimitz* was commissioned in 1975, the first of a ten-strong class of nuclear-powered 'super-carriers' capable of embarking around 85 aircraft and free from the need to refuel at sea. For all that, several much older, conventional carriers, including *Saratoga* and *Constellation*, played major roles in the conflicts of the late 20th century and even into the early 21st.

The supersonic Grumman F-14 Tomcat took over from the Phantom as the US Navy's fleet air defence fighter, serving from 1974 to 2006 alongside, from 1983, the McDonnell (now Boeing) F-18 Hornet multi-mission fighter/attack aircraft, capable of up to Mach 1.7. The Grumman A-6 Intruder, which had entered service in 1964 as the jet replacement for the Douglas Skyraider, remained in service well into the 1990s, and a specialized variant of it, the EA-6B Prowler, provided electronic intelligence gathering and enemy radar jamming capability.

Hardly had the Cold War ended in 1989 than carriers were once again proving their importance, this time during Operation 'Desert Storm', the liberation of Kuwait from Iraqi occupation in 1991.

Mark 'Wiggy' Bennett, RO1 (G), HMS *Invincible*
Communication with the Editor

We sailed to America in 1980, when Prince Charles and Lady Diana got married. The captain, Mike Livesay, apparently was invited to attend the wedding but for some reason the Admiralty wouldn't let him go – I suppose because we were on our way to America to show the ship off. We took about twelve or thirteen days to steam across so we had a 'street party', probably similar to those that took place all over the country to celebrate the wedding. I recall we had a Lady Di look-alike competition; the winner looked nothing like her but I remember the prize was a case of beer. We dressed the ship with bunting and flags similar to Navy Days.

After we arrived in Virginia we were doing 'Colours' one morning, when we put the ensign up. The colour party also included an Admiral, the usual group of officers and a little Marine band: all very formal. The ensign should be a size 12 – quite a large flag (the bigger the ship, the bigger the flag). The actual size of flag which was bent on was a size 4 which was considerably smaller than the usual size 12! So there we were, all standing there in our best bib and tucker, trying to impress the Americans with *this is how the British do it*, and the

Admiral was *not* impressed. All the communicators' leave was stopped. They got it a few hours later in the day, but it cheesed a few people off.

Commander Tim Gedge, AFC, RN, 809 NAS
Communication with the Editor

I started my Naval career in the 1960s flying Sea Vixen aircraft off carriers, and then in the 1970s I flew the F-4 Phantom. Both these very large aircraft imposed most exacting requirements on ship operations while flying, required constant training by pilots to retain the high level of skills necessary and suffered from significant weather limitations in terms of sea state and visibility.

Very few of these limitations applied to the Sea Harrier where you could stop and hover over the carrier's deck and land in your own time. The level of pilot skill required was a fraction of that with a conventional aircraft and not only that but the fuel reserves necessary in case a conventional aircraft approach was missed and the aircraft had to 'go round' again were minimised. In an aircraft capable of landing vertically there is no need for 'go round' fuel reserves: in the Falklands we operated down to absolute fuel minimums, literally down to a minute or two of flying time before engine flameout.

When launching the Sea Harrier in high sea states and when the ship was pitching the pilot could simply time his launch so that he exited the top of the ramp as the ship pitched up. You could not have done any of this with a conventional aircraft carrier where aircraft have to land and then stop using arrester wires, where aircraft launch using catapults along a flat deck and without the benefit of a ramp, and where fuel reserves, measured in tens of minutes, have to be carried in case of a missed approach or landing

THE FALKLANDS CONFLICT

When Argentine forces launched a successful invasion of the disputed territory of the Falkland Islands in the South Atlantic on 2 April 1982, only one of the Royal Navy's new carriers, HMS *Invincible*, was in service. HMS *Hermes* had to be hastily recommissioned as flagship of the Task Force sent to retake the islands. Both carried Sea King helicopters and just 20 Sea Harrier VSTOL jets with which to provide air cover for the Task Force and the ground forces. It was completely lacking in Airborne Early Warning capability because in 1978, with the decommissioning of the old HMS *Ark Royal*, the Fairey Gannet had been withdrawn from service. The Navy had been obliged to depend upon land-based AEW assets, but those did not reach the Falklands. In eleven weeks a completely new system, using the Mk. 2 Sea King helicopter, was created and rushed into operation in the war zone, but during the period of vulnerability the Argentines sank six ships and caused damage to others, resulting in deaths and injuries and the loss of essential equipment.

Captain, later Admiral Sir, John Jeremy Black, GBE, KCB, DSO, HMS _Invincible_
IWM Sound Archive Reference 13445

At 0400 in the morning I was home in bed and my duty officer rang up from the ship and told me that I had to be ready to sail by midday on the following day – that would have been a Saturday lunchtime.

I recall one [of the crew] came back from Canada; one chap who was motoring through Germany heard on his car radio that we were being sent and turned tail and drove back to the United Kingdom. Funnily enough, some of the most difficult people to get at were those living in Portsmouth, but in fact we got everybody back before we left the United Kingdom ...

I was due to give an 18[th birthday] party for my daughter, and some hundred of her closer friends were due to come from all over in order to have this party in the ship. And throughout the forenoon I had the principle that Drake finished his game of bowls and Wellington had a ball on the eve of Waterloo, so why shouldn't I have a dance? However, at about lunchtime I came to the conclusion that we were going to be ammunitioning all night and it would look inappropriate in a press photograph next day in the _[Daily] Mirror_ if, at the same time sailors were passing ammunition, some of the younger blades of Hampshire were flying around in their dinner jackets. So I shifted the venue.

But ammunition came in particular from Germany before we sailed. A particular type of Sidewinder missile, which we didn't have in the Royal Navy, was held by the Royal Air Force in Germany, and it was deemed particularly important ... It enabled a Harrier to fire head-on to its opposing fighter as opposed to coming round the stern.

People really galvanised themselves. They had an objective with which everyone agreed, everybody understood the urgency, and everybody did it ... In normal life that is seldom the case.

We didn't actually sail until Monday morning ... I came on board ... The commander-in-chief, Admiral Eberle, came to call on me and wished me well and so did my own Admiral Reffell, and I was sitting in my cabin, which did not have a view over the dockyard, and so I didn't get the flavour of what was happening everywhere until I set off from my cabin to go to the bridge to sail. Now I typically arrived on the bridge five minutes, four minutes, before we slipped, and it took a little while to walk there from the other end of the ship. It wasn't until I started on my journey and had the odd glimpse of the dockyard that I suddenly saw all these people collecting with banners – all sorts of groups, not just dockyard maties ...

When we slipped the ship was facing the wrong way so we had to go up harbour and turn out. The _Sheffield_ – or was it the _Southampton_? – manned and cheered ship for us as we left, and suddenly there was the side of the Harbour swarming with people. Well of course I had sailed out of Portsmouth many times in my life and I hadn't imagined it would be any different ... until there, suddenly, were all these people. I have to say that I had an immense feeling of responsibility at that moment, but implicitly they were saying: 'on your way, good luck, go and sort this out and we will be delighted to see you back.' Which is fair enough, except at that time we didn't know what we were going to do, we had no idea whether it was going to be a diplomatic solution, military solution. We had had no idea whether we could achieve it, whatever 'it' was, and I felt this burden very heavily.

Flight Lieutenant David H. S. Morgan, DSC, RAF, later Lieutenant Commander, RN, HMS *Hermes* from *Hostile Skies*

Morgan was on exchange with the Royal Navy, converting to the Sea Harrier with 800 Squadron NAS, when he was sent to the Falklands. Like a number of other pilots, he had never taken off from or landed on a carrier.

Before leaving Yeovilton I had been briefed to make absolutely sure I would be able to land on board before jettisoning fuel down to landing weight. Apparently, carriers had the habit of telling you to dump fuel and then changing their minds and expecting you to hold off for another half an hour. So when the call came, 'Yeovil five zero, dump down to landing weight and Charlie immediately,' I politely requested confirmation that the deck was clear. This confirmation came in what I considered a rather unnecessarily curt message. Oops, I thought. Just made myself unpopular – not a very auspicious start. Without more ado, I dumped down to 1500 pounds of gas and was just about to start my approach when a further call came: 'Five zero, change of plan. Hold off and endure.' Sod's law had operated.

Despite a large floating crane in his way, Morgan managed to land safely and started to investigate the carrier.

The bunks were really very comfortable, being quite long and more than wide enough for the average person. They also had large mahogany leeboards to stop you being thrown out in a heavy sea. The later carriers of the *Invincible* class had settees that converted into extremely narrow bunks. Not only were these uncomfortable, they were so narrow that seat belts were required to keep you from ending up on the floor. They also had a mechanism which tended to unlock in a heavy sea, and numerous people woke up to find themselves incarcerated behind the back of a settee with no means of escape. This was known universally as being 'clam shelled'.

I spent that afternoon finding my way around the ship. It was a confusing warren of passageways and hatches containing a bewildering array of pipework, damage control equipment and signs. There were no signs to guide you and apparently no maps either; it was just a case of learning where the essential places were.

I quickly discovered that there were a number of spaces it was essential for an aviator to be able to locate. The No. 2 Briefing Room in 2M with its adjacent aircrew refreshment buffet (referred to universally as the ACRB or Greasy Spoon) was to be the centre of our operations. The wardroom, with its dining room and bar, was the social centre of the ship, and up in the island were the bridge, operations room and Flyco.

Hermes had been designed as a fixed-wing carrier capable of carrying two squadrons of jet aircraft. To this end she had spacious accommodation for both personnel and equipment, unlike the newer *Invincible* class, which had been designed purely to take helicopters. This gave her a cavernous hangar with large workshops, a vast expanse of armoured flight deck, and more importantly a very spacious wardroom with a very large bar. On *Hermes* the compartment in which the bar was located was large enough to hold the entire ship's officer complement in comfort and still have a game of mess rugby.

Mark 'Wiggy' Bennett, RO1 (G), HMS *Invincible*
Communication with the Editor

For evening entertainment a film was usually shown. Prior to each film there would be a bit of chat and banter by the Schoolie Officer and his crew who helped out in the CCTV studio, generally covering the day's events, what's planned for tomorrow and daily orders, and things like that.

I recall one night there was a 'mystery guest'. He was silhouetted or something like that and asked questions. You could usually figure out after the second question or so who it was going to be. On one occasion it was Prince Andrew. He was giving his views about how long he'd been on the ship and how he was finding it. I can't remember how the interview got round to it, but he was talking about how he celebrated Christmas with his family, and he said something along the lines of 'We all sit down for a meal like any other family and we all have jokes and fun at the end of the day'. Of course, he was asked: 'What sort of fun?' He kept referring to the Queen as Her Majesty, whereas most of us would have said 'Mum'. And he just said Her Majesty was chasing people with spray-string. We were all thinking: 'no, *can't* be true; the Queen wouldn't do things like that.' But then we thought, 'why not?'

801 Naval Air Squadron Engineers, HMS *Invincible*, Falkland Islands, 1982
Communication with the Editor

How were the aircraft maintained? The Fleet Air Arm had a Technician and Mechanic structure which was much different from the Royal Air Force and totally different from that employed by the United States Navy.

At the time of the Falklands conflict, the structure comprised four aircraft direct trades – Airframe and Engine; Electrical, which also looked after the weapons and navigation system; Radar, responsible for the radar and radio systems; Weapons Electrical (the old Armourers). The Squadron operated a watch keeping maintenance system of which the Mechanics were the largest element. Each watch had approximately 35 personnel comprising a Chief Petty Officer in charge, a mix of 9 Senior Technicians plus junior Mechanics. A Mechanic 'plane captain' was allocated from each watch to a particular aircraft, which not only engendered a healthy rivalry because each Mechanic wanted his aircraft to be the most available to fly, but generated a thorough knowledge of an aircraft's idiosyncrasies.

The shift Technicians were from different trades and like the Mechanics were expected to both diagnose faults and play an active part in rectification. Whereas the Royal Air Force had eight to ten trades directly involved with aircraft maintenance and more supervisory personnel, naval aviation could not (and still cannot) afford such a degree of trade dilution and non-productive personnel because of the ship's limited amount of accommodation space.

Invincible loaded at Ascension Island

Captain, later Admiral Sir, John Jeremy Black, GBE, KCB, DSO, HMS *Invincible*
IWM Sound Archive reference 13445

What I remember most clearly was that one of the features, whilst we waited there at anchor, was storing by helicopter from shore, and we had something like 25 helicopters in the circuit between the airfield on Ascension and my flight deck going round and round and dropping stores; I've never seen a sight like it in my life: simply amazing, and wonderfully controlled as they just swung round in a circle dropping off their tons and tons of stores.

We left rather hurriedly because someone thought there was a submarine in the area and that was a fairly cathartic moment ... It was a moment of realisation by the sailors. Up to that moment 95% at least of them – the ship's company – thought that we would not fight. I personally had told my wife before we sailed that we would fight ... Suddenly it came almost in a day, things had changed, and I by this time was living in the bridge area and seldom was able to get too far below. But my Secretary, who was an extremely able chap, kept me in the picture, and he told me at that stage that there was disquiet in the ship's company because they came to the conclusion that they were going to fight ...

So I determined to address them on the television which I did that night for 30 minutes, and my theme was: *this is what they have got; this is how we're going to tackle it; this is the military response to it, and, broadly speaking, don't worry about it because I reckon we've got this alright.* I was really going out to calm the scene by trying to explain it ... I had prepared what I was going to say and this I did for 29 minutes. Then it suddenly dawned on me at that moment that I needed to sign off and I had not thought through, ahead of time, my signing-off phrase ... I was thinking as I was talking towards the end of my piece, and I decided to use the sailors' vernacular and so I signed off by saying: 'And as far as I'm concerned we'll piss it.' Which is very much a sailor's term for winning, be it a football match or whatever.

I then left the studio, which was way down in the ship, to climb about seven or eight decks back to my cabin, and amazingly that talk, and in particular that line, absolutely set them up ... I should think about eight or twelve sailors of different hues stopped me between the studio and my cabin saying words to the effect of: *you're right there, sir, we'll piss it*! And this became then a phrase that we found on shirts, on mess deck doors. I even got a present from them subsequently on which was *we'll piss it with JJ* (because I was always known as JJ by the sailors).

801 Naval Air Squadron Engineers, HMS *Invincible*, Falkland Islands, 1982
Communication with the Editor

As the ship sailed farther south the pilots noted that [an] aircraft's dark sea-grey upper surface and white anti-flash under-surface presented a 'twinkle' effect during in-flight manoeuvring. This was deemed hazardous and a directive was issued to re-spray the aircraft underside and all equipment that could be attached to the wings to match the upper surface. The turnover rate of air was sufficient for this to be done safely in the below deck hangar, and the standard achieved meant that most of the aircraft were not re-finished until the next major overhaul.

To increase availability, the Aircraft Engineering Authority in the United Kingdom authorised a significant reduction in scheduled maintenance requirements and the complementary documentation. However, this did not sit well – either with us or more especially our Squadron Air Engineer Officer, Lieutenant Commander Dick Goodenough, Royal Navy, a gentleman much respected who had set, and expected, very high standards from us. So, following discussion with the senior Technicians, and the approval of the ship's senior Air Engineer an amended policy was adopted by him.

Without seriously jeopardising flight availability, one aircraft each night was subject to a thorough check of all systems and equipment in the security of the hangar. This included fresh-water washing to remove salt deposits and restoration of surface finishes thus minimising the effects of corrosion; checking and charging pneumatic and hydraulic systems; lubrication of flying and engine controls, undercarriages and hinged panels; vacuum cleaning the cockpit, cleaning instruments and consoles, polishing the canopy and windscreen – and finally preparing the aircraft for flight. It is understood that the Sea Harrier squadron embarked in the Flagship, HMS *Hermes*, embraced the minimum maintenance policy – with some detriment to serviceability and availability of their aircraft.

To be prepared for problems such as battle damage, the maintenance teams constructed sheet metal frames and patches and manufactured wiring looms for radar, radio and electrical systems. Later this proved invaluable when an aircraft suffered both structural and wiring loom damage after anti aircraft fire yet was airborne again within hours. Post conflict assessment deemed the repairs satisfactory for the remainder of the aircraft's life. Items known to be susceptible to the adverse conditions and essential for flight operations, such as the weapons and navigation systems 'black boxes', were held ready in the flight deck office so they could be changed whilst the aircraft were refuelled and rearmed. The Squadron workshop personnel worked tirelessly to supply serviceable components and circuit boards.

Commander Tim Gedge, AFC, RN, 809 NAS
Communication with the Editor

As the Task Force headed south, reinforcements were being prepared.

I had handed over command of 800 Squadron some weeks earlier and thought it very strange and in some ways unfair that I was now involved in the process of sending my old squadron off on real operations with me not with them. This was, however, short lived and I was brought back to the Naval Air Station at Yeovilton where I had been based for some years, to form another Sea Harrier squadron as a back-up to those already deployed.

I was given 21 days to form and train this new team, commissioned as 809 Naval Air Squadron; in the event we deployed just over three weeks later with eight aircraft, flying down to Gambia and then on to Ascension Island. The MV *Atlantic Conveyor* on which I had carried out trials two weeks earlier was in due course at anchor off Ascension and we landed aboard without any problems. For two of my pilots, just transferred from the RAF, this was their first ever landing on a ship!

After a 12-day passage to the Total Exclusion Zone (TEZ) we transferred four of my aircraft to *Hermes* and the other four including me to *Invincible*. In both ships the aircraft and pilots were integrated into the squadrons already aboard, although I did manage to retain 809 Squadron identity to some limited extent.

One of the huge benefits that the Royal Navy enjoys when flying from ships is that the difference between wartime and peacetime flying is minimal. An aircraft carrier exists to provide a base from which flying operations can be conducted. People do not go home in the evenings or at weekends: ship's routine is geared up to provided a wide panoply of facilities whenever it is needed. The biggest change from peacetime flying was the tempo of operations and the fact that all of the ship's company were dressed for action, kept their anti-flash gear and respirators with them at all times and were well prepared for any eventuality.

In the wardroom, officers helped themselves to food as opposed to being served, but this did mean that meals were generally available at extended times as opposed to a rigid routine. The seat cushions in *Invincible* were put away as a fire hazard so the wardroom chairs were slightly less comfortable! But generally the habitability was little changed. Life in *Hermes* was a little less comfortable as the wardroom ante-room was used for sleeping by some, there being a real shortage of accommodation space.

After a day's flying you could eat as well as we ever did, the bar was open if required, and films were shown in the evening. So, for those not night flying, either not qualified or who were not programmed, there was some scope for relaxation. My requirement was that any pilot would be capable of flying if required: it was entirely up to each individual to ensure they were ready if required. Some days we had mail deliveries with news from home. The mail would be dropped by parachute from the RAF Hercules aircraft flying from Ascension Island. These very extended, and in some cases record-breaking, missions were the lifeblood of the fleet and provided everything from mail to essential stores and even people. Mail sent from the ships would be loaded on to ships and then transported the four thousand miles back to Ascension by sea. There were no satellite telephones in the warships, so news to and from home was inevitably somewhat drawn out. Amazingly, the system worked extremely well, a real tribute to planning and ingenuity on the part of so many.

801 Naval Air Squadron Engineers, Falkland Islands, 1982
Communication with the Editor

There was one major problem with the aircraft navigation system, which was not programmed to operate in the southern hemisphere, an amazing oversight by the manufacturer. The remedy was to fly in new components. This was no mean feat and required the crew of an RAF Hercules aircraft to fly 4,000 miles from Ascension Island, identify and find the ship in the combat zone and parachute drop the items as close by as possible, then return all courtesy of a huge in-flight refuelling operation. On a lighter note, on a later parachute drop the crew of the Hercules was seen 'mooning' on the lowered ramp!!

Humidity at over 100% and dripping moisture was an ongoing problem particularly in the aircraft cockpit. One solution was to cover the consoles with 'cling film', much to the bemusement of the chef's in the galley who found aircraft maintainers 'borrowing' the odd roll or two.

Commander Tim Gedge, AFC, RN, 809 NAS
Communication with the Editor

Throughout the war the Argentines managed to keep an air defence radar operational in Stanley and could, therefore, plot our aircraft on passage to and from the carriers. They could not, however, see to low level and so we all invariably climbed out from and descended to a common point that changed daily at distances of up to 100 miles from the carriers. This in order to fool the enemy about the carriers' position.

It obviously worked well but did of course have very significant penalties on our fuel reserves. Transiting at low level where fuel usage is much higher for up to 200 miles each sortie and sometimes not in the right direction did curtail our time on task in the Operations Area over the Islands themselves. But much better to suffer this penalty than to not have a base to return to at the end of the sortie!

Mark 'Wiggy' Bennett, RO1 (G), HMS *Invincible*
Communication with the Editor

We didn't use local time; we stayed in Zulu time [GMT] almost from the moment we left until the conflict ended. The signals used to start off at midnight and number through 'til the following midnight when they'd start again, and it's the only time I've ever known it go over a thousand in a day. I remember the Chief RS Len Jones commenting he'd never seen that before, and like other departments we were constantly on the go. It's so instant now. *Then* it was teleprinters, similar to those that brought up the football results on the TV – and that was the pace at which they worked. There were about twenty of us on shift at a time. Eight or nine in the main communications office, three in the Ops room and the rest on the bridge. Due to the sheer number of signals being sent, as you can imagine, there was a restriction on what could and could not be sent, but in amongst all that was going on we still managed to send one from Prince Andrew saying he'd run out of Buckingham Palace notepaper and requesting some more.

We had a number of newspaper reporters aboard, from the red-tops to the broadsheets, and twice a day they were allowed to send a signal. Their reports were usually typed up on their little typewriters – remember this is pre-word-processors! So we had to retype up from their typescripts, and they were very wordy, very lengthy. The content and style varied noticeably between the red-tops and the broadsheets. The same story was very different in the style and tone that they told it. Some of them, especially from the red tops, made you think: *well that isn't quite what happened,* or *that isn't true.* They tailored it to the audience. I do remember this one tickled me: Able Seaman so-and-so was quoted as saying: *Oh I'd like to get the Argies. I'd like to kick 'em in the 'ead.* And I thought: *Well I know him; he wouldn't say things like that.* Towards the end we used to dread sending the reports because they were so long to retype up. The journalists just wanted to be off the ship so their paper could say its reporter was the first into Port Stanley.

801 Naval Air Squadron Engineers, Falkland Islands, 1982
Communication with the Editor

Improvisation was frequently required to keep aircraft serviceable. A control column bearing was changed with the aid of a Sea King helicopter wheel-bearing puller, a bench vice and the assistance of a welder. The spare bearing was supplied by parachute. In peacetime the column would have been removed and sent away for repair. The vital windscreen wash system was repaired by the simple expedient of adding a bonded washer to the valve body. The wash system had never worked on the Royal Air Force version of the Harrier. The avionic trade was equally imaginative in solving problems including the use of plastic skin from the sick bay and drying out 'black boxes' in the galley ovens, and the use of bathroom sealant provided from the shipwright's department to seal joints on the aircraft to prevent moisture ingress. The ship's company thus feeling that they were contributing to keeping the Sea Harriers airborne.

Flight Lieutenant David H. S. Morgan, DSC, RAF,
later Lieutenant Commander, RN
from *Hostile Skies*

The weather was no friend to the Task Force.

Down below in the hangar the maintainers used the lull in the fighting to carry out vital work on the aircraft. The conditions were appalling and great care had to be taken to avoid being injured by being thrown against machinery in the heavy seas. In the wardroom, the scene of so many evenings of pageantry and elegant dining, the heavy mahogany tables and chairs were upturned and secured to the deck with rope lashings. The large mirrored back wall of the bar had been covered in plywood to avoid splinter damage and now sported stencilled outlines representing our successes so far. People sat around in their blue action dress, white overalls or flying suits, their highly coloured cummerbunds having given way to webbing belts carrying life jackets, gas masks, survival suits and shell dressings.

Since the sinking of the *Sheffield* [on 4 May by an Exocet missile] the ship had been kept at Condition Zulu, with every hatch and watertight door fully closed. This made moving around a slow and difficult process with every door requiring eight clips to be knocked off and then re-secured. The hatches between decks were too heavy to be easily opened and were fitted with smaller kidney hatches which were tight at the best of times and required anyone wearing their survival equipment to wriggle and squeeze in order to pass through. The heavy metal hatch had to then be pulled back into place and secured with three clips. Many a finger was trapped and many a knuckle skinned passing through these hatches but we all knew that they would be essential to stop the spread of not only water but also smoke and fire if we were unlucky enough to be hit. The rate at which smoke had spread in *Sheffield* had been a salutary warning to us all.

On 25 May, HMS *Coventry* was hit; later that afternoon an air raid warning was sounded in *Hermes*.

As I arrived at the briefing room pilots were running up the ladders to man all available aircraft and the deck was shuddering as the ship came up to maximum speed to allow full manoeuvring. There was an eerie calm among those few of us left below. I became acutely aware that we were sitting at the precise centre of the ship's radar cross section, which meant that if the missile came in from the starboard side it would explode directly beneath my feet.

Christ, what a silly way to go, I thought.

A couple of minutes later John Locke calmly informed us that an Exocet radar transmission had been detected and that we were under attack.

'Estimated time to impact, three minutes.'

The next minute dragged into hours as I stood in the corner of the compartment, my feet spread and my hands on the bulkhead to steady myself. I imagined the nose of the missile coming inboard. What would it be like? Would I be aware of the impact before the 380-pound warhead exploded? Would the overpressure kill me outright or would the fireball suck the life out of me? Perhaps it would hit the stern and we would survive. The old girl was built to solid Second World War standards after all, not like *Invincible,* whose plates had been bowed by rough seas. If the missile exploded in the hangar there would be one hell of a conflagration but at least the blast would be dissipated. We might lose a lift though.

'Estimated time to impact, two minutes.'

I wish he would shut up! You can take the dissemination of information a little too far.

'Estimated impact in one minute. Brace! Brace! Brace!'

Feet spread, knees slightly bent, leaning towards the bulkhead, antiflash pulled right down over the eyes so that only the minutest part of my face is exposed. Waiting, waiting. My dread of dying in a fire is palpable; the smell of burnt flesh hangs in my nostrils.

One minute – nothing. Two minutes – still nothing. My thoughts began to slow down. Perhaps we had been successful and deflected the missile. Perhaps the chaff rockets and decoy helicopters had done their job. For a few minutes everything was calm and then suddenly there was a tremendous roar, followed by another and then another. Missiles roared overhead as *Invincible* engaged a low-level target to the north. Chaos reigned and it was some time before the phones began to ring again and we started to get some information.

We suspected that a ship had been hit but no one seemed sure which one. I experienced mixed feelings: on the one hand I was incredibly relieved that the *Hermes* was still in one piece; on the other I was desperately concerned to know what had happened. I began to feel the onset of survivor's guilt without even knowing whether anyone had been hit. Looking around the compartment I could tell that others were thinking the same. We all felt the desperate helplessness, the inability to have any influence over events taking place somewhere close to us but removed, almost in a different dimension.

The Exocet hit the container ship *Atlantic Conveyor,* destroying almost all her valuable supplies and helicopters.

801 Naval Air Squadron Engineers, Falkland Islands 1982
Communication with the Editor

The fourth aircraft loss, on 23 May, was a waste and again something which would not have happened in peace time. The aircraft was in the launch position on the aft end of the flight deck when the ship turned hard to starboard and naturally rolled to port. At the same time a Sea King helicopter was coming into land to starboard of the aircraft. The combined effect of the ship rolling and the downdraught from the helicopter caused the aircraft to pivot on the centre main wheel, and because the deck was saturated by the dreadful conditions it slid, with brakes applied, gently towards then over the side of the ship – at which point Lt. Cdr M. Broadwater ejected. He was recovered by helicopter but was returned home with spinal damage.

Commander Tim Gedge, AFC, RN, 809 NAS
IWM Sound Archive Reference 16782

On May 24 Gedge was on CAP.

It was late in the the day, it was dusk, sun was setting, dramatic landscape and suddenly it was apparent there was a lot going on: there were enemy aircraft around. It wasn't quite apparent where they were at that stage and they were being called by the direction teams in the ships that they had indications that an attack was coming in, and quite suddenly everything started happening.

I remember seeing another pair of Sea Harriers [800 Squadron's Andy Auld and Dave Smith] coming down at my left-hand side, two or three miles away and then it was apparent that they were going for an enemy target. I remember seeing over my left shoulder an aircraft hit and explode. I think that this was the first time I had actually seen an aircraft explode at quite that range to me. I mean, it was a mile or so away from me, and it was sort of highlighted in the setting sun. It was a very dramatic picture in itself – both dramatic and horrific. In the event there were several aircraft shot down at that stage … That sort of thing is over very quickly, and then we all went back and landed on board … Thankfully we were not losing aircraft ourselves.

27 May
We knew that one of the Air Force Harriers had been lost and the pilot had parachuted down and was thought to be on the Falklands [Squadron Leader Iveson] … And over the radio I remember hearing someone using yesterday's call sign, which seemed strange. We realised actually that this was the chap, who had been shot down the day before, calling on his emergency radio. Now at that time there was very very thick cloud – weather was extremely poor and we were trying to let down – there were enemy aircraft known to be around. I remember letting down through holes in the cloud, trying to get down to low level, trying to get in behind where we thought the Argentine Skyhawk aircraft would be and eventually hurtling through the space between the ground and

the cloud, probably less than 100 foot thick. The chap who had been shot down, I remember him saying to me after the event that he had heard aircraft. He had gone out (he had been hiding in an Argentine hut) to see what was going on and he had been confronted by an Argentine aircraft flying past at a very low level, very fast, and then within a few seconds by a Harrier aircraft chasing it. In fact the Harrier aircraft was myself, but we never did actually get onto the Argentine aircraft.

801 Naval Air Squadron Engineers, Falkland Islands 1982
Communication with the Editor

Pilots identified that one particular aircraft was showing signs of power reduction to the point where replacement was the only option. Utilising the only spare engine on board, this was done on 31 May at night because the Argentineans had never attacked at that time. Changing a Sea Harrier engine was not easy. The aircraft had to be lifted clear of the deck in a supporting frame, the undercarriage retracted and the wing removed from the fuselage by being lifted about fifteen feet clear. The latter operation was particularly dangerous at sea and to minimize the swing, personnel had to hold it steady with lashings. However, this was not entirely safe, thus the ship had to be maintained on a steady course in a direction that lessened the effect of the sea state on pitch and roll movements. This was not ideal in a war zone and only done after full consideration of the potential risk from below (submarines), above (aircraft) and at sea level (ships). The work was completed in record time and the aircraft successfully test flown late the next day. As luck would have it, the aircraft was shot down later that day by a ground-fired missile, one of four Squadron aircraft lost during the conflict. The pilot, Flight Lieutenant I. 'Morts' Mortimer, ejected and survived many harrowing hours in a dinghy before being rescued by one of the ship's Sea King helicopters. He was returned on board to much cheering and relief. Despite being a member of the Royal Air Force, the pilot was very popular and gave a spirited response to gentle taunting from his 'plane captain'.

Commander Nigel 'Sharkey' Ward, DSC, AFC, RN, 801 Squadron, HMS *Invincible*, 1982
from *Sea Harrier over the Falklands*

On 5 June, Ward was informed that *Invincible* and two missile-carrying ships would sail close to the south-western tip of West Falkland, within easy range of both the Argentine coast and radar, in an attempt to lure out the enemy air force.

I launched, flew to the west of Cape Meredith at low level, and then climbed to high level for the transit west. When I reached the newly agreed CAP station I called, 'Trident Leader, on CAP.'

Once there my Navhars platform toppled [Navigation Heading and Attitude Reference System failed] and I was left with no Head-Up Display references, no navigation assistance, and no radar stabilisation. This is certainly not my night, I thought, and began the routine for the airborne realignment of the Navhars system. If it wouldn't realign then the recovery on board would definitely not be easy; nor would any night combat.

The Navhars realignment worked fine and I settled down to the task of searching for contacts on the radar that would indicate to me that I had 'company'. The Argentine coastline was clearly visible on radar, and as I ran towards it from my CAP station I looked up and saw three red orbs in the blackness ahead. Were they after-burner plumes from Mirages? There was no contact at all on the radar, and I was too far from the ship for any control. Shit! Better watch them to see how they manoeuvre.

They didn't manoeuvre, and slowly I realised that I was looking at gas-burning waste-pipes on the coastline, the bright flames condensed by distance to dots in the sky.

The Argentine pilots didn't want to play. No one launched from the shore bases and at the end of my planned cycle on patrol I turned to the east and waited to hear Steve Thomas's check-in call. 'Trident Two, top of climb, en route CAP.'

'Evening, Steve. Nothing doing up here at the moment. See you when you get down.'

I was in descent towards West Falkland before I was able to make contact with the ship. 'Loud and clear, Trident Leader.'

'Roger, likewise.'

I was just updating my Navhars system on Cape Meredith with the radar when adrenaline started to flow. I had picked up a large slow-moving target ahead at low level. Could it be a Hercules on a night supply run?

I decreased height rapidly and throttled back. 'Do you have any friendlies in my area? Over.' 'Negative. But we do have one Sea King out of contact to the north-west. Probably south of you.'

'Roger.' I couldn't take any risks by firing at an unknown target. Maybe it was the Sea King. I was now in thick cloud and approaching to within 2 miles of the contact. It was very slow. I tracked it down to quarter of a mile and then flew past to starboard, very close. Whoever it was, they would know that they had had company.

The remainder of the flight was uneventful. A low-level transit to the ship and a simple recovery to the deck. Charlie Cantan was preparing to get airborne as I grabbed a coffee and went aft to my cabin. My confrontation with Wings had depressed me more than a little, but I tried to put it out of my mind.

Nothing had changed; there was still a war to be fought and that took priority over everything else. I was asleep as my head hit the pillow, unaware of the drama that had just begun in the air.

Charlie had been launched and Steve Thomas had recovered. But the low cloud was getting lower, and fog was a strong possibility. Wings called Robin Kent to Flyco, but before he arrived there the fog had set in. Charlie was on route to the CAP station at high level when he was recalled. Flyco was lucky that he was still within radio range.

But, having steamed into the fog bank, *Invincible* was unable to get clear of it. Areas that had been clear a few minutes before were totally socked [closed] in. Even the far side of the flight-deck was not visible from Flyco. The fog was as thick as you could get.

Charlie returned to the ship with plenty of fuel and set off down the slope for his first recovery attempt. He entered the fog bank at a little over 200 feet and from that point was able to see nothing outside the cockpit. He started his transition to the hover but had to throw it away and accelerate past the ship. He was very close because in Flyco they heard the roar of the Pegasus pass down the deck – but they didn't see him at all.

As he climbed out through the black murk and into the still moonlight above the cloud, Charlie knew that if he didn't come up with something he was going to get his feet wet. Picking him out of the water might not be so easy either. But he had been a Sea King helicopter pilot before training for the SHAR and decided to adopt the last-ditch profile for getting a helo back on board in fog.

'Flyco, will you put on a searchlight, please, and shine it vertically through the fog. I'm going to find it above the clag, hover alongside and then descend down to the deck.'

'Roger. Wilco.'

The searchlight was soon doing its work and Charlie found the diffused glow easily above the fog layer. The next bit wasn't going to be so easy, but it was his best bet. He transitioned to the hover, steadied next to the searchlight's glow, and then carefully selected a moderate rate of descent down into the gloom. It was a totally disorientating experience and he flew it brilliantly.

In Flyco, they first heard the noise of the jet, and then out of the clag above the deck appeared the Sea Harrier with the rear nozzles glowing red-hot in the night. Charlie touched down and relaxed into a ball of sweat. It was a marvellous demonstration of airmanship and aircraft control. His skill had definitely saved the aircraft and the whole evolution was undoubtedly Air Force Cross material.

The three ships sped eastward and before dawn were within spitting range of the Task Group. Perhaps the AAF had taken some message from the exercise, because within forty-eight hours the Mirage IIIs started showing themselves again by day over West Falkland.

801 Naval Air Squadron Engineers, Falkland Islands, 1982
Communication with the Editor

As the conflict progressed it was clear that night attacks would be unlikely, so a small permanent night watch was established. The majority of Squadron maintenance personnel were divided into two watches. Those off-watch manned the hangar to rectify defective aircraft, and those on-watch manned the flight deck for flying operations. The watches were rotated at regular intervals. A small number of the off-watch personnel were retained in the hangar, whilst the remainder manned fire and emergency damage control teams throughout the ship – in some cases deep in the bowels. Although of vital importance, it was an irksome duty especially when under attack. On completion of off-watch time personnel went to the flight deck for on-watch time. At no time during this punishing routine did personnel falter – a tribute to their professionalism and dedication. At one period we were launching a pair of fully serviceable Sea Harriers every twenty minutes on to Combat Air Patrol. Figures later showed that we had achieved a staggering 98% availability, not only a reflection of the tenacity of our maintenance team in dreadful conditions, but also on the wonderful capability and reliability of the British-built Sea Harrier and of course the stamina of our pilots.

Commander Tim Gedge, AFC, RN, 809 NAS
IWM Sound Archive Reference 16782

8 June
Another event that is imprinted indelibly on my mind is the time when the ships – the landing ships – were attacked in Fitzroy [Cove] and set alight and there was a huge loss of life and a lot of people burnt. We heard that something was happening and I remember arriving on the scene there and providing combat air patrol over the top of these two ships and seeing this horrific situation of ships having been set alight glowing red in the middle. I mean it was a most awful sight, looking down on it from above, and difficult to imagine quite the scene ashore ...

Lieutenant Commander David Morgan, DSC, RN, 800 NAS, HMS *Hermes*
from *Hostile Skies*

During the evening of that same day, after the attack on *Sir Tristram* and *Sir Galahad*, Morgan was on evening patrol in the area and keeping an eye on a landing craft belonging to HMS *Fearless* as it made its way towards Fitzroy. Suddenly he spotted a Skyhawk fighter, low over the sea and heading for the landing craft.

I jammed the throttle fully open, shouted over the radio, 'A4s attacking the boat. Follow me down!' and peeled off into a sixty-degree dive towards the attacker. As my airspeed rattled up through 400 knots I retracted my flaps and pushed to zero G to achieve the best possible rate of acceleration. Dave Smith wrenched his Sea Harrier around after me but lost sight of my machine as we plunged down with our airspeeds rocketing from the economical 240 on CAP to well over 600 knots, as we strained to catch the enemy before he could reach his target.

I watched impotently, urging my aircraft onward and downward, as the A4 opened fire with his 20-millimetre cannon, bracketing the tiny craft. My heart soared as his bomb exploded a good 100 feet beyond the landing craft but then sank as I realised that a further A4 was running in behind him. The second pilot did not miss and I bore mute and frustrated witness to the violent fire-bright petals of the explosion which obliterated the stern, killing the crew and mortally wounding the landing craft. All-consuming anger welled in my throat and I determined in that instant that this pilot was going to die!

The world suddenly became very quiet. I was completely focused and acutely aware that this was the moment for which all my training had prepared me. I had flown many hours of mock combat against all manner of fighters but this was the defining moment. As I closed rapidly on his tail I noticed in my peripheral vision a further A4 skimming the spume-flecked water, paralleling his track to my left. I hauled my aircraft to the left and rolled out less than half a mile behind the third fighter, closing like a runaway train. I had both missiles and guns selected and within seconds I heard the growl in my earphones which told me that my Sidewinder could see the heat from his engine. My right thumb pressed the lock button on the stick and instantly the small green missile cross in the head-up display transformed itself into a diamond sitting squarely over the back end of the Skyhawk. At the same time the growl of the missile became an urgent high-pitched chirp, telling me that the infrared homing head of the weapon was locked on and ready to fire.

I raised the safety catch and mashed the recessed red firing button with all the strength I could muster. There was a short delay as the missile's thermal battery ignited and its voltage increased to that required to launch the weapon. In less than half a second the Sidewinder was transformed from an inert eleven-foot drainpipe into a fire-breathing monster as it accelerated to nearly three times the speed of sound and streaked towards the nearest enemy aircraft. As it left the rails the rocket efflux and supersonic shock wave over the left wing rolled my charging Sea Harrier rapidly to the right, throwing me onto my right wing tip at less than 100 feet above the sea. As I rolled erect the missile started to guide towards the Skyhawk's jet pipe, trailing a white corkscrew of smoke against the slate-grey sea. Within two seconds the missile had disappeared directly up his jet pipe and what had been a vibrant flying machine was completely obliterated as the missile tore it apart. The pilot had no chance of survival and within a further two seconds the ocean had swallowed all trace of him and his aeroplane as if they had never been.

Commander Tim Gedge, AFC, RN, 809 NAS
IWM Sound Archive Reference 16782

We spent a lot of time on deck and waiting in the aircraft ready to launch should something happen, and then of course there were the lengthy transits when you were flying in relative safety into the air patrol area. Then there was a period in the combat air patrol area where you were working at a very high level and waiting for something to happen, trying to follow any sort of indication that there were enemy aircraft around. Then there was a period of transit back and landing back on board the ship, generally speaking.

The most number of missions I flew in a day was four. Generally we were flying twice or three times in a day, although there were periods of total inactivity. And this general pattern of events continued. The last time I actually flew was four days before the end of the war when I was ordered to go ashore.

Argentine forces surrendered on 14 June.

801 Naval Air Squadron Engineers, Falkland Islands, 1982
Communication with the Editor

Finally HMS *Illustrious* relieved HMS *Invincible* for the voyage to Portsmouth 166 days after leaving – which remains the record for a British ship to remain at sea. The ship's company lead by the indomitable Captain J. J. Black, Royal Navy (and the maverick Sea Harrier Squadron commanding officer 'Sharkey' Ward), returned as probably the most effective, efficient and close-knit group of British sailors in a warship since the Second World War, or dare one say the days of Admiral Nelson!

Mark 'Wiggy' Bennett, RO1 (G), HMS *Invincible*
Communication with the Editor

We were apprehensive because we'd been away for so long, and we didn't know what to expect. We'd seen in the papers how, when the *QE2* came in, and the people from the *Sheffield* and other ships, they got a fantastic welcome home, but we weren't in the thick of it as such because we were basically just a deck for aircraft.

The morning that we were entering Portsmouth was really foggy so we thought that we'd sailed all this way and, on the last day, nobody was going to see us – and as we were coming in, the fog just lifted and it was a bright, glorious day. We were doing 'procedure Alpha' which is when the ships company is lining the upper deck when a ship leaves or enters port. We were all the way round the ship, on both sides, and there were just absolutely loads and loads of people. I particularly remember that at the submarine base HMS *Dolphin* there was a banner that said *Welcome back skimmers* (the term *skimmers* is given to those who served on surface ships).

Prior to returning to Portsmouth we had to what seemed like repaint a fair part of the inside of the ship as the Queen was going to come on board. We'd been away all that time, going through all that, and the last thing most of us wanted to do was to end up chipping and painting and polishing ship again. No doubt the Queen thinks the world smells of fresh paint!

Commander Tim Gedge, AFC, RN, 809 NAS
Communication with the Editor

If we had not had the Sea Harrier with its Short Take Off Vertical Landing (STOVL) capability in the Falklands war we would have been very severely limited in our capability to operate aircraft for much of the time. The Argentine aircraft operating from airfields in a quite different weather zone would have been able to exploit our weakness here. Without the STOVL capable Sea Harrier we would have lost the war

MORE ROUTINE ACTIVITIES

The end of the Cold War in 1989 did not mean an end to the need for Anti-Submarine Warfare capability. For the Royal Navy, the platform of choice was the Westland Sea King helicopter (now superseded by the Agusta Westland Merlin).

Commander Jason Phillips, 820 Squadron
Communication with the Editor

Despite the end of the Cold War, all navies continued to practise Anti-Submarine Warfare.

The peak of the Cold War was just before my time, really, in the 70s to mid 80s with our carriers designed to provide the AS screen that was going to protect the US carrier battlegroups. I am unashamedly an ASW warrior. We did an awful lot of ripple flying: we fly 24/7 for weeks at a time, flying three aircraft so that two are always on station out there to protect the force. You would have helicopters in a screen and primarily we would do active screening.

There are two forms of anti-submarine hunting: active and passive. *Active* is where we go out with SONAR, effectively a microphone on a large piece of electronic string. Press a button and it goes *ping*. If there's nothing there, the *ping* goes, that's it; if something's there, you get a return, but with a different sound. The disadvantage is that, when you ping, they know you're there. That's where the anti-submarine community get their nickname from: we're *pingers*.

Passive is where we drop sonar buoys. These are drainpipe-sized tubes. They splash into the water, an aerial pops out the top of the water, a little bit of electronic string goes down. It just listens, so if it hears anything it then transmits that up to the aircraft, and by having a pattern of buoys, you know you've got something. So that's how it was done in the Cold War, operating with towed array ships. We'd launch from a carrier, and there'd perhaps be a ship with a towed array, which is effectively a big microphone on the back. They would get a bearing, and there'd perhaps be a submarine over there. We would launch and go and drop sonar buoy patterns. And many happy hours were spent flying from a carrier at night. When you ripple, all you do is sleep, eat, brief, fly, eat, sleep, eat, brief, fly. There are legendary stories of people getting up at seven-o-clock and walking into the ward room in all sorts of kit, even night dress – and it's 7.00 *A.M.* – you do completely lose track of what's going on. The rule is: unless someone wakes you, you don't get up. We don't do that so much now because we don't have the squadron size or the people to do what we did in the past when we had nine Sea Kings and 15 crews probably whereas now we have hopefully up to six Merlin and eleven crews. We do ripple but maybe for a week at a time but you are on the edge of your limits there because you do get extremely tired. Your work pattern goes completely because you're not just night flying or just day flying. It's only when you walk out to the flight deck you find out if it's day or night, and it can be a bit of a culture shock.

The size, speed, versatility and on-board resources of a carrier make it the perfect ship for responding to unexpected civilian as well as military emergencies.

Frank Beierly, Chief, later Senior Chief, (E8), USS *Abraham Lincoln* (CVN-72)
from his unpublished diary

Log of Activities of the USS *Abraham Lincoln* Aircraft Carrier – 1991

Sunday, Jun 9
Never happened, International dateline.

Sunday, Jun 16
Heard a volcano in P.I. [Philippine Islands] blew named Pinatubo. Flew off 29 aircraft to Kadena AFB to make room for possible evacuation of Clark AFB/Subic dependents due to eruption. Papered acft [aircraft] on roof to prevent ash damage. (The aircraft that didn't fly off the carrier and stayed on the flight deck we actually wrapped in barrier paper – heavy brown paper – to protect them from the ash that was still in the air, especially when the winds picked up.)

Monday, Jun 17
Arrived P.I. 1400. Picked up 2100 evacuees/180 dogs due to volcano eruption, departed 2200. Air filled with ash, en route to Cebu. Looks like a moonscape out there. Everything is covered with ash, amazing, like a *National Geographic* moment. Never seen anything like this, like chewing on sand, in eyes, ears.

Tuesday, Jun 18
Transiting to Cebu, a baby was born on the *Roanoke* today.

Wednesday, Jun 19
Arrived Cebu (Magellan Bay) approx 0800. Evacuees begin departing ship via CH-53 [Sea Stallion helicopter]. Slow process. Clean air.

Thursday, Jun 20
Last CH-53 left 0100. Departed Cebu at 0500 we are heading back to Subic to pick up more evacuees. The *Midway* should be there tomorrow, now a part of operation 'Fiery Vigil'.

Friday, Jun 21
Arrived in Subic 0600 for second run. Scheduled pullout is 1300. Took approx 3300 people. Pull alongside *Midway* for vertrep [vertical replenishment]. *Midway* will finish evacuee run today. Raining hard. Muddy.

Saturday, Jun 22
Arrived Cebu 0730 with verified 3200 evacuees. Departure by helo should take 14–16 hours. Abraham Canetta, 6 lb 8 oz was born onboard today at 1630. They say *Midway* took 1400 evacuees aboard on the 21st and will not have to return.

Sunday, Jun 23
Last helo departed 0300, rumors abound. Next? Pulled anchor 0800. Headed north. Aft berthing compartments are trashed. Hangar bay still smells like wet dogs.

THE FIRST GULF WAR

The Iraqi invasion of Kuwait took place on 2 August 1990, and when UN resolutions requiring Iraq to withdraw its forces were ignored a broad-based coalition led by the USA was authorized to end the occupation by force. The Task Force of primarily US Navy ships, including six carriers, was sent to the Red Sea and Persian Gulf. After a period of working up, while diplomatic channels tried to end the occupation peacefully, hostilities began at 0300 hours on 17 January. A massive bombardment of targets in and around Baghdad was carried out using Tomahawk land-attack missiles launched from surface ships and submarines, and strikes by the carrier aircraft. During the 43 days of the conflict, US Navy and US Marine pilots flew 30,000 sorties, some of them 700-mile round trips.

**Lieutenant Commander, now Rear Admiral, Mark I. Fox,* VFA-81
Squadron (The Sunliners), USS *Saratoga***
First published in *Foundation*, Fall 2004, © Mark I. Fox
**Lieutenant, later Commander, Barry 'Skull' W. Hull, USN, VFA-81
Squadron (The Sunliners), USS *Saratoga***
Extracts from unpublished letters to his parents, brother David and sister Nora
**Stephen W. Daniels, AQCS, USN Ret, Flight Deck Coordinator, VFA-83
(Rampagers), USS *Saratoga***
Communication with the Editor

USS *Saratoga* was bound for the Mediterranean, with plans for a Christmas visit to Marseilles

Fox
Old 'Super Sara' made what must have been a record-setting transatlantic crossing for a 34-year-old carrier. We arrived in the Red Sea by mid-August,

---

* At the time of printing, Rear Admiral Fox has been nominated for appointment to the rank of vice admiral as commander of Fifth Fleet in Bahrain.

relieved USS *Dwight D. Eisenhower* (CVN-69), prepared for the worst.

From a glance at the map, it was obvious we'd need a lot of external tanking support to conduct combat operations from the Red Sea. In early September I got my first taste of the time and distance involved when I led a flight of six CVW-17 aircraft to the eastern side of the Saudi Peninsula. Five hours, several refuelings and a couple of piddle packs later, I climbed out of my *Hornet* wishing it had a relief tube and a more comfortable seat …

Hull

25 October

We flew a tough hop last night. We were scheduled for an air wing strike (simulated). That includes most of the jets from our carrier. We rendezvoused with the large Air Force tankers and did our thing getting gas. Only problem was, there were over fifty airplanes in a small piece of dark sky and it was hazy and very gusty and cloudy. Our tanker track took us directly through a thunderstorm. I didn't know they had those things here until last night. That's the first time I've tried to tank off a KC-135 in the middle of the night in the clouds with five of my squadron mates all flying tight formation so we don't lose each other in the goo. Add to that a whole bunch of other KC-135's close by using small altitude splits with other jets doing the same thing and it was scary! For those of you who have flown at night you know that sometimes you can't see the clouds until you get in them, and that's very bad when you are flying formation and all of a sudden your lead disappears. The heart races and the palms sweat and you hope to God he pops through a hole so you can see him and tighten it up a little before you go bump in the night. You can't be rough with the stick though and turn away because right off your wing is a guy doing the same thing to you that you're doing to your lead, just trying to maintain.

12 Dec

… we were landing to the south this morning. BRC (base recovery course, Nora) was 163 degrees and it put us looking right in the sunrise. When we CAP we have to stay there until our relief shows up. This puts us late for the recovery because now we have to fly back to mom (the boat, Nora) and sometimes she is a long way off, and on top of all that we have to find her. The boat doesn't radiate and even though it seems like it would be easy to find an aircraft carrier it's not. Usually we fly back at around twenty thousand so we can see farther and find her and then come down for the recovery. Air Force guys don't know anything about this stuff. They just know how to kick out their pretty little parachutes to help slow them down on, what is it?, ten thousand feet of runway. Gee, how demanding. I'm flying with Coop, my wingman, and we both spy the carrier about the same time. I'm in the lead but unless you're within a few miles of mom you don't fly tight formation so you can look around and work the aircraft systems. In tight formation, if you're flying wing position, you don't even look inside the cockpit. You just glue your eyes to the other jet.

Don't want to go bump. The boss (Air Boss, Nora, he sits in the tower like at an airport) called up and said, 'Hey Sunliners, come on down.' He told us he had a clear deck for us, and 'Charlie'. That means land now. So we circle around to lose some altitude and then line up on final bearing, we're three miles from the boat doing about 400 kts and down to break altitude, 800 feet Nora. The sun is dead in our eyes but I can tell it's a carrier with the flat top. Something doesn't look right though, it seems so much bigger than normal. About ½ mile from the ship I go, 'Uh oh, hey Coop, guess what?, wrong ship.' About that time I look to my right about two miles and see the *Saratoga*. The boss comes up on the radio so everyone can hear and says, 'Hey Sunliners, we're over here, come on over and land.' Then he goes, 'Attention all aircraft, the *Saratoga* is the southernmost carrier'. He had a little smirk in his voice when he said it.

Fox

Shortly after we re-entered the Mediterranean Sea via the Suez Canal in early December, I became operations officer. We pulled into Haifa, Israel, for some much-needed liberty and wondered whether we had passed the mid-point of the deployment.

One bright spot for me was Priscilla's last-minute decision to keep our planned Christmas rendezvous (albeit a bit farther east of Paris). She arrived in Tel Aviv with an adventurous group of wives the day before the ship pulled into Haifa. I managed to get off the ship early and met her at Ben Gurion Airport for what turned out to be a very bittersweet but memorable visit to Israel. After a wonderful reunion, Priscilla and I drove to Haifa to leave our recall number with shore patrol, then returned to enjoy a leisurely meal in the old port city of Joppa. About 0230 we were awakened by a phone call in our Tel Aviv hotel room. Thinking the J.O.s were playing games when I first answered the phone, I was stunned to learn there had been some sort of a boating accident [22 December] and that there was a general recall to the ship.

Hull

27 Dec 90

Dear Mom and Pops and Sports Fans,

Merry Christmas and Happy New Year again. I suppose you have all heard about the death of twenty-one of our sailors. It was a nightmare out here and lots of confusion and a real mess. The story is that a liberty boat was returning to the ship. Our young sailors are required to be back to the dock by midnight. Only on special occasions do we allow them overnight liberty. The seas were very rough and about 150 yards from the carrier a wave came over the back and swamped the boat. Apparently it went down in a matter of seconds. There were many guys trapped downstairs. Some of them were able to make it out but many of them died. Several of the guys on the boat were in our squadron but luckily they all survived. Their stories are pretty scary though. One guy talks of being on the top of the boat when it went over. That should have been the safest place because most of those men were thrown clear. However this sailor got his foot caught and was stuck going down with the boat. He figures he was over thirty feet under when he finally got loose and he had to jerk his leg so hard he actually thought he pulled his foot off. He's on crutches. I asked him if the cold water shocked him. Most people didn't even notice the water was cold until on the surface and huddled with other men. We're talking a serious adrenaline rush. Most were rescued in under thirty minutes but already many of the guys were almost dead from exposure. Another guy I talked to said he had fallen asleep downstairs and woke up as his head went underwater! I know, I get chilly bumps thinking about it too!! One more thing about it and then enough of this stuff. It seems when you fly for the military you develop intense habit patterns and tend to do the important things just the same way every time. I think this tends to make me a little superstitious. For instance, on my preflight I always kick the tire (way back when I saw either Pops or Buck do that) even though it does no good and I also kiss the nose of my jet and give it a little pat. Seems I fly better if I carry out this little superstitious ritual.

Fox

I can't remember a time I was so tired, saddened, discouraged and frustrated. A forbidding sense of impending war filled the air; my ship and air wing had lost 21 young men in a terrible tragedy (fortunately, my squadron had escaped without loss); I'd had fewer than two hours sleep in the past 36 hours; and was again separated from the love of my life after having been only briefly together. When we parted, we were unsure of when we'd see each other again. (The rumors were thick that the ship was getting underway.) As I kissed her good-bye, Priscilla, half in jest, told me that she didn't want to be like Natalie in Herman Wouk's *The Winds of War*, inadvertently getting herself caught in a war zone!

The new year found us back in the Red Sea, putting finishing touches on the four carefully planned sequential strikes that would open the campaign, as well as making other contingency plans. The 15 January 1991 UN deadline for Iraq to withdraw from Kuwait drew steadily closer with no diplomatic progress toward a peaceful resolution.

My journal entry summed up my feelings:

10 January 1991 ... I am at peace, mentally and spiritually. My prayers continue to ask for a peaceful solution, but if war does occur, to be strong, courageous, and filled with extraordinary awareness and judgement in combat.

We received the execute order late on the 15th; the first strike would launch late the next night, with a time on target (TOT) of 0300, Thursday, 17 January 1991.

A fellow Sunliner department head, LCDR Scott 'Spike' Speicher, was originally scheduled as a spare for the first strike against the Iraqi air defenses near western Baghdad. He approached me and said, 'MRT, I've prepared all my life to fly in combat, and I don't want to be on the sideline when this thing starts. Can you shift the lineup around so I can count on flying this mission? It's important to me.' I told him I knew exactly how he felt, and promised to talk to Skipper Anderson about it. Spock agreed to the shuffle and moved Spike's name from the spare to the list of go aircrew for the first strike.

16 January 1991: The execute order has been received – CVIC has exploded into a controlled frenzy of polishing strike plans ...

A variety of moods, emotions and feelings – Relief that we at last are going to act; concern and fear of the unknown. Bravado, camaraderie, introspection, fatigue ... a blend of many conflicting emotions.

Thoughts of Priscilla, William, Collin, Mason and Abigail – What a cruel place this world can be. God protect them from the rancid and ugly evil that causes wars ... This is clearly going to be very intense for the foreseeable future ...

Daniels

As the flight deck coordinator for VFA-83 Rampagers flying the F/A-18C Hornets, my job was to be the eyes and ears for *my* squadron to the ship on the flight deck. I was constantly roaming the flight deck where my squadron aircraft were located from the bow area to aft portion of the flight deck. Of all my time working the flight deck during this cruise, this night had gone smoother than all the previous nights. There were no problems as I watched the aircraft being started and the pilots and plane captains go through the numerous checks on the aircraft. I was constantly on the move from one end of the flight deck to the other constantly checking the aircraft status and to be sure the plane captains remained with their aircraft until they were handed over to the flight deck director (Yellow Shirt). My fellow flight deck coordinator of VFA-81 and I stayed in communication with each other via portable radios if we saw problems with each others' aircraft. This saved each of us from trying to be everywhere at once on the four acre flight deck. We also shared information and technical advice and lent each other a hand when needed.

I was ready for the launch to begin as the ship turned into the wind and the first aircraft were being positioned on the catapults. The magic ballet had begun. The yellow shirts with their yellow lens flashlights directed Hornets, Tomcats, Intruders, Vikings, and Hawkeyes to their various holding positions near each of the four catapults. The white vested Troubleshooters gave the aircraft a once over for the half a dozenth time as the red shirt Ordnance man checked the various types of weapons installed on the aircraft. While the ship steamed into the wind, the plane guard Sea King helicopter was launched to take its position around the ship until the last aircraft was launched. The aircraft were hooked to the catapults; the Troubleshooters gave the aircraft one last visual inspection from nose to tail and took their positions near the horizontal stabilizers as the jet blast deflector was raised from the flight deck.

The Ordnance people then removed the safety pins and armed the weapons. The catapult officer, nicknamed the Shooter, with his yellow lens flashlights directed the pilot to increase engine power and finally light the afterburners for maximum power. Now most catapult officers or Shooters have their own style of motions when it comes to launching an aircraft. Some like to go through gyrations with their arms and legs like a police man directs traffic, while others are stiff like a classical music conductor. It does not matter how they go about their task, once the shooter's flashlight beam pointed forward, within 3 seconds the aircraft was launched into the starry early morning sky. Within twenty minutes all the launch aircraft were airborne.

The Red Sea air felt cool without the heat of the jet exhaust. The flight deck had an empty look about it. Despite the several aircraft parked around the island structure, it reminded me of the end of a sporting event and the crowd had quickly left the parking lot. Now we waited. There was very little to do with two-thirds of our squadron on a six hour mission in to Iraq.

Hull
31 Jan 91

The first night in downtown Baghdad [16/17 Jan] was about as scary as it gets. If you've seen the video of that night you get a feel for what it was like. From my squadron there were six Hornets launched, and many more aircraft from the rest of the squadrons on the *Sara*. It was a dark night with not much of a moon but it was clear. During the brief I remember being really nervous and it got even worse just before walk time. On the flight deck you could sense the seriousness of what we were about to do. None of us had ever been in combat before. Once I got in the jet I calmed down a lot. Back to the old familiar Hornet and control of the situation, I hoped. We launched and headed east and joined on the tankers. They dragged us close to the Iraqi border. Each of us had a similar but separate mission that night so there was no formation flying to be done over Iraq. Finally it came time for us to depart the tankers and head into bad guy country. We were on our own to proceed to individual launch points even though they were closely located. I remember getting uptight all over again, especially as I looked out on the horizon and saw the first bombs going off. Now I really got nervous. The reality of the situation sank in, at this instant. Quickly that fire on the horizon was directly underneath and all around us. There was a low fog and misty deck. The Iraqis were launching flares and they lit up the night sky and the mist. If you shine a flashlight through clear air you only see where the light lands, but if you shine it through smoke it lights up the air. That was my impression. We have electronic gear in our jets telling us of radar locks and missiles fired at us and stuff, can't get too specific again Nora. That ole *I'd have to kill you if I told you* thing just won't go away. Ask David, let him kill you. Anyway, my warning gear was overloaded. I tried to make sense of it but I couldn't absorb all the information. I saw missiles launched in my direction and that is a fear I will never forget.

Apparently they didn't guide on me but at the time I didn't know that. The flares allowed me to see the missiles even when they burned out because of the way the night was lit up. The AAA was everywhere. The videos on the news show that pretty good. I didn't know you could put so many bullets in the sky. Soon the first missiles from us were launched. Nobody told me what to expect so when they went off I thought it was more bad guy missiles and about jumped out of the cockpit. Somebody yelled over the radio our call that a SAM was in the air but we quickly realized it was one of ours. Someone told us way back if we didn't check six [watch our rear] in practice we wouldn't do it in combat. When I find him I'm going to tell him he's a fool and doesn't know what he's talking about. Everyone on that mission came back with a sore neck from jerking our heads back and forth, checking six. The instinct of survival, I've felt it pretty good now, I think. One thing contributing to my fear was not exactly knowing where my priorities should be to protect myself. Doing this for real was new even though we practice all the time. We kept hearing reports in the news questioning the ability of the American pilots. Reports of how the Iraqis are seasoned combat veterans and junk like that. Now I know for sure there are no pilots in the world like U.S. pilots. Don't even mention Iraqi pilots in the same breath. That sky was lit up like I couldn't believe. I was scared to death. With so much for my brain to process, and with the pucker factor (I stole that from Buck) pretty high, I wasn't sure if I was looking in the right direction. Do I study the radar for the air threat, or check my gear for the ground threat, or just say the heck with it and look outside? I tried to do it all but finally I couldn't sort out all the information on the electronic gear so my head came outside. If a missile was on its way I thought the best chance was to see it and avoid it. I got to the launch point and let em rip, that felt good, and then headed south. There was much more running through my mind but the main emotion was fear. Scott Speicher was shot down that night. As I checked back in, headed south, our skipper asked over the radio if anyone had heard from Spike. I said no but since he was the last one off the tanker, figured he must be behind us. Hopefully he is walking around in the desert and we hang on to that thought until someone tells us otherwise. We know he was hit, we saw a fireball in the sky that we now know was his jet, but pilots survive those things and hopefully he did too.

Daniels

After a dozen cups of coffee and a dozen trips to the head, it was time to get back to the flight deck to recover the returning aircraft. The sun was still below the horizon, but the early morning sky began to take on a light blue color with yellow streaks of sunlight above the horizon. The Red Sea was calm and took on an almost glass appearance. A FOD (Foreign-Object-Damage) walkdown was conducted on the flight deck by all those on the Deck to look for any material that could damage an aircraft engine or injure a person. As I checked my watch I heard the faint sound of a jet engine in the distance and saw several

387

small specks in the growing light. First came the Hornets and then quickly followed by other aircraft of the air wing. They flew down the starboard side of the ship and one by one did a sharp left bank to begin their approach to the aft end of the ship. I tried to count the number of F/A-18s as they flew by, but the sky seemed to be filled with airplanes and I lost count. I walked up to bow area of the flight deck and took my position between the bow catapults with my fellow flight deck coordinator of VFA-81. The F/A-18s were the first to land. As the Hornet released the cable from the tailhook, the aircraft was directed to the de-arm safe area where any weapons were pinned and made safe on deck by the Ordancemen. Once this was completed I signaled to the pilot of the aircraft to give me a status of the aircraft, so I could relay the status to my maintenance control below deck and the ship's flight deck control in the Island. One by one I went through the signal process until all my six aircraft were accounted for and reported their status. I walked among the aircraft to see if the plane captains were properly chaining the aircraft down and just being another set of eyes looking for anything missing or out of place. The pilots were excited as they greeted one another. I could see their flight suits were wet and their faces covered in perspiration. Many greeted me with a strong hand shake and a pat on the back. I then noticed my fellow flight deck coordinator still standing between the bow catapults. When he saw me I gave him a shrug and he pointed his index finger in the air ... he was waiting for his last aircraft to come aboard. One by one we both watched as the Tomcats, Intruders, Vikings, and Hawkeye landed on the flight deck hoping an F/A-18 would be mixed in with one of those groups. When we saw the Sea King slowly approach the landing area from the port side and about to land, we knew something was wrong, one of his airplanes was missing. He then told me it was Lt. Commander Speicher. Word spread quickly throughout the ship about the missing F/A-18. As days turned into weeks, we continued to launch aircraft to attack targets in Iraq. It was always a relief to see the same number of aircraft that had been launched a few hours earlier were returning to the ship, but Lcdr. Speicher was always on my mind.

Fox

After a short, restless night, I woke early and called the ready room to find out how the first strike had gone:

17 Jan 1991: The first strike from Saratoga *is complete, and Scott Speicher in 403 is the only guy who did not return. No mayday call, no comm – I can only pray that he diverted, or in worst case, ejected, and is now hopefully to be picked up.*

A distant sense of dread of losing a friend – small things hit me as being suddenly presumptuous – putting my laundry out this morning, for example, presumes I'll be back to get it back.

I am ever so aware – now more than ever – of my total dependence on God's grace. I am choosing to be strong and courageous ...

Briefers, aviators and onlookers filled CVIC for *Saratoga*'s first daylight strike brief, a complex, 36-plane attack against an airfield in western Iraq named H-3. The CVW 17 strike included an F-14 MiG sweep, multiple HARM shots, multi-axis EA-6B jamming, a deception group launching airborne decoys, a stand-off weapon axis delivering Walleye glide bombs and finally (the element for which I was the spare) six Hornets going straight up the middle, flying right over the airfield to drop 2,000-lb. Mark 84 dumb bombs on various targets in the airfield complex. I watched the ship's meteorologist's hands shake as he waited his turn to brief the weather. Although CVIC was cold, I knew his shiver wasn't caused by air conditioning alone …

The only way for me to prepare for this strike was to mentally put a knife in my teeth and literally hope and pray that I would actually fly in it. Although I knew I would fly a combat sortie later that evening, I wanted with all my being to participate in this strike as well. I didn't allow the smallest thought of, Gee, I hope nobody has any problems with their jet to creep into my mind. I was prepared, mentally, emotionally and spiritually to plunge into combat …

Soon after launching as an airborne spare, I realized I was going to fly on the strike. My fellow Sunliner department head, LCDR Steve 'Ammo' Minnis (also my roommate and Naval Academy classmate) had a problem with his aircraft's mission computer that forced him to abort the mission prior to the rendezvous, so I took his position as Dash-3 (the second section lead) of the six-plane Hornet element …

We crossed the border just below the contrail level at 30,000 feet, going as fast as possible without using afterburner – approximately 0.9 Mach (about 600 knots groundspeed). It was clear the Iraqis were airborne. Snatches of the E-2's bandit calls referencing 'Manny' crowded into my mind as I tried to keep a mental plot of how the strike was developing. The quantity and intensity of transmissions over the strike frequency increased, and my attempts to keep the big picture faltered as we continued north. A series of streaking contrails to our left grabbed my attention until I realized they were caused by HARM antiradiation missiles headed toward the target. After a brief jolt, it was comforting to see visible evidence the strike timeline was working …

Seconds after selecting the air-to-ground master mode, the E-2 controller, LT John Joyce, made the call that finally registered: '400, that bandit's on your nose, 15.' Now that was a call I understood! I immediately went back to the air-to-air master mode by selecting Sidewinder and got a lock on a head-on, supersonic Iraqi MiG-21 about nine miles away. I wanted to kill this guy as soon as I could, but couldn't get a good tone, so I kept caging the Sidewinder seeker to look down the radar line of sight. I heard the Sidewinder's distinctive growl at the same time I saw the speck of the Iraqi fighter, and squeezed the trigger. The missile fired like a passing train … then simply disappeared, which produced in me quite a visceral reaction. Although vaguely aware we had smokeless Sidewinder rocket motors, I wasn't prepared for the missile to just go away. Over my career, I had fired several Sidewinders against drones in various missile exercises, but all of them left a telltale white plume that always led to the target. This one just vanished!

Things were happening really fast; our relative closure was over 1,200 knots, and the MiG was getting bigger. Assuming the Sidewinder wasn't working, I thought to myself as I selected a Sparrow, 'Well, he won't get away from this,' and squeezed the trigger. This time I clearly watched the missile streak toward him. While the Sparrow accelerated, the MiG briefly disappeared in a bright flash and cloud of black smoke, then emerged, still nose on, but trailing flame and smoke. The Sparrow hit the doomed fighter with yet another explosion, but incredibly, there was still an airplane there, albeit clearly burning, decelerating and descending. As he disappeared under my nose, I rocked up on my left wing to watch him pass about 1,000 feet below me. The front of the Iraqi MiG-21 was intact, with the rear half enveloped in flames. The pilot didn't get out. I passed through the black smoke from the first missile impact as we continued toward the target.

Mongo's excited 'splash one!' shifted my attention to the left where his kill was marked by a huge smear of flame and smoke. Bouncer's much calmer 'splash two' gave me the impression that the first explosion on my MiG was caused by one of his missiles. 'Oh well, Bouncer beat me to the draw ... At least I'm still alive and didn't jettison my bombs. Maybe I'll get an honorable mention for shooting a burning MiG.'

There was no time to savor the kills. We were entering the heart of H-3's SAM defenses, and I was still aware I wasn't carrying the pod designed to counter the SA-6. Almost immediately, we got radar locks on another group of airplanes slightly west of the target that were initially nose on, but began to slowly turn to the east. The peculiar thing about these bogeys was they were extremely slow, about 0.4 Mach, (or about 200 kts) at 23,000 feet! Whatever those guys were doing, I didn't like the situation at all. 200 kts at 23,000?! This time there were no bandit calls from the E-2, and we had no indications of who they were. They must be some kind of bait, trying to lure us into a trap, I thought, and started doing deep six checks for about the next minute.

Satisfied no one was sneaking up from behind, I refocused my attention out ahead, and had a no escape Sparrow shot on whomever I was locked on, with a flashing shoot cue to remind me. By this time he was basically tail-on to me, and I was closing fast. But at my right two o'clock was H-3! To chase the bogey down would mean I'd have to fly past the target in a predictable stern conversion in order to visually identify him, and I was lugging 8,000 pounds of bombs around ... not what one normally carries in a VID [Visual Identification] scenario.

'Well, I came here to drop bombs on the target,' I thought as I reluctantly broke lock and switched to the air-to-ground mode. I jinked left into the 100 kt. jetstream, then reversed right and rolled in. Unable to see the earth-covered bunker that had been my original target, I quickly picked a secondary target, a big hangar with a white roof, and made the sweetest dive bombing run of my life.

Determined to see where my bombs hit, but unwilling to rock up on a wing like a big predictable grape, I built in a series of peeks back at the target into my off-target jinking plan. Glancing back the first time, I saw my four 2,000-lb. bombs falling together like a small school of fish. I then noticed the dust and smoke kicking up all over the airfield from AAA batteries shooting at us, and the crazy zigzag corkscrew smoketrails of dozens of hand-held, heatseeking SAMs streaking into the sky. Spectating too long, I resumed jinking with a renewed zeal. (I discovered jinking doesn't need to be taught. It is a very natural act under the right circumstances. The real key is not kill so many snakes in the cockpit that you bleed yourself out of airspeed.) My next peek paid dividends; it was a beautiful sight to watch those bombs explode on that hangar! I came off target also hopeful of finding the bogeys we'd let escape prior to rolling in, but never saw them.

We got back together and headed south as fast as we could make our jets go. As we passed abeam the area where we'd run into the MiGs, there was a final reminder of our encounter; two columns of black smoke rising up from the desert in the same relative formation they'd been when we shot them down.

Still convinced Bouncer or someone else had put that first missile into my MiG, my hopes began to rise when we checked each other over for battle damage and I saw that only Mongo was missing a missile. I was more certain that it must have been my Sidewinder that caused the first explosion after all, but I put it out of my mind for fear I'd bolter when I got back to the ship.

I had a low-fuel light when I plugged into the KC-135 south of the border. The boom operator kept pointing to the empty missile station on my right wingtip and giving me big congratulatory smiles and thumbs up. Feeling fully alive and relieved to have successfully completed the mission without loss was simply overwhelming. What a hop!

The return to the ship was uneventful. Even if I'd been absolutely sure I had the kill, I was in no mood to do anything extraordinary (like a victory roll in the break) upon return to the *Saratoga;* I'd been raised in the Light Attack 'quiet professional' school, and it just didn't seem like the right thing to do in light of Spike's loss last night. I did manage to get aboard my first pass with an OK-3 wire, ending the most eventful and demanding flight of my life.

The post-strike debrief in CVIC [Combat Visual Information Center] was like the locker room of a winning team in a championship football game. *Saratoga*'s C.O., CAPT Joe Mobley, gave me some good-natured ribbing about firing a Sparrow into an already burning airplane. I shrugged and smiled, 'I just wanted to be sure, Skipper.'

I was still in my flight gear, debriefing in CVIC, when preparations for the next strike brief began. Plunging into the mental preparation for another strike was a tonic. Tonight's strike was also against H-3, but this time the A-6s were attacking at low altitude in the darkness, with a robust SEAD [Suppression of Enemy Air Defenses] effort to suppress the radar guided SAMs in the target area.

The brief, man-up and launch went smoothly. I took it as a good omen that I was again flying Sunliner 401, the airplane in which I had the MiG kill. When we got to the tanker tracks, however, a wide band of broken and layered stratus clouds made the tanking evolution very difficult. The five KC-135s, spaced about a mile in trail and stepped up 1,000 feet in a stair-step fashion, each had four or five Navy aircraft flying formation in and out of choppy, turbulent clouds. It was a vertigo-inducing environment, and at one point one of my wingmen, LT Bob 'Kong' King, said on the back radio, 'MRT. I've got vertigo' at the same time I watched a set of aircraft lights prescribe an arching barrel roll over the tanker on which we were flying formation. Thinking it was Kong, I snapped at him to level his wings and 'get on the gauges'. His reply was 'MRT, I'm underneath you flying column.' I watched whomever it was recover from his unusual attitude and rejoin ...

Our A-6's low level attack did not fare well against the Iraqi's withering low altitude defenses. One Intruder, Raygun 510, flown by Lts Bob Wetzel and Jeff Zaun, was shot down not far from the target. (They were both captured and held as POWs until the end of the war.) Another A-6, AA 502, was badly shot up by small arms fire and AAA, but managed to limp into Al Jouf, a Saudi divert field. The overcast layer had prevented me from seeing any of the of the target area fireworks from my vantage point as a HARM shooter, but I still had vivid recollections of the scene from earlier in the day.

Knowing we lost an airplane and crew made the flight back to *Saratoga* especially long. After I finally trapped aboard at 0115, I wearily made my way to CVIC to debrief the flight. Reflecting on the day's events, I mentally rode the incredible rollercoaster of the previous 24 hours. Going to war ... Spike's loss ... launching as a spare ... the MiG kill ... the tough hop tonight ...What a day! I wrestled with the thought that if I hadn't helped Spike fly on the first strike, he'd still be aboard, greeting me with a smile and wisecrack. I built a mental wall against his loss, and refused to surrender hope that he was still alive ...

I flew 18 combat sorties into Iraq and Kuwait, and even with that relatively small number of missions, I could write a book describing those experiences. Flying through someone's rock-hard jet wash in the dark as I crossed the border into Saudi Arabia after a KTO [Kuwait Theater of Operations] strike; rolling in on the phosphate plant at Al Qaim, unsuccessfully trying to ignore the incredible sight of glowing yellow and orange streams of AAA rising slowly in the darkness; watching a refinery and oil storage tanks disappear under an angry, dark red explosion that blossomed up thousands of feet; flying through the surreal daytime darkness caused by smoke from the oil well fires; playing traffic cop with 12 low-state [low on fuel] Hornets as we discovered we had one KC-10 with a single hose instead of three KC-135s.

Hull

Now you might be thinking we don't drop many bombs. The Hornet is so accurate we don't need to carry as many. Our targets are generally more difficult and precise, because this is the strength of the Hornet (not even bringing up the awesome fighter capabilities). In one hop our squadron shot down two planes and a few seconds later rolled in on the target. The jet is amazing. Stuff I've personally hit are ammo dumps, bridges, radar sites, command and control centers, baby milk factories – oops – tanks and trucks and other equipment of the Republican Guard, airplanes parked at airfields, etc. There is news about killing civilians. I can assure you straight from one of the guys actually doing the bombing, not someone telling you third hand, that we make every effort not to hit civilians. Not because we are told not to drop on them, but because I'm no vicious killer, along with my fellow pilots. Put yourself in my shoes, would you want to drop bombs knowing they were killing Iraqi citizens who possibly don't even support the terrorism of Hussein? Even if they do support him their children are just like kids everywhere, who cares about this political mumbo jumbo? Aw, I hate to get into all this stuff. Those of you who know me well know I'm not that way. I just saw the poster and wanted to fly.

Fox

I was preparing to lead my fifth strike when the war was unilaterally stopped. Although much has been written on the wisdom of how and when the war ended, I was overjoyed. My birthday is March lst, and I couldn't think of a nicer gift. Like a leaky tire kept inflated by the heat of rolling, I didn't realize how weary and tired I was until the cease fire was announced, and promptly went to bed for about 12 hours.

Hull

2 Mar 91

Dear Mom and Pops and Sports Fans,

Well what do you know, the war is over. Iraq finally called it quits. Can you believe the job our ground forces did? It was awesome. Know why it was awesome? Because of the outstanding job the pilot types did before they rolled through …

The feeling on this ship is great. You can see it when you walk down the passageways. Today is a no fly day. Haven't had one of those in a long time. On the flight deck the footballs and joggers and suntanners are out. Now we're just antsy to sail west. There will be many things I'll miss once we return. This cruise has made the pilots like family. Many will be leaving VFA-81 shortly after cruise and that will be sad. There is an unspoken commitment to each other. We sit around and complain, but if an outsider badmouths one of us look out. I guess I can criticize family, but no one else can. I'll also miss these insincere form letters, telling stories and letting everyone know just what a strange brother and sister I have. There is really only one side of the argument, mine. I'll also miss the flight time. Once home our budget has been cut, and flight hours reduced, so our proficiency will drop tremendously. Ports were few and far between, but they were fun. There are many things I won't miss. The fear of combat. Losing some good friends. One has been shot down and one is a

POW, Scott Speicher and Jeff Zaun. There is another pilot unaccounted for, and also another POW from the *Sara*. I wasn't close to them, and I'm glad, it makes it easier to take. I sure won't miss living on this boat, trying to sleep through cat shots [catapult launches], trying to deal with the idiots at the post office, standing alerts at all hours of the night, spending month after month away from home, and taking showers where not only the cold hot water runs out, but all the water runs out! We've made the most of our living conditions, however, and once you get used to them, it's not so bad. Maybe it will help give a better appreciation of how good we have it in the states. Gosh, will eating Nora's cooking have me dreaming of meals on the boat?

2
Send a Carrier: 1993–2010

The ending of both the Gulf War and the Cold War left what proved to be unfinished business; the decade kept the carriers of several navies busy with conflicts in Yugoslavia, Afganistan and Iraq. And there was a major change in the composition of crews and squadrons.

US women had gained the right to serve in combat ships including carriers in 1978. Although women in general had been flying aircraft almost as long as men, the first woman naval aviator, Barbara Allen, gained her US Navy wings only in 1974. She never saw carrier service because not until 1991 were female US aviators allowed to fly combat aircraft, and it was a further three years before the first of them became carrier-qualified. The Royal Navy admitted women to combat ships in 1990.

Following the end of World War II, Italy's navy was not permitted to operate fixed wing aircraft, so when in 1985 the Marina Militare commissioned its first light carrier, *Giuseppe Garibaldi* (the smallest in the world), it carried ASW helicopters. The treaty restriction was lifted in 1989, allowing the embarkation of a Harrier squadron, and in September 2009 the much larger *Cavour*, 27,900 tons, was commissioned.

France had commissioned its first new-build carrier, *Clemenceau*, in 1961 and a sister-ship, *Foch*, in 1963. *Clemenceau* was decommissioned in 1997; three years later *Foch* was sold to the Brazilian Navy. By this time the only nuclear-powered aircraft carrier outside the US Navy was under construction, and after some teething troubles the *Charles de Gaulle* was commissioned in 2001.

BOSNIA

While most nations of the former Warsaw Pact and the Soviet Union managed a relatively peaceful transition to independence, Yugoslavia fractured along racial, historical and religious fault-lines, rapidly descending into civil war in 1992. The conflict was at its worst in Bosnia, and the United Nations deployed a protection force to what was rapidly becoming Former Yugoslavia. In October, in an attempt to stop airborne attacks and the movement by air of men and weapons, particularly by Bosnian Serb forces against Bosnian Muslims, the UN passed Resolution 78, prohibiting all but UN-authorized flights. This was comprehensively violated. In March 1993 the Muslim town of Srebrenica was bombed, for which the Serbs were blamed. Operation 'Deny Flight' was set up to forcibly interdict unauthorized flights, with NATO aircraft tasked to enforce it. UN safe-havens were created in towns including Gorazde and Srebrenica. Aircraft from NATO carriers stationed in the Adriatic carried out much of the reconnaissance, close air support and air defence, but throughout the conflict they were hampered by the UN's Rules of Engagement.

Lieutenant Commander, now Commander, Henry Mitchell, 801 Naval Air Squadron, HMS *Ark Royal*
Communication with the Editor

At the end of 1992 I had just taken over as the Air Warfare Instructor (AWI) of 801 Naval Air Squadron, Sea Harriers, and we were part of the *Ark Royal* Carrier Air Group at that point. In January '93 we were suddenly told to embark, proceed to the Adriatic at speed and be prepared to support whatever was going on in Bosnia. We had seven Sea Harriers initially, and the normal Air Group of Sea King Mark 2 AEWs and Sea King Mark 6 ASW helicopters.

So we rushed out to the Adriatic. I seem to remember embarking in some pretty dismal weather off the Isle of Wight only to have a microphone thrust straight into my face as soon as I landed on the deck, asking 'What are you off to do?' I made some trite comment without having the faintest idea what our task was. We arrived in the Adriatic, and politically it was good that we were there. The practical reality was we weren't very sure what we were going to be expected to do. One of the liaison officers up at the Air Operations Centre came on board and told us that they were thinking of using us for close air support, which didn't necessarily surprise us, especially me as I was the AWI – I'd been wondering myself, trying to provide some sort of guidance as to what we might be doing. But the aircraft was procured as a fleet air defence fighter in the North Atlantic; it had a limited low-level reconnaissance capability: the F95camera; its weapons system relied on whatever we were dropping bombs on being largely at sea level; it was generally optimised for a low-level shallow dive angle.

So we find ourselves then over Bosnia. Being expected to go into Bosnia and go over land (for which the radar was clearly not optimised) and carry out medium-level reconnaissance and close air support – which most of the pilots couldn't spell let alone do – in steep dive profiles, for which the bombing sight was not optimised, came as a bit of a challenge. It fell to my responsibility to rewrite the entire tactic manual almost overnight.

On top of that we had a requirement for anti-surface warfare tactics to provide some kind of capability against the embargo-busting ships, and in that domain (having spent most of our Cold War days trying to develop the most covert long-range, unseen, over-the-horizon targeting techniques) we suddenly found ourselves in the Adriatic in a dense shipping situation where, first of all you didn't need to use covert tactics. The longer away you'd fire your missile against, potentially, an embargo-busting ship, the more likelihood there was that that missile was going to catch several targets of opportunity en route. So we had to swing from an ultra-covert, generally at night, to an ultra-open, short range procedure.

UN approval for flying over the land was not forthcoming between January and August 1993 while *Ark Royal* was in the Adriatic, but new tactics were developed and then tested out in a major NATO exercise off Italy before the carrier left for home.

We did all the work up and all the hard work rewriting the documents, and then we met up with our sister squadron in Gibraltar (800 Naval Air Squadron). We had a lot of equipment that was required by *Invincible* and so we joined up with her and had a particularly good run ashore in Gibraltar. We ended up in a bar until very late at night singing squadron songs and that sort of thing round the piano. It was particularly memorable for another reason. Most of the time there's close competitive rivalry between squadrons of the same aircraft type, for understandable reasons, as well as Carrier Air Groups and Carriers themselves. This was an unusual situation in which we were all in this boat together. 801 NAS had developed all the tactics and we'd fed as much as possible to 800 NAS as they were working up, before they came out. It was an opportunity to get our heads together, and we handed over what we'd got, and they would take them on and refine them further. So it was a Force effort rather than an individual squadron effort, and it gave rise to a jolly good piss up. So *Invincible* went on with 800 Squadron and then started flying immediately over land over Bosnia …

We came back in January '94. Now things were beginning to hot up a bit. We brought out 8 aircraft this time, and more aircrew, and got very quickly into all the procedures that we had generated and which had been refined by 800, and we took on the next stage. Very rapidly we started establishing a very good rapport with the forward air controllers on the ground, and the reconnaissance photos that we took were fed back to the CAOC [Combined Air Operations Centre] and provided extra intelligence. We analysed them on board and sent them back as an assessed product to the intelligence organisation. We were also flying air defence, so we were doing all three roles. We were out there for six months, which was months longer than anyone else – everyone else would rotate every six weeks or so, which provides limited continuity, and no real engagement with what was going on on the ground. They do their flight once every two or every three days then go back to their hotel and sit around the pool – all too remote for my liking.

One of the benefits of the carrier in the Adriatic was that we were a hell of a lot closer to where we needed to be in the first place than all those who were sitting in their hotels in Italy, who had another 60–100 miles to transit before they even got to where the ship was, let alone where Bosnia was. So there was always a bigger call for the tankers for the land-based facilities than there was for the carrier-based facilities.

Some of our missions were four to four and a half hours: that was the air defence mission, because you would use the tanker for in-flight refuelling. Most of the close air support and reconnaissance missions were an hour and a half or so. We'd go in for the close air support – you never knew quite who you were going to speak to or where you were going to be working, but you had to be very adaptable.

The only maps we had of the area were those generated by the Germans in the Second World War, printed on a different scale to that which we'd all trained to use, with subtly different marks for different things. So we got accustomed to that quite quickly, but because the Harrier didn't have a moving map in the cockpit our version of the moving map was a stack of 32 options in your right leg pocket. When you were told where you were going, you'd get out these 32 maps and rifle through them 'til you found the one that was relevant to the area you would be working in, and of course we didn't have an auto pilot. Sometimes you had a hunch you were going to be sent to Gorazde or Srebrenica or Banja Luka but most of the time you didn't. You'd be given a nine-line brief of the target with a grid reference, so as you were transiting up country trying to work out where you were, you'd first of all have to find the right map for the right area and then decipher the grid reference – all on a scale which was rather smaller than the one you're used to reading. All that, and you're also trying to fly a naturally unstable aircraft. Your wingman can see your plane wobbling. It's a bit like trying to smoke and make a phone call in the car while you're changing gear …

With the air defence role you have a four-hour window to provide coverage throughout Bosnia, or in the southern half, or wherever, so you get airborne, you enter the country and once you're down to a certain fuel state you need to tank, you then exit, tank, and come back in again. You keep on doing that, and if anything happens in that four hour window you can be vectored on to investigate by the AWACS* airborne control aircraft which was patrolling up and down the Adriatic. Might have been the E2, might have been the US Navy E3. But either way they were looking over into Bosnia. But between the Adriatic and Bosnia you've got a string of mountains, which means that quite a lot is in shadow of the radar and in those days – the technology is better now – there was limited capability, if not nil capability, for them to pick up low-level moving targets in ground clutter, so occasionally they would get a sniff at something. They'd see a quick 'skin paint'* and they'd vector an aircraft. So the air defence role was relatively straightforward and, to be honest, a bit of a break from the support and reconnaissance.

In the recce role we would be given target coordinates – generally they'd generate about ten targets. We had no automatic mission planning system, we didn't have a moving map. Nowadays there is a system of drag and drop, and somebody else programmes the targets into a computer. Those days, it was a basic colour photocopier with A4 paper, photocopying 10 different Initial-Point-to-Target maps, one for each of the targets, and photocopied three times: one for the lead, one for the wingman and one for the standby,

* Airborne Warning and Control System.
* A radar indication caused by a radar signal briefly reflected from an object.

because, for every two aircraft, we briefed up and manned a third. Provided the first two went, the third pilot would shut down, and he would then rotate back into being the wingman or lead in the next sortie. It was frenetic. I think we had a commitment to fly twelve sorties a day so 18 cockpits had to be crewed though only 12 got airborne. On top of that we continued night flying training.

We tended to do a week on, a couple of days off; as the senior pilot, each of those few days off I'd gather all the bits together – who was having to go to the dentist on Tuesday morning, somebody else who was ill and unfit to fly, or whatever it might be … It would take me most of those two days to sort out the matrix of who could do which one of the sorties or be a spare. The reconnaissance sortie planning timeline was about 8 hours before you even got airborne, because it was all totally man-draulic: getting the maps, writing it up, sticking them together, writing up the IP-target run, plugging in the hand-held yachting GPS that we had on the dashboard as a modification, and it was definitely warfare in accordance with the manual of Heath Robinson, but great fun, very busy and professionally very satisfying, despite all the constraints. We ended up by producing what was a record of 576 sorties in six months, which for that number of aircraft wasn't achieved in the Second World War. It was intense. It was tough for the maintainers and they did a sterling job, and of course there were lots of weapons fits as well.

Lieutenant, now Commander, Jason Phillips, 820 Squadron, HMS *Ark Royal* / HMS *Illustrious*
Communication with the Editor

We didn't fly any sorties over Bosnia; we went to Split regularly where we had to drop personnel off, or stores. The majority of our tasking was in support of the operations going on in Former Yugoslavia, particularly by the Harriers that were flying air patrols all the time, which was why the carrier was there then. So I was out there, initially on *Ark Royal*, in 1994 and then went back out again with *Illustrious*. Primarily we flew stores around the fleet. So, although based on the carrier, we would end up with the squadron having some aircraft on the carrier, and some on the fleet auxiliary. *Fort Austin,* as I remember, was one of the bomb-and-bullet carriers. Every week the fleet auxiliary would go in towards Bari, which was where the Air Head was. Stores would be flown into Bari, and we would fly all day long picking up stores from Bari and flying them out to the *Austin* and it would go back to the fleet. We would sometimes do eight hours of flying, maybe three aircraft at a time, distributing stores primarily to the carrier. Although there were lots of other missions flown including numerous surface search and ASW exercises it's the loadlifting that we did mostly. We all got a medal – but, if you ask any of the ASW helicopter crews who were there, they reckoned that it was for cabbage carrying in the Adriatic because that was what they felt that we were doing. It was a great time to be on the carrier because it was very busy, it was flying combat missions so it was great to be part of the excitement.

Lieutenant Commander, now Commander, Henry Mitchell, 801 Squadron, HMS *Ark Royal*
Communication with the Editor

Because of the multi-role nature of the aircraft, even though we might have been tasked for air defence, we always carried the recce camera anyway, internally, so we could be retasked in the air for reconnaissance, and frequently were – by General Rose himself on one occasion, and we also carried a bomb to be able to help out at short notice in close air support. It certainly illustrated the validity of having a multi-role platform that could swing from one role to another in the air. Because we were carrying missiles, a recce camera and a bomb, as the temperature got hotter and hotter – and we didn't have the bigger engine in the Sea Harrier – the margin got thinner and thinner, and in the height of the summer we ended up by coming back targeting our minimum landing allowance as our landing allowance. Normally you'd have a minimum landing allowance and then a buffer and you'd generally come back with a bit more than the buffer. In a VSTOL aircraft your thrust needs to exceed your weight. If you're taking rather too much weight, your thrust effectively is reduced. We ended up having to reduce it just to maintain the capability that could be on offer over Bosnia. We had to trade our fuel margins to almost nothing in order just to make do. Now if there was poor weather forecast we wouldn't do that; we would remove the bomb and just declare that we were going to fly reconnaissance, as opposed to reconnaissance and attack, but if it was a nice day you could pretty much guarantee that there would be nothing from the ship or the weather to prevent us from getting on board when we needed.

We had to change the approach slightly in that normally you would negotiate a Charlie time – a landing-on time. In our case we would give them a rough gauge as to when we would be able to land on board, but when we got near the ship we would go around and around to effect a procedure that 'I'm going to land when my fuel is right' – as opposed to 'I'm going to land on a time'. If you had landed on the target time you might have too much fuel (in which case you're too heavy), or too little (in which case, you flame out) ...

Because the maps were pretty ancient, the ground commanders had limited benefit of mapping. In any case, a map wouldn't tell you whether a bridge had been knocked out by the warring factions, so normally Commanders would have to request a task for an aircraft to take a photograph to determine whether that bridge was passable or not for their operation in a couple of days time. While we were floating around in the air defence role, and generally at the end of every close air support mission as well, we'd just do one circuit, or a couple of circuits perhaps, of a particular area, say Srebrenica, and take some medium-level photographic coverage. Not good enough for intelligence value but very good and hugely appreciated by the guys on the ground. Wouldn't tell you whether the bridge had been dropped [blown up] within the last 24 hours, but very recent compared to 1940s maps.

Commander, now RADM, Mark I. Fox, VFA-81 (The Sunliners), USS *Saratoga*
Communication with the Editor

In early February 1994, I was XO of Strike Fighter Squadron (VFA) 81, an FA-18C Hornet squadron assigned to Carrier Air Wing 17 embarked aboard USS *Saratoga* (CV-60) operating in the Adriatic Sea. *Saratoga*, underway on the last deployment of her 38-year career, was just beginning to conduct flight operations in support of Operation 'Deny Flight', a NATO operation enforcing a U.N. no-fly zone over Bosnia-Herzegovina.

On 4 February 1994, briefing for my first operational 'real world' flight since Operation 'Desert Storm' three years earlier, my wingman (LTjg Colin 'Rainman' Farrar, USN) and I covered the details of our 'Deny Flight' mission over Bosnia – callsigns, frequencies, carrier procedures, the route of flight, potential diverts, communications, air-to-air and air-to-ground tactics, fuel management, etc. To put Farrar (a young 'nugget' aviator flying his first tactical mission on his first deployment) at ease, I emphasized he needed only to execute the basics to conduct the mission (mainly keeping sight of me!) and predicted it would be a routine and uneventful flight. Boy, was I wrong!

Although cold, rainy and raw (typical February weather in the Adriatic) the man-up, launch, rendezvous and flow into the no-fly zone over the Balkans went smoothly. The 15,000-foot overcast layer over Bosnia-Herzegovina was a tactical concern, since we had to fly below it in order to visually identify potential targets on the ground. Accepting the risk of operating beneath the overcast, we flew at tactical airspeeds and maintained a sharp lookout while conducting our mission.

After completing an extended aerial patrol of Bosnia-Herzegovina, we climbed above the overcast, decelerated to a more gas-conserving airspeed, started heading to the southwest egress point and began shifting our focus toward going 'feet wet' and returning to the carrier. We had just enough fuel to get back to the ship for a normal recovery.

Then, an unexpected call from the Combined Air Operations Center (CAOC), relayed by the AWACS – '*Quicksand 61, stand by to copy words: proceed to (Sarajevo), check in with Disney 06 on amber 4, Chariot sends. Do not delay.*' (Translation: Our flight's call sign was Quicksand 61; we were given grid coordinates of a location that turned out to be in the heart of downtown Sarajevo; Disney 06 was a French (NATO or UN) Forward Air Controller (FAC); amber 4 was Disney 06's radio frequency, and 'Chariot' was the Air Force general in command of the CAOC, located in Vicenza, Italy.)

Surging with adrenaline, I confirmed the coordinates, thumbed through the kneeboard package to find the right frequency, and took a couple of deep breaths to keep the excitement out of my voice before acknowledging the unexpected directive. This sounded urgent, and there was no idea of what kind of situation we'd be dealing with.

We descended again below the overcast, accelerated to tactical airspeeds as we headed to Sarajevo, a large city in nestled in mountainous terrain, and checked in with Disney 06, the French FAC. Sarajevo, once a beautiful city that had hosted the 1984 Winter Olympics, was wracked by a protracted conflict between the newly independent Bosnian government and the besieging Serbs. The Frenchman described an ongoing firefight in the heart of Sarajevo, located south of a large stadium north of town and asked me to 'make simulated bombing runs' on the area.

A couple of things to consider:
First, both 'Rainman' and I had just enough fuel to return to the ship as planned, and since high speed tactical maneuvering would consume even more gas, I instructed 'Rainman' to stay high, conserve fuel, keep a sharp lookout for groundfire directed at me and sing out if he saw anything unusual. No point in having both of us on fumes.

Second, even though this pop-up tasking would delay our return to the ship for the scheduled recovery, we had to support the French FAC, even though it wasn't clear exactly who was shooting at whom on the ground.

Sarajevo sprawled beneath me in gray winter colors as I overbanked my Hornet, rolled into a 45 degree dive, pointed my nose at the troubled neighborhood, and preemptively pumped out chaff and flares to defeat infrared missiles or radar guided AAA (anti-aircraft artillery). As I pulled out of the dive, jinking and maneuvering the jet, the FAC came up on the radio and said in a cheerful French voice, *'Thees is very good!! Zey have stopped shooting at each other… and now zey are shooting at you!'*

'Great!' I thought – 'This is about the craziest thing I've ever done in my life!' After making several more dry dive-bombing runs / shows of force from different directions during the next fifteen minutes, the French FAC was finally satisfied, passed his thanks and told us the firefight had died down.

Several thousand pounds of fuel below my fuel ladder, I began a max range climb profile heading back toward the Adriatic with Rainman faithfully tied on, passed the mission report to the AWACS, then began coordinating with our own E-2 to let the ship know we'd either be late or have to divert to Bari, an airbase on the east coast of Italy.

Complicating our situation was the fact that Bari's weather had degraded in the last few hours and was right at or below approach minimums, with freezing rain, low ceilings & poor visibility. Not a viable option. Looked like we'd be coming back to the ship one way or another … but we'd need some airborne gas to make it.

Our E-2 masterfully coordinated the effort to get gas headed our way, and an S-3 tanker actually met us before we went 'feet wet' over the Adriatic. Rainman and I tanked as the S-3 dragged us back toward *Saratoga*. Still relatively low on gas for such a foul weather day (but thankful to have gotten back to a more reasonable fuel state ... and even more thankful my nugget wingman calmly plugged the tanker during a critical phase of the flight) our return to the ship was ultimately uneventful – other than the fact that we disrupted the flight deck's cycle and aircraft respot by recovering back aboard almost an hour late ... I later had to explain to CAG and the CO of the ship why we had been so tardy.

After the flight, Rainman and I debriefed the various phases of the mission; I was impressed by his poise and level-headed demeanor, especially for a young aviator on his first operational flight. Having badly blown my prediction for an uneventful flight, I was thankful my inexperienced wingman executed the basics very well.

Post Script: On 5 February 1994, a mortar attack on a market near the Sarajevo neighborhood I'd flown over the day before killed 68 people and injured hundreds more. As a personal participant in the unusual flight, I was a bit skeptical of the press reports that described the attack as retribution for the 'aggressive maneuvering of NATO jets over Sarajevo in early February.'

Lieutenant Commander, now Commander, Henry Mitchell, 801 Squadron, HMS *Ark Royal*
Communication with the Editor

Then in April it gradually heated up. In February some F-16s shot down several Bosnian Serb aircraft .In April Gorazde flared up and the Serbs encircled Gorazde firing Triple-A [Anti-Aircraft Artillery] down into the town and it was all getting very messy. The locals were turning on the UN because they had been promised that the UN would come to their rescue and protect them and they didn't see a manifestation of that. The Sea Harriers were on task – they were on air defence task, actually, and suddenly the CAOC wanted some aircraft to go over to Gorazde, and the Sea Harriers were the nearest – again the benefits of being a swing role aircraft – but the ground elevation exceeded what our weapon settings would allow us to bomb against. For some reason, and none of know to this day why it happened, neither aircraft could get a radar lock on the target which was the only way – and best way – of priming the weapon system for accuracy and to meet the stringent collateral damage constraints at the time. It was to support a soldier who was basically holed up, while triple-A fire rained down on him, while he was trying to call in close air support on a tank which was making its way to a position which could have been threatening to the inhabitants of the town. And in the process of that the 2 Sea Harriers kept on going round and round to try and provide a level of support but failed to get a weapons solution. Rules of engagement prevented either from dropping a weapon unless able to do so because of the risk of collateral damage. In the process of that, one SAM narrowly missed him. The next time round one of them hit his aircraft from which he ejected safely. He was recovered by the Bosnian Moslems and soon handed over to the British soldiers in Gorazde who regarded him as something of a spare hand – here's a gun, come and help us out! – and then eventually he was looked after by them rather than the UN monitoring officers. Things had come to such a head that the British decided they were going to walk out and they walked out almost between the Bosnian Serb and the Bosnian Moslem lines at the dead of night and were collected by a French special forces helicopter.*

The whole command and control thing was all a bit toothless anyway because it was under the control of the UN and the rules of engagement were hugely constraining. There was one occasion when a tank appeared out of a farm building and had a shot at some UN personnel up near Banja Luka or the Bihac pocket, I think, and a request went through Sarajevo for use of close air support. That process at the time required the request to go to UN headquarters – a completely different time zone – to the Secretary General Boutros Boutros-Ghali, himself. By the time they got the answer it was the following morning if not midday and the tank was not going to oblige the UN by waiting for trouble … Aircraft were almost immediately in position to help out but the ROE would not allow them to do anything until hours, even days, later.

SOUTHERN WATCH AND SOMALIA

Lieutenant Keith Gallagher, Bombardier Navigator,
USS *Abraham Lincoln*
published in *Approach Magazine* in November, 1991; by permission of the author

On 9 July 1991, four days out of Singapore and bound for patrol duty in the Gulf, Gallagher was in the rear seat of a Green Lizard KA-6D aerial tanker on a refuelling mission above USS *Abraham Lincoln*. Without warning, his ejector seat partially fired, leaving him with his legs inside the aircraft and the rest of him in the airstream. His parachute deployed and wrapped itself around the tail of the aircraft.

Murphy's Law says, 'Whatever can go wrong, will, and when you least expect it.' (And, of course, we all know that Murphy was an aviator.) Murphy was correct beyond his wildest dreams in my case. Fortunately for me, however, he failed to follow through. On my 26th birthday I was blindsided by a piece of bad luck the size of Texas that should have killed me. Luckily, it was followed immediately by a whole slew of miracles that allowed me to be around for my 27th. Not even Murphy could have conceived of such a bizarre accident (many people still find it hard to believe), and the fact that I am here to write about it makes it that much more bizarre.

---

* See *No Escape Zone*, Nick Richardson, Little Brown & Company, 2000.

We were the overhead tanker, one third of the way through cruise, making circles in the sky. Although the tanker pattern can be pretty boring midway through the cycle, we were alert and maintaining a good lookout doctrine because our airwing had a midair less than a week before, and we did not want to repeat. We felt we were ready for 'any' emergency: fire lights, hydraulic failures and fuel transfer problems. Bring 'em on! We were ready for them. After all, how much trouble can two JO's get in overhead the ship?

After my third fuel update call, we decided that the left outboard drop was going to require a little help in order to transfer. NATOPS recommends applying positive and negative G to force the valve open. As the pilot pulled the stick back I wondered how many times we would have to porpoise the nose of the plane before the valve opened. As he moved the stick forward, I felt the familiar sensation of negative G, and then something strange happened: my head touched the canopy. For a brief moment I thought that I had failed to tighten my lap belts, but I knew that wasn't true. Before I could complete that thought, there was a loud bang, followed by wind, noise, disorientation and more wind, wind, wind. Confusion reigned in my mind as I was forced back against my seat, head against the headrest, arms out behind me, the wind roaring in my head, pounding against my body.

'Did the canopy blow off? Did I eject? Did my windscreen implode?' All of these questions occurred to me amidst the pandemonium in my mind and over my body. These questions were quickly answered, and replaced by a thousand more, as I looked down and saw a sight that I will never forget: the top of the canopy, close enough to touch, and through the canopy I could see the top of my pilot's helmet. It took a few moments for this image to sink into my suddenly overloaded brain. This was worse than I ever could have imagined – I was sitting on top of a flying A-6!

Pain, confusion, panic, fear and denial surged through my brain and body as a new development occurred to me: I couldn't breathe. My helmet and mask had ripped off my head, and without them, the full force of the wind was hitting me square in the face. It was like trying to drink through a fire hose. I couldn't seem to get a breath of air amidst the wind. My arms were dragging along behind me until I managed to pull both of them into my chest and hold them there. I tried to think for a second as I continued my attempts to breathe.

For some reason, it never occurred to me that my pilot would be trying to land. I just never thought about it. I finally decided that the only thing that I could do was eject. (What else could I do?) I grabbed the lower handle with both hands and pulled – it wouldn't budge. With a little more panic induced strength I tried again, but to no avail. The handle was not going to move. I attempted to reach the upper handle but the wind prevented me from getting a hand on it. As a matter of fact, all that I could do was hold my arms into my chest. If either of them slid out into the wind stream, they immediately flailed out behind me, and that was definitely not good.

The wind had become physically and emotionally overwhelming. It pounded against my face and body like a huge wall of water that wouldn't stop. The roaring in my ears confused me, the pressure in my mouth prevented me from breathing, and the pounding on my eyes kept me from seeing. Time had lost all meaning. For all I knew, I could have been sitting there for seconds or for hours. I was suffocating, and I couldn't seem to get a breath. I wish I could say that my last thoughts were of my wife, but as I felt myself blacking out, all I said was, 'I don't want to die.'

Someone turned on the lights and I had a funny view of the front end of an A-6, with jagged plexiglas where my half of the canopy was supposed to be. Looking down from the top of the jet, I was surprised to find the plane stopped on the flight deck with about 100 people looking up at me. (I guess I was surprised because I had expected to see the pearly gates and some dead relatives.) My first thought was that we had never taken off, that something had happened before the catapult. Then everything came flooding back into my brain, the wind, the noise and the confusion. As my pilot spoke to me and the medical people swarmed all over me, I realized that I had survived, I was alive.

It didn't take me very long to realize that I was a very lucky man, but as I heard more details, I found out how lucky I was. For example, my parachute became entangled in the horizontal stabilizer tight enough to act as a shoulder harness for the trap, but not tight enough to bind the flight controls. If this had not happened, I would have been thrown into the jagged plexiglas during the trap as my shoulder harness had been disconnected from the seat as the parachute deployed. There are many other things that happened, or didn't happen, that allowed me to survive this mishap, some of them only inches away from disaster. These little things, and a s-hot, level headed pilot who reacted quickly and correctly are the reason that I am alive and flying today. Also, a generous helping of good old-fashioned Irish luck didn't hurt.

The pilot, Lieutenant Mark Baden, received the Air Medal for landing the plane safely on the *Lincoln* within six minutes of noting the emergency. Others on the ship were also recognized for responding so quickly to the need to get the aircraft down.

Between the end of the First Gulf War (Operation 'Desert Storm') and the start of the Second Gulf War (Operation 'Iraqi Freedom'), carrier pilots flew patrols over the north and south of Iraq to establish no-fly zones and protect vulnerable groups such as the Kurds (Operation 'Southern Watch').

Lieutenant Loree Draude Hirschman, USS *Abraham Lincoln*, 1995
from *She's Just Another Navy Pilot*

The first two weeks of flying in the Arabian Gulf gave me a hint of how difficult our summer was going to be. The heat was so intense that every aviator was drenched in sweat before even boarding the aircraft.

Air conditioners in the S-3s don't work until the engines are running, and temperatures inside the sun-baked cabins commonly exceeded 110 degrees. Haze clung to the horizon; it was like flying in a bowl of milk.

Each night catapult launch propelled us into a wall of total darkness. The horizon was non-existent, and we had no references except for our instruments as to which way was up. If we were lucky, the ship would be pointed toward an oil platform and the orange flames would hint at the horizon. Even that could be disorienting, however, and I made it my practice not to look up from my instruments until we were a few thousand feet into the air. Then I could usually see the stars above. The haze would accumulate only around the horizon, so I could pick out constellations and see whatever portion of the moon was in phase. Each approach to the carrier at night was a vertigo-inducing blur.

On daytime flights we scanned the sea for ships, submarines, and sea life. I had heard that the gulf was full of poisonous sea snakes, and I saw plenty of them from the cockpit. Sometimes there were just a few, but occasionally I would see hundreds of them swirling together in giant, frenzied balls.

Lt. Larry 'Jedi' Anderson sensed that the snakes made me uncomfortable, so he regaled me with imaginary tales of the snakes' ferocity. He said they could unlock their jaws and bite people on the eyes. And he told me they were known to jump six feet out of the water and come down in aviators' life rafts. He said he wanted to fly with me as often as possible while we were in the gulf because sea snakes preferred women; if we ever bailed out, he said, the snakes would chew me up but leave him alone. Jedi was only displaying his twisted sense of humor, but the snakes were definitely creepy.

After each flight I tried to cool off with a cold shower, but water demand on the ship was so high that they frequently cut off the flow entirely. Or they eliminated the cold water and left only steaming hot water, so it was common for us to go to bed tired and sticky.

I got to fly an S-3 over Kuwait on a refueling mission, and it seemed like the first time in months that I had flown over land. The terrain itself was so barren and featureless that it was hard to imagine why so many wars had been fought for control of it.

I looked down on miles of blackened oil fields that the Iraqis had set afire during the Persian Gulf War three years before. It was an amazing sight. There's a term in warfare scorched-earth policy for the practice whereby a retreating army ruins everything in its wake in an attempt to deny its opponents any resources. Scorched earth had always seemed to me a figurative term, but this land was literally blackened. Every inch of it was charred and lifeless, and the desolation extended for miles in all directions.

At the same time, a savage civil war in Somalia had led to unsuccessful UN intervention. In January 1995 it became necessary to organise the evacuation of all UNOSOM peacekeepers – the majority of them Bangladeshi and Pakistani – by sea.

Several nations contributed ground forces while the naval component of Operation 'United Shield' was made up of US and Italian ships, with ITS *Garibaldi* as the one aircraft carrier. A preparatory exercise, Operation 'Somalia 3', took place off the Kenyan coast.

Sottotenente di Vascello, now Capitano di Corvetta, Gian Battista Molteni, Harrier pilot, ITS *Giuseppe Garibaldi*
Communication with the Editor

South of the Equator all pilots, including the rotary wing branch, plus the special forces drawn from the men of St Marco and Consubin* began taking part in a series of ops briefings on the current situation. During that working up period, and for the first time in my career, I was introduced to the concept of Combat SAR.

At 0430 the following day, 50 miles off the Kenyan coast, the MMI's first Combat SAR was set in train, and I was tasked with the part of a downed pilot in need of rescue. We assembled in COC [Command and Control] for the pre-mission briefing. The Commander opened a map, scale 1:250,000, of the Kenyan interior and I noticed that it was strangely monochrome. It represented the expanse of land that flowed from the savannah to the equatorial jungle close to the Zambezi river ...

The various experts began to debate as to the precise spot at which the pilot should be released. However, though called to the briefing, I had no right to say anything, and nor had the helicopter's commander, who restricted himself to asking for co-ordinates so he could plot his course. Just then an old comrade from my days at the helicopter flying school gave me a look that I interpreted to mean he was glad that *he* was not the one facing the unfortunate fate of the pilot who had been shot down. It came to the point when the various arguments were crisply interrupted by the voice of the commander who pointed to a spot on the map with his finger and said: 'that's it'.

It was still dark and our Sea King was ready with the APU [Auxiliary Power Unit] on. The helicopter's consoles gave off that familiar reddish light that make the atmosphere around those special forces ops so fascinating. I climbed aboard with my camouflage kit, armed with map, compass (no portable GPS units), knife, emergency radio and ... a 9-calibre pistol. With me came an escort of two men from the St Marco regiment who would keep me company and who, more to the point, were armed a bit better that I was and would have a better chance of getting me out of any trouble.

We took off to the east and, trying to escape the light of the sun rising behind us, we arrived at the coast and began to climb above the course of the Zambezi. The starboard gunner opened the door as we were flying low, and I couldn't believe what I was seeing. Zebras, hippos bathing ... it was like a day-trip to the zoo, and a day trip it really was. After flying up river for half an hour

* The S. Marco Regiment are Italy's Marines; CONSUBIN is the Comando Subacquei Incursori.

we turned right and for about ten minutes we flew over a thick forest of trees rather like our coastal pines but taller and thicker. The map showed only an expanse of green, damnably like the landscape. At one point a gap opened up beneath us; this was the clearing that the experts intended for the CSAR operation. They dropped me off, hardly bothering to put a wheel down. Trust my old college friends!

The two marines from the St Marco had wisely brought along a package containing 12 water packs. Soon afterwards the noise of the departing helicopter faded away, leaving the place in unnatural silence.

In fact, after a month on board, accustomed to all the noise of the ship, that quiet seemed troubling and heightened the sense of abandonment. It reached a peak when the silence was interrupted by what seemed like the roar of a big cat followed by a rustling from what might have been a python ready to attack. Fear does strange things to you, and now my St Marco friends did not look so well armed, and they betrayed almost as much anxiety as yours truly.

We had to start the trek to reach the spot appointed for the rescue. It wasn't far away, probably less than 5 kilometres, and we had 10 hours in which to do it. We decided to get it out of the way immediately. We set off along the path, water packs firmly strapped on shoulders. We took infinite care over every footstep, paying obsessive attention to the grass we disturbed to avoid to avoid further unpleasant surprises such as scorpions, snakes or deadly spiders. We arrived at out destination six hours ahead of the appointed time. All this time our surroundings seemed to be taking on a less hostile atmosphere and we were getting used to them. But just as when you think you're in control of the situation, something crops ups.

The trio suddenly found themselves surrounded by local villagers.

They produced their traditional weapons in the shape of bows and arrows. When one of them nocked his arrow I have to confess that the sweat froze on me and my hand closed on the Beretta. We looked at each other and all three of us shared the same concerns and the same awareness that there was nothing we could or should do. As the men moved, they made a lot of noise; the sounds did not seem to indicate hostile intentions, but neither were we reassured that they were harmless. The chap who had nocked his arrow shot it into a tree trunk, then another, then a third, as if wishing to show off his skill. Proud of his expertise he turned to us and we understood from his gesticulation that he wanted us to have a go. We declined, but he insisted – until he had the brilliant idea of bartering: his bow for my pistol!

The trio were guided away from the malaria-ridden village by the local policeman. The time for the rescue arrived and Molteni's minders left him on his own.

I never saw where the helo landed, and, truth to tell, I don't recall seeing anyone approaching me. All I do remember is a strong grip on my neck and finding myself face down on the ground, my pistol taken from me and a knee planted in my back.

'What was the name of the sheepdog you had when you were a kid?' yelled a voice in a heavy Sardinian accent. In my confusion it took me a few moments to realise what was happening to me. Then the penny dropped: I realised they were demanding the password and I had to remember the procedure. My bewilderment was due to the fact that, while it was just an exercise, the violence of the attack which had caught me was enough to make me think it was real. Moreover, the pain in my back was real enough. I knew the reply and shouted 'Spazzola', certain that this would bring down the curtain on the performance.

On the contrary, all I got was another pain, from a blow between the shoulders by what could have been a rifle butt.

'I'll say it again: what was the name of the sheepdog you had as a kid?' the Sardinian voice shouted again. I repeated the same answer, knowing I could not be wrong because my dog, when I was little, really *was* Spazzola. After giving the same reply for the fourth time – there was no other that I could give – I stiffened in order to resist the umpteenth blow. However, he just turned me onto my back and shouted in my ear:

'But was he a *sheepdog*?'

I remembered then, that he wasn't ... But that bastard of a Sardinian commando deliberately split hairs to trap me, and expected me to realise it. So I finally told him that he was *not* a sheepdog and, trussed up like a salami, I was dragged to the helo.

The atmosphere was the same in the aircraft. Throughout the flight the Sardinian was surly towards me. I was hoping for someone with common sense to say that the exercise was over, likewise all hostilities, but it did not end until we were back on board when I was allowed to buy a drink for everyone in the wardroom. Including the Sardinian.

So I finished my equatorial adventure in front of the camera belonging to the small group of journalists responsible for the ship's television news. And when the Chief Armourer came to collect my pistol I told him, for a joke, that I had swapped it for a genuine set of bow and arrows, with a Kenyan tribe I'd met that day. You can imagine the reaction of the senior Petty Officer responsible for the ship's small arms.

The actual evacuation of UNOSOM personnel began on 27–8 February, and all forces and UN personnel were evacuated at a cost of one slightly concussed US Marine.

WOMEN ON BOARD

Life on board carriers was characterized by a 'work hard, play hard' ethic, particularly among the embarked squadrons. The culture, however, began to change with the arrival of women.

Commander Jason Phillips, 820 Squadron, HMS *Illustrious*
Communication with the Editor

I remember on my second carrier deployment we had swapped from *Ark Royal* to *Illustrious*. There is a piano in every carrier bar, and on this deployment we took one with us and kept it in the hangar initially. I think the CO had always known it was going to happen, because one night there was a wardroom party and he gave the order to destroy the piano that was already there – but no implements were allowed to be used, only fists and feet. Next day there was the replacement piano in the wardroom – even with a brass plaque on it: 'Presented to the wardroom HMS *Illustrious* by 820 Squadron'. Classic Fleet Air Arm style.

On the *Invincible* class there are thoroughfares right round the ship only on Two Deck and Five Deck. Two Deck is immediately below the flight deck, where the accommodation is. The Two Deck 'dash' is a legendary run normally made in just anti-flash (white hood and gloves) and footwear, nothing else, and the aim is to run around Two Deck as fast as you can without being captured. Obviously there is the risk of people jumping over the hatch coamings as they are running and so getting the classic 'hatch rash' – which is when you smack your head on the top and are often found unconscious or bleeding heavily while wearing only anti-flash.

In the past there was little to do in your cabin apart from work, write letters home, sleep, or perhaps listen to whatever music was available to you. Now cabins will be decked out with X-Boxes and there are all sorts of leagues set up. All ships have some form of fitness room, the bigger ones will have a CV suite, a weights room, or, tucked away in corners, they'll have a rowing machine. While I was away on a six-month deployment last year, all the traditional interdepartmental sports were on, whether it was 'it's a knock-out' tug of war, deck hockey, bucket-ball volleyball – and it's quite good on a carrier because they can lower the ramp half way so you've got a ready-built court without, hopefully, the ball disappearing over the side every five minutes.

There are the usual pranks, including swapping ranks when people joining the ship go to see the Commander. I heard of one ship where the EWO on board played the Commander while the latter played the EWO, and they also had a female officer involved. In the middle of the interview the supposed 'EWO' came in. They ended up having a mock fight, which stunned the interviewee, and, in the midst of it, out of the Commander's shower came a female officer wearing a bathrobe – which made the interviewee wonder what the hell was happening on this ship.

We held Quiz nights, often involving a theme which required imagination to manufacture some form of fancy dress. I remember one great evening when in the 'Guess the Film round' the Squadron had made some short clips parodying the Hollywood blockbusters to assist in guessing the title. The best one was *Titanic*, where one of the more portly observers – male –

played Kate Winslet's role. They managed to find a dress for him, which concerns me somewhat! He was filmed on the brow of the carrier with the *Titanic* music. There were various other scenes from the movie. In the scene where Winslet was being sketched, he was in the Captain's cabin just with his longjohns on. I think they asked the Captain if they could use his cap for filming. So he was in there, naked bar his longjohns, laying on the settee, with someone drawing a big fat stick man, with the Captain's cap covering his privates – which was a nice touch. There's another scene in *Titanic* where Winslet and DiCaprio have sex in the car. There are a variety of vehicles kept in the hangar including a minibus. They steamed up the inside of the minibus, got unseen people wildly rocking it – and we in the audience saw a pair of feet in the window, and a pair of feet in between them – and then *another* pair of feet appeared. It was a classic night of entertainment.

Commander Henry Mitchell, RN
Communication with the Editor

The Cold War days consisted of endless Cold War exercises, which were fun with very demanding flying in some very demanding conditions – in the Arctic in the dead of winter, for instance. Much more demanding than flying nowadays in the fair weather of the Mediterranean and the Gulf ... I suppose there was a requirement to let off steam after you've survived a landing when the ship is pitching and rolling – as you come round the final turn and see the propellers coming out of the water you know you're in for an interesting recovery.

But that started changing, and about the same time, in the early '90s, women started coming to sea and it started making the wardroom a more couth place, or with the odd exception less couth; also, there was a transition to wardrooms getting hi-fi systems and so on. It became less of the CAG: highly competitive squadrons standing around the piano singing squadron songs loudly and rudely focussed at the other squadrons' limited attributes, and lighting became slightly brighter, hi-fi system on in the background, and males and females – everybody starting to get a bit politically sensitive. I suppose it was a question of tiptoeing around some of the tulips we hadn't bothered to tiptoe around (or were even aware of) before.

The newspapers were frequently gossiping about salacious events during the period focussing on the transition of having women at sea. There were a few incidents, which of course made it to the front page of *The Sun*: HMS Sin-vincible, HMS Lust-rious and HMS Lark Royal. It was easy headlines, so I suppose we were all a bit sensitive, boys and girls, about that, but professionally it made not a jot of difference and I think socially it was an improvement, probably – certainly less raucous than before.

Senior Chief, now Command Master Chief, Kathleen A. Hansen, USS *Kitty Hawk*
Communication with the Editor

Hansen worked her way up through the technical grades.

I was a young, in-trouble teenager, and my mother steered me toward the navy because I needed some discipline. Secretly she hoped the navy would teach me how to cook and sew. I never did learn how to cook and sew; what I did learn was how to fix her toilet, which was worth more to her. I wasn't one for administrative-type work. In junior high and high school I took welding, woodworking and small-engine repair. I believe those classes influenced me to go into the engineering and repair fields. When I joined the navy in 1979, the rating of hull technician (which involved the fabrication, installation and repair of all types of shipboard structures, plumbing, sheet-metal fabrication, carpentry and piping systems) had just opened up for women.

By the time I got to the *Kitty Hawk* in 1997 I was a senior chief petty officer and was assigned as the repair division leading chief petty officer. I had about 200 sailors who worked for me. Hull technicians were not the only rating assigned to the repair division; there were also machinery repairmen and women (skilled machine-tool operators who made replacement parts for the ship's engine auxiliary equipment, such as evaporators, air compressors and pumps) and damage controlmen and women (who were responsible for ship stability, fire fighting, fire prevention and chemical, biological and radiological [CBR] warfare defense and who instructed personnel in damage control and CBR defense methods, as well as damage control equipment and system repair).

The *Kitty Hawk* was going to Japan in 1998 to replace the *Independence* (the navy rotates a new aircraft carrier to Japan about every 10 years due to maintenance). We had approximately 300 women on board, which was less than 10 percent of the crew; but the *Independence* did not have any women assigned. The *Kitty Hawk* met the *Independence* in Pearl Harbor. Some of the *Independence* crew, supplies and equipment were cross-decked over to us. After a couple of months in Japan, some of the *Independence* sailors confided in me that they had been worried about working with women, but in a short amount of time, they realized that it wasn't an issue at all. Often women worked harder because they thought they had to prove themselves.

The chief engineer on the *Kitty Hawk* was kind of a rough guy at first. It felt like he didn't believe a female holding the position of leading chief petty officer for the repair division could do the job. Again, just like the male *Independence* sailors, within a very short amount of time we were great allies. After a few months the chief engineer told me I had changed his opinion of women in the engineering field.

While the first women to serve in front-line ships were determined to show their male colleagues that they were their equals, they also had to correct misapprehensions outside their navies.

Lieutenant Loree Draude Hirschman, USS *Abraham Lincoln*, 1995
from *She's Just Another Navy Pilot*

We hosted a group of foreign dignitaries in Singapore one evening. We displayed a variety of airplanes and equipment on the Lincoln's flight deck, and some of us were assigned to stand there and answer questions from the visitors. It was fun to meet new people and show them around. They were usually in awe of what they saw.

I'll never forget one of the comments from a Pakistani government official, though. He asked Heidi, a female flight officer from one of the EA-6B Prowler squadrons, what she did on the ship, and she explained that she operated the electrical, radar, and weapons systems on combat jets. Prowlers are used for electronic warfare, and their powerful systems can jam enemy radar and fire antiradar missiles.

The visitor's eyebrows arched up, and he seemed pretty impressed. Then he asked how many men were on the ship and how many women. She quickly gave him the answer: about five thousand men and five hundred women. He looked at her sympathetically and in all seriousness said, 'You women must get very tired.'

Heidi kind of shrugged and said, 'Everyone works hard on the ship, so everyone gets tired. But the women don't get any more exhausted than the men.'

'But you must be more tired because you service all of the men,' he explained.

This guy thought our collateral duty was to provide sexual services for the men on board! My jaw dropped, but Heidi did a remarkably good job of calmly explaining to the gentleman from Pakistan that we were not for hire and we didn't get tired – at least not that kind of tired.

Abraham Lincoln and its battle group soon entered the Indian Ocean and steamed west, a few hundred miles south of Sri Lanka.

I took off just before sunset for a three-hour flight, and the sight of the stars emerging from the purple sky was spectacular. It was amazing how many stars were visible on a clear night in the middle of the ocean. The sun had long since dropped below the horizon when I approached the ship to land that night. But the diffuse starlight made the *Lincoln*'s silhouette almost as crisp and clear as day, and I could see the outline of the ship several miles away.

Because of the lack of satellite coverage in this part of the world, we weren't able to make telephone calls from the ship. But even without phones, navy rumor continued to operate at full speed. The last time we spoke, Harry [her fiancée] said that he had heard all the way back in [NAS] Lemoore that the female pilots on the *Lincoln* were flying poorly. People who thought women shouldn't be serving on combat ships or flying front-line jets were quick to believe what they wanted to believe.

A NEW MILLENNIUM

The terrorist attack on New York's 'Twin Towers' on 11 September 2001 led to the invasion of Afghanistan by the US and supporting nations including Britain, France and Italy (Operation 'Enduring Freedom') with the aims of destroying Al-Qaeda bases, capturing Al-Qaeda's leader, Osama Bin Laden, and overthrowing the Taleban regime in favour of a democratically elected government. On 18 December 2001, four ships of the Marina Militare, including the carrier *Garibaldi*, sailed from Taranto for the Indian Ocean to take part in the operation The 88-day deployment set a post-war record for an Italian warship. While the Italian Harriers and the French Super Etendards from *Charles de Gaulle* supported coalition ground forces, the helicopters had other roles.

Tenente di Vascello, now Capitano di Corvetta, Marco Casapieri,
Marina Militare, *Giuseppe Garibaldi*
Communication with the Editor

The air component at the heart of the Italian strategy comprised a number of AV8B Harriers and embarked helicopters. Among the latter on board the *Garibaldi* were two SH3D Sea Kings of the 1st Gruppo Elicotteri di Luna, reserved for special operations. At that time I served with the 4th Gruppo Elicotteri di Grottaglie and, to be more precise, I was part of that elite band of pilots of the prestigious Nucleo Lotta Anfibia (amphibious combat service). Of the 3 months in the Gulf (out of four in total for the deployment), I particularly remember a mission that in several respects proved to be something out of the ordinary. It was one of many support activities carried out in conjunction with the boarding teams during their checks on suspicious merchant ships,

The freighter was rather large, but nevertheless it was decided to intercept at night, using surface vessels rather than by helicopter. The helicopter was given the covering role: a sniper was on board, overseeing maritime operations and in contact with the boarding team on the ship. For us it meant shadowing the freighter sufficiently closely to see what was happening on board. We were all using Night Vision Goggles – NVG. There was something suspicious going on: if the freighter isn't cooperating as it ought to, is it hiding something?

In the end, we pulled back after about 5 hours, having been close to opening fire on more than one occasion, and with the adrenaline pumping. The flight commander, myself as co-pilot, and the rest of the flight crew returned to the carrier. We had flown while wearing NVG, without a single break, something that had rarely or never happened in the past.

The three-month stint in the operations zone passed fairly quickly and it was time to go home. The crew was thrilled: we had left behind the stress of the mission with the knowledge of having done a great job. All tasks were performed successfully, the MMI (and all Italy) had once again demonstrated its readiness and determination to be proactive in international activities. Our fixed-wing aircraft, flying missions of 6–7 hours, requiring three or four in-fight refuellings, had done their part by providing essential support to the ground troops deployed in Afghanistan. All the crew had worked well and with professionalism, without incidents or trouble ...

But a few days before their scheduled arrival at Taranto in mid-March the carrier began to receive information about the suspicious behaviour of a cargo ship, *Monica*, apparently heading for Italy. It was being shadowed by vessels from the Port Authority and Customs (GdF) and by the frigate *Perseo*.

It was about 0115 when the commander of *Perseo* informed us that the crew of the merchantman had agreed let the Customs people board the ship. They reported that the holds were crammed with hundreds of people. It was then obvious what sort of cargo the ship was carrying, and we realized that it was not possible to search the ship. In that context there was, therefore, no need to insert a team by helicopter.

We were still passing the information to the leader of the SOF [Special Forces] team when we picked up a message on *Perseo*'s frequency '... our people inform us that there is a woman who has just given birth and is in a serious condition, wonder if you can winch her off for emergency transfer to hospital in Catania ...'

We looked at one another, our faces half hidden by our visors and illuminated by the pale green light of the NVG. 'What do you say?' I asked my comrade ...

We contacted the GdF patrol boats who confirmed that their people on the freighter's deck would give us every assistance. We asked them to switch off their searchlights and the lights on the freighter's deck so as not to damage our ability to obtain horizontal references. However, they were unable to do this in the short time available because the GdF personnel on board were unable to take control of the lighting system and set up a suitable configuration. Also, the sea conditions and the safety of those working on the deck of a merchant ship required adequate lighting. We had, therefore, to accept this compromise.

We were confronted by an interesting situation. The wind had veered northerly, the ship was almost broadside to the sea – which was still southerly – and it rolled at the mercy of the waves which were breaking over the port side. The first detail I noted was the crowd of people huddled in the bow and near the stern (we learned later from the newspapers that there were 922).

The freighter, the general characteristics of which we had been able to study, was a typical cargo ship, about 75 meters long. Holds amidships, superstructure aft, and a low forecastle with a mast. The main obstacles to hovering were the two masts, but there was enough space between them, however, to permit hovering. It was easy to pick out the GdF staff on the deck, ready to receive us ...

The co-pilot took the controls because we were approaching on the port side and the superstructure was on the starboard side, the opposite side to my seat. During the turn I checked again the selector height of the hover coupler: 200 ft ... I looked for the horizon: nothing – completely dark. However, it was just possible to discern the shapes of the coastal mountains. We made the final turn and came in on a northerly course. The pilot nicely decreased the speed and, in consequence, the altitude of the helicopter in line with the descent plan produced by the semi-automatic coupler to bring us 50ft above the ship. We lowered our NVG. They were not much good for keeping the trim level, but they were useful for discerning what was going on beyond the lights of the motor launches. From my side I could see in the distance the coastline which provided a minimum reference. If you kept your eyes on the instruments it was possible to maintain a hover.

We realized now that our danger lay in getting into a 'vertigo situation' ... caused by moving lights in a dark scene without depth. The masthead lights rolled to the ship's movements, and the floodlights on the deck did likewise. By looking at the deck and the masts you could easily fall into the trap of fixing the hover by those references and so lose the correct position relative to the real horizon.

When we had reached the hovering position just out of 'ground effect' above the freighter's deck, the winchman and I began the safety checks with respect to distance from the superstructure, and we directed the pilot to the deck. The optical illusion effect, causing visual disorientation, was very strong and the pilot and I had to swap command several times during the operation. The moment I lost the fixed reference points, I handed the controls to him and set myself to recover those fixed references, such as the mountains over on my left, in order to regain a correct sense of the horizontal. He did the same. I can't remember exactly how long we could maintain control, I think it was about 30 seconds each. However, despite the continuous change of command, the operation proceeded smoothly. On our first descent we released the stretcher and then returned to hovering over the deck. The team on the freighter were quick to lay the patient, who was clutching her child, on the stretcher. Later we found out that the child was a baby.

Finally, the team on the deck gave us the okay to hoist the stretcher on board. This required two manoeuvres to bring us back into position: first, proceed horizontally between the masts and then descend vertically to working height. As a matter of fact, we had to decrease the hovering altitude to give the stretcher enough slack on the deck to avoid it jerking when the ship rolled. The awareness of having people on the hook made us more determined and our little routine of changing command became almost second-nature.

I've no idea how long the whole operation lasted, probably only a few minutes, but you wouldn't have thought so, given the tiredness we experienced at end of the mission.

Then the aircrewman reported to us that the stretcher was attached – personnel standing clear, ready for recovery. We began to winch the two patients up. When the crewman reported that the stretcher was free from all obstructions, we began to move slowly forwards, gaining altitude so we could get the stretcher well clear of the ship and take up a position upwind of the freighter at the safe height of 200 feet ...

'100 ft, 50 ft ... hook's at the door,' then 'stretcher aboard and door closed. Ready for takeoff.'

That was the best message ever given me by a crewman. We could depart from the scene and release the tension. In the back, the doctor and a qualified member of the SOF took care of the woman who was clutching her newborn baby. Our people reported that mother and child were in good health, but we nevertheless flew to Catania at our maximum speed ...

Once the helicopter was switched off, weariness swept over me, and when I took off my helmet, I realized I was soaked in sweat. At the same time, however, I felt proud to have been part of the crew who had just completed the demanding mission. We hugged and slapped one another on the back as we climbed out of the aircraft. As is often the case with me after particularly tiring operations, I looked at the helicopter, now silent and motionless on its spot, almost smiling at the thought that a few minutes before it was a living machine, under our control, on board which I had gone through some particularly nerve-racking moments.

We crashed out for a few hours' sleep before being back in the air around 0600 for our return to the *Garibaldi*, which had waited for us before entering port and holding a ceremony to mark our return from Operation 'Enduring Freedom'. The following day we returned home with the rest of the crew, happy that the '24 hour kit' had once again proved equal to the task.

Together with our doctor, mother and child reached hospital in a good state. Some days later we learned that the mother had named her baby daughter 'Marina' in memory of the crew who who had helped them on the night of their arrival in Italy.

On 18 March, *Monica* was escorted into Catania. Her human cargo consisted of Iraqi Kurds who had paid smugglers to take them to Germany via Italy.

Lieutenant de Vaisseau, Marine Française, *Charles De Gaulle*
Communication with the Editor
French Navy policy forbids serving pilots to be identified.

The carrier was exercising off Sicily. The evening patrol consisted of 6 Super Etendards Modernisés (SEMs) and 4 Rafales. I was the No. 4 Rafale. At the weather briefing, the Met Officer confirmed that it would be a dark night – no moon and a blanket of cloud around 2,000 feet covering the whole sky. Moreover, the wind would be light with a fair swell caused by the strong wind that we had encountered all day. The conditions thus combined to make the recovery a tricky business. In the event of being unable to land on because of technical problems or bad weather, there was an emergency landing strip at Sigonella in Sicily to which we could divert.

The patrol was catapulted off; the flights went off without a hitch. On returning from the mission, the 6 SEMs were advised that they would be landing on first, followed by the Rafales. All our apprehensions were confirmed. We observed the bolters. The pilots had to open the throttle and go round again. If you boltered, you had to wait; if you had to wait you had less time to decide to divert. The carrier warned the Rafales that they would not land on until all the SEMs were down. We were ordered to conserve fuel. We all had the same quantity of fuel, and so the landing order remained that of the patrol. I would be the last to line up.

In view of that situation I decided to take advantage of the waiting time by going over the charts, in case I had to divert to the nearest aerodrome. Unfortunately, however hard I looked through the documents I had taken on board I didn't find them. Then I remembered very clearly having seen them before the launch and putting them next to my log book. They were, therefore, back on the carrier just when I needed them up here in the cockpit. A feeling of great loneliness swept over me. I knew the ground frequencies in the Rafale's database, but not the approach path. What would happen if I had to divert to Sigonella ?

My pals lined up to land on, and got down. When it was my turn, I lined up knowing that I only had one shot because I didn't have enough fuel to go round again.

Less than impressed with my experience, I shared it with everyone at the debrief so that we could learn every possible lesson and avoid another pilot finding himself in that position in the future

Recent years have seen changes to the composition of carrier air groups in some navies, making them more flexible.

Commander Jason Phillips, 820 Squadron, HMS *Illustrious* / HMS *Ark Royal*
Communication with the Editor

We used to have Carrier Air Groups, CAGS, so I knew, for example, that being on 820 Squadron as a Sea King ASW Squadron – a 'pinger' – we would go on board with 801 Squadron, Sea Harrier fighters, and 849 B Flight, the airborne early warning Sea Kings. We were always together and would wear the badge of the CAG with the carrier's emblem central and her Squadron numbers round the outside.

We now deploy as Tailored Air Groups, TAGS, which allows greater flexibility by deploying the exact aircraft package for the task – if the deployment doesn't need jets they won't go, but if there is a submarine threat then more ASW helicopters will go; similarly, if it is a jet-heavy deployment then it would be prudent to take fewer ASW helos and more jets.

THE SECOND GULF WAR

On 20 March 2003 the US-led ground invasion of Iraq began under the US codename Operation 'Iraqi Freedom' (The British code name was Operation 'Telic'). Five US carriers including USS *Constellation* were stationed in the Gulf at the time, and massive strikes were launched against Baghdad the following day – known as 'Shock and Awe' – in support of the troops, who secured a rapid military victory. HMS *Ark Royal* was also present, ready to land and support her contingent of Royal Marines. Before and during the operation, dust and sandstorms caused problems for aircraft maintainers and serious dangers for aircrew.

Commander, now Captain, Chris Alcock, Commander (Air), HMS *Ark Royal*
Communication with the Editor

We had one of the ASACs* up on a training mission in preparation, on 13th March, just before the war started, and we had notification of a dust storm or sandstorm coming through. We'd been given a time it was going to hit us, but all the aircraft were due back on board, so no problem – however, it came through much faster and with much more ferocity than was forecast, so we made the decision to divert the helo to one of the Australian ships, *Kanimbla*, because we had their weather forecast and they told us 'we're blue,** it's clear …' However, before the aircraft got there they told us that the storm had hit them and they could not see a thing! So we were in a situation where the aircraft was chasing ships (with an ever decreasing fuel load) in an attempt to get to one before the storm hit, and all we kept getting over the radio was 'Oh, sandstorm's with us now!' I was standing in the ops room, listening to the aircraft talking, and we were just making decisions second by second in an attempt to get the a/c safely on deck … any deck. I was continually being asked by the Captain, 'Where's it going now?' and I was desperate to give him a certain answer, but the dynamics of the situation was just not letting me!

In the end it landed on one of the American frigates with a very small flight deck, actually in the middle of the sandstorm. It arrived there with almost no fuel left and with no visual references. The pilot and the observer did a fantastic job to get it on the deck. We did seriously contemplate at one stage that the a/c may have to ditch alongside a ship; we worked up a contingency plan but never had to execute it – thank God! The guys did an absolutely

---

* Air Surveillance and Control Systems.
** Weather conditions at night are colour-coded in the sequence: Red Amber, Yellow 2, Yellow 1, Green, White, Blue, Red being the worst and Blue the best.

brilliant job, and they received a commendation for it, quite rightly so. It was night, so it was even worse.

The guys and girls maintain the aircraft particularly well, and when we do environmental work they condition the aircraft to work in sand, etc., because sand *does* get everywhere, in the bearings, etc. But they'll protect the aircraft, and increase the servicing schedule – if needed – to make sure it takes that into account. We recovered the aircraft the next morning and when it came back it was completely brown, just a brown aircraft.

Commander, now RADM, Mark I. Fox, commanding Air Wing 2, USS *Constellation*
First published in *Foundation*, Fall 2004, © Mark I. Fox

Ready Room Five was crowded – standing room only – for the late afternoon strike brief on 21 March 2003. A hushed atmosphere and unmistakable feeling of 'This is it' filled the ready room as the journalists and aviators crowded in for the brief.

I briefed the strike earlier than normal to create a time margin and establish an unhurried atmosphere of clinical, calculated and deliberate professionalism. Only lightly touching on the momentous nature of our undertaking, there was no need for any, 'Rendezvous with destiny', or, 'Win one for the Gipper' comments. Everyone's head was in the game tonight.

For me and my element, the launch was smooth, the flow to the tankers exactly as planned, and the weather was, for the first wave, very workable. Having worked carefully on this plan, I knew each element by call sign as they checked in. Using night vision goggles (NVGs), I watched the multiple dozens of aircraft launched from three carriers and several land bases proceed to their tanker tracks over and into Iraq as if we had practised it a dozen times. It was like flying over New York, Chicago or Los Angeles on a busy night, but with no air traffic control center to coordinate and deconflict flightpaths. After all the effort to build simple airspace rules in the previous weeks and months, watching the first strike smoothly unfold was a beautiful thing indeed.

With tanking complete and our element formed, I worked the time-distance problem to Baghdad with a northwesterly 120 knot jetstream adding variables to my calculations. About 100 nautical miles south of Baghdad, the high overcast layer receded to reveal a dark, clear night. F-15Cs, flying combat air patrol west of us, left high contrails that paralleled our northbound flightpath.

Baghdad, a city the size of Detroit, was faintly visible on the horizon to the naked eye, but brightly lit in green hues when viewed through NVGs. As I looked east, familiar geography emerged. The Tigris and Euphrates Rivers were defined by the cultural lighting of Iraq's southern towns and cities. To the west, the empty expanse of the desert was marked by an occasional light visible only on goggles. Up north, things were heating up. Prowlers began jamming and cruise missiles started exploding, kicking off the most impressive fireworks display I have ever seen. Dozens of unguided surface-to-air missiles gracefully arced upward, some exploding well above our altitude, others snuffing out in mid-flight. Hundreds of AAA sites around Baghdad punctuated the night sky, their muzzle flashes sparkling like the scattered flash photography at the end of the Super Bowl.

The graphic light show intensified. All over Baghdad fireworks streaked skyward, and the rate of bright explosions blossoming on the ground accelerated. It was like an extended climax at the end of a Fourth of July fireworks display, with countless explosions both in the air and on the ground.

Not everything was going as planned. While working to get to my JSOW [Joint Stand-Off Weapon] release point on time, I was simultaneously figuring out a way to get all the strikers to their targets in spite of emerging lapses in the Super MEZ [Missile Engagement Zone] suppression effort. A flight of Hornets carrying anti-radiation missiles had been delayed during tanking and was out of position to fire pre-emptive HARMs in support of a JDAM-carrying Tomcat division. The Tomcats, on timeline, would be in the heart of the Super MEZ without a key element of suppression. To delay until the HARM shooters arrived would run the F-14s low on gas, add to their exposure in the Baghdad area, and otherwise disrupt the strike flow. Of all times to rely on the Iraqi defenses being confused and saturated, this was the night. I told the Tomcats to press on to their targets as planned without the HARM support.

Baghdad's fires and the building crescendo of explosions were almost too bright to view through NVGs. The Iraqi defenses were spectacular but ineffective. None of the SAMs were guiding, no one had any indication of being illuminated by fire control or target tracker radars, and the vast majority of the fireworks were in front of and mostly below us. Still, co-altitude AAA bursts and SAM trajectories rising through our altitude kept our jets in constant maneuver and our eyes out of the cockpits for the entire attack.

Having never launched multiple JSOWs before, I was relieved when the third consecutive 'thunk' indicated a normal release of my last weapon. Wrapping up into a hard right turn, I glanced straight down from a steep angle of bank and was intrigued by a series of sparkles arrayed below in grid squares. Fascinated by the spectacle, I stared at barrage fire from a unique perspective, directly above hundreds of Iraqi troops deployed along the roads of Baghdad's southern suburbs, firing their weapons straight up in the air. Safe in a sanctuary well above the firestorm, I thought to myself 'This would be a bad night to go low.'

Heading southeast on a tangent away from Baghdad, I leaned left and took a last look at the epic scene, our attack vividly marked [by] continuing series of explosions blossoming throughout the city. Contrails formed behind our jets as we climbed up to the high 30s to egress.

Departing central Iraq in our 'egress altitude block;' we passed waves of attacking jets in their preplanned 'ingress altitude block,' headed toward Baghdad. When we approached the Iraq/Kuwait border from the northwest, we could see evidence of the coalition ground attack into southern Iraq marked by flashes of gunfire and explosions. Although not as vivid or graphic as the sights of Baghdad a quarter hour before, the fact that soldiers and Marines were advancing into Iraq was momentous.

Post-strike tanking and return to the ship was uneventful, with all aircraft accounted for. Trapping aboard close to midnight, I was very pleased that *Constellation* and CVW-2's first combat flight operations in 'Iraqi Freedom' culminated in a 'gold star,' (no bolters or wave-offs) Case III recovery. A small point, but with great professional satisfaction!

The Royal Marines operation was, of course, coordinated with that of the Coalition partners. After her Royal Marines had made their opposed landing, *Ark Royal's* helicopter squadrons provided continuous support by ferrying food, water and ammunition ashore and maintaining continuous air surveillance. A mid-air collision in the early morning darkness of 22 March resulted in the deaths of all seven crew members, and devastated the carrier's closely knit complement. Shock and grief notwithstanding, they continued to deliver essential services to the Royal Marines and provide vital air surveillance with the remaining Sea Kings and crews.

Commander, now RADM, Mark I. Fox, commanding Air Wing 2, USS *Constellation*
First published in *Foundation*, Fall 2004, © Mark I. Fox

On 25 March, after trapping aboard in the midst of a terrible sandstorm at sea that produced near zero-zero ceiling and visibility, I, with *Constellation* commanding officer Captain John 'Fozzie' Miller's consultation and concurrence, recommended to Rear Admiral Costello that we knock off flight operations until conditions improved. Minutes later, the CAOC's US. Navy 'night O-6, Captain Gary 'Craze' Mace, called with an urgent and compelling request: 'We think the Marines are going to get 'slimed' (a chemical or biological attack) tonight. We really need you to launch a quick reaction strike in support of the Marines. We have the target coordinates for your GPS weapons. All the ground bases are socked in and no other carriers are flying. You're the only ones who can launch right now.'

My pre-war desire of having the CAOC choose CVW-2 for a really hard job had been fulfilled in a way I could never have predicted. Only minutes after deciding to stop flying because of the sandstorm, I not only reversed my previous recommendation but urged that we increase the size of the next launch to support the CAOC's request.

The soul-searching moment for Captain Miller, me and ultimately Rear Admiral Costello defined the concept of 'operational necessity.'

We accepted the risk that we might lose aviators and aircraft based on the need to support the Marines ashore, and we launched the strike.

We continued to fly through the night and into the next day in the most difficult conditions imaginable, ultimately recovering all aircraft without mishap. I was very much relieved when our fly day ended with everybody in one piece.

The success of the air strikes facilitated the initial military victory and the consequent toppling of Saddam Hussein's regime. *Ark Royal* continued to take supplies ashore, and on one occasion a Chinook returned with an unexpected cargo!

Commander, now Captain, Chris Alcock, Commander (Air),
HMS *Ark Royal*
Communication with the Editor

We had an uninvited guest on board: a dragon lizard, which climbed into the tail of a Chinook and flew back. It's about about five foot long.

The weather was hot, so they were doing lots of servicing on the deck early in the morning. About six-o-clock, I was wandering down and all these boys are going to this Chinook, and then they all ran out. My handlers are laughing their heads off, saying: 'there's a big lizard down here, Boss.'

Then one lad on board – we called him 'Saudi' because he'd lived in Saudi Arabia said : 'Oh, it's a dragon lizard, sir.'

'Really?'

'Yes, eats fruit ...'

'So it's not going to eat anybody?'

'No, sir.'

We kept it in a big box and fed it until we could fly it back ashore. Great thing about a carrier. You can ask any question, pose any problem, and somebody will know the answer.

3. A Role To Be Proud Of

Command Master Chief Kathleen A. Hansen, USS *Ronald Reagan*
Communication with the Editor

Hansen became only the second woman to be appointed as command master chief of an aircraft carrier, and in that capacity she joined USS *Ronald Reagan* in 2004.

The command master chief is the most senior enlisted sailor on a ship. I'm the liaison between the enlisted crew and the captain, but I'm also there to help mentor the junior officers. The leadership triad (commanding officer, executive officer and command master chief) is like a tricycle. The captain is the big front wheel; the executive officer and CMC are the two little rear wheels. If one of us is off kilter, we go round in circles.

I encounter good and bad all day as I walk around the ship, making sure sailors' pay is okay, checking that they have had career development boards, and sometimes dealing with people not getting along – the list of things I deal with is long. Do I miss the hands-on work of being a hull technician? No, I do plenty of repairs to my house when I'm in port. Even as a command master chief I find that sailors are curious about my prior rating. As a hull technician I fixed things; as a command master chief I have a much harder time fixing people. As command master chief at sea, I never forgot my old rating, and I would stop in at the repair shops to chat and see how everyone was doing. Often someone would try to get me to weld a little bit.

When you're the command master chief, everybody knows who you are. You have no time to yourself unless you're sleeping. A carrier command master chief gets a stateroom. Staterooms are normally for officers; they vary in size, holding from one up to 15 people. For the first time in my career I was not in a berthing compartment with all the other females. Enlisted sailors sleep in berthing compartments (or bedrooms) holding from 15 to as many as 250 with triple bunks. It was a big deal to have my own space with so much privacy.

I'm a creature of habit; I would be up and in the gym by 4:30 a.m. Most of the time sailors knew that was my time – an hour or an hour and a half in the morning to get my work out in before starting my work day. After the gym I would shower and head to the chiefs' mess to eat breakfast. Even when I was eating, business was conducted. People had to catch me when they could; I was on the move all day long.

I'd walk around the ship most of the day. In order to know the sailors, I had to be out with the sailors. You can't sit just behind your desk. I would tour the ship from down in aft steering up to the bridge. After a while people got used to me popping in unannounced.

In the evening, a ping-pong table was set up on the forward mess deck. Two or three times a week I would stop by to play a game or two on my way up to my stateroom. No matter how long the line was, the sailors would let me jump in and play. That was always fun and a big deal to the sailors that I would stop and play ping-pong with them.

You could call the command master chief the school principal or the cruise director on a ship. The average age of the sailors is between 18 and 22 – they're very young. If they were at home they'd be hanging out with friends and going on the Internet. So we have to have events to entertain them during their off time. We had poetry reading and karaoke on the mess deck, as well as volleyball, basketball and sumo wrestling in the hangar bays, provided there were no aircraft. No matter where you went on the ship at night, work was going on 24 hours a day. While I didn't sing karaoke and didn't participate in some of those events, sailors always appreciated that I showed up, supported them and cheered them on.

I always believe that if I lead and mentor my sailors, I'm automatically going to be successful. Shortly after I left the *Kitty Hawk* I learned I had made master chief, and the first thing I did was send an e-mail to my division officer telling him to thank all my guys for making me a master chief. Right then I knew I wanted to be a command master chief. The first woman to be the command master chief of an aircraft carrier was a friend of mine, Beth Lambert on USS *Theodore Roosevelt*. She's now retired.

The *Ronald Reagan* was built in Newport News, Virginia, and commissioned in 2003. In 2004 she was to change home port to San Diego. The *Ronald Reagan* coming home to California was a big deal, and everyone was praying the former president would live to see his ship pull in. Ronald Reagan lived in California, where he'd been governor before he was president. He was in the late stages of Alzheimer's. He passed away when the ship was halfway home, as we pulled into Rio de Janeiro for liberty.

During that cruise we held our crossing-the-line ceremony. Thes e shellback ceremonies used to be about bullying and humiliation. The first time I crossed the equator was on an amphibious ship – it was a rough, raunchy ceremony. This tradition has changed for the better and if done right can make a crew become a really powerful team. I've participated in and been in charge of many crossing-the-line ceremonies. They involve a whole script about King Neptune and cleansing the ship of the 'polliwogs' (people who haven't crossed the equator before). It takes years to build a ship because the crew comes and goes. The sailors are really not a team until the first time they go on that cruise.

We went through the Straits of Magellan in June. The *Ronald Reagan*'s a huge ship and it seemed like we were so tiny, a postage stamp, compared to the Andes Mountains and the glaciers. This two-day voyage through the straits was the highlight of my career. When we came out into the Pacific Ocean, there were about 16-foot seas. In this huge warship, we barely felt the ship rocking and rolling.

In the end, I don't want to be known as a good *female* command master chief; I just want to be known as a good *command master chief.* Occasionally I have worked with men who believe women should not be at sea or in the military. The navy is all that I have known for 30 years, but I'm sure this is also the case in some civilian jobs. I have had a great career. The navy is a great organization and very diverse.

Commander Jason Phillips, 820 Squadron
Communication with the Editor

I deployed for the first time as a CO last year [2009]. When I walked out on the deck and saw my aircraft all out on the line, all flashed up, I thought: 'these are mine'. It's a very special moment indeed.

Flying on to the ship is always good, particularly when you embark in numbers; it always looks impressive, and the clue is in the title: aircraft carrier. Until the aircraft turn up, arguably it's 'just' a ship. So it does make a great difference when the air group comes on board and it 'becomes' a carrier ready to project air power from the sea.

Instrumentation and engineering is more advanced than ever before, but nobody can design out the unexpected malfunction – or two – or the element of risk. It is then that the professionalism of the highly-skilled ship's company and/or squadrons really matters, and in that respect nothing has changed.

Capitano di Fregata David Fossati, Marina Militare,
Flight Captain EH-101, NO. 2-02, ITS *Garibaldi*, February 2007
Communication with the Editor

Even if – difficult as that would be – I ever forget the emotions and fear I experienced on that occasion, I am absolutely certain that it will be impossible to forget the great surge of professional pride that ran through the whole crew at the end of the incident.

The mission, which took place at night, saw us take off from the *Garibaldi* in our EH-101 to complete a sonar search for a vessel acting as an OPFOR [Opposing Force] as part of a major air-sea exercise in the Gulf of Taranto.

The first dipping positions were at a distance greater than 40 miles from the mother ship. Such a distance, even if it was well within the operating range of our powerful, relatively new and thoroughly trusty helo, seemed to be impossible to bridge on the return leg.

Once we reached the position assigned to us for the exercise we began to dip our active HELRAS [Helicopter Long Range Active Sonar] at the maximum depth to make a bathyvelocitygram, to get a complete picture of sound propagation at that depth. Everything was going to plan, and at 2134 hours the transducer was raised to the optimum level for searching, in this case a depth of 1,000ft, in order to get the expected range of 9 miles, which would give the best opportunity for a good detection.

Around five miles to the NW we had an AB 212 [helicopter] in support, call sign 'Tiger', in visual/radar search; we also had a good radio link with the tactical controllers on the frigates *Espero* and *Euro* and with our carrier, *Garibaldi*; this was almost luxury.

Our second round of dipping, still in the same position, began at 2147, with the sonar immersed to 1,000ft, but just after the first two *pings* the sonar system developed a fault which we picked up immediately. We had to stop the search and I had to order the emergency shutting down of the sonar and its recovery on board using the auxiliary winch. This was at 2157.

This fault, although difficult to deal with (we could not be sure transducer's extendable hydrophones were definitely in their closed position until they had surfaced and we could physically see them) was actually very lucky for us. We signalled the tactical controller of our intention to interrupt the mission and break off the dip as soon as we had the sonar on board.

I am still asking myself today what would have happened if the sonar had worked properly, at a depth of 1,000 feet right up to the moment of the emergency that followed. Had things had gone to plan, we would have continued our search and found ourselves dealing with an engine that was cutting out and with a transducer submerged at great depth .

With the sonar still in recovery phase, actually passing 270ft on its way up, my co-pilot and I were suddenly aware in our headsets of the pre-programmed, soft, gentle female voice (whose computerised task was to break bad news in a kindly way via the voice warning system) saying 'WARNING'. It meant that there was an unspecified major fault, and her tones were not remotely reassuring to us.

'*WARNING* – what on earth???' I asked the co-pilot as I looked for something more specific on the alarm panel and tried to hold the helicopter centred over the sonar that was still in the water.

'*WARNING*? what's going on?' I repeated.

'Dave, there's nothing showing on the alarm panels or the warnings,' my co-pilot, Andrea de Natale answered.

A few seconds later, and while the sonar continued to come up, but was still 150ft down, Andrea told me a light had come on: 'OIL PRESSURE NO.2 ENGINE' indicating the oil pressure was plummeting and the temperature was rising. Very bad news. The engine was giving up.

I thought about cutting the sonar wire – in my pilot's mind it had become nothing but a troublesome, submerged excrescence – so we might be able make a dash for the ship, squeezing the last gasps out of the dying engine, but then I considered the favourable wind that was assisting us with twenty knots from dead ahead, and the value of applied torque equal to 75%, on three engines. I made two quick calculations. 75 times 3 equals 225; 225 divided by two equals 112.5, or the power which the two remaining engines should have once No. 2 has failed. We should still be within our limits. 'Andrea, we can try *not* cutting the ball … Everyone happy with that?' Okay.

The engine is still holding up; the sonar ball at last emerges from the water. The sonar umbrella – fortunately closed – is 'in trail' - swinging above the water, hanging from its wire – the engine pressure is close to zero. We start to pass from hovering to forward flight, with the sonar spinning. The flight crew are ordered to continue the sonar recovery procedure. The handbook dictates that the last three metres of recovery be carried out by manually operating the winch because that same transducer fault prevented the normal electro-hydraulic recovery of the sonar into its internal housing.

At the same time the crew are ordered to prepare for ditching without warning.

Andrea signals: 'All stations PAN PAN PAN'. According to previously agreed procedure, our friendly Tiger is shadowing us as a precaution; our intention being to make for our carrier to execute a running landing, while anticipating the engine would cut out at any moment. An accurate forecast, as it actually died 15 seconds later, with the helo, by now in forward flight, climbing to above 500ft – a more suitable altitude for a twin-engined transit.

'MAYDAY MAYDAY MAYDAY' is Andrea's next transmission, obeying the procedures. He is watching me as I run through the procedures in which we are continually drilled for just such an emergency. For his part he carries on with his checklist, turning the transponder to emergency and also giving me first-rate back-up according to crew-coordination procedure. The three aircrewmen play their part too. A good team, working together.

After an interminable flight at 2,000ft we contact Flyco, by now 10 miles away and ask what the chances are of making a running landing with touch-town on No 5 spot and rolling onto 4 and 3.

'Base recovery course 270, mother is making 19, steady and ready for recovery …' It's Paolo Lazzaretti from the carrier.

Garibaldi's wake is clearly visible in the night, and by now she's 8 miles away, landing lights already on. The illuminated path lets us descend in safety, following the green beam. They are ready to recover us. We fasten belts, and even consider the chance of restarting No. 2 engine, but quickly abandon the idea, given the mechanical nature of the fault. Running landing, chocks and lashings for us. Landing on a ship at night is not a simple affair but on this occasion the surging adrenaline heightened concentration while the continuous practice in night-landing gave us the sensation of something routine. The thinking and the what-ifs come later.

On 12 January 2010 the Caribbean island of Haiti was struck by an earthquake measuring 7.7 on the Richter scale. Three days later a US carrier was on station, to be joined during February by ITS *Cavour* on its maiden deployment.

Candice Villarreal, MC2, USS *Carl Vinson*
Communication with the Editor

We arrived off the coast of Haiti January 15, composing pictures in our heads about the things we imagined we'd see when we got on shore. The ship was charged with a new kind of energy; we were nervous, we were afraid of what we'd run into, but mainly, we were excited. We were excited to get there, excited to make a positive impact on a less fortunate nation. Our boots hit the ground running from the moment we arrived with an intensity none of us knew we possessed.

I flew by helicopter over the trash-laden waterline and through the thick smoke suffocating the island. There were about six of us – five medical personnel and myself, there to document everything. It was real. We were there, it was happening, people were dead, they'd lost everything. My heart hurt for them.

We landed in a small clearing adjacent to the Killick Haitian Coast Guard Clinic in Carrefour, and the four or five hundred yard walk up to the clinic was intense and gruesome. Hundreds of bleeding, wounded Haitians covered the ground, waiting to be seen, on sheets, doors, mattresses and even wheelbarrows that their friends and family members carried them in on. The dirt and gravel covering the ground was soaked in some areas with blood, with various bodily fluids and with dirty water from the UN troops' makeshift camp.

The moment they saw us carrying medical supplies, they knew help had arrived and it almost sent them to a sort of panic. They scrambled for our attention, hungry and dehydrated. They moaned, cried, wailed, pulled on our clothing and gestured with their hands toward their wounds or their wounded loved ones with a heavy fear in their eyes, and all I could do was offer them a bottle of water and shrug and motion to them that I wasn't a doctor. I felt guilty.

The smell of the dead bodies placed under the shade, of feces, urine, gangrene, wounds and infection festered and infiltrated everything, and I tried not to vomit. It hung in the air and assaulted my nose, absorbed into my clothing and embedded itself into the mask I wore.

Our sailors set up shop in the clinic, which was an empty room with a couple of folding tables used to treat patients on. Directly in front of the building's side entrance was a raised cement slab our docs turned into a makeshift triage with about 25 to 30 patients lined up, waiting for medical evacuations. We were flying their children in our helicopters and taking them to our aircraft carrier for more intense treatment in our facilities. They didn't know where we were taking them or when they'd see them again, but they trusted us to help and let us take them anyway. After two days of amputations, tourniquets, medevacs, screams, bandaging and splinting, our team reduced the number of waiting injured to about 75, and they were still coming in. We fed them, kept them hydrated and cleaned them up. They appreciated everything and the tense atmosphere was slowly easing.

On my last day there, a worried woman carried in her eight-year-old son. He didn't have any visible wounds, but ended up taking his last breath and passing away before us. I can't remember having a harder time keeping myself together than when I watched one of our chaplains kneel over him to administer his final prayer, with one hand resting on his smooth forehead and the other closing the boy's eyes for the last time. After he was covered and carefully laid in his place under the shade, the chaplain consoled his mother, who shook her head and wept. And then she thanked us.

For a woman who just lost her own flesh and blood – her little boy – to turn around and thank us for what we were doing when it was too late for her own child just took the breath out of my lungs. She had bigger things to worry about, to think about, than thanking us for our help two minutes after she witnessed the death of her young son. She'd lost everything. We saved many but couldn't save him, and she thanked us anyway. And when she did, the look in her eyes between each falling tear told us she meant it.

I wrote my mother an e-mail telling her about it all, and she said she was sad because I've seen so much in my life. I only said one thing to her in response: I have never been prouder to be a part of anything than I was on that island.

Tenente de Vascello Andrea Pingitore, pilot, ITS *Cavour*
Marina Militare

During Operation 'White Crane' off Haiti the Italian flagship kept a helicopter at 30 minutes notice for emergencies. Although writing in the third-person, Pingitore was the helicopter pilot.

13:10, a Sunday in mid-February. Although this is a public holiday, support activities and help for the Haitian people continue unabated, while the warmth of the sun coupled with the high humidity make operations even more difficult. Loudspeakers throughout the ship call relentlessly: 'Medevac, Medevac, Medevac.'

The crew of the emergency helicopter (TV Andrea Pingitore, STV Lovascio Luca, Domenico Vitale C1, C1 Anthony Camporeale) go immediately to the ship's Operations Centre to gather all relevant information. Two children, one-and-a-half and twelve years old respectively, are in a critical condition. The on-board doctors classify both as 'Alpha Cases', i.e., requiring action within one hour of the request for assistance. Just enough time to quickly brief the crew before they run to the helicopter that is ready to take off. At 1320 the helicopter is in flight with the medical team and all the equipment necessary to rescue and stabilize patients on board. Both were victims of a car accident and both suffered severe trauma to the skull. With no time to lose, you just airlift them for a CAT scan and emergency surgery.

The return flight to the *Cavour* with the two patients is made is at full speed, trying to avoid even the slightest vibration, which could prove fatal. After just 15 minutes flying time the helicopter SH3D lands on the flight deck and the children are rushed to the hospital for emergency operations. After a few hours they are pronounced out of danger.

Epilogue

A century after Ely's historic flight, nine countries operate active carriers: USA, eleven; Britain and Italy, two each; India, France, Russia, Brazil, Spain and Thailand, one each. Another ten vessels are under construction or being rebuilt: they comprise China's first three aircraft carriers, three for India, a second for Spain, the first of a new *Gerald R. Ford* class for the USA – and HMSS *Queen Elizabeth* and *Prince of Wales* for the Royal Navy. Other navies including France and Russia are considering their own medium-term options in a rapidly changing world that has been hit by economic recession and in which nobody can predict with any certainty exactly what kind of military conflicts will have to be resolved in the future or what means will be required.

Aircraft carriers and the aircraft that operate from them are expensive, as are the many highly-skilled personnel aboard them. There is a very long lead time between the signing of the contract and the commissioning of the ship or the entry into service of a new fighter or helicopter. Critics have argued that too much is invested in them, that the loss of a carrier to enemy action would be a catastrophe for a fleet. It is perhaps not surprising that at various times over the past century different governments have viewed them as luxuries or irrelevancies. Nevertheless, as their past record demonstrates, they are arguably the most versatile and potent means of projecting a nation's power overseas, enforcing UN resolutions and keeping open essential trade routes.

The carrier is, however, much more than a powerful warship. Wherever it is sent it remains a strip of superbly-equipped sovereign territory. In international waters it acts as a self-contained air base independent of the consent of foreign governments whose policies may change or who may be subjected to pressure from neighbouring states. It is true that its old adversary, the submarine, has become ever stealthier, but modern ASW, along with AEW and anti-missile systems, has become correspondingly more sophisticated. 'Mother' and her brood of rotary and fixed-wing aircraft are likely to remain a cornerstone of naval policy for decades to come, because, in the words of US President Bill Clinton during a visit to USS *Theodore Roosevelt*: 'When word of crisis breaks out in Washington, it's no accident the first question that comes to everyone's lips is: *Where is the nearest carrier?*'

Bibliography

This list comprises the books quoted in the text and a few others that readers may also enjoy. All are worth reading, and this author is particularly fond of Jack Thomas's wonderful poetry collection, *The Lonely Sky and the Sea*, Hank Adlam's honest and humane *On and Off the Flight Deck*, and Theodore Taylor's extremely moving biography *The Flight of Jesse Leroy Brown*. The Fleet Air Arm Songbook is something of a treat, too. Publisher and date refer to the author's personal copy.

Abe, Zenji, *The Emperor's Sea Eagle*, Arizona Memorial Museum, Hawaii, 2006

Adlam, Hank, *On and Off the Flight Deck*, Pen and Sword Maritime, Barnsley, 2007

Atkinson, Tex, *From the Cockpit*, John M. Hardy Publishing, Houston, 2004

Baldwin, Sherman, *Ironclaw*, William Morrow and Co., Inc, New York, 1996

Barringer, E. E. , *Alone on a Wide, Wide Sea*, Pen and Sword, 1995

Booth, Rear Admiral Peter B., *True Faith And Allegiance*, C.R.B. Publications, Pensacola, 2004

Brand, Stanley, *Achtung! Swordfish!*, Propagator Press, Leeds, 2005

Brown, Captain Eric 'Winkle', *Wings On My Sleeve*, Weidenfeld & Nicolson, London, 2006

Dannreuther, Raymond, *Somerville's Force H*, Aurum Press Ltd, London, 2006

Davies, Richard Bell, *Sailor in the Air*, Seaforth Publishing, Barnsley, 2008

Duncan, Dr Doy, *Abandoned at Leyte*, Phoenix International Inc., Arkansas, 2002

Fleet Air Arm Museum of the Royal Australian Navy, *Flying Stations*, Nowra, NSW

Fleet Air Arm Songbook, printed by The Fleet Air Arm Officer's Association, London, no date

Fuchida, Mitsuo, *Midway*, Ballantyne Books, 1986

Gillcrist, Paul T., *Feet Wet*, Schiffer Publishing Ltd., Atglen, 1997

Hanson, Norman, *Carrier Pilot*, First Futura Publications, London, 1980

Hirschman, Loree Draude and Dave Hirschman, *She's Just Another Navy Pilot*, Naval Institute Press, Annapolis, 2000

Hough, Richard, *The Longest Battle*, Pan, London, 1987

Johnston, Stanley, *Queen of the Flat Tops*, Ace Books Inc., New York (no date)

Jones, Albert H. and Michael H. Jones, *No Easy Choices*, Square One Publications, Worcester, 1994

Kernan, Alvin, *Crossing the Line*, Naval Institute Press, Annapolis, 1994

Lawson, Captain Ted W., *Thirty Seconds Over Tokyo*, Penguin Books, Washington, 1945

Layman, R. D., *Before the Aircraft Carrier*, Conway, London, 1989

Morgan, David, *Hostile Skies*, Weidenfeld & Nicolson, London, 2006

Poolman, Kenneth, *Escort Carrier*, Secker & Warburg, 1983

— *Illustrious: The Fight For Life*, Cerberus Publishing, Bristol, 2007

Richardson, Nick, *No Escape Zone*, Sphere, London, 2009

Romanelli, Lieutenant Commander Otto, *Blue Ghost Memories*, Turner Publishing Company, Paducah, 2002

Rossiter, M., *Ark Royal*, Corgi, London 2007

Smith, Peter C., *Eagle's War*, Crécy Books, 1995; www.crecy.co.uk/

— *Task Force 57*, Crécy Publishing, Manchester, 2001

Taylor, Theodore, *The Flight of Jesse Leroy Brown*, Avon Books, New York, c.1998.

Thomas, Jack, *The Lonely Sky And The Sea*

— 'We Rode the Covered Wagon', in *Proceedings*, October 1978, US Naval Institute Press, Annapolis, MD

Vercken, Vice Admiral Roger, *Au Dela du Pont d'Envol*, Alerion, 1995

Wallace, Gordon, *Carrier Observer*, Airlife, Shrewsbury, 1993

Ward, Sharkey, *Sea Harrier Over the Falklands*, Cassell Military Paperbacks, London, 2003

Winton, John, *Carrier Glorious*, Cassell Military Paperbacks, London, 1999

Woodward, Admiral Sandy, *One Hundred Days*, Fontana, 1992

Wragg, David, *The Escort Carrier in World War II*, Pen and Sword Maritime, Barnsley, 2005

Young, Desmond, *Rutland of Jutland*, Cassell, London, 1963

Useful websites

Every carrier has its own website, sometimes more than one, frequently providing eyewitness material, so these are not listed individually with the exception of:

www.usscoralsea.net

www.ussgambierbay-vc10.com

www.cv6.org

Britain's Small Wars, www.britains-smallwars.com

www.thenavysvanishinggeneration.com

Korean War Project, www.koreanwar.org

www.maritimequest.com

www.flightglobal.com/pdfarchive/index.html (comprises all available back copies of Flight magazine 1909–2005)

Credits

Extract from *Navy Times* used by kind permission of Army Times Publishing Company; transcripts of IWM Sound Archive Recordings used by kind permission of the Imperial War Museum; extract from Richard Griffin's memoir used by kind permission of Diane Rayburn; extracts from usscoralsea.net used by kind permission of usscoralsea.net; extracts from the diary of Erskine Childers used by kind permission of Trinity College Library, Dublin; extracts from private documents deposited at the Fleet Air Arm Museum used by kind permission of the Fleet Air Arm Museum, Yeovilton; extracts from the files of the Covered Wagon Association used by kind permission of USS *Midway* Museum; extracts from *Au-Delà du pont d'Envol* used by kind permission of the author; extracts from *Eagle's War* used by kind permission of Crécy Publishing; extracts from material in the Special Collections Dept, J. Y. Joyner Library, used by kind permission of East Carolina University; extracts from *Crossing the Line* used by kind permission of Yale University Press; extracts from *The Times*, 22 May 1991, used by kind permission of News International; extracts from *The Emperor's Sea Eagle* used by kind permission of Arizona Memorial Museum and the author's family; extracts from *Proceedings*, October 1978, *Midway* and *She's Just Another Navy Pilot* used by kind permission of Naval Institute Press; extracts from *No Easy Choices* used by kind permission of the authors; extract from the Jack Stout Collection used by kind permission of the Library of Congress; extracts from *The Longest Battle* used by kind permission of David Higham Associates; extracts from *On and Off the Flight Deck* used by kind permission of Pen and Sword Books Ltd; extracts from *Sea Harrier Over The Falklands* used by kind permission of the author; extracts from *Abandoned at Leyte* used by kind permission of *Phoenix International Inc.*; extract from *Achtung! Swordfish!* used by kind permission of Propagator Press; *Swordfish – LS 384 (The Dingbat)* used by kind permission of the author; extracts from *Wings On My Sleeve* and *Hostile Skies* used by kind permission of the Orion Publishing Group; extracts from *From The Cockpit* used by kind permission of the author; extracts from *On Jesse's Wing* used by kind permission of the author; extract from Brian Ellis's interview used by kind permission of Rowland White; extracts from *True Faith and Allegiance* used by kind permission of the author; General Art Bloomer's letter from Brigadier General William A. Bloomer Collection, used by kind permission of Emporia State UniversityArchives, Emporia State University; extract from *Flying Stations* used by kind permission of the Fleet Air Arm Museum of the Royal Australian Navy.

Extracts from Private Papers in the Department of Documents, Imperial War Museum used by kind permission of the IWM and the following copyright holders:

G. R. Grandage, Mrs Barbara Grandage; Commander F. A. Swanton, Mr H. S. Swanton; C. H. Bridge, Mrs A. Proffitt; K. Morris, himself; C. P. Wareham, Mrs Beryl Wareham; E. V. B. Morton, Mrs A Morton; M. G. Haworth, Ms Penelope Salter; J. Needham, Mrs C. Jackson; E. E. Barringer, and Mrs L. Barringer.

Index